MY MOTHER'S DREAMS

Dear Rose
We are happy to
have you out there.

Be blessed
always:
Bamurangirwa
31 / 1 / 2014

MY MOTHER'S DREAMS

PATRICIA BAMURANGIRWA

Matador
9 Priory Business Park
Kibworth Beauchamp
Leicestershire LE8 0RX, UK
Tel: (+44) 116 279 2299
Fax: (+44) 116 279 2277
Email: books@troubador.co.uk
Web: www.troubador.co.uk/matador

ISBN 978-1783065-585

British Library Cataloguing in Publication Data.
A catalogue record for this book is available from the British Library.

Printed and bound in the UK by TJ International, Padstow, Cornwall
Typeset in 11pt Bembo by Troubador Publishing Ltd, Leicester, UK

Matador is an imprint of Troubador Publishing Ltd

BRIEF AUTOBIOGRAPHY OF THE AUTHOR PATRICIA SINZI BAMURANGIRWA

I was the last born in a family of six children. Three among them were boys (Rusingizandekwe, Mpanumusingo, and Kambanda) and three girls (Kantamage, Kankuyo, and I, Bamurangirwa). All my elders used to take care of me probably because I was too young compared to them. I was a little spoiled girl. My dad was a man of strong character and a hard-working one. He used to work together with those he hired for any kind of work. He used to dig his entire garden or build huts; therefore, he was harsh to his children as he wanted them to imitate him as far as working was concerned. He used to do everything possible in taking care of his flock. In case someone did not do the right thing according to his standard of living he or she was expecting to be seriously smashed. Seriously thus he was known as a clean person, a hard-working man and someone who knew how to entertain others.

People were not bored wherever he was as they were listening to him and laughing. Moreover, his talk was full of teachings, which attracted people and friends to him. My mum was so lovely and gracious in everything. Once she knew that a child would be punished, she advised to hide for a while until dad forgot about it. That made us love her more than our dad. We used to respect and listen to her even though to respect a parent in our time was a requirement no matter how he or she behaved towards you. No child objected before his parents, what is known today as the right of children. This was part of the culture that a child had to learn in his early age.

My dad never punished me, not because he did not try but my elders used to protect me. Sometimes they used to hide me with my elder brother Rusingizandekwe who was married and lived not far from home. In those days, relatives used to live closer as the parent was the one to provide the plot for his children. As the result of my father's hard work, he had one of the biggest forests in the area that existed until 2000. According to what I was told by people there, it will still remain there for a long time, as the trees planted are not destroying the earth.

Some people used to respect us as we were classed amongst the rich in the area. As a matter of fact, people who were highly considered were chiefs but when they used to visit our area they used to sleep over in our house and this made us esteemed in the community. I liked cows so I used to spend much time taking care of calves as I thought that my brother called Kambanda who was younger than my elders, was doing other jobs during the day. After a while, I came to realise that he was going to school like other neighbours' children of his age. I was surprised and decided to start going to school as well even though I liked to be a shepherd.

When I started my primary school I was five or six years old but the school nearly refused me because I was so small, short, and slim that they did not want to have me at school. Fortunately, my mum insisted that my younger brother who was maybe eight years older than me, would be taking care of me. This included taking a packed lunch for me made by of sweet potatoes and milk, as I liked this kind of food too much. Even though the teacher refused to have me at school, my brother pleaded, as they did not have a fixed age of admittance, then, I was accepted as long as my brother would be taking care of my needs. In the assembly, we used to line up according to our height. So, I used to be in front as I was the shortest at school. At the end of school, my brother used to take me back home. However, in the beginning he had to carry me in on his back as most of the time I was asleep while going to school as it was early for me. After a while I became used to the school system and became able to do things without the help of my brother. Moreover, the teachers loved me, as I was intelligent. In fact, I passed the final exam, and passed from year one to year two. Unfortunately, I had to move near home, as year two was not near home. Year two was far, around ten miles, which I had to walk by foot in the area called Inyamabuye. My new school was not only far from home but, at the same time I did not go with my brother who used to take care of me.

I had seen other students fighting or being beaten by others. As far as I was concerned I never fought with anyone or was beaten, as I was under the protection of my brother. Therefore, in my new school I had to develop a survival system in order to protect myself, as I feared being beaten. I used to take lemons and oranges as we had a big garden of fruits and I gave them to those I identified as fighters so that they may protect me in return. I studied many months at Inyamabuye because my old sister called Kantamage wanted me where she was married and at Musasu.

It is at Musasu that she enrolled me in year two. My first teacher called Martin loved me as I was intelligent and polite. In order to learn about religions and become Roman Catholic members which was compulsory, our teachers used to take us to Kiruhura Parish, called Kiruhura Mission at the time. The Roman Catholic Church was at the time the only one in charge of the education of the country and its population. They were also in charge of knowing the welfare of the population and they were preparing to rule the entire country. The easiest way was to start by teaching children, as I saw it. Anyhow, teachers used to take children (students) to the mission so that they may repent of any wrong-doing. The priest was sitting inside the room and each child had to repent through a small window. Then, he would forgive by giving a punishment of reciting some prayers written in a prayer book or memorised as it was a requirement. Before leaving, the priest had to touch children on the forehead and we were told that it was a way of blessing us. None had to stand before the priest finished performing the giving of the so-called 'blessing'. Obedient children were chosen and integrated into the group of Xaverian that was like the scouts for the Roman Catholic Church. I remember one of the songs that says: 'when angel and priests are walking on the road, I will first of all greet priest with respect, yes all respect belongs to him'. I did not understand the relationship between the priest and the angel except that I came to realise that they wanted the priest to be above everyone and everything, so that he can be taken serious by Rwandese.

The priest who used to receive us in the parish was a Rwandese called Fr Alfrail Sekamonyo. I am not sure how he came to realise that I was an intelligent girl, but he made me his friend. Most of the time after having our Penitence, he used to take me to his house that was behind the church. Once in the house he used to feed me with special food I never ate at home. The only food I knew was eggs but it was fried. He took interest in me to the level that he came to visit my brother-in-law where I was living. He recommended him to bring me to church and gave him the exact time he should take me as he told him that I was intelligent. I was so happy, not because the church was interested in me but I was more interested in his food. Otherwise I could not accept to go each time to Kiruhura as it was too far.

At the end of the exams I became once more the first in year two. My teacher called Martin was happy and encouraged me by giving me one franc. I bought some eggs and hid them in one of our jugs hoping that they would increase; then, we would be eating eggs on a daily basis like the priest. After a while the entire house smelt and no one knew what happened until my sister discovered the jug. She took it and threw everything far from the house. Then, she asked me if I had any idea of where the eggs came from. I explained everything to her and the plan I had, then, she laughed and explained to me how eggs can be found or where they come from. I became homesick, and especialy I missed my mother, I needed to see her so I told everyone that I wanted to go home. They pleaded with me that they would be taking me home to visit during the holidays but I refused as I wanted to live with my mum. The priest said that I could go as long as I would continue to study and attend the church even though he would miss me. I did think a lot about the nice food given to me by the priest but before going I asked him the name of the food. He told me that it was called bread.

When I went back at to Nyamabuye, the school had already improved as they had the full primary school. By this I mean from year one up to year five. Among the teachers I remember are Mr Deogratias Bitahurugamba and Mr Mathew Misago. I still remember Deogratias because he taught me for many years. As I moved from one year to another he was moving with me as well. I was a cheeky girl at school to the level that I used to make others laugh in the classroom while I myself was not laughing. Sometimes the teacher used to ask why they were laughing in the middle of the session and the classmates told him that it was Bamurangirwa who was making them laugh. As I was very serious, the teacher used to be on my side saying that it was impossible that I disturbed the class, as I was always serious. Most of the time other students used to be beaten except for me as I was not laughing. The teacher moved me from the middle to the front chairs saying that they should not lie on behalf of a serious girl.

At the front I was sitting with a timid girl Mukakalisa, but in the end I made her laugh as well. What I used to do was imitate the teacher as he was writing on the blackboard. If he turned around I would quickly sit back down so that he would not catch me doing anything wrong. My teacher loved me despite being cheeky as he used to tell other students that they should be ashamed of following a small girl like me when they were so grown up compared to me, and I always had better marks than them. I was not too young but my height and stature showed I was too young compared to others of my age.

There were some girls who were elders such as Nyombayire and others. On some issues that they were ashamed to ask the teacher, they used to tell me to ask for them. Normally I did not fear to ask any questions. Most of the time the teacher used to tell me to ask her after school, especially if I was asking about sexual issues as I was not ashamed. For instance, at that time teachers or parents could not talk about sex either at school or at home. Sometimes when I went to talk privately with the teacher, he used to send me to ask the grown-up girls. When I came out of the classroom all the girls came around me, as they wanted to know what the teacher's answer was. When I told them what the teacher said to me, they were only laughing as they said that the teacher already knew that they knew about all sexual issues. After all, the grown-up girls explained to me what they were asking the teacher.

I did my test allowing me to start the secondary school in 1960 as it was being done in year five. The test used to be done at the area called Kiruhura. Our teacher called Bitahurugamba took us there but he told us that he would not be in the classroom because he would be in charge of other students. However, he told me that in filling the form I had to choose to be a sister in a Catholic school. That way I would not fail the test. I asked the teacher if to perform well in my test was not enough to pass, instead of filling in to be a Catholic sister. He told me that I should fill it as he advised and change to whatever I wish to after passing the exam. I said to myself that the essential was to answer most of the questions, that was one of the reasons that made me leave my country on 20th October 1961 running away from the mass killings and the burning of houses. Many fled, the young and the old alike. Newborn babies were born on the roadside. Most people thought that they would be back after a few months but I have been outside the country for thirty-four years. I have been in four countries living as a refugee during these thirty-four years. How did I manage to live life as a little girl until I got married and had children? It is a very long journey full of suspense, sadness, joy and discovery.

MY JOURNEY AND LIVING

FROM NYANZA (RWANDA) TO D.R. CONGO

When we left home it was in the evening between 6:00 and 7:00pm. Wherever we went we were walking because we did not have any other option and we were used to walking. The only problem we had was my granny who was not used to walking and she was too old to walk. This made us walk slowly as a way of looking after her but those who were young carried foods to be used in our journey and some mats to sleep on once the grown-ups were tired. As we could not carry enough foods, our parents chose to take only sorghums flour as it could be used to cook porridge and breads. Few other foods were taken but we remembered to take paraffin's lamp and a gallon of paraffin. The lamp was used only if we were walking into darkness as no one had a torch.

My parents did not know where to go as they had two sons who were refugees since 1959 when King Rudahigwa died. When our elder brother called Rusingizandekwe fled to Congo he was nearly cursed as my parents said that there was no reason for leaving the country. His in-laws went forth and took his wife but the family pleaded and they agreed to leave their first boy called Emmanuel Rusingizandekwe. Everybody who left during this period was treated as foolish but they had seen the trouble coming before the great massacre. The other son Mpanumusingo fled to Uganda in 1959, where his uncle Karekezi, and he who came to be his brother-in-law, Ngamije, had fled earlier when the forced work was introduced to Rwanda. They refused to beat others and to be beaten; therefore, they fled towards East Africa. Having people outside made our parents not know which country to go to

1

first, even though there was not a straight choice of the country as many had to walk during the night as they feared being killed. However, because we had a boy, our elder brother, with us, our parents had chosen to pass through Congo before going somewhere else in case Congo was not accepting them.

The only possible way of reaching Congo was to pass by the city of Nyanza, for two reasons. First of all, we had my brother Kambanda who lived there, and there was no way we were to leave him alone, he had to come with us. Secondly, cars were not to be found everywhere in Rwanda as they were very few. That is why we had to go to Nyanza hoping that our younger brother would find us a car that would take us to Congo. In the preparation of leaving, my parents sold a few cows for a cheap price as they knew that the car would need to be paid for. We went at Nyanza without any problem as many knew the way because some studied there and others used to attend the Roman Catholic Church during special Christian feasts such as Christmas, Easter and so forth. After we reached Nyanza, my parents were very thankful for those who advised them to leave and recognised that even those who refused to hide my father were right as we might not be alive if we delayed our journey.

Once in Nyanza we came to realise that many people from all over the country had been coming to seek refuge there. Many who came to Nyanza had varied reasons from each family such as fear, following others or fleeing from serious menace of death and so on. Those who were living on the border with other countries were lucky as they did not have any loss as they were crossing with everything they had. We were taken in to a place prepared for misplaced people. There was clean water to drink and people were free to cook food even though the place was crowded daily and nothing was prepared as far as sleeping was concerned. Each family had to sleep outside and on the soil or on a mat for those who had one. Fortunately for us we had to spend only one night in this common place as our brother took us to his house the following morning. However, we did not last as we feared the worst to happen even though we thought that we would be outside of the country only for a short time. The major problem was the lack of cars to take people where they wanted to go. The transport on at the time was lorries that were very controlled during the day. The only way of going out of the country was to travel during the night. We were lucky as our brother lived at Nyanza and knew a few Arabs who had lorries to hire. These lorries had two conditions: First of all, people had to pay all the money needed in advance. Secondly, the lorry was given a number of people to take; unless the number of people required was complete the lorry was not going anywhere. Therefore, no one had a precise time of going as it was dependent on finding the car.

As I said before, my brother who lived already at Nyanza was commissioned by my dad to find a car as soon as possible that would take us to the border of Congo. It took him only one day to find that car even though they told us that they had many conditions. Indeed, once in the car, there would be no stopping on the road and no smoking at all, and we had to be prepared to travel in the bush. As a child I was so happy to be a refugee as I knew that at least I would discover another country and I would study again and in a foreign country we would be eating like a priest and we would be wearing shoes too. I have seen shoes with priests too, and liked them but can't get them. However, my mum was so sad since we left home. When I tried to ask her why she was sad, the only answer was to tell me that I cannot understand as I was a child, but wandering is bad, especially being a stranger in a foreign country. I told her that we would not be strangers as we would meet our brother. She remained quiet but was seriously worried. Around 7:00pm my dad and my brother came and announced to us that it was time to go. The car was not coming here but they led us in a bush near a road where they told us to sit quietly and the car would come. My dad and all my brothers went, leaving us sitting in the bush. They had spent more than two hours and we began to worry. Among all the people my mum was very worried as she began to say that she wished she was given some money as she could help in case something wrong happened. At that time no woman was allowed to make the decisions of the family as the most important

3

burden of families had to be the man's responsiblilty. While sitting some cars passed and none of them stopped. Then came a car with a lot of noises. We thought that it was the shooting as we had never heard any guns shooting. Mum told us to come in front of her saying that if they should shoot it is better that she died and her children could run away and reproduce again. We began to cry saying that we did not want her to die, fortunately nothing exploded again for at least an hour. Then, a lorry came and stopped closer to where we were hiding. They began to speak but we could not understand as it was a foreign language that afterwards I came to identify as Swahili. When they were talking, we became very quiet because we were very scared thinking that they were coming to kill us. After a while we heard Kinyarwanda and we become interested to follow the conversation. Then, my brother Kambanda called us and we went to the car. Young boys helped us to get into the car. The car stopped four times in order to take other families, then; we were told the regulations to follow all along the journey: no smoking in the car until reaching the final destination. The car would not stop anywhere except where the drivers would change themselves.

Our journey began as the driver said to hold on firmly because we were now leaving. It was a hard journey as the road was too bad with many holes. Only young people were laughing and enjoyed it as they were praising the driver each time the lorry was throwing people each side of the lorry. As for women and children, they were falling all over the place to the level that some began to vomit but the car did not stop at all. Grown-up people began to silence young ones saying that it is not a time of rejoicing but of sadness. They answered that the essential is to be alive and forget all the bad things we are facing. My mum began to tell Kambanda how they heard a shooting and thought that people were shooting at us. My brother told her that it was a tyre puncture on the car that was passing before them. After a long journey, an old lady began to ask for a light as she wanted to smoke. She was told that it was prohibited to smoke in the car and even if they wished, there was no light for a cigarette in the car. She told them that they should be polite instead of lying to her as she could see a big light in front of the car. People began to laugh because she was talking about the headlights of the car. In the end the man in charge of the people on the back of the car agreed to give her the light. Normally they used to smoke tobacco from the garden and it was so strong. Once she inhaled the first smoke, all the people around her began to cough maybe because we were packed the way Kenyan minibuses were packed. For instance, before Kibaki people were saying that a minibus never gets full (matatu). The consequence of the smoking was that many if not all of them began to vomit on people's heads and everywhere. Apart from the smelling of tobacco it was the first time most of the people got in a car. We tried to stop the car but it was impossible because they said that if there was anyone who died it was better to check when they arrived as they could bury him instead of throwing him on the road. We warned you before, said the man in charge, the car has to continue as we can get killed by for stopping. We reached at the region of Gisenyi at dawn. We did not reach Gisenyi as we were left on the way because the driver said he was not allowed to cross the border and was not willing to be known as someone helping Tutsis to flee. He could easily be killed as he could be taken as an enemy of the country. The driver told us to go straight on and we would see the border but he told us that it would be good if we could cross through the bush instead of using the border.

After a while, we began to see those coming out of the car. Some were from the same family but could not know as each one was planning to go quietly without telling others. Each family was hidden in the bush and no one was allowed to talk as we were avoiding attracting or being heard by killers. For example, I met with my cousin called Kantanga who was married and her family but we did not know that they were in the same car. So many people found their relatives, friends and neighbours. Men agreed that they would go first and check if it was easy to cross the border and then they would come to take the women and children and those who were ill as they could run away in case of any attack. Few people came back after twenty minutes and told us that it was not far, we could cross the border without any problem as no one was in the bush. We had used around thirty minutes and yet we were very slow because of old people.

Once we reached Congo, we appreciated the country especially the field that looked green and big, just the place prepared for a lot of herd. The Lake Kivu was fantastic to be seen as we had never seen any lake before. The only problem was young men who were protecting the lake or the city. They were wearing khaki uniforms and were so kind and concerned by our situation. In running away, we were easily categorised in four parts. First of all, there were children like me who knew that we were running away but we were happy as we were discovering a lot of things we could never had a chance of knowing if we were at home. We felt that foreign countries were better than home. Indeed we had seen many beautiful houses that we knew as western houses. At home we had seen very few in our parish but in Congo we saw many, therefore, to be a refugee was good for us as children. Second, we had a group of parents who were crying all along that there was no place like home. We could not understand why they were mourning but they were telling us that we would know what was bad about being refugees in a short time. Lastly, there was a group of old people who did not know why all of that had to happen, why we had to go outside of the country and why the King was not doing anything to prevent people going outside of the country.

As for the children we went far from our parents and began to play. Those young men in uniforms brought to us some bananas that we enjoyed as we were already hungry. As I was very curious I asked my mother who these people in uniform were as they looked strong and similar. I was told that these young men were the soldiers watching for the security of the border. We were desperate to taste the water of the lake in order to know if it was the same as our water. So, I asked one of the soldiers if we could drink the water from the lake. He agreed but told us that no child was allowed in the lake as it could swallow us. He went and brought us some water but we did not drink from it as it was too salty. When we fled we were with an old man who was a gentleman named Kabango son of Ruhilika who used to live at Kibika, which was not far from our village. He fled having a Rwandese hair style called *amasunzu*. He asked soldiers if they could give him a piece of land where he could bring only two cows so that his children could have milk. All of them were laughing as they felt that he did not understand what was going on. Soldiers told the old man to bring his cow and take the land he wanted.

He straight away told one of the young people, "Can you run after that thing that brought us so that I may send them to bring at least two cows." It was explained that it was impossible to catch the car and it was too risky.

We left the border and went towards the city of Goma in Congo. We found other people in another kind of uniform. I was told that they were soldiers even though they were wearing camouflage. This group was not as nice as those we left at the border. We had two problems with them. First of all, they were speaking only French and Swahili and yet very few among us knew those languages. Thus, we did not have enough communication and that became the first thing to tell us that we were now in a foreign country. Secondly, these soldiers were interested in having girls that they wanted to marry and yet we could not let anyone among foreigners as we did not know where we were going. Moreover, Rwandese had their own hair style known as *amasunzu,* that differentiated girls from ladies who married. Before leaving Nyanza, drivers told parents to shave every girl, otherwise they would be harassed on the border and this is what made the soldiers angry as they could not identify any girl. Some were asking if all the ladies were married or can they can have some. All the boys divided all the ladies among themselves to the level that some were claiming three or four ladies to be their wives. Some were showing their sisters and others did not even know each other but they were just protecting every lady who was not accompanied. This was so because we were told that Congolese soldiers were forcing Rwandese girls into marriage. Soldiers were asking why you married many ladies. Is it because you did not want to give us some of your daughters? People told them that it was because they knew that they were going to suffer outside the country, therefore they needed people who will help them to support all the pain.

We were taken to a place prepared for refugees. It was a big house having a big field where children were playing. Grown-ups were just there receiving newcomers and showing us the place. What was strange to me was to see ladies cooking beans outside in a kind of pot I had never seen before. What was very strange was to see that the pots were not even covered and I wondered how beans would be cooked and ready to be eaten. Some of the people found there were people we knew before, therefore, we felt welcomed. They took us inside the house that was too big but seemed to be empty with small bags beside each arranged grasses. They told us that each one had to find a place where he would put his stuff and that would be his place. The next thing was to cut grasses in order to make a bed like others. We were told that wherever you prepare will be your place until you leave for another place or house.

What was good in this refugee house was the unity among all the people and how they were helping each other in everything. For example, no food was provided in this camp but people used to buy everything. Thus, those who came before were showing newcomers around and where to buy what they needed and how much to spend on what they wanted. We were shown where to sit as children and old people, while others who were strong were taken to be shown where to get long grasses that would make a bed. I never knew the rest as I slept while parents were still talking. When I woke up I did not know if I slept only one night or two.

My first evaluation was to know that the camp had many serious problems. First of all, when I asked my mum for milk to drink because normally I liked milk, my mum cried and told me that I had to forget all about milk. When I asked if I could use the toilet, I was told that there was no toilet and I had to go in the bush. The problem of using the bush was that wherever you were trying to use had been used by others. The consequence was that sometimes when you were sitting you found that you were touching *mavi* of others because you could not see what was down as the bush was so high. Moreover, wherever, you stepped was full of *mavi* and yet there was no water to clean yourself. This made people smell and no one had an immediate solution as one could spend days without water. As for old people, they had more problems than other people. For instance, they were ashamed of doing their deed closer to the camp. As they went far, most of the time they were lost and young people were in charge of searching for them. Sometimes they were found in the evening, very tired and hungry. Many people died because of this kind of situation. Those who were the most affected were old people and children even though some young people died as well.

The other serious problem was the cooking. People did not have enough pots to use. People were waiting for those who had pots to finish cooking so that they may use the same pots. It was understandable that some were cooking very late in the night sometimes one pot could go around many families. Imagine the situation of those who had small children without having utensils. Children were crying until their mothers began to cry as well, and this was the beginning of knowing how bad it is to leave your country and home and live in a foreign country. Everything was so strange from what we used to do and worse, the situation seemed not to be addressed, as more people came more hard times we were facing. We were so lucky because we did not last long in that camp. My brother-in-law Kantamage's husband who was there at Goma before us had found a house for my family. His neighbour gave us a house for free as no one rented the house at that time. The house was so nice and had a bathroom inside, first time to see flush toilet that made us forget a bit of the misery we tasted. We remained in that house until we went to find our brother Rusingizandekwe who was living far from Goma. There were young boys organised and in charge of finding separated family. Once they found a family they were uniting them. As for us they told us that our brother lived at Nyabyondo and told us how we could go there. But on the day of our journey Kambanda became very sick and he was admitted to the hospital. Those young people were not discouraged but gave us another week until they took us. We met our brother at Nyamitabo and he took all the family to his place. Once at his home my parents decided to use the food brought from Rwanda as they felt that we were now safe. Unfortunately, all the food was spoiled because the paraffin spilt in the food and no one could eat it. It was sad to think how people carried the food on their heads, at the end it did not help. We all regretted about our sorghum flours as we used it normally for many things such as making porridge, drinks and breads.

I can't explain who organised people as I was just a child but as I keep thinking I presume that politicians did it. For example, was there a group of young people who had to go everywhere Rwandans were settled in order to give them information of what was going on in the country and other part of Africa where Rwandans went to live in neighbouring countries. They used to be the link between families and unaccompanied children. Moreover, they used to tell people where to go and make a good living. That was how many people knew that in Uganda and Tanzania they could live peacefully and find many Rwandans who fled before the King was deposed. This was because people were not settled in one place or region. Even those who had chosen to settle in Congo could not know what was happening elsewhere as Congo was so big. Moreover, that was the only means of communication as no telephones were in use in our part of Africa. They used to walk several miles just to bring news and to know what was going on and sometimes to bring some money that a family may send to their relatives or vice versa. Sometimes by luck they could get transport on lorries. Grown-ups among them used to go to other parts of Congo in order to know what was new and communicate to those in charge when they came. No one paid these people, it was kind of patriotism, if it was paid I should have heard someone say something about it. But they had chosen to help those who newly came from Rwanda as they were lost and were outside of the country for the first time. Indeed, they had done a great job because there was no way people could know how to find their relatives in a big area especially those who were too old and unable to walk. It was these young boys who made it possible for us to meet my brother Rusingizandekwe.

Life was not easy especially in the city of Goma. This city was big and most of the people living in the city were clean and the city itself was clean and had a lot of lights even on the roads. As for me it was a kind of paradise as I had never seen this kind of city in my country. I wished we lived in the city but those who came before us told my parents that the city was expensive and good for those who work.

For example, old people used to struggle as they fled without enough money. Sometimes they used to see young boys who were smart. Old people could approach them and ask, "Young boy do I know you from somewhere?"

When the young man answered politely that it was possible, the old man would ask, "What is your father's name?"

"It is so," he would start, "yes I can guess because you look alike. Do you know, your father was a good man and he was my friend we grew up together? Or we were together in many different things. I hope you are good as well as your father. Where is your father for the moment?"

"He died," or, "he went far," or, "he did not want to live in the city as he had cows, he went to live in the countryside."

After knowing all the information, the old man would tell the young man what he used to do with the father. He could end up by telling him that he hopes he is like his father and say, "Let us go in a quiet place that I have seen." As young people were polite they normally used to accept anything a grown-up said. Once in a restaurant, because that was where the old man was taking the young man, the old man would order meals and drinks and would tell the young man to order as well what he wanted. After finishing the meal, the old man would tell the boy to pay so that they may go.

"Thank you anyway, I can see that you belong to your father and have taken all his character, I appreciate." At that time boys used to spend unplanned money or sometimes they did not have any, therefore, they were forced to leave a jacket or something else that they would redeem once they paid the money back. When the young men discovered that it was becoming a used joke, they changed the game. They agreed to be wearing suits as there were some restaurants in the city that accepted only those who wore suits. When an old man proposed them to go in a restaurant, they told him that they knew a nice place. Once on the door they would accept the young man to get in, not the old man as he did not have any suit. He would explain that he needed to get in because his son was in already but they would ask him to go and wear a suit that he did not have or wait for him when he came out. After waiting for so long as the boy was not willing to come out he would go, and that was how the joke finished because they realised that young men had discovered the trick.

Those who went to live at Bibwe were lucky because the U.N..H.C.R went to their rescue and began to give them what they needed as refugees. People were living by what was given to them without working as they said that they would go back to Rwanda soon, therefore there was no need to waste their strengths. However, after spending some few years the U.N. started to stop some of the help they were giving them, and they started to go and work for food and so on… they began to realise that it was not easy to go back as soon as they thought. Therefore, they began to organise themselves and began to create some jobs. People began to dig and plant foods instead of relying on what few they were receiving as refugees. Moreover, for the sake of their young children, they started to build schools and churches. Those who were teachers back home began to volunteer as school teachers, while others such as Catholic priests and pastors began to teach spirituality in their churches. They thought that it would be good to keep the moral standard of their children and keep their hope high through church teachings. Some found it too difficult and chose to go back to Rwanda as they said that instead of dying as refugees, they preferred to die at home.

After my brother Kambanda came out of hospital we began to plan how to go to my elder brother's place. As my dad kept asking about the elder brother we came to know that he was living in a place called

12

Nyabyondo. There was a lorry that used to go there in order to buy food for selling. We took the van as we were a big family composed with many children and the in-laws, grandmother and ourselves. We were told to stop in a place called Nyamitabo and ask for my brother as he lived not far from this place. Moreover, many people used to meet in that village in order to know some news from Rwanda, or the news of relatives separated or lost. My interest was just to go quickly as I missed my brother and I wanted to see him as soon as possible.

NYAMITABO

On one hand we were happy to go and meet our brother Rusingizandekwe. On the other side we were sad to be separated with the lady who was so good to us. Receiving a family of more than ten people in the city without even knowing them is something to be praised. Apart from having the house that she did not rent, everything else such as electricity and water were to be paid. According to what my parents were saying, she refused us to contribute to any cost except that from time to time we would shop for some food even though she used to give us food as well. I used to sleep with her in her bed. You may think that she was waiting for us to come and therefore, prepared rooms for us.

When we went up in the lorry that took us both of us were so sad. Our lorry was so slow because we stopped many times. We did like it because wherever we stopped, parents were told to buy something to eat for the children. We have eaten many things, they said that it was too cheap compared with what we used in Goma. The journey was long but we were not too tired as we had to stop many times and had a lot of fruit during the journey. The first thing we had seen once in the area was to be a surprise, we met many people not only from our country but also from our neighbourhood. We felt at home as all the people received us very well. It was like when we reached Goma because the people we knew and those we did not know before were kind. In brief, people were very united in this foreign country to the level that those who were worried became calm. Those who received us told us to bath first as they did not have an issue with water and then they gave us meals.

My mother said to one of the ladies, "It looks like you were waiting for us."

The lady said, "We are used to receiving Rwandese and there is no shortage of food in Congo. Have a rest and do not worry, because tomorrow you will have your own house as we will talk to the owner tonight and your son will come soon as he keeps coming regularly to get news from the newcomers."

Most of them had two bedrooms and were built on two lines. We slept. The following morning we were shown houses. All the houses were built on trees and mud: but covered by iron sheets even though few of them had cement on the floor. Separated by a road in the middle that had a lot of dust, each house was facing another. Nyamitabo was a nice place in many ways, such as the view and its mountains that were inhabited. When there was a lot of rain, the mountain could be dismantled and taken away. Probably because the soil was becoming so soft. What is true is that there is not much sunshine in the area. There were a lot of cheap foods for those who used to buy or those who were choosing to work and get given it. Working was easy because they were not given hard jobs. The only problem was to carry the foods and bring them home especially when it was given from the top of the mountain. People were not used to carrying heavy loads and it was a descent that made the knees shake up. Sometimes we thought of letting the loads roll and getting them once down the hill but it was impossible as we needed the food. There was clean water not far from where we lived and to fetch water was one of my jobs, and to keep small children. Sometimes I used to accompany my older sister to buy things we did not have at home. The only major thing we missed was milk as there were no cows around. The only cows we could see were a bit far and people told us that they belonged to a man called Bucyana. All his cows were the same colour and they told us that they were European.

To be in that part of Congo made us forget that we were in a foreign country, because almost every person was speaking Kinyarwanda only and those speaking our language were calling themselves natives of that area. Those people were a mix of Tutsi and

Abakiga, even though Abakiga was the majority. We never believed that we were in Congo as most things there looked like Rwanda. The only thing that reminded us that we were not in Rwanda was that there were no cows around and the area was too green; I never played or visited anybody. The only time I went out was to go and fetch water, or to take care of children. Sometimes I could hear other young girls asking why I did not play with others. There were grown-up ladies and young girls of my age sitting in groups in front of their houses chatting or treading hair. They used to call me to join the group, but most of the time I refused. By curiosity I went to see what they were doing in girls' heads and found that they were just treading. They offered to do it for me but I rejected the offer as we had never done it before back home and I didn't understand yet why they did it. Some thought that my parents were tough on me, but the real reason for not associating with others was to remain with my grandmother, as I did not want to leave her alone in case she wanted something. She was too old and had no strength for going out like others. She was more than happy to see me at her side and I liked how she used to tell me Rwandese culture and how to grow older.

Like many parts of Congo, Nyamitambo had many refugees. People used to fulfil their wishes and make them a reality. Most of the time they used to spread false news among other refugees. Maybe they wanted to be famous or to get very well known as a liar while knowing that they were deceiving themselves. They were so serious, so no one had the idea of questioning them. These people were classified into two categories. First of all, there were old people who were talking because they were *abatesi,* the ones who were spoiled by soft life, and thought that they should not be in a state of being a refugee. Therefore, what they wanted was to go back to Rwanda without any delay. To come up with a date of going back and how they would go was the right thing to spread and no one could oppose their thoughts. They could not believe that they would spend so much time outside of their country. For instance, they used to tell young boys or their children not to buy clothes because they would buy nice ones at home, as they would be going very soon. Some used to say, "Prepare my clothes because I want to wear them next month at home," as if they were sure of their return date.

Secondly, there were scholars who used to invent false news that many people believed and spread so quickly. They used to bring different news but all of them used to say almost the same thing. For example, they could motion the leaders of their party which was seen to be Tutsi's, UNAR (Union Nation Rwanda). They would say that Francois Rukeba went to Kampala to meet King Kigeli as they had to meet Rwangobwa and Mungarulire, then they went to Dar es Salaam as Michel Kayihura was bringing an accord signed by the U.N. that allowed everybody to go back to Rwanda. Everybody should be ready to go back soon. No one questioned how he knew the news, as he did not go away nor had he got a radio. Others, when they saw just a plane passing, they could tell you that, so and so are coming from Brussels and are going to meet in order to take us back home and so forth.

There was a man who said that King Kigeli was given rule of the whole world! No one questioned how it came that the king was given the world without being in his own country. In reality, he listened to the radio in Swahili. As he did not know Swahili properly, he said what people wanted to hear the most. The radio said, 'habari za inchi zote za kigeni', meaning 'news of the world', but he translated the way he wanted. These kind of lies made many poor as they refused to be integrated in the society as they thought that they would soon go back home. They were given a free garden that they refused as they hoped to go no later than a month. Some were given seeds to plant but threw them away or did not plant them properly as they said that in the time it took them to grow, they will be gone already. We came to realise that all news was false after years, then, we began to become humble and settled down. People began to work to the level that some became richer than the natives themselves.

Our house in Nyamitabo had one room and one sitting room and had no cement or any beds. Our bedding was made of grasses that we used to take out early in the morning, so that if we had visitors, they may find a place to sit. This was done in the sitting room where my parents used to sleep with some children. While that room was being used, the other children were still sleeping with my grandmother, including myself. We used to remove the grasses from the room once a week as we did not want to disturb Granny. All visitors used to sit on mats given by friends we met in the village. Once, when I was going to bring children inside the house so that they may eat, I saw a man coming my way. He was tall and very clean so I thought that the man must be rich. When he called me I felt intimated so I went back a bit but stopped as I thought that he may ask me something. Then, he asked me if I was living in the area, I said yes and showed him my home. He asked me if I came recently after my parents came. I told him that all of us came together.

He asked me, "How come I have never seen you, when all others I keep seeing as they have spent enough time here."

"I do not know, but I do live here," I told him.

"What is your name?" he asked me.

"My name is Bamurangirwa," I told him.

"Bamurangirwa who?" he asked.

"Call me that name because the other one is not important as it was not given by my parents."

He was surprise and said, "But you have a Christian name I believe."

"Yes, I have it, but I do not like it because I do not know its meaning." So, I told him that I was taking the children home as they are waiting for them.

He told me that he was the owner of the houses and he knows my parents. "Ask them permission and come back so that we may have a talk, I will wait for you in my garden which is near here," he told me.

Once at home, I asked my parents if after eating I could go and have a talk with the owner of this house. Everybody laughed and asked me, "What house are you talking about?"

"This house we live in," I replied.

They laughed more again and asked, "What are you going to talk with a grown-up about? And how do you know him?"

I told them how I met him and what we spoke about, then, they gave me permission to go and meet him.

I found him in his garden and told him that my parents gave me permission so that I may spend time with him. "Tell me now why you refuse your Christian name and what is that name?" he asked. I realised that he just wanted to know my second name and why I rejected it. I told him that the other name is Patricia.

"You have a very nice name, why do you not like it?" he said.

"This name may be nice for Europeans, but not for us Africans as we do not know its meaning and its origin," I answered.

"I do not understand what you are saying because I have never heard anyone thinking like that before, and yet you are a small kid."

"The reason for rejecting my Christian name is because those who brought those names came with a wrong motive. They said that they came for religious purposes and gave us names but the reality was something else. It was not necessary to give us their names, but what they did was brainwash us. In fact, they told us to have their names so that we may be like them, knowing that it was impossible, and we lost our culture by imitating them," I told him.

He began to look around as if he was searching, ensuring that no one heard what I said. In a low voice, he said that he had never heard anyone criticising religious people. He went far from me, like two metres, and then came back and held my hand. We began to walk without saying anything until we reached a big tree that fell down. He sat down and pulled my hand until I found myself sitting down beside him. Looking at him, he was like someone who was afraid of what I said as people used to look at religious people as holy.

"But where have you been before? Because as I said, I have never seen you before," he asked.

"I am home, but I like to be with my granny because others go out and I do not want her to be alone."

"I did know that you have a granny in the house but do you not feel bored when other children are playing outside?"

"No," I said, "because no one forces me, I just choose to be with her."

"The old man and his wife are your parents or relatives?" he asked me.

"They are my parents," I answered.

"How come you have these kinds of thoughts when you have parents?"

I smiled and told him, "It is because I have parents who can teach me."

He replied, "I am not saying that your parents are not intelligent, but people say that orphans grow quickly in their thinking."

"I am not intelligent, I am the youngest amongst all my family so all of them are my teachers," I told him.

He began to tell me his life as if he forgot that I was just a small kid. He said, "I came when I was a grown-up even though I was not married. I came with my uncle who did not want to be chief of the village because it was too demanding and he did not want to get involved in the Rwandese system at the time. The natives did not live in one place but I have chosen to remain in this place since I came. I spent much of my time working in the garden and building these houses you live in. All my family have been baptised and me as well. I am surprised to meet someone who is not happy about religion and yet you are just a small kid. I am not sure if you can tell me why you do not like religious people."

"Wait," I told him, "because I need to tell my parents that I am still with you in case they want me."

I went and told my parents that I was still with the man in case they wanted me. They told me that it was no problem, I could be with him as long as he wanted. Then, I went back to the man who told me that I was so quick. "But did you tell them who you are with?" he asked.

"Yes, I told them that I am with the owner of the house," I answered him.

"I refuse to let the house be my name, like you who refuse your name, my parents did give me my name too," he went on, "my name is not my house." He told me his name which I don't remember. He asked me if my sister was at home and if I could call her. I went running and told my sister Kantamage that the man wanted to talk to her. She asked me what it was about. I said that I did not know, as I did not ask him. She stood up and came with me.

"I think you are asking yourself what I am doing talking to a small girl like this. I was happy to listen to her as it was like being at school according to what she was saying." My sister began to laugh without saying anything. Then, he told my sister to follow him so that he may show her a garden where she could get anything we wanted at home, all the time we lived in the village.

"Wait until he comes back," she told me.

I was sitting there waiting for him. When he was back he asked me if he took too long, I said not. He began to talk to me as someone talking to his friend, not a stranger talking to a child.

"I have just shown your sister a garden of sweet potatoes and yams," he said. "My children will be bringing to you some beans and I think this can help any Rwandese to live."

"Thank you so much," we said.

"I can see that your family is rich because no one can run away with a big family like yours if he has no means," he said.

He sat down again and asked to tell him what made me hate the church. I said, "Without accepting the church we would not be refugees and I could be in school. What I have discovered is that you have to accept everything white people say otherwise you will be in trouble. The religious people are the ones leading our country, or police to their masters, and yet they are foreigners."

"Until now, I did not understand what you were saying as you are talking like proverbs," he told me.

"Ask my dad as he can explain better than I do," I said.

"I will definitely talk to him but you can tell me what you know as well."

"Most of the time I kept questioning why these people were allowed to bring their gods because we knew who God was as we used to worship Ryangombe, and knew that God is above anyone and everything. I do not know why they have allowed them to lead us without knowing who they are and their real plan. If they did it in the way they were telling us, by now we could have still our king and our peace in our country. Once I asked my mother why they just followed them so quickly. And my mother told me that white people did not give them time to know them, as they imposed everything once in our country. They taught us that we don't know how to pray and even if we do, we invoke a false God. We were deceived and accepted their God, thinking that they knew better than we imagined. It was easy for them because they knew our language and our culture. Therefore, it was a matter of time to take advantage of us."

Then, I told him the story of Kayondo and Nturo, where one time in Nyanza both were invited by priests to show them a film according to their Catholic religion, they showed them pictures of angels, Jesus Christ and his mother Mary, after they showed them Shitani, as they were calling it.

According to these two men, Nturo and Kayondo, on the way back they were discussing what they saw, when Nturo told Kayondo that the priests were saying the truth all along, when they were telling them that Jesus and his angels are good, and Shitani and his followers are bad. "Have you seen how they are beautiful, with good dresses, and what Shitani and his followers look like? How they can scare anyone?" Nturo said. That is when Kayondo told his friend to wait when Shatani's followers came, and hear their side of the stories too, at this time they can't know which is behind all of these stories. At this time we can be too quick to judge with stories of one side, we don't know what happened between those men or where they came from, and we don't have any reason why we can believe everything they told us.

He began to laugh but at the end he began to think about it. He said, "I think I need to research about what you are telling me and observe seriously Catholic priests and religions in general. Do you mean if you are given a place of being a sister or your brother to be a priest you can't accept? On one side it is not good to send someone you love to work with these people because it will put him or her into a prison and only work for them, but on the other side it will be good to be with them so that we may know them as well. It is a way of becoming a scholar and gaining wisdom from them as they have what we do not have in terms of wisdom, we too have what they don't have. It is like opening a door that will help to disorganise their government in case there are those who do not fear them. Some may even make themselves stupid so that they may become good spies. In terms of African wisdom, elders keep saying that, you need to be far from your enemy, but if you are able it is good to be closer to your enemy. This helps because he can't kill you the way he wants or when he wants as you keep watching his movement." Then, he told me, "I feel like I am in a school even though I have been baptised I think you have your own reasons for hating the religions but maybe especially the Roman Catholic Church. I wish to see you when you are a grown-up in order to know your life and what you are doing."

That was the end of our chat as I went home leaving him sitting in the garden. At home they were still talking about him and how he was helping us.

After a few days I saw our landlord coming towards me. I was waiting so that I may greet him but behind him I saw someone who looked like my brother Rusingizandekwe. I began to tell to myself loudly that he looked like my brother but at the same time I realised that indeed it was him. I jumped on him while crying so that everybody at home heard me and came running as well. Since he left home he had never written any letter. We never believed that we would meet him again. I was beside him as he went around greeting others to the level that I forgot to greet our landlord. When I looked towards him he was happy looking at what we had been doing and how happy we were. I went to greet him as well, "You have seen your brother and have forgotten me," he said.

I told him that I did not forget him but I was so surprised to see him. You can see that even grown-ups reacted like me. All of us entered the house together and began to talk and ask him some questions. He told us that most of the times he used to meet our landlord because he knew newcomers, as people looked for him so that he may give them houses to rent. On that note, he said that he was going so that we may talk to our brother. "Let one of you come with me so that I may give him food for your visitor," he said.

My dad offered to go with him, "Let them remain doing other works," he said.

We remained and asked him several questions but I never went far from him since he came. As far as I was concerned I did all of my jobs before he came. In fact, I had fetched enough water and we had enough firewood for cooking and the children were sitting with us. The rest of the jobs belonged to my sisters and my mum. Therefore, I was asking many questions until my mum told me to stop because others wanted to talk to him as well. "You would think you had a place where you kept questions to ask him when you saw him," she said. My brother told her to let me talk because I would get tired and questions would stop. That is how it happened because I was tired and began to ask Mum if there was some work so that I could help but there was nothing for me to do.

The landlord's children found us in the same place he left us. They had a big jug of 'Urwagwa' (alcohol made from banana) and a basket full of beans. They said that our dad sent these for the visitor but we would not sit as we had things to do. Mum told them to thank their dad so much on her behalf, so they left. This kind of beer was well known in the area of Burundi, Tanzania, Eastern of Congo Rwanda and Uganda where it is made in a factory and is known as 'Uganda waragi.' It was one of the beers that was much esteemed in the village and was made for grown-up people as it was strong. They continued to drink until my dad came. They began to talk about our landlord saying how he was a good guy full of mercy. At this point my brother began to tell us about his journey.

He informed us that he lived a bit far away in a place called Nyabyondo and he came to take us so that we may live together. My dad asked how the place was.

He said, "It is a long story but it is a good place with a lot of food even though there are no meats, and you can't find peanut so that you can make a sauce, but people do not care. The natives don't live in one place as they move a lot. They live in the same houses like these except that they are covered by grasses and are round. If you find an empty house you can live in it without paying and no one will ask you. They speak Swahili and Hunde. There are bushes everywhere made of bananas, yams and trees but there are no animals. These bananas and yams have no owners. If you decide to live in place everything you find there belongs to you, and no one claims anything."

"Are you serious? You can dig and reap in garden for free?" all of us asked at once.

"No one digs in garden because everything such as bananas and beans grow by themselves, your work is just to reap," he told us.

We told him that if what he is saying is true, there should be vegetables somewhere. "It is possible," he said, "but I have never seen vegetables, but there are lots of bananas of three kinds. Some we mix with beans, some we make bread with and others we make beers and we have plenty."

"Tell us how you can make bread from bananas?" we asked.

He said, "They put banana in the sun until it is dry; then, they make flour from it that they use in making a kind of bread which you eat when it is still fresh. This bread has no taste and you do not need even to struggle in mashing because once in the mouth it goes itself, it is called 'ubuliga'."

"It is understandable that it does not not taste because banana itself has none," said my dad.

"In that village, the only drink is from banana and we drink tea but there is no milk as they do not have cows and no sugar," he replied.

"That is why they do not have meat," said my dad. "Lack of meat affects only Rwandese not the natives."

"Why?" we asked.

"They go hunting and every animal killed is meat and they get fish in the water."

We asked again, "You mean they do not choose what to eat as far as animal is concerned?"

"Correct," he said, "imagine that they eat rat and when they find chenilles in trees they praise God, in the river they catch even crabs and eat them."

"What is that?" I asked, as we never used to fish.

"It is something small that is hard and has many legs," he answered.

When he saw that we were surprised he went on, "They dig even mountains in order to catch forums which they eat as well, moreover, they eat snakes and monkeys."

All of us swore at the same time and Grandma asked him, "Did you share food with those kinds of people?"

"Grandma, can we despise people who accept us in their own country instead of them despising us? Since you are not yet Guhumana (a kind of skin disease she thought they might get because of mixing with them), you will not get any sicknesses at all." Then he said, "There are no shops in that area. Therefore, you do not wash with soap or eat salt. We do have things we need because that area has tea plantations and people come to sell what we need. What is good is that each family has someone working in the plantation."

My brother Kambanda asked, "What do they do exactly in tea plantations?"

"They plant tea, dig in there or reap and others work in the factory. The only problem that we have is to get clean water. This is because people piss in the water and wash themselves in the same water."

"Do they, women and men wash together in the same water?" I asked.

"Both," he said.

"How can a grown-up go in the water and mess up?"

"The grown-ups are the ones going in deep water as they can swim," he told us.

"Is it the same water that they fetch and use for the cooking?"

"Of course yes, they believe that because their river flows, it takes away unclean stuff, but many among them have *ubuheri* skin problems and I think it is the consequence of unclean water and what they eat."

My older sister, who usually was a person of few words, asked why the people can't dig toilets.

"Maybe if the government teaches them they will do it, but for the time being they do not have any toilets. What is too surprising is when they see those shits while fetching water; they push aside with their hand so that they may have water. Moreover, when women give birth they take a big jug to the river so that they may have a bath. Then, they fetch water in the jug and take it back home."

"Where they get the strength to go to the river and fetch water?" my mum asked.

"Even our ladies ask them the same question, but they laugh at them saying why should we not have the strength when we have already been separated by the weight of the child?"

My dad said, "Those are real women instead of ours who have been spoiled." We had a general laugh but we were thinking quite a lot about the issue of water so that anyone could see on it our faeces.

We asked him if they had accepted that kind of situation to the level of settling down. He told us, "For us, we do not use the river's water because we have chosen to use waters from wells."

All of us were relieved and said, "Well water is so wonderful."

He said quickly, "The only problem is that the wells are on a mountain, the problem is when it rains and it rains most of the time, the place becomes so sliding only children fetch water there."

I said straight away that I would be fetching the water each time. They began to laugh but I am not sure if they were happy or it was just a way of thanking me. Then we asked if there was Rwandese in that area.

"You may think that we live in Rwanda," he replied, "but all of them come just to make money and then leave for another place or another country. I think it is right because no one can live in a place like that except for natives."

We left all questions aside and began to ask him about the journey and how to plan it. "Talk about the journey tomorrow, as he seems too tired," Mum told us. We agreed and he slept.

27

Early in the morning we began again to talk about the journey. My brother told us, "There are some lorries that can take us there but no one knows when to get one as it can take one week or a month but if we decide to walk we can be there in two or three days"

Because of Grandma and Kambanda who was recovering, my dad asked if we could have places to sleep in case we were tired.

"Yes," he said, "because natives are so good and give houses to anybody when he is a traveller. Therefore, it is good to go because since we came I have never seen any car passing by."

All of us agreed, "Tell us only the day we should be ready," we said.

He said, "We are not waiting for anything else, let tomorrow be the day of telling our neighbours and thanking our landlord, then, the following day we will go."

We did as we said and began to tell everybody that we were leaving tomorrow. We told our landlord as well and we offered money for the rent. He refused by saying, "Use the money for your journey as you will need it." He told us that he would give us banana juice that we could use on the journey. We were very sad to be separated with our kind landlord as he treated us as his own brothers and sisters, but we had to go.

THE JOURNEY TOWARDS
NYABYONDO

We were used to waking up early in the morning and when we were told that we were leaving very early, we decided to clean the house before going, which we did. This journey was simple compared with the previous because my older brother told us not to be overloaded with many things as we would be given what we needed once we were there. We had already given away almost everything we had and began our journey. We were advised to walk slowly because of Grandma who could not follow our quick walk. Kambanda and Rusingizandekwe could understand a bit of Swahili while I had learned French at school even though I did not like it and my French was not that good but could talk.

In the dawn we were already far and we began to meet other travellers on the road. In all the stories that my brother told us, he forgot to tell us everything in detail. We were surprised to meet grown-up people men and ladies semi-naked. They did not wear anything at all apart from a small piece of cloth that seemed to hide their private parts only. It was very strange for us to see a lady having her breasts uncovered and all of the legs being uncovered even though it was the same for men. Our first idea was fear, thinking that they were mad people. "They are normal," our brother told us, "it is just their style for those who have a long journey." Kambanda and I began to laugh and to look at them closely. Grandma and Mum told us not to laugh as they believed that they were witches, and by laughing at them we were running the risk of being killed. What was worse was to meet a fat lady, or a lady who was pregnant. Most of the time, they were having heavy loads on their backs, which seemed to be supported by their big bumps. The baskets longer than themselves were held by ropes on both sides that were round and tied on the head. In order to maintain the loads right it was necessary for them to bend a bit and that made us laugh as we looked behind them.

The other thing that surprised us was the loads a lady could carry. These were pieces of wood, the same size as if it were done by machine. However, it looked like whole trees in pieces that the ladies did carry and some had children on the chest. We could not imagine a strong lady among us carrying a half of it. Rusingizandekwe told us, "Every lady goes in the bush to cut the trees. After the tree is fallen she will cut it in small pieces that she will carry on her back. Even if there is no one to help them carry the loads they will still carry it as they have their own way of doing it. However, anyone could like them as they were so willing to help anybody, and were naturally full of love."

In summary, it was a lovely journey for us who were young but for grown-ups, especially our grandma, it was a hell as everything was strange and she was not used to walking a long distance. She was normally a quiet lady and did not complain even though she was at the limit of her strength. In looking at her, I remembered what my mum used to tell me that to be a foreigner was a bad thing.

On the other hand we were looking at the country we were reaching as a paradise, as we could see big land that had never been touched and the possibility of developing big agricultural farms. The land looked like it was always green as if they had never known sunshine. Moreover, the people were so friendly to the level that we loved Congo just for that. All along the road they were giving us banana alcohol. As there was not a soft drink we were given alcohol to drink as well even though they were saying that it was strong. But they could not let us suffer from thirst. The consequence was that all children were drunk and parents too, but for us it was a fun journey that we enjoyed more than all other journeys.

We had reached a village called Gashebeli where they decided that we would have a rest and therefore spend the night there. There were a lot of western cows in that area; therefore, we enjoyed a drink of milk after a long time as the only thing they gave was milk. They also had clean water from the tap and were really civilized, but we did not stay as we had to go where my older brother lived.

We continued our journey and nothing changed as we still had alcohol all the way. There was only one straight road that made children run far from us but we did not care as we were told that cars could pass after a long time, even months, in order to take tea as there were many tea plantations in the area. We were told as well that people were kind towards children, so we were not prevented to run. When the grown-ups were tired, Rusingizandekwe told us that we were no longer far and he showed us some mountains saying that we were going exactly to those mountains. As there were many corners sometimes we could not see children. Suddenly we heard many people talking that made us worried. I began to run towards the children as I felt that I was the sharp one despite the drunkenness. I found all the children sitting surrounded by grown-ups who were so smart, looking at their clothes. All of them were wearing very clean shorts and shirts that seemed new to me. It was quite a long time since we had met people wearing clothes. There were around six people asking the children questions. All the children were discharging themselves in the road to the level that you may think that they were in a competition. All the way they did not do it because they used to ask us permission and we used to take them in the bush, but I concluded that it was the effect of alcohol.

As I was the first to reach that place it was necessary to talk to those people. They were talking Swahili that I could not understand a word, but I thought that they may speak French, then, I began to talk knowing that I was making mistakes but I was forced to talk. My parents came but I continued to talk my French so that they would understand that at least I was clever as they did not know any word of French. After a while I informed them that my brothers spoke Swahili. At this point they began to talk to my brothers and welcomed us in

31

the area. We thanked them and continued our journey but everyone was praising me as I spoke a western language. It did not take long before we reached my brother's place. Except for my granny and Kambanda, the rest were not tired. The first thing we discovered was that all Rwandese did not mix with the natives as they had their own place distinct from Congolese. Everybody from Rwanda was living like brothers and was helping each other.

We were very well received and found that they had prepared everything needed including cooked foods. As they saw us being surprised, they told us that they knew that my brother had found us because normally he never took long but he told them that if he took longer that would mean that he had found his family. He told them that because of the old people, he would give them at least two or three days of recovery before starting the journey. This would take him at least one week and that is how it happened and that is why they were able to cook for us.

People we met there came from different part of Rwanda, but they received us as familiar people. We did not sleep all the night except for Granny and Kambanda who were not feeling well. We were talking about our journey and what we faced and how we behaved in several situations. Each one had his own experience, some made us laugh others were very sad and made the parents tell all children to go and sleep. It was not a lovely place, especially for children and grown-up people because they were ill several times. Maybe it was because we had never had varieties of foods that could help the body to fight sicknesses, therefore, many were dying.

After Kambanda was healed he chose to go back to the city of Goma together with my sister Kantamage. She left behind three children namely, Rwikaze, Batsinduka and Rwabukambiza. Rusingizandekwe Emmanuel son to my brother Rusingizandekwe went to his parents, his home was not far from ours. Mpanumusingo and Kankuyo were in Uganda that is why my father decided to go and see what Uganda looked like, having in mind that we would have to leave this area. My mum became worried as she became responsible for the family without any man around, Kantamage and Kambanda went too. I told her not to worry, there was nothing I hated like seeing my mother being sad in any way. So I told her that we had the wife of my brother Rusingizandekwe, who was so good. She used to say that her in-laws were perfect family to her like her, Mum and Daddy. I told my mum that two of us would be able to take care of young children.

The area was slippy to the level I used to fetch water four times before I reached home because all the way I would slip and pour out all the water.

There was a banana tree which was rooted and was almost everywhere down there, and there was mud too, all of that was bad for slipping but the banana tree was worse than the mud, because it took me from the top until when I reached the banana tree to stop me. Sometimes when slipping made me become late I was angry, but for who? For nobody. And at the time I did not see it as funny.

Our area had no free food, we had to go to work for it, but the work was simple, and you would be given a lot of food, but the problem was to carry it in that slippery situation, so I had to go with someone to help me in case I fell down. One day my mum wanted to go with me and I refused as I didn't wanted her to fall down, before it was brother's responsibility to know what we would eat, but the time came when I thought that I had to take over and be responsible, and let him look after his family. Yes I knew that my mum was happy with everything I was doing and that is what I wanted to see her happy, but on other side, my mum was sad because she saw that I was doing too much concidering my age, she saw that I had no time to be a child. Many times she was complaining telling me that I carried too much. I was killing myself. I was telling her that was OK with me, when I knew that was not OK.

Sometime after, I had to put what I was carrying down as I was feeling dizzy and had to go quickly to hide myself from Mum and start vomiting. I felt that I was going up in a slow motion way, like if something inside me was pulling me up, I felt like that inside my body. I knew that was because what I was carrying on my head was too heavy for me, something I couldn't tell my mum, and something which I would do again and again. I knew if she knew that, it would kill her, she wouldn't be happy at all, to see her last born do that, because of her, and her grandchildren, who still had their parents.

After the problem of fetching the water, I told my sister-in-law to leave it for me, that I would take that responsibility for them too. I believed that any grown-up person if they fell down it would be a big problem, to me it was not like that, this made them happy, both Mum and them.

One day I asked my mum's permission to go with my sister-in-law to see how they did the tea plantation, where they were working. Men were digging, while women were reaping it, so my Mum gave me the permission.

There I asked them, if I too could reap with them. They told me that it was no problem, I was inside the tea plantation with them, and I did it, helping my sister-in-law. Back home Mum was worried to see that I took a long time to come back compared to what she was expecting, but I came with firewood from there, and I told her that I was helping my sister-in-law, and she said that was no problem.

There I saw other children my age who were working with their relatives, since I had never seen or heard anything like school there, there was nothing else they had to do. I told Mum that I saw children reap the tea leaves, and asked if she would let me go and work too, so that we could buy small things for ourselves which Rusingizandekwe was buying for us, and I could go to work for food on weekends, fetch our water in the morning time, and for Rusingizandekwe's home at evening time, she said that if I think that I can, then there was no problem.

That is how I started to work, we had to wear plastic paper behind our dress, or torn clothes, because when we reaped the tea, the inside of the tea trees was making the dress become very wet and easily torn. We had to put the big long basket behind our back in its holder with rope which was on our head, the way they carried all of their things, especially women.

We were packing some food to take with us, I became used to

34

taking care of my family and it seemed that I was the head of family, Rusingizandekwe raised his family. At home when I was home I wanted to help Mum with everything, we had clean water more than many in that area, but when we fetched it in our container, the water was going dirty from the top of mountain because of the raining.

One day all of my sister's children got skin disease only on their hands, 'ubuheri', and I saw that it made Mum feel very sorry for them and she was uncomfortable, she was using warm water and using some piece of small clothes to clean them, so I had a very foolish idea. I thought that I would help her, when she was not there I wanted to do it quickly before she came back. I planned to clean the children to the point that they became better there and then, I wanted to give her a good surprise. Since I always saw her use warm water to clean them, I thought that if I could use hotter water then they would be cured at once!

I boiled water then I gave them orders to go to the line. I got the piece of small clothes, the first one came and since I was not able to touch the water for a long time I had to do it in a quick way, because it was burning me! But I still thought that they had a problem and it would be cured! The children had to follow the order, and I was excited the way I was going to surprise my mum when she came back and saw that her grandchildren were cured! So I burned them one by one, they were crying a lot and instead of being better, all their hands were burned so they had wounds!

I was surprised to see the result of what I did. Mum was shocked, when she came back, when I told her why I did it, and how I did it in a quick way because it was burning me. I explained everything, that I also wanted her to see that they were cured when she got back. She laughed at that, she said that I didn't have to worry, because she saw that I was too worried.

But after a few days they were OK, and Mum was making fun of it by saying that to take care of burns was better than that kind of skin problem that they had before.

After few days, first my sister Kantamage came back from Goma, and soon our father also came back from Uganda.

We were happy to get them back, he told us how he got Kankuyo and Mpanumusingo with their family, and how he saw life there, he told us that both Mpanumusingo and our brother-in-law Ngamije, Kankuyo's husband, were working in Masaka Hospital, our brother-in-law was manager in department of cleaners, and Mpanumusingo was head of electricians in the kitchen department, to me they had a better life there, he told us that they were very happy to hear that we were still alive.

Big problem there was in Nyabyondo was the kind of food we could get, it was poor and couldn't help old people and young ones under ten years. So because of that, Rusingizandekwe's son whom they had soon after they reached there, Rutagand, was three years old when my father came back from Uganda, he had already passed away, caused by poor food. And their daugther Mukakimenyi who was still breast feeding, also was not in good shape, because her mum had nothing in her breast to feed her. So the food there, was just to eat so that you felt that your stomach was full, but full with nothing to help your body.

I felt very bad to see that even their daughter might die and I thought that I had to do something to save her. I had an idea, there was another tea company which was far from where we were, they liked to work where we were working because it was near. I had the idea of going there because that company was more rich than where I was. I heard that that company had a hospital and car in case their patient needed to be taken to the big hospital in Masisi. You could buy whatever you wanted from there, even things which were also not easy to get anywhere, like soap, salt, just small things, so I thought that maybe they could help my family in the way of medication. With hope that my parents would allow me to move there, when I told them about my idea they were happy, but on other hand worried if I could manage by myself to go all the way every day.

"Yes," I told them, "that is no problem."

They would not refuse anyone who wanted the job, what you had to do was just go to the director of the group, and talk to him. When I reached there the director was a Rwandan man. He registered me and told me to start. I was dressed like them, the women there, they were almost half naked just covering their chest and short skirt which their stomach was outside, which I thought to be the fashion, the money which was left from what I bought was given to Mum to keep. Money did not mean anything much, only to foreigners who wanted to save for their journey when the time came.

After a few days they started to give us milk at 10:00am, they were boiling powder milk in a big container and all of the staff had to go and be given milk to drink. First day I went home and told my sister-in-law to get me a bottle, I thought that I would ask the man who cooked it for us, who also was Rwandan, if instead of drinking mine, he would give it to me so that I could take it back to Mukakimenyi. My sister-in-law give me the bottle and when the time of having our milk came, I took the man aside and asked him if he could give me the milk I had to drink to take it home, he looked surprised and confused, he had to ask me again and again. I told him the same thing; he asked me why I chose not to drink the milk there like everyone?

I told him that we had a child who was sick at home, he seemed to be sorry and felt sympathy for me, I think he thought about a child of my age having that idea of sacrifice for others. He told me that was OK, I could drink with the others as much as I wanted, and he would be giving me some to take home too, and he asked me if I had anything with me to take the milk home in. I showed him the bottle I had which was like one litre.

One day this man who cooked milk, called me and took me aside, and asked me, "Now you have seen how we cook the milk here, if I gave you powered milk, could you show home how they should cook it?"

I said yes, then he told me to tell home to give me something which he could put it in for me: at that time Mukakimenyi was started to change and look much better.

I went home very happy that all of my family were going to start drinking milk, when I told them this good news, all of them were very happy but then the problem came to be something to take to carry this powered milk!

They tried even the neighbours, but nowhere had something which was suitable to put milk, and I believed them, because they needed this milk. Being people whom their culture was farming cows, they knew how good milk was to their health in general.

The pots they had were big and turned black and had nothing to cover them, no plates, we were eating using big wider things where many times we were sharing, no cups they saw that things we were using to drink water were not good enough for that. After trying very hard they got a small cup and they washed a piece of cloth to cover it, and I took that one. When I gaves it to the man who cooked the milk, he asked me if they could get something big. I said, "Yes, they tried but can't find anything big than that." He looked to be sad for that; he started to give me milk every day.

After some time my grandmother was not well and I told them that it would be better if her and my mum could share milk with Mukakimenyi, something which Mum and Grandma refused by saying that it was better to let it be for the child only. Mukakimenyi was becoming better and better every day, after a few days, when I was on the bed holding my grandmother trying to give her something to drink she was not drinking and she wasn't talking, when I told my mum she came and put her back to sleep and she announced to me that my grandmother had passed away. I was very sad because she was my best friend; she passed away because she had no proper food to help her.

Where I was working started to give us salt, soap, tea leaves and sugar for free, because I had this for free now, and since I thought that I knew something concerning health, I thought that if Mum would drink tea with lots of sugar and with a lot of tea leaves inside, it would help her, and if she used a lot of soap when she had a bath. I believed that all of this would help her to be better. But she went ahead by refusing to share her granddaughter's milk, this was the mentality of the old people at the time, that the young ones were more important than them. Sometimes when I was telling her things like that she would just laugh and thank me, but on the other hand she was looking sad, when I asked her what the problem was, she had never told me what it was. Maybe because she knew that I couldn't do anything for it, she was sad to see where she was in that bush of Nyabyondo, and see that life there was too poor and maybe she also saw that her life was ending, and the thought of leaving me there in that bush at the age I was. Even though I had other family members, I was sure like any normal parent, she would like to guide me, until I had my own family.

I was sure she had doubt if she would be able to manage to survive and be able to reach Uganda to meet her other children after it was a long time since she was with them. I heard her telling my sister that she couldn't say what she wanted, because there was nowhere we could get it from, and my sister when I asked her said that it was fresh milk from a cow, she wished to have her life back, the life she used to have. She had hope that if she reached Uganda she would be alright, I wanted others to help me to force her to share milk with Mukakimenyi but they didn't, maybe because they knew that she couldn't, so we were almost ready to prepare ourselves to start the journey to Uganda.

My daddy told us that was a good country and they had a good life and Mum was saying that even if she could see her children and die after, she could die happy Mother. I came to realise that my mum was more worried about me, maybe because I was her last born who was still young. After hearing that her children in Uganda had a good life, she had big hope that as soon as I would be with my elders in Uganda, I would be alright in all ways. One day I heard her tell Kantamage about it. But the journey had to be postponed because of relatives who wanted to go with us.

After few days my mum started to be sick and weak, I was reminding my sister a lot of sugar and tea leaves and to use a lot of soap but when I was asking what also had to be done they would laugh at me but not fun laugh or happy one, it was sad smiles. I saw that there was a problem, but when I asked them what I could do, Mum was always telling me that I was doing more than enough, what I did was only what I could. When she started to be so weak I asked all of them including her if where I was working would say yes to admit her to the hospital would it be OK? All of them said that it could be OK.

Next morning I went to work as usual, but I had to ask where the office of the manager was before starting to work, I wanted to go to tell him about my mum and ask him if he could help her.

I got where the office was and outside was many people, the office was where the factory was, and all of the people there were dressed well, no one was in that small piece of old cloth which is only between their legs, 'urubindo', and I was dressed in my dress I work with, which was half dressed like the others there. I had my long basket on my back which I used to reap the tea leaves with, which was past my head and down my bottom. There was only a small part of my legs which you could see, if you were behind me, meaning that if you came from behind me from far, when I was walking, you could think that was that basket which was walking. Now I asked the staff where I could get the manager and they showed me his office.

I knew that both my names were hard to the people there, one day I said that my names were not easy to primitive people, in Kinyarwanda. Which made 'capitan', our director, that is the name we were calling him, the name of his position, he laughed a lot saying that he didn't know that I could be a comedian if I wanted to. But when they asked him what I said, he told them something else.

So I was not worried how I would talk with the manager, I told myself that if I was going to be able to make him know how to say my names then other things would be easy.

I stood outside of office, and after some minutes one of the man came out and asked me my problem, but before I answered him I asked him if he was the one who was manager, and he told me that was not him. I asked him if manager was there, he said, "Yes, he is inside." He tried to ask me to instead tell him, that he too could help me. I told him that if he was not the manager then I was not going to tell him, because it was only him I came to talk too.

He smiled a little smile, and told me to wait, that they would call me. His smile was like to tell me, you a little girl, half dressed with a basket which is bigger than you, how can you try to choose between officers? What difference do you know between us anyway, and in general how much do you know? I see that you are just a little girl who knows nothing and now you are here trying to surprise me by arguing with me. Try to tell me that you know a lot!

After few minutes, they called me and I was inside the office, the man who was outside was the one who showed me who the manager was, because there were three men, the manager of that factory was a dark young man, tall, slender, very smart, he welcomed me with a wider smile. If he had not sharpened all his teeth he was very handsome, but that was my view, to them I thought that might be part of beauty or culture.

He seemed to be a good person, the way he welcomed me with a smile and he showed me where to sit, in general according to his position, we knew people like him to be ignorant to small ordinary people like me who were in front of him, if he wanted to, I could be nothing, nobody at all. He was opposite of where I was sitting, he showed respect to me, maybe he was happy to see a small girl who could insist only to see him because he was the one who she came to see!

"What do you want me to do for you?" he asked me.

I told him, "I am a worker in your factory, and my parents they are old, now my mum is very sick, if your factory can help my mum by giving her treatment?"

"Look girl, they are no reasons why this factory can't give your mum the treatment needed, tell me now where you are, they are on the road so that I can give you a car and take her to the hospital, and if you want to take her to Masisi too, I will take her now," he answered

I thanked him so much, but I told him that where we were was too far from the road, but people were going to carry her and take her to the hospital. About taking her to Masisi, it was not me who could make that decision, but when I had asked my elders if they chose to take her to Masisi, then I would come back and tell him.

He said that there was no need to come back, he was going to write a letter which I would take to the hospital when I took her, and if my elders chose to take her to Masisi then they would take her from there, because he would tell them about it too in the letter.

41

Where we were was between the bush, they chose to take her to the hospital near there, since Masisi was far and transport was a problem, to visit her can't be easy, she was admitted in hospital the same day.

It was my father who stayed with her, others were just visiting her every day, and I would see them in the morning before I went to work, and evening when I got home, all the time when I asked her how she felt she was telling me that she felt alright, and since it was me who was seeing her after others went back home, they were asking me how I left her, and always I was telling them that she was OK, because that is what she told me.

One day when I reached home they asked me how she was, and when I told them that she was OK, I saw that they were surprised and I asked them why they looked to be surprised, they told me that when Rusingizandekwe come back from the hospital to see her, he told them that she was not well, then I was confused, because I knew that she told me that she felt good.

Next morning when I went as usual before I went to work, I had to talk to her first, but this time she looked like she was sleeping, when I asked my daddy he told me that the whole night she didn't sleep, so I said if she didn't sleep, then, let me not disturb her, I would talk with her in the evening.

I went to the other patients around to say hello to them, there were few others in that room and I said hello to them too when I was there to see my mum.

Evening time when I came back she was awake and I went straight to where she was, and I greeted her, but her voice was weak so I had to put my head near her to be able to listen, I asked her how she felt and she told me that she was OK, but this time the way she was talking, made me doubt if she was OK as she was telling me. I asked myself why her voice was weak and she spoke slowly! Then she asked me why I didn't talk to her in the morning.

I told her that my daddy told me that she was just sleeping since she didn't the whole night, and I didn't wanted to wake her up. I asked her how she knew and she told me that she saw me go around talking to others, but couldn't call me back, then I thought that she might be in bad situation, but how was not understandable to me. She looked to be too beautiful, more than I had ever seen her, and she was sweating a lot too. All of that was confusing to me. I didn't want to believe that she was in a bad situation because I didn't want her to be in it, I asked my daddy if I could spend the night with them, and he told me that was impossible because they did not even have something to cover myself, I didn't want to leave her so I slept with her, she was sleeping and when she woke up and saw me in front of her she was asking me why I was still there.

"I don't want to go and leave her but they refused me to spend the night there," i told her. She said that they were right and I had to go.

I asked her if she forgave me because I didn't talk to her in morning. And she said yes she understood that I thought that she was sleeping. I don't have to worry for that. She asked me to take the money she was keeping for me which was in her pocket. I asked her, "Why can I take it? Do you feel that you will die?

"No my child, it is just because I am here," she answered. I thought that since she had a weak voice, to take that money from her, showed that I believed that she might die, or on other hand, it was like giving the green light to death to come and take her.

"No," I told her, "I can't take that money." She didn't know what to do to make me take them and she didn't know what I had in my mind, why I refused to take the money.

I said bye to her and told her that I would tell people at home that she was talking slow with a weak voice.

"No," she told me, "just tell them that I am OK."

OK then, me too I believed that she was OK, because she said so. At home when they asked me how she was, I told them that she was OK. I didn't mention that she was talking with a weak voice since she told me not to say so.

Next morning everything I was doing I was do it quickly and

wherever I was going I was running. I was lucky when I went to fetch water I didn't slip even once. So at hospital I didn't see them, other patients, didn't say anything and I didn't ask them, I went everywhere I could reach outside without seeing any of them, then I met my father outside, I told him that I failed to get them anywhere, and he told me that he knew that I would have that problem.

"Where is my mum?" I asked.

"Now you have no mum!" was the reply. "Go home and tell them that she passed away."

I didn't say one other thing I didn't even feel that I was sad, I just felt nothing, I didn't know how to feel at that time.

I turned to go on the way home, in my head was one sentence, 'now you have no mum', which was like someone telling me these cruel words over and over.

Since that time I didn't talk to anyone I hadn't even been with other children, and I didn't cry either. I was always doing what I was supposed to do, I was always by myself; I liked to hide myself in the corner somewhere in the bush near the hut or behind it. When I was there I was thinking nothing. At her burial time, I was standing aside like soldier, looking at them very carefully for whatever they were doing, how they were in a hurry throwing the dust on top of her body, and wondering why they were in that hurry! When they finished they put their tools on their shoulder and turn their back and went. I think no one would remember where I was standing because all of them went and it was only me who was left there standing looking where my mum was sleeping, and knowing that time will come. I would go and maybe go forever not even to come back to see where she was sleeping. Time came when I too went, but very slowly, I was turning my head now and then until I was out of that bush.

But still I didn't cry and I did not remember to ask myself why. And I had never seen tears because of losing my beloved mother. The lady I loved so much and who loved me in turn even more than that. And I didn't know why I didn't cry for her. I was like that for some time, without talking to anyone until one day when my sister came where I was siting, and asked me why I was by myself those days. She was trying to show me that I had her, I didn't have to worry myself and be too sad that way, when she told me, "Bamurangirwa you have me I will be your mum don't worry."

Without a second I talked and told her that she would always be my elder sister not my mother and I used a high voice. A voice which was the first time to hear me talk in that horrible way not even to other children. She didn't know what else to do, maybe it shocked her because normally they knew me as a child who had respect for old people, couldn't answer back to them. She turned and went without trying to say another word, something I came to regret after some years, thinking about that behaviour which maybe hurt her more when she was trying to help me.

One day I was coming from work alone when that thought of the day when I lost my mum came back to me. I wanted to make a very loud noise and talk it over and over but loudly as many times as I could. I knew that once you died you were gone, not like before when I thought that to die was like to sleep for some time, but my two relatives who where in Nyabyondo before her, Rutaganda and my grandmother didn't come back again, meaning that, even my mum would not come back either! No I didn't want to believe it then, I felt that I had a headache and pain in my stomach, I felt that maybe I was going to die too, I thought that if I could be lucky, I could die there and then. I wanted to cry in a loud voice but no voice came out. I didn't want life without her; I didn't know how I would manage. It was like my head and my heart were empty, that my world and life were nothing to me now alone without her. I wished that it was me who died before her that was always my wish. I was young, alone; I believed that from no one, nowhere, would I ever get her love, not anyone in my family or outside. Forever she had gone, with her love for me finished.

I remembered one day we were in our normal conversation when I was begging her, after my relative died and I saw that they didn't come back, I told her that I wished that I would die before her. At that time she turned to me and looked serious and told me that I don't

45

have to think like that, "It is always good when parents leave behind children," she said.

I told her that my problem was that I didn't believe that there was anyone who could love me like her.

And she told me that I deserved to have the long life because I would get a husband and children who would love me, and if my husband was a bad person my children would love me, and I would be happy to have a life, because it is good to be alive. When I was thinking all of that, I heard something which was too loud, 'paaaapaaaaaa', a part of noise and then I saw myself in the air, that is the last thing I saw. Yes I was in the middle of the road, but that road you could stay a month without seeing any car on, so was like I had forgotten that it was a road. The driver also was not careful since I was in the corner, maybe if he was more careful he wouldn't have had that accident.

I didn't know other things; my last thought was that I was happy that I had died.

Time came when I woke up and one of my arms and one leg was tied up on the top of the bed, where I was sleeping with people around the bed as if they were waiting for me, maybe to see if I woke up or if I had died.

My sister, brother, and my father, all of them were there and when I opened my eyes they came near me, bending to the bed and they were talking very slowly. They asked me how I felt and I asked them what happened.

I felt that my head was very heavy and they told me that I had car accident that is when I realised that I was in the hospital. When I looked at myself I realised that one arm and leg were as though they were not mine any more, I covered my face and I was in deep thought asking myself why and how I got in that accident when I always went by myself on that road! I came to remember everything by myself, then I started to ask myself why they felt sad according to the way I saw their faces. Was it because we lost our mum or was it because I had accident? Or was it the thought that they had almost lost two people at the same time? I thought that they might be sad because we lost our mum, since

I count myself as nothing, and I wished that the car had killed me at last and so I would be away from the cruel life which might be ahead of me, life without my mother.

Now without my arm and leg, who was going to be patient enough to take care of me? No one.

I was in the hospital for two months, when I started to walk with a stick they asked them to release me, and they prepared for the journey to Uganda, if they ran from there, they had enough of that area.

FROM CONGO TO UGANDA

To get transport was a big problem, they wanted a car to take us to Goma but when they got the car which reached Gashebeli they said that they couldn't miss it, since they had people in that area. The time came, and they put their bags on to their heads, we went up to the road, where we were going to wait for the car to pick us from there to Gashebeli. I was on my own, alone, and quiet, but in my heart I was talking to Nyabyondo, I was asking Nyabyondo how it felt to see me go just like that alone without my beloved mum, my good and only friend in life, I was telling Nyabyondo that it had no kindness, can't even feel sorry for me, is cruel enough to have that gut to do what it did to me when I was still young, when I still needed her guidance in all areas of life. I needed all her intelligence. I wanted to be like her in life, now without her I would not be recognised by anyone. I was going to be nobody. If she was there, I would be her flower, and be able to be a flower to others too.

I told my mum that it was not my wish to leave her there, between that bush, if I had my independence, I could be there with her where she was sleeping. "You are not in that bush alone my mum, you have your mum there with you, both of you loved each other, and chose to be together wherever you were, and with your grandson too, but I promise you mum, if I am alive, I will be the good person you would like me to be, no matter what, I will love myself and others, and respect myself too and others as you once told me, and I will talk about your beauty and good personality, your relatives who didn't get chance to know you. I will tell my children if I have them, the way you were beautiful outside, but inside you were more beautiful that you had a golden heart. I don't have your picture on paper, but I have it in my heart, I see you everywhere I am, and that is how it will be always, my beautiful Mum, with shining black skin, tall, medium weight, good figure, fine soft black long hair, which at last, you gave me part of it."

I came to remember that if it could be the case, Nyabyondo could beat me, it could say that it didn't invite me, I came by myself, and it had power to do whatever it wanted in its territory, and I had to follow its laws and culture, and maybe tell me to turn that case to who made me go there.

I was standing somewhere alone, they were busy putting bags in the lorry and they were acting as though they had forgotten all about me, and I didn't care. After finishing the bags they started to take care of the children, that is how Kantamage saw where I was. When she reached me she was shocked to see where I was, I was alone and quiet, but tears were down to my chest, she asked me if I felt pain anywhere, but I told her that I was only saying bye to Mum.

She looked sad and she held me and she told me that she was there and I didn't have to worry. She will be my mum, but without even a second again I told her that she couldn't be my mum, she would always be my elder sister that is.

Yes, she wanted to genuinely comfort me, but I think she noticed that I was not the easy child to say yes when is not yes. I cried a lot that time all the way; I cried the tears I didn't cry before. And I heard someone say that was good to let me cry which they did. But if they said it or not I was crying anyway. It was only me who could stop by myself without being told.

She took me where others were and all of us were inside the car which was the lorry, normally supposed to be for luggage, they sat up with the luggage and I sat with the driver. The ones who were on the top covered themselves with a tent because of raining, and when we were down at Gashebeli other children were asking me what I saw on the way and I told them that I saw a beautifully green country again.

They divided us into families at Gashebeli to look how people there looked, how they were beautifully shining, and questioning where we came from, you ask yourself why someone could even think to go to Nyabyondo. It was like two different countries

We were given milk, something we had last time when we were there, on our way to Nyabyondo, next day we got another lorry to Goma, lorries were the only transport you could get, if you were lucky.

When I saw myself sitting with the driver, I thought it was special, on other hand, I thought that was good to have the problem with my leg. On the way the driver bought me the bread without anything to eat it with. Which I did not mind and thought that is how it was supposed to be, since we couldn't get the type I saw with the priest. I was still remembering that kind of bread, last time I had seen it was whenthe priest gave it to me at Kiruhura Missionary.

I thought that I was lucky I got a special gift to take to my brother and sister, I thought that they didn't know it, like many, and since I was by myself, the driver didn't mind if I ate it or not, he would think that I chose to eat it after, with the other children, but my plan was to hide it up to Uganda no matter how long our journey would be. Already they had told us that we might be on our way even two to three weeks.

I put it carefully in the paper where it was and hid it inside my bag where I was sure that other children would never touch.

In Goma we went to the different families, and they started to struggle to see how they could get transport to Uganda. We didn't know what time we were going to be there, though they wished that by luck it could be quick since life there was expensive, they had to buy food not like where we were.Still, the lorry they got was the lorry which would take luggage past Uganda to other countries, the driver told them that unless they were ready to go with the luggage and be aware that they might be on the way for a long time, because sometimes they stayed on the borders for some days, but since there was no other choices, they said yes, and we prepared our journey to Uganda.

There were almost twenty people with all of us. They sat with luggage, only me, because I was sick again, I was with the driver, they were making fun of me because I was speaking the native language clear, it was me who was translating for them, they were saying that in Uganda it was me who would help them too. Since I picked up languages easily.

So me and the driver communicated easily I was speaking Swahili too. The driver was Muhunde man, meaning that I was speaking his two languages. He was a good man, he was talking to me telling me things on the way, buying me some food, and sometimes I was giving some to other children who were with the luggage on the top.

But whatever I was doing, my thoughts were with the gift I was taking to my sister and brother in Uganda. I had not yet checked where I put it. I feared to do that in case other children saw me and went to see what was there when I was not there and found out what I was hiding from them. I only had a hope that was still there.

Our journey was long but good, we had a lot of food, sometimes the driver was the one who would buy for all of us when we were on the border of Congo and Uganda, *matoke* was coming from Uganda side, which was cheap so was no problem. It was a warm place, we were sleeping outside where the car was, it didn't mean that we were comfortable, we wanted to reach where we were going, we were there for two weeks, then the driver got the papers he was waiting for.

On Uganda side he didn't get any problems, we were there one day and at night we started our journey to Masaka.

My father told us in advance that when we knew that we were almost going to reach Masaka, we would see somewhere with stars of many different colours that had fallen down to the ground when we looked to the big village. At that point all of as asked him at once with surprise, what that meant, how could stars fall down from the sky? We had to ask him what that would be. And he told us that it was lights of different colours which were in town.

He was telling us many different things which he had seen in Uganda, all of the things seemed strange to us, the driver didn't stop a lot, we were on the way the whole night and like 5:00am we started to see many stars, my daddy was telling us. And yes he had described them very clearly to anyone who could see lights for the first time, that is what she or he would think, that the sky had fallen down. We reached Masaka early morning, my father was our director, but our driver knew where the hospital was, so he took us to the front of Masaka Hospital, and he turned his lorry and he was gone.

Then daddy told us to sit next to the big trees which were in front of the gate and wait for him, after a short time he came back with a small car, he told us that the car would take the bags and the weak people, I was one of them so he would come back with that car and go with the rest by walking.

That is what we did.

I went with the first group, I was very happy to join my people again, after a long time, now in Uganda with them, and I had big hopes of my future then, though I lost my mum, now I had my sister and my brother again with me. At Mpanumusingo's home, all were still sleeping. They woke up and we were hugging all of us with happiness, it was like a dream come true, to be together again, though we missed our mum more now. After a short time the ones we left were there with us, my leg and arm were not bad at that time, I could walk by myself without any support, they told us first to wait for tea, when tea came it was like the one I had with Fr Sekamonyo! Almost everyone was surprised and they were asking if they had milk to make tea.

They said that they had a lot, they came with a wide plate full of sliced bread, when I tasted the tea it even had sugar! When in Nyabyondo before to go to work in a rich company, no one knew sugar, they only drank tea with tea leaves, my heart thought about the gift I came with for them, I thought that even though they knew about it and they have them, I thought that still I would give them their gift and explain. After tea I went to check where I hid my gift but when I opened where it was, there was a bad smell which welcomed me, the gift had turned to be like sponge covered with white cotton! I was confused and disappointed, I threw it far, and I didn't tell anyone about it.

They sent a message to Ngamije's family, that we were alive.

Next day when I woke up my sister Kankuyo was there waiting for me, when I came she greeted me with a lot of emotion, she was very happy to see me. She left me when I was still too young, and she met me when I was almost a teenager, she was turning me here and there, to see clearly how I looked, and sometimes she was crying, it took time for her to let me go where the other children were.

The way she looked, it showed me that she had a good life, as I thought after my father told us how he saw them. Mpanumusingo's home was a big home, a big good permanent house of six rooms, big compound which was in Rwandan style, and had other small houses inside with still a lot of space, one was in Rwandan's style, built by tree and covered by grasses, which he told us that he was waiting for our father to finish. With big land too where they could get food from.

Because even the compound was in Rwandan style, Ugandans were coming to see his home, and some tried to show that they knew much about Rwanda, and they were telling others that the way he built his home was how Rwandan kings built theirs! But to this point, Mpanumusingo was telling some who asked him that it was how all ordinary Rwandans built their homes. His home even had no security, but no one was entering without having an appointment.

When Kankuyo came she wanted to go with me and I wanted the same thing.

At her home, Ngamije was a tall man, too light skinned, you could think that he was Arab descent, with a small long face, small long nose, he was too handsome, quiet man, with a lot of politeness, kind, with few words, who was loved by everybody. Something which normally is impossible, he had three different homes, but in one big compound, one for his elder wife, another one for young wife, who was my sister Kankuyo, and between his wives was his sister. All of these homes were permanent good ones, and he had houses for rent in the same compound, they looked to be a good family.

The majority of workers who were under him were Rwandans and a few Burundians, they nicknamed him the name of Mutware, meaning 'chief', so that was the name which was common to many who knew him. They had big land where they got food from, and Kankuyo tried everything to see that I was happy, every time she was asking me what I wanted and what I didn't, sometimes she was asking me what I missed so that she could get it for me. Sometimes when I was telling her some of the things I missed she was crying, maybe because I was telling her normal things, which no one would think that someone could miss.

She managed to feed me whatever I missed and be satisfied, but my heart wanted to go to school, I believed that they were waiting for me to reach there and without wasting any time they were going to put me in school. Ngamije's home was near Kitovu Mission and all of the students in that area were going there. Ngamije's old wife had girls my age who were students, so because I came to be permanent there, I thought that Kankuyo and Mpanumusingo shared us between themselves so that they could easily help us. Kantamage and her children were at Mpanumusingo's side, and I was at Kankuyo's side, Mpanumusingo took Kantamage's children to school when I was waiting to be put in to school by Kankuyo.

One day after I saw that no one had said anything about it, when I was in a good conversation with Kankuyo, I asked her, "Since I see Mutware to be a good person, can you ask him to put me in the school?"

But the answer I got shocked me and made me to feel so upset.

She told me that I was too old now to go to school. Something I didn't even think that they could think, since there were a lot of children my age, who were in school and I always saw them! If I was too old, now what? What do they suggesting to do for me?

Then I started to doubt if they loved me or they hated me. I wondered who I could blame at this point between Mpanumusingo and Kankuyo, since I could not count on the people I came with from Congo. Because they had nothing. No one was better then, because though I was in Kankuyo's responsibility, Mpanumusingo also had the right to ask her about it and they could solve that problem if they wanted to, but they didn't want to see it as a problem, they were comfortable to see me sitting at home.

Instead Kankuyo taught me housework including cooking, because I had never cooked before, my work was to get food and firewood and water, the rest of the work was for Mum and Kantamage, but sometimes I was helping with some housework when I was at home but not cooking.

The first time when Kankuyo asked me if I knew how to cook, I lied and said yes, because I feared that she might refuse me to cook, and I didn't wanted to sit doing nothing, but all the time I was cooking, we were going to sleep without eating anything, because I would make it burn or I would make it half cooked. In front of her husband, she was very ashamed, and thought that I was ashamed too, but when she turned her head to look at me I didn't show any sign of shock or shame. After, she was confused, she asked me again if I really knew how to cook, then I told her that I lied and I told her why.

So she started to teach me, and I was always in charge of the housework, because she always had many visitors. Since they were neighbours of schools, and school children in Uganda at that time had uniform, I was seeing them going and coming back from school. It gave me a bad heart to see them every day when I was not with them, so I told them that I wanted to go and stay at Mpanumusingo's home, but I didn't say why I went there, but I would come back as a visitor.

I went to Mpanumusingo's home after some days without being told anything. I decided to ask him and hear what he was going to tell me, when I asked him if he could take me to school, he told me that he would think about it!

Think about what? About that I have to study, or that I don't deserve it? If he told me that he didn't have money, fine, but to think about it. I did not understand it, time doesn't wait for him to think! What was he thinking? I was wasting enough time and would not like to waste more if I could help it. I was confused with my brother and my sister, I didn't know what agenda they had for me. I had no one now, meaning that it shut my hope of being able to study, maybe not that time, or not ever, if not forever then, what next? There was no one to answer me for that.

Then I was wondering if this family, which was my family, who I had wanted to join with a lot of hope that they would be happy to see me, and happy to build my future, now this is how they welcomed me. Were there are any other ways that I could have a hope that they would do anything in my future? Nothing.

I believed that if I came with our mum, they would have done it without any question, because Mum loved me and she knew that was my wish to have a good study, and they loved their mum and respected her, so she would have told them and they would done it no question about it, just for her. And they would have done anything to make her happy, including that. It made me miss my mum more than before.

I never asked Mpanumusingo or Kankuyo about it again, and they didn't say anything again concerning that point, the chapter was closed. No one was ready to carry the burden of building my future and that was it.

But even though my permanent home was Mpanumusingo's, I was here and there to Kantamage's home or Kankuyo, when they needed my help, maybe a child was sick or they had a visitor who was sick or they got a new baby, anything. So I was their helper or their houseworker. Rusingizandekwe was in the countryside, Mpanumusingo was somewhere called Kasijagirwa where Obote built barracks for his soldiers, which was on the way to town, near the town of Masaka, and Kantamage was near Masaka Hospital which was near to town. You didn't need any transport to town, so it was very easy for me to visit her at any time I went to town or from town.

One day came a message that Kankuyo wanted to see me, I went, and because it was early Kankuyo asked me if I could wait for Mutware as he was the one who wanted to see me.

To spend the night there was no problem, what I didn't want was to be there every day.

Evening time, Mutware came back, we greeted each other, and he told me that Kankuyo refused to give me his message, and in my heart I asked myself what kind of message she was afraid to tell me, I was waiting patiently.

All of us were quiet he was the only one who was talking. He started to tell me the message, by telling me that he knew me to be a good girl, who couldn't shame anyone. There was a lady Mrs. Sentongo who was his coworker, her house girl had run away from her recently, and she needed someone to help her, he was asking me if I could go and help her.

At that time in Africa up until 2000, a house boy or girl was known to be a job of law people, which was hard work, you had to work many hours, wake up very early in the morning, and sleep very late, and law payment was between £10-£15 per month, or less. You slept and ate with them if they gave you that respect, and if they had a heart, but to many it was normal for their house girl/boy to eat different types of food from their boss, and not sit with them at the same table.

Because it was normally known that that kind of job was for only poor people, you worked like slaves, since there was nothing else they could do, and they were too poor so had to do whatever came their way. And they had no qualifications to support them.

I had to give him an answer otherwise it could be seen as ignorance, at the time the kind of job someone had was like identity, to tell people who do not know you what kind of person you are, that is why some people who were working far from their families, sometimes would lie about what kind of job they did, so that they could be able to get the respect they needed. Some people thought that only jobs in offices were good ones, but after they came to know that businesses were better than offices.

I thought that they told me what they had decided, and saw that I could do it because I was doing nothing, and it was them who told that lady that they had a girl at home who could do that for her.

I told them that I would give them an answer tomorrow, and they seemed to be worried that I might refuse, when maybe they had assured her, they were trying to tell me how good she was and I told them that it was OK, we would talk the next day.

At night I was crying. I had to make a decision and grow up. I saw that I had no chance to be a child, I was a child when I had my mum, now no one wanted to see me as a child, so I had to grow up and think as any grown-up person, because I was on my own.

They had a neighbour who had a child, girl of my age, who was my good friend. Mukabagira was in primary school in Kitovu, there were five children, a sister and three brothers, their father passed away back home in Rwanda. They came to Uganda from Rwanda soon before us, they had a medium life according to the standard of life at the time, and all of the children were in school there at Kitovu.

Any time when I was in Kasana for any reason it would be our chance to see each other again, because we knew that she couldn't get time since she was a student and her mum wouldn't let her come by herself to see me on weekends. I wanted first to see her tomorrow after school, and tell her and listen to what she would say, then after her views I would know what answer to give them. When I was with her, I told her everything and what Mpanumusingo told me concerning school fees, and after listening to all, we were quiet for some time. She was the one who started by telling me that at the moment, it was good to say yes for whatever they saw that suited me, so it would be better to go to the lady and see if I would be able to work for her, whatever time I would be able to. Since I didn't need money for anything at the moment, because wherever I could I walked, I would try to save, and after we would see that the money I got might be helpful somehow. She would try to ask maybe if there was somewhere I could go to college for anything so that I could learn and pay fees using the money I would have.

And I thought that to be a good idea, after a short silence she told me her story, that their mum told them that soon some of them were going to quit the school, because of school fees. When she was saying this, she looked so sad, but her elder sister Ingabire who was the first born in the family, said that she would do whatever to see that her young sister and brothers would go ahead with their studies, she was the only one who would go out if it needed to be.

Then we were asking ourselves what she would do, but we coudn't get an answer. All of that time when we were talking, sometimes we were laughing and other times we were crying.

Evening time when I told my sister and my brother-in-law that I would go to work for their friend, they seemed to be happy, next day I went with Mutware and when he show me Mrs. Sentong she seemed to be happy.

Her home was near the town, her house was big and clean, she had four children, the space between them was one year. The last born was one year-old.

Only one girl, the first born, was walking, all of the other three were crawling or pulling themselves with their stomachs.

Their mum told me that she had a hope that even the others would walk, because the one who was walking was like them before, and when you looked at them they looked to be OK, they were very beautiful children, it was easy to look after them.

The big problem was when they discharged, sometimes where they slept or in what they were dressed in, and most of the time they were doing it at the same time! They had nothing to prevent this, no gloves to wear on my hands, it was like taking care of disabled people who also didn't talk. Normally I loved children, and I loved to see clean things wherever was possible, now would I be able to manage that? It was a big test, the time I was alone at home I had to do everything concerning housework then, she had to teach me some other things, how she wanted things to be done. In general Mrs Sentongo was a good person and maybe she liked me, or she saw that I was a good house girl, but anyhow, she treated me nicely. Apart from having to face that dirtiness with my bare hands every time, other things were no big problem because when she was at home she was doing what I left behind.

One day she asked me if I knew how to read and write. I said yes I know, and again she asked me if I knew English, maybe because they told her that I came to Uganda not long time ago. I told her that I didn't know it. She bought small books without asking me, and she told me that the time she was at home she would be teaching me.

She started to teach me English and she was happy teaching me, she said that I was a good student, and I was happy to see that there was someone who could see that I needed to know more things than what was ahead of me. On the other hand, it made me more sad, because that was not the right person to have that sympathy towards me. I thought that she might not be happy to see that I didn't get chance to go to school, but she couldn't say or do anything about it. She was happy to have me to take care of her children and her house if I was a good house girl to her then that is what she was looking for.

I wanted to know English not like when I was in school when I hated French, but she had very little time, she wanted to do it for me but sometimes she couldn't get time for the whole month.

I was there for one year, my family was quiet, like they had put me to one side, and maybe they thought that I was happy for the situation I was in. I was still having some kind of fear about my life, I saw that Mrs. Sentongo was still good to me, but to clean her children couldn't be my future, and it was not a life to stick to. It was only my father who sometimes was visiting me, and some of my friends including Mukabagira. I told Mukabagira that I was tired of it, and I had no idea how I would go since Mrs. Sentongo was still too good to me, and I wanted to go without hurting her, maybe she was good to me in a genuine way, or was she just to trying to hold me there? Whatever the reason, I had to try to see if I could get other ways for myself.

Always when I was talking with Mukabagira about my life I could see how it was hurting her, but there was nothing she could do, she was only telling me to be patient and never lose hope.

One day my father came to see me as usual, but at that time he also came to tell me that he was going up country to get work to do instead of sitting in his son's home when he could do something better than that.

Then I got a new reason, I didn't want my father to go there by himself when I was there cleaning that dirt every day with my bare hands in the name of that small money. So I told my father, luckily in Kinyarwanda since it was only two of us who understood the language, to tell Mrs. Sentongo that he wanted me back, he didn't have to tell her his reasons, I was his child, and he had the right to say anything concerning me. In African culture, it doesn't matter how old you are, you are to be controlled by your parents or your elders.

Time came when he told her and Mrs. Sentongo kneeled down, according to her culture, as a Ugandan lady, she had to talk with a man when she kneeled down, that time she was crying uncontrollably. She put her arm up, showing him a sign, and said to him that if someone was to lend you a bangle, and come for it, if you gave the person your arm to make it easy for the person to take it from your arm. "So I would like to stay with Bamurangirwa for a long time if possible, but she is your daughter, if you want her then that is how it has to be," she said.

I felt sorry for her, but that is how it had to be, I had to go to help my father.

Mukabagira was told me how to save my money using the post office, so all the money I worked for, ninety-eight percent I kept.

My father chose to go to the village called Buwenda, because there were other Rwandans, in that area, almost all of the native people there were step sisters and step brothers, according to their stories, there was a man who was rich and had many wives, so he had many children, but he left big land with coffee trees for all of them, which held a big part of the economy in the country at the time. It can show you a good example of how Uganda was ahead more than many parts of Africa at least where I had seen before. They had roads, there was still dust but they had them, it was easy to reach the home of each and everyone, and they had the electricity in their houses. Something they didn't have was clean water, and telephones or TV, although no one knew or heard anything like TV in Africa at the time, but at least if they had clean water, to me they would be the winner to self-improvement.

Concerning foreigners, Baganda people were proud of themselves and knew that all foreigners were behind them for everything, sometimes they thought that they couldn't even share with them the same table, they talked like many African people at the time, the foreigners that they gave a lot of respect or maybe fear to, were white.

When they wanted to show you that they trusted you or that you did the right things, you heard them call you white person, or say that you were like white person, sometimes someone who was telling you that, had never seen a white person!

At that village many had their own cars, Rwandans and Burundians were people who were coming to work for them in big numbers from many years back, so they knew them and some could speak their languages, but they would put them in categories of very law people, the people only who could work for them and be paid no other businesses they could deal with them.

At the time after 1959 when our people started to go outside of our country in big numbers, that changed their mentality completely concerning Rwandans.

No 1: it took us a long time to make Baganda believe that we too came from Rwanda and we were Rwandans, especially in villages. It started when they saw us talk the same language with their workers, that is how they asked us how come we understood each other? When we told them that was because all of us were Banyarwanda, sometimes you could see that they would start arguments, that can't be! That we must have come from somewhere else, not the same place where their workers came from, leave alone to say that all of us were Rwandans.

All of that, I thought that the reason was because the workers were caring for the work more than themselves, in other words, in terms of taking care of themselves, there was a problem.

And they were doing whatever their masters told them to do without questions.

The reasons they were giving us, why we were not the same as their workers, was that they knew Rwandans and Burundians to be dirty people! When they feared us and gave us a lot of respect for how we took care of ourselves and how we looked in general.

Some Ugandans at the time, especially in the villages, could tell that when you said that you were Rwandan you were abusing yourselves, that is something like shame, or someone could ask you, how many miles between Rwanda and Tutsi land!

At that time since villages had that mentality, they used to treat their workers the way they wanted, sometimes like slaves, they had to change it slowly after seeing that was not easy for them to do the same to new Rwandans, people who came after, because when they abused them or showed any sign of ignorance, many were telling them off! Though they were in their home and working for them, it didn't mean that they had the right to treat them the way they wanted, I saw something like that many times, between the lady Nakamate and my father, this lady was a very good person, but many times there was misunderstanding between her and my father because of languages, and my father had heard stories before that native people had a lot of ignorance to foreigners. So I thought he was standing by, in case she would try to ignore him in any way. I had to be between them for translations when my father was already angry and starting to ask Nakamate many questions. Like what she thought she was, just because he was in her home she didn't have any right to do this and that to him or his children!

At that time some marriages broke up because natives wanted to get children with our people, once I asked Nsereko, one of the richest people in that area, he was brother to Nakamate, and was an educated man, and had other reasons to be a respected person too. He used to travel in Europe, he had big family, but he had mistresses of young Rwandan girls. I asked him why they ran after our boys and girls? He told me that Tutsi's children are beautiful, and smart in many ways if not all ways.

He went ahead, and said, "We think that we know Rwandans, but we have not yet seen the proper ones, when they are left alone to forget their wives, when the women leave theit husbands, the way I see you, in the future, you might even become our leaders."

I asked him why he thinks that way.

"You people you are too smart," he said. "That is how it was like in other neighbouring countries to Rwanda, where Rwandans went in big numbers since 1959, it was the same thing concerning their point of view to younger Rwandans. There were big numbers in intermarriages more than ten percent of native people in Uganda as any other neighbouring countries as I said, who married Rwandan girls, there were many different reasons why they wanted these girls for themselves, and the girls had their reasons why they went with them, but the big reason on the girls' side: was to survive, to see that they could help their families to have a better life. They did that inside and outside of their country. To be successful for that, they used their culture of respect, politeness and beauty, and since they knew what they were doing, it was easy to be successful, sometimes they were in marriages without love at first sight, some of them had to learn to love after, that I can call a kind of sacrifice, but most of the time they got what they wanted. Tutsi girls slowly came to be recognised also with white men, and to the point where intermarriages became international."

Where we were, there was a lot of food, which we got by working for it, not buying it, I had to go around to see if there was someone who would tell me what to do to get food from them, because that was the women's job, since I saw that Ugandan people liked to be clean and I too was a clean girl, so it was easy for to me to prepare in advance what I would wear when I went to find food, so I had to make myself look clean as much as I could, comb my soft and long black hair, and look like I was going to visit someone, this confused some of them and they asked me what kind of job they could give me, since the job for food, was to dig in their banana plantations.

Nakamate was a lady who gave us a house to live in, which was one of her good houses, when other workers were in small huts, so she had a lot of respect for my father, sometimes she gave us food for free, and she was good enough to see that I was still a child who was acting like a housewife, so when I had visitors she volunteered to be responsible for them until they left! When the time came to go to find food outside, sometimes people would enjoy to see me in front of them and ask me questions about me, and sometimes they would give me simple work, or feel sorry, or sympathy. Some others asked me to touch my skin or my hair, something like that, when I was alone it made me laugh when I thought about it. Or sometimes they simply liked me and gave me food for free, and others wasted my time and told me 'no work no food', when it was too late to try somewhere else!

After getting to know them, I had to ask them before not to waste my time, if they had work to give me or not, and when they told me that I didn't have to worry, then I sat and went ahead with their conversations, they looked to be innocent people who had never seen any kind of problems, sometimes they asked me a child like me how come it was possible to come out of my country up to there, or asked me what I did to look the way I looked, that was a common questions to us.

When on an unlucky day I was to meet someone who would give me somewhere to dig but when I looked how big it was, and sometimes it could be late and I couldn't try somewhere else, at that point I was not sure if I would be able to finish, but I had to try, if I did not finish the same day, then I had to come back the next day, that day she would give me half of my food.

And when I met a good person and the gave me a lot of food, then to carry it would be the same problem like Nyabyond's, it would be too heavy for me, but I had to carry it instead of coming again, I would take all but after I put it down from my head, I would feel that I was different person, like if I was growing up slow. Buwenda, I was with my father and his two young grandchildren, Mpanumusingo's children and I, so my responsibility was to know what we would eat, and to cook. The money my father was working for he was saving all of it, we were not at Buwenda for a long time, we were there for two years. My father got the money he worked for and he had other money he saved before, he gave some of it to Mpanumusingo to go to Tanzania on his behalf and buy land for him there, because he wanted to move and be settled there.

He wanted to go there and be able to farm cows as before back home in Rwanda; he wanted to be where he would be with Rwandan neighbours too. But I didn't want to go to Tanzania, I had no specific reasons to make me like Tanzania or hate it, I was not happy for my father to leave me with other member of my family, but at last I had Mukabagira.

I think I loved Mukabagira because she had a lot of my mum's looks, and height, but more than that she had a good heart and she gave me ideas which made it very clear that she wished me a good future.

And also I liked her because her beauty had not given her green light to think that she was better than others.

She was too beautiful, she had height, a good figure, and when you looked at her if you didn't know her before, you could think that she used some make up on her face! Especially her eyes and her lips, when she smiled you wished that she would go ahead for some more time.

We went back to Mpanumusingo's home, waiting to go to Tanzania, though I didn't want to go there but I had no other way, at Mpanumusingo's home, Mukabagira came to see me and she told me that she knew some charity in town where they taught English for free, though, they were not busy, but it was better than nothing, at last it could help me have a reason to go out.

When I told my father about that charity, that is when I knew how much he was not happy to see me doing nothing, the way he was telling me that it was much better to stay and at last learn the language, he looked to be sad when he was saying it, somehow I was confused why he didn't tell his children to do something about it? But maybe it was because he saw himself to be a burden to them and hoped that that they could do it without being told.

I was happy to see that he was happy for that, on the other hand I was not happy to see him go to Tanzania alone, though he had another relative old man who would go with him. This couldn't be reason enough to let him go alone when I was doing nothing. I was happy to get a good reason not to go to Tanzania at that time. When my father reached Tanzania, by being a hard-working man, he was a big farmer and he was an example in that area to the foreigners and native people as well, people were coming at his home to work for food, that is how he got a young Rwandan woman and married, the lady he came to have three sons with her, Rutabulingonga, Gahenda and Sinzi Rukara, when I heard that he got married I was very happy, I was sure that my father now was settled and had a happy life.

At that time my life was only guessing and hoping, saying maybe tomorrow, this and that, I was waiting for that thing people call luck, when and how I would get it, I couldn't tell. I started to go to the charity twice a week for one hour of English and one hour of knitting, it helped me a lot, I had a chance to meet new people, when I was coming from study I had to pass at Kantamage's home until evening.

These foreigners who were coming to Uganda, were in three different categories.

There were some people who were coming to work for money and go back home without waiting to work for so long, these kinds of people would normally like to come back many times when they saw that it was necessary to build up themselves.

And other ones who believed that it would be easy for them to get a lot of money as soon as they put their foot in Uganda, people who wanted to become rich quickly.

These kinds of people, most of them when they reached Uganda and saw that it was completely different with what they had in their mind, they became disappointed and became drunker or disappeared and got women who many times were single mothers, and forgot about back home, their family back home sometimes thought that they had died.

Third group were people who came and saw that they would not be able to manage to work in coffee, tree, or banana plantations since they had no experience of digging, and these kinds of people they would go to ask for work with cow farmers so that they could deal with cows since that is what they had experience of. These people they were nicknamed as Balalo or Bararo to Ugandans, meaning the people who look after cows or cow boys.

In that time up to 1970s the kind of Ugandans who were rich, in Buganda most of them were rich because of coffee. And even if some were educated, there were few who would struggle to look for office jobs, and they thought that to be in the army was not their responsibility.

I thought that it was because they grew up with rich family and they saw other work to be hard work, or to be for poor people, they thought that the army was supposed to be a job for North Ugandans.

HOW I MET ALEX

Both Mpanumusingo and his wife went to Tanzania to visit their parents, since both of them were leaving there, at that time when I went to college I had to come quickly without staying at Kantamage home until evening, because I was responsible for everything at home including the young children, though I had Mpanumusingo's brother-in-law Karoli, an old man who was there in case we wanted anything and he was like our guide.

One afternoon when I was at home, having just come back from college, through the window I saw two young men walking outside the gate. I didn't bother much about them since I used to see people admire our home.

When I came out of the house going to the kitchen, I was surprised to see that the same young men were still outside of the gate and when they saw me they knocked the door of the gate, and I had to go to see what they wanted, I thought that they wanted to ask me something, maybe to direct them somewhere.

It was first the time I had seen them: after greetings was question time.

"What can I do for you?"

"We are your visitors."

I had to ask them again to be sure if I heard them correct. The same question, "You are my visitors?"

"Yes we are your visitors."

I looked at them carefully they were good-looking men, well dressed, well behaved according to the way they talked, and at that time there was nothing to fear of someone just because they were a stranger, by thinking that if you welcomed him or her, the person couldn't give you any kind of problem, instead, if you cannot welcome the stranger, anyone could see you as someone who had strange behaviour.

Old people were teaching young ones to welcome strangers and listen to them, in that way you might save them somehow.

I told them to wait for me to come and open for them.

I showed them where to sit, after a few minutes, I asked them if I could give them a cup of tea and both of them said yes.

Luckily I had tea in the Thermos; I came with three cups and gave them tea while I was having mine, sat down and waited to hear what they wanted me for.

Those men were almost the same size and the same height, tall like six foot or more maybe between ninety-five to one hundred kilograms, but looked strong like sportsmen with short haircuts.

One who was talking to me a lot had light skin, long face, small long nose, big white eyes, white teeth one in front was broken a little, and you could think that he broke it purposely because it made him look more handsome when he smiled.

I asked them what I could do for them, he told me that his name was Alex his friend was John, and they were soldiers, Alex went on by telling me that he came from Busia district in Uganda side, in Samia, most Samia people I knew were dark-skinned and I asked him if there were Samia people who were light-skinned, and with a wider smile he said yes, they have him, and all of us we laughed at that. I told them my name and waited to hear their story, it was my first time to be near any soldier, and like many at the time, I believed that soldiers were bad and harsh people, the way they were talking I saw a big difference with my thoughts, because of their politeness.

When I asked them who sent them and what they wanted me to help with, Alex started to tell me why they came to see me.

Alex said, "You know Bamurangirwa. I have seen you sometime back, passing front of our barracks, and I wished to talk to you but I was not sure if you can stand in middle of the road and talk to me, I started to come behind you and wanted to know where you came from, I started to come with friends and wait to see you when you were out of the house, also I didn't manage to talk to you. I didn't know how your relatives would take it. And now I saw that you are by yourself and say that it is my time to talk to you; I just wanted to know more about you."

It surprised me a little and showed me that soldiers were like any other human.

"Because you saw me alone, that is why you talked to me?"

"Yes, but also it was a matter of trying, I knew that there might be a possibility for you to refuse to talk to strangers."

I told them that if I knew before that they were soldiers I wouldn't have opened for them. And all of us we laughed at that, and they said that they were clever, that is why they didn't say it before.

It was his time to ask me some questions. "What connection is there between you and this family you are living with?"

"The gentleman is my brother."

"Where they have been in these days?"

This question surprised me and I laughed at it. Before I answered him I had to ask him how he knew each and everything happening at my home!

"You mean that you come here every day and you know most of everything happening here!?"

"Yes, when I am here I just come to pass without stopping many times, sometimes when I am lucky to see you outside, I go back home satisfied."

"They went on a journey to visit our parents," I told him.

"And they left you here alone?"

"I am with the children, they are at school soon they will be back, and we are with the brother-in-law to my brother too."

"What if they meet us here?"

"There can't be any problem, you will introduce yourselves."

"And tell them that we are soldiers?"

"Yes." Together they went ahead by saying that they couldn't say so because people knew soldiers as bad people and they feared them, maybe I hated them too, I just couldn't say it now. They went ahead by trying to tell me that was not all soldiers who were bad people. To that point I told them that I heard people hated and feared them, but without knowing about them and I said that I would fear them yes, in the first place, but not hate them, because I had never been near a soldier and I knew nothing about them, and I just couldn't hate anyone without a reason. But now I saw them like any other people.

They asked me if it would be OK for them to visit me next time. I told them that it was OK. And they asked if I could see them off. I said that was no problem too, outside we were walking very slowly and John was ahead of us we were walking almost together and he was trying to pronounce my name which was not easy to him and the way he was trying was good to hear, it was like a little child who doesn't yet talk properly.

He was by my side looking down in front of him.

"Bamurangirwa you are so beautiful can I ask you something?" he asked me.

"Yes ask me anything," I told him.

"I might not have the right to know about you but I would like to know if you have a boyfriend or maybe you have a fiancé, I also might not like your answers, but it is better to know whatever it is."

"What answer you would like to have from me?"

"That you have no one at this moment." He was still looking in front of him and it seemed that he had forgotten that he had someone who was waiting for him and he looked to be serious that he was saying something he had thought for some time.

"I have no boyfriend or fiancé at this moment," I told him.

At that second he turned quickly and looked down at me as if he didn't believe me or he was surprised, and he asked again the same question, "You said that you don't have a boyfriend?!"

He was like he was talking by himself, he was talking non-stop without waiting for any answer, he went ahead by talking by himself.

"How can it be?! Can I be that much in luck to have you? The way you are talking is if you can let me be your friend and if can be possible be everything to you, I was afraid to think that when I got a chance to talk to you, if it would happen, that as soon as you knew that I am a soldier you will never talk to me again. If I heard correct it means that you can welcome me then: and if so you will never ever regret to know me. To you now it might look to be so soon but, to me, not soon because I had you in my mind in my heart for quite some time now, today is a dream come true."

At the time he was telling me all of that I didn't say anything, after he touched me on my back, but for a short time, maybe he thought that might show me that he didn't give me enough respect. I looked at him only for a short time because my eyes were too weak to look at him for a long time. After listening to all of the sweet words he was telling me.

I didn't know him yet, but the way he looked, the way he dressed, his height and his masculinity with soft and sweet words, which he was speaking in a very careful way full of politeness and respect, made me feel that I liked him, and I wanted him to hold me for so long, though I couldn't tell him.

I thought to myself that yes I liked him, and I was sure that nothing could touch me, to be able to hurt me when I was with him. I saw he could be enough and a good guide to any lucky girl.

I didn't want to go back, he was the first man to tell me those sweet peaceful words, I wanted to listen to him forever. His words showed me that they were genuine love which had no reason, especially when he told me that he loved me at the time he saw me, but he was not sure if he would see me again in the future, or even if he would see me, if I would talk to him... I felt his love into my heart and wondered how anyone could survive without love. But only a true one, not a materialist one.

In that very short time, I didn't remember my past alone, without him. I saw him like I had been with him all my life.

He went on by repeating the same story, "You know Bamurangirwa when I saw you at my free time I was escorting you, and when sometimes you turned your head back, I wanted to tell you that we are together, but thought that might scare you. But I was always happy to see you in front of me, though I was scared in case when you would meet a man who would show that he might be your lover or more than that, but I was aware of that too. Luckily you didn't meet anyone yet. I already know all of places you go I have escorted you almost everywhere, but I didn't ask you where you come from." This was a question and I had to answer him.

"I come from Rwanda."

"I know some Rwandans came in recent years because of the war."

"I am one of them." He looked to be quiet for some few seconds.

"Let me go and you too go back to wait for the children I will be visiting you if it will be OK with your family."

"When you have time you can come, my family they are not bad people." He gave me his hand to say bye, my hand in his, was like a child's in a grown-up's, we held each other for seconds in silence, I forgot to make any sign to let me go, in that silence he let my hand go, but used both his hands to hold my head and force me to look up at him, he was looking down at me for some time but I didn't manage to look at him.

I closed my eyes, I was shy like any girl should be, he let me go and before he turned to go, it was like he had forgotten something.

"Bamurangirwa do you think that your family can be happy to see you with a non-Rwandan one?"

"Why you ask me that? We will talk next time, go home but please remember that I am here for you, if will be possible always."

I turned to go home, we were not far yet, but I had to go and do housework.

On the way home I found myself thinking of Alex non-stop, wondering how strong love could be, with it came no time to think of any other thing, like where the person came from, wealth or any other thing, you could only be there, thinking and wishing to be with that person, thinking of him or her to be yours and feeling that person to be your peace. I turned my head back and our eyes met and we went ahead after, we went where we were going.

73

Where fear of the army was, went proudness that it was them who protected us to be able to be in peace. Without them a country can be nothing.

When Karoli came back I told him about my visitors, and he was surprised to hear that I had visitors from the army. He asked me his tribe and when I told him that he was Samia he didn't like it, but didn't say much, I was aware of that.

I went ahead to tell him that he would come back the next day in case I had not yet come back, since he would be at home the whole day to welcome him for me. It was time for questions between me and him.

"How will I know him?" he asked

"He will introduce himself; even though today was the first time I saw him."

"How did he know here?"

I told him how he was following me. And it seemed to surprise him and he told me that he loved me, I didn't have to hurt him.

We laughed but deep down I meant it. I didn't want anything which could hurt Alex.

Karoli and I used to chat a lot as if we were the same age, he went ahead by asking me a lot about Alex and I was telling him what I was supposed to tell him, I didn't know him much yet, but I liked the story because it was like a good movie which was going around in my mind, and which I didn't want to stop.

Next day was my college day, from college I didn't stop to Kantamage's home, and they thought that was because of the children they could be by themselves in case Karoli was not there so to them I was a good girl, they didn't know that I had a new reason, that I had Alex.

At home I was alone even Karoli was not there, and I did my normal housework but that time I wanted to finish what I had to do so that I could be free when he came. Karoli come back and I give him something to eat, when he come where I was, he made a joke to me by asking in case Alex did not come, if I would become sick, but I didn't want that joke, I thought that in case if he couldn't come back again it would be shame for me in front of Karoli, and I regreted telling him about it.

After some time Karoli came in the kitchen where I was, looking at me smiling then I stood looking at him, but I was serious. He was jumping here and there, and I wanted to tell him not to be like he was enjoying me.

I asked him once more to tell me what was going on, he was looking surprised or happy, finally he told me to do what I was doing quickly because my visitor had come, that he was going to be with them and we would talk the rest later, he meant that he would see if he was a good person or not.

After a short time I went to the mirror for some minutes and then after to be satisfied I went inside to greet Alex. I was happy to see him again but on the other hand I was nervous, inside the house, Alex came by himself without his friend, after I went to greet him and to introduce them to each other, I asked him what could I give him and he said what I had, I chose to give him orange juice.

After that I left him with Karoli and I saw that they were comfortable together, it made me feel relaxed, time for him to go back, Karoli came where I was with the children, and told me that my visitor was going, we escorted him but I reached near and left Karoli to push him ahead.

Time came after the children went to sleep, when Karoli and I were having our dinner he called me, and I knew he was going to tell me about Alex, I wanted to hear his view about him.

He started with loud laugh and after he said that I was lucky girl to meet a man like him, no one would know that he came from that tribe! I asked him why and he simply said that he looked good with good behaviour.

I didn't say anything to that point since I believed that everywhere there were people with different behaviour and looks. Even he the first time he didn't know where I came from and he didn't mind, that to him was not the point.

Karoli went on by telling me how good Alex was, and he told me that if I had anything I would want him to help with, to be free to tell him, since he would not like to see that I missed him, maybe to be my messenger. I laughed and we went to sleep.

After that Alex was visiting me regularly when Mpanumusingo and his wife came back they were already like family friends. One day when I was escorting him he asked me, to tell him when I would visit him, and maybe because I had not had that in my mind, that he would ask me to visit him, it shocked me and he noticed it, he asked me why it shocked me and I said nothing, he went on to say that maybe there was a time I had visited a man and he did or he tried to do something bad to me.

If so he assured me that I would be safe in his home, if I could trust him but if I couldn't it would not change anything, it was not a must to visit him when I didn't feel free and happy to do that, and he would escort me back up to home if I would come, he went ahead by telling me that if there was any man who did something to hurt me, if he could meet him, he would pay for that and it would be his last time to play with girls.

After long conversations I thought that to refuse his invitation would show him that I didn't trust him, to go with someone like one of my friends, is the same thing, then I would go by myself after college.

When I told him, it shocked him, he didn't believe that he heard correct and I had to repeat, he seemed to be happy and since I didn't know his home he told me that he would meet me on the way, I told him a time. And we parted.

At night when I was thinking that I would visit Alex I had two thoughts, one I was wondering if it was good idea to say yes, or if I put myself in a dangerous situation to go to a soldier's house. I left the rest for God and told myself again that sometimes we do mistakes when we see that they are mistakes, and we call God after to see ourselves in the middle of the danger, like we are giving God a test.

I had a lot of questions some of them I got answers and others had none, or saw them to be childish.

When I came from the college I didn't stay for long on the way not even Kantamage's home when I was near their gate I saw two young men come where I was, from in front of me, it was Alex and his friend John.

We greeted each other and they were in front of me, I was behind and I started to ask myself again where and why I was going, I tried to look calm as much as possible.

Inside the house was small but clean with a few things which were in order, both men sat one side and they showed me where to sit, another side opposite, it was Alex who asked me what I would take but I told him that I was OK, something both of them refused to hear and told me that in their home visitors had to have something, then I chose milk which I got. They tried to make me busy by showing me the photos, and coming up with different conversations.

After one hour, I told them that I would like to go home and Alex asked me if I wanted to be home before Karoli, and I said yes something which he supported and thanked me for visiting him.

I was out waiting for them, they came out with a big bag, it was John who had it, and I thought that they would go somewhere after to part with me, I saw that when we started our way home they didn't lock the door, and when I asked them why, they told me that they didn't have a thief and didn't even have anything they could steal, at that all of us we laughed.

At my home I showed them where to sit but before they gave me the bag and told me that they were my things they only need back the bag.

It surprised me and I had to ask them again they looked to each other with a smile and I went in the room, inside were many tins of things, food and different beers.

But a part from the tins there was a big paper bag which was not heavy and I opened it in quick way, when I saw what was inside, I threw it on the bed as if I saw snake, that is an animal many people fear.

After a short time I picked my gift again, it was two dresses which had different fashions and everything was different but they looked to be too expensive. It shocked me because it was the last thing I would even guess that I could get from him, it was not any kind of gift which was in my mind. I felt shy and nervous. I didn't know how I would thank him, to go back where they were was not easy but I had to go.

Back in the sitting room they were not bored, they were acting like they used the house, it was like somehow home to them, when I was there all of them looked to be happy and they were waiting for me to see how I would take it, it was a big test and they knew it.

I was speechless and I saw that they were enjoying seeing me like that.

I had to say something anyway, I questioned them. "How can I thank you?"

"Are you happy with it?"

"Everyone I am sure can be happy for beautiful gifts like that, it was a big surprise."

"If you are happy then I am happy."

I thought it was good to try the dress for him, and I asked if they would like me to see me wearing them.

"Yes thank you. I would like to see you wearing them but it would not be easy for me to ask you to do that."

I dressed the first one. I tried to make myself look more beautiful by combing my hair again, when I looked in the mirror I saw that I had changed a lot, is like I was someone else. I thought that the gift would surprise all my family. I stared to ask myself when I would wear them and where I would go where would be a good enough place to wear them. In front of them I went straight near of Alex and he was turning me here and there like he was making it straight, he was touching it everywhere, and to get something to say I asked if I looked smart, and he said that I looked fantastic. I didn't want to leave behind his friend, so, I turned to him and asked him if it was true, I looked that good, and his reply was that even the person who wore it is beautiful. The second dress was more beautiful than the first one, after wearing it even I myself, noticed that I was too beautiful.

In front of them they looked to be speechless too, and they looked to each other with very short words, which I didn't understand, and I had no time to know all of that, seconds later Alex stood up and held my shoulders when he looked down at me, it was like he was talking to himself and said, "You are so beautiful Bamurangirwa." All of that was making me too shy, I thanked him again and went back to change into the one I was in before, when I was back they told me that it was their time to go back and I escorted them for a short distance.

They went. I was home with surprising gifts waiting Karoli.

After our dinner I told Karoli that I had a lot of stories.

"Alex's stories?" Karoli said.

"It must to be his?"

"Yes now Alex is our headline."

"I visited him."

"You did what?! You are telling me that you went at his home?"

"Yes I had his invitation but I didn't stay for long, he was with his friend, and they escorted me up to here. But there are more stories." I told him that without giving him time to say anything; in case he said what I didn't want to hear.

I went in the room and came back with the bag of things he was too surprised and said that we would use some of the food he brought us for some time, and since he knew that I didn't drink, it meant that the beer was his.

"OK," I said, "you can even start now to drink."

He told me, "You know Bamurangirwa this man loves you, you have to know that."

He was not yet to know about the dress, I went inside and came back wearing one of the dresses, when Karoli saw me he held his mouth as a sign of being too surprised.

"Bamurangirwa you want to tell me that this dress, it was Alex who gave it to you?"

"Where can I get money from? Yes it was him." When he was still drinking, I went and put on other one and when I stood in front of him he stood up and said a word to show big surprise which in

Kinyarwanda called it 'kwirahira', someone metioned the name of an important person to him or her normally who give him or her a cow, he held his mouth for second after, 'kwirahira', and it was question time again.

"This man you know him before or?"

"No I knew him from time I told you."

Kalori said, "This man he might have some worry that he will not get you!"

At night I didn't sleep most of the time I saw us together when I wore one of the dresses and Alex was putting me in front of him, by putting his wide strong hand on my back, I wanted that movie in my mind to go on and on and on.

Next day evening he came back alone without his friend, I was at home and I didn't know if he would come but any time I wanted to see him, I welcomed him as usual to show him where to sit and gave him something to drink.

He moved from where he was and came near where I was sitting, one of his arms went round my shoulder and the other one held my cheek he put my face up to look at him, I closed my eyes after a few seconds I had his teeth on my cheek, he bit me but in a soft way, he let me go.

At that time he went back to where he was and all of that time we were in silence I saw that there might be something wrong. After one minute in that silence he put his hands on his face and his head down on his knees, I was confused, didn't know what is going on if he had somewhere where it hurt him, it might be worse, then after I came to know that was is crying!

I didn't know that men also could cry, on top of that, this one was a soldier, with his height, the way he looked to be that strong and everything, the way he look I had no idea that there could be something which could make him feel soft and sad enough to cry! To me that was strange, but I saw that he was human too, I wanted to go and hold him tightly but I was not brave enough to do that. I had to wait and see what it was, when he took some time in that position, I had to go near him and try to find out what it was, with a hope that was not a kind of sickness which comes up.

There were only two of us, I had to be brave and go to try to see if there was something I could do to help.

I held him so tightly, and he put his head on my shoulder and seemed relaxe but both of us were still in silence, after one minute he had a handkerchief with a soft smile he was apologising to me by telling me that he was weak.

He stood up and held both two pockets of his trousers and walked slowly around the sitting room. I waited and looked at him in that silence.

After seconds he turned and sat near me, he called my name in short to save time. I turned my head and we looked to each other.

He said, "I have something to tell you. Number one: our work many times we are aware, can make us do something we are not happy with, like take us anywhere any time when there are reasons, now I come to say that I am going and to ask you one question."

"Where are going and which question do you want to ask me? And when are you going?"

Alex said, "I can't say that you are the first girl I met, but you are the first girl I loved as soon as I saw you without waiting to know more, and I always have peace in me when I see you and want to be by your side forever, and be in that peace in my future, if by luck you too have the same feeling towards me. As I told you I have no power, my boss has rights on me to change me any where any time as I said, so now they want to send me to America for a course of between one year and two. I have only two months I am going home to say bye to my family, and I want to hear what you say, so that I can know what to tell my family. My boss expected me to be happy, normally this is good chance, but because of you I can't be happy to see that maybe I might lose you."

On my side soon after to hear that he was going, I felt sick and I assumed all things had changed; they were going to turn in a bad direction. I saw that I might have a hard test in front of me. After his talk he waited for my answer, in that confusion he noticed that I changed: but anyhow I had to tell him something then I asked him his question again.

"What I want to hear from you is to hear you telling me that you love me enough to be my future wife so when I will be with my parents I will be proud to tell them about you."

I said, "You mean you're still doubting that I love you?"

"I might know that you do, but please I would like to see you say so Bamurangirwa."

"Look Alex I love you be sure of that."

"Are you happy to be with me in all of your life as I am happy to see you on my side?" Alex asked. The question was strange to me and I was quiet for some time, and he had to repeat it.

Yes I wanted to be with him forever, I said yes I was, in a weak voice and I felt weak too. Had a lot of doubt now, many questions in less than a second.

He held me and hugged me so tightly for some time, he was shaking, I think for that time I was stronger than him. After he let me go, he looked to be so happy and relaxed, as if we were in front of authority, and we were putting our signs down on the papers saying 'yes I do'.

Alex said, "What I am worried of is your brother."

"What about him?"

"He will not giving us his blessing because I am not Rwandan."

"I didn't see that, if I tell him that I love you and I want to be with you it is my choice then. I don't think that can be any problem since is my life. Your background can't be a point to me, so it will have to be the same to him."

"What do you think about the old man?" He meant my father. I told him in brief that concerning that point that my father was someone who didn't understand some families which chose or forced their children to marry because of different tribes, where people came from. That he was better than many including brothers.

He looked to be happy and asked my address where he would be passing my letters when he was still with his parents, and I gave him Mpanumusingo's box number of his office, since that was the only address I had to give all my friends.

Alex said, "When I will be back I will talk to him and see if he will arange us to make a wedding so that we can go together."

"We can't have wedding without my father," I said.

"To bring him is very easy; according the way you talk about him he will come no problem."

It was my time to ask him some questions. "Now what about your parents what do you think they will say about a Rwandan girl?"

Alex said, "To me there is no problem even my mother is not my father's tribe she is Kenyan, concerning you to be Rwandan, I will not be the only one who has a wife from Rwanda, there are a few and it can be respectful to us as a family, because with some reason we love and respect girls from Rwanda." He went on and said that the other thing which worried him, was in case they refused us to marry and go together. He said, "You know it might a be long time, I don't know if you can be patient and wait for me."

"At that point it is me who can be worried that you will see other girls."

"Forget about other girls I have seen many before, don't even think about them. I know about the dowry even us we give them to our girls. I will give them whatever they will ask me, I will make sure to see that they are happy, I have other plan, but I will say this when time comes."

"You can tell me now no problem."

"It is that I will build a good permanent house for your father who will be happy with, and know that he has a beautiful daughter." He was smiling when he was talking about the last words, and I smiled too. He took some pictures of me and left.

I didn't tell Karoli any of this. I said that they would know when the time came.

When he was at his parents, he sent me letters telling me that his parents were happy for him, and they liked me a lot, now next was to

83

come back and talk with my brother and see the next thing. I told Karoli that if he wanted to talk about Alex fine, but he had to leave that story for me to tell his sister, meaning that he could tell Mpanumusingo if he wanted to.

Soon after Alex went, after two days Mpanumusingo and his wife came back.

Next day Mpanumusingo went to work, after my sister-in-law and I were alone finishing what normally we had to do in the morning time, at that time it was a good time to sit down and talk about this and that, including talking behind the backs of other people and friends.

I started my new story, the story of my Alex; I told her each and everything. I enjoyed telling her because she was acting like she was hearing a kind of interesting story, and I liked her for that. She was silent only listening to me sometimes she was holding her mouth, a sign of surprise or clapping her hands. After finishing my story, I came with the dresses to show her, when she saw them she was acting dumb, only she said that no time is a short time, whatever time is, things could change in other directions.

And again she said that we had to pray for this man, or for everything concerning this good news so that nothing would come between us and disappoint him.

Alex's time to come back home came, I was at home with my sister-in-law after sitting down, I made introductions that he is my friend Alex, and she is my sister-in-law Urutundi. We had a brief conversation and Urutundi excused herself and went to the kitchen, when she went Alex asked me if I told them about us, and I told him that I only told Urutundi and she would tell my brother.

Alex said, "Can you call her for me I want to give a message myself to your brother and go I don't want him to meet me here before she has told him; I want to get an appointment to meet him."

I was in front of the kitchen Urutundi used her hands as a sign of calling me near her, when I was there I told her that Alex wanted to talk to her.

Urutundi said, "Why do you think he want to talk to me?"

I said, "He wants to give you Mpanumusingo's message."

"I can see that this young man he means what he says."

She stood up and told me to come with her and I refused by telling her that it was her who he wanted to see not me, instead I would do what she was doing.

She made herself ready to go inside, she was there for some time and when she came back she told me that he wanted to go. Inside Urutundi said bye to him, and told me to see him off, when we were outside, he told me that he would be back the next day, that Urutundi told him in good time to see Mpanumusingo, and he hoped that the meeting would go on well. I didn't go far with him. I wanted to hear what Urutundi said about him with hope that she would support me. Back with Urutundi I wanted to hear her side as soon as possible after to sit down.

Urutundi said, "Bamurangirwa there is nothing I can say, it is not understandable, love is too strong and sometimes really blind, what does a man like Alex want with a short girl like you?!" Both of us we laughed at that. I was proud to have a man who anyone saw as really a man, then I told her that I wanted to hear their conversations with my brother.

Urutundi said, "He wants to talk with your brother, to him, even if he can get the green light to make a wedding tomorrow he can be happy."

"And what do you think, how will Mpanumusingo take it?"

Urutundi replied, "I don't see why cannot give him the green light, he wants to do things in an open and respectful way, that is a man anyone would be happy to welcome in to their family." To me in my heart I didn't want other thoughts which were coming in my mind that maybe Mpanumusingo would make excuses because he was not Rwandan.

Next day Alex came with his friend John in an army car, Mpanumusingo and Karoli were waiting for him. Urutundi wanted me to go and greet them but I refused by telling her that that day they

85

were Mpanumusingo and Karoli's visitors not mine, but on the other hand I felt that I could faint in front of them because I was shy and nervous. When they came they were welcomed by Urutundi, Karoli and Mpanumusingo, they had some beers which they brought with them. To Rwandan people that was something important to offer respect to visitors, unless if for some reason they didn't drink, their time to go came and they went without seeing me.

When they went Urutundi told me that she would tell me the whole story the next day when we were free.

Even before that, I was sure that Mpanumusingo when he saw Alex, who was almost the same height as him and the same light skin, only Alex was stronger than him. That concerning the look he would not have any excuses, unless if he was going to make the excuse that he was a soldier and not Rwandan, because I knew him like many Tutsi, they had that problem, they had a kind of racism and knew themselves to be superior for everything: no one else who could be this and that, even looks, had to be a Tutsi to be handsome or a beautiful girl, brave, sharp minded and some knew to give others funny names, and yes I knew that the majority of Tutsi had that problem. That was their mistake as when I believe that everywhere else people had some mistakes concerning their nature. So I had a good reason to worry about my brother, I wished that my father could be there.

At night when we were having our dinner, Mpanumusingo went ahead to try to make fun of me by talking about soldiers, that it shows that I am too brave to be with a soldier… sometimes they were laughing but I didn't say anything, but I still had doubt about what would happen, I had to wait when Urutundi would tell me, at night I didn't sleep well, I had many different questions, and different pictures of how it would be, when I will be Alex's wife, and in case for some it might not go well. I saw myself to be still in Mpanumusingo's prison, he had the power over me. I had to be an African girl, Rwandan girl, who had to be under my elders for everything concerning my life, concerning my future, so it was a matter of waiting and hoping.

Next day when our time came Urutundi started to tell me stories, how they came, how they welcomed them, that time they came with a lot of different type of beers, that Alex wanted to come with his friends next week and meet our people: so that we could pass the first stage of our culture concerning the wedding, so after a few days came the wedding day. She said, "Something your brother was against by saying that is too soon, and when he went he told us that if he said yes it can seem that he is tired of taking care of you, but he assured him that no matter how long he will be there he will gate you here, you are going to wait for him and Mpanumusingo is not going to give green light to any other man to marry you."

She continued, "He asked permission to go with you in town to get a college for you, and he will pay, again his friend John when he's here in Masaka he will be coming to see us, Mpanumusingo say that is no problem, by going with you in town but Alex was not happy about that waiting matter. Mpanumusingo told him to pay for the first term so he would pay the rest. What do you say about that?"

I said, "It is OK," but to me was not OK, I didn't see good reason for that pride that kept me there, and saying that he would even pay my school fees, why didn't he pay for it when I was begging him? I was upset now; I had a lot of questions in my mind, what if he was there for long time and met another girl? What if by bad luck I met a mad man who raped me and I become pregnant? And would he really pay those fees? But I was not brave enough to do otherwise. I had to pretend that everything was right.

The day Alex had to take me to town he came home, and he waited for when I made myself ready, I chose one of the dresses he bought for me and I choose the best one since I didn't know when I would wear it again, I didn't know when I would be with him again. After, to see myself that I was OK to go in front of him, I first I wanted Urutundi to see me and she told me that I was not the same Bamurangirwa she was with a few minutes ago. That I looked too beautiful.

When I was in the sitting room Alex looked a little shocked and he stood up and came to where I was to welcome me, and he touched me on the shoulder and looked down at me and in a low heavy strong voice said, "You are beautiful and you look so smart." I thanked him without looking up at him, we were out, first we turned and said bye to Urutundi, who was there waiting for us to go. Alex held the passenger door and show me a sign to go inside, after I sat he started the car and we left.

At the college he paid three months before, he made introductions to the teachers and they gave me some papers to tell me about the college, and we went outside but we didn't get inside the car, he took me in shops and told me to choose the dresses I wanted, I told him that was not necessary I had enough and I meant it, but he insisted then I chose a few. "Good or let me choose for you," he said. I didn't want him to think that I was greedy, I choose a cheap one, after he took back all that I had chosen and he was the one who was choosing for me.

Since Kantamage was near the road, we passed there and I made introduction: Kantamage asked us what we would like, I told her that we were hungry but Alex was in a hurry, and Alex told her that he didn't take me to the hotel to eat, he thought that I might not like it. So I told Kantamage to give us milk which she did, she gave us milk in a big mug and we were OK and ready to go.

At Mpanumusingo's home Urutundi gave us some fruits, after a short time Alex said that he was going, but Urutundi wanted him to wait for dinner, but he said that he had to go, at that time he said bye and I saw him go.

When we were by ourselves I told Urutundi what happened and showed her what he bought for me, then Urutundi said that it was as if I was not his fiancé, it was like he wass leaving back his wife!

Since there was no other communication he didn't come for a few days and I didn't know what was going on, we were in the kitchen when children came telling us that we had a visitor, inside the sitting room was Alex and John, Urutundi insisted to give them something to drink, they had told us already that they were in hurry.

They stood up and we saw them off, but Urutundi didn't reach far, she excused herself to go back for the children, and John said that he had someone who was waiting for him at home, we were left by ourselves.

It was 24th March 1968, evening time, that time with Alex after Urutundi and John left, Alex came near me and held my hand, we were walking very slowly, hand in hand in silence, then after one minute Alex called my name when he looked down at me, and my body and heart felt his eyes without having to look up at him. My heart and my body, all of me, had fear that I might lose him, he broke the silence and started to tell me what he had to say.

He went ahead, "Bamurangirwa I am going but please know that I am going on my behalf and your behalf and our future family, please don't break your promises, I am worried that men will show you many different things – they might use the same eyes I used to see you and do all they can to change you."

I told him that it was me who had to be worried that women would take him from me, and he told me what he told me always, that he had seen many already, he turned to me and hugged me so tight for seconds, one arm holding my face and made me to look up at him, I was closing my eyes and within no time his lips were to mine, and I wanted to be there forever, it was for a very short time and he let me go, he put one hand in his pocket and the hand came up with an envelope, he gave it to me. I asked what it was and he said that I would see what it was after, he said bye and we parted, he went on his way and I turned back.

When I was going I was turning my head to see where he reached but any time when I turned our eyes were meeting because he too was turning until when he reached where we couldn't see each other.

I told myself that I would tell no one about that letter, I hid it under my bed and came back and went ahead with normal housework. Whatever I was doing, in my heart was the letter, time came to go to sleep, quickly I got the envelope, opened it, and inside was a letter and money. I didn't bother the money; I was in a hurry to read the words he told me.

Dear Bamurangirwa, as I told you before I am going on behalf of me and you, on behalf of our future children, I can say that because of thinking about you maybe I will fail, but no, I believe that it will make me work too hard so that in the future I will be able to take care of you in the way I am planning to, and our future children can be happy and proud to have parents like us. I will take very good care of you Bamurangirwa that is a promise; everyone who will know you will see that you are the luckiest girl in the world.

That money, just keep them, it will be helping you in small things so that you will not go to your brother to ask him for the money soon.

I will be sending you a letter many times using addresses you give me because we don't have other ways of communication, try to reply as soon as you receive them, so that I can know that you received them, at times I will know how I will be sending you more money, maybe I will use John at times he will be there. Some religions say that wife comes from the side of man, but me I see that one is head, other one is heart, so since this is two important parts of our body, no one who can survive without one of these parts.

Love you forever.

Yours, Alex xxxx

After got to America we went ahead with our communication, I had to get a letter from him once a week or twice a month, yes Mpanumusingo was giving me all my letters and I had no one else to pass my letters to. I had no reason to think about it. John went ahead to visit me, after three months I sent him my report from college, I was passed with good results; I was happy and proud to send them. I was able to use a typing machine very well and knew a little English but to write it was still a problem, according to the level I was at it was OK.

When he saw my result he was happy too, and sais that even if he has enough money, but I still wanted to have my private businesses or find a job, or join any other course he would support me, he liked hard working people and he saw me to be one of them.

To that point I said that I got the man I was looking for.

I saw him to be the man of my dreams, the man who was able to help me to help my people when it was needed, in that way I would even be able to go to see our family we left in Rwanda.

Only I was sad because I saw that I was going to be someone when my mum was no longer with me.

I got a letter from him telling me that he wanted to surprise me, to come to visit Africa for a very short time, but things changed, he would not come, still it made me happy. I was taking some of letters to read together with Urutundi, the person I had to read all of my letters with was Mukabagira but when we came back from Buwenda, I heard that she was in Kampala with her sister Ingabire, both were married and rich and they had kept their mum in another situation of life, a different life style to what she had before. And I knew that I couldn't get permission to go to Kampala.

I knew that when Alex came, I would be free and I could go with him to visit Mukabagira, and everywhere I wanted.

John came to tell us that we would not see him again as they gave him a transfer to Mbarara, to me that was not good because he was there for me in case.

Our communication went well until after five months, when I first waited for his letter for the whole month, something which was strange to me. Mpanumusingo was still giving me letters from other friends, I asked him if he didn't get letters from Alex yet for the whole month, and he said he didn't get them yet. I told myself that I would not ask him again because if there were no letters then there were no letters. I was sending letters to him as normal asking him what was going on there and if he was OK or what. I was confused with millions of questions, John was not there, and he was the one who could tell me what the problem was if there were any. I was not wife to Alex yet, if I was wife, I would have a right to go to the boss and ask him, but now I couldn't go to the army's boss to ask him about his soldiers, telling him that I was just a friend, he would think that I was completely mad!

I changed a lot for everything, in conversations, housework, everything went slowly. I was not the same even my health I started to feel like if I was sick.

But no one asked me what was wrong with me, or if I needed any help. I was on my own; my prayers were that wherever he was whatever he was doing everything would be alright. Time came to go back home after I had no fees. All the time when I was alone I was crying, sometimes crying in a loud voice asking my God what was happening to me: and why? But God didn't tell me anything. I was angry with them now more than ever, seeing that if it was not for their pride, I would be in America with the man I loved. Again I wished that I had my mum, she could get comforting words to tell me, and I was sure that some other things would happen to me anyway, or if I was with Mukabagira, she could understand what I felt and at least she could be there for me.

It showed me that they would fight everything they could to make me a better person, the reason I did not know why, when normally they had to fight for whatever possible way to put me in a good position. I felt bitterness and hatred. I wanted to go somewhere far from them, anywhere, but far from them. I had heard stories that when someone had a misunderstanding between him or her with their family, but without proper reasons, when this person had a bad life in the future, the family would say that they knew it, that he or she would be useless, but when this person had a better life in the future, they would say that they knew it, that he or she would be a better person and come back and be friends and forget or pretend to forget all that happened in the past. That is what will happen to me, and I would be better than them, I didn't know how, but I would. I had that hope. My mother told me to love myself and always have a hope, I had a hope.

WHEN I MET NYIRASOKO

Time I was sick of sitting at home with houswork and was not comfortable with people who I was with. It forced me to go back where I was before the charity, it was a matter of passing time and meeting people, one day when I was coming from charity as always I had to pass Kantamage's home, in order to reach where I was calling my home, Mpanumusingo's. Someone knocked the door when we opened it was Kantamage's child, I was in the house only a few minutes, it was like the child came soon after I left, and what surprised us is why they didn't give me the message instead of sending the child soon after I came from there, so when we asked the child what happened, he told us that his mother wanted me to go back to her home!

We tried to ask him what happened and he told us nothing, and said that maybe the visitor who came is the one who wants to see me.

When we asked who, he told us that it was a lady but it was the first time they saw her. I couldn't refuse but I was tired, and was too hot, I went but I was not happy. I also went with slippers thinking that would show them that I was not ready to go anywhere.

At Kantamage's home was a lady, it was my first time to see her, when both of them saw me they seemed to be so happy. It confused me why they were happy this much, what was going on here? I asked myself.

She looked to be a very rich woman, just to see how she was dressed, from the scarf she had on her head, handbag, shoes, the dress which was known because it was latest and was only for rich woman, because it was very expensive.

Kantamage did introductions, that this lady was Nyirasoko, young sister to ex-wife to Mpanumusingo, who married a Muganda man at Butambara area. "Have you heard about her?" they asked me. And I had heard about her. I said yes. I wanted them to tell me what they had to tell me in brief. I didn't want more stories concerning her. Only from the few minutes I was there already I didn't like her, the way she was talking in a way of showing off, trying to show to anyone who was there so they could know that she was rich, in my nature I hate to show off for anything.

After a short time my sister called me and took me in the room, she asked me, "Have you seen Nyirasoko?"

The question to me was meaningless and a surprise, "Yes," I said, "I saw her."

Kantamage said, "How do you see her?"

"She is like anybody," I said.

At this point she looked to be excited and she told me that it was her who wanted to see me.

Again I had to ask her if she wanted to see me, why she didn't come where I was instead to bringing me back in this sun, I asked her. And she was looking at me to see that I might be happy but she was disappointed because I was angry.

"Can't you see how rich she is? She can't be able to go up and down that mountain with this sun!" Since I saw that she expected to see me happy for all of that, I chose to keep quiet, because if I had to talk I had to ask her why she didn't come with her car? And to behave the way she does, did she think that would going to help her in anything?

I think it surprised her to see me quiet without questions, or it made her happy, but after I asked her why she wanted to see me when she didn't know me yet?

Kantamage said, "She seems to be relaxed and has got something to say, look serious and happy, you know Bamurangirwa, you can't know how God works, this is to show someone who knows her people, to think of us and want to keep good bond between us as family. She wanted you to go with her and know where she lives, so that you can take us next time and we can be visiting her."

"Must I go with her today?" I asked.

Kantamage said, "Yes it must be today because she can't spend the night here, she was not ready for that as she has young children."

"I can't go back to make myself ready and to get a dress and shoes? If she can direct me I can go by myself next time, I can't get lost."

Kantamage looked to be very happy and also looked like she was trying hard before I changed my mind, she told me that normally I didn't like long dressed but I could choose from any of hers.

"What about shoes?"

"That is no problem you will be in a long dress, no one will notice that you are in slippers," she said. I had to say yes, I was wondering why all of this was happening, all of that was strange to me but there was nothing else I could do, I had to go and see what it was, I told myself that if they thought that I might be there even for two days they were going to be disappointed: because I have to come back the next day. It was like they had kidnapped me then.

My sister was happy and she put aside the work she had been given to do.

"I am going, but I will be back tomorrow," I said.

"That is no problem," my sister said.

"Give me some money for my transport back?" I asked my sister.

With big surprise she asked me, "You think that someone like her can't afford that transport?!"

Because I respected my elders, I had to do it, and be kidnapped, go somewhere I didn't know, without even a single pen in my hand, because I was angry, I had to choose one of her best dresses and most expensive of all her dresses, which she wore only on big occasions, with a hope that she would refuse and try to give me another one, so that I would have an excuse to refuse to go too, but she was very clever, I think she knew why I did it, without any word she said that it was no problem. I could wear it if that was what I wanted. All of that was surprising me but my heart couldn't tell me more. I thought that my sister saw Nyirasoko to be too rich, and that is why she was trying anything to praise her, because there are some people who give a lot of respect to someone only because they see that person to be rich. I was not that kind of person, to me people they are the same, you are rich today and maybe tomorrow you might become poor, and someone who you would see down because she or he is poor could become rich in no time. But Kantamage was my elder sister and I knew she loved me, so I had to respect her because of that reason.

I had already known that Ugandans were very clean people, their body, what they wore, food, and their houses too.

Most of them had a kitchen separate from the main house, because they used firewood for cooking the main house had to have some bedrooms and a sitting room. Sometimes they put some kind of beautiful grass and put full mats there so that was a place to sit for themselves and their visitors. Each time you sat on the mats or grass they put food down in the middle of you, the food must have been matoke and some other things like meat. The matoke they cooked by tying them in banana leaves, and putting them on the pot and cooking by steaming them.

And when eating they also might not need plates if they chose not to. The main thing with the cooking and eating up to now in some areas was banana leaves, that style was important, it was seen to be a good culture and hygienic.

I started my journey with Nyirasoko, we were using public transport and she didn't get the car which passed near her home according to her stories, and we were forced to go with any we could get since it was late so we walked the rest of the distance. When we were out of the car we started to go in silence. I was angry because of the unnecessary journey I was on, I would not get a word to talk with her, she still had her kind of words she had before, in a show off way. What made me not understand her more, was that she seemed like she was trying to teach me Islam religion, though she was talking by herself, something which to her seemed to be no problem. I had no idea of that religion at all, so I didn't know what she was talking about, but since was not telling me directly, and was just mentioning Islam only when she was shocked with something. The away I knew at that at the time was because we as Rwandans, if you mentioned someone who was important to you especially who gaves you a cow, as I said before. I thought that Islam was the name of her important person, or otherwise she had something wrong.

We reached at her home 9.00pm, her home was a good place, top of the mountain, looked to be a relaxing area, a lot of green banana trees, big house coved with iron-sheets, which outside looked to be a good house, with small hut kitchen, a hut curved with grass, built with a few trees which had a little mud between them.

Outside Nyirasoko made a little shout to let them know that she was there.

I heard inside the house noises at that time the door was wide open with children, who were fighting to come out, each and every one wanted to be number one to come out, and there were many young children around four to ten years old, some of them looked to be the same age, you could think that they were twins. I was asking myself how all of those children could be of one woman, and it was too late to say that they were neighbours, because it was too late to be out of the home, so they must be her children. They looked dirty, their body and their torn dresses, only one old boy who looked like he was my age, he was the only one one who was clean and smart.

We were inside the house in the sitting room, the floor was dusty and dirty, with torn mats, that is where the children sat, there was one old long bench that is where I sat. Fifty percent of that room was dry coffee, after a short time there came an old man, tall and dark, looked clean with a long white dress. This was respect dress to Ugandan men, 'kanzu', especially in the countryside, which I came to know was the dress for Arabic men too. He had a small white hat which afterwards I came to know that it was a sign of Islam religion to men. I thought that might be their neighbour. Nyirasoko knelt down to greet him, according to Ugandan culture, I started to ask myself how I was going to greet him but, I chose to greet him while I was sitting where I was, kneeling was not my culture, and I was not supporting it. After a short time he went out but I already knew that he was Nyirasoko's husband according to the way I saw how he went up and down inside the house.

They came with tea for both of us, tea which I had last time in Nyabyondo, it was different in that it had sugar, they didn't ask me if I took sugar or how much. We started to drink our tea, when they came with a small basket which was old and dirty, inside were pieces of bread which looked like they used their hands to cut. I saw the room the way it looked, I saw that basket and the way they had cut their bread, all of the things which were in front of me were strange and dirty, including their children. I nearly refused to eat the bread, but I thought that they might think that I was trying to show them that I was more special than them, and I didn't want to be seen that way, so I ate. Nyirasoko was busy in the kitchen, but as soon as we reached home her children told her people who came looking for her, and said that they would come back to see if she was back.

After our tea, when Nyirasoko came inside the house, two children came, after greetings they told her that their mum asked her to give them her scarf because she would go somewhere early in the morning. I saw Nyirasoko get out the scarf she had on her head and just give it to them like that without even putting it in some bag! I thought that was a shock to her, for the children to ask for it in front of me.

What was worse was that her head looked too rough, you would think that she stayed days without combing her hair.

After a short time, around five minutes, came another two children and also after greeting, they told Nyirasoko that it was the third time they had had to come, and their mum wanted her dress and shoes back! I turned my head to see if there was someone I could give a wink to, I saw no one. I wished that I had Mukabagira who I could tell this movie to, I was disappointed to keep it for myself only. But I would keep it for her whatever time I would see her. I said at last if these children had not mentioned these things by name maybe they could leave them to Nyirasoko, but maybe because they were tired of coming many times or they didn't see anything wrong by that.

Nyirasoko went to the room and came back with a small paper bag in her hand and put inside the shoes which were still in the sitting room in front of us! She gave them the paper bag, they went

I wished Kantamage was with me. What I didn't know the end of was the handbag. I did not know if was hers or not, but what I saw was more than enough.

At that time the old man came back and went in the room which was opposite where I was sitting, he called one of the children, and after the child came back he told me that his father wanted me to go in the room!

I had to ask him again to be sure that I heard him correctly, and yes, he said that he wanted to see me. I thought that he couldn't hear well, but I would go and see. I was walking very slowly, telling myself in case the child didn't hear correctly what reason could I give that had made me to go to his room?!

In front of the door I asked him if he called me, and he said yes, he was sitting on the bed looking at the door like he was waiting for someone, the room was small but very clean. There was cement on the floor and a new good colourful mat, you would think that the room was not inside that house, the double bed was covered with a new bedcover, the walls, everywhere, everywhere and everything in that room looked to be new, and he had a big hand lamp, when other rooms were using small things, the kind of tins they put pieces of old clothes and paraffin in and turn into lamps, which were went out easily and had bad smoke.

I stood still, and waited to be told what he want to tell me, at the same time I was asking myself why they couldn't make the whole house look like this. In that room there was no chair and he show me a sign to sit on the bed near him, something I refused, by telling him that was OK for me to stand. I was in a hurry to hear what he had called me for. He insisted that I sat on the bed, and since I wanted to hear what he wanted to say, and wanted to get out of his room, I sat, but not near him. After I sat he came near me and he started to touch me, pulling me on his side, I thought that the old man might be crazy then, I held his arm and pushed it very far, and told him to say what he wanted to say so that I could go.

The old man asked me if I knew why I had come.

"I know I escorted your wife so that I would know how to get here, and so I can direct others to visit you next time," I told him.

"They told you nothing else?" the old man asked.

"Nothing at all," I told him. I had to ask him now what the problem was, I had to be told.

The old man looked surprised; he started his story about why I was supposed to come. I was quiet while I listened to him; sometimes he seemed as though he was talking to himself.

"I am surprised to see that they could do this to you or to anyone else, how could they bring you here by kidnapping you? She had to ask you if you are happy to come, and if you are not then you didn't have to come, this is not what we agreed before you came."

He didn't try to touch me again he was sat still only talking. "I had a second wife, native girl from here, she is the mother of those young children, and recently they didn't get on well together and she went, and since I have to have two wives, she is the one who came up with idea that she would go and bring a girl from her family. I saw myself as a lucky man.

When he was still telling me this story, I came to see why my sister tried all means to see that I came, she believed that as soon as I saw how rich he was, I would not say any other word, which was wrong. My wish was to be with a man only because of love, not other reasons. I started to think what I would do if he raped me, he might even be helped by his wife. Still I could go back. At the time many believed that when a girl spent the night with a man, she was his wife and that was the style, some people used to force girls into marriages by kidnapping and raping them.

He went on, "I thought that I was going to have two Tutsi wives which in front of the villagers here and my relatives I would have a good reason to be proud, and on the other hand I would have peace at my home since my wives would have an understanding between themselves and have peace in my home. I was sure that she was organising it before; I didn't know that she was coming to kidnap anyone. I am disappointed. Now let us talk by ourselves and see if we can reach some agreement can you marry me so that we can go back home after, as husband and wife?"

I said, "I understand what happened is not your faulty but, I still can't get married now, I need my time too."

The old man said, "I can understand maybe it is because I am too old for you."

"That is definitely not the reason, yes I am a girl, but to me the purpose of life is not only to get married, I believe that I still have time, even if I do get married someday, I do not want to now." I had to try not to hurt him more than what his wife had done already.

"I can't blame you, if that is how you see things, then, that is understandable, when are you going back?" he asked me.

"Tomorrow," I said.

He said, "Can't you wait and be here for few days?"

"No, at home I told them that I will be back tomorrow."

"OK, go with peace. I can't be lucky enough to get a girl like you." We said bye to each other, and I went back in the sitting room, when I was at the door, I met Nyirasoko coming into the kitchen from outside. Since seeing the picture of children coming one by one to take back their mum's things, she was ashamed enough, and was not looking directly at my face.

I was not going to tell her anything I had seen her behaviour to be abnormal, her husband called her into his room, and she went inside, in my heart I wished I could tell her to go and explain how and why she brought me here, the crazy woman.

I was wondering why she thought that I would be good enough at her home, it made me want to be happy, to count there as being my future home. Or perhaps she thought that because I came from the family where once her sister married and I was younger than her, it was that easy to bring me and make me her servant.

I started to worry that I would get not be able to be transported but I was determined that with or without money I would go by whatever means, but I was not going to spend another night there.

After Nyirasoko spoke with her husband she brought our dinner which was matoke mixed with ground nuts, to me it was good food, to them it was just food which had been cooked in a rush, because of the short time they had. The proper one way to cook that type was to tie matoke in banana leaves and cook it by steaming them, for a long time, more than two hours.

The time to go to sleep was other drama, I spent the night in the same bed with Nyirasoko and her baby who was still breastfeeding, in her room which looked like a store. To know where to put my feet was a big problem, so to reach where the bed was from the sitting room was not easy. Sometimes the light would go off and we had to stand still there and get matches to light it again, it seemed that she keep everything there, as soon as you went from the sitting room, you started to see different things everywhere down there, including trees. Up to her bedroom, we slept together three of us, Nyirasoko, her baby and I. I was awake, waiting for morning to come so that I would be out of that situation. At around 3:00am, I heard the baby cry but I didn't know where she was crying from, I was sleeping on my side the baby was the other side, her mum was in the middle of us, I waited to see if her mother would do something, but I realised that she was in a deep sleep, so I woke her up. When she was awake she was in shock, the baby was crying and she was not in front of her, she was not on the bed, she was under the bed!

Quickly she went to find her in the dark, in between all of the things, it was not easy, it took some time to get her out from under there, that is when I found out how she made a bed to be big enough for three of us. She tried to join other trees to the trees which made that bed, by putting them between the bed and the wall, but she didn't manage to make them good enough to hold the baby until the morning. Again it was a big shame to her, she tried again and we slept.

In the morning before everything, I told her that I wanted money for transport and that I wanted to go early.

102

Nyirasoko said, "Just wait for some time we have a neighbour who will pass through here, he will give you lift so that you can have time at least to have tea."

I had no one to speak to and I didn't want to sit doing nothing, though I didn't even want their tea, I also didn't want it to seem that I thought I was too much to her.

I went outside to sweep their ground, which was big and wide, I thought I had heard a story that in Ugandan culture, women didn't sweep outside because it could bring bad luck, I told myself that even if it was true, then I would do it and they would have to stop me. The tea we had in the morning was like what we had at night, but there was no bread, after tea I asked her when their neighbour would pass,

She told me, "Up to now he hasn't passed yet, he will not go anywhere."

"OK now," I said, "give me transport so I can go."

Nyirasoko said, "Where we got to get cars is too far to walk, you need someone to take you there, so let us go to our other farm to get food for cooking, then we can cook, and after eating someone will escort you."

I said, "But I don't want to wait for food, and I can't get lost, I remember how we came, there is only one way."

Nyirasoko said, "Come with us then, you will go when we will come back."

I had no money, if I had, I would have gone straight away when I woke up. Even though I said that I could go just by walking alone, it was impossible, it was far, but I didn't want to show her that I had fear, though I assumed that she knew.

I had to go with them.

It was far and we had to pass a bush with some small trees which tore up Kantamage's dress. I did not mind much, there was a long mountain we had to go up and down to reach where we were going, it was a big farm where there were banana trees which were like bushes. It was not clean in the way that other people's houses were, I was wondering what she wanted to show me there.

We were at home between 2:00pm–3:00pm. I told her that I wanted transport, I turned out like a song.

"No no, you can't go without eating first," she told me. I didn't know if I was happy with the offer, she was preparing to cook in a good way, that Baganda style which could take between one hour to two or more. Though it could be something which would take a short time, I didn't want her food, what I wanted was to go.

So I saw that she wanted to make me talk bad, because of my anger I was not feeling hungry.

"I don't want to wait for food," I told her. I didn't know if she didn't realise that I wanted nothing from her home. I only had one problem, how to get away from there, or if she thought that she could trick me and tie me there!

"But it is too late you can't get transport," I saw that she was now trying to scare me, something which would not work.

"No problem I will go," I said.

I think she was thinking of what she could do to shut my mouth. I had no idea why she wanted me at her home. Then she came with a new idea, I am sure she believed that if she told me then I would keep quiet.

"I don't have money; I am waiting for my husband," she told me.

It shocked me, and since it was the first time she said that, I didn't believe her, automatically I thought that it was one of her tricks to try to keep me at her home. Yes, I couldn't walk, but if it was necessary then I would go, and spend the night at a police station which I saw on the way when we were coming, and the next day, I could go very early in the morning by walking, and maybe I would get a lift on the way.

I decided to try and go and see if she would let me go without offering to give me money for transport.

But then I told myself to be patient and try to talk with her in a diplomatic way, without showing anger.

"But the truth is you knew that I would go today, since last night and early this morning we were talking about this point, you were telling me to wait because of other reasons, not because you didn't have money for my transport. Even your husband, at night I told him that I would go today, so it is not something I just came up with just now, I think he should have given you that money before he went, and because I don't know when he will come back, and since I will not spend other night here, then I will go by foot."

I said that and then I stood up and went out to show her that it was no joke, she saw that I was serious, and she stood up quickly, she looked surprised, and she told me to wait. I went to wait for her on the road, meaning that with or without her money, I was going.

She came quickly and give me 40 Ush, which was a lot of money at the time and was including a fine for all of the problems she had made me pass through, because of her low mathematics. I didn't thank her, again she told me that it was late and it would have been better to go the next day. I told her that I was still going. We said bye and she turned with a lot of anger and shame, and disappeared into the kitchen without sending greetings for home or giving me a little push, and I went with a worry of the time, I knew that it was late and I might not get transport.

Yes I had money, but that didn't mean that I wouldn't be in trouble, because of the time. I was aware that anything might happen to me, but I still had my idea of the last solution being the police station.

To reach the main road which came from Kampala where I had to get my transport was a long distance, it could take me the whole hour or more, but I had to try. I was fit, being hungry was not affecting me anyhow, I tied my dress up and started to run, it took me half an hour to be on the main road.

There were many people in different groups, I started to go near the groups to see if I could get one that was going to Masaka, so that I could share with them. All of them were going near, all of them had the same worry concerning time, that to get transport was not easy, the cars that came from Kampala at that time might have no space for more pasengers, it was a matter of trying. Especially the one which was going to Masaka. I had to forget, people there told me.

Some people started to give up and go back home, I had no home to go back too, yes the police station was a trustful place, but I had to try first as I said. Now I had undestood that the time was over, and saw some people leave, what next?

I knew that if I could get a lift from the city centre to Masaka, I would be OK. I could walk to Kantamage's place, walking at night was not dangerous, instead of worrying about the people you could meet on the way who could hurt you, they could help you by escorting you to where you were going, but that didn't mean that you could just go on the road at night time without good reason.

Since I was there, army cars were passing from Kampala to Masaka or Mbarara, I thought that I could try to ask the army for a lift, that was not easy but I was going to try, because almost everyone had a kind of fear of soldiers, yes even me, but meeting Alex helped me to know them to be like any other people. There were the good ones and the bad ones, to be a soldier was a job, which in fact made us see them as brave and heroic, and they deserved to be loved. I decided to try and see if they could give me a lift, even if they were going to Mbarara, they could drop me at Masaka.

If they came again I would try, and if I could get one, by luck I would meet a good person. I had some fear in case it would be a bad person and being soldiers it could be worse still than I had that thought.

Army cars started to pass but I was scared, I asked myself if the soldier took me and raped me, who would be to blame? It could be my own fault but still I started to put my arm up as a sign of stopping a car, a sign of asking for lift, people around me started to look at me. The drivers were not seeing me trying to stop them or they had no time for me, and I was telling myself that I was lucky letting them go, and that it was much better, I would go to the police station, I would go tomorrow, I was forced to try and stop them!

The one that I tried to stop, which I decided would be the last one, drove ahead up to the top of the mountain, and stopped for a second, and then came back, and where I was he stopped. The people who were around there quickly went far from me, they went far so that by bad luck the soldier couldn't think that it was them who had stopped him, to them it seemed criminal.

Where they stood, their eyes were on me, in their hearts I thought that they were telling me to wait and see, it was me who called the soldiers. They believed that I knew them, I might have been their wife or girlfriend. After the car stopped, five soldiers with their uniforms and guns in their hands jumped and stopped on the ground at once. I saw them come from the top inside the tent, and at the front where the driver was, it was a big lorry, no one asked me anything, it seemed that they had no time to waste. One told me in Swahili by showing me where to pass, 'pita hapa', and carried me and put me inside, it was only me and the driver, all of them were back inside the car, all of that happened in one minute or less! I told myself that this was how soldiers had to work.

As soon as I saw them step down at once with their uniforms and guns, all of my fear disappeared, I told myself that it was my arm which made a sign to make them come back, I had better be strong and see what would happen next. Both of them were tall men, maybe six foot or more, and big, maybe more than one hundred kilograms, and strong too. I heard others call the driver David, a handsome man with light skin, he was tall and big, he looked very strong, and look to be between twenty-five to thirty years old. He was only looking in front of him and did what he had to do, no more, no talking, nothing. I was waiting for questions like my name, where I was going, or why I stopped them. When we reached Masaka that is when he asked me where I was going, in Swahili, that was the first time I used the Swahili I got from Congo, I told him I was going to the same place they are going, I asked if they were going to Gasijajirwa barracks.

I had a hope that when they were at the front of Kantamage's home, I would tell him to leave me there, but they didn't pass that road. He passed the other side and he was dropping the soldiers one by one at their homes, when he dropped all of them he went to their barracks, when I saw that he had brought the car back to the barracks, I knew that it was finished now. I was going to be what he wanted me to be to him, his bosses saw me coming with him willingly at this time of night, what could I say? Nothing at all. He didn't ask me anything, because he had the power over me, he didn't need any of my ideas, at the gate he stopped and within a second around the car were ten soldiers, with guns. I heard a loud voice from the distance say something, after it finished the man sitting by my side also said some other words in a loud voice too.

He took the car and stopped it, he came out and came to where I was and opened the door, he put his arm up as a sign to carry me from the car, I gave myself to him, so that he could put me down, when I was down I didn't know which direction he would recommend me to take. He had a big torch in his hands and he showed me a sign to go ahead in front of him without a word. I told myself that since he didn't say anything, I would go to the gate and see if he refused me and showed me his direction.

I went to the gate and he was behind me, I chose to go to Kantamage's home because it was closer than Mpanumusingo's, I turned and after around five minute we were at Kantamage's home, I showed him where it was and he stopped and told me to go. I went without looking behind me, his torch was on, you would think that was the city council's light. I reached the door and knocked, when they opened it that was when the torch went off! I didn't even thank him. I remembered that I had to do that after the torch was off, my regret was that I would never see him again to thank him, but I only said, "God, my God, our God, bless him a lot. Amen."

Inside Kantamage's house there was another drama, firstly the door took time for me to open because when she was asking who was knocking, I was quiet until she decided to open and see who I was. Her home was near Masaka hospital, sometimes the Rwandan staff who at night just when they saw that nothing needed them, they were coming to her home so that they could tell stories to push time. So that time there were two in the sitting room enjoying their stories, when she opened. I passed in front of them like lightning, and went into the bedroom, they were asking themselves if it was Bamurangirwa they saw, and if was her where had she come from at this time of night?! To Kantamage it was a difficult test, it was shame to her, to see her young sister out at that time, when she had no explanation to tell them where I came from, to her too, it was also a big confusion as she believed up until that time that I was a bridegroom.

I sat on the bed, Kantamage came in front of me, she was trying to ask me, she looked confused and scared, but she didn't get any response to all the questions she was asking. We were looking at each other, she went ahead and tried to ask me what had happened, but I was quiet I was only looking at her, she was where I was for minute, and went to where the visitors were the next minute, when they asked her anything concerning me she had no answers, and she had no place where she could be steady then, not where I was or where the visitors were.

So her visitors were also worried, they knew me to be a good girl, with respect for people in general, it was not like Bamurangirwa to pass them that way without greetings, and to be on the road at that time of the night.

They were telling her to come back to see if she knew what was going on, that is why she had a problem, because when she was with me I was dumb, and when she was with them she didn't have anything to tell them. She wasn't brave enough to tell them where she was expecting me to be and how I went there.

The way I was sat, and the way I was looking at her non-stop, with the tiredness, hunger, and anger, I think I was near looking like a ghost; she had to protect me so she had to say something to her visitors. In the end I didn't know what she told them, or if she told them anything at all.

The time came when she remembered to ask me if she could give me something to eat. I said yes, that was the first and last word which she got from me that night. She went in the kitchen, soon she came back with beans mixed with cassava and milk, it was good food to me, I was lucky.

What she had as leftovers, I ate until morning. Concerning my journey, I didn't tell her anything until after twenty years had passed, Nyirasoko didn't come back at all.

I didn't blame my sister for that, she believed that she was helping me according to the culture, at that time they believed that it was better to be a wife to someone even if you could divorce, otherwise no matter how old you were you would still be under your family.

MY JOURNEY TO TANZANIA

After being disappointed and believing that I had no hope to have Alex as my future husband as I had expected, I went to talk to my elder sister Kantamage with hope that she would understand and feel sorry for me.

I told her everything that happened and her answer to me was very simple, that I would get another one, so, to her it was no problem. I realised that she didn't understand me as I expected. Meaning that I had no one to talk to, my problem was only mine.

There were times I seemed to have health problems, and once Urutundi asked me if I had to go to hospital, but she never asked me what the problem was, and I had no reason to tell her anything. I knew how she would take it, and I thought that I had to try to eat something because no one else was going to bother.

I started to be with other people and going to college, one day when I was coming from college, I passed Kantamage's place as usual, and when she saw me she was overjoyed that she was lucky enough for me to come, because she had visitors she wanted me to help to take care of them.

When I asked her who there were and where they come from, she told me that they were our relatives and they stayed in Mwanza Tanzania.

After hearing where they came from, I was interested and I sat down helping her and asking the visitors each and every thing about Mwanza.

My big problem was my lack of education, whatever I wanted to be, it was possible. They told me about my Rwandan family, Mr Rugamba on Kirumba Street in Mwanza. I wanted to record each and every thing they were telling me, without being able to write any of it I trusted my head. As soon as I heard about the life there, I got an idea of the place, and told myself that if I had to go, I would go there.

I wanted to go far, far away from my family, anywhere. When I asked them if it was easy to study there, they told me that depended on what you wanted to go to college for, and the money you had. Yes, always, everywhere, for anything, money money moneeeeeey, forever about money. They told me that in Tanzania you could do anything to get money, you could even sell vegetables and so on. They didn't mind who you were, or where you came from.

When I reached my brother's home, his wife told me that she had my message but I thought that I didn't hear her correctly, I had to ask her again, and she repeated the same thing, that she had my message.

I listened to her, she told me that as my brother nowadays didn't hear me talk about Alex, and he assumed that nothing was between me and him, he had a Rwandan man who he wanted to marry me!

I had no interest in their story, because it showed me that they were doing all of this with the intention of giving me a man from my country and my tribe. To do what they wanted and when they wanted. It showed me their power over me, and that they were using me to make them feel powerful and happy for themselves.

I asked her very few questions to make her happy, not that I had any interest to know anything about their story.

It showed me that they didn't know me at all, because they thought that I would say yes to whatever they said, just because I gave them respect, they also believed that I was someone who could be directed in everything, the way they wanted it! So they thought that they could put me anywhere they wanted, when and how they wanted to. It said to me that, they were very wrong, and I was going to disappoint them in a way that I didn't know yet.

I was very angry, and since I couldn't say anything, because of my culture of giving our elders respect, I was talking to myself in my heart.

I saw that they treated me like girls of past times, where they were taken by their elders when and where they wanted, they had to choose their husband for them, and they had no right even to know their future husbands.

There were two different stories I had heard of marriages of before. I didn't know how they came to have the confidence that they could treat me that way. Maybe because they saw that I gave them respect, because they were my elders I had to say yes, yes to whatever they told me to do. One story I heard was that girls were covered everywhere, and they couldn't say anything. I thought that I didn't know if the bride and bridegroom were happy about the situation, in most cases no one knew each other before the wedding, sometimes even the boys, it was the parents' responsibility to put them together.

After being a bit civilized, they would not cover them, but when the time came for the bride and bridegroom to meet as husband and wife, in their private time and place, it was like war. They had to wrestle, and since the houses had no doors and they were grass houses, around them had to be young men, friends of the man who had married, in case they had to come to his rescue if the girl was too strong for him.

And whatever happened, for the friends of the girl, as with friends of the boy, in the different time and place, it would be big news the next day. To me I was wondering if the first night I could call it the first night of marriage or the first night of rape.

Now I was I asking myself which plan they had for me. Would they plan to take me according to the time of covering or wrestling?

She told me that his name was Kagabo, he was the neighbour of Ngamije and was working at Kitovu Missionary.

I was wondering how they found Kagabo so soon! I confirmed that Mpanumusingo had something to do with Alex's disappearing, since it was only him who was between our communications.

I saw it like they saw me as a burden to them and they didn't want me to have a man of my choice so they wanted anything in any way for me but it had to be their way, to get me away from them.

I was very sure that no matter what, I was going to find a way out of that problem, and I was going to shame them, concerning our culture I was very careful and might have used one side of it for my revenge. I wanted to shock and shame them.

I believed that I would go, yes, but I couldn't just go without seeing my father because he was my friend and I also liked him for always he fought for the girls' rights. I knew that if he was there it wouldn't have happened like that.

To me he was much better than young ones who called themselves educated.

At night Urutundi came to my room and she told me that they sent a message to our father to tell him about me and Kagabo, and he gave them the green light to go ahead with what they had to do before the wedding, he said that he would only come to the wedding. And the first ceremony would be on the coming Sunday, so I could tell my friends to come. I told her that my friends would have no time and I wouldn't be able to get in touch with Mukabagira, so they could call their friends, it was OK with me. But I lied, it was just because I was not happy with it and I had nothing to tell my friends about. The day of the ceremony, I wanted to hide myself somewhere, but I didn't know where, and I didn't want them to know that I didn't want the marriage, so I had to be patient.

On Sunday they were very busy here and there, on my side I had to relax and only make myself beautiful. But I helped Urutundi a little with the cleaning, but when I saw them very busy and looking very tired, somehow it made me laugh. According to Rwandan culture at the time, they only had to have many different beers and the visitors would come with other beers, but there would not be anything like food.

So there was no problem of cooking.

Their friends were there in Mpanumusingo's big house which was full of people. Men had to be in their room, and women by themselves in other room. After discussion between the men, they sent one person to tell the women what they said, and ask them their views, though most of the time women couldn't change what the men said. Normally at the time, the men had to go back without seeing me, but I asked myself if they were going back without seeing me, it would be wrong. I wanted them to see me in an abnormal way, so maybe they would be aware and know that I was trying to show them indirectly that I didn't want that man or marriage. I had to pass in front of them even if only for a second, I knew that I couldn't get permission, it was me who had to find a way of doing that. When I saw that women were busy because they were happy and some were drunk, I jumped and passed through the sitting room where the men were. I passed there like lightning and went through another door, I went outside and came back to where the women were.

Now to anyone who saw me I knew that I would make them ask questions.

Women thought that I came from the kitchen and they were complaining why I didn't say what I wanted, so that they could do it for me. They thought that I did what I did because I gave them a lot of respect didn't want to ask them to do everything for me. In the second I passed through sitting room, that was when I saw Kagabo. I knew him, not that they did any introduction, but because he was the only one who was there who I didn't know before.

I saw how he was dressed and remembered hearing someone say that he was a drunken man. But whatever he was, even if he was someone who looked in classic way, there was no way I would accept him. Yes I knew that my wish was to be with a man only because of love, but also I knew that I could be with a man when I saw that he could build up my family somehow, like many girls in my generation, but still it had to be my choice. Or could I be with a man without love if I was in trouble of some kind,? Whatever could be said for that point, it had to be me who had the right to choose.

At night, Mpanumusingo and his wife looked relaxed and happy; it was time to discuss the wedding. Mpanumusingo asked if two weeks was OK for the time of the wedding. His wife answered quickly that three weeks was a good time. "What about you Bamurangirwa?" he asked me. I told him that it was no problem; only I asked them to let me go to see my father first. Mpanumusingo told me that he was thinking the same thing, that the money was no problem any time I was ready, he would give me the money. I told them that I would go the day after next.

The next day when I told Kantamage that I would go to see our father she told me that she would give me a child to go with, so that I was not alone. And it would make him happy to see his grandchild after a long time. I asked her who she would give me, and she said that she would give me Ilibagiza, because her brothers were in school, she was four years old. All of my family trusted me with their children because I was their childcare.

The next day was the day of my journey with Ilibagiza, they directed me everywhere I would pass, and they told me all of the problems I might get on the way.

I reached to the border of Uganda and Tanzania. From Uganda side Mbarara, we had to use the ferry in Kagera River to reach the side of Tanzania, we were going to mountain Rwabunuka which was very difficult to pass in any way, by walking or by car, and it was high with many many corners

It was almost time for the bus to start and there were no more places for passengers to sit, so because I had a child, they gave me the place which was supposed to be for the cow driver, in front next to the driver.

So where I was I saw clearly outside, the mountain with terrible corners. When you are in the car, and know that you are a nervous person, it is better if you do not look outside the window. Some they were vomiting because of fear, to look outside you couldn't imagine how you were going to survive from there, it was worse when you saw parts of cars which had fallen down there. Some other people, who had used that way before, were telling others to be calm, that it was no problem, and others were just laughing. From the border it was not far if the road was good, it could take between two to three hours, but at that time even I had no watch, I think we took more than seven hours.

Where my father was at Karagwe Kayisho, it was well known, he had built a permanent house, and he had married a young wife, Nyiraromba. At their home, they had other people who stayed with them, in that area they knew him for his hard working. His home was already strong and he had a people who were working for him, some native from that area. I was not surprise at that, I knew him for two things, to be a very hard working man and very clean too. They were surprised to see that I had managed to come with a child, but they were very happy. I was there for three days, it was me who was going for water, their water came from far, other times we went to visit neighbours, or we were at home asking my daddy stories, because I liked his stories.

After I gave him Mpanumusingo's message asking him if he would still come to the wedding, he told me that he would not be able to come, he would come after for visiting, because at that time he had a lot to do. Since I was not brave enough to tell him the truth, I also didn't want him to come for nothing and be ashamed when he was not the one who caused the problem. If I knew that the wedding was a proper one, then I would have told him that I would wait for him until he had time to come. When it was time for going back, they took us to the bus and we started our journey, but on our way, our bus got a problem and they took a long time to try to do what they did so that we could go ahead with our journey.

Where I was sat, I was with a young handsome man around twenty-four years old, and he was helping me hold Ilibagiza, especially when she was sleeping because she was too heavy for me, and I asked him if we reached the border late what would happen? He told me that any time a bus from Uganda or from Tanzania came late, passengers had to spend the night that side, there were houses for visitors, and I didn't have to worry, he would help me with that. We reached the border very late and he told me that there were a few rooms and it was first come first served, so he had to go to get a room for me, and he would come back for me after, and he would only stand in the window and call me, since they wouldn't allow him to enter the bus again. I wanted him to help me, I relaxed because I saw him to be a good person and kind.

The driver, who was a mature man, was out when he came back, he saw me still inside the bus, and he asked me where I was going, I told him that I didn't know where to go, though I heard that there were some rooms there, and there was someone who was going to get one for me. I told him. He asked about the person who was going to get the room for me, who was he to me. And I told him that I forgot to ask him his name, that I met him on the bus. He seemed to be surprised, and he told me that the rooms that I was told about, were not proper ones. He said, "When you are out you will see very well who is inside. They are not somewhere a girl like you can spend the night. And that child, she is your young sister?" I told him that the child was my sister. Then he asked me if the young man I told him about. who was helping me,was the one who he saw outside. He tolded me the way he looked, according to the description, I told him that sounded like him. Then he told me that if that was the one who was helping me in any way, he was not a good person, he saw him with a group from a gang who were well-known in this area. He told me that he had to lock the bus, so no one could enter the bus without his permission. So I didn't have to go out, he would go out for whatever I would like to have from the shop, and he would guard me to take the child to the toilet!

At that point I was confused about who to believe, but I had no reason to trust the young man. I asked myself if the driver did spend the night somewhere else, then if what he told me was true, they would find a way to enter the bus and they would harm me and the child.

I believed the old man couldn't harm me in any way; if he was there then I would be safe. After a short time the driver went out and he locked the door, when he was away. I heard outside where I was sat someone calling, "You girl you girl," and banging, banging the bus very hard. I looked out, it was that man I was sat with. "Come out," he was asking me, "what are you waiting for? Come I got the room for you and the child, come before the driver comes back so that it can be easier for me to help you with your things, open the bus for me from the inside then I will come to help you." Then I told him that I was not going anywhere, that I would spend the night on the bus. I thought that by telling him that I was not going out he would just go. I had no idea that he would insist.

He started shouting saying that I had to come out, that they would chase me out, that I didn't have to lie to myself because there was no law of passengers to spend the night on the bus, so they couldn't let me stay inside. I didn't say anything again. I heard him calling others and telling them that I had refused to come out, and I heard them telling him, that they would wait for me so I could be chased out. I was very surprised to see all of that, and hoped that the driver was going to spend the night inside the bus. I believed him then, but I was not going to tell him about it, since I saw that he knew them more than I.

After a short time the driver and his cow driver came back with bags in their hands, they gave me some of it and told me that there was food for me and the child, with something to drink. I asked to give them back their money, and they said that I didn't have to give them anything, what they wanted was to see that I was OK with my little niece. After our dinner they took me outside to the toilet, then the driver told me to choose where I would be comfortable with a child, and he was going to sleep on the front seats.

Ilibagiza and I went to the last seat. We had good night, in the morning he took us to have breakfast in one of the cheap restraurants which were there. After we finished our breakfast, he escorted us to the border. I was tongue-tied and didn't know how to thank him. As soon as I reached the other side, in Uganda, the bus came and we were inside. The road in Uganda was good, so it was no problem on the way, when we reached home, they were very happy to see us back.

I gave them the message that our father gave me. And told them how Daddy was with his new family there, and how he had a strong and clean home, but for Mpanumisingo and his wife, all their hearts were concenting on the wedding. I didn't know if they were happy because they were going to show their power of being responsible for it, or it was because they were sure I was going to be away from them, out of their way and their rules. I came to guess something new, which was very bad and made my pain of disappointment worse, after some time my body was relaxed, we were talking like friends at that time, and they had a lot of smiles whenever we were talking. There was a lot of laughing, a laugh of happiness, like a happy family, and they reminded me that I was tired. I had to go to sleep, indeed after a long, long time I began to get sympathy from them. Before I went to my room, Mpanumusingo went to their bedroom, and came back with envelopes, and my heart jumped a little, thinking that one might be from Alex, which could save me from all of that mix up. I had to go though in case it was Alex and I could try to explain everything and he could help me to find a way out of it. I had to read them in my room. I said goodnight and left, but when he was giving me the letters, he told me something that was in one of the letters, and I thought that it was a joke, since we were friends, according to the way I saw them and what they believed. When I was in my room I started to check them one by one, to see where they came from before I read them. I thought that Alex's letters were stacked somewhere and now they had come all of them at once. They all came from my other friends, what surprised me more, was to see that what he told me was true, indeed the sentence was in one of the letters.

When all of them were still neatly closed, I was confused because I had a very strong belief and I assumed that he was opening my letters all along, including those from Alex, and he was not giving them to me because he didn't want me to be with him, for his own reasons. I was angry and felt that I would go any time from that day, but it was good to go when there was only one week left before the wedding. I got the idea of going back to my father and telling him the truth, and telling him that I had moved there to be with them. I knew that he couldn't say no, and he understood me more than all of them. But I had heard many stories before and most of the time, women were not happy with the children of their husband, so what if his wife saw only my bad side and it was uncomfortable. Which would make the whole family unhappy, me and my daddy. I thought that it was not a good idea because it could destroy their happiness.

There and then, I remembered Kantamage, her visitors from Mwanza and our conversations, I felt happy and relaxed.

I decided to go to Mwanza. I thought it was a good idea because it was far and they wouldn't know where I was and they would only see me when I wanted to. Even the relatives who were there, there was no way they could give them information, since at that time communication was not easy. I had some money which I had worked for when I was at Sentongo's home, and the money Alex gaves me. I had 100 Ush with me, at the time that was a lot of money. I had some money in the post and the three countries were still using the same money, they were still in unity as East Africa: Kenya, Uganda and Tanzania. So I could go to the post anywhere I went. That money was enough to push me for some time. Yes, I knew that I might not see beautiful things on my way ahead, but God would help me. If I wanted to survive, I had better hope for the best.

IT WAS 10 /1/1969

I was preparing for my journey to Mwanza. I wanted to go very early so that no one could meet me on the way, and I wanted to be far away from my brother and his wife's home by the time they woke up. I had to go by bus from Masaka Uganda to Bukoba Tanzania, then from Bukoba by ship through Lake Victoria to Mwanza. To go somewhere that I didn't know was like commiting suicide, like marrying Kagabo, so it was better to commit suicide and die where my family wouldn't see how I died.

I was angry and sad. Angry with my family, especially Mpanumusingo and Kankuyo who didn't try to help me have a future by putting me in school, and now wanteded to force me to marry. I saw that there were times in life, when the worst times could show you the true colours of the people who you thought cared about you. I had strong anger to the Catholic Church and their masters, who made me go out of my country at that early age, and made me lose my mother because of the horrible life she was in. By losing her, I believed that she took a part of my life, a big part in fact. It was sad because I didn't know if the decision I made would take me to heaven or hell. Then it was the time to ask myself, why me? Why me? Why all of this mix-up, and until when? I didn't expect an answer from anywhere or from anyone. I had only to carry on and go to Mwanza. But I knew that I would miss the children terribly. I had a strong bond with them, they were innocent, I loved them. I decided to go to the family that I heard the visitors talking about, who I had no connection or relationship. I didn't want to see a relative be more important than anyone, who maybe had understanding and kindness. I had to be in a new life, with new people.

If I was a good person I would meet good people, in my life ahead of me, I had to have patience, respect and love to others, I would try not to lose my confidence and hope, and I would know how to keep the secrets of others when it needed to. That was my mother's last words to me. I would go to Rugamba and ask him to let me in and take care of me together with his family. There would be big questions between themselves and my relatives there, about why I had chosen them.

In Mpanumusingo's home where I was sleeping, it was a house which was separated with a big house where him and his wife slept. It was inside the compound, it was for children and sometimes visitors. So there was no problem waking up in the morning and going. I was almost on my own. At Masaka, there was one bus which passed there from Kampala every day go to Bukoba. There was not exactly time for that bus to stay at the bus station, so I had to be there very early in the morning, with a hope that it would come early, because buses there, at that time, seemed like they didn't have a timetable, they could even come in the evening or miss completely. To me it was again like I was a new refugee. I was running from Uganda. I had lost all my hope in Uganda, study, Alex, and now I had a good reason, I was running from a forced marriage.

I woke up one of the children who was a grown-up compared to the others, Son of Rusingizandekwe Boniface, his name Rusingizandekwe Emmanuel who was killed in 1994 in genocide in Rwanda, he was young boy at the time. When he woke up, he looked at me, and at the bags I had and the way I was dressed, then he was confused, he saw that I was going somewhere far at that time of night. The children had started to use some of Kiganda words, in a respectful way, they could't call me by my names, he called me 'senga' which meant auntie. "Where are you going? It is still night auntie." I didn't have much to tell him, he was too young to understand any of it. He held me and started to cry telling me that it was night. I didn't have to go at that time, or he asked me if he could come with me.

No, I told him he was too young even to escort me at that time of night, so I tried to calm him down by telling him that I would be back. I was out and he locked the door.

From Mpanumusingo's home to the bus station it was three miles or more, for almost two miles I had to pass between the banana plantation. It was dark, I could only see in front of me where I was passing. I was not thinking of anything which could make me scared of the night; all of my thoughts were about the bus, and the journey which was ahead of me. It was as if it was a normal walk, I had to pass in front of Kantamage's home, when I reached there, I looked to Kantamage's home, which was only a few metres from where I was standing on the road which was taking me to the bus station to Bukoba. I stood there for a few minutes asking myself if I could go without seeing them and saying bye to them, since they wouldn't be able to make me change my mind, it was better I just went, since I knew very well about the many questions which they would give me. So to avoid all of that, I chose to go without passing through her home. I knew it would have been a big drama too, because she had a visitor, our cousin Kamucyera. I didn't want any of them to know anything until I wanted them to know it. Apart from the questions, I also knew that they wouldn't believe me one hundred percent that I was going by myself somewhere I didn't know. They would think differently, they could think or tell me that there was some man with me, to say no wouldn't help much to make them believe me. Maybe they would think that I found out that I was pregnant and that is why I was running away. Better to let them say all of this when I was not there.

Let them be left with questions of why and how, and then some of them would come up with rumours about why I did it, and maybe how I did it. I left for the bus stop, all of the people who were there were still sleeping, some on the floor others on the benches which normally are for sitting. There were always people who spent the night there because of different reasons, but for most of them it was because of transport. Many were passengers who came from far, because there were few who could afford to go to the hotels. I went near a woman

124

and sat there, and waited for her to wake up. When she woke up, first, it was time to say good morning and I saw that she had a watch, I asked her the time and it took her some seconds and then she told me that it was near 6:00am. From that time then we started conversations, after a few minute it felt like we had know each other for days. I started by asking her if she spent the night there or if she had just come. The answer was yes she had spent the night there and she came yesterday, the bus didn't come from Kampala yesterday, so they was hope that it might come that day.

It was her turn to ask me, she asked me if I had just come.

"Yes," I said, "I just came; my home is not far from here."

"Where are you going?" she asked.

"I am going to Bukoba," I said.

She said that she was going to Bukoba too, that was where she was living. She said that she was lucky to have someone with her.

I told her that it was me who was lucky because it was my first time to go to Bukoba so I needed someone to direct me. She said that she had not reached town exactly but she knew all parts of Bukoba, if I told her where I was going she would direct me. I told her that I was going to Mwanza, and then she said that was easy because the ship's always went late at night, and it was near where the bus station was. There were many people who went to the ship, so anyone could direct you and if you were scared to ask there were taxis which were cheap, you could pay a few shillings and it would take you.

She went ahead and told me that now she was not worried, if we could not get the bus she had someone who could take her home so that she could get a good rest at last. I said quickly that it couldn't be a good idea for us to go home, because we didn't know the time of the bus, so even if the bus did not come I was going to spend the night there. And she said that it was a very good idea. When it was 9:00am she told me that bus looked like it might come late, so it was better to buy some breakfast, and to me this was a good idea. I was hungry, we bought tea and cassava. At 10:00am we heard someone calling passengers for Bukoba, we stood up running to where they showed us that the bus would stand. We were inside the bus sitting, after a short time the bus started the journey. We went, when we were almost out of Masaka, I turned my head and looked behind me, I wanted to wave and say bye to Masaka and bye to Uganda but I said it in my heart. I said bye to Masaka, to my family, and that I was angry with them but I didn't hate them. Because I couldn't hate my mother's children, she wouldn't be happy with that, I knew that she loved her children, all of us in an equal way, and I loved my mother, and we were very good friends, so, I couldn't do anything which she wouldn't be happy with if she was here.

I didn't understand how they treated me, if they hated me or if there was only a lack of understanding, and maybe they were unable to look back and see that if they had managed to give me an education, they would not only be helping me, they would also have helped themselves as a family in general. I would also help my country Rwanda, because I knew that Rwanda would always be my county. Home is a point, one day, or always, things come and go, things change in this way or that way, but home remains to be home forever, no matter what. I wanted to have children and take good care of them for my country and for the whole world in general.

We had good journey, at 5:00pm the lady reached her village and she told me that it was only a short time before we reached the town of Bukoba, and she reminded me that in case I wanted to ask someone anything, it was better to go to women or old men, it was not good to trust everybody in town. She told me that I was in luck because I came on the ship's day. After a long journey up and down in mountains we reached town of Bukoba.

To look at Bukoba at that time, first I compared it with Masaka and I saw that Masaka, though it was a small town, was good and clean, more so than Bukoba. Bukoba was the town which was between mountains. The bus station was a big place which was made of dust, around were some good hotels, and other small ones which didn't look clean, unlike the big ones which looked to be very clean and modern. I wanted to feel relaxed for a while, I knew that the good ones might be expensive but I choose to go there anyway. Outside I saw women, the way they were dressed, I thought that it was uniform. All of them were dressed in two kangas or three, a kind of good soft material, one down from the waist to the middle of the legs, another one, on the top around like a scarf, or some of them covered their head with it.

After a short time, there came another group of women who dressed in black and their dresses were from head to toe! Some of them were too wide. I also thought that they might be wearing some kind of uniform, because of different jobs, but I was wondering why they had chosen black as their fashion. I couldn't help it, I had to ask someone about them, there was a young girl who was standing near where I was, I asked her what kind of job those ladies did.

She asks me, "Which ladies?"

"Those ladies in black uniform," I told her.

She gave me an answer, but with a big smile, she told me that it was not uniform, it was the dress of Muslim women.

The first thing I did when I came out from the bus was to go where they were selling newspapers. I wanted to have it in my hand, I was reading, the newspaper was in Swahili, I knew Swahili because I got it from Congo, I thought that it was somehow different but I had no problem understanding what I was reading. At that time, I had seen enough outside, it was time to enter inside and eat something. Inside the staff were clean and seemed to respect customers, I enjoyed the meal which was 'matoke', fresh banana and beans, I had cold milk to drink.

Outside since I didn't want to give myself any more trouble, I went to where a taxi was standing and three men all came out at once, and said that they would take me where I wanted to go. I talked to one, who was near where I was, and he was the first one to talk to me anyway. I saw that they had no order guiding their job. He asked me where I was going. I told him that I was going to the ship, I asked him when the ship started its journey. He said between 8:00pm–9:00pm, I told him that it was still early and that I would come later, and still was him who was going to take me. He told me that he thought that

I knew that the ship was not going anywhere until the next day. I had to go back to sit down and think about what I would do next.

The dress I had chosen to put on was one of the best I had, one of the ones that Alex had bought for me, which was black and looked very expensive, I chose that one because I didn't want to look cheap on my journey, and it would take time to look dirty. I looked respectful, like a child who came from a wealthy family. Since I had no idea of anyone in Bukoba, I had to spend the night in the hotel, which was no problem. I trusted the one I saw in front of me, but I was in no hurry, so I sat outside and went ahead with my newspaper to kill time.

Where I was sitting came a young man, he was handsome and he sat down near me. I had already seen Rwandans there and now I knew that here also there were some of us. He was tall, slender, light-skinned, with short soft hair, he didn't talk to me and I didn't ask him anything. I thought that he looked Rwandan but I decided not to talk to him, the lady on the bus from Masaka told me that it was not a good idea to talk to young people, especially men. After a short time in front of us came an old man pushing a bicycle, when I saw him I thought that he was his father, he looked like him somehow, he came and stood where we were. The young man stood up, as a sign of respect, and greeted him in Kinyarwanda, they started to talk to each other. When I heard that they were Rwandans and in fact he was not his father they only know each other, I decided that this old man was the person I was going to talk with, but I was not going to interrupt them, I was going to ask him something. At that time I pretended that I was reading, by bending my head down to the newspaper and keeping quiet. Even though I was bending my head, my two eyes were on them. When they finished their conversations the young man turned and left. The old man started to turn his bicycle. I stood up in front of him, I did it so quickly like a soldier.

I started by greeting him, and it was his turn to ask me if I knew him somehow or if I wanted to ask him something.

I told him that I had just moved there and it was my first time to be in Bukoba, I was on my way to Mwanza and they told me that the ship was not going today.

Without me having to ask, he helped me by asking why I was going Mwanza? It was a question to me but before I gave him any answer he went on, "For sure the person who directed you has directed you very well because, it has to go today, but since it is missed today without question it is going to go tomorrow. You are going to school?" he asked me. I said yes very quickly, at that point, I could see that he had already helped me to make up a very good story. That was the only thing I had to say on my way; to everyone who was going to ask me why I was going to Mwanza.

Again he questioned, "In Mwanza who are you going to be with?"

"My brother," I told him.

"They choose for you to have study there?" he asked me.

"Yes my brother there has done all that is necessary concerning my study," I told him.

He went on by telling me the timetable of the school, that some had already started, but not all of them yet. I kept quiet, I had to talk less and be a girl for a few minutes, he would see me as polite, but to me that was because I didn't know what to say to a stranger, a respectable man, and I liked him because of the way he was talking to me. I went ahead and asked him to direct me to a good hotel where I could spend the night. To give me an answer, it didn't take him even a second, he told me that there was no need to direct me to the hotel, that his home was not far and there were other children my age, if I knew how to sit on the bicycle, we could go together, then he would bring me back the next day for my journey to Mwanza.

He didn't ask me if that was OK with me, he assumed that I was happy with the offer, which he was very much right about. I was happy to spend the night where I would have other people to talk to. I thanked him, he took my bag and tied it to the bicycle, I knew how to sit on the bicycle from back home in Rwanda when Mpanumusingo sometimes gave me a lift on his. At his home, there was a very good view, it was a wider area which looked new, there were not yet many people moved there, it was a very green area on the top of the mountain. On the top of that mountain, which looked new and very fresh, I felt that there was even different oxygen which made me feel more alive and relaxed. I felt happy to be there and think that whatever time I was going to be there, I could say that I was happy to get that chance. I liked everything about that area, he was the one who had a house there, it was a good area for everything for farming and cultivating. I saw other homes a bit further from his home. He was still building his houses where they were sleeping, and where the cows slept. When we reached inside the house, before everything, he remembered that he didn't know my name yet. "Girl I didn't even ask you your name, mine is Murangira what is yours?"

"My name is Bamurangirwa," I told him.

He had told me before, that no one would be at home at the time we reached there, his wife took their older child to school, and some of the other children were at their grandmother's place, he wanted me to be aware in advance, that I would see others when they came back from grazing the cows.

Inside the house there was a carpet made of a type of dry soft grasses, which was in very good order and looked clean, and sitting on it felt like soft like a mattress. He started telling me the history of those grasses, he questioning me but on the other hand he was teaching me. He started by saying, "You young people, when you see grasses like this, you think that it is clutter for these people over here?" Without waiting to hear my answer, he went on telling me that even Rwandans before were using these type of grasses like that, which was the responsibility of girls since they were the ones who had to take care of the cleaning of the home. But I had seen that in a few homes back home in Rwanda and I had seen it in many homes in Uganda, but I didn't say anything in front of him, I tried to be a girl of very few words as much as I could.

From that time Murangira was not calling me a girl as before, and he was not bothered about asking me my other names like many other people did. He was satisfied with that and I liked him for that. I heard him calling me from outside, I went out quickly to hear and maybe see what he was telling me. When he saw me he told me to prepare myself as he wanted to show me where the bathroom was, so that I could have a bath, but also he said that he had to check first if there would be enough water. When I heard him say that, I told him that it would be better for him to show me where they fetched water from, so that I could go for water before. He seemed to be surprised and told me that I was tired I would have to leave that for the other children, they would do it when they came back. I insisted, and after a few minutes he looked happy at the idea, and with a smile which said that to be young was good. He went behind the house and came back with a container, he gave it to me and showed me where to go. And he told me that when I came back I should just have a bath and have rest. It was down the hill, I went passing between the long beautiful grasses, which had a little wind, a wind which felt peaceful. I told myself that if I could find a way of changing the story, I could ask him if I could stay be there at least for a little while longer but that was impossible, I had to go to Mwanza. When I came back, he told me that one of his children who was at home already, had warmed water for me to have bath. I had my bath and dressed. I came out and saw how all of the children were waiting for me as if they knew me already. Or they wanted to see that visitor they had heard about, to see if I was the way they had been told. We started chatting and laughing there and then, I almost forgot my problems. I thought that I was lucky to meet Murangira and gave myself hope of what was waiting for me ahead, it showed me that it could be mighty good.

We had our dinner, 'amatoke', which was the main food in that part of the country like Baganda, fresh banana almost like what I had at my lunch, I slept and I got a very good sleep.

In the morning Mr. Murangira told me that I didn't have to be in a hurry, the ship was going at night. The time to be taken to the ship came, it was not easy between us, it was not easy to part with the children even though we were only together for that short time. And Mr Murangira took me where the ship was, there were many other passengers, and he told me that I didn't have to be scared of anything because all of the people I saw were passengers who were waiting for the ship. So he told me all about the journey, and he remembered to tell me that it was good to see someone, who he could go near and talk to, then we said bye to each other, but before that I thanked him a lot. Then Murangira was gone and I was on my own with other passengers.

I was excited about that area; I looked around here and there, around Lake Victoria, it was like I was there for a holiday, to see the beauty of Lake Victoria and the mountains around it. Many people were inside the fence where there were two big houses, which looked to be offices, outside the front of the houses there were a few cars which looked to be the staff's cars, because many cars were outside the gate, between that gate and the shops, but there was only one house which was open and had staff inside who were going in and out.

Again when I was coming from Murangira's house, I chose to dress up, like I was going to a party. I changed to another dress, which was the best I had, that was my time to look excellent. I believed that most people judged others concerning the way they dressed. Normally I liked to dress nice when I could. I wanted to be judged in a respectful way on my journey. I didn't want to be seen as a young girl who had ran away from her family, and didn't even know where she was going, what she was going to do, or what was waiting for her.

I saw where they were selling newspapers and I bought one, newspapers at that time were good to me in many ways. Normally I liked reading but that time I didn't want to feel alone, and again at the time, some people who saw someone with newspaper, they put you in a different category. It was still morning time; Murangira had to go to do his things which was the reason he had to bring me at that time. I had a long time walking and looking at that beautiful area. I sat down, I wanted to see what my newspaper said first, and then I would go around before to see who I could talk to and try to make a friend. I finished my newspaper and put it down, after short time I decided to go behind the houses and have a good look at the lake, my bag was not heavy so it was easy to go with it everywhere. When I stood up I heard someone calling 'girl' in Swahili. I decided to turn my head and see if it was me who the person was calling. Yes, indeed it was me. The man was sat near to where I was, he was looking at me and he asked me if I could give him the newspaper for some time.

I gave it to him and he started to read, after some time he turned his head and looked at me, and asked me if I was waiting for the ship. I said yes.

"Where are you going?" he asked.

"I am going to Mwanza."

"Are you going for study?"

I changed the story since I didn't know who he was and where he was going. I told him that I was going to visit my sister who had married there.

"She is married to Sukuma man?"

I thought that I hadn't heard clearly; I had to ask him again, the answer was the same! So I had to ask him what he meant by saying 'Sukuma man'.

The word sukuma, in the languages I knew, meant to push.

First he smiled a little, and then he told me that Sukuma was one of the Tanzanian tribes which were native of the Mwanza area. He went ahead and said that it showed him that I didn't know Tanzanian's tribes.

I said that I only knew Wanyambo and Wahaya he said that Tanzanians had many different tribes.

"What is your name?"

"My name is Bamurangirwa."

He repeated my name in a very clear way which surprised me since I was only used to Rwandan people and some people from parts of Uganda like Ankole, it was usually them who couldn't say my name without a struggle first. Before I said anything he asked me if I was Rwandan. That was a big surprise; I asked him how come he knew I was Rwandan?

"Because of your name," he said.

He told me that he was working in Rwanda and he was there for some time, he knew a lot about Rwanda and its people.

He went ahead by telling me how Rwandans were very good people in many ways, that he loved them. At that point where I was, I felt proud and happy to hear that my country, my people, still had good things in their culture which someone could see in them. After a short silence he told me his name without being asked. "My name is Yusuf I am Nyamwezi from Tabora," he said. Again we kept quiet but on my side I turned my head and looked at him waiting for an explanation, or I thought he was still going ahead with his story. When I didn't say anything, but was still looking at him non-stop, he thought that I didn't hear him clearly, so, he had to repeat.

It was like my eyes had asked him without me talking. "My name is Yusuf, I am Tanzanian, and I am Nyamwezi from Tabora."

That was when I knew that before I had heard him clearly.

Again in the languages I knew, 'mwezi' had another meaning which was moon. So it was my time again to ask him if Nyamwezi was his tribe or if they was any kind of connection with him and the moon in any way.

He was confused and I had to try to find a way to make him understand my question. Sometimes I had to use signs, like showing him the sky…

Again that made him laugh a lot, but he tried to explain that like Sukuma, Nyamwezi was one of Tanzanians's tribes, Nyamwezi was native of Tabora and he was one of them.

Yusuf had a lot to do by teaching me about Tanzanians and their culture, though he seemed to be happy about that, because he had got something to do which made him busy. I told him that it was my first time going to Mwanza and he told me that I wouldn't get lost if I knew the name of where I was going and the name of the road. He told me that the journey by ship was part of his life, because he passed there many times so he knew all, if I was tired we could go around and leave our things no problem, there, there was no one who could steal. I stood up quickly I was tired indeed, I wanted to go around, I was relaxed with Yusuf then, I saw him to be a quiet and polite man. He decided to go first and ask about our transport. He told me that the ship was there for almost a week and didn't know what the problem was, he was in the hotel and since he had hope that that day the ship would go. He gave back the key, and he said that to get a room was not easy because of the many passengers, so he was wondering in case the ship couldn't go, what was going to happen. I didn't say anything. I only hoped that we would go. I didn't know what to say. So when he went to ask about the time of the tickets, they told him that they didn't have permission yet to give them to the passengers.

We went for our walk, and we came to pass the front of the hotel, he told me to go inside and get something to eat, it was evening time and I was hungry, so it was a good idea. Inside the hotel was a good place and it was clean with polite waiters. After we relaxed ourselves on the table, the waiter came to ask us what we wanted, I told them what I waneted, and it was Yusuf's turn, when they asked him he told them that he would not take anything. I turned my head and looked at him as if it was the first time I met him, I saw that he was a black man, not very handsome, around five and a half tall, maybe around seventy-five to eighty-five kilograms, he looked to be around twenty-eight to thirty-five but he looked like he was tired or sick.

I had to ask him what was wrong with him. Then he told me that he was fasting.

We were communicating in Swahili then, the word in Swahili was 'nimefunga', meaning that he had put someone in prison! Again I was surprised with him, I had to ask him until I understood what was going on, but at that point I was aware that there were a lot of strange things ahead of me, it seemed that it was beginning here with Yusuf.

No doubt about that.

"You said something like prison?"

"No I said that I am fasting Lamathan." To me this sounded like he had put Lamathan in prison, which still didn't make sense, even if he was a boss somewhere, somehow, and gave Lamathan a punishment, then why was he punishing himself? Maybe it was necessary to punish Lamathan, but he was a normal, kind person and he felt bad for that.

I thought that if it was me, it would be very easy, I could give an order to let him go and then talk to Lamathan and tell him that he had to change his behaviour. Now I was determined to ask more, though it was not easy, I asked him, but on the other hand I was not sure if I was giving him any ideas. I then told him that if putting Lamathan in prison was not comfortable to him, then why couldn't he let him go? When I gave him that idea, I was looking straight in his face waiting for my answers.

At that time all the tiredness he had, it disappeared, and he was laughing uncontrollably. I kept quiet now waiting to know what he was laughing at, what was funny here. After looking like he had relaxed, he turned to me now, first he said that he couldn't blame me for not knowing anything about Islam, because in my country, Rwanda, the Islamic religion was not common.

So he started to tell me some things concerning that religion. I was interested to listen to all which he managed to tell me, because all of it was new to me. He gave the waiter who came to clear my table the money, and he came back with the change.

I gave the waiter the money, and he asked me why I was giving him the money, and I told him that I was paying for my lunch.

He said that I didn't have to, he had paid already. I asked him when and why? His answer was simple that he was happy doing that, I told him that I thought the money was to buy something to go with, so he could wait for his right time to eat.

"No, this week I was here I was by myself, but now to be with a beautiful respectable girl like you, to me is worth more than money, only to be with you walking together around, was an honour to me. So I will come back when the time comes." When his time for eating came, I escorted him and I was still full, but he asked for milk for me without even asking me, maybe he had noticed that I liked milk. After we went back to the ship, but when we reached there, outside there were only very few people and he told me that I didn't have to worry, because if they gave the tickets when we were away, we would get them when we were inside the ship.

But when we asked the people, what they told us was a completely different story. They said that there was no journey again! Some were back at their home or with friends or at hotels, the few who who were there would spend the night there outside. Now what about me? Or what about us? Me and Yusuf. I would not be able to go back to Murangira's home, I was sure they would welcome me but I didn't even know where it was. So I was confused, perhaps I was going to spend the night there outside like the few others.

"Can I try to see if I can get hotel?" Maybe. Yusuf was the first one to tell me we could go back and see if we could get rooms. We went but everywhere we tried was full, I came up with idea, I asked him if we could go back, if they could be any chance to see staffs. It was time for questions which I didn't expect.

"Staff for what?"

"Just to try and see if they can help."

"Help in which way?"

"For this problem we have of where to sleep."

"How come you have had that idea? What do you think they can help?"

"I don't know, it is just a matter of trying, most things you just have to try and see."

He said that maybe they were still there, we went to see. We asked a watch man if he could show us to the director, and at that time he pointed to the man who was standing outside the office. We went to where he was standing, and greeted him.

Yusuf started to talk and I gave him time, "Sir we went to eat late because we were fasting, and when we came back all of the people were gone and the few who were left told us that even today there was no journey. We can't get a place in the hotel too, and outside there is no taxi so we can't go to town to try and see if we could get hotel there. Now can you help me please where can my sister and I spend the night?"

The director was a quiet man and listened with respect, even before he gave us an answer, I liked him the way he gave Yusuf a chance and listened to whatever he told him. After Yusuf's story, he said that it was understandable, to get a hotel was not easy, and his car had a problem, he had to take us in to town there we could get a hotel. Now the director, when he was talking, sometimes you could see that he was talking to both of us, or to Yusuf, or to himself.

"It is understandable, to be with a sister like this one, you have to worry; now what I will do, it is good and you are lucky, normally you can't get me here at this time. I will give this girl the keys to my offices and she will be the leader of that place tonight, if she would like you to sleep there, it is up to her, my office has two rooms but no doors, and if she will not want you there then she will have her reasons, there will be no arguments. Do you hear girl?"

"Yes Sir thank you very much."

At that point the man who was standing with him laughed a little and Yusuf also laughed. The director was still giving orders, he told the man who was standing beside him, "Go, and bring the mattress for this girl. What I don't have is something to cover yourself, and another mattress in case you want to give your brother place a to sleep. You man you will know how you will sleep, we men we can handle any kind of problems." They gave us the mattress and he told us to go for whatever we wanted in the shops, he would wait for us and then he would give me the keys when we were ready. We went to get something to drink later, now Yusuf was my brother, brother who I met a few hours ago, I didn't know if I was going to trust this brother or not.

When we came back he remembered to tell us, he showed me the keys, there were many together. He said, "This key is the only one, no one else has them, if maybe some people see you lock the door and come to disturb by you knocking or telling you any kind of lies, in case that happens don't listen to any of them. My home is far from here I will come tomorrow morning. So you will give them to me tomorrow."

He took us inside, and showed us the rooms, and told Yusuf again, "If your sister doesn't want you here you better go out before I go, there are times when we have to give girls the full respect that they deserve."

He managed to answer him with one word, "Yes. You are right." But he looked at me, a short look which was a look of asking me, 'should I go or I stay'? I didn't say anything; I had to have a few words, like a respectable girl who was with her older brother and old man too. After the director went, Yusuf didn't asked me for the keys though even if he had tried I wouldn't have given them to him, it was me who was in charge of everything concerning the house until the morning.

After the director left it was our test time, especially me. I saw it to be a test to me because I was confused about what I was going to do with Yusuf. There was silence for a few minute then it was Yusuf who broke it. It was the time for the suggestion and the decision.

"Will you let me spend the night inside the house?" he asked. Before I gave him an answer he went ahead with talking. "Or if you feel that you can't trust me enough to let me sleep here then I will understand and I will sleep outside. It is your decision which I will respect."

I saw how he was ready for anything, and knew that I had that power. He was a man, if he wanted to come up with violence at that time, it would be easy for him to do anything to me, but he was still the same man I was with a few hours ago, polite and respectful towards me. Then I thought that to put him out was not a good idea, I had to take the risk and let him sleep inside.

I had one mattress and I had already made the bed, so I told him that he would sleep inside.

"In this room? Or are we going to sleep together, since there are no other mattresses?"

"That could be far more than I trust you. Just be there in your room I will be in mine," I told him.

I hoped that was just a way of trying, like any man, but hopefuly l I wanted to believe that he was not the kind of man who could rape girls. I didn't know what I should do in case he turned out to be a monster. I only had to have hope.

As soon as I slept I was in a deep sleep. I was very comfortable, it was a warm place so I didn't need something to cover myself. After midnight, I heard someone knock on the door, I didn't know when the knock started, at first I thought that I was dreaming, then I was listening, it was clearly someone knocking, and the more time passed, he knocked more and more in louder voices!

I remembered all that the director had told me and then saw that these were the people he was talking about, luckily he remembered to mention about this problem, otherwise it would have become a bigger problem. The solution was to keep quiet. After he saw that no one cared he started to abuse us, and banged the door very hard, so hard that we thought that he was in our house. He tried to say many things, that he was the boss who wanted something and so on. Then after he saw that no one responded he left, it was quiet again and I went back to sleep.

I didn't say anything not even to Yusuf.

It was the morning after, we woke up, and got ready to go out. I saw where the director was and I went there to give him the keys and thank him again, and also to tell him that he did very good by telling me about the people who might come and knock. He was happy that I didn't open the door, and said that he knew that things like that could happen.

Yusuf asked me if I was ready to go for breakfast so that he could escort me, and I was ready, when I was having my tea he told me that he was with me the last time because in the ship there were a lot of people, and he wouldn't get chance to be with me again, because there would be high competition. I asked, "Competition for what?"

"Most of young men will try to be near you and to be your friend."

"Why me? I don't think that I will be the only girl on that ship."

"The way you look, and the way you dress, there will not be many like you."

He went ahead with the story, "but Bamurangirwa?" I turned my head and looked at him waiting, wondering what special thing or new thing he wanted to tell me.

"Thank you. Tonight, because you didn't open the door, it showed me that you are a respectable girl who comes from a good family, but the way you look can be enough to judge you for that category."

I asked if there was anyone who would open for someone who they didn't know at that time of the night. Especially after being told that I might get people like them coming. At a place that I didn't know anything about. I thought something like that would be madness? He said that some girls don't think that much. They think about the danger after they are in the middle of it, and the rest it is thought about when it is too late.

FROM BUKOBA TO MWANZA

That day we were lucky, they told us that we would go, and any time they would give us the tickets. People were lining behind the window to be given their ticket, but others were lining where the ship was. When I asked why they were going without buying their tickets first, I was told that they wanted to be the first to enter the ship, so that they could get a good place inside, and those who wanted to go inside without a ticket got them inside the ship.

Outside the ship there were two lines, one line which was next to us, there were two young men who were looking at me as if they knew me somewhere, I tried to think if I knew them too, but couldn't remember seeing them anywhere. They looked like Rwandans, most Rwandans, especially Tutsi, most of them they were tall, slender, with light skin and soft hair and a long face. These young men looked like each other, you could think that they were twins. Inside the ship there were so many people, but I was still on the window looking at the water in the lake, it was beautiful the way it was wider and so on. Again I felt relaxed, like I was on a good holiday. I was by myself there, when I heard someone beside me say 'muraho', greetings in Kinyarwanda, I didn't know if is was me who the person was talking to, or someone else, but I turned my head in surprise since I had no idea that there would be any other Rwandan apart from me on the shipm, especially not someone who knew me. The person who greeted me, was one of those young men, who were looking at me outside the ship. To see that it was only the two of us there, I knew that it was me who he was greeting and I turned back and returned his greetings. I asked him how he knew that I spoke Kinyarwanda.

He told me that not only did he know that I spoke the language, he already knew that I was Rwandan!

I was again surprised and I asked him how?

The answer was that when we were outside they though that I might be Rwandan and when they were talking about it, the person who was with them told them that, yes, I was Rwandan, that he knew me and where I was working as a doctor in Masaka Hospital!

I told him, "I am not working there and I am not doctor, maybe the person saw me with people who work there or when I was there for treatment." He said that they would have been surprised if I was a doctor and I had finished my studies because I looked to be still young. What surprised me was how someone could only see a person, and know where the person was working and even know the position! Just because maybe he or she saw how the person looked and how he or she was dressed!

That I understood of some of people at the time, some people when they were far from their home, where no one knew them, they started to give themselves different high positions, so that they would be respected for that! We talked about our journey and they told me the same thing, that to reach where I was going was easy.

When I was outside the ship, I saw that the ship was very small compared to the people who were waiting to enter inside it. I was telling myself to wait and see what would happen. I was still standing at the window when I lost Yusuf. After satisfying my eyes by looking at that water, I decided to change position and go somewhere else. I didn't go far from where I was then, in front of me was a hall, it was a big place, which had many people. On some sides there were benches and people were sitting on them, others were standing, all sides had doors, there were rooms, and on some other sides there were stairs which showed the upstairs, there were other places which were maybe bigger than that, and had many rooms. Some people there had radios and they were singing with the radios, some were eating, others who were standing looked like their minds were still busy somehow. There were others who were passing the doors, others coming from the doors, when others opened the doors, some were going upstairs, there were some who came down from upstairs too.

It was a busy place indeed, it was like being in the market.

Many people who were there were women and children, you could think that they had been there for days, the place was dirty and I thought that might be the reason why other people didn't feel comfortable to be there for a long time.

I thought that it could be a good idea if first I went round and saw the difference, then that is when I would know where I would choose to sit. Then I chose to start with upstairs, on my way I met a lady who was alone standing on the stairs. The lady looked to be very smart, she had nothing on her hands.

I told myself that it was a good idea to speak to her and ask her more about our journey on that ship. Greeting her showed me that she spoke better Swahili than I, but the way she answered me and the way she spoke to me in general was in a respectful way. It showed me that she might be a kind lady, something gavee me the confidence to go ahead and talk to her. After greeting her, she responded also saying that I was her sister, 'salam dada yangu', then I said that I was asking her if she could help me by explaining about the ship because I didn't understand.

"What do you not understand?"

"Everything, I see people in many different positions, and doing different things, sitting, singing, eating, standing, and going up and down. I don't know if it is going to be like this until morning, and I don't know if there are any laws here which people have to follow. Like that place where there are so many people, even passing between them is not easy. I don't know then why it seems to be OK to them to make that place dirty that way. That is why I am trying to see first the other places and see if there is somewhere that is different."

First she laughed and said that she could tell it was my first time in the ship, and I said yes it was. She told me to follow her to where she was going, I followed her and we went back where I came from at that place where there were a group of women and children, where they sat as if they were at home. She told me that one group were her people who she came with, they came from the same village and they were going to the same place. "So here was where I left my things, I give them yours too. And come, I'll show you around this ship, to me it is like my home because I am on this journey many times. This old woman is my people back home."

I gave them my things too. When I turned she was there standing waiting for me. Then we started to go, but at the same time in a second I turned and thanked them and said bye to them. By doing so, it seemed to make them happy, they said bye back to me with wider smiles, and told me, "Go my children and enjoy."

After she started to tell me about inside the ship. "Here inside the ship is very wide and big, something you can't imagine when you look at it from the outside of it. So I am going to take you everywhere. When you feel tired or hungry just let me know."

I felt relaxed and happy now, like a child who is with his or her mum. A part from being my director she was also my guard, I started to enjoy my journey on the ship, it was as if she was there waiting for me to give me that wonderful company. First she chose to take me upstairs, it was on top of the ship, and then I was standing on top of that water. First I only stood for a few minutes in silence only looking here and there, it was another world, different from what I knew, I was in a world of water now, on top of it. It was like I was not there, she gave me time by keeping quiet and when I turned she was looking at me, maybe she knew that I was surprised or I was happy or I had other kinds of feelings, strange feelings, everywhere I turned my head, I was only seeing water. I didn't ask but I thought that maybe it was because it was night. The way she looked at me, she seemed to be happy, I think because she saw that I was very happy. I liked her more then, she gave me her hand with a sign that now we had to go somewhere else, I was holding her hands. The wind started to be too much and was too cold.

I didn't mind the many other people who were there, some were standing, some sitting and others sleeping and covering themselves with tents. But on the other hand I liked their conversations. I didn't ask her anything there.

It was time to go to show me where there were rooms, and she told me that she had two rooms, hers and her sister's. She didn't know why but her sister had missed the journey so she would give me hers. So we had to collect our things and go to our rooms and first have a rest. We collected our things and we were in our rooms now sitting down, that is when she started to tell me about her in brief. But first I asked her how much she paid for the room so that I could give her back the money, and she refused by saying that it was not necessary to pay back that money. I thanked her then; and we went ahead with our stories. But before that she remembered to ask me my name in a surprised way, "We have forgotten to ask each other our names! What is your name?"

"My name is Bamurangirwa."

"Mine is Karungi," (meaning someone who is good in all ways). To me she suited her name, she was too good, and she was beautiful too, and very smart, so she was good in all ways. She said that she had to have a room because on the ship she had to sleep, otherwise she couldn't survive because, she said, "The ship is my life, which is where I am many days, more than I am home."

It was my time to ask why, I asked her then.

"Why are you on the ship many times?"

"I am business woman between Mwanza and Bukoba and sometime Dal es Salaam, since I divorced with my husband that is what I do."

I looked at her in silence for some seconds, and then I asked her what happened between them to divorce? I felt sorry for her then.

I think she saw how I asked her in a serious way, and she had to tell me something. "You know Bamurangirwa you are still a child, you don't know yet problems between men and women and problems concerning marriage in general. You can call yourself a lucky person,

146

when you love and are loved back, and have a chance to be with the person you love. Someone who loved and was loved back had very strong things happen in him or her, but someone who was disappointed by the person he or she loved did not. Sometimes you stay with it for all of your life, regardless of what happens to you in that time, happiness or sadness, it depends. It can be worse when you trust someone and think that person you love loves you in the same way. There comes a time of big shock when it comes, a time of betrayal, a time of hate, a time of change, the change of life, and the time of breaking your heart, and all hopes you had. It can be too heavy to carry, and sometimes you feel ashamed in front of the people you knew, you don't know how you will be able to tell them about the disappointment."

I was listening to her then, I said, "That can be cruel."

"Yes," she said, and went ahead. You could see her when she was talking, it was like she was talking to herself, and, I saw that she was still carrying the pain of what her ex-husband had done to her. And she seemed to have truly loved him, a genuine love.

"My ex-husband left me with two children, and now it is only me who takes care of them." When those people, her time, the time of betrayal came, they couldn't have time to think or bother.

I thought that she might love her ex-husband as much as I loved Alex. Where our room was, there were other beds, after a short time, a young man entered our room and greeted us. "How are my sisters?" he asked, and I saw that was the respectful way of greeting in Swahili. He asked us if it was us who were his neighbours? I kept quiet and let Karungi deal with him. He started to introduce himself, "My name is Kasaija, I am a business man."

Karungi broke the short silence, maybe she waited to see if I would say something, then Karungi started by telling him our names, and on top of that, she also told him, "Bamurangirwa is like our visitor because it is her first time in the ship."

Kasaija said, "She is with us. So Bamurangirwa, feel free to ask us anything, to us this is like our second home, and don't worry you have good guides." I thanked him and both of them together. Kasaija told us that he was hungry and he was going to eat, so if we too had not yet had our dinner, we could go together. I was hungry, but I still kept quiet so that Karungi could decide. At the same time Kasaija stood up and stood at the door, meaning that he was waiting for us. When Karungi saw that I didn't say anything she knew that I had left it to her to decide. "Bamurangirwa, let us go with him, also we were on our way there, so there is no need to refuse to go with him," she said. I stood up and we went to the hotel, to reach there we passed many corners, it was not as near as I thought, it showed me how big the ship was, with many different places. It was a big hotel, clean, with clean staff, and looked like other mordern hotels. The chefs had good clean uniforms. They had few clients. One of the waiters came to where we were sat, and asked us to give orders of food and drink that we would like to be served.

All of us chose chicken and matoke, Kasaija seemed to want to have conversations, he was trying to tell me this and that, and I was only giving answers to the questions, but said no more, as he liked. So he told me that the ship would reach Mwanza very early in the morning and he was going to be there almost the whole day, so he would escort me to where I was going. I thanked him but the truth was that I didn't want to go with anyone; since I didn't know the welcome I would get from Rugamba's family. They gave us drinks and I asked for tea when Karungi and Kasaija asked for beer, we had a good and long conversation, after some time I asked Karungi where the toilet was, and she told me that the staff would direct me.

When I came back our food was there and when we finished the waiter came to clear the table. I asked the waiter how much it cost, it was Kasaija who replied that I didn't have to worry about paying, I could buy something for them later. I tried to insist at last that we could help him and he refused, something which I was not comfortable with. I saw that even though him and Karungi were strangers, I didn't understand why she looked to be comfortable with it. So I too gave up and thanked him. When Kasaija was telling me all of that he was looking at me with a little smile. A smile which told me that to him it was a very small thing to pay the bills, on other hand it was like he was telling me that if you are a man and you go somewhere with women, then, it is your responsibilty to pay no matter what. Even when women have more money than men. I thought that is why Karungi was confortable. I thought that it was like that then, like Kasaija who we had met there, and maybe we would never ever see him again, it was part of colonising and brainwashing which women did to men, which can be bad on both sides sometimes. Men had to do this and that, just because they were men. When it came to women also, it was the same thing, women had to do this and that because they were women.

We stood up and started to go back, Kasaija went ahead of us, Karungi and I were at the back following him. Karungi came near me, she started to talk to me by asking me how I saw Kasaija. My answer was a question also, "How I see Kasaija, in which way?"

Karungi said, "For everything, in general, and what about his looks?"

Then I thought that she had some feelings for him and I didn't have any reason to discourage her.

I told her that he was handsome, tall, good looking and with a good smile.

"And he's generous too," I said. Then I had to ask her how she saw him, by that I would know why she had asked me that kind of question in the first place.

When I asked her how she saw him, she gave me a quick answer, "He is a good looking man, and he has a lot of money, and it seems that he can give away that money easily." I saw that she was waiting for my comment, then I had to say something.

I said, "Maybe he has the money, and can give it away easily I can't know about that." She went on by telling me that he was sending a message to me through her to tell me that he wanted me.

She went ahead by questioning me with an idea, "So Bamurangirwa, what if you go to try and see how it goes?"

"Try what?"

Karungi said, "If you will argue with that, he will get another room, and you will spend the night together. So we can see each other tomorrow. Me too, when I get someone I will go. In this ship when the girl gets someone she calls it a day, and she counts it to be a good journey depending on who she got."

It was a big surprise to me, and I told her, "It is better to tell him no. Although I don't hate him, I don't have a reason to hate him, I can't do that either, I don't have reason too."

She looked to be surprised and asked me again if that was the only answer I had. And I said sorry, that was the only answer I had. When we reached our room, Kasaija asked us if we could escort him to where he was going. It was Karungi who asked him where he wanted us to escort him. Kasaija said that whatever it was, it was only in this ship. Then Karungi stood up without any other questions.

I was not yet tired and I enjoyed everything in the ship, so I told myself that there was no reason why I couldn't use this chance to look around and be happy at this moment since I didn't know what tomorrow held for me.

He took us in the bar, inside the bar were few people, after sitting down, Kasaija asked us what we wanted to drink. Karungi told him that she was going to have any kind of beer they had. "What about you Bamurangirwa?" he asked.

"Any kind of soda they have," I told him.

He didn't like my answer and he tried to insist that I could at least drink one bottle of beer, but I told him that I had never drank beer and it was OK with me to drink soda. He went to bring us our drinks and we sat down and started to drink, listening to the conversations of others while we had ours too. In general we were enjoying being there. Before finishing our drinks he called Karungi to go with him to bring the other drinks, they were there for some minutes talking and when they came back Karungi excused herself to go to the toilets, and when she went Kasaija asked me why I didn't want to spend the night with him. He asked why I hated him. I told him that maybe they hadn't given him my message in the correct way, that my message was that I didn't hate him, it was just that I couldn't do what he asked me to do.

He looked serious and he asked me if I had a particular reason, and I told him that it was only because to me, it was not time yet to share a bed with any man, and I was not in a hurry for that. After telling him that he looked relaxed and said that he understood me now, and he gave me respect for that. He went on by telling me, "Bamurangirwa, if I had a sister who respected herself this way I would be very happy and proud of her, we are not used to meeting women like you on this ship. No matter the age, old or young, as soon as you talk to her, she follows you as if she was waiting for you to come."

He continued, "So don't worry, from now on I will guide you as your brother, I will direct you to whatever you need here, and I will escort you where you are going there in Mwanza as I told you before." I didn't see Karungi again from that time, we went back to our room and it was time to reach Mwanza. He showed me where to have a shower and it was a good idea, he told me that there was no hurry. I took my time, so that we could go at the time we wanted to. Sometimes when I was in the rooms I forgot that I was in the middle of the water unless I looked in the window, that is when I remembered that I was still in the world of water.

After finishing what I wanted to do, he took me to the hotel, and we had our breakfast and again he insisted on paying for everything, then it was time to go and find Mr. Rugamba's home.

IN MWANZA TOWN

After going out of the ship I went to the side of it and looked at that wider water I was travelling on the whole night, then I turned my head to look at the town. It was small but not like Bukoba and it was clean compared to Bukoba. It was down around the mountains which had many stones, some would say that someone came with them and put them there in order, some places there were many small stones and in other places there were big rocks.

They were no houses in those mountains which was understandable, I thought that people there would be unable to get food or water if they went to live there, but I saw houses down the hill. We started to go in front of us, it was still early morning. I saw a small group of women, they were dressed in black like the women I had seen in Bukoba, but some of these ones had not only covered their head, they had also covered their eyes! What a surprised it was to me that they were going with others without any problems, so I had to ask if it was also because of their religion and how they managed to see front of them.

I asked Kasaija and he told me that they were Muslim and for the ones who covered their eyes, exactly in front of their eyes was transparent enough to let them see clearly.

I told Kasaja that I was going to visit my sister and her family and now I didn't know how I could refuse for him to come with me; to him he was doing me a favour. To me, I had a lot of doubt about the welcome I would get, and it would be better if I could be by myself. Kasaija took me where the taxis were standing and when I told a taxi man where I was going he said that it was near. We were inside the car and after a few minutes we were there, the taxi man told us that this was the road so if I could start to ask then it would be better to ask, Kasaija told him that it was our first time going there.

I told them to stop there so that I could go by myself to ask first, I saw the children outside of the house near the road playing, the children I thought might be Ethiopians or mixed Arabic, they had too light skin with long hair, but I promised myself that if they didn't know the people I was looking for, their parents might know. But still I would first try by talking with them in Kinyarwanda and seeing if they could be Rwandans. When I reached the children I greeted them and they turned back my greetings clearly, when I asked them who their parents were they told me that Rugamba was their father.

Within one minute, before asking them if there was anyone at home, some of them were inside the house already and I saw them come back with a tall light-skinned lady who I assumed to be their mum. I turned my head to where the car was to see that they were able to see how this lady was going to look at me, I was sure that she was going to look at me with eyes of surprise with a lot of questions. After greeting each other I started to talk before her. I told her in brief why I was there; I didn't have to wait for her questions. I told her, "I am your visitor and in the car there is someone who I met on the ship with my things." At that time my heart was running quickly while I waited to see what she was going to say.

She said that I had better go and tell my friend to come with me so that she could give us something to drink first.

I knew that I might never meet Kasaija again in the future, but I wanted to part with him in a respectful way.

I went back to the car and asked the taxi man how much, he told me that he had been paid already, again I was so surprised, I didn't understand why Kasaija did all of that for me really. I told them that I had found the people I was looking for. So Kasaija said that if I had found them that was good, he was going back with the car. I told him that if he was not in a hurry he could come with me. Afterwards he could go back on foot since I saw that it was not far. It was a request.

He said that if that was my wish then fine, he was not in a hurry. We went, the lady took my things and she was in front of us as we followed her, inside she showed us where to sit and she gave us tea with bread, we were hungry because we had our breakfast earlier. When we finished we thanked her and Kasaija said that he had to go. I said to the lady, "Let me escort him so that I can know the way by myself".

She said, "That is a good idea."

I escorted Kasaija and when we reached a place where there was market, I told him that I had better go back, we said bye to each other, and I thanked him once more again. Though I had no words to use to thank him enough, he said that it was his pleasure to do what he did to me, and he couldn't say that he would ever see me again, but he wished me all the best in my future.

I thanked him once more again, but in my heart I knew that I needed those prayers more than ever. I parted with Kasaija and I went inside the market, I bought some food and vegetables for cooking and when I reached home, I give them to the lady and I saw that she seemed to be happy with that. There and then she started to show me her kindness by telling me to come so that she could show me where to have a shower and after I could sleep, we would talk later. I thanked her for that kindness, but I told her that I had a shower in the ship and I slept too because I had a room, it was better if she could show me something to help her. She told me that there was nothing I could do to help her, we could talk if I didn't feel tired and I could tell her about my journey. She was the one who started to tell me about them and I was listening.

She said, "My name is Kwezi, here I am with my co- wife, her name is Kanzage, you will see her, she went to cultivate, we have a place for digging which is the council's property. She is here with her children so we are a big family, the owner of this house is the old lady from Burundi, her name is Haziza. We have our neighbour who you will like and she is going to like you too, because she likes people like you. We call her by her daughter's name as Mama Jowa."

I thought that was enough for that time, and it was my time to tell her who I was and why I was there. But I wanted to ask her first how she saw me because she said that Mama Jowa liked people like me. First I told her my name. "My name is Bamurangirwa, Patricia you can call me which is easier for you. But before I go ahead with my story can I ask you something?"

Kwezi said, "Yes, ask me anything." I asked her the question concerning Mama Jowa and how she had seen me.

Kwezi said, "Mama Jowa likes people who have understanding and are clean like you."

"How can you judge me so soon?"

Kwezi replied, "Some other things don't need a lot of time to know."

I told her all about my story, from Alex to Kagabo and my entire journey from Mpanumusingo's home to her home. She was listening to each and every thing and when I finished my story, she said that I had a very good reason to run from that forced marriage, that no one at that time should be taken in that situation, when on the the other hand they were being told that it was their life, it was their future. She went ahead telling me a story concerning problems like that of forced marriages, and she told me that I didn't have to worry. I would survive there, people didn't do anything, no one would interfere. "Since they believe that they have all the powers on you."

The way she was talking, and the way she was looking at me, it made me feel relaxed, because I saw that she understood me very well, and she felt sorry for me too. I needed to meet someone who could understand me that way. And she was encouraging too. Kwezi looked happy talking with me, and she seemed to have a lot to tell me, on my side I was happy with listening to her, I wanted to have someone who would be happy to see me around, especially her, if that home was her home, I needed her recognition and for her to see me as a good person to be with. Their house was a big house with a few rooms which were on the line and there was a big corridor between the rooms which was dusty but inside the rooms some had cement, some were part of the house, it looked like they were still doing some finishing. After all of that she told me that I didn't have to worry and I would be OK, she went on with a lot of encouragement, by telling me that I would get something to do, and I told her how I knew her and why I had chosen to come to her home. I saw that all of that made her feel happy to be chosen according to the way she looked at me, she insisted that I had to relax now and things would be fine. She said that they would help me wherever they could, it was a long time since I had anyone telling me those kinds of words which were supportive and full of encouragement. According to the way I saw her now, it was the opposite of the thoughts I had before. Normally I knew that for most of the people who lived in the towns, it was not easy for them to be genuinely happy to welcome visitors, especially when those visitors showed that they might be at their home for a long time.

Kwezi went ahead giving me ideas and tried to see that I felt relaxed. When I told her that my wish was to go to college for something, she said that it was a very good idea, but to be able to do that would depend on what I would do to give me enough to pay for my fees. In my heart I said, yes money again, everywhere, for everything, forever money would be a leader.

They had one big room which they had divided into rooms using pieces of clothes One more thing which gave me confidence with her and her family, was that she didn't show any worries or complain about their small house and big family.

After a short time I heard outside someone called her, and asked her who she was talking to. "I have a child, our visitor," she said. She told her to come and see me, but she said that when she was already stood up and told me to go where she was and say hello to her. I stood up and we went outside behind the house. Behind the house looked to be a good place, more than inside. There was a big space with small stones down all over the place, and some places had been cemented, it was a big wider pavement where Aziza was sat, there was also a tap for water and toilets. They were doing most of their things outside like cooking.

Aziza was an old lady, she was black and big like 200 kg, she was wearing a lot of clothes, two kangas which she tied from her waist, but the kangas looked to be too small for her, they were not covering her enough, maybe that is why she had another two dresses on inside, which were longer than the kanga, and one more kanga on top from her head. On top of all of that was a big black dress which I already knew was for Muslim women.

Her black dress had a small rope which was tied on her head. To me, the way I saw her, she looked like she had a long time without having a bath or washing her dresses, something I didn't understand, since she had water outside, unless she was dirty by nature. We greeted each other and Kwezi told her that I was her young sister who came from home, and I was going to stay with her. It seemed that she was happy to have me there and she liked me, otherwise she wouldn't have given me that respect. Back inside with Kwezi, I didn't ask her why outside of the house she was like that, I had to keep quiet for some other things, I couldn't come the same day and start to tell the people I met there that I knew better than them about this and that, or start to show them their mistakes, if I was better then it would show by itself. Maybe the way I saw things was different to others.

Later there came a beautiful mature lady, she had light skin but not like Kwezi, she was slender and a bit shorter compared to Kwezi, with long soft hair. When I saw the way she looked, it was like some of the children there and she came inside like someone who was entering her home, before introduction I already knew that she was Kanzage. I stood up to greet her when Kwezi was telling her who I was. She told her, "This girl is our visitor from Uganda and she has come to stay with us." She looked at me with a smile and welcomed me more again.

Afternoon came a tall man around six and a half feet, or more. He was brown like Kwezi and I stood up and greeted him and then sat down, Kwezi told him who I was, like the way she had told Kanzage. We had our lunch and afterwards I was tired, but I kept quiet, because the way I saw it it was their room and I didn't know where they would tell me to sleep out of the the three beds which were there. "Bamurangirwa?" Kwezi called me.

"Yes," I said.

Kwezi said, "Go to that bed and have a rest if you are tired."

I was very happy and soon after I went to bed I was in a deep sleep until the evening. When I woke up, I was alone inside the room, but I heard people talk outside, so I went outside to where I heard them behind the house they were sat on the pavement. Kwezi was with a lady who looked to be forty to forty-five years old, light skin but not like her or Kanzage, wearing two kangas one from the waist down to her feet, the other on the back. She wore a short sleeved shirt and slippers, all of them looked to be new, her hair had a good style, more than Karungi's, and she had white teeth which had spaces between them, she looked beautiful and very clean. It was Kwezi who started to tell her, "This is my young sister Bamurangirwa, who I was telling you about. Our parents wanted her to come and be with me."

She turned to me and told me, "This is Mama Jowa, who I was telling you about."

We greeted each other and Mama Jowa who was talking with her beautiful smile welcomed me strongly, she said it in Swahili to be better understood. "Kalibu Sana," she said, meaning you are very much welcome. When they called any woman by name in that way, 'Mama so and so', anyone knew that the name belonged to her child, so, Jowa was her daughter. It was partly out of respect but up to the end I never knew her real name. And I didn't ask. Mama Jowa asked Kwezi if they had made evening tea, Kwezi said no, and told her that normally they didn't make evening tea. In one minute Mama Jowa was stood up and told me to come, so that we could share tea in her room. I was confused then, yes I wanted tea but I was supposed to depend on Kwezi not Mama Jowa, if I left, Kwezi would see me as greedy, if I refused, Mama Jowa would think that I didn't have respect for her. Since I was still standing, then, I just went ahead and stood there.

Mama Jowa was inside her room, I was still standing where I was, Kwezi thought that I went with Mama Jowa, later when she turned and saw me there she was surprised and asked me why I was still there. I didn't have any answer, she told me to go, said that now Mama Jowa was waiting for me, I got official permission and I went. In her room everything looked to be clean and in order, after finishing our tea I thanked her and we talked a little, I told her that I was going out, she told me that she would always like me to come and share with her her meal, morning and evening! I didn't say anything, I went out but I didn't tell Kwezi what Mama Jowa said. The next day when we were almost having our breakfast, we heard Mama Jowa calling me, but I pretended I didn't hear, it was Kwezi who replied on my behalf. And Kanzage told me to go by saying, "Bamurangirwa, just go, this shows that Mama Jowa likes you."

Kwezi also noticed that for some reason I was not free for going to share Mama Jowa's food with her, and wanted to give me freedom by telling me, "Bamurangirwa, if Mama Jowa is happy to share with you, any time then you may go, there is nothing wrong with that."

Mwanza is a hot place; there are a lot of mosquitos. I didn't know anything about mosquitos before then, after three days I had rashes all on my arms and face. When I was out Mama Jowa asked me what happened to me and I told her that I didn't know. She told me that it was the mosquitos that bit me, I had no idea. Then she offered me a net which she had in her suitcase. I didn't know how to thank her. For more than half of my life there in Mwanza, it was like it was Mama Jowa who was responsible for me in many ways.

In three weeks I already knew all about them, their character and behaviour. Then what I had to do, was to get all of them accordingly, and make them my friends, I managed to do so up to the end, even Lady Bibi Haziza, as they ware calling her. I liked to iron my clothes, so I decided to take responsibility for Rugamba's and all of the children's clothes, to wash them and iron Rugamba's together with mine, since the children's clothes didn't need ironing, it was just Rugamba's and mine.

Apart from the children who were calling him daddy, others were calling him by his name, so I started to call him chief , 'Mutware' since I was not able to call him by his name and I couldn't call him daddy. To me it would be like a loss of respect for him, it surprised all of them including him, and the first time he asked me why, and I told him that I was not comfortable calling him by his name, he looked happy with the idea, after a few days all of them started calling him chief. Where I came from, in my family I was the youngest and I had to give all of them respect as my elders. On the women's side there was no problem concerning that point, because all of the people were called through their children's names, it was part of the culture in some parts of Kenya and Tanzania as a sign of respect for mothers, and sometimes fathers. The landlady, since I came to know that she had never had any children, they called her only Bibi, not directly by her name Aziza, again this was a sign of respect.

There were four words my mum left with me, which helped me most in that big family where I needed to be friends with all of them, and I needed them to see me as a good child. I had to be good as much as possible in that stranger family who welcomed me with their open arms.

Self respect.

Respect others.

To be kind to others.

To keep secrets.

But kindness was my nature, I loved other people, I was not happy to see someone with a problem or in an abusive situation. I wanted to be fair for both of them. So these three ladies, Kwezi, Kanzage and Mama Jowa, each of them wanted to be closer to me than others, neighbours believed that I was sister to Kwezi, but to some outsiders Kanzage was telling them that I was her sister, also Mama Jowa in front of visitors was introducing me as her younger sister. The one who was there wanted to show that I was closer to her than everyone. This was a big test to me, I didn't want to lose any of them and I knew that losing one could cause a big problem between all of us; I had to be very careful then.

When Rugamba had something to do, which maybe his wives could do, they looked to each other to see who could be the first to do it. I would ask him to give it to me so that I could do it.

I was going to Mama Jowa's every day, many times for different reasons, when we had conversations, somehow we were like the same age, we were talking about this and that, laughing a lot more than I did when I was with the others. So we went along together and that was no problem to the others, they were happy for us to be good friends, and it was OK with them. But before I went to her room I had to first see if I had done what I had to do in Rugamba's house. And I had to ask Rugamba if he had something he wanted me to do for him as well as his wives. By doing all of that in that way, it made me feel that I was paying them back, it was the only way that I could pay them back for what they did for me. Sometimes when there were dirty dishes I had to clean them and do some other housework.

After some time I came to know that Munyaburanga could no longer care enough for his old wife Kanzage, sometimes when it was only the two of us, Kwezi and me, there were times when she would only give food to her children and leave alone Kanzage's. Although I didn't like it, I had no power to do anything, not even to tell Kanzage what happened to her children when she was away. And I couldn't tell Kwezi directly that what she was doing was not right. There were times Kwezi tried to tell me that I didn't have to be washing the clothes of Kanzage's children, she said that I gave myself a lot of things to do. But I refused by telling her that it was OK with me. Aziza and Mama Jowa believed that I was related to Kwezi and they would not talk about her in my presence, but the time came when they started talking about her mistakes in front of me. It was like they were sending messages to her through me so that maybe she would get an idea which would help her change her behaviour, but I wouldn't tell her anything.

Both Kwezi and Kanzage, each trusted me in their own ways, and both were telling me about the other, and telling me about their problems. I was in the centre then, of both of them, which is how I came to know that each one thought that I was her friend more than the other, and they had confidence because no one heard anything, anywhere, about what they had told me.

That is why I believed that each of them knew that she was the only one who was telling me her secrets.

I was like the husband of three wives.

One day when I was with Kwezi she told me that the first time that Rugamba saw me and heard that I was going to be with his family he was worried that I was not going to be able to manage the life they were in. In fact, I managed to handle his family in general, so now he believed that I could handle any kind of life anywhere I could be.

Kwezi was abusing Kanzage's children when their mum and daddy were not at home, but after she came to realise that I was not happy to see that, she changed, she was giving all of them food or whatever together in the same way when I was there. If there was something I had to do for the children, I was doing it in an equal way, it made the children love me, and when they wanted to take them somewhere, sometimes they would refuse, saying that unless they went with me too! Their parents gave me respect for that, it made them have a lot of trust in me. I thought because of their children they loved me more too.

Mama Jowa, most of the time when she wanted to go somewhere she liked to ask me to go with her, so one day I thought that if I asked her to come with me somewhere maybe she would not see that I was losing respect for her. My bed was only wires, and the net she had given me was starting to be torn apart because of the wires, also I was not comfortable sleeping on wires, but I saw that they didn't have any mattress to give me so I had to be patient.

I wanted to go and buy a mattress, I asked her and we went together and came back with a medium mattress, I used some of my savings. In that time I was there, more than one month, on Sundays I was going with Mama Jowa to the market which was up the country twenty miles or more away, and which was only on Sundays. There were cars which went there, and business people were going there to get things for their businesses. Mama Jowa was getting tomatoes from there and putting them outside of our door and selling them. She liked to go there every week.

One day on Sunday we went as always, she was paying for my transport. I think she just enjoyed my company, though I enjoyed being with her too. When we were there I noticed that she had two bags, it was different, as before she would always go with one bag. I asked her why she had come with two bags.

Mama Jowa said, "I realised that one bag is not enough per week." She bought tomatoes and came back, when we were at home; she called me and gave me one bag telling me that these tomatoes were mine. She told me to take them to my home which was Rugamba's house. She said that I had to start to sell them and what I got from them would be my capital, I would be going there every week and when I had a reason which would make me not go, she would go and buy them for me, and the same to her in case she needed to send me to buy for her. She surprised me and I thanked her but I thought that I had not thanked her enough, she had done a lot for me in many different ways, sometimes I was just looking at her, and saw nothing. I saw that what she did I took it to be too much. Then she broke the silence with her beautiful smile by saying, "It is OK Bamurangirwa, don't worry I am happy to do it." Meaning what she did for me, that was an introduction to the tomato business, from next week; I would be a business woman, and would see where it would take me.

The next day it was Monday afternoon, to the door came three men and they told us that they were officers from the government: and they went house to house looking for people who didn't know how to read and write, that they started a project of teaching them. They were asking all of those people who would like to come to school. It would be near to where they live, and would be for free. They also wanted someone who knew how to read and write who could volunteer for teaching.

I asked them if they taught English but they told me that they didn't yet have that programme of teaching, since no one needed it. I told them that I could teach how to write and read but I too would like to learn English, they said that could be a good idea, they didn't have anyone who was interested yet for English but they could get me a teacher even if it would only be me, maybe after some time there might be others who would be interested to learn it. Mama Jowa didn't know how to read or write and I asked her what she thought. Mama Jowa said, "I don't want to know all of that, I don't know it and I am OK. I don't miss anything because of that."

I wanted her to know, and I saw that it was not going to be as easy for me to convince her as I thought, but I had to try. Then I told her that if I would be a teacher she could be my student and I would be teaching her when we were at home also, so that she would learn quicker than others. They had to come back after two days to see our decision, then I told Mama Jowa that if she would go then, I too would go, if she would not go then I would not go either. I told her that I would ask Chief's permission and I was sure he would allow me to go. Then I saw that Mama Jowa seemed to be happy with that and had confidence and she said that she would go. I told her that in the future she would see the difference between knowing how to read and write, and not knowing, and I promised that she would be happy for that. At night I asked Chief's permission, when I told him the reason he seemed to be happy with the idea, and he told me that it was good, at last I would have something to take me out of the house. It was every evening for two hours. I had no teacher yet, I was a teacher and all of my students were older than me, most of them were women with their families. I had only two men. Even if I was young to them, they gave me respect as their teacher, and in turn I knew that if you think that a teacher is a good person, and maybe they are your friend, it is easier to understand what that teacher teaches you. So I made them my friends, in my lessons I gave them ideas and sometimes asked them for ideas too.

I was encouraging them and trying to see that they had enough confidence, at home I was teaching Mama Jowa. The director came to tell us about the time when the founders of the project would come from Dar es Salaam to give the students a test, and they wanted us to prepare how we would welcome them, we thought that it would be good if we could prepare some songs and dancing to welcome them.

I asked them to give me one teacher who would help me to organise all of that, and they did it. All of the songs had to be concerning Ujama Nyerer's system, a communist way of ruling. In that area my students were number one, and it was Mama Jowa who was number one in the class. Our photos were among the pictures which the founders took to their offices according to what they said. And they put them on the wall, they didn't give us the copies and we didn't ask them. But all of us were happy about that. I didn't get the teacher for myself, when I asked them about it they seemed to have almost forgotten about it. After my students were number one, the gifts they gave me were to two teachers, one for English, and the other one was a European lady who spoke Swahili and they told me that was my visitor.

That lady told me that she had come to ask me if I would like to know how to make some kind of handbags, she had one which looked so nice and she opened it, got another one out which she had made and it was another which was nicer than that, she said that she wanted to teach me to make those bags. I was shocked to see it, but to hear the idea that I would know how to make them. I had some kind of fear on my face and she noticed me, and she tried to give me confidence that I could, she went ahead by telling me that by knowing how to make them, it might help me somehow in the future. They were bags made of nylon rope, which were different curls. I thought that if this was something which was done by people, then why not me, I told her that it was OK, I would take the course.

She told me that if there were others who would like to join it would be fine. But no one wanted to join courses for English or making bags, no one was interested; I was only me who was a student to both of them. I asked my director to change my timetable, after talking with my students, so that I could get my time also.

I was busy then, when I didn't have something to do concerning my housework, I went creative, or I had something to do concerning my school, and when I was not at home my tomato business was still doing well. Anyone who was at home was taking care of it, that is how Mama Jowa was doing it too. So everyone was happy to help. Then I was happy with life somehow.

I was friends with both of my teachers, but I was sometimes angry with the teacher of bags, when I made the bag and had almost reached the end and she saw some mistake sometimes it was in the middle or at the beginning, she was telling me to take it off all, up to where the mistake was. But afterwards I realised that it helped me to learn quickly, because I feared that she would tell me to put it off, so I was very careful. After knowing very well how to make them, I started to make business with bags. I gave myself a timetable, enough to make my beautiful bags, in the time I was making them; I had to sit behind the house on the pavement. Sometimes I was designing new styles or mixing the beads.

After finishing them I put them outside and started to sell them. My bags were the first to be seen in Mwanza, so I got a big market for them. After one to three months many girls, especially girls in the offices, or in high schools, since I was hiding myself while I made them, they thought that they had come from somewhere else far away. I had money then, sometimes when I was getting a lift to the Sunday market, I started to help Rugamba's family for food stuff, I was happy that I was not useless and that I could do something for the people who helped me.

One day I came back late and I was tired and hungry, it was Kanzage who was at home. I think when she saw me she noticed that I was hungry and we said hello, but she seemed to be on the way to going somewhere, after a short time she came back with a small bag in her hands, she opened the bag and she took the milk from it, she put it in the cup and then she gave it to me. The first time I thought that it was some kind of mistake, I knew that she didn't have money, and if she had money then she also had her children to feed and not me. I didn't get it, her arm was still in the air, I looked at her in a silent way with eyes full of questions, yes, she knew my questions even in this silent way. She told me to have the milk, she said that she went for it only because of me. And yes I knew her to be a very kind lady; if she was a rich person then no one would have any problems when she was there. I drank the milk and felt much better and thanked her, also I asked her why she had done that. She told me that she saw that I was hungry, and that was understandable.

"Mama Jowa and Kwezi were not at home since the morning, so I thought that since morning you had nothing."

Yes, since morning I had nothing but I didn't tell her anything, I let her take the things the way she saw them, I didn't have to go into details of my day concerning that point. I only smiled a little smile, which was more to thank her and I was surprised that someone could have sympathy for me that way; I was happy and grateful for that. As anyone, I needed someone who could show me that sympathy and love. I was only doing what they told me to do, sometimes, they were just indirectly refusing to do housework and when that happened I was doing it, it was like I depended on both Rugamba's family and Mama Jowa. So Mama Jowa took very good care of me willingly, she was happy to see me happy in any way she could. And instead when I was buying food I was not buying it for her, I was buying it only for Rugamba's family. I couldn't afford to contribute to both of them and maybe it would look funny, so I left it the way it was and Mama Jowa didn't show any sign of complaining. If I was to choose I would have to choose Mama Jowa, but it was only me who sometimes had confusion, after I realised that between themselves Mama Jowa and Rugamba's family had no problem at all with the way I handled them, tI relaxed.

Kanzage started to talk like she was talking to herself, on the other hand she was telling me that she was always happy for me, and she liked the way I handled life in general. She told me about her brother who she said was like me in many ways, in that he was hard-working and she said that people like us we gave confidence and hope to others. In her case, she said that people like us were the hope of the future, we would be the contribution to go back to our home no matter what time it would take. I asked her where all of that hope came from, and how we could give other people that kind of confidence. She started to tell me her story in brief, where her family were in Bibwe Congo, that when they reached there in late 1959 and early 1960. They survived with everything the U.N. gave them, but the U.N. had to give them time, after which the help would stop and they would have to

167

depend on themselves after that time. They gave them seeds and showed them part of the land where they could grow their food, but to this, Rwandans, like many other Rwandans in other countries where they were, it was like abuse to them, to tell them to grow food in a foreign country.

To the special old people, they didn't understand why they should grow food in a foreign country, they believed that soon they would go back to their home, so the different seeds of different kinds of food were not used the way that they had to be used correctly, and they were telling the U.N. officers that the food for some reason refused to grow. But then the U.N. had to finish as it was their time to go. Rwandans were still in foreign countries and suffered in many different ways without the U.N.'s help. Because of the hunger, they had to work for food and they decided to start to work hard and stand on their own feet. They did this and it ended up that they went into the forest and bush and made the place a better place to stay, and after that they had a lot of food, good houses and better school. It was them who built the school and got teachers for themselves, they built the school for their children and the churches, and the ones who were teachers, pastors, and priests back home started to do the same to their people in the countries they were in as refugees. Again like other Rwandans who were in other countries many were even better than the native people, and they turned native people into their workers. She finished her story by telling me that in that area you wouldn't know that it was Congo, as they made the area like Rwanda, concerning culture and language. The women copied Congolese women's way of dressing, the 'kitenge', maybe because it was a good respectful way for women to dress, which covered their body down to their feet and was a good colourful material. Up until the 2000s, this had almost come to be African dress to women in some parts of Africa far from Congo, but they managed to stick to their way of life at least ninety-eight percent without copying anything from the native cultures.

At that time I knew the town very well, so I didn't need anyone to take me anywhere. The money I came with from Uganda was already gone, but I had money because of my small businesses of tomatoes and making bags. I had money and sometimes I was saving enough, so had no worries concerning that point. One day I went to town to buy a slightly bigger mattress, more than for me, this was for the children, because the one which they were using, was very old. When I reached home and gave it to them, all of them were very happy, children and parents, and it made me happy too, I saw that it was a good idea to do that. Mama Jowa and Bibi Aziza were good followers of their religion Islam, when it was Lamathan time, time for fasting, they had to do that. In the day time when they sometimes didn't have things to do, during times like that, Mama Jowa chose to chop firewood, as I said before Mama Jowa was a very beautiful lady in all ways, including the way she dressed, it was easy for any man who met her to admire her.

One day when she was where she was doing her firewood cutting between Bibi Aziza's house and another neighbouring house, she had someone telling her 'pole nakazi', which meant well done. That was part of the culture of Tanzanians, in a Swahili language the same as in Baganda culture which had it in their language too, it was a way of encouraging their people for working. She didn't know where the person came from, because it was only me who was going to get the firewood which was ready to put where they had to be ready to sell them. And since was no way for passersby, and the voice was a man's, it shocked her a little. According to her story, she had to stand and see who it could be, who was talking to her, and when she turned her head, she saw the handsome man who sometimes she saw on the road with others or alone. It was the man who started to introduce himself by telling her that his name was Seleman Hawang from Tabora, and the neighbouring house was his brother-in-law and that is where he was living. He told her that when he looked where someone was cutting the firewood and he saw that it was a woman; it attracted him since he knew that it was a man's work, since it was a hard job, but being as it was a woman he decided to go and help a bit. So Mama Jowa was grateful for the offer, after a short time Seleman asked her a little about herself and told her that he would like to visit her one day, but Mama Jowa as a human being and grown-up woman, she noticed that he was trying to make a kind of friendship between themselves and she knew that she couldn't encourage it. She told him there and then, that he was too young for her, and to her it could not be possible to have that kind of friendship, but she had a young sister with her. She thought that when he saw her he would like her, it was me who she was talking about. Mama Jowa came home to tell me that it was my time to pick firewood, and I thought that it was a kind of joke because it was so soon, when she saw that I didn't believe her, she had to tell me how it happened and told me that she got the help from a stranger, a handsome young man. We went together, when we reached there the man stopped chopping the firewood and looked at us. Mama Jowa told him that this was her young sister, Bamurangirwa. Our eyes met for a few second and we greeted each other, and he told me his name. I came to take the firewood, but I didn't go back again, I waited until Seleman was finished and had gone. Why I didn't do as before and pick the firewood as soon as I came, I don't know why. I thought that maybe I wanted to be there and see him chopping firewood, but I didn't want any of them to find out that was what I thought.

At night, from nowhere, I was thinking about Seleman. He was tall and slender but a medium build, light skin, good smile, well dressed, he looked decent and smart, and he was a good-looking man in many ways. The feelings made me think about Alex, for the first time since I was in Mwanza. There, twenty minutes walking distance, was a family friend with Rugamba's family, and they had children, girls of my age. Since they were in school, at weekends or holidays, I liked to be sent there for some messages, because that was a good time for us to have our chat, or for them to be sent to our home. Sometimes when we escorted each other, we would stand in the middle of the way and forget to go ahead because of the stories.

It was on a Sunday when I was coming from their home, these girls were escorting me and we were standing in our position where we would always stand and talk about our stories, before we said bye to each other. After seeing that the time was going and we had been there for so long ,as always with a lot of laughing, we decided that it was time to go, we said bye to each other. They went their way and I went mine.

Within no time I saw a bicycle in front of me, when I looked up it was Seleman who was looking down at me, I had almost forgotten about him, but when I saw him I felt kind of nervous, I had to try quickly to fight it so that Seleman wouldn't notice that. I was the first to greet him.

"Where do you come from?" he asked me.

"I come from where they had sent me for something," I told him.

"You come from that girls' place?" he asked me.

That surprised me. I asked him, "How do you know about them?"

"I saw them; I was waiting for them to go."

Silence…

Seleman said, "Where are you going now?"

"Home."

"Do you know how to sit on a bicycle?"

I said yes, at this time he didn't ask, it was a command, "Sit, I am going home too so we can go together."

I was too nervous I couldn't say anything. I didn't need that help, home was near, but I thought that to refuse might show that I had a primitive character, so I decided to accept the offer. Now I had the question of how I was going to sit, there were two positions, to sit behind, looking at the one who was riding the bicycle, with the legs apart, which is seen to be a man's style. Or I could sit behind but with only my side opposite to the person who was riding the bicycle, that way the legs would be together in the same position, and this was seen to be the women's style. So which one was I going to use? Before I asked myself, he was the one who showed me where and how I would sit, in front of him between his arms and in front of his chest. I didn't know if that was how he knew to carry people or if it was because he wanted me in his arms and his chest, or he was worried that I could fall down and that was the way of protecting me? Yes, I felt safe and protected in his arms. I didn't say anything, I was sweating and trembling, I didn't know if he noticed it or not, on other hand the distance was short, we were home, but I wished the journey was longer, a part of me was nervous, but I felt peace in his chest between his arms. When we were at home, it was at the front of the house and he asked me if I could pass the home so that I could see where they lived, and he told me that he was staying with his brother in the room, maybe it was a way of telling me that he was single. I thanked him but refused to pass by his place, by telling him that I would visit him next time. The truth was that I wanted to go and sit down and talk to him for hours. The problem was that I had heard the story before many times that women were not allowed to directly show their feelings to men, if they did, it could be a reason for the man to think that the woman had something wrong with her, the proper way was to let the man struggle by trying very hard to show their love to the woman.

I didn't know why or how people had started that belief, but that was what many believed, women had to behave if they wanted to get full respect as women. To me it was meaningless, why men could be free to tell women their feelings and women couldn't. Since I didn't know the history of how it started and, I knew that I couldn't change the mentality of people, I had to keep quiet and behave like other women who needed proper respect, by showing what I saw to be good behaviour in front of Seleman, and being a girl with very few words. When I said bye to him, he gave me his hand and I gave him mine, he seemed that he didn't want to let me go, he was not bad to me either, when I looked up in his face I saw him looking down at me in quite a serious way, and he looked like he was far from where we were. I had to talk again telling him bye, and then he said yes, and told me to send greetings to others at home. At home I went ahead with what was my responsibility, but whatever I was doing I realised that I thought about Seleman every minute I was not with him. I thought that it was not quite right to start to think of him that way, I didn't know him enough yet to allow myself to think of him. So I tried to get him out of my mind.

On the other hand, I thought that it could be a good idea if I could get other good friends too, I thought that it was not a good idea to go ahead hurting myself by holding Alex with me forever when I now already knew that I would never see him again. But also I had to be careful since I knew that love could hurt in different ways. After two days, it was evening time and I was inside the house when Mama Jowa called me. I came out, she was standing with a young man who it was my first time to see, when I was there both of them were looking at me, the young man was looking at me from head to toe, he seemed to have a lot of questions for me too. I had the same questions, but before I asked mine, the man asked me first if I was Bamurangirwa.

"Yes, that is me," I said. Mama Jowa was still there quietly standing and waiting, she was looking at me, that young man who I didn't get time or remember to ask him his name, was the one who had to tell me why he wanted to see me. If Mama Jowa seemed like she was waiting for something maybe it was to see why this man wanted to see me.

"I have your letter," finally he told me. Before I could ask him where he got the letter from he didn't give me any chance, he went ahead by telling me that he had to go back with the answer, but he decided to go and come back later to get the answer. I said that was a good idea, so he had better come back in the evening for a reply. Since the messenger looked to be in hurry, I didn't get time to ask him who gave him the letter, it was not really necessary, since I was going to know where the letter came from soon after opening it. Mama Jowa was looking at me with a little smile, her face was full of happiness as if she knew what the letter was all about. I went like wind to the room which was still empty and locked the door, then I opened the letter. I had to start at the bottom to know where the letter came from, it was signed, 'yours forever, Seleman Hawanga'!

I didn't go ahead, I put it aside and waited, keeping quiet for some time, asking myself many questions without answers. I was holding the letter in my hands which was written by the hands of the man I wanted to know if he could have any feelings towards me, now he told me that he loved me, what else now? I had to be brave and read the letter. I opened it again and now started from the beginning.

To read the letter was not that easy for me. Since I knew that I was on my own, I was reading one line and sometimes jumping here and there, or covering my face with my hands like I was shy, or happy. Other times I had a big smile or a big laugh, and told myself many different things. I was giving myself ideas, I tried to calm myself down, or give myself counselling to take it easy, I acted like I was with someone else, and sometimes I remembered that I was acting crazy, and I told myself to concentrate on reading the letter not craziness. I was delighted but I knew that if I was going to welcome Seleman into my heart, into my life, then I had to know that this new chapter I was opening was a delicate chapter, which could be a struggle and needed to be handled with care. I knew that in Mwanza, no one was to blame, it was going to be between me and Seleman, so I had to grow up and see each and every thing in a careful way concerning the business I was going into, the business of love, which is hard when it has any complications, and which is simple, sweet, peaceful, lovely, when it is in a good and normal position. At that good time of love make you feel alive and loved, and forget where you were in life without it, and wonder how anyone could survive without it. It is is easy and sweet to enter in the house of love, but hard and can hurt when you are parting with it. His letter was a short letter with few words but strong enough to turn me in another direction. But I had to know that if I wanted to stay normal, I didn't have to trust one hundred percent.

Dear Bamurangirwa,

I loved you as soon as I saw you, but when I was with you on my bicycle I was thinking of you every minute, I can't help it, I had to tell you Bamurangirwa, that now I am in love, the love I have towards you is strong enough to stand in front of everything and fight anything which can stand front of me, it is strong enough to dry the Ocean. I can fight any thing which can come in front of me wherever it can come from, in the air or in the earth.

Maybe you are in love with someone else, please if so let me know it, I will understand, but if you are free and you are able to visit me, *please I am inviting you to my home tomorrow evening so that we can talk more.*

I promise you that you don't have to fear me, I can't harm you, instead I would like to have a chance to guide you Bamurangirwa.

Yours forever,

Seleman Hawanga.

I wanted to go, but I didn't want Seleman to see me as if I had a lot of independence, meaning that I had no respect for my elder sisters. I wanted to show him that I could only go when I had permission, and also I wanted to show him that I was not easygoing. I was not someone who could go at the time he told me to go, I wanted to give him time to struggle because he was a man, I had to use that mentality of the majority of other girls. So I had to give him an answer and tell him that I would go when I had time.

When I was at home I didn't want to sit doing nothing, before knowing how to make bags, in my free time I liked to make tablecloths which were very beautiful and I had many. So I decided to write very few words and put one in the envelope and send it to him with my letter of reply. But I didn't know how and when I would give him exactly as a time, on the other hand I thought that what I did was madness, it was too soon, but the messenger was gone. I was about to visit him, he would just have to wait when I told him and I would try to keep quiet unless he asked me again, meaning that I had to wait and see if he would struggle more than that.

I thought that I was very brave to be able to do so.

I promised myself that by giving him a gift so soon, I knew that it would sound like a crazy thing to do, so I would never tell anyone, not even Mama Jowa. The next day, in the evening one of my girlfriends came home, and I was very happy to see her not only because I would get a good story with her, but also because by luck when I escorted her I might get chance to see Seleman. When I was escorting her it was as if Seleman was in the window looking outside, you might think that he was waiting for me. I heard someone calling and I turned my head, it was Seleman who was in the window, we greeted each other, and he said that when I came back from escorting my visitor he would be there because he had something to tell me, it was a request. I said yes, I would pass there.

But the way I was talking to him with big ignorance made even the other girl ignore all of it, she didn't even ask me who the young man was, and that is what I wanted. I had no story about him yet. When I came back he was still there, and he came quickly to where I was, the first thing he did was ask me when I would come, and I told him that I didn't know. Something surprised him and he asked me if I didn't know then who would. He tried to give me ideas by telling me that if I feared him or my sisters I had to trust him one hundred percent, then I could ask my sisters permission since at his home I would be safe, then we agreed that I would go the next day in the evening time. At home I had a problem in my mind of what I would wear, how I would behave in front of him and so on.

The time to go came after a long decision in my head of how, or what, would be. I went and I knew where I would pass where Seleman would see me before I asked anyone. I didn't want to ask or to talk to anyone before seeing him, just because I was too nervous. At their home inside their compound there were men who were playing, there were more than five, sitting around the short table. All of them were looking down, when I saw them I stood still in one place and the first man who saw me, looked as if he had turned to stone, he was looking at me without any words, or turning his head anywhere else, so we looked at each other for a few seconds, both of us silence. It was as if he had seen an alien, then all of them they had to turn their heads and see why he was in that position. Because I felt nervous and shy I didn't know if Seleman was there or not, and I didn't know how or who to ask, so I had to greet them according to the culture. To the person who came, my legs were trembling and I was not sure if I could get my voice to talk, I thought that it was ridiculous to go ahead and keep quiet. Then Seleman was there and he stood up as soon as he saw me, then when I saw him I got my voice back and I was able to talk and I greeted them, both of them returned my greetings at once, like they were in a singing competition, all of that happened in one minute.

Seleman was in front and I was behind in his room, it was a big room, with one double bed and a small table in the corner, on it there was the tablecloth that I had sent to him. He sat in the bed, and welcomed me a second time, he was sitting when I was still standing, I didn't know if I had to sit, where was I supposed to sit? In a silent way I questioned, but I only had to wait. He saw that I was confused and tried to make me understand by saying that they didn't have any chairs yet, so I could sit on the bed or he could go out to find where he could get a chair.

I saw that it was not necessary, I had to sit. The door was open, outside were people and other rooms of other people and their doors were also open, so I thought that I was OK, I didn't have to worry. Soon after Seleman went to the end of the bed and slept, he didn't say anything, in that silence, I asked myself what was going on here, to get a visitor and sleep and just keep quiet! Then I had to turn and see at last the position he was in. He was asleep with his hands covering his face, when he heard me turning, he turned his head and his eyes were red wiping tears, and he apologised. He explained that he was very weak when he was in love, he started to tell me how he saw me the first time, talking about my beauty, saying that he had never come across anyone as beautiful as me, it was like a long beautiful song, which I didn't want to end. I was telling myself in my heart that the men I had come across, were the men who could easily cry, or maybe all men could cry. I remembered Alex when he cried like it was yesterday.

He went on with his song that he would like to be at my side every minute, but he still feared my sisters, he didn't know yet how they would take it if he was coming to my home every time he would like too. All the time I was with him, it was like the same story repeating the same thing over and over. He remembered to say that even if there were other girls who might be beautiful like me or more than me, his eyes would never see them. That the love he felt towards me was a lot, enough to fight for anything which could be in front of him, if it came from the air or from the earth, that it was enough to dry the ocean. His words were like good poetry in person, he repeated some which were in the letter he sent me, it was like a good romantic song, Solomon's song, which I didn't want to end. I came to remember Mama Jowa telling me that I had to hold him tightly, because he was so handsome, many girls might fight for him, and then I counted myself to be the lucky one. I thought that I might be very beautiful if a man like him was telling me all of those sweet words, and if that is how he saw me, it is true what they say that love is blind.

Since I sat on the bed I was in one position, like the first African followers of catholic churches or other foreign religions years ago. Holding my arms across my chest all of that time. After some time he held my hand with the arm on his side and asked me if I was not tired by putting my arms on the same position. I said that it was OK, he put my hand on his and you could think that it was a child's hand in a man's. Compared to his, my hand was very small. He thanked me for the tablecloth, and at that point I had something to say, I asked him if he liked it, and he said that not only did he like it, it even shocked him, he had no idea I would ever give him any gift, it was very beautiful.

We saw the door open in a wider way, it was the slender girl, the dark and beautiful one, she stood in the door, quietly, just looking at us. She seemed to be someone who stayed around there, she was holding a comb in her hand and looked like someone who was at home, even the way she was dressed, since it was a big building with many rooms for rent. And she called Seleman to come for a walk. He told her that he had a visitor so he couldn't go anywhere. She came and sat beside me for a short time, all of us were quiet, and she said bye and said that she was going by herself, she was gone. Seleman looked worried, he asked me if I thought that woman to be his, I told him that I thought nothing about her. I told him that I thought her to be just a friend and neighbour. He started to tell me a long story, that he didn't want anything from his side which would ever hurt me, that he wanted to be frank to me from the beginning from there and then. He told me that the lady was a neighbour some time ago, and they were friends and it ended. "So maybe she was around there and she saw us and she wanted to come and see you clearly, now she saw you she will never come near me because I am sure she can't compare herself with you," he said. That was the story. I didn't have to worry about her she was no longer important to him anymore, he wanted me to be sure of what he told me. He went ahead by saying that even if he came across another one hundred beautiful women he couldn't see them, even if there came someone who gave him a sign, he could do it now and then. I was not saying anything and he asked me if I was upset because of her. I said, "I am not upset with anything, I only want to go back home."

"Why so soon?" he asked me.

"I told home that I would not be out for long," I answered back.

He wanted to introduce me to his sister, he asked me if I could go to say hello to her.

"Not today," I said. I said no because I saw that it was too soon.

Seleman asked, "Why not today?"

I said, "I saw a lot of people outside, and I would like to pass here through another door without having to go back there."

Seleman said, "If that is how you want, will you come tomorrow?"

"Maybe," I said.

Seleman said, "Tomorrow I will take you there to greet my sister."

I kept quiet and left, he escorted me and said bye and that was the end of my first visit to Seleman's home. It was only Mama Jowa who knew where I went, when I was at home afterwards, changing what I was wearing, I went to Mama Jowa's room. When she saw me she waited to do what she was doing, and she showed me where to sit as if I was her visitor, all of us we kept quiet, looking at each other's eyes, her eyes had a lot of questions, she seems that she wanted quick answers if possible without wasting her time. She was asking me because she was sure I knew what she wanted to hear from me. That is what I did; I started to tell her each and every thing because I had to tell her, so that I could ask her ideas, since there was no other who knew yet about me and Seleman. After telling her everything, she said that as she was

179

always telling me, he was a good-looking man. I had to try, but that didn't mean that to look good with good height meant that you could be good at everything. I had to be careful and remember that I didn't know him enough yet, I didn't know about his culture and behaviour in general.

My English teacher got transfered and they didn't give me another one, but later I heard of a place where they taught English, but people had to pay, and I decided to go and see because I believed that I could afford to pay my fees. The college taught many different things, but at that time they had no vacancies for English, and they told me that when the time came they took students for English only from other courses instead of taking others from outside, so it was not easy to get a vacancy from outside. They said, if I wanted to get in next time, then I had to take any course there and they would put me on waiting list. I took that idea and registered myself with accounting, because I liked mathematics, yes I would have liked to go ahead with it, but I had a problem with it, because all of the work was in English. So maybe if it took a long time to get in to English, I would have to let it go, until I had learned enough English which could help me with all of that.

The relationship between me and Seleman was becoming very strong day by day, we had to see each other twice a week. Sometimes I would go to his home or he would come to my home. All my people and neighbours already knew that we were girlfriend and boyfriend, at his home too all of his relatives and their neighbours knew that. My college was every afternoon from Monday to Friday, my responsibilities at home went ahead as they were before, I even went to cultivate. The days I would go for digging I had to go early in the morning, on the first week I didn't see him to tell him that I had started college. Because of the short time, I thought that we would see each other only on weekends.

One day when I was coming from college I saw him in front of the shop which was our neighbour's, it was on the way I called the main road. When he saw me he stood up, and I too stood where I was. I wanted to meet him too, we met in the middle of the road and I told him that I wanted to see him to tell him all about the changes. He asked me where I always went that he saw me go and come back from everyday, and I told him everything. He seemed to be happy with the new changes, and told me that he would like to ask me if on Saturday I could come to his home, because there were relatives he would like to introduce me to. I said that I would be there. He also asked if when he had time, would it be OK with me if he came to wait for me from the college. I told him that would be so kind of him, he had no car, but was near enough so that he didn't need another kind of transport unless he wanted to, and it was close. Just to come and be together on the walk back, I was happy with the idea. I wanted him at my side every time it was possible. Seleman once tried to have me in a gentle way, as man and woman without force, and I told him that my wish was to engage myself in that life only when I was married with the man who was my husband. He respected me for that.

The next time we had a conversation he told me that he wanted to hear from me if I loved him enough to take him as my husband and be with him forever in all my life. He wanted to hear that with my own words. It surprised me, I didn't expect that question. I asked him why.

"Bamurangirwa, it is only you I want beside me in all my life, please let me know about you."

It was a kind of proposal. I told him that he didn't have to worry about me, yes I loved him. He was overjoyed.

After that our conversations were only for him to ask me when the time would come that I would like to take him home or if he would deal with my sisters there, at his home. My answer was that we would know at the time what and how we would do it.

According to where we were in our relationship, even if I had no engagement ring, we counted ourselves as engaged, the ring was not important, what was important was our hearts. No one even thought or talked about the ring, it was not in any of our cultures and we didn't have to rememeber it anyway. The Saturday came, the day when I would go to his home to meet his visitors. His sister, Emma, I thought that in her own way she liked me, one day she asked me if I would give her my photo, and when I gave it to her, she hung it in her sitting room, it was the only photo that was there in that room. It showed me that all of us were family, that is how much love and respect they had for me. Before I left I went and looked in the mirror many times to see if I looked perfect enough to be in front of Seleman's visitors, I had to check myself from head to toe, then I was sure that I looked beautiful enough to be front of anyone. I thought that Seleman was waiting for me, when I was still outside he came out to take me inside, he seemed shy, that helped me. When we were inside he showed me where to sit, and it was the old people who first had their time to meet me, and they introduced themselves by telling me that some of them were uncles, and others were aunties. They told them that I was Bamurangirwa, who they had been looking at in the photo.

So according to the way that they were looking at me with respect and happiness, I saw that they had been told a lot about me. I didn't have any words to talk with them. I kept quiet, I was only answering the questions that I was asked. I had nowhere to look as all of them were looking at me as if they had given a test, like the time came, when I had gone, they would ask the relatives to say how they saw me, sometimes they were talking in their own language. Seleman noticed that I was not comfortable, and told them that we were going and I said bye to them. Seleman was in front of me and I was behind, we went in to his room and we sat on the bed since it was only the bed which was inside. After a few seconds, he turned to me and held me on my back and then held me with both his arms very tightly, we were in silence for a short time, and then he called me by name as if he had come from somewhere. Still holding me, he told me that he loved me so much and now more than before, because all of his family had confirmed to him that it was me who they would be happy to see with him in the future. Now I didn't have any reason to doubt him, he wanted me to surrender to him and let us see each other as wife and husband, because now even if I became pregnant he would be there for me. I told him that at that moment he was better to forget it, if we were going to be wife and husband then he had to be patient and wait for that time.

Little he knew that no matter how much I loved him, I couldn't risk that much. I knew what the consequences were if I became pregnant in the situation I was in. The words I had heard from my mum, that as soon as you gave yourself to the man in an easy way, most of them would lose respect for you, and I needed both, full respect from him, and my peace. I had to know that if I gave myself that full freedom, it could mean that I was engaging myself to a life of having children without proper futures yet. He was not upset with that, instead he apologised and promised me that he would never give me a hard time again, since he was older than me he would be helping me and guiding me, not stressing me, so: I had to know that I was in good hands until our time came and again he respected me more because I respected myself.

After all of that he started to tell me about his life. He had a daughter he had with his girlfriend who was taken care of by his mum. About his business, he told me almost everything about him and his family, he said that he wanted to tell me all about him and his family instead of waiting and me getting it from outside. I assumed that he wanted me to tell him about me, I didn't know what to tell him then, if I told him that the family I lived with were just strangers, and because I was angry I ran away from home, I didn't know how he would react. I didn't know yet how I could tell him about me, because according to the way people thought, children and girls no matter how old they were, there could be no reason that was enough to make them run away from their family. They had to keep quiet about everything, and it could be much better when they closed their eyes and went ahead with whatever was in front of them and that was that. Which to me was ridiculous, there were no African people who could understand it at the time, at least not many. All of the time he was telling me his stories, he was still holding me, he put me to his chest and I was like a child in their father's chest. He promised me that from now on we would be looking more on our future, and that idea of joining college was the best idea. He told me that according his businesses of importing and exporting, sometimes he had money and sometimes he was short of money, he had an idea of supporting me for fees, but only when he came back from the businesses trip which he was planning soon.

I was very happy to hear that he was so happy with my idea of joining college, to the point of supporting me through it. That was the kind of person I was looking for, someone who could encourage me and support me in my studies. Seleman could be Alex? I was asking myself, but there was no answer, only I had to wait and see about tomorrow.

I was lucky that day as we didn't get time for my story, and it seemed that he didn't even care much; maybe he thought that he knew me enough. Yes I knew that the time would come when I would have to tell him much about myself, and I would have to tell him the truth no matter what, if he was going be my husband. After all it was not the shame that I wanted to see, what I did, I tried to fight for my rights, and the family I was with took good care of me, all of them, apart from Bibi Aziza who saw everyone in a business-like way, the rest were trying to see that I was happy and show that I was on their side, and show me that they were happy to have me with them. I had to be proud of it, Seleman told me that he would go to Congo (Zaire), maybe for one month or two for the business, and when he was back we would start the process of our marriage. According to African culture, it was me who would direct him with what to do, where and how I wanted it. When he looked at me in my face he saw what I was like if I was not with him, and he asked me if I had any problem with what he was telling me and I told him that it was because I was concentrating on that, and he was happy so he went back and he relaxed on my shoulder again. But the truth was that my thoughts were with tha questions I had, questions of the life I had, which were still secret to him. All of that time I was speaking only when he asked me something, and all of his family knew me as a polite girl with very few words. And they liked me for that too, but I knew that concerning that side, they didn't know me at all. He said that he had one more point to talk about it, and he asked me if I knew that he was Muslim.

"Yes, I know because of your name," I knew some of the names of Muslim people already since I was there in Mwanza.

Seleman said, "I don't know if it will be easy for you to change and join me in my religion."

"The truth to me about religions is that I don't know yet which one is better than the others, and if there is one, which is a better one and has more than the other ones, then in that case I don't know why I can't go from one side to another side, if I can know what I am looking for in that side, then fine, I can easily come." It was his time to listen to me and to say something if there was anything to say concerning that point. Since their home was on the way, he saw me sometimes on Sundays when I went to the church, and he asked me if I knew the difference in religions and what I wanted to get out of them. "When you go to the church on Sundays, why do you go then? Do you just go without knowing why you are going there? he asked me.

"Yes I am Catholic, but it was my parents who took me to be given the name, they had their reasons, I believe that they were brainwashed at the time. I was a baby and they gave me the name of Patricia, I don't say that it is the name which took me to the church, also that name is not important to me, I can change it if I want to, or just be without it, even though I don't yet know the meaning of it anyway. The reason why I go in the church here on Sundays, is because I am a stranger here, and there is nowhere you can get people together at once like in the churches, so I just go there to meet people to know them, and maybe I can find a way to know their culture and characters. I just like to mix with different people, I believe in God and believe that God can hear me anywhere, not only in a particular place, and I think even the religious people say so, that God is everywhere."

"You are still young, where and how do you have all of that from?" he asked me.

I always didn't want to go into religious stories, and I saw that to make things short was to change the subject since I saw that he didn't know my background yet. I needed a long time to try to tell him all of that; I thought that it was better to tell him only at the right time, if that time would come.

At last he asked, "Do you believe that there is a hell and heaven where people go when they die?"

I answered, "No, I am sorry I don't believe it, but I support the preachers, to teach people is a very good idea. I wish that the majority of people could believe it, so that it would reduce big numbers of bad people, since many can try hard to be good to others, it they can get that benefit after they die. But instead I believe that all of that, heaven and hell, they are here in our planet, you can be in heaven when you have what you would like to have, a happy life in general. And hell when you are in a miserable life in all ways. Though on the other hand I believe that there is life after death, which I can't say anything about (it is one of those things which is beyond my understanding). I don't believe that there is anyone who can say how it is, to me there is not enough evidence why I should believe anyone about that. Since I believe that my people are intellectual in their own way, according to their history, how they were reading their life in many different ways compare to modern life we have it now."

I continued, "Our parents believed that there was life after death, people don't change when they die, they are still in the same position, happy or sad, if you were happy in life, or had a miserable life, that is how you will be in the other life then, 'ukuruta imusozi niyageze ikuzimu arakuruta', meaning that if someone was better than you in life, even after death they will be better than you. So since I don't have a way of doing any research about life after death, to me, it is better to be me, without other reasons of this or that. I love people, I don't like to see anyone with a problem when I can help. I do what I can, when I can, simple, not because I am preparing myself for better life after I die, I do what I do only because I am always happy when I am surrounded with happy people, and when someone does something good to me, I feel happy, so maybe that is why I'm always happy when I do good things to other people when I can. I think it is my nature. And I believe that it is enough to give me the confidence to mix with society. And concerning religion, if I am to choose, I can choose the one my great parents believed in, but I think that can't be a problem anyway: when we knew each other in the first place we didn't ask ourselves before about it, so we will get a solution when the time will come."

After all of that conversation I felt very relaxed in my mind. I saw our wedding, a lot of people outside, and I wanted to talk in a very loud voice and tell him that our wedding day would be my heaven. It was like I was sleeping, he held my head with both his hands and made me look up to him, he called me by my name and I replied with a weak low voice. He asked me to look at him because I had closed my eyes, he asked me to do that for him, it was not easy for me, I was shy about looking him directly in his face, but in the end I did, and he was there, he was looking at me, with a soft smile and again he asked me if I loved him enough to be his wife. I kept quiet and he had to ask again and again, I gave him the reply but on other hand it was like a question, which was much easier for me. "What else would my answers have to be? Did you think that I would have changed my mind in this few days? Yes I love you for whatever it can take."

Seleman said, "This is the only time I have to be sure where our relationship stands before I go. I want to go on my journey with a good heart and I promise again that I will never ever hurt you, just let me know when you see me, about any kind of mistakes."

I had almost forgotten that I had to go back to where I was supposed to go, where I called home, I thought that I was lucky he didn't ask me about myself, I told him that I had to go and I asked him to say bye to his family for me, and he offered to escort me. The time for Seleman to go on his business journey came, we sat for many hours, alone, talking the same story over and over, sometimes laughing, sometimes crying, and he was asking me or begging me to be a good girl and to think of him when he was away. He wanted me to know that wherever he would be, whatever he would be doing, his heart would be with me, and what he went to do was for us. I gave him all of my promises. I told him that he didn't have to worry about anything, I would wait for him no matter how long he was there, but inside my heart I had a question, would I ever see Seleman again? Even if I would see him again, would he still love me like now? At this time I remembered Alex again, because when Alex went, that was the end of us. I had a fear that it would be the same with Seleman, that when he came back, if he did, he might not be the same Seleman.

After Seleman left, his sister Emma was very good to me, she was coming to visit me many times, or coming and taking me to her home, she wanted to see me happy. I was close to her and saw her as if we had been together for years, she was a good lady, kind, and maybe she liked me in her own way, or maybe on the other hand she was guiding me because she wanted me for her brother. Sometimes she would come up with the topic of Seleman, the things that she had told him before he went, that he would always have to remember that he left me behind. The last time I was with him he gave me 500 Tanzania money, telling me that would help me somehow, since he didn't know when he would be back, and now I joined the college so he had to leave something with me. Seleman went, and behind I went ahead with what I was doing before, housework, my business of bags, and going to market on Sundays, and sometimes going digging as before, nothing changed. The time came when I thought that it would be better to quit the college, I saw that I was wasting my time and money, since I was not understanding what they were teaching, so I could wait when I was outside, and just check every time if they had a vacancy for me.

To think about Seleman made me feel happy, one time I remembered when he told me that he went with his body but he left his heart with me, and I thought that it was him who went with my heart. After one month his sister gave me a letter which was a piece of paper with few words and she told me that it was a letter from Seleman. It was not in the envelope and had no address so that I could write back to him. I was happy but I had questions, why was it not in the envelope, why was there only a few words, and why no addresses? Something like that, anyone could write it. I was asking myself questions and I gave myself answers. About my letter not being in an envelope, I saw it to be that he wanted to show his relatives that he was still thinking of me. Why a few words, I saw that was because he was on the way coming back. About the address, still that was because he was coming soon so there wouldn't be enough time to reach him where he was in case I wrote back to him. And when we were together he knew that he was going to tell me a lot of words, the words I would like to hear about our life, about our future.

It was in June 1970, on a Tuesday evening, I was coming from college in the middle of the road and I saw a beautiful lady coming to where I was. She said hello and told me that she wanted to go with me she said that she didn't know that I was in that college. I told her that I was happy to: to have someone to go with. I asked her if she knew me from somewhere, and she said that she thought that I knew her too. I said that I didn't know her unless I had forgotten her, she introduced herself and told me that she was renting a room in Seleman's sister's building. She said that her room was opposite Seleman's, and she had seen me many times there, and she came from Bukoba, she was there with her husband and she told me that her name was Peace. She looked to be a very beautiful young lady, with light skin, medium height and weight, and from the way she was talking I saw her to be a kind and loving person. She asked me how long I was in that college.

I told her, "I have been there for a few months now, but I think that I might quit soon."

Peace said, "Why because of money or?"

"Not because of money, I wanted to learn English but at the moment there is no vacancy for it." I told her what they told me about getting the vacancy for English, and I told her that it was something I thought to be business language. "I don't understand what they teach and I am wasting time and money," I said.

Peace said, "If your only lesson is English then I will help you."

Was it me who had to ask her how?

She said, "You will be sitting with me so that I can be helping you." Most of the time I was with Peace, going to college and coming back from college with her, and sitting with her. I became used to being with her and I saw her to be a very good person. When my time came to quit, I told her and she also told me that she was quitting, when I asked her why she told me that her doctor told her to relax and her husband didn't want her to go ahead with college too, because she was four months pregnant.

I told her that it was a very good idea to do what the doctor said. After it had been three and half month since Seleman had gone, I got another letter from Seleman which was like the first one. Emma, his sister, as before told me that he was coming soon and always she was telling him not to look around at other girls. I didn't ask her how they communicated.

SELEMAN COME BACK FROM CONGO (ZAIRE AT TIME) WHAT HAPPENED BETWEEN US?

G o ahead and read, see the mixed life some of people pass through. It was 10th September 1970 when I was sitting on the balcony behind our house I was sitting down and Mama Jowa was sitting up making my hair. Since I had no idea yet that Seleman had come back, when I saw him I thought that it was someone who looked like him, but I had to ask Mama Jowa if my eyes were correct and she told me that she had seen him before, but she wanted to finish my hair first. I kept quiet, because I gave a lot of respect to Mama Jowa, but I wanted to jump and go where he was standing and give him a big hug.

I thought that he did want to come to where we were because he was waiting for us to be in our place with our own time. After Mama Jowa finished my hair I tried any way I could to make myself beautiful and put on a new dress which Seleman had never seen, and I was sure that I looked perfect. I went as quickly as I could and I went directly to his sister's house, since I thought that all of them had to be there. Yes, all of them were there and Seleman was sitting in the chair which was near the door, his back was on the side of the chair, his legs were on the other side, maybe because he wanted to look where his sister was. His legs were straight in front of him, on top of the chair his arms were in front of him. I greeted all of them in the same way, I knew that hugging was not in their culture, and I knew where and when I would hug him, when we were in his room. Since they didn't know that I was talkative, I chose to be that way, and told myself that if I was going to spend the rest of my life with them, then the time would come when they would see that side. But that day I had to talk in a careful way by asking him about his journey. I was there for about ten minutes, we were still talking, but Seleman was only talking to me when he was answering what I asked him, and he was still sitting in the same position. After some time I saw myself, it was as if I was lost in words, and I decided to go and come back next time, and I assumed that he was still tired. I told them that I had to go home, it showed in the eyes of his relatives that they were confused and ashamed, so he said that it was better to go and come back the next day, and we would talk, but at that time he was still tired. Back home, I was asking myself many questions, why this behaviour, I had no idea of the reason, maybe it was because I didn't go to greet him when he was standing in the road? Maybe it was because someone told him some rumours? But how could that be when I was still good friends with his relatives? Could it be only ignorance without any reason at all? Maybe he was with other women where he was, and now he can't see me any more? I had a lot of questions without answers, and I decided to believe that he was still tired.

Next day, when the time came, I went and he was in his sister's house. I sat for a short time and he stood up, I stood up too, we went in his room, and we sat on his bed. We sat on the bed and I waited for stories, and hugs and many words, sweet words, that he missed me, that he was not sleeping because of thinking of me, but he sat a bit distant, no hugs or talking. I waited, there was silence, he took his white shirt which was on the floor and talked as if he was talking to himself, but also telling me. "This shirt is still wet because of the rain."

"Where did it get the rain from?" I asked him.

Seleman said, "Some of the rooms of this house are not good, they are leaking even where I didn't know it before, I saw it last night when I was sleeping with Rose."

"Who is Rose?"

"The girl who came here the first time when you came here and I told you that she was living here before, nowadays she has moved here again."

It was a big surprise to me, and I thought that he wanted to hear what I would say, but I chose to say nothing. All I had in my mind was that he was going to welcome me with a lot of stories concerning our future, now it was completely the opposite. In one second I thought of a thousand or more words. I thought that his sister knew him, maybe that is why she was always worried about our relationship, and she had no way to tell me the truth. I thought that by telling me this story, he might want me to act in a funny way, and if so, I was not going to say anything at all, I was going to take it as if I didn't hear anything. I didn't make any comment about it, and as always my words were very few, so we talked less. I only wanted to push time and go without doing anything which showed my anger, I wanted to surprise him in case he was waiting to see drama. I acted as normal as possible, but the time came when I couldn't pretend any more, and I told him that it was time for me to go back home.

He said that it was good for me to come and see him. On my way home, I thought it was a good idea to start struggling to move him from my thoughts, from my head and heart. Which I knew that was not going to be hard, yes I loved him enough to be his wife, but not enough like the love I had for Alex. I had no one to tell, not even Mama Jowa. I saw it like shame, so I had to handle it in my way. If he was my husband it would be different, I had to get older people to help us, by seeing who was wrong, and trying to put us together again, but now we were nobody to each other, it was so soon to promise myself that I was going to forget him there and then, but I knew I would, so I told myself to be at home some few days and see if he would come to see me or if he would not. And one time I could go there and see his situation, maybe it would be the last visit to his home. I once saw him on the road with Rose, and told myself that there was nothing any more that I wanted to know. Then I decided to go once more, though I had no reason why still I wanted to go, when I knew very well what I might see or hear. Now the question I had was that I wondered if Seleman rejected me maybe because I didn't allow myself to go to bed with him. But to that point I was very happy that I refused, I said that even if I didn't refuse, it wouldn't change who he was and even without having to have his fatherless child, it was also good to think that at last I still had my pride. If he liked to have many different women at once that is how he was. I thanked my mother once more again, for her good advice which helped me a lot. I believed that to go to bed with a man, didn't mean love, they were two different things, and I couldn't make the love be there when it was not.

I made myself ready to go, I was not happy by going there, you would think that someone had taken me by force. I decided to go only to Seleman's room, not his sister's, because she couldn't do anything about it, even making her feel sory for me couldn't help anything. And I didn't want sympathy from anyone. When I reached Seleman's home, Peace was outside, we greeted each other, and I asked her if Seleman was in, and she told me that he was inside, she was standing in front of her door. I turned to enter Seleman's room, and the same time, I heard Peace pulling my clothes without talking. I turned and she said in a very low voice, "Seleman he has visitor with him." I asked who the visitor was.

"The girl who is with him many times."

Since I had promised myself that it was my last time to go there and I came to say bye to him, I would still enter and do what I came for.

Then I told her that I would still go inside as it was my last visit to his home, since that was why I was there. To her, she seemed to see that danger was coming, so, it was better to go out of the way, she entered her room as quickly as she could. When I stood behind the door I knocked without having an answer and I decided to try to push a little and see. The door was locked from the inside, so I had to go back home. When I was on my way back I asked myself why I insisted on entering inside the room when I heard that he was with another woman. I had no answer but I saw that was a crazy thought, it was good that I didn't managed to enter the room at all. What if I was inside and was only faced with their ignorance, there could even be a possibility of one of them trying to harm me. I had no time to think about all of that, and I hated myself for that, maybe I wanted to make them feel sorry for me, or to make them feel more happy because they hurt me? Was it a meaningless thought to have in the first place?

I didn't close Seleman's chapter. I knew I could not count on him to be my friend, let alone to be my boyfriend or fiancé. But still I had a job to do with him, because I had to get revenge, though I had no idea how I would do it, but anything which would put him down and make him see that I was not the person who he thought I was. Someone who he could just hurt and let go. I would get something maybe which would shame him or make him feel down, in the way he wanted me to, if not more.

After two days the children came inside calling me and told me that I had a visitor, my heart jumped a little thinking that it was Seleman who had come to ask forgiveness, though I had no forgiveness for him, but I would be happy if he did. Outside was Peace and she asked me if I had time to make her hair. I told her that I was free, even though I was not an expert in that, unless she didn't mind, I told her.

Peace said, "I don't mind, just make the way you can." We went behind to the pavement and we sat down, I started to make her hair, and to Peace it was her time to start telling me what she came for. She had come for stories, something which showed me that many times it was not always, when I saw women outside making their hair or anything which made themselves busy in group: they had two reasons to be there, to do what they were doing and to talk many different stories about other peeeople who were not with them.

Peace started to ask me about that day, and told me what happened after she ran inside her room. I told her all that had happened. And she told me that the girl had destroyed him with black magic. Soon after finishing her sentence I laughed in a loud voice for many seconds, but I saw that I was laughing alone, and when I kept quiet she was serious, she asked me why I was laughing, what was funny?

My reply was also a question, "How could she give him that black magic? In the food or was it in an injection?" I laughed again.

I think she noticed that I was not joking or pretending and she asked me, "Bamurangirwa, you want to tell me that you don't know that there are things like that?"

"This is the first time I have heard a story like this, so I thought that you were trying to cheer me up. Now if you are telling me something you know then tell me, because if there is magic which can make people hate others, meaning there are others which make people love others, then there is other magic which can make people love them too?"

Her answer was very strong and she looked to be happy, maybe because she saw that I had started to believe her story, she wanted to go ahead talking about that black magic, but to me it was a waste of time, and I told her that it was not easy for me to believe it, so it would be better for us to talk about something else, we were wasting our time.

Peace said, "It is OK, I am only seeing it that way, because it is not normal the way he turned out and changed suddenly, when before he was telling everyone the way he loved you, he was not here and you were close with his family, so everything is not hard to understand. I saw him with that girl as soon as he came back, but I didn't want to tell you, I doubted that would believe me."

I told her, "It is better to forget his story now, I know already and I am no longer counting on him as anybody to me. So let us talk about other things. I will be OK without him." I started to ask her questions about her, without any reasons in my mind at all. I just wanted us to get something else to talk about, when we were still together.

"You told me that you come from Bukoba, which part of Bukoba do you come from?"

"I come from Kamacumu, but most of my life I was in Kenya, there was where I went to school and where I met my husband, and got married, my husband was working there."

"Which part of Kenya?"

"Nairobi."

"That is where your parents live?"

"No, it is my Auntie who is living there."

There was silence at the time and my mind was up and down. Peace, like many around there, didn't know my relationship with the family I stayed with, and I had no reason to tell her, but according to my situation, concerning the relationship between Seleman and I, it was not a secret to her, and I thought that maybe if she knew what was going on in my mind. In those minutes, I saw myself like I was going to go around Africa, if not around the world, just trying to reach where I would get love and peace. Kenya cames into my mind there and then. My business of bags was started to go down, I couldn't promise myself that in the future I would be able to afford the fees. And Seleman I had no hope with, he was good enough to show me who he was early, now what else was I waiting for there in Mwanza? Nothing, it was time to go, but where?

Kenya, now.

I didn't want to be useless wherever I was, I wanted, and I wished that if I had a family with a man from any part of the world, no matter what, my children would know their origin, that I came from Rwanda, and they were going to speak my language, because I would do whatever I could to ensure that my children knew and loved my country, their country. And I would be telling them a lot about their origin, and about our family who was still there. I sent my father a letter before, telling him where I was, and so I had to send him other one telling him to wait for my new addresses. And at that moment I had no news which I could tell Mukabagira concerning her; I had to wait until I had proper news to tell her. Again it was like when I was coming from Uganda, when I was again, a refugee, running away from my family, running away from forced marriage. Yes again I had no one in Kenya, and I didn't know anything about Kenya, it was like commiting suicide. Just a girl to go on her own, it was not understandable, even to me, not exactly, but I had to go.

It was Peace who broke the silence by asking why I was quiet and

I told her that she had to ask why we were both quiet? We laughed at once together for some seconds. I started to show her the reason for my silence.

I said, "Peace can you tell me about Kenya? I always had a wish to visit that country, but because I had no one there I didn't put that into plan yet. Now I have you, if you think that your auntie can welcome me as her visitor, then I can think about it."

She seemed to be surprised, the way she asked me.

"Bamurangirwa that is very hard."

"How is it very hard. which side? Is it your auntie's or on the other side? And is it something we can get a solution to?"

I asked her that because I didn't want to give her a chance to make things so hard when maybe they were not, it was like I wanted to remind her that many things can get solutions. I was almost insisting rather than questioning. I had a fear that she might say that it was impossible when I wanted it to be possible.

Peace said "Not concerning my auntie, she is OK with that, I know her, she loves me, she wouldn't see my friend as a burden, and the way I know you already you can't be a burden to anyone."

"What is hard?" I asked her.

"It is transport, it is a lot of money because is far," she told me.

I had confidence in that, I knew I had enough money for transport even if I didn't know yet exactly how much, but I was sure that at least I could afford the transport anyway. Maybe, I could go by air, but I wanted to use a way many ordinary people used, because, I wanted to save some money which I could use for some time when I was there, if I was going to go. Though I was sure that I was going to use that idea, an idea which I had less than fifteen minutes ago, the whole situation was crazy, but I started to feel relaxed as if my head and heart were the right way, and in those seconds I felt like I could see that picture, the picture of my journey, I was happy then.

Peace went ahead by telling me about her auntie, "The area where she is, there are a lot of people and everyone knows each other. " So I couldn't get lost, as it was easy to get to her.

"Everyone says that it is far, which kind of transport do passengers use?"

"Most of the people use the ship, few go by air, but all the ships don't reach there, it is only Victoria which reaches Kisumu, and from there you get a train to Nairobi."

I was listening, she went on, "In the ship there are many people, when you reach Musoma you will already have friends, some who are going where you are going and maybe know my auntie."

Her stories were encouraging. "Like you, it is easy since you know how to talk with people, you can just go near a woman who comes from Bokoba, and you can know them by listening if they are speaking in Kihaya or Kinyambo, that is the the person who can take you to her. If you really decide, just let me know when. I will give you a letter to take to her and I will put her name and her addresses on to the envelope, that will be enough and it will be easy for you to get to her. Remember to buy a few things you will use on your journey." I thanked her for the idea and encouragement.

Now I had the last question, "My wish is to learn anything, so do you think life there is easy and I can get something to do, so that I can afford fees for a course? And in life in general, will it be easy to support myself?"

Peace gave me answer like she was aware of my next question, it didn't take her even a second. Yes, I told myself, she knew the place indeed, it did not surprise me to get an answer so quickly.

She said, "You know girls like you, you are still young and beautiful it is very easy, you will get a job and you will learn what you want, there is a lot of money there." Then things were almost good ahead of me, I thought, I still had a very small question concerning the kind of job I could do. But when I asked the question I didn't get a direct answer: again she seemed like she was repeating what she had said before, that there was a lot of money and my life would be easy and a good life in the way I wanted it to be.

I thought that I had wasted my time coming to Mwanza, if I had known anything about Kenya at that time instead of Mwanza, if I had gone to Nairobi by that time, I could have improved myself a lot. I started to regret the time I wasted in Mwanza.

It was time for Peace to go to her home, everything was in line, I was sure that I was moving to Kenya now, it was only a matter of time, I told myself that it might be true that everything had a reason. My craziness to insist on seeing Seleman turned out to be my way to Kenya! But I still had questions concerning the job there in Nairobi, Peace said that I was young and beautiful, fine, if that is how she saw me, but still what did that mean?

I got an answer by myself to both of my two questions.

No 1: Because if it was to put a girl in a shop, maybe the boss would want the good looking girls, maybe it was looks, or being young, one of those things, or both. So that could be one of the reasons, to increase customers, and being young is good because you can work in a quick way here and there, that is also understandable. I thought of Peace as being the answer to all of my problems, and without any notice I hugged her very hard, and thanked her. I told her that I understood that it was not easy to send someone to your relative who was in town, knowing that I might go there and depend to her.

The way I thanked her, the way I was happy, it surprised her, she told me that she did nothing.

But I knew that it was a big thing to me, it came at a good time, to give me a new way of life, a new step, to start a new life, a life which I didn't know what kind of life it would be, how I would handle it, and if this struggle would end, how and when would it end?

Questions and questions in my head were again a lot, but not being able to have even one answer, it was a matter of hoping and waiting, with determination of being the good person wherever I was, and doing the best for myself and others who were around me when I could, the way I could. She tried to make me have more confidence by telling me that she would send her auntie a very good letter, the letter which would be my recommendation.

Now it was time for me to decide which good time to move from Mwanza.

At that time Mama Jowa had already moved from Bibi Aziza's house to another neighbouring area. I still had to give myself time to see if I would find a way to have my revenge on Seleman. And to do something to show Rugamba's family my appreciation for all that they did for me. Men in Tanzania at that time had something similar to Ugandan men, they loved women in a way of respect, many times a man who was driving couldn't pass a woman on the way, especially when she was carrying something or when it was raining. or simply if he liked the lady for some reason, he would stop his car and ask her where she was going and in a respectful way sometimes he would request to give her a lift. He would take the lady wherever she was going, sometimes without even asking her, knowing that he might not even see her again in the future, but that was no problem to him, they were just happy to give that kind of help to them.

And there was nothing like fear that they were strange men who could harm you in any way, at that time, anyone could say that people were still innocent. When a woman made a move to stop a car, just to show a sign of asking for a lift, without question it was only a few cars which could pass her, but normally the car was going to stop and take her no matter what. On my side I always refused that lift, because of respect for Seleman. I knew that as a man, I couldn't just believe that he was someone I didn't know, our relationship was more important than to enjoy strangers's lifts, but I thought that it was the first move I had to do. And I planned it, I knew that it was going to be very easy, and I knew that people liked to think about riches for whatever they saw, to him he would hate to see me with get a lift in a car, a car which looked to be expensive, to him it would be like abuse, like I was telling him that there are men out there who even have more money than him.

Because people thought and counted money for everything, even sometimes for relationships, anything, always. It would show him in another case, that he had done a favour to me to let me go. I was sure that would hurt him. I started to choose only expensive cars to ask for lifts and I would ask them to bring me home, since we were neighbours, so that he would be able to see me and neighbours would talk.

I knew that some people would feel happy to see that their partner was only stressful, when it was them who had taken the first step to break up the relationship, they didn't like to see their partner move on, and it hurt them more when they moved on with a better partner than them in any way. Every time when I went out even if I was not far, I had to come back with a lift i a different expensive car, so I was sure that it confused him, but what was important to me was to show him that other men could talk to me, even the rich ones. I had all confidence that in that short time I would do enough to hurt him, he was going to be surprised how I got all of the men and only the rich ones. Some other time, when Seleman and his brother saw me coming with a car they were coming out so that I could see that they were there and they saw me, maybe trying to stare me out, or they thought that I still gave them any respect, little did they know that I was doing that purposefully just to show them that, yes I could do it. I could hurt him too. And when I saw them I came out of the car very slowly holding the door, and trying to talk with this man, I thanked him and made it out to be long conversation, which would last almost one minute. I wanted to show everyone that we knew each other, and the gentleman who gave me a lift looked to be happy with the way I thanked him, and maybe thought that he had met a polite girl who had a lot of respect. There was an old man who was coming to visit Mama Jowa many times, he was like fifty years old, according to Mama Jowa he was her family friend for many years. On that day he came it seemed that he didn't know yet that Mama Jowa had moved to another place, so he had to knock on Rugamba's house to ask them. They told him that she had moved and it was only me who knew where she had gone, and he asked them if they could give me permission to go with him and show him where she was living.

He was a respected person so they told me to be ready and take him.

I came inside the car, we had no other conversation between

ourselves, and it was only me who was talking when I was directing him. The gentleman was not saying anything, only following my directions, and that is what I expected him to do, to keep quiet and only follow what I was telling him, since it was me who knew where we were going.

But to my surprise, I started to see that he was not following my directions any more, something which I didn't have in my mind at all. Somehow it shocked me, though I had a lot of respect for him, but it was necessary to ask him where he was taking me! When I asked him he told me that we had almost reached there. After some time we reached somewhere which was like a bush, the place in the distance, it had a few shops which was where he stopped, and I thought that he came to buy some gifts for Mama Jowa, but why here, when we passed a lot of shops, I had to wait and see. If the person I was with was a woman, I would think that she came to get some kind of grasses for medication for her children, I knew some people didn't want to take their children to the hospital when they had some problems; they prefered to go to the bush and get some grasses they knew instead.

He stopped the car then, most of time he was silent and I knew that it was time for me to hear why he brought me there, he turned to me still in a silent way, it seemed that he had come from somewhere else, that we were not together and if he was carrying something heavy, he looked to be short of oxygen. I had to ask him what the problem was, but when I opened my mouth to ask him he was already covering mine with his!

He kissed me for a long time without a word, I was in his car, I didn't even know where I was, I had to take it easy with the hope that he had no intention of raping me, otherwise I had to be very careful and see his attention and know my next move. After all that kissing, he seemed to be relaxed, and he told me the long story of how he loved me since he saw me, but didn't know how to start and said that he knew that I was too young for him and he didn't want to break his respect in front of my family, but that was the only chance he got to be with me and he would never get any other excuse, to bring him at our home since Mama Jowa moved. What he wanted was to tell me that he loved me, that he was a grandfather and he still had children like me, and he would not like to destroy my life as he wouldn't be happy to see someone destroy his child's life. But the only thing that he promised me was that what he had done was not going to happen again, he only wanted permission to let him see me when he had the time, only to see me gave him some kind of peace. That is why I came here and now we were going to see Mama Jowa. He waited for my answer, to give him the green light to be visiting me or to see me in any way which would suit me, or I couldn't let him see me any more. I had to give him the answer, after we will be apart, no other way of sending my message to him.

My mind quickly showed me that he was a good man to use for my problem, the problem of revenge, making Seleman feel down and hurt, the old man was old but he was the man anyway, he had the best car in the whole of Mwanza, his new car was a Benz, at that time there were very few people who had Benz there. He was a very clean person and his car was also clean, so this was the right man then, only I had to be very careful, I didn't wanted Rugamba to think that I was losing my respect, and I didn't want to hurt this man also. At that time Rugamba was working at night, all the good things concerning my revenge on Seleman came at the same time. I had an idea that since I couldn't talk with Rugamba about a story like that, I would tell his wives why they were going to be seeing me with that man. It would be night time and I also wanted his wives still to have trust in me, so I was going to tell him that I would like him to come home, that we would be having our conversation when he stood there, when we were in his car, we were there for a long time depending on the time he had, because he had to go to work the next day.

That would be even easier for Selemen and his family to see that I had a man who had a new Benz, I hoped that they remembered that he came into my life as my rescue, from the dark sadness they wanted to put me in, and he was even better than them in the way concerning wealth. I told him the timetable of how and when he would be seeing me, he was very happy. I told him that it was because I didn't want my brother-in-law to see us together, when he would change to working day times we would wait then, and be at the front of our door because my sisters sometimes wanted me for this and that. He said that the way I gave respect my family made him love me more. I wanted to laugh at that then, he seemed to be relaxed and he said that anything I said he would follow, hoping that it would make me feel comfortable with him. He was the one who was talking, telling me different stories and telling me all of the things that the first time were hard but after some time, even my family saw that he was a good person, and some things would change by themselves, it would be a matter of time, and he promised me again that he would not ever do anything again against my wishes.

At Mama Jowa's we didn't stay for long, soon after having tea he told her that now he knew where she was, he would be coming by himself but he wanted to take me back. So he would start to come to see me from the next Monday. Back home, when I was inside, the children told me that I had a visitor, still my heart jumped a little, asking myself if it could be Seleman who maybe had come to say sorry because of the cars which had been seen driving me, if so what would I do, could I ever trust him again? I had that doubt, no I couldn't, but I remembered that the children knew him, and I asked them if they knew that person, and they said that they didn't know the person. When I asked if the person was a man or woman, they told me that it was a man. When I asked them if he mentioned my name, they told me yes he knew me, since they told me that he was going to come back I had to wait and see who and what he wanted.

It was between 6.00pm–7.00pm, when the children told me that my visitor had come back and he was waiting for me behind the house. The children held my hands and they took me to where they left him, when I saw who he was, I almost fell down with shock. I took him to the pavement and showed him where to sit down; I too sat and waited. What could be so important to make Seleman's brother-in-law come to my home? I had seen Emma's husband few times because most of time he was at the work or maybe sleeping and I had never bothered to ask anything about him. I saw him to be a man of few words, all the times I had seen him I had not spoken to him any other words apart from hello. And I thought that even if we met on the road he wouldn't recognise me, because he was always looking sideways or down. Then, I thought that Seleman was shamed enough to come in front of me to say sorry, and he sent him on his behalf, but I had to wait and see. I asked myself why he would send him when he knew that I was a friend of his sister, why he didn't use her I had no idea.

He was the one who started to break the silence by asking me why I didn't come to his home these days.

"I come, it is because you are at work when I am at your home."

Silence.

"Again, or you don't come because of Mama Vitu?" he asked me.

With surprise I gave him an answer with a question, by asking why and how Mama Vitu would be a reason to refuse me to go to his home?

Mama Vitu was a lady who was our neighbour, the one who was the owner of the shop which we had around there, she was with her husband and her children, so to me it was not understandable at all how she could come into the conversation, he had to tell me. He told me confidently, maybe thinking that was going to be a big point to me.

"That is because these days Mama Vitu and Seleman they are friends," he said.

I had to say something. I told him that I didn't know that, but still it couldn't be a reason. "I come anyway, it is because you are not at home most of the time," I said,. He had no reason to tell me anything concerning my life, or even anything between me and Seleman, let him think what he thinks that he knows.

Maybe he thought that he was going to be the first one to tell me that story, I talked without anger. When he saw that it was nothing to me, he went ahead to try to make it be a big point.

Again he called me now by name, "Bamurangirwa, you mean that you are OK to have Mama Vitu as your co-wife?"

Now I was angry, I asked myself what he wanted from me, the good thing would be to tell him off then, so that would be the last time he would try me, if that was what he wanted. So I could be the last person to tell useless stories, or he would think twice before. I went ahead by telling him that Seleman had the right to have any friends he wanted, and I couldn't call any of them my co wife because I was not yet his wife, I too was his friend and I had every right to be friends with anyone I wanted.

He tried again, "I thought that you didn't know about Seleman's behaviour; it is hurting me to see what he is doing it to you."

I had to try to show him that I didn't need his empathy. I said, "I think that no one is an angel, me too, maybe, I have my behaviour which is not, so if I can handle the way he is, then no problem".

He saw that things were not good and as easy as maybe he thought, there was silence. "I just wanted to say hello then I can go."

"Thank you," I said.

"I am going," he said that when he was stood up already.

I just say OK still sitting where I was, say hello to others.

And he was gone, where I was sat I knew that he was not going to think to come back ever again; I knew that I did a good job for him.

I didn't have many questions about my visitor, I thought that there might be a misunderstanding between him and his wife, so he didn't want to take the wife's side and he was not happy to see me and Seleman together in his future. Or what he said was true and maybe he didn't know about Seleman and Rose yet, and then he might have felt sorry for me, which was wrong. Even if I was married to Seleman, not him, who could come to me to give me ideas, he could have told his wife to come to me which was a more respectful way, unless he wanted a way to tell me that he loved me the first time he saw me, and I was the most beautiful girl he had ever seen, like every man, men's language.

At night they realised that they didn't have the children's milk, and Kanzage's child had just stopped the breastfeeding, so it was not easy to keep her at night without milk. I told them to let me go and see if the shop was still open, they seemed to be happy about that idea, and they gave me money with the hope that the shop was still open.

I went running, the shop was near, it was almost in the same compound, it was only because there were different buildings, with different owners. When I was on my way I almost reached Mama Vitus's kitchen, her kitchen was a big one, they were still doing some finishing of it, it had no door and it had a big wide window which had nothing in it, there was someone who standing there alone and quietly.

The person, when he saw me, he went inside the kitchen through the window! My mind quickly jumped to the story I had just heard a few hours ago.

I went to the kitchen then to see who it might be, with the idea that if it was Seleman I would be able to shame him. I would talk to him just to show him that I saw him. I stood in the window, it was not too dark, I could see him, not very clearly because he was in the corner, but we were looking at each other. I greeted him and he kept quiet, I repeated again, again he kept quiet, now it was like I was enjoying him and making a fool of him. Then I asked him many different questions to make myself happy, like, "What are you doing here?"

"What are you waiting here for? And why are you hiding yourself? What is the problem??" I went ahead to enjoy him, "Ooo my God, since when did you become dumb?" Maybe he saw that I was not going anywhere if he was quiet, and he came near me, that is when I realised that, the whole of his body was shaking. I didn't keep quiet then, again I greeted him, again I said, "How are you Seleman?" And now he answered back, I repeated the same questions, "What are you waiting here for at this time?" I think he wanted to see me go from there, and he said that he was waiting for someone, but he was looking at me, you would think that I was Mama Vitu's husband who was there, he was scared to death. And I enjoyed every minute of it. I wanted to laugh, to see the way his eyes were looking at me in a non-stop position when he was shaking, as if he wanted to beg me to go and leave him alone, in case someone was waiting to come and meet him there. But he was in luck because I didn't want the shop to close before I bought the milk. In a hurried way and in surprised voice, I asked him, and I wanted also to tell him that I knew who he was waiting for, in a brief way.

"Ooo poor Seleman, I thought that it is not true, on top of all of that you mean you see a married woman too, poor you, here in her home when her husband is inside! You are too brave!" I went running and got the milk, back home when I saw the picture of his long legs on top of him trying to go inside the window, I laughed and when I heard my sound come out, I turned it into a song, so that no one could ask me what I was laughing for.

On Monday at 7:30pm, the Benz was outside; I was looking through the window as I didn't want him to knock.

I was ready to go, to be with him outside at any time. I was finished everything I had to do. So since that was my last chance to get revenge on Seleman, I had to be sure that I was using it in a proper way, to enter the car was taking me around a minute, so that if Seleman was around he could see me clearly, without any doubt.

Inside the car, I was beside him and he looked to be in a quiet, peaceful, happy life. We talked about this and that, I was hoping that he would not kiss me again, but I loved the way he was clean, himself, and his car, you could think that his car didn't pass in the road past other cars pass as it was clean outside and inside too.

On the other hand I was proud to be seen with a kind of person like him.

MY JOURNEY FROM TANZANIA TO KENYA

At that time in our conversation he said in a surprising way that other girls preferred to go out and see different places and different people, but he didn't understand why I was happy just to be in one place. I said that as far as I am with him then I am happy where we are. And I want to be near in case my sister wanted me for something.

He asked if we had some empty bottles so that we could go to buy drinks for the children, I told him that I had to go and see. Inside the house when I told them what I came for, all of them looked surprised, they gave me empty bottles and they put them in a bag. Back in the car, he started the car and we went to the shop, he told me to go inside the shop, he asked for the drinks, dry beans, sugar, breads... He bought many different things like someone who was buying stuff for his big family, and wanted to buy things which would last for some time, some of the other things were around five to ten kilograms, when I told him that was enough he told me not to worry.

He shocked me with that, I was happy and at the same time I was surprised and I felt ashamed to see him do things like that, because I knew that he was doing it to make me happy, and I didn't want him to spend anything on me. Back home I told him that I had to go inside to tell them to come and help me, when they came to see the things which were inside the car, they were surprised and they didn't know how to thank him. To them it was the first time they had something which could be used for at least one week without having go back to the shop for the same thing.

We were there then I saw that it was the middle of the night, and I told myself that he might be in Mwanza by himself without his family, he didn't tell me anything concerning his family, and he didn't ask me anything concerning mine, maybe he thought that he knew. So at that time I was lucky he didn't ask me anything on my side at all. He looked to be satisfied with the way things were. I had no intention of asking him more about himself, he told me that he had to let me go to sleep, I said that he too needed to go and have a rest because tomorrow he had to go to work, and he asked me if he could come back the next day. I told him that all of the week my brother-in-law would work at night and if he had time and was happy for it, he could come every day that week no problem. We said goodnight to each other and he was gone, when I was in the car and when I was going inside the house, I was looking here and there to see if there was anyone in Seleman's side who might have seen me in the Benz. I saw no one who had seen me, but I said that the whole week was a long time, if he was going to be coming; they were going to see me.

The next day at the same time my Benz was outside, I went, but in my heart hoped that the things he bought yesterday were not bought for me too, so they would not give him power to use me in any way he wanted or wished too.

I felt sorry for him, when I was thinking why I put him there, and maybe he saw me as a young innocent girl, when I was there using him! I thought that maybe if he knew he could be surprised and probably he wouldn't like it, so I saw that it was not easy to know someone exactly for who he or she was, it was only luck to meet a genuine person for everything.

After some time I saw Seleman with his cousin at the front of Mama Vitu's shop, that shop had a city council light in front of it, and there were some good flat rocks which people liked to sit on, and they were there without moving, as if they wanted to be sure it was me who was inside that car. I thought that even if we were here until tomorrow then, they were going to be there too! I felt comfortable and listened to the stories of my old man, he was an expert for stories, you could think that he had a story book in his head. Then he asked me if the children had milk. I told him that I thought they had it, but he insisted by telling me that to look after big family like that was not easy, it was better if we went to get something for them. I thanked him but now I wanted us to pass in front of Seleman where they sat, so that they could see me very clearly and be sure if they were not yet. I told him that we would go to the other shops, he said that we were going anywhere I wanted to, so he turned the car and we passed in front of them then. I saw the way they were standing by to look at us, in my heart I was satisfied, I thought that my work might be good, and I did it the way I wanted it to be.

When we came back I called the children to take the things inside, again, he bought many different things as before, after a short time, Seleman and his relative came and passed near to where we were. After a short time they came back and passed near there again, and they were just walking very slowly and they went to their home. I hoped that it hurt them as I wanted it to.

The day he went home earlier.

The next time he came back, I was inside the car, so we started our conversations as usual, but before we got far with our story he had a request, that he would like to ask me if I could greet him in another special way. I asked him which one he would like, at that moment he turned to me and he was putting me in his chest with a big hug which was very strong and tight, it made me short of breath, but I tried to hold him as hard as I could, though I was not strong like him. After he held my face in both of his hands, and forced my head to look up in his face for a few seconds, and then kissed me on the forehead, and I was surprised and happy at that. I asked myself how he came to know that I didn't want him to kiss me on my lips again!

When the time came to go I said goodnight and started to open the door, but he told me to wait. I waited, he looked like he stood up a little, and he brought the thing which was in the chair behind us, and told me that it was mine. I asked him what it was, he told me to go and said that I would know when I was inside. It was a big paper bag and it was heavy. I told him that it was not necessary to do more than he had done, what he did was enough already, as if I could tell him that I was not there, he didn't have to do anything for me, for sure I didn't want him to spend anything, but I had no way to tell him. I asked if I could open it there and he said that it was OK if I wanted to. I opened it then I looked at the gift and then to him. I had nothing to say, it was too much for me, it was a very beautiful dress which looked to be very expensive, he noticed that it was too much for me to.

He was the one who broke the silence by calling my name, "Look Bamurangirwa, take the gift, it's yours, don't worry, I am happy by giving you the gift because I love you. It is not surprising when you love someone you can give that person even a car like this or a house that you see in the city. So it is the usual thing to do, when you have things to give, and you have someone you are happy to give it to. What are the things anyway? Things are for what? Are they for making us happy when we have them? And only when we are lucky enough to have people who can be with us, to share them? We come in to this world with nothing, and we go from it with nothing." He went ahead by telling me that he didn't know what he could do to make me know that he loved me. I tried to assure him that I knew, he had to relax and not to spend any more, he was a very good person and I appreciated the things he had done for me.

We said goodnight to each other and I went, as always he was starting the car after seeing that I was inside the house.

Before I had thought that I didn't have to tell him that I was going, I saw that it was not his business, but that dress made me change my mind and I decided to tell him. I didn't want to see him do a lot for me when maybe he thought that somehow he would be with me. Inside the house everyone was surprised to see the dress, I saw that he might have had some idea that maybe he wanted to use his money to win me, so that he could have me as his mistress or his wife, one of the two, so I had to stop it before it went too far. Otherwise, if I could just keep quiet, when my time came to go, when he came he would only get the news that I was no longer in Tanzania. He would see me as evil, since he wouldn't be able to see any reason why I could just go like that as if I was running from him or I was conning him. I had two weeks left. I had to ask Rugamba's family to tell me everything they wanted me to help with before I left. Inside the house when all of them saw the dress everyone said many different words, saying how good and beautiful dress it was.

The next day, when I was going to the shop I meet Seleman's cousin, and he stopped me, we greeted each other. After a short time he was the one who started to talk, "I am lucky and happy to meet you."

"Why lucky and happy to meet me?"

"I just want to tell you how you made Seleman a very angry man and you disappointed him; nowadays he doesn't even sleep thinking about you, wondering why you are doing what you are doing to him."

"What have I done?"

"You speak with a lot of surprise, you mean you don't know what you did?!"

"Not at all, I don't know."

"You think that he didn't know that it is you who was in that Benz yesterday? If it was not for me he would have done bad things, but I told him not to lose his temper. We came to pass near where you was so that he could make sure by himself, to see that if what they tell him that these days you have a man who is driving a Benz is true. And he saw it by himself. I kept quiet; again, he went on. On top of that you even passed in front of him with the Benz just to show it to him! Again I kept quiet, only looking at him."

He waited for any kind of answer from me, when he saw that I was saying nothing, he told me that he was going. I gave him a little smile which was telling him that he had better not waste his time, as I was happy already now, I knew that I had done a good job. I said nothing, only I said OK. I didn't like to say something which I would not want to say. And I knew that silence hurt more than words. I saw the way he seemed to be surprised, how I was careless for them, and maybe he thought that they had pushed me to the level to do what I was doing. I showed him that I knew what I was doing and I was happy and proud of it. And they didn't have to pretend to try to expect any more respect from me when they knew who started all of that. First of all they had to know that I too deserved respect.

I had a lot to tell him but I chose not too. I had no case with either one of them anyway, and why waste my time telling them what they already knew. I was doing what I wanted to do, and now I was successful. I was happy about that and surprised at the same time, to see that I had done it and I had managed to do it from the begining. I was not sure how after everything Seleman did to me, he could think that I would still count on him for anything. So I knew that silence was a strong weapon, it shows ignorance and it hurts, but I knew that they knew why I did what I did.

The only thing that maybe shocked them, was that they didn't expect that I was capable of doing that, on top of that, to have a man with a car, not any car but a new Benz! I was sure that it surprised them. And they wanted to see me the way that they thought they knew me, a quiet and shy girl of very few words. When I came from the shop, we had our breakfast, I told Kanzage and Kwezi that I had something I would like to tell them. They talked almost at once, saying that they were free and I could tell them anything now. I told them that I was going in town but I was coming back soon, so we would talk when I was back.

I wanted to buy something for them but since I couldn't afford to buy something good for all of the children, I bought just small things for them to make them happy. But for the grown-up people, I bought three pairs of kangas for Kwezi, Kanzage and Mama Jowa, and I bought a nice shirt for Mutware. When I came back I asked them if they were ready and they said that they were waiting for me, they sat down and they put themselves together, it took them around two minutes to put themselves together and look to be steady and ready to listen. I gave them time; all of us were silent waiting what for what was coming. I was waiting to tell them the news which I was sure was going to be new to them, and would maybe shock them, and they were waiting for what I was going to tell them, and they had a lot of guessing trying to know what it was before being told.

I started by thanking them for the way they had welcomed me, and all the ways that they treated me up to that time, that they took care of me in general like their daughter or sister, which was very true. I also asked them forgiveness for whatever maybe I did which didn't made them happy, and I told them that now it was time to go somewhere in another country, that I was going to Kenya, and I just wanted to go there to see where life there would take me. Since I knew that they would ask me some questions, I told them some of the things I thought they would ask me before being asked, to save time. I told them that I didn't know anyone there, it was like the way I came to Mwanza, all of this was a matter of trying, trying to see where was better.

I gave them their gifts and I gave them Mutware's, and that was all from me, and I told them that before I had to go I was asking if there was anything they wanted me to do for them, maybe somewhere they wanted me to finish digging, or anything I could do for them. When I was telling them this story, one was holding her cheek, the other was holding her mouth. They were looking at me as if I was talking very slowly when they wanted to know quickly the end and why I had made this decision. When I finished they looked shocked, surprised, and sad too, I told them that I had got someone who would welcome me.

Kwezi laughed and told us that when I started to tell them she thought that I was telling them about me and the old man. I told them that I didn't know him yet and I didn't have time to wait to know him more, both of us laughed but they had tears in their eyes. They said that it would take time to get used to life without me, and that they were sure that I would be able to manage life everywhere I went, with everyone I would be with. When Kanzage and Kwezi started, they gave each other time to talk, what they said was almost the same. It was not them who were good to me, it was because I was good to them and good to myself too, as a point of respect, I respected everyone and I respected myself too.

No one can be loved or be respected when can't respect herself or himself. I thanked them once more again. It was time for my old man, I was ready, I already had it in my mind how I would tell him my story; I had to lie to him. Although I hated lies, but I was in a life of lies and lies. I didn't know when this life of lies would come to an end, so when I was beside him after greetings and talking about the sun and rain, I told him that I had something I wanted to tell him. He asked me if I wanted to tell him when we were on the way or after when we were back, he went on, because he wanted us to go to get the children's milk. I told him that I would tell him any time he would give me permission. He said that he wanted us to go to the shops in town so I could tell him any time I wanted. He turned the car and we passed in front of the shop again. Selemen was there, looking at us, which was good to me.

In town, he left me inside the car and he went and came back with meat, maybe four kilograms and gave it to me, he went back and came back with other things to give me one by one, and I was thanking him every time he was giving me whatever he came with, and he asked me if I wanted anything to drink. I told him that I could have any kind of soda, he asked me if I wanted us to go inside or if we should have our drink in the car? I told him that in the car was OK. He came with sodas and some snacks, we were in our car now in a peaceful way, looking at each other when we were waiting, he was waiting to hear what I had on my mind and I was waiting to tell him that I was leaving him for good.

Inside the car, we were sitting in a quiet, peaceful way, he was looking at me and I saw that he was relaxed. He told me that now was the time I could tell him what I wanted to tell him. I started by thanking him and telling him that I was happy to know him and be with him. I tried to thank him by saying that it was not easy to thank him, I thanked him for everything he had already done for me. I told him, "I just thank you in general for your generosity, what you did for me was not because you have money, though yes you might love me, but still the big reason why you did it is because you are generous enough to be happy to do it. But I am only very sorry to have all of this good time with you, when the time is very short…" At this point he interrupted me.

"What do you mean by short time?"

"Short time to be here in Mwanza."

"Are you going somewhere else?"

"Yes next week I am moving to Kenya!"

I had to tell him the same story which I told Mama Jowa since they talked to each other. Mama Jowa didn't know any more than what Kwezi had told her, that I was her young sister, and that was how it had to be to him, we were using the name only old man, which on the other hand, Muzee was a name of respect even to some of the other gentleman, you could use it when they were still young, but it could only be used to show respect for them. In some parts of Africa, you could use nicknames like that to some people all the time and be comfortable with it.

So concerning him we had two reasons to call him Muzee. Muzee continued with his questions, but he was already looking shocked and surprised.

"Do you have relatives in Kenya?"

"We have a brother and he is not happy to see me here doing nothing."

"What are you going to do there then?"

"I don't know what he has planned for me, maybe he will take me to the college. I had no reason to go without telling you. I didn't want to go as if I was running from you, and also I had to let you know how much I appreciated all you have done for me."

Muzee looked relaxed after that conversation and he thanked me for being able to tell him about my journey. "You know Bamurangirwa, I have to thank you because if you chose to keep quiet and go, it would be you to nothing to you, but this shows me that still you have what I have seen in you, understanding, politeness, and respect. Thank you so much, this is not your fault to go to another country, since it is not you who planned it, it is God, so go and see what God holds for you there, that is what we Muslim people believe. I will be Arusha from that day, but I will see you before you go. I know the timetable of the ship."

It was the first week of January 1971, on a Monday, I went in to town to buy a suitcase I would use for my journey. I had to finish all of the digging which was left. I had to go to tell Peace to write a letter to her auntie, and I had to go to Mama Jowa. And I had to go back for my ticket for my journey after all of that. It was time to go to see Peace come and she was at home, she showed me where to sit and after greetings and drinking the tea which she offered to me, I told her that I came to see when she would get time to write a letter for her auntie for me. When I told her that she seemed to be surprised, and she said that she was on her way to come to ask me about my Benz man, now why was I going when I had a strong man like him?!

I laughed, but Peace looked serious and she asked me why I laughed when she thought that it was a serious thing, according to the way outside talked about it! She went ahead that she thought that I had changed the plan of going anywhere.

But my laugh, I think it was maybe a laugh of proudness, or it made me happy to hear that my man was the talk of the area; I think it made me more to feel satisfied.

Peace was still looking in a surprised way, and then asked me why I was laughing when she thought that it was a serious thing I was in.

I told her that it was just a game, I did show them that I could, and it was possible! At that point we laughed together. Peace said that it was not understandable to her. "Just because you are angry, there and then you get him, and not any man, only the man with new Benz? Or you had him before and you kept him somewhere to wait for your right time?"

"I think we can put it in that way," I said.

She told me that she would bring a letter for me and I went back.

The day for me to see Muzee came and I was on my way to town to get my ticket for my journey the next day. He told me that he was in hurry we had better go together, inside the car he told me that he was going to leave me in the office, and the next day he would be busy so I could get a taxi to take me to the ship. I said that it was OK, in the ship's office we said bye to each other for the last time, and he gave me the envelope and wished me all the best in my future. I thanked him once more and then Muzee had gone in his way and I went in mine. When I opened the envelope, inside was his picture in a black suit, his address in case I wanted to send him a letter, his names and 500 Tsh. When I was back at home, Peace came and she gave me the letter and 50 Tsh to help me on my way, I thanked her and she was gone. Inside I remembered that I had to go to see Mama Jowa, when I reached her home she was on the door opening, and she said that I was lucky she had just come back, she was not there since the morning.

After telling her everything, she was not surprised like the others she seemed to be happy and she started to give me some advice, and told me that I was still young, it was good to go somewhere else and see if that was maybe where my future was. To try when I still could. I gave her the gift and told her some words of thanks as those I told Rugamba's wives. Yes Mama Jowa was too good to me indeed.

She was happy for the gift and though she was not as surprised as Rugamba's wives, she showed signs of being sad.

She peppered the tea and after told me to drink it, I told her that I had to go as there were some other things I had to do.

She gave me the bag and I held it with surprise, she said that I had better open it and see what was inside. I opened it and inside were body soaps and face cream with body oil! It surprised me more, how she even thought about it. She told me that even if I was going to my brother's home but he had a wife, in that case his wife would see that I was a girl who respected myself, who didn't come to be a burden to her for everything, at least not there and then, it was OK even if I had bought the same stuff. She said that she would miss me a lot, she escorted me, when we were in the middle of the road we said bye to each other. I had some kind of scare that I was parting with people I had been with for a long time, and in a good way in all ways at all times, the people who gave me hope and encouragement in everything I was doing, the people who were happy to see me around them and were proud to see me as one of them. I had some strong sadness, something which was heavy at that time was Mama Jowa, who cried in a very loud voice. I didn't waste any time, I started exactly at the same time and we cried together then we hugged each other, we cried for maybe one minute, and after, she told me that she would never ever forget me, because I left her with a good gift and she would die with it, I left her when she knew how to read and write.

Back home Kanzage and Kwezi called me and they told me that they didn't have anything to give to me. Aziza refused to give them back their money which she had, and I told them that they didn't have to worry. I had enough money which would help me for some time, that money would help them in other things, I knew that they were telling me the truth and it was not necessary for them to give me anything.

In the morning it was my journey day, Rugamba called me and thanked me for the gift, and told me that he wanted to say bye and to thank me for the gift, and he apologised that he didn't have anything to give to me. I told him that what they had done for me was more than enough, I thanked him too. We said bye to each other and he went where he was going, the children already knew that I was going somewhere, some were asking me when I would be back, others were asking me if I would take them with me.

To make things easier I told them that I would be back for them. The car was outside, Kanzage and Kwezi were taking the things to the car when I was trying to calm down the children who were crying, their mothers were crying too, but I was trying to be strong because I was determined to do it. Down in my heart I was crying to see that I was leaving them, thinking how they had taken very good care of me, trying to do everything to see that I felt happy and comfortable. I was inside the car and the car turned when my head was on the window, our eyes looked at each other and I started to cry too. I waved to them and they waved back. I was going to the ship, the ship which was going to take me to Kenya.

To start a new life, a life I didn't know how and where was going to take me, I knew that this idea might again be commiting suicide or would it take me to heaven quickly? If Kenya was going to be my heaven.

After a few minutes I started to think about what I was doing, and I laughed to myself, asking myself if this journey meant that if, and when, I was upset with something I would be moving from one country to another. If so then by bad luck I might go around the world searching for love and peace until I saw myself coming back to where I started at the beginning, so help me God.

I had heard a little story about Kenya, that it was one of the countries which white people, like any other part of Africa, had colonised. But they seemed to have a hope that they had it for themselves forever, that it was almost like Congo DRC, Kenya and S.A, where black people had their schools, their areas and so on, where they couldn't mix with whites in many different things. This went on until the Kenyans said that enough was enough, and stood up to fight for their independence, and fought by themselves using a group called Maumau. In the area of improvement I believed that Kenya was different from other part of Africa, at least where I had already seen.

I was not new to the ship, though I only suspected that the things I saw on the ship from Bukoba were not the same as what I was going to see on the ship which was going to Kenya. I thought that the passengers to Kenya might look like well civilised people.

I chose a nice bright dress and I knew that I looked smart enough to win respect for that matter. And I had one small bag which I had just started to make and I left it in the mid-way, so I would be making it on the way, so that I could keep myself busy, maybe when I was by myself.

Inside the ship I thought that there would be no people who looked like the ones I saw in the ship I came in from Bukoba. Where I was, there were not many people yet, and there were many empty benches to sit on if I wanted to, and it was still early so I decided to sit down and wait. I had a lot of time to go around on the ship, I chose to sit in the corner alone, and go ahead making my bag. After a short time came a small group of young men, and they sat the other side, but not far from where I was. After some time they were coming in small groups, sitting there but in different places, one group had one who was an expert in stories, he was like a comedian, the way he was capable of making people around him laugh at whatever he said.

It was as if it was a kind of job he was doing to keep them busy and happy, other groups started to move to where he was, one by one until all of them sat together and became a big group. It seemed that they knew each other, but apart from those young men, others were also joining them because of those stories.

I pretended that I didn't understand what they said, but I was just trying to make myself look unique from others, otherwise I wanted to go and join them. Where I was, I was laughing and when I looked down to my bag, there was a woman with them. I came to think that even though it was still early, it could be better if I started to ask them if they knew where I was going. I wanted them to be the first to talk to me not me to start to talk to them, so I was sure that it would be one of them who would come to see this bag, or simply come just to make me talk. I already knew that one of the ladies was neighbouring with the comedian, where they came from at home, so he was talking in Swahili in a loud voice to see if I would show any sign of being able to hear what he was saying, but he didn't get any sign at all, so he was confused. He didn't know if I knew Swahili or if I was just ignorant to them. I didn't even turn my head to look where they were. Then he called Kalikwera and asked her, "Kalikwera what do you think about that girl?"

Kalikwera replied, "Which girl?"

"That one who is sitting alone in the corner, I think it is her first time to travel on this ship and maybe someone lied to her and said that to talk inside the ship had to be paid for in advance." All of them laughed at once and still I turned myself to stone.

Kalikwera was not very happy with that. "But you people, what is the matter with you? She didn't do or say anything to you. What do you want from her? Leave the girl alone."

The young man told Kalikwera, that was what he didn't want, in fact the big problem was because the girl didn't talk. He turned to the group and asked them, "My friends, what do you say concerning that girl? If you tell me to leave her alone I am going to do that, but only you have to show me the good reason for that, to leave her in that situation without even knowing her problem, it might be that she is dumb, because I tried to say things to see at least if she can laugh but she didn't. Maybe someone told her that she had to buy two different tickets, one for travelling, the second to give her permission for talking and laughing inside the ship. So it can be like that, to leave her in that situation cannot be helpful to her. I want to be able to help her then, and also I can't go all of this way with a girl like this one without trying to talk to her in any way, it is not right." All of them were laughing a lot at that, they told him that he was right, it was better to try and find out my problem. So I was aware that someone was coming, since I hadn't turned my head, I didn't know what Kalikwera looked like. I heard a voice greeting me and I turned to look at her and to return her greetings too.

She sat down and said that I was making a good bag, I gave her the bag so she could see it properly, and I showed her how I did it to show her that I was not a bad person. At that time one of the young men came and also sat down with greetings, he asked me if I was going to Musoma. I told him that I was going to Kenya, then he said that was too bad, if I was going to Musoma he would have taken care of me. I told him that I was going to Kenya. "That means that you will go with Kalikwera," he told me.

I said, "If that is where she is going, yes." I was happy that they helped me by talking to me, they came one by one where we were until the whole group was with us.

In my heart I told myself that I was a winner, they came to where I was. I kept the bag now and I joined them in conversations.

We were laughing together now, and sometimes you wouldn't believe that it was me who was dumb! Because my voice was on top of all of the others and the comedian, as I was calling him, you could think that he was the leader of all of the others, because most of the time he was the one who was talking and many times they were doing what he was telling them. Then he asked me my name. "My name is

Bamurangirwa," I said. He said that his was Gakuru, and he told others to tell me their names too, which they did, he said that I would go with Kalikwera because she was going to Kenya too. I knew her name before, because I heard them calling her, after some time, there came a girl and Kalikwera told me that her name was Aida. Gakuru said that Aida came for a walk, it was our time to go, otherwise we might become stiff because of sitting in one place for a long time. I was the first to stand up, I didn't want to part with Gakuru and Kalikwera, a few men also came with us, we went around the ship then, one of the men said that he was tired so it would be better if we sat down, but Gakuru refused to believe him by saying that he was not going to listen to him until the girls said so, he asked us and both of us said yes at once.

Then Gakuru said that it was better to go to the hotel to sit there while we had something to eat. In the hotel, he said that all of us could eat whatever we wanted and he would pay, and he turned to one of his friends, and told him that he would pay for the drinks, and asked him if that was right and it was OK for him too. At that time it was OK with me to eat and drink when strangers paid for it.

I had that experience on the first journey on the ship from Bukoba. I was a girl who was supposed to be treated by strange men for free, just because I was a girl.

After our dinner we went back to where we were, after maybe one hour the young men told us that they had reached their destination, and said bye to both of us. I knew that we were in Musoma then, all of the young men went out, they were soldiers according to how some of them were dressed. We started to feel bored and that is when I remembered that I had to ask Kalikwera where I was going.

I laughed at that, thinking that in case we had to be with Gakuru for our entire journey, I was going to listen to him and forget about it.

I went near Kalikwera and told her my problem that I needed directions; she said that it was no problem. I just told her where I was going and asked if she knew where it was, there was no problem and she would do anything to see that I got there. I got the envelope and

225

showed her, she held it and said that the lady I was looking for was her neighbour in Kenya and back home too, she went ahead by telling me that she had a niece who was called Peace, who had grown up there and had just been back to Tanzania to finish her study and get married, and she went with her husband.

I told her that it was Peace who gave me the letter.

Then I relaxed, I saw that my journey to Kenya was full of luck. I didn't want to be away from Kalikwera again, and she didn't want to go anywhere without me either. She introduced me to many other ladies and told me that all of us were going together, but a few were going to Mombasa, and others were with going to Nairobi.

Now was my time for questions, "Kalikwera how long have you been in Nairobi?"

"I have been there for four years."

"How do you see life there?"

"It is very good, it is a simple and nice life especially for girls like you!"

"Why girls like me?" I asked her.

"Because you can't be there without a job."

"Meaning that as soon as I will reach there I will get job?"

"Yes you will!"

"What kind of job is there that is easy to get?"

"Any job, it is you who will choose."

I thought that I was lucky to go somewhere and just choose the job I wanted! When I thought about all of those women she introduced to me, some were young girls who looked like they had just finished their secondary school, and even the old ones were good-looking women. Then I told myself to calm down, there was no need even to ask again about jobs since I saw that all of them had the same answer. I was going there so I would see by myself, and yes it was an easy and a good life and that is why all of them went there. As always I thought that Kenya was like a white person's country, I believed that no one could be poor in those countries.

There came one of the youngest girls in the group who looked my age, and she was with me everywhere, so I asked her if she had been in Kenya for a long time and she said that she had grown up there. I tried once more again to ask, I promised myself that it was going to be the last time. I asked her how she saw life in Kenya. Her answer was that in Kenya they was money and that was what everyone wanted.

"It means that there is no problem getting a job?"

"No problem at all, to those who want it."

"Meaning that all of these women have a job there?"

She answered like my question was meaninglessness, "Of course how could you be there without a job!"

"What kind of job is easy to get?"

"You don't have to worry, you will get job."

I said that I was not going to ask that question to anyone again in that ship. Maybe they were housegirls and they felt ashamed about it, to me if they were paid good money there was no problem with it, I would work and save so that I could go to college for something.

When reached Kisumu, Kalikwera held my hand and told me that it was time to go to the train which was taking us to Nairobi. Outside of the ship I turned my head to each side to see the Lake Victoria again. Now in Kenya, the people who were there were too black like the Sudanese people I had seen in Kampala, they were tall and some were big but strong, some had no shoes, others had clothes that were torn and some looked dirty, and I was confused. I asked myself if I was in Kenya or not yet. Then I asked Kalikwera if we were in Kenya. "Yes," she said. I said nothing, but there were others who were very smart and clean, who I thought might be directors of something there concerning fish, which I saw to be the only work that they were dealing with. If this was almost a town, and then what would I see if I could go in to the villages? What I saw there was no different to the other countries that I came from.

I thought that maybe in Nairobi, because it was the capital, it might be different. I believed that when white people came here to Africa, they took the whole continent in the same way, they had the same intention of why they came, nowhere was favourable. The life of the

African people was uniform so they had their agenda, now if so, in case we were not happy with the life we had, we had our Africa, and it was us who had to change it. Or if we were satisfied then we could sit down and keep quiet, because to sing a song of history and only blame others would not work. Maybe we thought that we were making people be sympathetic and feel sorry for us, but this would not work, it would never take us anywhere.

Inside the train Kalikwera showed me the room where I would sleep when I felt tired. She was telling me everywhere we reached, but sometimes I was just saying yes without paying attention or knowing the names of the places. The time came when Kalikwera told me that we had reached Nairobi! My heart jumped and I opened my eyes wider, as if I wanted many eyes to see more clear, outside there were women with the same dress as I saw Bukoba and Mwanza, the black dress, long from head to toe, I already knew about that dress. Here there were big numbers who dressed like that, so I thought that I was going to be near Arab countries then. I believed that I was not going to see any Rwandans, I might have been the first one to go there.

They got taxi cars, and each had the number of passengers who could fit in it, it showed me that they were neighbours, because they told the taxi man to go to one place, something I saw to be a good idea because if they were together then they would never feel alone, and it would help them not miss home so much. On the way where we were passing, my head was outside the window, my eyes were just open non-stop, the road was dirty, the houses were like in other towns in countries where I came from, but I realised that we were not in the city centre exactly. After I came to see something which shocked me a little, we were on a dusty road, there were very small houses which were together and they were mud houses, this was the first time I saw a place like that. Some of the people on the road were like mad people concerning the way they looked and their dirty dresses. I told myself that I didn't have to ask, I just had to look and keep quiet.

There was six in the car and when the car stopped it was between small mud houses, which were in a line and between some of them there was just a small space to pass. One lady who was outside standing on her door saw us and came jumping here and there, she was very happy to see us, and she took us inside her house, the first thing they did was call others, and they came in a big number. All of them looked happy and wanted to know the news from back home where they came from, which showed me that they must all come from the same area as I thought before.

Inside the house there were two beds, one was small and the other one was a double bed, there was no chair and there was no space to put the chair anyway, there was only room for her to put her things, like a stove in the corner and a few other things. I thought that some other things might be kept under the beds; on the floor was a plastic carpet, but in general she managed to keep her small room clean.

So all of us were sitting on the beds, the ladies who came to get the news from home, we gave them their letters and some went, others came back with tea and snacks, we was started to have tea already. All of them who I saw were young women, at last the oldest one could be over forty years, but there were none older than that to my guess.

I didn't want to think about what would happen if I could't get to Peace's auntie, what could be, what could I do, it came in my mind once but I didn't like it. They started to go one by one, and then one remembered me and asked "What about this child?" Kalikwera told them who I was looking for. They said that they were going to tell her that she had a visitor, after ten minutes, there came the old lady who looked older than all of those who I had seen before. She was tall and dark but with a good figure, with a long face, a big long nose which made her face to look beautiful, wide big lips and big eyes. She had a medium chest, a small waist and big hips with long beautiful legs, but the legs had become so soft to show that she was too old. She looked around sixty years old or more, she greeted all of us with her heavy voice. I thought that when she was young she was very beautiful.

After a short time she asked about her visitor and they showed her where I was, and at that point I stood up and greeted her. She told me that her name was Rose and I told her that mine was Bamurangirwa.

I went in my pocket and I gave her the letter, she looked behind it and she seemed to be happy, she didn't open it, she put it in her pocket and sat down. After two minutes, she told them that they had better take her visitor so she could have a rest. She thanked them and we had gone, she was the one who carried my suit case, her home was not far and after a few minutes we were there.

Her house was like where we were, the house was the same size, and had the same look, the only difference was the things which were inside.

She told me that she wanted to give me tea then sleep and she wanted me to have a good rest. She said that I could have a bath at night since in the day time I couldn't have somewhere to do that, and she tried to see that I was comfortable, because she said that Peace was her child, she had grown up there, and I was her children's age, so I was in good hands because she was a mother too. She wanted to give me tea, but I told her that I had a tea where I was, and she insisted, I too wanted tea again, but I didn't want to be seen as greedy. The tea was already ready, and I asked her how and why all of them made tea ready for other people when they were alone? She told me that they knew the day of the train from Kisumu, and they knew that there was always a possibility to get visitors from home. She told me that she had a lady neighbour, her name was Zena, who was Rwandan, she had a girl my age, her name Zulia. She would go to tell her so that I could go to play with Zulia when I woke up. After having tea she showed me the bed and she covered me. I didn't take time to sleep; I didn't know how many hours I slept. I heard people talking when I woke up, and downstairs there were four people sitting, there were two women and two men, they had a conversation in Swahili. When I was preparing myself to come down, Rose told me to come and greet people who came to see me, and we could talk in my language. It was them who started by telling me that they were waiting for me. I asked them why they didn't wake me up, and they said that they didn't want to do that, they wanted to let me have enough rest. We greeted each other and we went ahead in all conversations in Kinyarwanda. After seeing her house I asked myself how she managed to take care of Peace in there. Maybe that was why there was two beds, so one was hers and now was going to be mine. After seeing that she struggled to get Rwandan people to come to see me, I thought that she had the idea of trying to get people from my country for me, so that by luck they would take me and I could be their responsibility. Or that I could get people from my home country so that I would have people to be talking with, to make me feel more comfortable. Whatever the reason was or whatever would come out of it, I hoped it would be good.

The first time my visitors came they were not sure that I spoke our language in a clear way since some of our children had lost it, it depended where and how they grew up. After they had heard me talking, they were happy with that. I too told them that I had doubts that I would meet anyone there who came from Rwanda, and they said that we were all over every corner of the world, it was only that in some places there could only be a small number so we couldn't be recognised.

One of them said that he would like to see someone who came directly from Rwanda and see how they looked alike. The other one told him that he was better to go to wait at the airport or where business people met then he would see them, all of us laughed at that. I told them my names, it was only the men who told me their names, one was Kagimbangabo and other was Rugira. Kagimbangabo had light skin and he looked to be between thirty-five and forty years old, and Rugira looked to be between fifty and sixty years old and had dark skin, he was slim and tall with few words. I didn't ask the names of the women. The food was ready, to me it was good food, it was matoke mixed with meat with some other things like tomato, she told others to join us but they said that they were OK. We finished and I insisted on washing the dishes. The time came when a woman knocked the door, she was a very beautiful young lady, had a mini skirt, and a nice blouse, she had a good figure and she was short, around five foot four. I wanted to look at her legs non-stop, but I wouldn't do that, I thought that if I had legs like that I would dress in a short dress always, but maybe she too knew that, that could be the reason why she dressed the way she dressed. She had white teeth which had spaces, with a long face which was a chocolate colour.

Many Rwandan women were still following their culture, after a girl got married, no matter what age she was, she had to dress in a long dress and she couldn't show her legs any more. So this lady was a modern one, she greeted us in general, and they returned her greetings, they also mentioned her name when saying, "Good evening Zena." So I knew that she was the girl who Rose had told me about, the problem was that when she came inside and she was talking to people, her face was tight. Then I asked myself if a beautiful woman like her looked to be angry with anything which was front of her, how could someone manage to be with her? I concluded that it was how she looked and might not mean that she had a bad heart.

She asked if the visitor they had told her about was me, Rose said yes that I was their visitor. She stood up, and said that she was still alone at home, but it was time for Zulia to be back, and she wanted to take me to meet her. She said that I didn't look like someone who came from the journey, but Rose told her that if I had a shower I should look more fresh, she said that there was no problem, I would go with Zulia to have a shower.

I just stood up and Rose told me to go, she said that it was near so I could come for my things later. Zena called me her child by telling me, "Come my child, and see myother child." Then I thought that she might not be the bad person I had thought she was just because of her stone face. I assumed that maybe I was going to live in Zena's place, maybe because she was Rwandan and she had a girl my age, and maybe she had a big house, they might have talked about it between themselves. On our way, no one was talking, she was the one who started by saying that to be young was good, if it was her who came from the journey she would look like a drunk or sick person, she asked me my names and I told her, it was not far and I started to feel relaxed a little.

At her home, her house was like the two houses I had seen before,

232

she had two beds, but what was different, where she was, in front of her room was a big dusty place. It looked like that was where the children of that area came to play and anyone who had car that was where they parked them. When the other houses were almost together with just small spaces between each other.

After a short time, a girl came with books in her hands, she stood still looking at me, in silence. Her mum was the one who said, "Zulia I brought other child for you." Zulia looked happy and confused, and she asked if I would be there permanently.

Her mum said that unless she told her no then she would take her back. Then Zulia told her, "Please let her be here. I will do whatever you will say."

Then she told her that I was her young sister who she doesn't know yet, and Zulia was too happy.

The way I saw it, I was older than Zulia, maybe a couple of years or so, she was a dark girl but she was not beautiful like her mother, but she had very good personality and she was kind too.

ZENA, ZULIA, AND I IN
PROSTITUTES' LAND.

How the discussion went between Rose and Zena I had no idea, but Zena was too good to me, there were times I thought that maybe there was some kind of payment between themselves concerning the taking care of me. Maybe because she had to do whatever she could, to see that I was in a good situation without any complaint because she loved her niece Peace. And I was her friend and had depended on what Peace told her about me. Or only Zena had heard about me, and she was one of the patriotic people who were happy to help their people, simple maybe because I was a young Rwandan girl who was on my own.

Zena called Zulia and told her, "You listen Zulia, Bamurangirwa is my young sister, and you have to give her all respect do you hear me?"

"Yes Mum."

"Whatever she will tell you and anything she will ask you, you have to talk to her in a respectful way, I repeat, do you understand?"

"Yes Mum."

I didn't like the way she was giving her those orders.

"Now take her to the toilet to have a shower," she told her.

"Yes Mum," Zulia said. I asked myself about that toilet where people went to have a shower! Zulia got a container to come back with water and we went on our way. I asked Zulia what kind of toilet was it where people go to have shower. And she told me that was the city council's, she went on by telling me that there was a tap so they could get water from there, they went there for everything, even for showers, but many got baths inside their houses because their rooms had that plastic carpet.

Zulia was very happy to be with me and she was begging me to stay with them and not to go anywhere. I didn't know if I should say yes or no. I didn't know yet what kind of life I was in, she told me that since she came she was alone apart from when she was at school, she hated coming back from school because she knew that she was going to be by herself. I was older than her but it was easy for me to get along with her, she held my arm and we ran outside the toilet, it was not far, you could see the building of the toilet when you stood in their door. We reached there, it was one big building with two different sides, one for men and the other one for women, outside was a tap, we left our container outside and we went inside, it was clean and we had our shower. On our way back home with water I told Zulia that the place was clean, maybe it was because that was where people went to have a shower, she said that the city council sent cleaners, but before they came to clean it sometimes some people made the place dirty, some they were mad or they were drunk and they didn't care. She told me that we could go slow, we had nothing to do at home, she was going very slowly then I told myself that if we were going to go slow then that was no problem at all, let me try to walk like a bride and bridegroom, the water we had was not heavy.

She told me that Zulia was not her name, she looked sad when she was telling me that her name was Umunyana, but when she came here her mum put her in the Muslim religion because she was already converted to Islam because of her boyfriend. She wanted me to call her Zulia, because that is what her mum wanted.

She looked more sad when she told me that she hated the place but she didn't have the means to go back home. I asked her why she hated it there, she told me that she hated it there because of everything, when she was brought her from home all she was told was lies.

I tried to ask her how bad the place was, but the only thing she could say was that it was everything. I had no other way to make her tell me how bad the place was or maybe the whole area was. I saw that she had a lot she would like to tell me but I thought that it was still early.

I told myself that this child wouldn't say that the situation here was bad when it was not, and it might be very bad according to the way she was talking. It seemed that she hated it to the point of going back if she had the means. The time would come when I would know what it was. I started to feel some kind of fear, fear of something I had no idea of. In that area the majority of people who were there were women, and the way I saw all of them, they were at home. I was wondering when they went to work or if they lived with more than one, and maybe they went to work in turn. When we reached home from the toilet to have our shower and bring water, the door of our house was locked, and I thought that Zena had gone somewhere and Zulia would open so that we could put the water inside. But instead she told me that we would put the water outside near the door and we could go around for a walk. I was very happy with the idea, because I thought that Zulia wanted to show me around.

We started our walk which was in no hurry, the houses as I said before were very small houses and they were almost together, so we were passing between them in a zigzagged way up and down. I waited for her and when she would say that it was time to go back. In most of the houses the women looked smart, well dressed, standing outside their doors or sitting. Some doors were locked and I thought that they were not at home, which was understandable. But there were many others who I saw outside their doors, so I had to ask why and how all of them got time off, or had holiday at the same time?

Instead of giving me an answer, Zulia had a long and hard laugh, after keeping quiet she asked me what kind of job they had told me they worked.

"No one told me anything, but I assumed that they worked anyway."

Zulia said, "This is no holiday, they are in work."

"There where they are standing or they are sitting?" I asked her.

"Yes, where they are sitting or standing they are working!"

"What kind of job?"

"A job I told you that they are working."

We reached home and the water was inside with bags of clothes. I changed after having a shower in the toilet. Zena was waiting for us and she looked happy, though her stone face was permanent, and didn't mean that she was a hard lady as her face showed. I saw that she was a kind and caring person according to the way she was talking to us.

Concerning what kind of the job the women there did, I saw that it seemed not to have a name, because Zulia too gave me the same answer I got from Mwanza, and on the ship and up to now it was the same answer, which was no answer.

She told us to sit down and have tea and bread and then she wanted to send us to Rose's place for something.

When we were out going to Rose's place again, she started to try to tell me her story which she seemed to have had for a long time, and she had no one to talk to. "You know Bamurangirwa, I hate this place and no one in my family comes to visit us, in case anyone comes and then can't go back without me."

"But in the first place why didn't you refuse to come?"

"She told us a lot of lies that this place is a good place, that she will put me in the school…"

"Then what, she lied?! I see that you are in school, so what do you want?"

"Just wait. It is because you do not understood; even I don't know why you came here!" At that time she started to cry, and I didn't know what to do, I didn't help her to cry, I only took her inside where people didn't pass as if I was guiding her, I gave her all the time to cry, I was feeling very sorry for her and for myself too.

In Rose's place, she was outside her door sitting in the small chair, she had dressed up in a mini skirt, and a sleeveless blouse which had the buttons open to the middle of her chest, all her big but nice legs were out. It showed me that she was an old woman, and it was the first time I saw a lady like her dress like that, she had hair which was like a hat. All her face had changed, every part of her face had different

237

colours, she looked like a completely different person than I had seen before, and her face looked a bit young.

I was in a hurry to be alone with Zulia, to ask her about all of that. Then the time came for me to ask her why Rose did that.

"Did what?"

"An old lady to dress like that in a mini skirt and top like that, sitting outside to show herself?!"

"It is because she finished what she was doing," she told me.

"And why has she changed her face?"

"To show that she is a civilized old lady."

"Do you know what she used to change her face like that?" I asked her.

Sometimes it was not easy to get answers to my questions and when the answers were hard to her, she was trying to change the subject, maybe because she was younger than me. I had no fear or shyness in front of her, and I wanted to know, so she had a problem with me many times. I had to insist until sometimes she had to just give me answers so that I might keep quiet. As soon as we reached home it was the first thing I told Zena, waiting to see how she was going to be surprised to hear how Rose had changed her face, and the way she was dressed. She told me that she knew, I kept quiet but I thought that it was because I didn't tell her that she was sitting outside, when she looked like that at her age! Zena was looking natural, as I knew other women where I came from, that were satisfied with their natural beauty.

When we were outside with Zulia, there came four girls, two were dressed in wide trousers, which at that time were in fashion, the other two had mini skirts which were shorter than Rose's, They had a lot of decoration on their faces, more than Rose's too. I looked at them with a lot of attention, Zulia also looked at me, preparing herself for questions. Zulia started to laugh when I was laughing, after some time she asked me what I was laughing for, I told her that I was laughing at what she was laughing at. I asked her if she saw those girls and the way they made good art on their faces? She laughed more, then I thought that maybe we were not laughing at the same thing. I asked her then, what she was laughing for, and she was laughing at me and the way I was looking at them. I was surprise to see that we were laughing at different things but it was OK, then I asked her why they drew on themselves on their faces, this made her laugh more. I realised that calling it drawing might sound funny.

She said, "Because they are going to work for money." I understood that I should ask no more questions concerning those girls. I assumed that they were sporting girls but it would have been much better if they could do everything concerning their sport after reaching where they did their sports.

I was sleeping with Zulia.

The next time Zena sent us to Rose for some messages, at Rose's home she was dressed like before, sitting in that small chair where she was sat the first time we sent to her. But the things that she was putting on her face now were more than she had done before. It was like the girls we had seen and what they had on their faces, I tried not to laugh. We said bye and we had gone, but as soon as we were away from her I started to laugh in a loud voice while Zulia was looking at me, I didn't know what was going on in me. She asked me, "What is funny?"

I asked her, "Is Rose a sport lady too?!"

She told me that she didn't understand what I was talking about, then I questioned her, "Didn't you see that she had drawn on her face like sport people?"

Then it was her time to laugh when she was asking me where I got that story from, who told me that people with that make-up were sport people, I told her that when I saw those girls I thought that they were going to play somewhere, and then she had told me that they were going to work for money. She laughed again when she was telling me that I must be crazy, to see things and just judge them that way without being told by anyone.

Then again I had question, "Then why do they do all of that?"

"To get money!"

"Money from where?"

"From men!"

"From men?! And those men from here they are mad or fools, or they have a lot of money to go throwing everywhere?"

"Yes they have a lot of money."

"And to be given their money they have to wear clothes like that and draw different colours on their face?"

"Yes."

After Zulia told me that men there gave money to women because of how they dressed and how they drew on their faces and seeing that all of my questions concerning what the women did in that area, including her mum, were the same, and there was no proper answer, I started to suspect that there might be something wrong, something which was abnormal. I decided to leave her alone and try to do the investigation by myself, then after knowing what was going on I would surprise her. But how was I going to do it? I only had to watch Zena and our neighbours, they were always there, they had no business of any kind which they were selling outside. It was only native people who had different business like vegetables etc… and at our home Zena never said that she was short of money, she always fed us in a good way, then I was wondering where she got money from. When Zulia went to school I was home with Zena doing homework, but most of the time I was outside, she liked to send me here and there, I knew all of the neighbouring places and when I was back and sometimes the door was locked, I had to go somewhere to wait until Zena came back because I assumed that she went somewhere and I had no key. Not even Zulia had a spare key, so to them it was normal.

I understood why Zulia was very happy to see me there, to have someone who kept her company.

Sometimes when we were on our way walking, when we passed between the houses and reached where the women stood or sat outside their door. When a man came, I saw that he just passed her where she was, and went inside the room quickly, the lady would follow him and shut the door, so at that point I didn't asked Zulia why, I assumed that she was the husband or boyfriend who came and he was in a hurry because they had only one room, and they had to talk and they needed their privacy, so they had to lock the door.

I liked Zena very much because she was treating me with a lot of love and respect in her way, but sometimes she was acting in a strange way. I had never liked to sit and be fed without having to do anything, so I didn't like when Zulia was not there, after finishing our breakfast sometimes she didn't want me to do anything in the house, even wash dishes or do anything, when I wanted to help and do something at home. But instead she was telling me to go to the toilet to have a shower or go out to play with other children. On the one hand I saw that I was lucky to be somewhere where I could do nothing, but on the other hand I didn't like to sit doing nothing, and just going out to play. Play, who would I play with? I was not a young child who could be out the whole day running here and there or playing with children of ten years old. I was a big girl who anyone could be happy to have at her home, letting me take care of her housework and allowing herself to relax, if I had no other things to do, and if I was happy doing it.

But Zena was happy to feed me and not see me inside the house.

She had never asked me my ideas, since I assumed that she might know that any young person who goes outside of their home country, is trying to get somewhere better than where they came from. What I didn't like about Zena was how sometimes she would make noises to Zulia without any reason, and sometimes Zulia noticed that it hurt me, and she was telling me that I didn't have to feel bad about it, because since I came things like that had changed a lot. Before I came she was even beating her, she thought of going back many times but had no way of doing that, when she was telling me this she looked upset and I hated to see her in that situation, sometimes she was crying. I thought that Zena was doing that to her so that she could make her depressed because she had that power over her.

My investigation was failed and still I had no idea what the women did. I tried once more to ask her, this time in a serious way.

"But Zulia, seriously what does your mum do for living?"

Zulia again seemed to be too serious and somehow upset, "You know Bamurangirwa all of these women here they do the same job."

"What kind of job then?"

"They open and shut the doors."

"That is still a job yes, but it is thought to be men's. The problem I have here is I always see them here, if they go to work then who do they work for?" But as I was asking this, when I was laughing, she was with me and laughing too then.

"They open and shut their doors," she was still laughing.

"If they are their doors then who is there to pay them for that?"

"When they lock the doors they clean the towels and I told you that there are men who give them the money."

"Clean towels! Where do they get those towels for cleaning every day? I don't understand the men here, I told you that they have some abnormality." When Zulia was coming from school she would come running because of missing my questions, and we started to laugh all the time we were outside. I knew that I was asking her serious questions but she saw it to be funny, so when she was laughing I was laughing with her with the hope that one day I would get satisfactory answers.

After our laugh she seemed to be relaxed and she looked at me and called me by my name and she looked more serious. She went ahead by saying, "You know now, let me not go ahead enjoying your questions and making fun of you. Concerning these women here, I realised that you know nothing at all, and I remember back when I came here it took me a long time to know what was going on here." I was quiet only looking at her ready for an answer, after all of that time and since this answer was hard to get, it might be something which I had no idea of. She went ahead with a word which seemed to be too heavy to mention, it took her time and I gave her all the time by going ahead and keeping quiet. We were looking at each other, I was scared that she was not going to let it out, something which had been inside her maybe for a long time, and something which maybe was killing her somehow, at last she could say it.

"These women, all of them in this area, they are prostitutes! The name of this place is called Magengo, it is one of the slums here in Nairobi, but here is like a part of these women."

I was in big shock, it was the opposite of all I had in my mind. I asked her to repeat what she had said, I thought that I didn't hear her clearly and wished that what I heard was not true.

"What? What do you say? They are what?"

I asked these questions almost at once.

"What you heard, that is how it is."

"You are telling me that they come here to prepare themselves to come and do that job?"

We were seriously talking now like grown-up people, her answer was yes some came ready for that, and others were kidnapped in many different ways.

"That is why sometimes I see men pass them like lightning and after women follow them!"

"Yes, it is them, they come to sleep with them and they pay them: 2 K.sh! Unless the man wants to give her more that is up to him, it is like a tip to her."

I waited, thinking that maybe she still had other things to tell me, we were very serious, you wouln't even think that it was us who were laughing in a loud voice before.

She went ahead with her story by telling me that I was lucky to meet her there, that when she came she had no one to tell her and it took her a long time to find out after passing all of those kinds of problems, when she didn't even know the other language and she thought that her mum hated her and that was why she didn't want her inside the house, and she was wondering why she brought her there, and now it seemed as if it was a bit easier for her since I came.

Then again I had to ask Zulia one more question.

"Zulia, in your view, who is the prostitute between these women and the men who come to gives them their money? The women are happy to use their body for a living, to use it in any way even if it is to sell themselves to any man they can get, no matter what or no matter who?! And they count themselves lucky when they get a big number of men in a day. To use their body for whatever they want in the name of money, they see it as their right. And both see that it is their right. Or is it the man who sometimes leaves his wife at home and goes to get strange women just because he has the money to buy them, when he can use that money to get mistress if he wanted another woman outside the marriage. To be faithful can be much better than all of that, but this man chose to be unfaithful to his wife, to make matters worse he does it with strangers, or does the same to his girlfriend, and is proud of it, because he knows that they will never know what he is doing outside. Now who is the prostitute between these two people?"

"Both of them are prostitutes, because they encourage each other. Maybe for the men, one of the reasons why some chose prostitutes instead of having permanent girlfriends is because they are not married, yet I think that they fear responsibility and they are happy to do that, maybe it makes them feel like proper men."

Now I was on my own with my thoughts, I had heard the word prostitute before, that was women who sold themselves to men, sleeping with them and the men gave them money for it, but I had never taken it seriously, as if it was something which existed at all. Now here I was! What next? I came all the way over here searching for peace and love, thinking that my luck might be here, now I slipped and I had fallen down in the hole, I didn't know how I was going to come out of it, I didn't know that I was going to the land of prostitutes! Did I come here to become one of them? Now would I be a prostitute, or would I go somewhere else again, maybe another place, or another country? What next?

I was listening when they had their stories about the big things they did back home, what they were building, and so on, but to me, I was never going to be one of them, no matter what. I didn't know anyone around there yet, but still I had to have hope. I was surprised to see that neither Zena or Rose ever tried to put me in training for prostitution. For whatever reason, they did not introduce me or try to force me to do their job. In my heart I thanked them for that, or maybe they were giving me time. Rose didn't forget me, one day she called me to her home and when I was there she told me that she wanted me to go to her home the next day in the morning. She said that there were Rwandan people who she had asked to come and talk to me and see if they could help me by showing me the way of getting registered with the United Nation High Commission as a refugee. Being registered by them meant that they gave support for different things, money for food and even support for studying.

I went back with big hope that God, my God, was still guiding me, I could see that I was going to get out of this hole of Sodom and Gomorrah. The next day I went by myself, Zulia was at school, but I told her to pray for me whatever she was doing, and she was very happy for me even though we didn't know yet what was going to happen. On the other hand she was worried that she was going to be alone again.

At her home when they came, I was there waiting for them. She told them that she was asking them to help me.

There had to be questions and answers.

They asked her what she wanted them to help me with. After telling them the kind of help she was asking for, all of them said that things had changed, it was not as easy as before. After they had gone, Rose was not happy and she told me that she would get others, that those people were the drunken people of the area. I saw that she was not happy to see that I was there doing nothing and she had no intention of introducing me to her job, which made me love her more.

The next day Rose came with a Rwandan woman, she asked her for the same help and she gave her the same answer, like what the men had given her. And this made me start to lose hope.

I asked Zulia to give me an idea, I told her that I had some money, and I was tired of sitting doing nothing, that I was thinking of starting to sell something outside, where others were selling their things.

"Here in Kenya it is not like that."

"It's not like what?"

"Kenyans can't let you do that near where they are selling theirs, people here they are racist, and that is one of the reasons why you don't see foreigners do any kind of business."

"What can they do if someone else did it?"

"They can do whatever, abuse and bully in many ways and you can go by yourself or they can tell you openly that you have to go."

"OK then what if I sell my things in front of our door?"

She laughed in loud voice and said, "It could destroy Mum's business, the men can't get where they want to go without having to pass where people are there coming to buy, and also when Mum locks the door they can steal your things." At that point we laughed together, we had a long time without a good laugh.

"What it means now, is that I have to be here running here and there in the name of playing?"

"Don't lose hope, I too have not lost it yet, you can't know about tomorrow."

WHEN I MEET NYILIMANZI

In that area there was a young man and his name was Nyilimanzi, he was one of the few people who were doing something, and he had respect for that. He was repairing different things in homes in the women's area. Drunken men, who had little free money which was a benefit from U.N..H.R, they spent their money on beer mostly, and they were not bothered themselves about doing those kinds of jobs. Even foreigners feared trying to do small jobs like sweeping, shoe shining…and others. Since they knew that they could be in trouble with native Kenyans, this made them lazy too, and it was a good excuse to become drinkers, after finishing their money, they had to start begging people who had jobs.

I thought that was because of two reasons, they feared native people because of their racism and hatred towards foreigners from other African countries at the time, and that situation of having a little free money that they had from the U.N. made them different to the other Rwandans who were in other neighbouring countries, there Rwandans were known to be hard-working people. But in that drunken way they had a strong unity, each month it was a must that some of them would go to prison because of different reasons related to being drunk. It was a law in the country to put away drunken people from the streets, especially at night, in the name of giving peace to society. Many saw it as a kind of income to the government, a way of getting money from people, and it was an easy way for police officers to get free money for themselves from people.

In prison, there was money that drunkards had to give afterwards to take them to court, which was known to everyone as 20 K.sh if the drunken one didn't make any arguments with the judge at the first hearing. But police officers always took someone to prison only if the person refused to give them a bribe, maybe because he didn't have money left to give them or simply he was too drunk to bother, something which was known as 'kitu kidogo' in Swahili, meaning small thing, this was how they used to call it when they asked for it. Sometimes policemen at night time could just stop people in the street, and ask them for 'kitu kidogo', even when they were not drunk, and if you had money with you, that was a bad day for you, it was better to go to prison and simply say that you were drunk, even if you had never tasted beer in your life. There was no kind of testing to see if you were drunk or not, and police had to be right in whatever they said.

People would sometimes make fun of police officers, saying that when their wives had no food to cook, and it was night time, they were telling them to get the pot ready for cooking, they were coming back with food, when they had no money themselves. It was a sure thing that they were going to get free money from passersby.

In the name of 'kitu kidogo', as far as he was in uniform and had a gun.

Since then, Kenya was among the countries which were most corrupt in almost everything, and everywhere you went, you had to be aware of 'kitu kidogo'. In all stages of life, like going to school for your children, to getting a job, to getting some important papers even passports, in different businesses too. And sometimes you could see someone borrow money to go to bribe people for this and that, or otherwise your things would be there without having to move anywhere.

So concerning this problem of 'kitu kidogo', it was like a business itself, if there were other people who wanted the same thing, and would be able to give bigger money than you, then it was you who would be a loser, you would lose your money and your time, because you would not be told that you would get nothing, instead you would be told to come tomorrow, tomorrow for months! If you were a woman sometimes an officer would want to sleep with you, to do for him what he wanted from you, he would try to show you, so that you would understand what he wanted from you, or he would tell you openly that he wanted to go out with you. It would be your choice, you could go with him or you would never get what you wanted full stop. Or simply you would be told the same thing, to come tomorrow, tomorrow, tomorrow, and that tomorrow would never come.

You could see when you went to the government offices, how people sat in the queue, someone could come in the morning and be told to come back in the evening. It could be like that for many days until other staff came to know you like you too were staff. Sometimes there was no other place where you could get what you wanted, so you would be there wasting the little money you had on transport, and sometimes the officer was not in the office for many hours. Some had systems, where they would go and leave their coat on their chair to show people that they were around, when they went about their personal business, and things like that. This was a kind of corruption, which made people sit in one place doing nothing, when they had different things to do, but you could see how those officers looked happy and proud to show people their power. If they would not give so and so what she or he wanted, then there was nowhere else they could get it from. I believed that behaviour like that was one of the things which would hold back our continent.

In Kenya, corruption was known to be everywhere even in the international airports, passengers were aware of that, until 2002 when president Mwai Kibaki promised his people and the whole world in general that he was going to fight and finish 'kitu kidogo' in all steps of life, something he did for a short time, and after that it was like it had been before, or worse.

In that area, when one of those drunken people was caught by the police, their friends had many ways to know that they had been arrested, most of the time they would be told by someone. Through experience, they knew when and where they would take him to court, and they would be ready to go there to give that 20 K.sh as a fine to let him free.

When they came back with their friend they had to go for a drink to celebrate getting him out, and sometimes they might catch them again when they came back home, this was their life, to them it was normal.

In the group of Rwandans which were in that area, Nyilimanzi was their boss because he had the U.N.'s money, and his own money, so when they finished their benefits they would go to him. And sometimes he was driving other people's cars as a taxi man; in general he was a hard-working man.

Nyilimanzi was a handsome young black man, tall, six foot or more, slender with black soft hair, they had nicknamed him Murefu, meaning tall person, some were calling him Somali because he looked like the Somali people.

Within no time he started to bring things home like food and give them to Zena by telling her that it was for her visitor, and Zena was very happy with that, one day Nyilimanzi came and asked Zena's permission to take us to watch a movie. She said yes, and we were happy because to go away from that area gave Zena time for her work, sometimes, if not all times, we had a stressful life, a life of running here and there always, when we came from the movie he asked us if we could pass his home and we said yes, because we knew that the more time we stayed away, the more time Zena had for herself.

At his home, his house was like the houses of those women and was in the line of other houses which were for the prostitutes. I think that is how all of that area had to be.

In his house he gave us food and drinks, since then he used to take us almost every evening. The movie was near there in the hall, and now it was our place of refuge, we would not go around that area anymore, and when he didn't come we were asking ourselves what had happened to him.

One day, Zena said that she wanted to talk to me, and when I went she told me that Nyilimanzi gave her my message, that he loved me and he would like to have me as his wife. When she finished she posed a little and started to talk again, "You know Bamurangirwa I don't see any

250

problem with being his wife, because he is not like those drunken men here, he can take very good care of you, so go and think about it, you will give me the answer after." I was confused then and surprised, before I wondered why he was doing all he was doing, and I thought that it was because he was our friend. I had no idea that he was doing it because of me, maybe because I had no feelings towards him that is why I had not had that idea before.

It seemed that Zena gave me the question and at the same time she was suggesting the answer for me!

I had many questions now, I was asking myself if maybe she was tired of taking care of me and probably wanted to put me aside. And she may have wanted to have her freedom back, and she might already have told him that I was in her hands so he didn't have to worry he would have me.

I saw that I hadn't had a chance yet to get to know other people from other areas, I had not even found a way of knowing those U.N. offices, and if Zena was fed up with me, if I refused her idea she might put me out. Next I would be forced to join them and start drawing my face depending on how good I would be able to draw it, and sit out waiting for numbers of men to sell myself to them. What choices I had now were either to go with Nyilimanzi or go with a thousand strange men.

I would go with Nyilimanzi, with the hope that still was not going to be my end, the time would come when I would come out of this place. I had no time or way of knowing his behaviour and I had no choice.

The next day when she asked me what I said about me and Nyilimanzi, I told her that it was OK, I would go. She was overjoyed and it surprised me, I thought that she might have sold me, because one day Zulia told me that women there sold girls, but still, I had nowhere to go.

Then she said that a small ceremony would be the next day so that other men couldn't take me. The only thing which I had seen which was good in him was that he was not drinking, since I hated drinking and violence, maybe because I had not yet come across any of that kind of behaviour before. In general my family had good behaviour, I had never seen my mother and my father arguing in any way, if they did then it was one of their secrets. Although my father did punishing the children, but to everyone I was like the queen. Then I told myself that I would see the other side of his behaviour, with hope that it would not be bad. I did not like to drink, I hated to see people behave in strange ways and make excuses for their behaviour because of beer. I told myself it was better not to drink at all, something which surprised my family and made them happy, for the youngest in the family to be the only one to decide not to drink or smoke.

I was a refugee in Nyilimanzi's house as his wife, I had run away to become a prostitute and hide myself in a prostitute's land. I had an idea that if Nyilimanzi was a good man we could build ourselves and move from there. I didn't like the place for everything, he was poor, but Rwandan, and young, and hard-working. He might have known that we had to look forward, and knew that we had to remember back home, but we couldn't do anything about home if we didn't manage ourselves first.

I would have married a non-Rwandan only for two reasons, the first for love and the second for money. Tutsi girls who went for money without love in the neighbouring countries like Uganda, Tanzania Congo, and Burundi were ten percent or more. After seeing how their husbands took very good care of them, with a lot of respect, by giving them peace and freedom, and trusting and believing in them, and loving their people, then the good behaviour of those men helped the women to learn to love them, they had what they wanted, like any other Rwandan girl at the time. It happened in big numbers, as I said before, the Tutsi girls used their beauty and good background, which helped them as well as their good behaviour, sharp mind and their beauty. Those who married non-Rwandans, many times were like survivors, it was a kind of war to save their people, that is how their brothers and young sisters were able to go to school and be in the high life. It was a kind of sacrifice, they had to do anything to see that their

252

parents were happy, they didn't know about prostitution and couldn't do it. Yes it was a big test in their life, if they wanted to turn themselves into prostitutes because of their beauty then maybe it would be easy for them, but still they needed their respect, and they didn't know anything about it at the time. They thought that it was dirty, something which was for non-respected people, up until now some of them saw it that way.

Before, Rwandans would see their daughters as second class, because at the end they would go and belong to other strange families and they didn't go to the front line. That was how it was known at the time, but after 1959, most of the families who had daughters were much better and happier than those who had only boys, and they won a lot of respect and showed that they could fight for their families too, even better than their brothers. For this, Rwandans were like others in many parts of the world, knowing girls as second class citizens, although it was still better compared to some other parts, because they gave them some kind of respect by saying that even at the end they could go to belong to other families, but that was also a strong way to build unity with wider families, and it was always known that women couldn't do hard work.

In Kenya there was a small number of Rwandans compared to neighbouring countries to Rwanda, and most of them were young. In the big cities, especially Nairobi and Mombasa, most of them were there in different colleges studying this and that. There was a lot of opportunity for study. Their daughters, like anywhere else, met non-Rwandan men in many different ways, some were in the family as househelpers, child care, and so on. In the end, the wife who was supposed to be their boss was out and the Rwandan girl would take over if the wife saw that she wouldn't be able to compete with that Rwandan girl. Others met in colleges, offices or through friends or when they went out at night, that is how they met white men too, it was easy to be recognised because of their looks.

When they saw that the men had what they wanted, but maybe the men had a bad side somehow, in their character or in other ways, and it was hard to manage, she would do whatever she could to change him on her way. It was easy to them, they would not use force, just through love, respect, and taking things easy. But at first it was not easy on the girls' side, with these non-Rwandan men, outside Rwanda and back inside Rwanda with Hutu men. Hutu men competed to have them, because as soon as the men saw that they had money, to prove it was to go out with a Tutsi girl. Although many times their parents and their brothers were not in a good situation, and they knew that they were doing all of it for their sake, but they were not comfortable with it, they still had their pride. You could hear them when their daughter or sisters were expecting to have a baby with a non-Rwandan husband, or some Hutu husband, they would say that they wished their daughter to have a child who looked like them and not like the husband. To our people, the look of some other people was a problem. And yes, in the first place a big number of non-Rwandan men wanted the Tutsi girls with the hope that they would give them good-looking children! The time came when the Rwandan government made a law that meant that any man who worked with the government didn't have to marry a Tutsi girl. They couldn't trust them enough in their life concerning political matters, and secondly, their daughters had no men to marry them. But still they had them as mistresses, and the men would take good care of their Tutsi mistress's family more than their Hutu wife's, and still they couldn't go out with their Hutu wife unless it was a government's ceremony.

After time, life came to be seen as normal to both sides. That was how it started, anyone who had a daughter could be proud of her more than before. In big cities like Bujumbura, Kampala, Dar es Salaam, Nairobi and Mombasa that is where they started to get Senegal men and others, some Kenyans too, but only those who were known to be money makers, that was the benefit. They had no full trust in Senegal men, not enough to let their daughters go with them to Senegal, they were worried about what could happen to them if they took them there, and yes it happened to some families when the husband didn't take the wife back in Senegal, but took their children. For those children who were taken by their fathers, some were kidnapped from their mothers, they would do whatever they wanted to them and their mothers would never see them again!

They were always happier when their daughters and their sisters married white men, they trusted them for everything, let alone money, to that point, they believed that white people were the money's creature. And to go with their daughters or sisters was not a worry to them, instead they saw it as a blessing, they were sure that they would be safe with white men wherever they would take them, more than Senegal or Nigerian men! Rwandan girls began to intermarry, they became international.

Many times it was only white men who had something to do in Africa, at that time, it was only them who had a chance to be in that part of the continent of Africa, because of different reasons. For most of those who were married to them, they did everything they could to give the in-laws a happy and modern life, like building good houses for them, giving them helpers at home, and allowing the young ones to go to school. Sometimes they would give them some kind of business to stand for themselves.

After 1966 and the fall of Kabaka Mutesa, Obote took over in 1966 since then Uganda was in the hands of North East Ugandans until 1986 when Museveni took over. At that time of twenty years it was the North men who had power, and it was North men who had Tutsi girls too. Like Kakwa, Lango, Acholi and Lubgara. You can call it what you like, gold digger, or survival, but we were blessed to be loved, and we reached our goals, and that was the war.

My wedding was a small ceremony, Zena looked busy and happy, and she was proud according to the way she was talking to everyone who was invited and making sure that they knew that I was her young sister.

Being at home with my husband was OK, but it could be happier if we were able to move somewhere else and he seemed that he was not that happy to be in that area either. Why he was there for such a long time I had no idea, the fact that it was a cheap area seemed to be a reason, but it was a very bad area too. He had fear that he might not get what he wanted to do in a new place and it could be expensive for him. After three months with him, he told me that there were Indian men in town who sold second-hand cars, he asked me to go with him and act as if it was me who wanted to buy the car, so that maybe he might respect me and trust me, and give me the car and allow me to pay him in resettlement. If he would give us the car he would use it as tax, and would pay the rest and save others. The businessman was not hard to convince, he told us to choose the car we wanted, I had the driver with me, Nyilimanzi, and we went with our car and he was my taxi man, and we had the money. It was me who was keeping the money inside the house, though I had an idea of telling him to save the money in the post office because that was what I knew.

Now I had hoped that we would start to look around where we could move to, that place was bad place in many different ways. Our house was in a line of another three which were for those women who were there for their business, the business of prostituting themselves, unlike Zena's place, ours was opposite a mosque. Between the mosque and our doors there was a small space which was a way for people to pass by, and when two people met one had to stop and wait to give the other space to pass first. It was a small line of drain which they made where dirty water passed from the mosque, and which we also used to pour the dirty water from inside our houses too.

We had a neighbour who had a big house with a big compound. Khadija, she was a business woman, she had many good houses which she was renting, she was there with her family, she was a respected lady in that area, my three neighbouring women would not go anywhere like me, not to fetch water or to go to have a shower in the city council toilet, or to the toilets at all. So about having water, there were people too high to bring water for them. Most of the prostitutes were not seen outside far from their houses, maybe they didn't want to go out and lose customers. Concerning having a shower, I was no longer going to have them in the toilet. I had started to have baths using a kind of wide container inside my room, but I still had to go to the toilet, I was always asking myself what my neighbours did.

One day, I came to see and know why my neighbours didn't bother to go out to the toilet at all. It was because they helped themselves to do everything in their containers, urine and faeces, and poured it in to that drain in front of our doors! I knew then that was what all of them did.

I too was only going out when I went to fetch water and when I was going to the toilet but only when I wanted to get rid of faeces, otherwise concerning urine – I started to use the container and pour it in that drain too. But the good thing was that the drain was in a very good condition, and all of that place was cemented up to the dust road, which we called the main road. It seemed that the drain was the work of the mosque builders, so all the dirty water was going without problems.

I had no friends, Zena and Rose had no time to visit me, sometimes Zulia would come to say hello for a short time. I was staying in for months without talking to anyone else apart from Nyilimanzi. I didn't want to be seen outside because men could see me as if I was on the work too. I was listening to the radio from morning to night. I came up with the idea of starting to make bags, or tablecloths, and bed covers, instead of locking myself inside that small room, sitting or sleeping and doing anything to protect myself from the men who came to buy women.

I had a hope that when I had been with Nyilimanzi for some time I would learn to love him, but I didn't, although I didn't hate him either. I had to go through the days and wait to see what tomorrow would come up with.

Kagimbangabo and Higiro were telling other Rwandan people who were in other areas that Nyilimanzi had a Rwandan wife. They started to visit us slowly, we had visitors, and I always had food to offer my visitors. I was very happy when I started to have people in my home, Nyilimanzi had no shame to see that sometimes respected people visited us there, what I had to do was to make sure that my small room was clean. I asked him to buy another mattress in case we would get visitor who came from far and would spend the night there, which he did. Sometimes people were asking him in front of me, how he got a girl like me and why he kept me in such an area, something which sometimes made him proud that people said that he had a beautiful wife, and other times it was embarrassing and he was angry saying that they would make me feel that he was not good enough for me. I didn't know when I would be in a different life, I was missing my family back in Uganda, especially the children, and my father in Tanzania, I missed Mukabagira too. I decided to tell them in brief how I was, whatever my life was.

They were happy to hear from me, I only told my family that I was alive and I was in Nairobi, Kenya, and was married to a Rwandan man. I told Mukabagira how life was in brief, she was happy to hear from me and she wrote back telling me that her husband had passed away but she couldn't tell me more in the letter. She told me that in a foreign land, no matter what, it was not your home, sometimes you would come across things which reminded you of your home. Nyilimanzi started to come home late at night, I was worried thinking that something had happened to him, he seemed like he had started some college and was going step by step. The next step, he started to come home when he was drunk, and go straight to bed quietly. I started to ask myself if I would be able to manage a drunken man.

But I had heard the stories from the elder ladies that proper women were the ones who could be patient with their husbands, fighting for their marriage no matter what, and keeping secret the mistakes they saw in their marriage. They said that men sometimes had different bad behaviour, and there were some which was worse, and it could be bad enough to break the marriage. If a man was not a drunk he could be a wife beater, or he could be a womaniser who was a cheater, or who would tie you at home and not give you money to buy food, or give you very little which was not enough, when sometimes he had a lot of money and he took the money to other women and to buy beer. Or when men had their wife working, they would command them to give them all their money, and be the one who would budget for everything. On the other hand they would do that by force in an

258

indirect way, the lady would say yes so that she could get peace in her home, or the man may have brainwashed her and she would believe that because he was a man, she had to do whatever he said or something else could happen... that was when he had managed to build some kind of fear in her head, this was a kind of abuse. And he would use her money to buy beer outside... or let her do everything at home alone, he wouldn't help her only because he was a man.

Then I told myself that so long as he didn't beat me, and he bought a lot of food, on top of that it was me who was keeping the money, whatever he was doing outside didn't matter much. I had to be a proper woman like others and fight for my marriage.

The next step was the problem of becoming insecure, seeing that any man could take me from him, from nowhere he started to be jealous with me, it was not understandable why he started to change. One time he would come home with his friends, after they went I would hear him asking me why so and so was looking at me too much, or why when I greeted him he had my hands for a long time! I chose not to answer such questions. When some of his friends came and left me his messages, when I gave him his messages, sometimes it would be a good reason for him to start his questions by asking me why he had come when he was not there, that he knew everything about us!

The next time when someone gave me his message there were big questions for me, whether to tell him or not, but since I couldn't tell visitors to keep quiet, and I had to tell him anyway, because when they would meet he would ask him about the message he left with his wife, so I used to let him talk, until he was tired and kept quiet.

The next step was when he came home and I was at the toilet, maybe fetching water or just going to the toilet, he would say that he knew that I said I went there as an excuse, but he knew that I was going to meet my boyfriends! For that point I was angry to hear all of those accusations, when I had never even talked with any other man in that area and I didn't even have that intention. I thought that maybe it was his way of scaring me, so that I would never think about it, but he was using the wrong way. I wished that none of his friends would talk about my beauty, especially when we were together, maybe that was what made him crazy.

The next step was to come home very late, but now it was with a high noise from afar, so that in that way I was hearing him before he reached the house. Inside the house he was not quiet like before, he was talking in a loud voice until he fell asleep.

I was feeling sorry for my neighbours and felt ashamed too. It went on and on and my neighbours waited to see if I would tell them about my problems concerning the noise they would always hear at night. Maybe they wanted to give me counselling or sympathy, but I didn't tell them anything. I was sure that they were surprised with that, maybe they didn't expect that I would be the person who could manage to be patient up to that level.

The next step was that when he was late coming back I had no worries, instead I wished that he would be there the whole night. I was worried about his noise when he came back.

The next step was when he beat me too hard, saying that he knew that I would leave him for another man and he knew that man already! Something which surprised me since I had never seen grown-up people fight or beat each other. I had only seen my father beat children to discipline them, but I had heard stories of men who were called useless men, who would beat their wives. So I saw him to be one of those useless men then, and I couldn't have children with him because I didn't see a future together, but I didn't have a way of protect myself from that, since I couldn't go to the hospital by myself without him.

Sometimes when I came from outside, men were coming with me to inside the room, thinking that I too was selling myself like the others, and I had to tell them to go back outside and make them understand, sometimes it was not easy. I had to ask one of my neighbours to come and help me. When she was helping me to talk with that man, she was laughing, but I was scared to death, because I knew that if Nyilimanzi saw him inside then it could be a big problem to me. He couldn't even remember that no real man would keep his wife in a line of prostitutes!

One day he was at home in the evening time and he was sober,

Khadija, who I knew only by seeing her outside and greeting her, knocked and she didn't wait to be welcomed inside. When she was inside the room, she greeted us and called him by name. "Nyilimanzi, I am hiring your car to take you out with your wife. I am not asking permission because I know that you can't give it to me, so I am commanding you. I want to take this young woman who you have already killed emotional, you don't deserve a girl like her, you know that."

I was scared, thinking that he would think that I had told Khadija about him!

I was expecting him to become angry, but instead he looked shy and down to earth in front of Khadija. I thought that sometimes Khadija would hear his noise when she passed in front of our door, or my neighbours had told her my stories. She seemed like she had that plan of taking me out before and she didn't give him time to talk. She went ahead by asking him, "How could you be comfortable to lock this child inside this room with a council toilet? This girl looks to come from a well off family, can't you see it and change the situation for the better?" I wanted to tell her that he also beat me, I felt like a lost child who had seen a parent after a lot of suffering, I wanted to hold her and not let her go without me forever. I wanted to cry and cry louder and tell her that too, but I was not brave enough to do that.

The good thing she did was that she said, "Look Nyilimanzi, even a fool can see that, this life is not for someone like her, it is not surprising to see that she can't tell anyone her situation, it is because she sees that there is no one who is on her level, who she can talk to."

All of that time he was quiet, Khadija saw that I was not moving and knew that I was scared of him and she told me to make myself ready. After a short time she told me again, "Look Bamurangirwa, just make yourself ready, if you come back and he has a reason to shout at you, I will take you and I will take more good care for you. It is me who volunteered to take you and both of you can drink and eat anything you want. I will pay for everything for you this evening, but just so your husband knows that I am doing all of this because of you.

I want to see you at least happy for a few minutes; I am going to tell my husband we will go together."

She went to her home, when she left Nyilimmanzi told me to make myself ready, by saying "You know Khadija, when she says something she means it, just do it quick in case she thinks that it is me who refused you to do so."

Khadija was the one who was directing him where to take us, we went many different places and all of us ate and we drank what we wanted, and we went dancing too. I was dancing with my husband or her husband, then she told me to sit with her, and told me that I didn't have to dance only with our men, also anyone who would come to ask me if I liked him. I had to feel free. That is why I was there. All of them were drinking beer, and I was drinking soda.

I started to dance with different good-looking young men with Khadija's permission, they were coming and asking her in a highly respectful way, if they could dance with her daughter, they were taking me and bringing me back to her.

Nyilimanzi came to where I was when Khadija went to dance and tried to make me drink beer, when I told him that I didn't drink beer and I had no reason to try it that day, he said that, then I could taste it and know how it was, and if maybe I became drunk then there would be no problem because I was with them. I refused completely then he gave up.

The time came when all of us wanted to go back but Khadija had to ask me first, if I wanted to go home. I said yes, I felt relaxed and happy, I didn't want to go back in that room, but I had to go. I thanked her very much, it was my first time to go to another area, let alone to go out in all of those wonderful places.

At home, my Nyilimanzi asked me why I refused even to taste beer. I told him that it was because I had never tried it, and I saw that it was not necessary to taste it since I was missing nothing.

He kept quiet and I thought that was because he was a drinker, he wanted me to be drinking together with him.

The next day I came to know that I was expecting a baby: I was not happy but I decided to go on and have my baby, though I would also go ahead by trying to see if I would be able to get away from him, from that room and from that area. Unless he would change and move from there, even if he could change and be a better man, but still stay there, it was not an area to bring up a child and it simply was not a good area for anything.

When he gave me a horrible night, in the morning he would go shopping for me, he would buy expensive dresses and a lot of food, and sometimes I had to give that food to my neighbours. Maybe he believed that things would make me happy and forget what he did at night, which was very wrong.

He didn't want me to have any friends, men or women, by saying that they can would teach me bad manners.

At that time he changed, he would not come late or makes noise, but he was still drinking and he would be drunker.

I had not yet had anyone tell me what I could do at the labour ward, I had only the stories which I had heard from my elders who said that when a woman was in labour, they had to be patient and wait, they didn't have to make noises or scream, because, that was the pride of women and it was the respect we had been given by God, for us to be a mother.

At Pumwani maternity hospital, I went to my appointment, and they refused to let me go back home. I started to get pains, but I had to keep quiet so that I could be a proper woman like my mother, but there were other mothers who screamed a lot, and I saw that it was because we had different cultures, and maybe that was how their aunties and mums had taught them. When I was calling the woman, a midwife who was there, to my surprise they were hushing me and telling me to keep quiet! Some were looking at me and shouting at me as if they could even slap me.

But they were going to help those who were screaming. The time came when it was afternoon and I couldn't even scream if I wanted too! I saw one young nurse who was not there before, I called her using a sign and she came quickly and started to help me, with her help I got my baby, and she told me that my child was big, and was a boy, but he didn't cry so she ran with him. She came back to give me full help and she told me that my son was too tired and they were helping him as soon as they finished they would bring him to me. I thought that if I lost my son, I could have killed those women who were there before her.

After a few hours my son passed away, and there came an Asian young man who told me that he was a doctor, I didn't know his name, he came to apologise. He said, "It was a mistake by our staff, it is lucky that you were saved."

My husband was good, we were together in the loss of our son, he was finished paying up the car and I thought that it was time to build ourselves, but it was his time to go back to his habits one by one as he had started before.

I told myself that I didn't know anyone yet who could help me and take me out of there, but if he would beat me again, I was not going to wait for another one, twice would be bad enough to make me go even without knowing where I was going again. Although, this time I would go where I knew I could go back to my family, now I was sure that they knew that I was not the same girl I was before who could be told to do this and that as they wished, I was no longer that child. I would do what I saw to be better for me first, if there was no fear of Nyilimanzi, I could stay there in Nairobi and try the U.N. business like others, but I was scared of him, that he would give me some problems or could even kill me.

He was in a group of all the known drunken men in the area, only he was better than them because he was always looking smart, had a wife and a car, and so he was their boss, and he was proud of that, so there were no more savings, most of the money was for beer.

The next step was to command me that I would be cooking for his friends every day, it was hard work but I was happy to be with people every day, with hope that they would be coming before he was drunker.

And it showed me that they had permission to come even when he was not at home. Their break time from beer was when they were in prison. When the time came of going to court for one of them, Nyilimanzi had to stop going to work, because all of them had to be there. I had to know about their timetables, concerning their court and prison dates, they were telling me everything because I was pretending to be sorry for them, and it was making them happy and they saw me as a good person. After trusting me and telling me about their times, I started to go round town which meant that I was able to give myself chance to know the town. I told myself that I didn't have to wait to be beaten again, it was better to go before.

I thought that a good day and time would be a day when they would have to go to court, they didn't know that their problems could be a profit to me. So I started to keep aside some money which I was saving for him, I started to tell him less amounts of money I had. He didn't bother much about that.

In the city centre of Nairobi at the time, on a roundabout there was a small shelter which the police officers would stand in and direct cars, they would use their arms to direct the cars. When Kagimbangabo passed one of the empty shelters in the city centre, he said that he was a good dancer before, and he could dance better than the policemen who stood there, so he stood inside the shelter and started to dance as a Rwandan culture dancer, using his arms here and there in the air, and there were big accidents which involved many cars because of him!

When the police officers came he told them that he was dancing better than them, and drivers wanted to dance with him using their cars, instead of going where they had to go. His case was far different from their normal cases, and they knew that it would be complicated and might take more time. I thought that had to be my time, I had to use that chance to go to Uganda. I was sure that they would have to be out almost the whole day.

The day came and Nyilimanzi went even without having breakfast by saying that he was late. I wanted him to go quickly and give me time to prepare myself. I helped him with his preparation so that he could go as soon as possible, and without forgetting anything which would make him have to come back.

After seeing that he had left, I started to prepare myself quickly. One of my friends had forgotten one of her long black dresses at my home, which she covered all of her body with, even her face when she wanted too. And I had planned that I would use it, I was hoping that she would not come to take it before that.

After dressing myself I covered myself with the black dress from head to toe, I was sure even if Nyilimanzi met or travelled with me, he would not know me, ever. I was laughing inside my black dress; saying that my black dress had saved me a lot. I didn't talk to anyone on my way in to town. I went to the train station and after being told that they had a train to Kampala the same day which would go in the evening time, I came back with my ticket. I started to pack my things knowing that in case by bad luck Nyilimanzi came back and found me packing he might kill me by believing that I was going to another man. He was talking about killing me whenever he was drunk, maybe he thought that he was showing me that he loved me so much by saying things like that, that if he saw me with another man he would kill both of us and then kill himself. Sometimes I was thinking that maybe he had killed in the past, or it was easy for him to kill. I wished to go out of his room, out of that area and out of Kenya.

After putting everything away in a proper way, so that he could get what he needed without any trouble, I went to get a taxi. It was near our home. I went and came with one, and gave one of our neighbours Yudita the key and that black dress and told her who she would give the dress to for me, and the key was for Nyilimanzi. Although we didn't talk, she looked happy, she seemed to understand clearly what I was doing. I knew that they felt sorry for me, even though we were not talking or anything, but you could know people in other ways, just by looking at them.

I went to the train, I knew that he would come later, by that time the train would be gone, when I was on my way, I was saying in my heart that this was a game I played to Nyilimanzi, it would show him that when someone is quiet it doesn't mean that the person is deaf or blind, or that person is stupid.

I went to the train station, I went where there were other passengers and sat with them, I bought newspapers. I started to read for the first time since I came to Kenya. I saw myself like I had been in prison, but my heart hoped that the train would come, and I wished that I could change time and it would go quicker.

The time came for the train to start its journey I knew that if he wanted to come he could reach my family, I was talking about them a lot, but I didn't see why he would struggle to come there, it would be better if he could be happy to have his freedom with his friends. In the train the passengers were clean and smart people.

In Kampala where the train stopped it was like the underground, it was a cleaner place than the train station in Nairobi, there were a few people who had different small businesses, and there were young men who did the business of carrying bags for passengers. One young man carried my bag and when we were out we started arguing about payment. I heard someone telling me in Kinyarwanda that he would help me! I was surprised that anyone would know that I was Rwandan in all of those people, I had to look up to see who this could be, I saw that the parson was Nyilimanzi, he was looking down at me with a little smile, a smile which was asking me if I thought that I was the only person who was clever. He was clever too, and now we were together.

I panicked for a short time and then told myself to be strong, that I was in Uganda not Kenya, he would go back himself without me, if he wanted his money, fine, I was going to give it back to him there and then. I had other money aside, and I still had a little money in my savings in the post. I was not going to be scared of him.

After deciding, I told myself to answer him and start to deal with him in a way which was going to surprise him since he had never heard me answer back to him.

I paid the boy, and it was him and I, he was insisting to help me; I asked him where he was taking me?

"Where that boy was taking you."

"This is my journey, I will handle it the way that suits me, I have no need for your help."

"Can you tell me why you came without telling me?"

"Because it was not necessary."

"I came to take you back home now."

"That is your home, I didn't leave anything behind, and if I am to go anywhere it will have to be my decision, not the decision of anyone else. Here I am home, although it is not Rwanda, but in Uganda I have my people here, so it is my second home then. Kenya has nothing for me, so you better go back to your home."

He looked shocked; I think he thought that I couldn't say no to him for anything.

He changed his story by saying that if I refused to go back with him, then we would go together to see my family, and see the next step from there! According to my culture, for a man like him who didn't know my family yet, I had to go to introduce him to them in good preparation which would be an official way.

But now I was going with him on which level? After failing to convince him to go back to Kenya and leave me alone, I tried to remind him about our culture, and he said that he would tell them that he came to know them and next time he would come to do whatever was supposed to be done.

I told him that I didn't want him to lie to them; I decided to be the one who would lie to them.

I knew the answers I would get from my sisters if I told them everything, that I was fed up with my marriage, that I was not going back with my husband, they would tell me to go and try, that was how marriages were. So I would have to be a visitor and tell them that we passed there to say hello but we were coming from somewhere else for business. And we would come back for an official visit.

And I would go back with him this time, I was going to show him that I could do anything, if he did not change and be the man I wanted, time would give me other ideas.

We had to reach Kantamage's home first, since she was the one who was near. We surprised her and she was happy to see me, she asked me if this man was my husband and I said yes he was, she did whatever she could do, like anyone who received visitors she loved and gave respect for. The next day, there came many people to greet us, I was lucky that my father was there, he had come to visit them too.

All of them including Ngamije's family and their neighbours and friends they prepared to meet us in Mpanumusingo's home, there was a party with different local beers,

When I saw how they were happy, I wanted to be happy too, and forget why I came. Yes I was happy, I wanted to meet Mukabagira before going back to Kenya. We were there for one week, and when we went back, many people, neighbours and friends escorted us for some distance, some were laughing, others were crying, others just in different stories.

I was missing them again and loved them more, though I had my anger towards them which I would have forever, but not hatred, they were my family, and there was no one else who could be them to me.

On our way back to Kenya I was happy that I didn't tell anyone that I was going to Uganda for good, there was no one who would see me to be a funny person, no one who knew my plans, not even Nyilimanzi or my sisters where I came from. It was up to me and it was my life, and I loved myself, with God's help. I would do whatever was possible to see that I could shape my life.

On our way back we didn't have any arguments, I thought that he had got enough reasons, we had good conversations like friends, and he told me that I was too clever. I did all of that to force him to go and meet my family, since I knew that he might follow me, that is why I didn't tell them all of the wrong things he did to me.

It showed me that he knew all of the wrong things he did, when we were at home he was telling everyone how my family were good and rich, and they treated him with respect. I believed that he was going to give me proper respect for that.

He told everybody that he would not drink again, he wanted to change himself into a proper person.

I normally had no conversations with Udita, but then I had to talk to her, I had to tell her about my journey so that she could also tell me what happened between her and Nyilimanzi when she gaves him his key.

The next day after we reached home I told her everything and she was laughing or she could have been surprised. After finishing my story she started to tell me hers, that when she heard that he came she waited so that first she could hear what he said, and gave him the key after.

When he saw that I was not there he made a lot of noise, saying, "I was just guessing but now I got her, and she will come by escorted with that man so that I will get chance to know him, she has done this many times, I was a fool for all of this time."

She said, "Inside my room I was laughing, then I came out and stood behind him and told him to have his key which Bamurangirwa gave to me. He stood up like he was carried up by electricity and turned to me like he was going to hit me. I was scared for a second, I knew him to be crazy and that he could do it by saying that it was me who made you go where you had gone. Then I blamed myself for taking it when I knew him, then he started to ask me where you had gone and I told him that I didn't know."

She continued, "He asked me if you had a car or if you were with someone, but I told him that I was inside so I didn't know, he started to ask the children and the taxi men, then that is how he came after you."

He changed, he was coming home early and he started to be with friends who were respected people, that was the time when the Rwandan king Ndahindurwa J Kigeli, who was living in Nairobi, came to know that I was sister to Mpanumusingo, one of his followers at the time in Uganda. Kigeli started to send his people to visit me, and a few times he was coming himself and that made me ashamed, for him to see where I could show him to sit, according to his height and his look in general.

He was too tall maybe more than seven foot, big, but handsome too, to the level that wherever he was passing he had people behind him who admired him, to me, he was a giant too.

After a short time I found out that I was expecting a baby and my doctor told me to see him regularly, I had to obey him because I didn't want to lose my baby again, and this time I had a hope that my husband was becoming a proper husband, because he was telling me that he had started to look for a house elsewhere.

When I was heavily pregnant, to my surprise he started to go back to all his old habits again, by starting with drinking and saying that no woman could make him not drink. I knew that he was telling me that I couldn't change him in my way, he had to be who he was, no matter how hard I might try. So I thought that he saw that I was on my way to becoming a mother, and it would not be easy for me to go anywhere, that was the thoughts of many people at the time, they had the belief that as soon as a woman became a mother, no matter how bad the man would treat her, she couldn't go anywhere, she couldn't leave the father of their child for the sake of that child. Some believed that women couln't take care of their child or children by herself or that it would simply be happier for her child or children to grow up with both parents.

On my side, I had to be patient and have my baby, then get away from him, because I would not like to see my child grow up with a father like him. I was sure that I would get away, and be on my own, there in Nairobi. I would not go out of the country, just because of one person again, when I saw that I could get what I wanted there. Now it was only a matter of time.

My doctor had already told me that I might have complications at the time of delivering my baby, so I needed one of my sisters to be there for me at that time.

It was Kantamage who came to help me and I had my beautiful healthy baby boy, Manzi. I had to be at the hospital the whole week, when Kantamage visited me she was telling me that they were fine, and when Nyilimanzi visited me he looked too drunk, and shouted to the nurses that they had to take very good care of his wife in a special way, something which was upsetting me, and I wished that I could be happier if he didn't visit me at all. You could hear him telling those women that I had a proper home, they didn't have to think that I was a simple woman… maybe he thought that I was happy with things like that, but they were my friends, because since they killed my first born, I knew that they could do anything to patients, and I tried to be their friends. Sometimes they were telling me things, some things that you could think of as being a test to me, but I was so simple to them, and said yes to whatever they said, because I knew that I was in their hands, and they had the power over me, and I couldn't take them anywhere for whatever they could do to me. Sometimes some of them were telling me that I was different with my husband, wondering how I managed him. And I was telling them that he liked talking and I liked keeping quiet.

One day one of the nurses asked me if she could see how good my home was, she said that she would visit me, I smiled and told her to come and visit me. I knew that she couldn't get the time. When I thought of my home with the one room and the drain of dirt in front of my door.

I said that the law classed people, sometimes they tried to put themselves in high class levels by forcing in a foolish way, like what he was doing here, when the proper way was to work hard and reach where you were admired, not by talking. From the hospital my sister Kantamage asked me if this was how my husband and I always were. When I asked her what he meant she told me that he came almost every morning and daytime and most of the time he was drunk.

That is when I told her the truth about our journey to visit them and why I didn't tell them as my elder sisters at the time, otherwise that was how we were.

Kantamage said that by not telling them because I thought that they might tell me to go back and try, yes I was right. I had to try and see if I could hold my marriage, but when she went home it was better to go with her since no one was helping me there, so I could come back when I was strong enough to deal with my home.

When we were talking, Nyilimmanzi pushed the door wider and came in looking at us without saying anything, after a short time, he came to where I was sitting, breastfeeding the baby, and pulled up my hair, looking angry, he was asking me why these days I looked too proud of myself, was it because I had a baby, or was it because my sister was there? If I thought that he wouldn't hit me then I was lying to myself, he could use only one hit using his leg or his arm and it would be enough to reach me and that baby. I stood up and stood in the corner in the same place, there was no corner anyway. When my sister started to say something, the door opened, and one of his drunken friends came in, surprised to see the situation we were in. Because he heard him shouting at us, he held him and took him out, and asked him if he was mad, "How can you shout at the mother of your new baby in front of her sister?!" he said. We heard him tell his friend that it was the mother of the baby, not his mother!

I thought that this was my time to relax, now I had nothing to say, I had to take it easy until I was able to be on my own. When he came back he greeted us and went directly to sleep, you could think that he was a different person, not the same one who had been there in the evening time.

In the morning I told him about going with my sister and he was happy with the idea. The time came for us to go there to Kantamage's home. I was a new mother who was treated with good care and I was relaxed. I was there for one month and Nyilimanzi came to take me back home.

He told me that he got a driver so the car could be useful, he was also doing other things because now he was serious about moving from that area, he knew that I didn't like it there. Already people were looking for a house for us, he was fed up of that place now. I wanted to believe him but on the other hand I doubted him.

I thought that when he was doing the right things, after time it made him feel uncomfortable or unhappy and it was not easy to know why he was doing that over and over again.

Back home, after a very short time, he started to change again and go back where he was comfortable, he was no longer doing anything, and he was not using the car either. He wanted to be a proper boss, to have a driver and be able to buy beer, they started to go back to prison, it seemed like they had a break since I had a baby. The time came when it was the real time to say enough was enough, how would I manage to leave him when I was scared to death of him, and how would I manage my life on my own. By coming back I thought that I had waited to know him much better so that I was able to make a final decision. The more time passed, the more I knew him, day by day. I had my baby Manzi, and my sister's daughter Ilibagiza Jane, she was still a young child and I had come with her, so that I wasn't on my own, I took her to nursery school. Khadija knew that I was back, I was there for sometime when we would meet outside and say hello, I never went in her home, and she never came in to my home and sat like a visitor and had any conversations with me, but for some reason she liked me a lot. In that area, it was only her who had a different life and was rich, according to standards, maybe that was why people respected her too much and maybe feared her, they knew that she could do whatever she wanted at any time she wanted too. At that time in Kenya, if you had money, yes you could do anything, it was the money which held some laws. And I thought that she saw me as a victim, and saw that I didn't deserve to be there in that life, maybe that is why she liked me.

And when she knew that something went wrong she couldn't get time to call the person to talk in private, but she would say it there and then so they were trying to be careful to her, because they knew that she couldn't keep secrets for them.

I think she saw Nyilimanzi coming inside the house, she came behind him, we saw someone push the door without knocking, it was her in her long black dress which she had on most of the time, which covered her from head to toe.

Inside she greeted me, "How are you Bamurangirwa?"

"I am OK thank you, how are you?"

She didn't say another word to me and she turned to Nyilimanzi, "Nyilimanzi I see that you are still sober, don't drink, I am going to hire your car and I will buy you a beer. I want you to be our driver, I don't want to be given another driver. Today I will take Bamurangirwa out, I will be here at 6:00pm. I want to come when all of you are ready."

Nyilimanzi said, "But how can we leave the children by themselves?"

Khadija said, "I know that they are children, I will come with someone to take care of them, don't worry about that."

Nyilimanzi seemed like he was talking to himself when he was asking me, "But what do you do to make people like you this much, when you don't even talk to them?!" I didn't say anything and he chose a dress for me to wear, and he chose one which was bought by Alex and still looked like new. I wanted to laugh and he said that he was going to get a car from a driver, it was better to make myself ready in time so that Khadija didn't think that it was him who made me be late.

He came back before Khadija, when he looked at me he asked himself now, "Where could Khadija want to take you when you look beautiful like this." I kept quiet and said that if it was not for Khadija he could change his mind and refuse me to go anywhere. It was going to be the second time I was going to go out, only because of Khadija.

By the time Khadija was there I almost didn't recognise her she was so beautiful, I was used to seeing make up, and she had it on but not too much like the women there, she held up her long black beautiful hair which was thick like Japanese hair and styled it by tying it up with flowers. She wore a long shining dress which featured her waist and chest, it was wide from the hips down, it was sleeveless and open, she had decorated it with a big pure gold chain, which was on her beautiful wide chest, with earrings in the same style, and many gold bangles, with a soft scarf which was on her back, which matched her handbag and shoes, she looked fantastic. She came with a girl who would take care of the children.

When she saw me she looked happy and it was like she was talking by herself, "You look beautiful, my child, you are happy and relaxed now let me take you from this prison you call a house." She told us to wait for her for a few minutes, she went back and came back with two gold chains, and one big bangle, all gold. She showed me one, and said that she would give me that, the other one she wanted me to wear and the bangle, but those were hers and she was just lending me them. She told Nyilimanzi, "Buy gold for your wife, every woman has to wear gold." She took out the fake necklace I had on, "You have to learn to take care of your wife as your wife is not like a prisoner or servant. I heard you have seen where she comes from, I am sure you have seen that she comes from a proper family."

When we were in the car she said that her husband was in front, me and her were behind and she spoke like she was talking to herself when she said, "Maybe Bamurangirwa has not been out since the last time, if so, she can't know if there is anywhere she will not like, she will have to tell me. You understand Bamurangirwa you will tell me OK?"

"OK," I said, "I will be telling you."

At the first place there were a lot of people and I was at her side, instead of sitting beside of my husband, she was holding my arm and with her that was where I felt peace. All of them were drinking beer, Khadija suggested that I have some type of soda which I didn't know about but it was sweet.

When they started to put music on, there came a handsome young man, you could think that he was Khadija's son, he looked of Arabic decent or a mixture, he was tall and strong. He bent a little in front of Khadija and asked her if she could allow him to dance with her daughter, she gave him my hand, he held me and we disappeared between dancers. I told myself that by dancing with this handsome man, it was better to be happy and forget Nyilimanzi and his house for the time, that is what Khadija wanted, and that is why I was there. Then I was in his chest, quiet and peacefully he asked me if Khadija was my mum. I told him that she was my friend, I told him that I came with my husband. He told me that he was lucky to see me with Khadija so that he was able to dance with me.

He took me back to Khadija after the second song, after some time Nyilimanzi said that we should go somewhere else, Khadija asked me what I wanted to do and I told her that if she thought it was OK then fine, we would go. She said that there was a lot of noise so we could go somewhere else.

We went to another place and there were a few people there. We had a drink then Nyilimanzi called me where he was, and he told me again that it was better to drink beer because I had a lot of soda, it could cause a problem in my stomach. When I told him that I couldn't, he tried to insist but I refused. And yes, I had no interest in beer anyway. I was wondering why he was insisting on making me drink beer, maybe that was his way of showing me his love or he had another reason. I told myself that even if I had to taste it then I would never do that when I was with him.

Khadija called me and told me to dance with her husband while she went to dance with my husband.

I went ahead dancing with different men with Khadija's permission, and the time came that all of us were tired, and Khadija asked me if I was happy, and I said yes I was so happy I didn't know how I could thank her, and I meant it. She told me that I didn't have to let Nyilimanzi scare me out. I had to see her as my mum and go to her for anything, she was telling me all of that when all of us were still in the car.

At home, Nyilimanzi said that he saw that I was going to be a reason to make people give him respect. I didn't say anything.

The next day he went out as always, some time later I saw the door open without knocking and I thought that it was Nyilimanzi, but when I turned my head I saw someone else. I didn't know the name, but sometimes I saw him, he was working with Nyilimanzi, he was a taxi man. According the way he was looking at me, I thought that even if it was some message Nyilimanzi had given him for me, it made him so happy. I stood up, after greetings I was looking at him quietly and waiting to hear what had given him the wide smile, and made him enter in the house like that. I even forgot that it was his first time to enter my house.

When he started to tell me, he was talking in a high voice, still with a wider smile. "Come out and see if the visitor I have is yours, I am in hurry," he said. I was behind him and out the door, down where the car was, I was asking myself where my visitor might come from. Uganda, Tanzania or somewhere else. Anyone that might have come looking for me from Rwanda was out of the question. The small dust road which passed down past the houses was near my room, because it was me who was at the end of the other rooms. Outside I heard someone from the car calling my name repeatedly, she was already coming out from the car, running to where I was, when I saw her I was speechless, wondering how she came and knew where I was, there in Magengo!

I was overjoyed.

It was Mukabagira, it had been five years since we saw each other, we met on the way and we hugged for many seconds, maybe one minute, quietly only our hearts were talking to each other, she held me tightly because she was stronger than me, because of her height and weight. After our strong hug that was when I started to talk to her, I was looking at her and turning her here and there, I wanted to see her clearly maybe to see if she had changed. I had forgotten about the taxi man, and he was good enough to forget his hurry and give us time for our greetings. When I turned to where he was standing, he looked to be quietly happy, just looking at us, he was there with his big smile which he had the first time he came into my room.

I apologised for making him late, and he said that there was no problem, it showed that we missed each other, he asked if we were sisters and I said yes we were. We paid him and he helped us to take the bags out of his car and he went.

She told me that she spent the night in Nairobi in the hotel, and before she came she went to ask my sisters how she could see me, and was not happy to hear that I had been there and came back without seeing her. I told her why it happened like that, that it was Nyilimanzi who came to tie himself to me, and she understood. We started our conversations, we had many, we didn't know which to start with, we had a short time because Mukabagira told me in short that, she had come for shopping for her wedding, and she came by air, she would be going back at night time. She told me about her, that she had finished her secondary school and gone to Kampala to her sister's home to stay with her. She told me about her sister and brothers, that her sister had done a lot for their family and she had a hope that after getting married she was going to help her with what she had already done. Some people thought that she too had married since she moved to her sister's home in Kampala because they didn't see her a lot in Masaka.

Ilibagiza had almost come back from school, she was in nursery school. I told her in brief what had happened to me since the last time we were together, and now there I was in that room. Mukabagira, to be in a position of being able to travel by air, and being able to spend time in hotels, showed me the level she was at now, and just the way she looked told anyone what kind of life she had. It was a big step to reach, and it showed me that it was good to have patience, and hope, so that you would be able to hold on and wait for tomorrow.

When I told her about the place and house I lived in, I think she wanted to give me a hope by telling me that "Although we are here at this time, what is important is to have a will of what you want to be tomorrow, if your husband will change and do the right things then, you will improve yourself, and move somewhere else, and be in another position." I told her that I doubted if I would be, we needed to have weeks for ourselves, but even this time was better than nothing, the short time we had we were laughing and sometimes crying. She told me that what was important in any relationship, was trust and love, with that and understanding each other you could be who you wanted to be step by step.

When you had a rich husband, if you were with him just for his money without love then maybe he would abuse you, there are times when you could chose a poor man who could give you peace.

The door opened without knocking and Nyilimanzi was inside, I introduced them and he told us that when he was at the taxi place they told him that he got a visitor, a girl who looked like an angel, and yes they were right, that was how she looked.

We laughed at that, by luck he was still sober. He went and came back with a car, all of us with our children were inside the car, he took her around to buy what she still wanted, and we took her to her hotel to pick up her bag, and then to the airport. She was gone, I was so happy for the first time since I was at that place, apart from the two times Khadija took me out.

I thought that at last Mukabagira had come when we had that small thing, a car, to take her around.

In the car on the way back from to the airport Nyilimanzi was talking about Mukabagira, how beautiful she was and saying that the man who was going to marry her had a problem. I asked him what kind of problem he would have?

"Like the one I have."

"What problem do you have? I don't see myself to be that beautiful and even if I am, I know that there are ones who are really beautiful, and I think that no one can compare me with Mukabagira."

"Can I ask you something?" he said.

"Yes anything if I know it I will answer you."

"When Khadija took us out, when I asked you to drink beer or even to taste it, you refused, what did you think?"

"Nothing, I only thought that you wanted me to taste the beer that is it."

"Then why did you refuse completely even to taste it?"

"It was just because I had never tasted it before, and I don't feel like I am missing anything."

"That time I gave respect to Khadija, if it was not for her, I should have come up with a bad fight there, when you were dancing with men and sometimes they were taking you far or talking to you. I was feeling very bad, enough to try and see if I could get a good reason to destroy your face completely so that no one could admire you in the future, and I could be sure that you are only mine alone forever! I wanted to beat you with the bottle in the face, but after you refused to drink even a little, so that they couldn't say that all of us were drunk. I was disappointed with that, you don't drink and no one talked to me, it was not easy to come up with any kind of fight, I saw you to be too clever and a lucky one."

I asked him if there was anyone who could do things like that just because of jealousy.

"Yes," he said, with a lot confidence and pride, "because I love you and I would rather die than see you with another man."

I told myself that I had to go before it was too late, I did not need any other evidence, I was done waiting to make sure that he had a problem and he would never change, I had to get away to save myself and my child.

I was used to him coming in the middle of the night, with high noise, I knew that it was him when he was still far away and I would start to worry, I didn't know what would happen as soon as he was inside. I regretted coming with Ilibagiza, for a child to see that behaviour was not good but sometimes I was not blaming myself for that, since I had hoped that he would change himself as soon as he saw that we were a proper family. I lied to myself then.

One night around 2:00am, I heard someone knock, knocking many times without saying anything, even when I asked who it was there was no response. After a few minutes he said that it was him in a loud, heavy voice, I opened, inside he sat down quietly, looking at me. I was sat opposite him, quietly, I didn't know where to look or what to say, his big eyes had turned red, I thought that maybe where he had been they had beaten him, or he had done something terrible there. I waited, next he took the big radio from where it was, and put it near him, then put it on, it was too loud, I felt sorry for the neighbours, I had shame and I was angry too.

He stood up and got a heavy sword he had, which had to be there to protect the family. The anger I had changed to fear, I was wondering what he was going to do with it, it was the first time I had seen him touch it, at that time he started to cut the radio repeatedly. My heart was jumping with high speed I asked myself if after the radio it was me or the children, I asked myself if it was better to go out and ask for help, or to call people from inside there, since to go out was impossible,

I couldn't even reach the door because of how small the room was.

He cut the radio until it stopped talking, soon after that; he slept there without any other words!

The good thing was that the children were in a deep sleep, maybe if they had cried it would have made him cut us instead of the radio.

The next day he was a normal person, you wouldn't even think that he was the same person who did that at night, any time when he had done foolish things, he could be a good person for some time after.

I told myself that it was better to use this break in time to return Ilibagiza home and then deal with him alone.

By luck we got a visitor, a friend from Uganda, I asked Nyilimanzi if we could send Ilibagiza back home and let her go ahead with her studies there. I think he knew that he was not able to take care of a family, so he was happy with the idea, he gave the lady money for the journey to go with Ilibagiza. I sent Kantamage a letter since she knew a little about Nyilimanzi, I told her that now I was determined to deal with him, and I was not scared of him. To think of the way he was giving me problems when I was in his room, he could do the same even when I was out of his life. I would not go out of the country just because of a sick man, unless I was sick myself.

I decided to stay there in Nairobi and make him believe that I had my right to have my life my own way, the only the problem was how I would do it.

Even though the child was only one year old, when he saw him you could see how he was scared, because of the way he was playing with him. I had a hope that the time would come when God, my God, would take us out of there alive.

It was one Monday in February 1974, it was the evening and it seemed too early for Nyilimanzi to come home. I heard outside his friends talking together at the same time in loud voices, and because they were talking in Kinyarwanda it showed me that they were telling me, and maybe they thought that their story would shock me and I would go out to listen to them. They were saying that Nyilimanzi had been arrested, and they would take him to court the next day in the morning,

I didn't ask them anything as maybe they were waiting for me to. I told them to pass me in the morning so that we could go together to the court, but deep down, I thought that it would be good for me if they could hold him for a while, so that I could have a break...

In the court they refused the fine and put him inside for four months, I was happy but couldn't say it to anyone. At the least it was going to be two months which was better than nothing. I would relax my head, I had money for using at home and the driver went ahead to use the car, one of his friends told me that he would take me to the U.N..H.C.R, so that I could ask them if they could help me to get him out of prison. I thought that they wanted him out quickly if it could be possible so that they would have someone to buy them beer. I said yes, little did he know that I wanted him there for a long time. The next morning he took me there.

There were a few queues going in to different offices, he showed me which one I had to go to. Where I was standing, behind me was a young tall Rwandan man who was talking to me, my child started to cry and he told me that since the queue was still long, I could go and sit down, deal with the baby, and only come when he was near the door. I thanked him and went to do what I had to do to my baby.

When he was near the door I went, but someone who was inside stayed there for a long time, people started to complain, that is when the man offered to help me by holding the baby, I thanked him, I was tired, he was a heavy baby.

At that office there were many people, most of them looked relaxed and happy, and they looked smart, some of them dressed in expensive dresses, I also met some Rwandans I knew a long time ago in Uganda. They had many different conversations, I saw that someone would go sometimes only to meet people and have free stories. I thought that this handsome man was well dressed, he must have been a good person to hold a baby even without knowing me, or he loved children, or he was only being kind.

But I was very careful how I dressed my baby and myself, I knew that I was going somewhere where there were many strange people, that is what my mum taught me, that before I went out firstly I had to double check myself and be sure that I looked perfect enough to go out.

So maybe he liked us because of the way we looked, whatever it was, it was a benefit to me.

After he held the baby he asked me if now he had the baby he could ask me some questions if I could give him answers.

I said that it was no problem and I would answer him.

He started by introducing himself that his name was Rutagambwa Alloys, then he asked, "What is your name?"

"My name is Bamurangirwa Patricia," I said.

"Where do you come from?"

"I come from Magengo."

Rutagambwa looked surprised and he asked me again, "Where?"

"I come from Magengo," I said again. I knew that people didn't want to mention that name; they preferred to say Pumwani instead. Because as soon as you mentioned the name Magengo, if you were a woman, people would see you in the picture of slums and prostitution, but to me whatever situation I was in at the time that was how it was then. I repeated where I came from. Rutagambwa told me that it was not my home, and I was not suited to being where I was telling him either, he didn't manage to mention the name Magengo.

"I am asking you where you come from back home in Rwanda."

I told him, "I come from Butare Kirwa, between Mwogo and Rusuli the well known rivers." He seemed to be shocked to hear that, and he said that it was enough and he looked so serious in what he was saying. When I asked him what was enough, he said that the area I was talking about was where he came from, and he didn't want to know more so that I couldn't be his relative! We laughed at that, and he asked me how I came to be in Magengo. I told him that I was there with my husband.

I heard him talk about a familiar name to me, when he was shocked as Kwirahira, he mentioned Rwegera.

Then it was my time to ask him a few questions, "This name Rwegare I heard you mention, is that your father or your master?"

Rutagambwa said, "Why?"

"Because if it is your father and you come from that area, you might be my relative, because I heard my parents talk about him many times, they said that his wife is my auntie, and he too came from the same clan of Abega." Since it was known that all branches of Abega came from one parent, he didn't talk again and when I turned to see why, he was holding the baby with one arm and with the other he was holding his chin, he was too surprised. When I asked him about what he had told me, I said that we would talk after to finish what we came to do, when I came out he told me to wait for him.

He asked me if it was my first time going there. I said yes, and he asked who came with me, I showed him Kagimbangabo, and he told him that he wanted to talk to me so it was better if we could wait for him because I was in front of him. And if he was in a hurry he could go and he would escort me to the bus stop. Kagimbangabo thanked him because he said that it was becoming late and he wanted to go.

I had to try and see if they could take out Nyilimanzi of prison, I couldn't refuse to do what his friends told me to do as his wife, I had to help him, unless I wanted him to kill me quickly when he came out, so I was praying that they didn't do anything for that matter.

Inside I told the officer why I came and he told me that it was too late, they couldn't do anything against the judge. They said that if I had come before the case was taken to the court, they would have helped.

Yes, inside my heart, I got what I wanted, my break. I sat near one group and went ahead listening to conversations while I was waiting for Rutagambwa, I didn't want to go back to that room, I was comfortable with the new people, the new place, and with the different stories.

When Rutagambwa came out, he told another tall young man who looked taller than him but looked alike, you could tell that they were brothers; we went out, the three of us. Rutagambwa introduced me to Senzage who was his younger brother. He turned to Senzage by telling him that he heard a story which he didn't want to hear alone.

It was time for Senzage to ask questions, he wanted to know about those stories and Rutagambwa asked me first if I was in a hurry, so that we could sit somewhere and talk. I told him that there was no problem with that, we went to a restaurant, he bought something for both of us to eat and drink, then he told me to repeat what I told him so that Senzage could hear it by himself.

I told them where I came from back home. That my father was Sinzi, son of Rutabagisha, and my mum was Bagore, daughter of Buhake, son of Bizampola. Again both of them talked at once, they said that my mum's name Bagore was short for Bagorebeza, which was the first time I had heard that, and I was happy to know. It meant good woman and beautiful woman.

Both of them mentioned their father's name, Kwirahira, and then there was a big silence, they looked at each other, then at me, and then in a surprised way they said that someone could pass her or his close relative without knowing each other! That day, I found my first cousins in Nairobi! That day was my good day and I didn't know how Nyilimanzi would take it, although I didn't mind much, what I knew was that him going to prison was the key which opened the door of a better future to me. I had my wish, I believed that to be on my own in Nairobi maybe was a reason to be scared of Nyilimanzi, but still I had to be careful, they started to tell me a lot of stories and history of our families. They knew more than I, especially my mum's side.

Rutagambwa, maybe because he was the oldest, was the one who was talking most, and he looked like someone who liked giving orders, but both seemed to be patriotic. They knew Nyilimanzi before; they used to meet in those U.N. offices.

They started to give me orders, on the other hand they were trying to make me feel that I was not alone anymore and that was what I wanted to hear from them. Rutagambwa told me, "Look now Bamurangirwa, how you came and how you ended up being there in Magengo and marrying someone from such a place, you don't have to go into details. It might be hard, but now we are here, put that in your mind. OK Bamurangirwa, you are understood?"

"OK I understand," I told them, "me too, I am happy to have you here." I didn't say anything concerning my problems, it was not the right time to say anything about my marriage, but I knew that the time was coming soon.

Rutagambwa told me to take the child home and have a relax, and they were going to take me home so that they could know where I lived.

They were visiting me many times from that day and I sent a letter home telling them that I was no longer alone. Back home they sent a letter to Rutagambwa asking him to be near me for whatever could happen, and they sent a letter to Nyilimanzi too, telling him that they were his brother-in-laws.

I thought that it would be good if I could go with my new cousins to visit him in prison, so that he could see that they were real family, who could be there for us in happy times and in difficult times too. I would not wait for when he was out to make introductions and tell him that they were my cousins who I had known when he was away. I thought that was a very good idea.

When I told them they saw that it was not a bad idea either. The time came and we were there, we were outside in the line with the others who came to see their people, all of the prisoners wore white shorts and sleeveless white shirts, with slippers made from tyres, they looked clean, but it was not easy to know who was who. They told us to wait outside the gate, and when they went inside, they took us to where we could see who we wanted to see. It was a small house of one room with a big window which had wires, police with guns came with him and put him inside the room when we were still outside the window.

I greeted him, but within seconds I could see that he was changed, he was not the same person who came inside, it was like where he was stood there was a fire. He was going around and around, his eyes became red, he even looked like he could cry, just because he saw that I was with those two handsome men. I thought that he should wait to be told who they were, but not him. I think he thought that both of them were my boyfriends, and I brought them to laugh at him, but still

287

I tried to tell him who they were, how I met them and their names but it was too late. It was like he was not hearing anything anymore, he heard only what his head told him, they greeted him and it was a struggle to answer them back.

After a short time he managed to ask me who these men were that I was with, and had I brought them there to see where he was! In my heart, I knew that if Mukabagira could see him now she would tell me to go when he was still there in prison, and when he came back he would get his room and clothes only, she would say that I didn't deserve that life.

Though we were talking in Kinyarwanda, anyone could see that we were at war, the policeman who was guarding him saw visitors coming with a war.

I felt ashamed for saying that I should take them, I didn't want things to be like that, I didn't know what I was going to tell them, I didn't know what would happen when he was out. No matter what I did, for the time being he would still be in prison, and that was the only picture he had, that back home I was with other men.

I was worried that they would fear him and despair.

It was Rutagambwa who started by saying that my husband was a sick man, why couldn't he wait and come home so that would prove what he thought was wrong.

Senzage said that maybe he wanted to scare them, so that they wouldn't be coming to his home, and if so, he said that until I stopped them visiting me, they would be coming any time as long as I was still there.

Rutagambwa said that men like him who didn't have politeness to strange people might be the men he heard about who beat women!

Senzage said, "Maybe he beats Bamurangirwa too, but she can't tell us, some women can keep secrets for their husbands until the end."

I didn't say anything, I knew that the time would come, I would tell them when l had to tell them.

I didn't visit him again, I was giving his friends transport and they were going on my behalf, the few days he was there were my good holidays. Rutagambwa and his brother went ahead to visit me until he was out.

In the first days when he was at home, he was acting like he was still thinking about where he would start. I gave him his letter from home, it was still in the envelope and still closed, the stamp showed where it came from (Uganda) and he asked me why I didn't open it. I told him that it was directed to him and not to me. He opened it and after he had read it, he looked ashamed, I think he saw that he had to learn to be patient and trust, he gave it to me to read too. It was greetings and they were making introductions between him and his new brother-in-laws who he had got in Nairobi.

He asked me if it was me who told home about Rutagambwa and Senzage, but I told him that it was not me, maybe it was them, because there was a time when they asked me for the address.

I think he thought that it was not going to be easy for him to treat me the way he used too, now I had my relatives near to me.

Between my new cousins and back home, the communication was good by sending letters, and they were visiting us at least once a week. They were telling me that almost every day they were in town, and since we were near the town for them it was easy to visit us.

So I believed that this was my strong answer from my God concerning my marriage.

When they came, Nyilimanzi was giving them respect, you could see him reminding me to see what I did for them like giving them something to drink… and when they went he was escorting them, but that still didn't change me, I still had my plan, it was only a matter of time.

Everytime my cousins got a chance to be alone with me, they showed concern that they didn't trust my marriage to be peaceful and successful, that gave me hope that even when the time would come to tell them, they would have no doubts that what I was telling them was true. Now I had them I would use them to get what I wanted, there was no other miracle I was waiting for.

That was when I realised that there was nothing important and which could be helpful like human beings. People were a way of luck or miracles to others, when on the other hand people could also be the cause of misery to others too. It depends who, how; and why.

Life is a game you play, sometimes you win, or you fail, but most of us we have to be in that playground, and see how our football will go ahead.

When Nyilimanzi was out of prison he was a good person and as always, I was confused if it was prison which shocked him, or if it was because I had my relatives, or if it was how he always gave himself a break by being good for some time and acting like a normal family man, but after a few days he would go back to his behaviour of being a street man. I had to wait and see. What I wanted more than anything was peace, and I was sure that I couldn't get it with him.

He acted like that for one month and went back to all his behaviour; one time he was asking me if I was proud and happy for myself because I had my relatives near. And in my heart I wanted to say yes I was, the next morning when my relatives came you could see him looking as if he was ashamed, knowing that he had been insulting me the whole night, you could see how he was saying things which showed that it was outsiders who lied to him about me about pointless things. I wanted to ask him if he knew that they lied to him, and ask him why he was listening to them, but I believed that no one was lying to him about anything, it was in his head.

And he was aware that I might come up with cases by telling my relatives this and that, so that they could put us down and give us counselling, and you could see him watching to see that they left without mentioning anything, because I didn't want any counselling or any cases. I didn't want any help concerning my marriage. I was only waiting for my time, time to go away from him forever.

The day I was waiting for came when my cousins came in the daytime and Nyirimanzi had just gone out, meaning that I had a lot of time for myself. I decided that this would be the day of telling them about my story. The story of my marriage to Nyirimanzi, only in brief, what they had to be told.

I was happy to see that the days of misery were counted. I already had hope in them, but until I talked with them, and was sure that they were the people who could come to my rescue, I was only waiting for when I would have a good time to talk to them and know where I stood. That would be the day.

After sitting down and to giving them something to drink, I told them that I had something to tell them, and they asked me if there was anything new.

I said yes I had something new to tell them but I was not going to tell them there, I had an appointment to take the child to the hospital, and I asked them if we could meet there. They said yes, they saw that there might be a reason we couldn't talk there, and if that was what I wanted they would be there.

At the hospital they were there before me, after I finished at the child's clinic, I was with them and they were the first to ask me about what I wanted to tell them. I started by telling them that I had a request for them, and it was a hard one, that was why I wanted us to talk where we saw that we were free. All of them looked at me as though they were telling me to say it quickly. "I wanted to tell you that my marriage is failing and I wanted your ideas," I said.

All of their eyes became big at once, then I made mine look in a soft way but I did not look down, because I wanted to look directly at their faces so that I would know how they took it.

It was Rutagambwa who started to talk first, he called my name but didn't wait for me to respond. He went ahead and said "Look Bamurangirwa, life between husband and wife is not something which is easy for someone to come between just like that, here you are with your husband and you had a child with him. In this country I don't think that it can be easy for us to come between you two, instead things like that could cause problems for us."

When he said that my heart jumped a little, I told myself that they were going to tell me that it was impossible to come between us, but I decided to be patient and wait to hear what was next. He went on, "But I am not saying that because of those problems which we might get through helping you can be a reason to be away from you. If you are not happy with this marriage, you must assure us that you have tried enough and this help you want from us is the last solution, or maybe you are just angry and you can probably forgive when your husband asks to be forgiven, which also is normal."

He continued, "We can't encourage you to break your marriage when we don't know yet the causes, but I think the good thing is if you can tell us the problems between you two, so that we can see if we can put you down and talk to you and see if together we can find a solution, and if it is something which you can't tell us we also respect that."

He kept quiet for a few seconds; then he asked Senzage his view. Senzage told him that there was nothing he could say before hearing what I was going to answer, so then they could know which direction to take.

The words Rutagambwa used were genuine words which could be used by a genuine person who wanted to help someone and wished to see that person in a better situation.

The questions were not as hard as I thought, I had the answers. I saw that it was my time to answer them in a clear way and truthfully. I put my head high and looked directly at them, ready to answer them. Firstly I thanked them for coming and listening, and according to the words Rutagambwa used, showing me that I had people with me who could try to do the right things when possible. Because they showed me that they were not just happy to see that I was on my way to breaking up my marriage, there was no one who could be happy with that, only when it was the last solution. By telling them the reason, I saw that it was not necessary. I could only tell them when I wanted them to help us to solve our problems, but now I was on the last step, it was over to me, finished, and had been finished for a long time, it was only a matter of time, now I wanted them to help me if they could.

There was silence for a few seconds, it was Rutagambwa who started to talk and he said, "If that is how it is then, it is better we don't lose time, let us see how we will put things in to practice. We can have time, any time, as long as we plan it. So since it is you who has a problem with time, it is you who will tell us about your time."

As always I was using their problems to my advantage, when they had cases concerning beer, they didn't know yet that when they had those cases they were a bonus to me, so I had a day and time of the case of one of them. I told them the day and time.

They told me that they would not come home, they told me where I would tell the taxi man, that they would wait for me there and if I didn't have money, it was better to tell them, so that they could give some to me.

I told them that I would get the money. I had to wait one more week until the next Monday, when he was doing his childish things, in my heart I was laughing at him.

On that day, I woke up early in the morning to help him and see that he could be ready to go as soon as possible. I tried to see that he did not forget any single thing, which could have made him come back.

When he went out I started to prepare myself and my child, but I was so scared, I knew very well that if he came back and saw the bags, he could kill me and my child, he would think that he knew where I was going, that I was going with other men.

I was not worried that I might not get my relatives. I had feelings that if someone put Nyirimanzi and I together, and asked who was clever, and who was a winner, I was sure that I could be a winner. He was going to be shocked again and now it was for good, let him find a woman who suited him and drank beer, but not me. After I finished packing I came with a taxi and put my things inside then again gave the key to my neighbour Judith, she didn't ask anything, and I didn't tell her anything, apart from telling her to give it to Nyirimanzi.

It seemed that she was happy to give me that help, for me it was a big help. After the taxi got straight to the main road, that was when my heart relaxed and believed that I was going. I told the driver to take me to Tusker, and he didn't ask me anything, which showed that he knew where I had told him.

We reached somewhere in the city centre, and he told me that we were where I had told him. I came out of the car and I didn't see anyone, which was when I started to be scared, if they were not there what would I do? I stood outside for a couple of minutes, I asked the driver to be patient, and he said that was no problem. I didn't see them, then I turned to go back inside the car, but I didn't know where to go, at that second when I was turning in the car I saw them standing up at once. When they saw that I saw them, they sat down again, like they were hiding themselves somewhere, it seemed that they were very careful of that matter, but they didn't come to where I was, so I knew that they didn't want to be seen with me by the taxi man, so I paid him and he was gone, that was when they came to where I was.

They got another taxi, which took us to their home, at their home there was one big wooden room which was good inside, they had one bed. They had four neighbours, outside there was a big compound which was not cemented yet, the toilets were outside but near there and they had a tap for water outside too.

They moved from the bed for me and my baby, and they were sleeping on a mattress. I knew that I was not going to pass only in soft ways ahead of me, but life was going to be different than what I had. And step by step things would be better. I would have my life back.

I told my heart to give myself time to see what would happen. I sent a letter to Mukabagira, and told her the changes in case she came and went straight to Magengo.

They tried to see that I relaxed my body and my mind, they sometimes didn't want to see me do this and that, sometimes they joked by reminding me that Rwandan men were known to be the few African men who took very good care of women and spoiled them when they needed to be.

After a few days, one morning, I was outside playing with my child, when I saw someone from afar coming to where we were. I didn't give it time to know who it might be, after a few minutes, I heard someone talk to me, I turned to see who it was, it was Nyirimanzi. I was alone at home but one of our neighbours was there, so, I didn't feel scared, because I knew that our neighbour would be there for me. He was looking at me with a little smile, as though he was asking me if I thought that he would not know where I was.

I knew that he might try different things to see that I would go back to him, but I knew too, that I had had enough, nothing was going to make me change my mind.

After normal greetings he asked me where the others were.

"Who do you want to see?"

"All of them."

"Wait for them, they will come."

"Why did you come here without saying bye?"

"Because I didn't need to be escorted."

"Now I am here so that we can go back."

"Back where?"

"I came to take you back home."

"This time is another time. I don't go anywhere with anyone, I go by myself when I see that it is the right thing to do, I came here by myself, when I see that it is the right thing to come back then I will do that by myself too."

"Please don't joke I am serious."

"I am too, it is you who is joking, to think that you can take me anywhere when you want to!"

He was calm, talking with respect to the level that even if you told someone his behaviour they could think that you were making things up.

He came three times with the same questions and was getting the same answers.

On the fourth time he came on a Sunday morning, when Rutagambwa and Senzage were at home and he came with four old men. We welcomed them, the time came for them to tell us why they had come. One of the old men asked me why I didn't go back to my home, that they were there to ask me what problem had made me leave, so that if Nyilimanzi had wronged me then there would be a fine paid to me, but they wanted to get a solution to whatever it was.

Nyilimanzi said that yes as they said he was going to give me whatever fine they would tell him, but he wanted me back.

I had to give those old men the respect they deserved, by sitting down and listening to them and talking to them.

"Is it true Bamurangirwa that when you came your husband didn't know?"

"Yes that is true."

"It shows that it was something which hurt you, which might be a good enough reason to make you do that."

"Yes I had it, but I am not going to say it here, or anywhere else, because it doesn't matter to me now, if he can change himself or not, so he can be who he wants to be, that is about him."

Those men looked shocked, and together said that was why they came. I told them that his behaviour was like a permanent disease which couldn't be cured, so there was no need to make them try to struggle for something which couldn't change in any way, yes he could say that he would change, but I was sure and he knew that he couldn't, that was a fact. He said that many times, he knew that.

They asked Nyilimanzi if he was following what I was telling them, and he said yes, he was listening. They talked between themselves, and they saw that there was nothing they could do to make me change my mind, and they went back with Nyilimanzi.

I told myself that now he saw that I was not playing any games any more, I was serious and knew what I was doing.

Rutagambwa and Senzage started to take me to the U.N.'s offices to see if I could be registered and do something for myself.

It was 20th April 1974, early in the morning, when Rutagambwa and Senzage prepared themselves to go to town. We saw the door wide open like someone had used something heavy to push it, we turned our heads to see what was going on, our eyes were looking directly into police officers' eyes, in uniforms and guns! By the time we were on the way to ask them what the problem was, thinking that they had come inside by mistake, they was busy looking here and there like they were looking for particular things which they came for.

After one minute, Nyilimanzi came inside with a wider smile, like he was telling me that now he had me! Now by gun! I thought that he was someone who was wasting his time and his money thinking that he could force anyone in to marriage! I saw that he had never got chance to know me, since all of the time I was with him the only word he knew from me was yes. For that point I felt sorry for him, because he seemed that he was in the game, playing football, but didn't know what kind of opponent he was playing with. I wanted to tell him that my goal was immune. It hurt me and made me angry to see that Rutagambwa and his brother were worried, and I had no time to tell them that they didn't have to worry, because it was nothing. I knew all of that was because of a bribe, you could buy anything if you could afford it.

They asked Nyilimanzi if it was me who they were looking for. "Yes," he told them that it was me.

They turned to me and asked me if it was me who ran away thinking that they were not going to get me.

"Yes it is me, now you got me, take me back then."

"That is why we came," they told me, "come with your baby and everything you came with."

Nyilimanzi was there showing them this and that which I came with and they were telling him, "Well done Nyilimanzi, you have to be careful that we don't leave anything here."

My cousins helped me to put my things together and they asked them where they were taking me. They told them that they were taking me to the chief of their area, and they told me that I didn't have to worry they would be there with me. I asked them how soon they thought they would be there. And they told me that they might be there before us, I didn't want to be far from them.

We were in a police car with my things, we passed somewhere and we stoped, officers went out with some papers and came back, we went ahead. I asked them where they came from, they told me that it was the chief of that area, they had to be given permission to take me from there.

I asked them again if they had passed there before they came to pick me up, and they said yes, that was how this job had to be done. On the way I had different conversations with the police officers, instead it was Nyilimanzi who didn't have anything to say, I think it surprised him. We passed Nyilimanzi's home and put my things inside, and started to go to the office, my relatives were there waiting.

Both of us went inside the office, the chief was an old man sitting behind the table and they showed me to him in a respectful way. "The lady is this one, we came with her Muzee." (Muzee in Swahili meant old, but on the other hand meant Sir.)

"Young woman is it you who gives my people problems?"

"Yes Muzee, it is me. We give each other problems, because I give them problems, and they give me problems too." He smiled, and showed me where to sit, when I saw him smile I thought that maybe he was not a bad person.

I was aware of what was going ahead, and had many different questions.

"Now young woman, who are these men?" the chief said.

"They are my brothers, Muzee."

"Do you want them here or do you want them to wait outside?"

"I want them here, Muzee."

Policemen saluted the chief and went out, the chief was an old man, maybe more than fifty years old, he was light-skinned, overweight, but strong. He was wearing a police uniform, with many stars on his shoulders, he read the papers they gave him, first when he finished he put them aside, in the room there was silence. He looked at us for a few seconds, and then called me in a respectful way, as mother of the baby, 'Mama mutoto', "Why did you run away?"

"Muzee, I didn't run away because I went in the daytime, and I went where I was supposed to go, to my family."

"To your family in which way?"

"Because I was at my brothers' home."

"How did you go? Who took you?"

"I went by myself."

"How did you know the place?"

"I was asking people."

"Now I brought you back so that you can go to your husband."

"I think that would be so hard of you, Muzee."

I was looking directly in his face and he changed a little, he looked angry and he asked me, "What do you mean by saying that? You see where you are and who you are talking to?"

I tried to tell him very carefully that I didn't say that by ignorance. "I see who you are Muzee, you deserve respect in all areas, I have to give you respect because of your age, you are like my father, and I have to give you respect because of your position too. But when I am telling you that you can't take me back to my husband, it is because the reason that made me to go is still there, and it is something which I believe is permanent. That is why I know that it is hard of anyone who could try to make me go back to him."

"I can understand that there are reasons why you are here in the government's office, we solve the hard problems that is our responsibility. I want you two to put together your marriage, that is why I called you here to help you with that."

In my heart I saw that because of the money Nyilimanzi gave him, he was trying to show him that he was doing the job, but I was sure he had seen that he would not change my mind. I had to be very careful when I was answering him. I knew that there was a place where I could get what I wanted in a better way, but all of that would depend on what I said and how I said it.

I was sure that Nyilimanzi thought that I was a coward. I would not be able to talk in front of him, but I could talk with the chief, he didn't know that when I was with him I was acting, because I had seen that he was sick.

I would sometimes pass my eyes over them in seconds in a secret way, I would see how Nyilimanzi looked very happy, and my cousins were very sad because they didn't know what would happen, but I wished that I could get away to tell them not to worry.

I was sitting directly in front of the chief as they had taught us since we were young that it was bad manners to look directly in the eyes of grown-up people. So I had to bend and look down until he asked me something, that was when I would look at him but I did not look exactly directly at him for long.

I told him that he could make me to go back because he had the power, if he could give me one of his soldiers to guard me with a gun, then yes I would stay there, but when I got a chance I would still go, and maybe that time they might never see me again!

He looked shocked and said quickly and strongly, that he couldn't get a soldier to guard me, he only wanted me to go willingly to build up my marriage, and not go by force.

I told him that it was something which I had tried and failed and I wouldn't be able to manage now.

The chief looked relaxed now, and he spoke to me now like a friend not like a chief. "Now Bamurangirwa," this was the first time he called me by my name, "can you tell me the reason for all of that and I can see if I can find a solution?"

"I said, "Look Mweshimiwa," meaning Sir, "I can tell you all of the reasons, but because he knows them he can tell you himself and see if you can find a solution, Muzee."

I thought that he was going to say all of his bad behaviour, and tell them to ask me to forgive him, but all of us were quiet. Then I told Nyilimanzi, "Tell Muzee now, tell him." It was like I was enjoying him now.

No one told Mweshimiwa about anything between us, not me or Nyilimanzi. He gave up and started to ask Nyilimanzi questions.

"Nyilimanzi, I am even wondering how you got this girl, she is your real wife, it is you who married her?" he went on talking to him, "she is too clever for you, I even don't know how you managed to be together for the time you were with her!" He asked him that and he was holding his chin as a sign of surprise, and Nyilimanzi gave him an answer quickly, maybe he hoped that he had got a proper answer to save him.

"Yes Mweshimiwa, she is my wife, it is me who is her first man and all of her family back home have seen me."

Chief smiled and shook his head in a way which said that he was dealing with a hard person who seemed deaf. He looked angry and told him, "Look Nyilimanzi, what you are telling me is completely the opposite of what I am asking you. What if this young woman met a crazy man and he raped her, she can't call him her husband, or if she had a boyfriend, she couldn't call him her husband just because that man was her first man."

He continued, "And if she didn't want to be with you without seeing her family back home, and she took you there, that is good. You can be her husband if when you were there you did all that we African men have to do to marry our wives, by giving their parents dowries. And if you didn't give them a dowry, yet you remembered to take her to the authority as you brought her here today, and have a certificate from us showing that you are husband and wife, then yes she is your wife. So if you have done one of those two things, we give both things respect and strong recognition. I know our African way doesn't have any certificate but it is recognised. But I am sorry, if you have done nothing, that means that she is not your wife, you were just friends. Which of those two things have you done?"

Nyilimanzi now looked cold and his eyes were red, the chief asked him again and he told him that he didn't do any of it.

Chief said that if he had remembered and asked him before, all of those problems of that day wouldn't have happened.

"In that case, this young lady is free to go anywhere, and do whatever she wants to do." To see Nyilimanzi, you wouldn't believe that it was the same person who was there standing like a boss, he looked as though he was standing on a fire going around and around. He didn't have anywhere to put his big red eyes, you could see that he was almost going to cry.

Nyilimanzi in all of those shocks he had, he told the chief that if he failed to have me back then he was going to take me back home to my parents. And he would leave with the baby.

The chief was the one who told him, "Look Nyilimanzi, I think you are a little mad. I told you that the mother of this baby is not your wife, how can the baby be yours?!" At that time in Kenya, they counted the children to be on the mothers's side, maybe it was not in writing but it was the understanding, especially to Kikuyu people. I think that it might have started when they were fighting for their independence, when in most families it was only the women who were responsible for many areas of life, at home and on the front line. But young children under ten years old had to be with their mum at the time. But now our time was different.

The chief went ahead, "Even if this young woman was your wife but now went on her own, there is no law in this country which would separate a child of this age from the mother."

Concerning taking me back home, it was me who told him that he didn't get me from home, we met there and we would separate there.

It was Rutagambwa who asked about my things, this surprised the chief, he didn't liked it, he asked why they came with my things when he told them to come with just me. Then he told us to go and pick up everything we came with. He asked Nyilimanzi if he would give us any problems and he said that there was no problem, we could go and pick them up.

I wanted to go to where the chief sat and thank him, when I hugged him, I saw that it was good now that Nyilimanzi had helped to bring me there in front of authority, so that he could hear for himself that I was free.

I saw him looking aside and wiping away tears, and I thought that maybe he was crying because I went away from him when I was alive and well.

We took our things and left, I went out of Magengo and away from prostitute land.

Now I had my freedom, and I was going to join others to deal with the U.N., how could I use my freedom and what I got from it and from the U.N. too? Go on and see that new chapter for yourself.

The author, 1969, Masak, Uganda

The author, 1974, Nairobi, Kenya

The author, 1974, Nairobi, Kenya

From right: Senzage, the author sitting down, Rutagambwa and baby
Manzi. April 1974, Nairobi, Kenya

The author and baby Manzi, 1974,
Masaka, Uganda

The author, 1975, Nairobi, Kenya

From right: Manzi, the author and Ilibagiza,
December 1975, Masaka, Uganda

The author, 1977, Nairobi, Kenya

Batsinduka, 1978, Nairobi, Kenya

The author, 1979 Nairobi, Kenya

The author, 1977, Nairobi, Kenya

The author's nephew,
Rusingizandekwe, who was one
of the victims of the genocide
against Tutsi in Rwanda 1994

The author, 1976, Nairobi, Kenya

The author, 1979, Nairobi, Kenya

The author, 1977, Nairobi, Kenya

The author, 1978, Nairobi, Kenya

The author, 1979, Nairobi, Kenya

Baby Manzi, 1974, Nairobi, Kenya

Muvunangoma in the early 80s

Muvunangoma and the author in
the early 80s, Nairobi, Kenya

From right: Ilibagiza, Gahongayire, the author, Batsinduka.
At the front is little Niwegaju.

1982, Batsinduka in London
as a Scout

Niwegaju and a friend from nursery
school, 1984, Nairobi

In 1980s Langata, Nairobi

The author and Batsinduka holding
baby Niwegaju, early 80s, Nairobi

The author, 1988, Nairobi

1988, Niwegaju on her birthday and me

The author, 1983, Nairobi

The author, 1981, Nairobi

Batsinduka and Niwegaju, early 80s, Nairobi

From right: Niwegaju, the author and Gahenda, early 80s, Nairobi

Ilibagiza and the author, 1986, Nairobi

Manzi, late 80s, Mombasa

Gahenda and Niewgaju, late 80s,
Nairobi

The author in 90s Nairobi

The author, 1996, Nairobi

Batsinduka and Kabanyana,
August, 1999

From right: the author's sister Kamashara, Batsinduka, Niwegaju, Muvunangoma and the author, 1999, Nairobi

Niwegaju and her friend in Rwanda cultural dress, dancing in Norway, 1998

Ilibagiza, mid 90s, Nairobi

From right: Niwegaju and Alfonci Mbayire, 1998, Nairobi

Gasengayire (sister-in-law to Mwavita), a survivor of the genocide against the Tutsi in 1994, Rwanda

Wedding day of the author's niece Mwavita Nyiramashashi who lost her husband in the genocide against the Tusti, 1994, Rwanda

The author's step brother, Sinzi
Rukara, 90s

Batsinduka and Niwegaju at
Kenyata airport. This was the first
time Niwegaju would be away on
her own, travelling to Norway in
the early 90s

From right: my niece Mwavita
Nyiramashashi, 1996, Bisesero,
Rwanda

Ilibagiza, early 90s, Nairobi, Kenya

The author's father, Sinzi, 1992, Toro, Uganda

From left: Mugwiza – First Secretary in the Rwanda Embassy in Kenya in 2004 – the author and Issa

Niwegaju, 2000, Nairobi

Manzi 2001, Mombasa, Kenya

The author, 2003, Nairobi, Kenya

Batsinduka and the author in 2000

Ilibagiza, 2000, Nairobi

In memory of Ilibagiza.
From the right: Batsinduka, Kabanyana, the author and Muvunangoma,
Langata, Nairobi, Kenya

Early 2004 to welcome Niwegaju to Batsinduka's home, Nairobi.
From right: Late Gahongayire, Batsinduka, Manzi, Niwegaju and
Muvunangoma.

Batsinduka and his wife at their
home for Niwegaju's party, early
2004

From right: Niwegaju and Late
Gahongayire at Niwegaju's party

From right: the author's sister Kankuyo, the author, Mary Rwamushayija, early 2004 at Batsimduka's home where they were welcoming Niwegaju. At the back on the right is Dina Kamanzi.

The author and Niwegaju at her party

From right: Manzi and Muvunangoma where they were welcoming Niwegaju at Batsinduka's home

From right: Batsinduka, Niwegaju in the middle and Batsinduka's wife Kabanyana in early 2004 in their home in Nairobi

Manzi and Niwegaju at her party, 2004

2004, Nasho, Rwanda

2004, Nasho, Rwanda

2004 in Nasho, Rwanda

The author with H.E. Paul Kagame, President of Rwanda,
2004, Kigali, Rwanda

The author, January 2005, London, Britain

The author and the Mayor of Birmingham, 2005

Some of the group at voluntary of hope gardening, 2012,
Birmingham, Britain

The author with her Angel Zimbabwean girl who
saved her from the street of Bury, Manchester 2005.
Shown is Trisha and her baby son with the author, in the middle

The author and the late Alfonse
Mbayire Mbandahe's family in
Glasgow, December 2004

The author and baby Cyusa, in the
authors's sitting room, Nairobi,
Kenya, 2004

On holiday in Queensland, Brisbane, Australia, 2014

On holiday in Queensland, Brisbane, Australia, 2014

On holiday in Queensland, Brisbane, Australia, 2014

Maina, the author, and Batsinduka in Nairobi, end of the 1980s

From right: the author, Princess Mukabayo, Kabudadali, Gorreti and others in Nairobi, Kenya, 2004

Niwegaju practising culture dancing with Liliane Mupende and others in Nairobi, Kenya in 1993

Next is me with Muthoni's baby Birmingham 2012

Niwegaju dancing with her friend at her party

The group of volunteers in Birmingham, Britain in 2012

Jane Kagenza, Gorreti and others at Niwegaju's party

Dina Kamanzi, Tedy Umuruta and others
at Niwegaju's party

Niwegaju and Nasri at Batsinduka's dinner at
his wedding

The ladies who sang for dancers at Batsinduka's wedding

Kabanda and Uwera at Niwegaju's party in Nairobi, Kenya

The author and her daughter,
Niwegaju, 2014 in Brisbane,
Australia

Uwera, Mutijima and Mahoro
children to Niwegaju and
Dylan Chown

Mukaneza, daughter to Manzi and
Edith Wangui

Cyusa and Isimbi, children of
Batsinduka and Kabanyana

Niwegaju and baby Uwera in
Preston, Britain, 2005

THIRD STEP IN NAIROBI

The hard and big job was to take me out of that hole, my cousins had finished it; the rest was mine now, what next? I had no income to have childcare, so I was not able to go here and there trying to see what I could get my hands on.

I saw that it was a good idea to go to my sister's and leave my child with them for a while, so that I could see what I was able to do to have my new beginning. In my new chapter.

I went to Uganda and I told them that I was no longer with Nyilimanzi any more. Kantamage was happy with that, because she was losing hope in him that he could change to be a better person tomorrow. I told them that I would be going back to Kenya and I wanted to try life there. She was the one who came up with the idea before I had to ask her, she said that it would be better if I could leave the child behind since I couldn't manage everything there by myself.

I was happy and my preparation to go was easy, but this time I had to see Mukabagira before going back to Kenya.

I wanted to be with her and give myself time with her, maybe a week or two since I didn't know when I would be free again. I didn't know what I was going to face, I wanted to tell her everything I had passed through, from Alex to Nyirasoko in Butambara, what I saw in Tanzania and up to then with Nyilimanzi.

I got to Mukabagira, the first night we didn't sleep at all, we talked the whole night. When we reached the funny parts we were laughing, and when we reached the sad ones we were crying, but the part in Magengo was the best part, she laughed more to hear how it took me a long time to know what was going on there, and the questions I was asking Zulia.

There was only one mistake that she said I made, and I too saw that she was right, it was a big mistake to do what I did, by forgetting to send the old man in Mwanza a letter when he had given me his address, and when his Benz did a very good job for me to be able to punish Seleman.

I told her that even Muzee in Mwanza, if he knew how Nairobi welcomed me then he could forgive me.

Mukabagira was now talking with anger when she was referring to Nyirasoko, she said that I was lucky to reach home safely, and the lady she was not a fool she was mad, to think that she could take a person like she would take something which she would put somewhere she wanted and do with it whatever she wanted!

To be old and non-Rwandan was not a problem, but to be poor and to be forced to be his second wife, that was a big problem, "So you did the right thing to come back," she said.

"I will marry a non-Rwandan only when he will be able to do what I want him to do to me and to my family. We are foreign here, our parents they come with nothing, no money, no land, some with no cows, they come with us. Now to many we are their present, and their future too, in many ways, and if we will use the capital we have very carefully, we will get what we want, whatever that will be, and even in the future we will be the strong sources to take them back home."

I had to ask her what capital she was talking about and she told me that she was talking about our heads, that we had to use our brains carefully for anything we did so that we were able to survive and help our families.

I asked her again if my story was the one which made her that angry.

"Yes," she said, "and it made me to remember the story my sister told me recently of the Rwandan girl, Ndabaga, of years ago."

"What happened to her?" I asked.

She told me, when she still looked angry about what had happened to Ndabaga, "It is a must to tell you about her, because what she did is our pride." I was listening and just looking directly at her.

She started by telling me that Ndabaga was one of our Rwandan girls who we had to remember in our history as Rwandan girls, she was one of our heroes at the time. Her parents had only her as their child, according to the understanding they had at the time, if you had no son, it meant that the family had no future, no one would give grandchildren to their side. For them, there was no one who would hold the family name in the future, because the girl would marry into a stranger family, and on top of that the girls would not go to the front line. When it was war time, and they would not go to help their father where they were in the master's home, they would go there on their father's behalf which was known as 'gukura igihe'.

So because of all of that, the family couldn't be happy like others in the community, many times they tried what they could to see that they could have sons, they tried marrying many wives when sometimes the men were helped by the first wife.

Back to the point of the master's home, the men had to go there and just live their permanently, sometimes they would come to visit their wives, until when their sons grew up and were old enough to come and be there instead of their fathers, that was when the man could be free to go back to stay with their family permanently again. Or by luck when the master liked the servant so much he could give him a lot of cows, and tell him that he was free to go to be the master himself to his village.

Now Ndabaga, by being only a child, she grew up without her father, and when she was asking her mother why her father was not at home, she was always told that it was not easy for him to come since she didn't have a brother to go to be there on his behalf. And her father didn't marry another wife hoping that maybe she might have them, so that was how it had to be, he had to wait until the master maybe gave him permission.

Ndabaga listened to her mother but she was not happy with all of

305

that, and she had to think harder about what she could do to help her father.

In the end she thought of a solution of how she would go and help her father! She decided that if it was only a son who had that chance to help their father, from then on she was going to change herself to become a man, and after being successful she would go and be there for him.

Ndabaga started to do all of the exercises she thought might help her to look masculine and she knew what men had to know and do, so in secret ways she practiced all of that. She started to change and her mother was worried for her, she didn't know what problem her child had.

And when she asked her she was telling her that she was fine. The time came when she was successful and got did she could do to her breast too, and now what was left was to go. She got herself a spear, bow, sword and everything necessary men had to take with them to the war for their protection. A proper young man at the time also had to go with their weapons sometimes wherever they went.

She was ready to go and she came in front of her mother when she was dressed as a young man who was going to war, that was how the brave men had to be everywhere there, they had to be ready for everything at any time, in case they were called for war, at any time wherever they were.

Her mother was shocked to see her in that way, she tried to say that she couldn't go ahead with her plan but it was too late, she was worried about her, in case they found out that she was a girl and it was a problem for the whole family, maybe they would say that they lied. She told her mum that she had to go, what she asked her to do was to keep quiet, she didn't have to tell the neighbours anything, because girls could be inside all the time, so if she was there or not, no one would know if they were not told.

People directed her and she reached their masters, she asked for an appointment to see the master, and when she was in front of him, the master asked her if she had come to ask to be taken as a new servant or if he had other messages for him?

She told him that she came to be there on behalf of her father and told him who the father was. The master was surprised and asked, "How come he has a son like you who looks to be a brave young man and he is still here?"

He said that she was not yet ready to come. They called her father and when he was there the girl stood up and greeted him with a lot of happiness, her father was surprised and confused, where had this handsome young man come from who was happy to see him and came to be there for him? He knew that he didn't have a son and he couldn't say a thing there, he had to go home and see what was going on there, maybe he had a son who he didn't know?!

At the master's home the daughter was the best at everything she was doing, and her master started to give her cows to show her that she was the best. With his other servants, the people loved her, she had to be together with other young men, and she tried to be very careful to see that no one would find out that she was a girl, that could be a big problem. Because of her braveness her master had given her many cows already.

Since they had no pants at the time, when they were doing their exercises, they were jumping, and one of her friends found out that she was a woman not a man!

When he asked her she said yes, that she had a reason why she did it, and she asked him not to say a word to the master, she would go and tell him herself. She saw that as soon as anyone knew the truth about her it couldn't be kept a secret anymore, so it was better to say it to the master herself and explain why she did it, so that maybe it wouldn't be a problem for the whole family.

She asked her master if she could talk to him alone, and when they were together she told him everything she had done, and how she did it, and why. Then she told him why she decided to tell him the truth about herself. And she told him, "Now, my master, I am a girl not a boy, it is you who will see what to do with me now."

The master was surprised with the braveness and patriotism of that girl. He looked at her and told her that he was going to do nothing to

307

her, instead of punishing her for that he gave her a lot of cows and servants, so that she could go back to her village and be a master herself and be happy with her parents.

When Mukabagira was telling me all of that, I was listening and she was serious, when she finished her story I told her it was too hard to achieve something like that. I thought that no one in our generation could.

She turned to me and told me, "Ndabaga was a human being and it was a long time ago when there was nothing much to help her, instead we can do better than her if we want to, we only need to believe in ourselves for whatever is in front of us. We have to stand up for ourselves and show our parents that we too, we can, as our brothers can or maybe better.

She continued, "This is not a competition with our brothers we are fighting for our lives and our family's life, and this time is our time to show our people our capabilities." After she finished telling me all of that, I told her that I supported all of it, but I had a question of how we could be successful.

She told me, "We simply have to believe in ourselves, as I said before, we can go as long as we have love for our people and we have a will, we will find a way to make them be happy for themselves and be proud to have us."

She went on, it was like her time to tell me her story because the first night was my time, so the second night was hers, and sometimes she was talking like she was talking to herself.

"You know Bamurangirwa, things can change any time and be completely the opposite to the way it was, up to now a lot has changed, we have good new things, a new life, which we had no idea that we would ever be able to have, and our lives have changed from ordinary low people, to the life of high class people. But in that new life," when she reached that point she kept quiet and she looked sad, or shocked, or simply thought of something which made her feel uncomfortable.

I didn't know what it was, she was on her own, I didn't like to see her that way, and I went near her, I held her so tightly. She was crying now, I saw myself crying with her though I didn't know yet why she was crying.

It took her some minutes to be able to talk, when the time came she was still in shock, when she was trying to tell me what it was. She called me by name but she didn't wait for my response, she went ahead and tell me her story in a very low voice, that she was planning to come to Nairobi to visit me and get a chance to see me, so that we could talk.

"I missed you a lot especially when I was having problems, many people I knew couldn't understand me. In our village they talk about us, saying that the girls have made their mum rich. That person who has a problem is the only one who didn't have a daughter, now they can't see me when I am in this house and drive this car, and see the other side of my problems, it is not easy to some to understand that there are other things that can hurt me when I have money. When you have money in front of people they believe that you have everything! When that is completely wrong."

She continued, "My sister, where she was in secondary school she was with Acholi young man, who loved her so much, but he was older than her, and he was Acholi, so my sister had no love for him though she didn't hate him either. When he finished his studies he was a top officer in the army, at that time, it was them who had power, he was the one who started to do a lot for our family. He bought a house for our mum, now she had a house in the area which we call mukizungu (white people's area). He sponsored our brothers at colleges, and all of us we forgot that the man was non-Rwandan, and we started to ask my sister what else she wanted from him, what else he could do to show her that he loved her. In the end, she married him and now they have a son."

"Still I had a lot to tell you," she said, she went ahead. "I didn't get time to tell you the story of how I came to meet the man who I was coming to marry. Where I was at my secondary school, where my brother-in-law took me, it was a boarding school and it was mixed with boys. That is where and how we came to know each other," now she was telling me this, again she looked deeply uncomfortable.

"He was a student from Rwanda, some of the Rwandans back home who could afford fees they sent their children there for study, we were friends for a long time until all of our people at school came to know about us. We promised ourselves to get married after our studies, his parents came here and met my family, and they arranged our marriage, that was before I came to Nairobi." At that point she kept quiet and she bent her head in her hands, she started to cry uncontrollably. I helped her, we cried for some time, though I knew that there was something which she was not yet telling me, I saw it the first time she started the story.

Something was not right, but I tried not to interrupt her. I didn't know what to do, to see her in that situation made me to cry too, but I had to do something. I went near her and tried to comfort her, after time she looked like she could talk and I asked her what had happened. She knew that I knew nothing about them because even my sisters had lost contact with them for some time, so they had no news to tell me about them.

Though I was only quiet and listening to her, now I had to ask some questions in a careful way which maybe could help; "Now Mukabagira, did the women take your fiancé from you?"

That question seemed to make her to talk, maybe to show me that he was good enough to be trusted. And she said that it would be better if some girl took him from her if he had stayed alive. "I am very sorry about that, what happened to him?" I asked. She put her head to my shoulder again and in a low voice she said that he died in a motorbike accident, one week before the wedding.

To hear that was a big shock to me, there was a big silence, she was the one who broke the silence and said as if she was talking to herself, "I can be sure that I will never ever again love any other man the way I loved Mucyo." It was the first time for me to hear her mention his name, she went ahead, that time she turned and changed position and looked at me and called me again, "You know Bamurangirwa, I can't lie to myself either that I will get a man who will love me the way he loved me. What hurt me most is that I didn't have his child, so that I could take care of a baby know that is Mucyo's child.

It was me who told her that he had gone so soon before the marriage could take place so she couldn't blame anything for that.

She was sitting on her own, we were not holding each other, and she turned to look at me straight and asked me, "You know I spent the night with him many times when I was still at school? He was asking me to do that for him, and I was hiding myself and going to his room and going from his room early in the morning, so no one would see me. But we did not make love even once, there were some times I was begging him to do it, but he was always telling me that it was a sign to show me that he had too much love for me, enough to give me all the respect I needed, that was to show me that he would be patient for anything which would come in front of me, in front of our life ahead of us. I loved him more for that, but to be in his chest and feel his breath and have him protect me with his strong arms was enough."

She continued, "I had my family and friends but no one who was like you to me, I missed you a lot at that time. What I passed through in my young age, I hope that in my old age I will have the opposite life, otherwise if life can only be like this then there is no need to be alive, because I see that it is like punishment. I wanted to die but I was not capable of commiting suicide, my family was worried about me they didn't know if I would ever be able to be near any man again."

"Kanziga, my sister, tried too hard to make me meet a young Tanzanian man who was working in Makerere University and we were friends for some time, his mother was Rwandan and father was Tanzanian, people used to tell us that we looked like sister and brother, but it was true, somehow we looked alike. This man was good enough to take it easy, concerning my behaviour, he liked to go back home to Tanzania many times because of his work, the time came of the wedding, but we knew that soon after the wedding he would go to America for some time for his work, so, he wanted to marry me before he went. So that other men couldn't take me from him when he was out of the country." At that I laughed a little, I said that the ring was not the thing which could make anyone be faithful to another, it was only the heart.

311

"He was here for three weeks after the wedding, and he was there for one year. When he came back it was Amin and his people who had power. When he came back we were happy to be together again, we missed each other and remembered that when he went we didn't even have enough time for our honeymoon, after a few days our two cars came from abroad, he had his, and I had mine, but at night we preferred to go in one and he liked to drive me, we were out almost every weekend, many times for dancing."

She continued, "He had the idea of waiting to start a family so that, first, we could give ourselves time to be happy. When I wanted a family there and then, so we didn't use any protection, and when I was tired and didn't want to go out, he used to tell me that my time to be at home was when I knew that I was expecting. And I saw that he was right. Any time when we were going out he liked to choose for me what I would wear. And one night he chose one of the dresses he came with from America. We went to two different places and he said that we should go to the last place then we should go home. When we were there, three young men came and stood in front of us, and started to talk to me, asking me where I came from, they said that in Kampala there were beautiful girls and I had not yet gone out to be seen with them, they asked if I was a visitor. I didn't say anything and they repeated the same questions, you could see that they were just wanting to fight because they saw me with a man, and still couldn't respect him at all. On the other side our friends were standing, quietly only looking, because Amin's men were known for their behaviour of fighting and sometimes killing, and they were feared by many, and when you met them it was easy to know them, because of how they looked and the way they spoke, they had their accent they showed off to everyone."

"They started to tell us things in their broken Swahili, when my husband spoke it perfectly. They asked if being a beautiful girl made me deaf too. So when I saw things were like that I told him it was better to go home, he held my waist and we turned to go. Where the others came from, we didn't know, there was around ten of them now, I didn't know where some of them took my husband, and the other ones took me somewhere I didn't know. They were telling me many unspeakable things, I didn't want to be a woman of one of them. Now I was going to be a woman for all of them. Where they took me there came men, I didn't know how many, they started to beat me up and abuse me in many different ways, and all of them raped me, I didn't know for how long, I even didn't know how many days I was there."

"From the stories I was given after by our friends, it was the people who were there when they took us, it was them who made our story known and our family tried to pass it on to some people who were inside the government to try and see if they could get us alive or dead. They got me like a dead person, and took me to the hospital. I was there for one month and came back. No one knew how my husband died, we have never got his body, though some of them say that they took his watch from him and they threw him in Lake Victoria."

I was so sorry for her, from the bottom of my heart. And I told her so that it was a terrible life she had passed through and I hoped that she had a lot of happiness ahead of her.

After taking a breath, I asked her about the other parts of her life, "How do you manage life in general with this good big house and good car?"

"This house my late husband bought it before our wedding, and this is one of the cars he bought when he was in America, he was putting two big shops for me in the city centre, you will see them, the good thing was all of the businesses went ahead, well up to today. And I am still having my job in the office, though now I am on holiday for two weeks, so I will have enough time with you."

After one week I went back to Nairobi, my cousins asked me why I left the child and I told them that my sisters wanted him with them for some time, and I had no good reason to refuse. I didn't want to tell them that I had the plan to leave him there, so that maybe they would think that I didn't trust them enough for everything. I also had the plan that after getting a few things which I could use, I would move on my own and give them their freedom, and maybe have mine. I thought that it was not necessary to tell them that at the time, and I thought that they would be happy with that, to see that I was going to stand on my own. If they had something they wanted to help me with that would be fine, they could do so when they could, but it was better to give them back their privacy, and me too, I had to go and have mine. What they had done was more than enough. I knew that what they did for me was something I couldn't pay back.

Now that was my time to see my capability of how I could handle my life, and yes I knew that it was not going to be that easy, since I had never been on my own, alone, and I knew that it would only be me and my house.

But I knew that I would not be on my own for long, I believed that after knowing about the U.N., and how they sponsored people for their studies, I would bring my nieces and nephews.

Though I was in Nairobi for four years, I was like a stranger in Nairobi and the life there in general. I was preparing to be on my own by trying this and that. I knew that no one would be with me all the time directing me everywhere.

Nairobi was the capital and a bigger city than anywhere I had ever been before, to know each and every place I needed to go, I was aware that it was going to be a little problem, and since I didn't know anything there yet, I had to go with what I heard people say.

One of stories I heard was that people there didn't help others, if they passed someone in a fight, they would just go ahead with their business and act like they didn't even see them, as though nothing was happening!

Where I had passed from my home, Congo, Uganda and Tanzania they had a habit I knew back home in Rwanda, of greeting each other on the street, without necessarily knowing each other and helping anyone who came in front of them on the street.

I was wondering about those things I was hearing people say, but I didn't understand properly if it was true, sometimes I thought that they made up stories.

It could be worse if it was a man who was beating a woman, even if they didn't know each other before, he could say that she was his wife, or his prostitute and he gave her his money! No one would think about investigating or intervening, nothing. He could beat you for whatever reason and go.

The Kenyan Government had just recently at the time given us small green books as our identity, with our name on it in capital letters as ALIEN, and they told us that we had to go with it everywhere we were, otherwise anyone who met a police officer when they didn't have it would have to answer some questions.

To me, I saw that this was not problem, that simple, I would put it in my handbag. I started to go to the U.N..H.C.R. They had different officers depending on what you wanted from them, one week after I started going by myself, in town, they pickpocketed the envelope which had my identity and the little money I had! I didn't know how or when they did it. And since I had not yet heard about pickpocketers, I was surprised to see that someone would touch the inside of someone's bag! At home when I told them with surprise because I was asking why and how someone could do that, they were laughing a lot to see that it was strange to me.

From that time after they pickpocketed me, when I was on the bus many times, inside the bus there were many people, and many times we had to stand up, so to be safe I had to remember to check so that I could see the kinds of people who were around me, to see if they looked like thieves or not. When I saw that they were old and clean men and women, then I knew none of them could be a thief, so I was safe. I thought that it was only the young men who looked to be dirty who were supposed to be pickpockets! After they took what little money I had many times, some other times, I was too shy to talk about it, I said to myself that where I passed was the same way others passed too. After I came to realise that even some men in suits could be thieves and some women were pickpockets too!

I said that was how to welcome me in the big city. It took me a long time to know how I had to hold my bag properly, and that I didn't have to trust anyone. People were making jokes about me by saying that thieves pickpocketed me always because of how I dressed, that they saw me and saw that I was foreign and I has a lot of money too, because I made myself look like a rich lady. And when someone else was pickpocketed, you could hear them say, "Today they thought that you are Bamurangirwa!" But since they had taken my purse money many times when it was empty or had very little coins, they might have known already that I was not rich. I thought that maybe the way I dressed attracted them the first time, I think that they came to see that I was a newcomer to the city, and still had the foolishness of villagers, and it was no problem, even if sometimes they didn't get a lot from my pocket, but wherever they could get it they would be helping themselves, until I woke up, and learned how the city people would deal with a situation like that.

They pickpocketed my ALIEN three times, immigration officers gave me another one each time but on the fourth one, they refused to give me another one by telling me that I was selling them to people who were in other countries and were coming to use them in Kenya. I didn't blame them, anyone could think that, they gave it to me after a long time and after a lot of struggle, helped by officers who came to my rescue there in those offices without 'kitu kidogo', Mrs Oyuwa and Peter Omaya, then I made a photocopy and kept the original at home.

By being someone who came from Rwanda and passed through those three countries which had the same culture concerning greetings to other people in the street, I liked it. In the streets of Nairobi, before I thought that was what people were supposed to do, but when I greeted someone, they were standing in one spot and turning to me like they were waiting for other words, maybe they thought I would ask directions, when I was waiting for them to respond too, but when I had no other words to say the person would look at me as if I was insane and go! I would go with a lot of confusion, after I decided that I would do no more greetings.

I had to go in to town almost everyday, and sometimes I could get greetings from a stranger maybe once a month, and I would see the person to be a very good person, because of that I would respond to the person in a special way to show the person my appreciation.

From the way I would respond, the person could see that I was more than happy to be greeted, maybe I was a foreign person who just came to the city, or there was some other thing which made me act that way.

One day I met a man, and he greeted me in a respectful way by saying good morning madam, 'Habali yasubuhi Mama', after seeing how I responded, he asked me the time, and when I looked at my watch, he too brought his head near to my face to check for himself. I let him check for himself so that he could go to where he was going. He didn't go anywhere, it surprised me to see that he was still in my direction, especially when he came near with me and we started to go together as people who knew each other!

I was preparing myself to go to visit my father. So I had money with me for that journey I had just come from the bank, I had heard stories that sometimes you could go with a thief into the bank without knowing that you were with them, and they would wait for their time to take your money from you.

I assumed that he was a thief and maybe we were together before without me knowing that. I was scared to death, he recognised that I was scared of him, and he asked me why I was scared of him. When I was in front of 680 Hotel, I thought of going inside the hotel, since he looked like a dirty man, maybe he would be afraid of going inside it, but I remembered that men could say anything to people, if the victim was a woman. I tried to go ahead as far as he would not refuse me to go where I was going. I had a hope that by luck I could meet a Rwandan who would save me, it could be their way to go and come back from one of the U.N.'s offices which were on Koinange Street.

I was scared enough to go anywhere he would tell me, if he wanted to do so, I should go. It was like he held a gun to my head! All of that was because I had in my mind that no one could help me no matter what. He was so proud to see how I was sweating and shaking.

After some time in front of us came a tall beautiful lady, who was dressed like me in a 'kitenge', a beautiful colourful dress, which was for non-Kenyan ladies at the time. We dressed ourselves from waist to feet, with a top which was part of it, and when you saw local women young or old, who dressed always in short dresses with their legs out, you felt yourself that you dressed as a lady enough to be seen as respected lady.

I told myself that she was going to save me, because I would stop her and talk to her, so this man would fear and go, and he would see that we might come from the same part of Africa. When she was near us I stopped in front of her and greeted her, instead of responding to me she asked me why I greeted her when I did not know her?! And to my surprise the man came and stood near me! When I had that question it was like she had slapped me in my face, and I wished the earth would swallow me. I turned dumb, but I had to try and see if this could be my chance to be saved by her, and I told her that I knew her in Kampala. It was a lie, a matter of trying. And she said that she had never been to Kampala and she said that if I knew her, who was she?! Before saying anything, the man apologised to her, and told her that since morning I was like that, telling people things which they were not understanding!

I thought that even if I just tried to tell the truth and ask her for help by telling her that I was in trouble, the man I was with was a stranger and I was scared of him, and he would still say the same thing, that I was mad. I was his wife…

But the lady had already seen that for some reason I was scared, so I thought she thought that we were corny people, the man and I, and she wanted to show us that she was not new in Nairobi, so we were not going to be able to steal from her however we tried. She had gone, it was me and him, he was still going in my direction, where I wanted to go and he was with me, sometimes he told me that I didn't have to be scared, that he was human like me.

I was going to Koinange Street, and I knew that normally you couldn't be in that area for five minutes without meeting any Rwandans or even Ethiopians who we used to meet in those U.N. offices. They could also save me, but what was a big worry to me was that no one was passing for all of that time!

We reached the market when I saw the office in front of me, where I was going, and I heard the man I was with say something like a sign.

Seconds after that around me there were around ten clean men, some were wearing uniform, working inside the market. They looked happy to see their friend with me, and they were talking in an unknown language to me.

At that time after seeing that I was between them, the way they were happy, I was no longer scared, the sweating dried out, I was no longer sweating or shaking, I was like a dumb person, only looking at them from one to another. I think even if they used some kind of weapon to cut me I wouldn't have felt any pain.

After being there for one minute, maybe they were still planning what better way to deal with me: I heard a voice calling my name and asking me what I was doing between those people, in my language, but I didn't even turn my head to see who might calling me. I thought that I was dreaming, and the voice called again and repeated the same question again in my language! Then I realised that even the first one I heard was real! And I turned my head and saw the two Rwandan girls Jose Bideli who later married Mr. Ntagozera, and her friend Alice Cyangabwoba. They were still waiting for the cars to pass so that they could cross the road which was there near where we were standing, and came to where we were.

When I saw them I started to be feel weak, sweating, and shaking again, the fear came back, but now it was more than double, I felt that I could faint, and I told them that I was with a thief and I had already passed away, that they had killed me!

Jose told me to hold on, they were coming to save me, maybe she thought that they had already hurt me somehow, but Alice was telling me that I was not dead yet, I was alive and they were coming to save me from them.

In very short time they were there, Alice was holding me when I was sweating and shaking and she went ahead telling me that I was alive when I was still telling her that I was already dead. After a few seconds I believed that I was really alive, and Jose, she was a brave girl, who had been in Nairobi for some time, more than all of us. Alice's job was to calm me down, Jose's was to deal with those men.

319

She started by asking if I had anything they owed me and they said nothing, and she went ahead asking them what they wanted from me then. At that time they had started to go back inside the market one by one, and they left the one who came with me at the beginning, he was the one now who answered Jose's questions. He told her that maybe their sister had some kind of problem, because they were just greeting me and I started sweating and shaking!

Then she told him that if he was asking me nothing then the game was over, and he went. I was sure they were disappointed, there was three of us now. I thanked them and they were in a hurry to get going somewhere, I said that even if they if they were in a hurry, it would be better to leave me where I was going and not in the street. They took me and left.

I had that shock still even after sitting down, they asked me what happened and I told them the whole story from the beginning to the end, and they told me that the problem was that I greeted the man back. I should have turned to see if I knew him first, and if I didn't then I should have left him, because in Nairobi normally they didn't greet each other, unless they knew each other.

I asked them how they came to have those bad habits, to mind their own business that much. And they told me that they got it from English people and it was not all parts of Kenya, only Nairobi. But I didn't believe them. I told them that it was not true because British people had also colonised Uganda and Tanzania and they were not like that, not even in their capitals. They told me that Uganda and Tanzania were too strong in some of their cultures, more than Kenyans

From that time when someone greeted me and I didn't know the person I had to show the person that I was a Nairobian lady, by showing the person a stone face before I left. It came to be a problem when my children became teenagers, when I met their friends who I didn't recognise yet, when they greeted me in the city centre, being teenagers they could be bad, more than old people, so I had to show them a double stone face! And when they met my children they were asking them what was wrong, what had they done to their mother when they were at home I was good to them. And when they told them what happened, it was a big surprise to my children that when they met me on the road I didn't respond to their greetings and on top of that I gave them very bad looks as if I was angry with them! When my children asked me many times, I told them to tell their friends to call me by name when we met, at last by using the name Mum it couldn't be easy for them to mention my name directly.

The last funny thing concerning those greetings in Nairobi was one evening when a man greeted me and I responded to him in a respectful way, but after I came to remember that I did that without checking first if I knew him or not! Then I turned my head and saw that I had never seen him anywhere, automatically my arms were on top of me, I was talking in a loud voice in my language, throwing my arms here and there like I was dancing, but the truth was I was scared, I believed that he was coming to catch me from behind, and I was talking like I was calling my God to protect me. I was sorry that I forget to check first to see if I knew him.

I had forgotten that I was midway in the road, and there were other people who saw me do such things. I told myself to turn my head and see where he was, if he was near me, maybe he was going to grab me! When I turned my head, I saw that the man who greeted me looked very shocked to the level that I thought he would never greet another person in Nairobi again, because I thought he thought that he had greeted a mad woman, and he was lucky he was not beaten.

He was still standing in the same sport and holding his chin, I felt sorry for him and I said that from now on I was not going to be scared any more. I was a proper Nairobian and I would be dealing with the situations the way they came, like everybody else.

After leaving my son with his auntie I came back, and started to deal with the U.N.. To make things easier, I didn't go as a newcomer, I went as someone who was there using the names Nyilimanzi had taken there before as his wife, so there I was, Mukaneza Winnie. This meant that I had my file there already, from that point things were easy to me. There were those small offices, and one main one, and you could go there only for really understandable reasons, you would need an appointment, sometimes it would take time to get it, people most of the time were going there to talk about problems which the officers didn't manage to solve, or didn't want to solve.

They were giving people benefits according how they were, if they were old, sick, or had a big family, but it was only a little money and some had no permission to work. So to survive with the little money they had, they had to go in cheaper areas like Kawangware, Kaliobangi or Dandora… foreigners liked to be together according to where they came from, so that they can't be bothered.

And it was known that most of the Rwandans were in Kawangware. This area was one of the places you could get the houses which were built in woods, which were for poor people, but there were some other refugees who were in the cheapest areas in ghettos like Kibera Magengo and Mathare, but there were only a small number of Rwandans who were in the ghetto, and that was unknown much with others, or there were only a few other Rwandans who knew where they were living.

One of the cultures of Rwandans was to do anything they could to see that they would be able to look excellent outside, by dressing properly. So since they had little money, the first thing they had to think about was dressing, then food came after. They didn't see food to be important, instead they liked drinking more than eating from the beginning. If someone talked about food a lot they saw that person as greedy, maybe that was why a big number of them liked beer, and some of them at the time would die because of drinking a lot of beer without eating properly, or beer was the reason to make them be only in one step forever. Maybe this came from history, because they would encourage children to drink milk instead of eating food since they were farmers and believed milk to be better than other food. Even in their sermons, like weddings, there was no food, all of the preparation for any sermons had to be different beers and that was it.

They were a few people who were using the U.N.. and getting a proper education, and those who were in colleges or high school they had high pocket money, and some of the young men might use that chance to get married because the girls were after them, because they were sure that after their studying they would get a better job.

But some were enjoying the money without going to school, thinking that they were clever enough to lie to the officers because they would bribe the teachers to send reports with good marks of their students, when the truth was that they didn't attend colleges at all. And the students who were in the colleges at that time, they were seen as rich, those who didn't want to be bothered with education, they would be leaders of other drinkers. When the rest who had little money would finish it and start to beg them.

I had already met many different people who told me different stories, how the officers gave them trouble in different ways, so that they coud get what they wanted from them, or simply because they didn't want to see them be successful. Some were jealous of them, especially women to women, just because of their looks and how they dressed, when girls or mothers went for something, sometimes what they wanted from the officer could be something which could be done in one day, but might take days, or months, or they would be given another course the opposite of what they were asking for. That was between the women officers and women refugees, but if an officer was a man, it was also another problem, because the man by bad luck would want to take her to bed before doing what she came to ask him for, when it was his job to do that. Or you would be there in front of his door for a long time and sometimes you would get nothing.

And it hurt more when it came to the studies of their children, at that time it could force some of them to go to the head office to ask for help. It would show the big bosses that their officers were not working the way they were supposed to be, in that case if they could see that you were a sharp person who could do that, it might save you trouble because sometimes it could cost someone his or her job. In that case you could get someone who would like anyone to get his or her right, and wanted people to be equal.

Many times they were favouring their officers, and when the

person was someone who already had anger with life, and knew his or her right, the person would find a way to communicate with Geneva. People like that were few, because many had fear that if they took another step they might cut out all of their support, or simply they didn't know how they could do it.

On my times it was those officers, the men and women, some came across as cleaner at first, when they were giving training the person who made the deal for them to come, step by step they became the officers. Sometimes without any qualifications, but just because they were relatives or they gave 'kitu kidogo', people like that, most of the time it was them who was too hard to refugees more than others.

I think that was because those kinds of people saw themselves in a position which they had never dreamed of, to see that they could be the key to shaping the future of someone! And now they could give themselves happiness but in the wrong way, by hurting others just because they could. And also people like that did not find it easy to deal with different people with different backgrounds and different cultures. Let alone to be head of anything. Many of them wanted to get high respect from their clients, which they would never get from many of them. Instead, sometimes they were beaten by their clients.

The way which they were treating foreigners was bad and made many people angry. Especially refusing the young generation a proper education by choosing them for courses which were the opposite of their choices! Something which made many of the young people hate going to colleges and turn themselves to beer instead. Ignorance like that happened to foreigners in many places, it was the situation of a refugee life, it was terrible to see someone being happy and proud to destroy the future of the young generation.

But on the another hand it was good, because it was helping these refugees, it reminded them that where they were, was not their home. When a child had done well in their exams, they were telling their parents that a refugee didn't have permission to join university! These officers were taking them to some colleges which did not have enough teachers or had unqualified ones. And sometimes it was their own or their relatives' business, and as far as the U.N. was concerned, they had money and they paid without a problem, so they were using them for their business and bribes. And they were trying hard to see that they sent as many of them as they could, because if they got many students they would get big school fees to divide for themselves, according to their deals and bribery. It didn't bother them if they had a good education or not, what was important to them was to get money from the U.N., they were using these children so that they could promote their business and themselves.

Things like that were going on every season, what you would be taking in college would depend where their business was, at that time, in my time, they were taking women old and young for dressmaking, that was where they took me too.

If you were a woman, and you were going to see an officer who was a woman, there was nothing else you could do, you had to go and see her, it would depend if that day was your lucky day, otherwise you would go when you were aware of what would happen inside that office.

When it was your turn, she would tell you to come in, after standing at the door for maybe more than fifteen minutes, and you would be in front of her when she was reading a newspaper. You would greet her, but there would be no response, or she could show you a sign using her head that she had heard you, and you would stand for five minutes, then she would tell you to sit down, and you sat. Silence, she was still reading the newspaper, you sat like that, in the same position, for ten minutes, this was forty minutes since you were standing at her door, and she was just reading the newspaper or magazine before she talked to you! When you sat you didn't know which position you should hold yourself, or where to look for that long time! Outside there were others who were waiting to see her, they were complaining that you took a long time with her!

Then she came back from what she was reading and looked at you without a word, but firstly she would look at you from head to toe, now you would start to talk and she would be answering without opening her lips, just using her head, as if she knew what you were telling her, or thought that you were talking about childish things, and you were wasting her time. To see her like that, would make you lose hope of whatever help you were looking for. Most of the time, when the situation was like that, you were aware that the answer you would get was one of two common answers, either it was impossible, or they would tell you to come back tomorrow.

And sometimes this tomorrow would never come. You would go for that particular thing for months and months, your neighbours would believe that you had an office job because you would go almost every day and many times you would go early in the morning depending what time they told you, or simply, you wanted to try and be the first to see the officer. And you would come back home in the evening time.

Those women officers had their reasons to treat other women, their clients, in such a way

No 1: they were jealous of them because of how they looked, and how they dressed! That was the reason that it could be too much for an officer sometimes and she would shout at you instead of listening to you, by asking you if someone who dressed like you had any problems, or if you were coming to show yourself off! And sometimes the dress you were dressed in, you had had it for years.

And you would try not to respond otherwise she could call security and throw you out, many times you had to be dumb, or say yes to everything. Those kinds of women, when they got a male client, many times they would do what was supposed to be done for him. Things like that forced many women to dress in rubbish, when they were going in those offices. But some of the officers, men or women, would simply do the opposite of how it was supposed to be done, to the majority of those who came to their offices, (simply because they were who they were). Unless they would do something to make them do a better job, in the way of bribing them, and they would give them a bribe from the small support they got.

After seeing all of that, I decided that I would never dress in rubbish or go with any male officer, just to be able to get what I was supposed to get.

But yes, I would try to bribe them when I could, to make shortcuts, or I would go to the head office when it was necessary. I couldn't avoid bribery when it was the culture of the country. But one day I got a big surprise when I went inside a German lady, a nun, Officer Louise's office. After having permission to sit, I greeted her, she was quiet and looked at me for one minute, and she didn't say anything, not even to ask me my names, and I waited to talk to her according to what she would tell me first. I assumed that she had to ask me my names first and write it down like any other officers, and I was trying to show her respect as much as I could. In that short silence she asked me if I had come to ask her for any kind of help. I said yes officer, in a humble way. I was almost starting to tell her what I had come to see her for, with an angry face she was talking a little with a high voice, now she started asking me how come I could dress in an expensive dress and look how I looked and come to waste her time to ask for help when there were the really genuine refugees who needed that help. I told her that the dress I was wearing I was given by friend and I was telling her the truth, but I was a genuine refugee and like others I survived with the small support I got from the U.N..

She was really angry now and she stood up and called the security to throw me out! She didn't know yet who I was; she didn't get time to ask me, I was not upset with that. I was surprised and told myself that I would go back to her office again, as far as she didn't write my names anywhere, but next time I would dress in a rubbish way and act miserable in front of her, and see how she would behave, or if she would remember me.

The next day I went to her office and she welcomed me, she greeted me and listened to me. I got what I went to ask her, and when I was out I asked myself what kind of habit was that, when you could be judged on the way you looked, did they want us to look like mad people? Or else you had a case to answer! Or she was someone who liked to see where and when people died first, before coming with aid, when they were capable of doing something to prevent the problems before they happened. I saw that, to them it was better to wait first to get enough work to do and it was easy business too.

Most of us, when we came out of those offices after seeing them, would say what had happened to us, so that you could be aware of what you were going to face, if you were next. We were nicknaming them, different names, related to their behaviour, or their looks, their behaviour towards us made us hate them. Some officers could hold you for the same position for a long time until the officer would go on holiday or when there would be some changes, and you would see a different officer, then it was your lucky time to move to another step, most of the time the new one was good at last for some time.

To the people who were forced to take their problems to the head office, though they favoured their workers, sometimes they were following up what was happening to them after getting a lot of complaints. And also in those male and female officers, there were few who were happy to do their job the way it had to be done to anyone who would come in front of them. Those who were genuine workers, most of the time they were not friends with their co-workers, because they were not happy to see what they were doing to people, or their co-workers themselves were jealous of them.

There were others who were naturally greedy for everything. One of them we had who was well known, was a lady who we knew as Mrs. Kamau. She was an old lady and too fat, more than everyone there, so we nicknamed her two names, one to us was like her first name, which was about her greediness, and the other one was like her surname, which meant her size. Although we were enjoying them, and making fun of them, on the other hand we were consoling ourselves. I was a good nicknamer, and they used to ask me which name suited so and so.

Some of them would not believe that we were poor, just because of how they saw us, and yes some of us were not that bad, some had children in countries and they were sending them money, or one member of the family had a good job, or simply they knew how to budget their small support.

If one of Mrs Kamau's clients support for some reason stopped, or they had other reasons and they had to see her, in her office, she would stand up and greet you with a big hug, and she would show you where to sit, and give you a tea, before telling you her problems, she was the first one to tell you hers! And after telling her why you came to see her, here you told her that your support had stopped, you had no money even to pay your rent, but she would tell you words which would show you that she wanted money from you, and if you had some which was extra to your transport, you would give it to her.

After getting money from you, she would start another topic, of how you looked and how you dressed. She would talk about you, from your shoes to your hair, and when she reached the necklace, or scarf, sometimes it would take her many minutes, still talking about it, and because you wanted to forge a friendship with her, and sometimes you had bought the necklace cheap from the street, you would take it off your neck and give it to her.

From there she would tell you how good she was, more than everyone in those offices, and your response would have to be that without her nothing good could happen to you, you knew that she was the one who was fighting for you in general. One day she told me how good she was and got a bible from her handbag and showed me, she told me that she believed in God and she couldn't go anywhere without it.

I told her that I had guessed that her generosity was not only nature; it was also included in being a good Christian. And that day was my lucky day, she did everything for me which had been on her shelf for months.

When I was with Rutagambwa and Senzage I started to get support from the U.N. and since I had the idea of moving on my own one day, I started to buy a few things one by one, and I thought it was good to buy fewer things but good material. I bought one good big mattress, and a few other things so that I could sleep on the mattress before I bought the proper bed. Rutagambwa and his brother were sleeping down just to give me respect, and they had their small old mattress which was made with cotton and because it was old it had been made into a ball inside and when they slept it was not comfortable.

At that time, soon after I moved from Nyirimanzi's home, Kantamage sent me her son Batsinduka, he had finished his primary school and had passed in a high level, but she didn't have school fees. According to the letter he came with, she was not comfortable seeing him sitting at home without going to school, so she was sure that I would try where I was, to see that he could go ahead with his study.

When I saw him, I knew he was a very good boy in all areas, he was a child who had respect for old and young, on top of that he was sharp in school, he had never been number four in school, he was always between number one and three, he was a lovable child at home and at school. So I was happy to try for him, knowing that if he was successful, it would be on behalf of all of us, if I was not able to help him, it would be a loss to all of us as a family.

One day I wanted us as a family to get a solution concerning Batsinduka. Senzage was new to life in Nairobi, and being younger that Rutagambwa, it was Rutagambwa who had to say something before him, so I told them why the child came and asked them where we could start in the U.N. to see that he could be recognised by them.

Batsinduka was outside playing with other children, Senzage and I waited to hear Rutagambwa's idea.

Rutagambwa gave me the answer to show me that he was the top of the home where I was, and if he wanted something to be done it would be done, and if he said no it would be a no. What he told me was completely opposite of what I wanted from him, and it shocked me, but it also gave me more determination to do everything that I thought was the right thing to do.

He told me that since they sent the child without asking us first, then what we would do was give him the transport to go back to where he came from! All of us said nothing, Senzage and I looked at each other, and I saw that Senzege too was not happy with his elder brother's decision, though he could't say anything. Our meeting was over and after Senzage came to where I was sitting by myself and asked me what I would do next. And I told him that I didn't know yet, he told me that it was not good to send him back before I saw what would happen first, he noticed that I was not happy either.

And I told him that to send him back before trying and getting a good reason why I should send him back was out, so I would try and see what would happen.

I told him that this was the same U.N. which didn't manage to protect me and allow me to be where I had to be in my country and get proper study. Now it was going to give Batsinduka proper study, maybe it would take time or it would give me some kind of trouble, but in the end it would be OK. Batsinduka would get means of study, I had that feeling.

Senzage smiled and told me that he didn't know that I could be determined to do something and believe in myself that much. He looked relaxed then.

I told myself that the time came to be me, and do whatever as me, without using anyone's mind, only when I saw that it was a good idea. I wanted to move on my own even before knowing that Batsinduka would come. Now I had him, the things I had to use in my home, I had enough, two spoons, two plates, two pots and two plastic cups.

The next day Rutagambwa came to where I was and asked me how much I needed for his transport back to Uganda. I told him that I would not send him back before trying. I told him that with a hope that he would not put us out because I didn't respect his idea, since then I was aware that he could change in any way if he wanted to.

Many times Batsinduka was at Angelina's home, my friend who was not very near, but to Batsinduka it was not a far walk from where we were. I didn't want him to be bothered, there was a boy there his age, Mitali, and Mitali had not yet started school either, so I got the house to move in, and Batsinduka would stay at Angelina's place before

I got what he would be using for sleeping. He was sleeping with another boy, Kennedy Ndahiro, at Rutagambwa's place, but Kennedy was in school in the daytime, that was why Batsinduka was going to be with Mitali in the daytime.

The time to say bye and thank them came, I told them that if it was not for them, it would not have been easy get away and come out of Magengo. What surprised me was that Rutagambwa was not happy that I moved, I thought that he would see it to be a good idea. I didn't know why, but I went anyway.

Rutagambwa came to see where I moved, he stood at the door and looked around in that one room with a few things inside, it was only Batsinduka and Ndahiro who carried them. It was him and I, he called me and asked me if I knew that being at his home was the reason I had managed to save the money to buy those things. I said yes, I knew that. He went on, "Because of that reason, all of these things are mine!" I didn't get to say anything, I told myself to wait and see what would happen next, but of the things which were there, I was worried for only three things; the mattress, stove and lamp, which was a big hand lamp, though the price of that mattress could buy all of the other things I had.

He went on talking, he was talking to himself, but I knew that he was telling me, "Now I have the right to take them all, but I will not do that, I will take some of them." Now I was asking myself which he liked more and chose to take away from me. I had to wait and see, he went on and told me that he was going home to send someone to take back that mattress! I wanted to scream and scream, and say that it was not fair to do those good things for me and help me so much and now do that to me!

I tried not to say a thing because if I said something maybe it would make a lot of noise, and neighbours would say that there was something wrong with the new person who was moving there.

I waited to hear that he would take the stove too but he didn't say another word.

I turned and left, I did not lock the door, when I came back my mattress was gone, and he sent me his old, small, cotton mattress, the same one which the cotton had turned like a ball inside. And I wanted to show him that I didn't need ignorance, and I would not sleep on a mattress like that in my house. I gave it to a child to take it back to him.

I wanted to show him that I was going a step ahead, not behind.

I was left without any mattress now. That night I slept on my clothes, the next day I went to my friend and borrowed a mattress, I got a new one, medium, which I used until I bought mine like the one which Rutagambwa took from me, a good bed of 300 K sh which was a lot to me.

It was Senzage who was escorting me everywhere, he was not happy with what Rutagambwa did to me, we were not talking about it. The time came when Rutagambwa was ashamed to come to my home to see how I had improved myself day by day, maybe he was jealous.

I had a neighbour, a Ugandan lady, she became my friend and I noticed that she was a good person, a person who could be happy to see others were happy. She was there for a long time and she knew a lot about the U.N., one day I told her my problem with Batsinduka, and she told me to give her time, she was going to think of the clean lies since those U.N. people hated the truth! I looked at her, the way she was talking without any doubt in her face and I believed that she knew what she was talking about, and I started to feel relaxed as if I would get what I wanted. I started to plan other names of young children I could say were younger sisters and brothers to Batsinduka, so that it would be easy for me when I wanted to bring another child after Batsinduka. I was going to use him as the key to others.

The time came and she called me and told me that she had got the clean lies; I said that as long as it was a lie which would not hurt anyone, I didn't mind. She started her stories and I was there in front of her listening to the Ugandan lady, we knew her as Narongo. So Narongo told me that she decided that she would take the boy in to the offices at the refugee council, and give him to those women, and tell them that the child had stopped her on the way, and asked her if she knew his auntie, that he had come from Burundi and he heard that his auntie was in Nairobi. She would say that when she asked him how he came he told her that there was a Kenyan man who helped him by bringing him with his lorry, that he had lost his parents in the war but he didn't know if they were dead or they were somewhere alive, so him and his young brothers and sisters were in the care of neighbours and since he was the oldest, he decided to come and try to see if he could find their auntie!

Being Ugandan they knew that we had some connections with Rwandans.

"I think that they will ask me to help them by staying with the boy and trying to find his auntie for them. Even if outside there will be Rwandans they will go to ask them for Mukaneza Winnie, no one will know her since they know you as Bamurangirwa Patricia, so it is not going to be easy for them to find someone who might know you, so they will need my help. That is how they do it. I will wait until the end so any time when they are out they will see that I am still there, so that they can't give him to someone else. And if it is going to be the way I think, then after some time, I will take both of you and tell them that I found you, and in front of them the boy has to look serious and sad. What you have to do is to put down the names and ages of young children and know that as soon as you tell them whatever you tell them you must stick to it because they might ask you the same questions after time, to see that you are telling them the same thing, because they have your file in front of them."

It was a Saturday, so the next day was the day of training Batsinduka, Narongo wanted to take him on Monday. On Monday they went and I was left at home just praying for them.

When they came back, as soon as they reached the house, they were laughing loudly before telling me anything, and their laugh gave me hope that they came with good news.

Narongo told me that everything went as it was planned, what she made up after was the name of the driver who helped Batsinduka, and she came up with an Akamba name, because the officer she was going to see came from the Akamba tribe. So she suggested that she might be kind and show her that most Akamba people were good people and would be as good to the boy as the Akamba driver was to him. She told me how the officer was happy for her help and asked her to go ahead helping them, by going with the boy for them, and trying to find out if she knew where Bamurangirwa Patricia might be somewhere around there, because she didn't have that person in her file. And she gave her some money to use to support the boy.

I told her that it was her money, but she refused and after an argument we divided the money.

After two weeks, Narongo took us and showed them that she had found me, and they started to give me Batsinduka's support, and told me to go home and wait, they were sending a letter to Burundi to see if what the boy told them was true, then after that he would start to go to school, and they would open my own file separate from Nyilimanzi's, that was where they would put Batsinduka.

And I would go to the head office to ask for an answer from Burundi after two weeks.

I went out of the office with big worries because I told him to tell them his real parents' names, and none of them had ever been to Burundi. And now our lies were not clean enough to win them, we forgot something, and we failed. They couldn't get a letter from Burundi telling them that they knew anything about him when they didn't!

Because I was too worried, I bribed one of the workers there in the head office to check for me if a result from Burundi had come and what it said. Though I thought that I knew what they would say, I was in a hurry to know it officially, so that I could know the next step I could take.

When I went to check the results they told me that Burundi had no information concerning that story and they would give the boy a ticket to Burundi. And they told me the day I would come with him and his bag.

I came back as a sick person. When I told Narongo she told me that I didn't have to be worried because he was not going to go anywhere! Even if they said so.

I asked her how. She said that they would give a security man his ticket; he was the one who would take him to the bus. That was how they did it. So we would wait for them and we would talk to that security man and ask what he wanted from us, 'kitu kidogo' a small thing, if he would try to be hard to us, we could give him 'kitu kikubwa' a big thing. And our boy would be here and we might know what we would do for that after. Again I saw that Narongo was talking with a lot of confidence, and I wanted things to be different, so I had to listen to her.

The time came and I took my Batsinduka to the head office. I was nervous, the security man took him inside the office, he was there the whole day because the buses were going in the evening time, and I waited, I knew the time and where buses which went out of Kenya stood, and I knew the time they might be there, but I was nervous because I didn't know how our plan would go.

I was by myself, waiting for them, the time came for them to come, and I went to talk to the security man. The man looked at me with a stone face to show me that he was doing his job, after he talked to me and I gave him 'kitu kidogo' he gave me my child and his ticket. I sold the ticket and went back with my child. I asked Narongo what was next, she told me that we had better wait for some time, because everyone said that the director was not a good person, especially to Tutsi. He was a Belgian man, maybe Narongo was right or maybe not, but I wouldn't trust the U.N. people one hundred percent, with or without being Belgian. We were going to try again anyway, that was when we would know the truth and see what we could do next. His contract was almost over, we had to wait for the new one.

At that time I already knew many places, and did everything by myself. I would always remember one day, one of my friends, Adela Madam, after seeing that I had a lot of trust in people, she told me that it was good to depend on myself for important things, that I didn't

336

have to trust anyone, so that I could know where things went wrong, since some people could pretend to be good to you when they were not. I didn't have to fear anywhere, it was better to go and try, if I was successful, fine, if I was not then that was it, instead of having fear or being scared of yourself. She had seen how I trusted everyone. And her idea helped me all my life, in many ways.

The life of the refugees and the U.N. and immigration business had particular people who were experts, they knew how to put stories in to good words and you couldn't go before you got them and sat together, and were trained until the stories were to satisfaction. Some were volunteers others were paid.

But me, I was happy with my volunteer. I had Narongo and she was enough. A short time passed, and they changed the director, but I didn't have to change the story. I only had to go and tell them that the boy went back, and the neighbour who was taking care of them was abusing them, and since he knew the way now, he came back by himself to ask me to rescue them, and now I couldn't tell him to go back in that situation.

That was how I did it and they told me to wait for two weeks while they were sending a letter to Burundi. I would come to see the answer, again I knew that they might be sending a letter this time but still the answer would have to be bad, because there was no one in Burundi who was going to favour me and lie. After that time, when I went back they told me that what the boy told them was true! And they apologised to me for what happened before, now what I had to do was to see how I could bring the young one who was in the hands of those neighbours! I thanked the officer who was talking to me, and went out. After I was out of their area, I sat somewhere and thanked my God, and told myself that the door of my blessings had opened. I was going to use this U.N. to help my family. I told myself that if a lie would not hurt anyone, and would help where help was needed, then that lie was blessed.

Everyone I told that story to didn't believe me, they thought that I sent a bribe to Burundi or I knew someone there! But I told them that when God opened the door of the blessings no one could close it.

In normal life I hated lying. If I was lied to by my friend our friendship was finished because I could not understand why anyone would lie. You should tell the truth, if you get what you want, fine, if you do not, that is it, but why lie, when sometimes you might carry it with you for all of your life, when maybe you had lied for no good reason at all. A good reason like this one, lying to the U.N..

But if the U.N. liked lies then I was going to learn to lie, and it would be them and me, I would see who was clever, them or me? They would only be powerful, but not clever. They told me to find a government school for him, they would sponsor him for everything, though he was finished at primary school in Uganda, they wanted him to go back to primary school there, even for a few years. He went to the primary school which was near where we were at Kangemi. I had a lot of trust in him. I knew that he was going to study, and he would get it. I didn't know what to do but to thank God, my God, to see that Batsinduka was wearing a school uniform; he was going back to school.

Now he was ready to go to school, I had to bless him in a way I believed to be a genuine one, which was to thank my great great grandparents.

I told him to sit down and he sat on the chair. I told him to sit on the mat and straighten his legs, he looked confused, but he did what I said. I went in to the corner that I called the kitchen, and came back with a mug full of milk and gave it to him and told him to drink. I was speaking my good words and thanking who I believed I had to thank. He drank and went to school. For himself, for his family, and for his country Rwanda, for Africa, and for the world in general.

It was my first time to be happy since I was in Kenya, now I knew that the next thing was to bring the other children who would be able to study.

But I needed a holiday before other things, I wanted to relax somehow, and I thought it would be a good idea to use that time to visit my father and come back and go ahead with what I wanted to do. I had no way I could pay back each and every person who gave me ideas, and helped me in different ways, what I had to do, was only wish all of them the best.

There was something I had seen with our people in general, maybe because most of us thought that we were poor, even when we were not, and when someone had a relative abroad, or a friend, the person believed that by being in a foreign land, you had to be rich, and make them rich too! So when you went to visit your family, that family and their neighbours expected that you would come with a lot of good things for them, including money. When some of them were not successful and were unable to go back with a lot of things as they expected, they saw it as shameful to both sides, the side of the one who went to visit, and the family who were visited. So it hurt them, sometimes when they went and they compared him or her to those who did this and that to their families.

And this family who were complaining had a farm, they didn't buy food or milk, and they had a house, sometimes a good one, but still they thought that their child had to do what the child of so and so had done. Few managed to tell them the truth about their life, where they were. If you were lucky, they would believe you, and feel sorry for you, but there was a possibility that they might not even believe you. They would just think that you were not a good child and you didn't care for them.

People like that could make their children fear visiting them, or force them to tell them lies. Many came from the culture that children felt that they owed their parents something, that they had to take care of them, with the belief that by doing so they would be blessed. That was something which built a lot of good feelings of unity and love, and became a source of love and respect in the family and society in general, love to your parents to the end. When young people knew that they were responsible for the older generation for everything, and from the love they received from them in advance, then they had the same love for them, at that things became easier for the young ones because they were happy to do that.

It was much easier before, when people had a good life in their home, especially when Africans were still gaining their wealth from animals and land, before money took over and was the leader of everything, in almost every corner of the world. At that time when a child was grown-up they would be given their own part of the wealth by their parents, and normally the family stayed together in the same area, it was rare for them to separate and go to different parts far from their people. Because of that, taking care of their old people was easy, and they were happy and proud to do that. But money came, and made everyone greedy, and there was no satisfaction for many and this become too much for some children. And slowly it might kill that love and unity which was between them, it could reduce hope and trust, and leave only a bond between some families. This could be dangerous to some good African cultures, like the culture of unity. Every child wished to be a good example to the village.

Like any other child, I wished to be the best to my family, especially to my father, and if it could be possible I wanted to be an example to the whole village too. I decided that as soon as I got transport and time to visit my family I would go. I would not wait for when I had money or things to take for them, because I didn't know when that time would come. So I would go to visit my father without taking any gift for him or other members of his family who were with him, and I would tell him all about my situation, and see how he would take it, though I knew him to be an understanding man for many things, more than many.

I was aware about problems with transport inside Tanzania at the time of Mwalimu Nyerere, you could spend double time or more of what you had to spend on the way because of poor transport.

After moving to my room, the place I saw as my home, at the end of the first month I budgeted for rent and saw what money I had left after everything that was necessary. I saw that it was not going to be easy to have enough for return transport, only one way was enough, I decided to go and hoped that my father would give me what I needed for the return. I was aware that his wife might not be happy with that, unless he knew how to talk with her, but I would go, I missed him.

I left Batsinduka a little money, he was going to be at Angelina's home, which was not far from his school.

I went on the bus from Nairobi to Mwanza, I had to spend time in Mwanza but I was lucky that it was the day that the ship Victoria was going back to Bukoba. At night I was on the water, in the morning I was in the city of Bukoba again, again I was lucky; I got a bus which would go to my father's village, which came once a week! I didn't get any problems on the way. Normally you could be somewhere a week waiting for transport or go with anything you could get, and because of bad roads, somewhere which would normally take a car six hours, could take ten hours or more. Inside the bus I was talking with other passengers to see if I could find someone who could direct me to my father's home.

I found his neighbours and we reached there at night, they were not yet asleep, they were still working with the cows. I surprised them and they were very happy to see me. It was the first time I met my stepmother. What surprised them more was that I had spent only two nights on my journey, they told me a lot about the problems they had in the country, especially on days when it was raining like that, because sometimes the rain could cut out the road. At times like that people would walk, or the cars could slip or cause accidents. Transport at that time was a big worry to them.

I told them about all of the changes in my life, and I told them that I would not be there for long because I left Batsinduka on his own. I also told them that I didn't come with any gifts, and I didn't have enough transport to go back either. They told me that I didn't have to worry about that, that they had money; instead they thanked me for having that heart and courage to come.

They had a strong home, a good permanent house with four bedrooms, they had big land and many cows, and they were better off than many native people.

The next day, they started to prepare different beers from their crops and bananas and they called their neighbours. It was a small party of thirty people, my father told them that he wanted them to greet his child who came to visit them for a short time, and she wanted to see their neighbours and also to say bye to them since she was going soon.

I stood up and greeted them and said a few words.

All of the villagers were farmers, there were some Rwandans who had big farms and were well known in the village like my father, or more than him. In the 1970s there came a law that meant that any refugee who was mixed with native people and not on the land which was separate from them, had to be given an identity and become a citizen of Tanzania.

Many Rwandans refused to become citizens of Tanzania by saying that it was to sell themselves out and it would confuse their children, they would stick to being refugees and be behind their King Kigeli Ndahindurwa and behind their country, Rwanda. In that, they would have to sell their property to natives and move to the refugee land.

My father was one of these people. For some, it was no problem for them to hold Tanzanian identities, as far as they knew who they were. Some of those who moved to refugee land were happy to go there so that they were able to have a wider area to be free so that they could farm a lot of cows.

Most of the Rwandans there had good strong permanent houses and good farms, they were in a good situation, you wouldn't know that they came with nothing. Some improved because their children had good jobs or were big businessmen, or their daughters married rich Tanzanian men or their children were abroad and they sent them money, or simply they worked so hard.

In 1959, Rwandans left their country in big numbers and they were well known because of three reasons. They managed to mix with local people in many ways, they had beautiful girls, and they were hardworking. This made them win a lot of respect in Great Lakes area and made them proud too.

I prepared my journey to go back to Kenya. Some of our neighbours who had children in Nairobi and wanted to send any messages to them gave them to me, and when the time came those who escorted me did that. I was to go to spend the night inside the bus because the journey started very early in the morning.

On the bus, I went inside to get a good place to sit, and came back to say bye to them.

I was happy to see my father again, and see that he was happy with his young wife, they understood each other, and had good neighbours who they had a big unity with, to the level which at first confused me. I had to ask him about them, I saw them give him a lot of respect, and since I didn't know all of our relatives, I asked him if those neighbours were by chance our relatives. He laughed in a long and loud voice and he talked, 'kwirahira', he asked me what would happen if we were in exile, another time like we were there already. How could I think that there was someone who could be lucky enough to meet a whole village full of relatives, in a foreign country.

Afterwards he looked sad and asked me, "Normally, I knew you as a good child who is social and patriotic, that country Kenya I think has changed you, maybe you are no longer socialising, if to see how I am with these neighbours surprised you. Don't forget that unity is a strong weapon, and that is where you find friends, in them some can be more than your family. Someone who is close to you, that is the one who is your people, that is one of our cultures."

The young men who escorted me told me that they had to go running because they saw signs of heavy rain. Inside the bus, around thirty percent of the passengers were Rwandan, the person who sat with me was a young man, a Rwandan. He was the one who was telling me stories, that the driver slept there in a small hotel, and early in the morning he would start the journey. He doubted if we would go since we might get heavy rain, the drivers feared the road when it was raining too much, because sometimes even the mountain could fall in front of you! But by luck, people got a lorry which would go to Bukoba or to Murushaka and it was a bit easier to get transport to Bukoba from Murushaka, easier than waiting from there.

I told him that reassured me in case the driver postponed the journey, I could go with the lorry. He went on telling me his stories, he was a good storyteller. He told me that he was born there, and when he was older and started to travel he was surprised to see the driver could drive in those mountains, and since he didn't know or hear anything about driving, he thought that it was the responsibility of the passengers to protect themselves by holding the bus and turning it in good positions, so without asking anyone he started to hold the bus in positions he thought were better for everybody. He was holding in front of him and believed that it was him who turned it from the wrong side, but he didn't understand why the others did not look bothered. To reach where he was going, his body was too tired, one day he told his mother that he was too tired because he was driving all the way by himself alone, no one helped him!

His mum was surprised since she knew that he had never taken any driving lessons! She asked him how. After he told her how he always did it and she laughed a lot and told him who the driver was. There were some mountains, almost like Rwabunuka, where the driver would tell passengers to walk and meet him ahead, drivers preferred to be alone when they thought that they could be a risk to their passengers.

The time came for our driver to come and it was still raining. He called passengers in case there were any who were staying in small hotels, but some feared travelling in such heavy rain, because they knew what might be on the way. The driver started the journey and we went for around two hours and he told us to take our bags and walk, he said that we would meet him ahead. The passengers who had big bags which they couldn't carry could leave them in the bus, but in case anything happened, it would be their choice. Because as the driver, by driving in that part it was like he was sacrificing himself, maybe because of money or because of helping society, I had no idea why.

I had only my big handbag, inside were a few things, only one pair of clothes for a change. I didn't want to take a big bag because I knew the problems I might get on the way. The dress I wore was long and brown with a flowered pattern, which I made by myself. It had a very good fashion, if it was dirty no one would know.

The young man told me that he was happy he didn't travel with a big bag. I told him that I was aware about the journey inside the country, because the people who visited there had talked about it.

I folded my clothes and we put out the shoes to who had them, because there was a lot of mud, we walked for more than half hour, we were there before our bus, we did that many times. The time we were in the bus on that mountain was less than the time it took us to walk. It was 5:00pm, and we thought that the driver would want to push and reach Murushaka, and then from there to reach Bukoba maybe it could be the middle of the night since there was a good road from Murushaka to Bukoba. That could have been what the driver would decide we would do.

But he told us that from where we were, the bus couldn't go any more steps from there! It was late evening, there were no shops, nowhere to sleep, we were hungry and tired. All of us decided to go ahead and walk, and go to Murushaka where we could get something to eat and somewhere to sleep. That was the only town in the area, and it was the only place you could get things like that. To reach there would take us hours, but there was no other solution, no other option, we had to walk. It would take between eight and nine miles to get there, by luck, the rain had stopped, but everywhere we passed either was muddy, or under water, or we had to pass through rivers.

Since that place was the only town they had around there, it was the centre of almost everything, transport etc... By the time we reached there it was the middle of the night. Because of the raining that day, many people were stranded there from different places, and they were going to different places too, and all businesses were closed. We could do nothing then, the only hope we had was for the next day, then we would have everything, we might even get transport to Bukoba from there.

So we decided to go to a big shop there, which had a wider balcony so that we could sleep there and wait for tomorrow. On the balcony we chose we met other people there who came before us, and with those people was one old man who was a neighbour to my father, and a very good friend to him, with his two young daughters, waiting for the next day to get transport to Kaisho, the village where my father was. So I was very happy to meet him there, I saw him like my uncle.

He was older than all of the people who were there, so we were calling him Muzee. There were many people and a lot of different stories, though some were too tired and slept as soon as we reached there.

All the time I was with Muzee and his young beautiful daughter, who was under thirteen years old, they were coming from Bukoba to go back home. When we decided to see if we too could go to sleep down there, we heard some people making loud noises and singing, all of us kept quiet and waited to see if we knew where they were. In a very short time, they were where we were. There were two strong men who had strong sticks in their hands, and when they saw us, they looked where we were for a few seconds and then they laughed loud, and said that they didn't know that there were other drunken people like them there, they were referring to us! They said that there was no reason to go ahead with their journey leaving us, they were going to spend the night with us, though with their stick nothing could happen to us on the way but there was no need to leave their other drinkers like them.

At 2:00am, they came and sat, they started to tell us many stories in a loud way, because of their stories, all of us were laughing since then. Even some who were sleeping were woken up, after a short time came another two men, we didn't know where they came from. These two who came after were well dressed men, each had a half bottle of beer in their hands, we didn't know if they came because of that noise or because the shop was on the road, it was in the line of other shops but that one was the one which was on the corner.

When they reached where we were, they stopped and quietly looked at us; then they first drank their beer, they were using the bottle to drink. The two men who came before kept quiet too, and waited to see what these new arrivals wanted to tell us. After a short silence one of those new arrivals said like he was asking us in a strong, angry and loud voice, "Who is this sleeping here?"

No one said a thing, he repeated his question but no one said a thing again, and now he asked if all of us were dumb, he was talking in Swahili. I thought that they were drunk, they would be tired and go, one of the girls told us that from now on she was dumb, to anyone

346

who asked about her it was better to say that was how she was born. She told us in a low voice that she saw that things might be tough, that made me laugh, but quietly. They went on asking the same questions and silence went on too.

The man who was asking finished his beer and gave a bottle to his friend, his friend went and I thought that he was going to follow his friend too, maybe all of us saw things in different ways but couldn't talk. The time came when I thought that he might be a thief and since it was known that passengers many times had money with them, we might be in danger here in case he had a gun, because things like that had happened before.

He went on talking alone, now he started to talk like he was trying to tell us why he was worried, and bothering us with his questions. "They killed a person here recently, and we said that no more could spend the night here, now look how many of you there are! Has the owner of the shop given you permission?" Wait I will show him who I am, at that point I thought that he might be one of the government officers if it was not the way of scaring us, because I didn't think that was the way he had to deal with that problem.

One of the two men who came before them he asked him, "You said that they killed someone here but it is you who is giving us problems now, when you came we were only in our stories, I think you saw that we were not killing each other. Can you leave us in peace now we are not killers?" That made some laugh. I think that it was what he was waiting for, anyone to say something, so that he could have an excuse to show us who he was.

We were with women who had babies and at first when the drunk men came they were crying because they disturbed them from sleep, but when the other men came suddenly they didn't cry anymore. After the man had to be told by our drunk man, he was very angry and told us in a high voice, now more than before, "All of you, with your identity in your hands."

We were in the line now and the first one, he asked him for his identity, and the man told him that he had none. The man said, "Ooo you mean you know to make noise here and you don't even have identity! What is your name?" He told him.

"Where do you live?"

He told him.

"What do you do for a living?"

"I am a farmer."

"Go there on that side," he told him, and went ahead asking all of us the same questions when he put us in different queues depending on who you were and if you had identity or not, but some of those who had the same identifications and qualifications he put them on the same side too, but some in a slow and peaceful way, others in a harsh way, and sometimes pushing, and kicking or beating them!

The girls, their father, and I, we decided to be the last because we were scared when we saw those kicking and beatings.

The time came, and one of the men who came before him, after interviewing him he kicked him, it was a big mistake. His friend came and together they told him, "We are farmers, and drinkers, as far as we are concerned, those two qualifications are well known and we are not violent, when we saw other people here, we came and we were with them in peace, until when you came. Now do other things you want with us, but don't make the mistake of beating us, because if you do it again, we are going to beat you up, and if we beat you, we will do it properly."

Then where I was I was happy and told myself that it was better to let them help us and make him be quiet with his craziness. I was wondering if that was how he wanted to be well known, as being respectable, from that time he didn't beat anyone again, he was pushing them. Now was our turn, he didn't ask anything of the children, and he put Muzee to one side without pushing. I was the last one, I gave him my identity, and he held it and looked at it for a second. "Where does this come from?" he asked me.

He had to read and see, but yes, I had to answer him, "I come from Kenya." It was like it was me who was carrying all the problems, or to come there from Kenya was a big mistake I made. He had got a job to do now, he seemed that he was going to deal with me. He jumped and spoke in a loud voice with many questions at once, but I had a few identities with me so I gave him one which I knew that even if I lost it it wouldn't be a big problem to me, because I didn't know anything about him yet, I was still thinking that he might be a thief who wanted to scare us first.

"It is you who we want," he said. "Where are the papers giving permission to enter Tanzania?"

"Those papers I will show them to officers, but in the offices, not here."

"I can see that you have ignorance."

"It is not ignorance, I think no one should give up a passport to anyone here on the street at this time of the night. Wait, you will know who I am. Can you give me my identity?"

"You are not getting it here and in fact not now. You Rwandans you see yourselves as if you can get what you want any time you want! Do you think that it is you who are our leaders or what?" I didn't say anything.

He told his friend to go somewhere and come with a car, after a short time his friend came back and told him that the car had some problem, he told us to go back and wait for him to get transport.

We went back to where we were, I asked others why he didn't give me back my identity when he was giving the others back to them, and they told me it was because we were still together.

Those two men who came before him told us that they better not take us to Kayanga because if he took us there they would not go.

I asked them why they would refuse to go to Kayanga.

They said that Kayanga was a police statation, and to be taken there meany that you were taken to be put in prison.

After some time, someone came, and he stood in front of where we were and called my name twice, no one said anything, then "Bamurangirwa who is going to Kenya," they were calling.

I had to say something now, "Who are these people calling me and where do you want to take me this time alone?"

349

"Not far, you will see, in one of these houses," he said.

"I am not coming."

"So I go back and tell them like that?"

"Yes go back and tell them that it is better to wait for me tomorrow."

When he went back I asked my co-passengers what they thought about these people who were calling me. And they told me that it was mad people who wanted to gives us problems until morning, when we were lucky they didn't get a car to take us to Kayanga.

I told myself that I gave them good reason to refuse, they thought that I would be easy just like that to go simply because I was told to go?!

I was talking to myself then. After a short time the same man who was there came back again, and called me again, by telling me that the boss was calling me now. I thought that it could be a good idea if all of us, as passengers, spoke in one voice, and said no. "At that time of night," said our co-passenger, "we're not going anywhere, wait for her tomorrow."

Everyone kept quiet, instead they started to talk to themselves, then I turned to Muzee, and said, "Uncle, say that my child is not going anywhere at this time of night."

Muzee told me, "Look my child, I have never talked to police officers in my life, I fear them, so I can't help you!" Some laughed.

Those drunk men who were quiet all of that time, I knew that they were Bakiga by tribe, they said so, and I knew them by talking, but I already knew that they understood Kinyarwanda, and we had seen that they were free to say anything they liked, so both of them told me at once, "We know the beauty of you Tutsi girls that always will save you, now go from this cold and wind, at least they will forget us until morning." Again some of the passengers laughed at that. Muzee told me to go, he said that there was no problem and I would come back.

But before Muzee said that, I was stood up already, soon after hearing what the drunk men said, and before even hearing the man who I was calling my uncle say what he said. I saw that it was only me who had to fight for myself, to fight for my right. No one else was there to help me, I was going to show that person, wherever he was, that he counted me wrong. God willing, I might teach him a lesson.

I went behind the man who they were sending to call me, and I had to be careful and know where I was passing in case I came back by myself. I was counting those houses, which was the fourth shop from where we were, he stopped and he showed me the door, I didn't say anything and I didn't take any steps. He seemed like he feared them, and couldn't go inside and couldn't knock, so he told me with a loud voice so that who was inside could hear him, again, that was the door to go inside.

The man opened the door and told me to come in, in my heart I prayed to come out well and alive from the house. I was going to enter at that time of the night. After my short prayer I went inside. Inside the house was big and clean, it was decorated with expensive things, near the door the man who was sat there was the one who was pushing, kicking and beating passengers a few minutes ago! He was the one who showed me where to sit; he greeted me with a lot of respect there! He was a polite man, completely opposite to the one who was kicking us! He looked happy, on his side was another younger man who didn't say anything, who was only looking at me non-stop as if I was a picture, and looked happy too. On the corner was a mature man who looked like a giant, he was sitting at a dining table eating meat, and yes I said in my heart that he had to eat meet through the night. No one said anything, after he finished eating he came where I was with a bottle of wine and a glass, he poured for me a full glass of wine and put it in front of me. There was no greeting, no asking me if I drank or not, there was an order to drink it, then he told me to drink it because he said that it would help me concerning the cold I was in outside.

Yes he was right, maybe because I sat somewhere warm, I felt at once hunger and tiredness more than before. After giving me wine he went back to where he was and he didn't say anything again, he too started to look at me as if someone had given him a temporary job to know each and every thing about my look.

I didn't mind their eyes, my thoughts were why they wanted me there. What I wanted was to be told and for them to let me go back where my co-passengers were, I prayed to get transport to Bukoba tomorrow.

After a long silence the mature man started by asking me questions.

"You girl, they told me that your name is Bamurangirwa?"

"Yes, that is my name."

"What do you say, to go back in that cold and wind or to be with us here?"

I didn't know if he felt sorry for me or if he had other reasons to ask me to choose between those two things. I told him that I didn't understand the question.

He looked to be surprised, and he wanted me to repeat, which I did, then he went on, by pointing to that man who was kicking us. I turned my head to look where he was sat, "You see this man, he is an immigration officer, and when he saw you there he came here and told us how he saw you. Now I see you and yes, I believe what he told us, that is how you are, and we think that you don't deserve to spend the night there in that wind and cold with Burundians and Bakigas!"

When he said that, it showed me that Tanzanians also had the same understanding like Ugandans at the time, to see some people to be lower class, wherever you would meet them no matter how they were, they had to be behind. To them Bakiga and Barundi were still that level. I believed that also Rwandans were at the same level with them, it reminded me how many times Baganda had arguments when we told them that we were Banmyarwanda. To them Banyarwanda at the time was lower class, not our class according to how they used to think because of their reasons. What pushed them so quickly from there and made them leave those behind, might be the way Mwalimu Nyerere welcomed Rwandan refuges in the 1960s, including how they behaved with them, (native people), without forgetting their daughters who played a big part in their lives. Mwalimu Nyerere was one of the leaders who welcomed Rwandan refugees in those years with a lot of love and respect.

I had to give the gentlemen an answer in a very careful way, since what he was telling me, was what that immigration officer told him, I would use Muzee who I called my uncle with a hope that was going to be an understandable answer. And make things be short. And I didn't want to be rude to him. I knew it was not his fault.

When I was starting to answer him he didn't give me time. I thought that he had finished the question but it was the beginning. He went on, "I have a young man here, my son, you are going to like him when you will see him, we saw that this as a good way to bring you over here, and I am sure when he sees you he is going to be happy too, any man who can have a chance to be with a girl like you, can't let it go." He was talking by himself, and other men who were there looked happy with what he was saying, "This house is your house, have a shower and relax."

He didn't ask me my view or to wait to see if I might have anything to say, it was like he was commanding me. He called the name with a high voice, and in came a very handsome young man who looked to be between twenty and twenty-five years old, tall like six foot, strong and big like ninety to one hundred kilograms or more. He was wearing a short sleeved shirt which was open from the neck to midway of the chest. All of his body was full of hair, apart of his face and hands, he had a good haircut, he looked like Arab descent or a mixture of Arabic or Asian.

To me he was a very handsome man, if I was in the market looking for men to buy, he was the one I would pick. When he came the man who was talking told him to greet me and go to prepare my shower or bath because I was too tired.

The young man looked to be a shy man, and he asked him, "Do you think that she is not hungry?"

And the man who gave commands told him that there was nothing they could do about it at that time.

Where I was, I was wondering how this man could believe in himself for his commanding and didn't have patience too!

353

The man didn't say anything now, not because he was giving me time to say something, but because he was finishing his duty of giving his son someone to spend the night with. Since no one else was talking, I saw that was my chance to say something.

I asked if I could say something and he said yes. I told him that it was not possible to sleep there, something all four men asked me at once as if it surprised them, even the one who was in the corner who I thought might be dumb, and he joined the others to ask me why.

I started to tell them my reasons; "I am with my uncle and my young cousins there, so if you are sorry for me being in the wind and cold, that is kind of you, thank you for that. But I will ask if you have enough space to bring them too, and if the space is not enough for all of us, then I better give this chance to my uncle and my young cousins more than I. I can manage that situation, but if there is space for one person then, I will choose my old uncle to come."

I took it as if they were sorry for me, not that they took me as an easy woman who was given a man to be with for that night, because I couldn't make my own choice, at least, not at that time.

They came up with another idea, and told me that now they would take us to Kayanga and come back with me, so that my uncle would think that they took me to the women's side.

I said, "OK do that", but I had my idea that as far as I heard that Kayanga was a police station, I was not going to come back, so I would not board any car again, I was going to surprise them there. I saw that they were treating me like a toy.

They gave me the man who didn't talk to take me where I came from, there they asked me what they wanted from me, and I didn't have to tell them that they wanted to give me wine and a handsome man, I told them that it was my papers, and even then, they didn't give them back to me yet.

After a few minutes, there came a car, a pickup, with that immigration officer, now he had changed and was harsh again, only talking in a loud voice, telling passengers to go inside the car. Normally I knew Tanzanians to take it easy and do their things in a calm, polite way, but he was acting different to the majority of other Tanzanians I knew.

He helped my uncle and children to go inside, and then after with all the others he put them in a rushed and rough way, he got a problem with the two Bakiga men because they told him that if he was taking them to Kayanga, they were not going, so they had to use force. I was standing aside and waited to see how he was acting, here pretending that he was doing his job.

After everyone was in the car he came to where I was and held my arm but he was talking rough to me, but not pushing me, and he put me in front, it was him and I and the driver. He and the driver were talking stories up to Kayanga. I didn't say a thing on the way, and I thought that the Arab man who was driving was angry to wake up, and normally the road also was rough, now the way he was driving the people who were behind were jumping up and down all the way, saying that they would get back problems.

When we reached there I saw the signs and the car stopped. I was the first to open the car and go out, the officer told us to wait there outside. He went inside to talk to them, the two men, they asked if they could let them go instead of spending the night there, it was better if they could go, they refused to let them go anywhere, then they told them that they were not going to spend the night in prison when they didn't do anything wrong. When they wanted to show them where to pass they said, "Now let us show you that Mukiga man is not joking, that is why we can't be far without our stick, we are going to beat you up and you will regret why you brought us here."

Yes they started to beat them seriously, the two soldiers who were there were beaten up and more soldiers had to come, they managed to take the stick from them, and they ordered them to put on their shoes and they were inside the prison.

It was us who were left outside standing, we wanted somewhere to sit down, even if it was there outside since it was not raining anymore, after some time they called us inside, and they showed us where to sit, there were a few benches where people waited, but those soldiers who were on night duty looked like they were good people or they were feeling sorry for us, one asked us if we wanted to sleep, he said that he could put aside those benches for us so that we could sleep down there.

We were happy for that offer, because down there was a clean place, I heard that the car which brought us was gone, I was not happy with that and I didn't know how the officer changed his mind concerning taking me back to the Arab man. I wanted him to go ahead with his plan so that I could get a chance to shame him.

We slept, and when some of us were in a deep sleep, I heard someone calling my name, but I thought that I didn't hear clearly, he called three times, I thought that maybe the Arab young man came there to pick me by himself!

The person was calling me in a low voice, but I told myself that wherever he was, I would show him that no one could treat anyone like rubbish. I was angry especially when I thought of the way I was tired since yesterday, how the whole journey was horrible. Let them give me a chance to teach them a lesson, I saw them like they were giving me some kind of punishment.

And they thought that they had rights, to do what they wanted to me, just because I was a woman.

He was calling me in a low voice, maybe he didn't want to wake up others. I wanted to know what was new now, and maybe after knowing it, I could get a little time to have a rest. I thought that I now knew that my fellow passengers couldn't do anything to help me, I was not going to be coward here at the police station, where they had to protect me.

I stood up with a lot of anger, I wished that it was not true, that maybe I was dreaming, that no one was calling me.

I saw a young man, a tall policeman with a uniform and a gun in his hands. Being a policeman with gun, I had to fear him, but since I was in the government's house and with all the tiredness, it was like I was committing suicide. I didn't care about anyone or what happened to me anymore, as far as knew that I didn't wrong anyone.

356

He told me that on the outside there was someone who wanted to talk to me! I looked up in his face and told him that I was not going anywhere, anyone who wanted to talk to me better come and talk to me there where I was, or wait for me tomorrow.

When he saw that I was more than serious, he looked to be surprised, and started to talk to me in a polite and calm way, so maybe he would tell me who sent him to me.

I turned to go back to sleep and he touched me on the shoulder but slowly, I turned my head to see what was new that he wanted to say. He told me, "You see I am staff here, and I am on night duty, here is the government's office, I can't take you to a wrong place, if you would not like to stay then, you will come back. I am here and I am not far."

When he went ahead to try and see that I would go where he wanted to take me, in that way of talking to me in a polite and calm way, while assuring me that nothing bad could happen to me, but on the other hand when I looked at him he had a very little smile like someone who knew what was going on there.

At last he saw that I was not that easy, as maybe they had told him. When we were still standing inside I saw that outside there were not any cars, so I knew that he was not going to take me back to the Arab man. I didn't know what it was now, I told him that whatever it was, I would not go outside of the compound. Quickly he said yes with a wide smile, I was confused, he was out and I was behind him, outside there was no one, he kept on going, then I told him that I didn't have to go far from there. I had a thought that he was the one who wanted to talk to me, then I told him, "If you want to talk to me, tell me what you want to tell me here."

He told me that it was not him, it was someone else who sent him to call me for him. "Why can't they wait to talk to me tomorrow?"

"You will come back if you want, it is in this house in front of us not far as you can see."

I asked him why he sent me inside the house at that time to see someone I didn't know, it was the same questions and the same answers over and over.

357

Then he saw that I was not happy with it, and I looked tired, I saw it in his face that he felt sorry for me but there was nothing he could do to help, he had to try to see that I went, he had an order to do it.

I came up with the point of my uncle again, like I was asking him for an idea, and said, "Look I am with my uncle there, how do you think it is going to look by me going away from them at this time?"

"OK if so, to protect your respect and his, I am going to tell them that I took you to the women's side."

"Then why can't you wait here for me? Since I know that I am not going to stay there for long?"

"Policeman told me, look now I am by myself; I can't be here for long just come back when you want to."

He went back to his job, and I went inside the house he had already shown me which was in front of me. Inside was one big clean room, which had only a mattress which was down with bed sheets, which looked like new ones, and a blanket. On that mattress, that immigration officer who brought us from Murushaka, was the one who was sitting on it!

He was sitting but one arm touched down on the mattress like if the other side was on the door looking as if he was waiting for any time that I would come. When he saw me he sat straight, he looked to be relaxed and happy with a wide smile as if he was waiting for someone who they had planned to meet there!

When I saw that smile all my anger came back and it showed me that he might be a fool, or he believed that I was fool. In my life I had feared fighting since I was child, but, at that time I didn't know what came over me. I didn't know where I got the strength from, I didn't give him time to say a thing even for one second, I didn't say anything either, automatically, I started to punch him with all the strength I had. I used everything, arms, head, legs, all tactics I saw on TV and in the books. I think it shocked him enough to think that maybe someone else had come, not the slim, hungry, and tired girl he came with from Murushaka! Or no one at all had entered his room and he might be beaten by a ghost; he was confused and shocked enough to make him helpless and not even try to defend himself.

I think because of that shock, that was why he didn't try to defend himself, otherwise if he did he would easily have put me down. And being a respected officer who well known in that area; it was shameful to him to scream or to ask for help, and say that a stranger woman who he called himself was killing him! So he saw that it was better to let himself die if whatever was beating him killed him, it was his fault.

Being in an empty room helped because we were not breaking anything or making any noise, the noise which was there, was only of my beatings. After seeing that he was like a dead body, I felt happy and relaxed, I wanted to scream and call everyone to come and see how I punished him, especially my co-passengers. I saw myself to be a brave lady, and I was sure that he would never ever try to play with any women just because he was a man.

I told myself that if he had a wife he would tell her that he had an accident then I smiled.

That was when I found out that all of this happened in the space of just a few seconds, my mind was full of anger, it was like I was sleeping, then I woke up and saw him in front of me still with all of his teeth out, because he thought that he had got me the way he wanted.

I knew that I couldn't beat him, only because I couldn't get that strength, otherwise if I could do it, I could even do more than that, only I couldn't kill him. Because I didn't want him die, even if I could be a killer and could find a way to punish him with death.

Because I was happy to know that he was alive and everywhere he would be, he would always remember that good lesson I gave him.

So since I couldn't do it better then I had to talk to him, he thought that I would go to sit where he was, I stood in front of him protected with a wall. He showed me a sign to go and sit, and I told him, "I didn't come to sit, just tell me what you want to tell me and I'll go."

"I know that you are tired come here and have a sleep."

"I am still on my journey, so I must not sleep on the mattress I will sleep where other passengers sleep."

"I was surprised now you want to say that your uncle will say anything here in a police station, he will think that you are in a women's side."

"I give my uncle respect but I didn't say that he is the one who protects me, I am protecting myself even now it is me who doesn't want to sleep here, not him who told me not to. Wherever I travel I am always by myself, no one who can say that can protect someone from things like this."

"I loved you when I saw you at Murushaka, when you said that you couldn't spend the night with that young Arab man because of your uncle, they told me to bring you over here so that I could get a good excuse to take you back, but they didn't know that I lied to them, where have they seen a man give a beautiful girl to another man? They think that I am mad?"

I was not talking but I wanted to tell him yes you are.

"I am not concerned with all of what you are telling me, if you saw me and loved me, did you also see that I am human or?"

"Yes you are what else can I see in you?"

"I don't think so, because you are acting to me as if I am a thing not a human, because a thing is something you can plan for in any way you want. I am sorry then that you put me in a category which is not mine, when I am on a journey I am not also going to pick men wherever I pass. I think you get the answer now can I go?"

"You mean you hate me that much, what have I done then?"

"To love and hate you I think I am not in that position, I don't have reasons for that. I don't know you, and I don't have time or reason for that."

"Come I will introduce myself to you and tomorrow I will take you to Bukoba."

"First of all forget about how I will go to Bukoba, where I go I don't manage just because I slept with men, I will go like everybody else." I had all confidence that he couldn't rape me in that government house, and if he tried I could scream.

"Or you want that Arab man because he is young and handsome?"

"I think you don't understand me, just give me my papers or if you don't want to tell me. Concerning the Arab man, he or you, to me, are the same. I don't have reasons or time to see and know how you look, and how anyone looks. We people, we see it in different ways, someone can see so and so, to be handsome or beautiful, when others see the person in a different way. We see things in different ways, the same as how we have different understandings, so the handsome men and beautiful women outside are many, I think you can't sleep with each and every one you meet then."

At that he laughed like to tell me that it was right, then quickly like he had forgotten that he didn't have to laugh or smile with me, in a second he changed himself with a stone face and asked me, "But you know who you are talking to with all of that ignorance? I can see that you believe in yourself wherever you are no matter who you are talking to, just because you have been told by everyone that Tutsi girls are beautiful. Me I am Tanzanian," when he reach that, automatically I interrupted him. I thought that even if I was going to give him an excuse to put me in prison so be it, all the same he gave me enough problems already, so enough was enough, I was not going to let him remind me again that I was a refugee in his country, I didn't have to be reminded by him, or anyone, ever, because I knew.

When I started to talk he kept quiet quickly as if it surprised him, maybe he didn't have the idea that I could do that, so he looked at me and listened to what I was telling him.

I started, "Eeeeee you surprised me sir, can you tell me, as me, here you are, you are with me, not with all Tutsi girls. What you are telling me now, I think, is not connected at all with what we were talking about, it seems that now you have changed the subject, and you want to remind me that I am a Rwandan girl, a refugee who is in Tanzania, and I am talking with a Tanzanian officer in his government. I am right? If so then, you want to remind me so that, I can be shaken and kneel down and say yes sir to whatever you say, so that I can go from here with peace or else what?"

I continued, "You are right, we are refugees who come from our country but we didn't do terrible things which can make us not go back in the future, it is only matter of time, and here we come with nothing, apart from our arms and our heads, we managed to mix with you people without any problems and now we have a better life even more than some of you Tanzanians. Go to my father's home and see how many Tanzanians he is helping and if you say something bad about him you will hear what his neighbours will tell you."

"We believe in ourselves yes, we have enough confidence that is why we are who we are. About that beauty you are talking about, it is you who sees it, but we first know that we have to trust our head and the beauty comes after. That is why my head refused me to say yes to someone like you, who wants something which you will talk about tomorrow, because you are who you are, no matter what, it seems to be stuck in your heart and head, that it is easy for you to get whatever you want especially to someone like me, a woman, a refugee in your country."

"Not to me then, some we protect our respect, and that is why sooner or later you will see, we will go back to our country."

"To know who you are, yes. I heard many times your position, that is why I am with you for a long time, because I am in the government's compound and I am with a government officer, whatever you do to me, you could be asked for it tomorrow, what if I postponed my journey and got your bosses and asked them about all of these problems you are giving me, if they allow their staff this behaviour when you have to be an example to your society?! I am sure the answer will be no, and they can't be happy with this story."

When I was telling him all of this, he was looking at me without any interruption. When I finished what I was telling him, he apologised and said that he hadn't planned to upset me that much, he touched in his pocket and gave me my identity, and said, "Yes, you are right, and I was very wrong. I put you in a level which is not yours, and I learned not to just be judging people as I think. Come and sit I am not going to touch you." I saw how he said it and I knew that this time he was telling me the truth, and he was regretting all of what he did. I was tired, I went and sat on that mattress.

He checked his watch and it was 5.00am. "I am going," he said, "if you want to sleep here, sleep, if you want to go where the other passengers are, I will take you." He apologised once more and at the same time he stood up waiting for my choice.

I chose to go where the others were, and he escorted me, I was inside, and he was gone.

I saw him to be one of the men who spent the night out of their home with other women, sometimes, strangers or prostitutes, and when they were not at home, their wives at that time they were worried to death, didn't know what had happened to the husband, and when he came in, either he would tell her that he had a lot of work, or he would come up with other lies. If he could not come up with anything, he would use violence to shut the wife's mouth, and in the end, some marriages it could be a reason to break up, just as you can imagine some reasons like that, which is like a wind, to cost him his marriage, when many times it was a good and steady one!

I went where others were sleeping and slept for a short time, it was time to go, for the people who were going to other places, but we, who were waiting to go to Bukoba, we were not in a hurry.

That day was 20th January 1976 I had to start to worry myself about rent, but the journey in Tanzania was a big problem I couldn't allow my mind to bother about it much. I was thinking about Batsinduka and the house he was in, hopefully wishing that I would be there at home in time.

So we had to go to the shopping centre Kayanga to wait there to see if we would get transport or not. They were not yet to send us out from where we were, so because it was a warm place we decided to be there for some time until the shops opened, so we could go and get something to eat. After a short time, there came a young man and he stood in front of us and he made a sign with his hand to call me. I had to be sure, so I used my finger to point to myself and asked him if he meant me, and he said yes by using his head.

I stood up, I had no fear, it was daytime now, and I was still in a police area, but I had questions of what this young man wanted from me now?!

363

When he saw that I stood up, he went back but was walking slowly, I was behind him, we were out when I was almost going to ask him where he was taking me or what he wanted to tell me, he stopped and turned to me, he looked at me for seconds both in silence, and told me, "pole sana kwa mambo yajana," meaning he was very sorry for what happened yesterday! I didn't know what he was talking about; I had to ask him what he meant happened yesterday?

He saw that I was surprised and said, "Don't be surprised, what happened at night between you and that man I was in the next room listening to everything, that room you were in, is my room, so that man asked me to lend it to him, which I did, but where I was, I was with my friend in the next room, we decided that we were not going to sleep until we knew the end between you two. The policeman, who escorted you to the room, is the one who was with me, and we have never seen a girl like you! A girl who can be in that test for the whole night without giving up! So we felt very sorry for you."

When he was telling me that he was smiling I think he was asking himself why they gave themselves that problem of staying the whole night without going to sleep. I didn't say anything, and maybe he didn't expect me to say anything.

At his home he showed me where he put a thermos full of tea, and bread with other things to eat with it, where the sugar was and a key, and where I would put it so that when I was finished I could lock the door and go. Tea made me happy, at the same time all of that surprised me, I thanked him so much, but asked him if there was a way how I could have a shower or a bath?

He told me that he didn't know that I wanted to have one, but it was no problem, he showed me where the bathroom was, and showed me all the necessary things, and told me to take it easy and feel at home, he was going to the church maybe he would see me again or not, and if he would not see me again, he wished me a safe journey and all the best in my future.

After waiting for him to go I was too hungry, but I had to be patient and have a shower first.

After having my shower I didn't change I didn't know where I was going to spend the night, so I had my tea and felt fine and forgot how I was a few minutes ago!

I said that the way someone could die quickly that was how quickly you could be alright too.

Back where my co-passengers were, we went to the shopping centre and all of us sat in front of one shop where there was a long bench. I was in that place without moving much, but others were moving a lot so I was taking care of bags.

Opposite was another line of the shops, between those lines was the road which was the main one, and that was why we chose to be there. So that it could be easy for us to get transport to Bukoba.

In that line of other shops opposite me was a man who was a dressmaker sitting at his sewing machine outside of one shop, he stood up and came to where I was, and greeted me in Kinyarwanda. It didn't shock me that he was a Rwandan or how he knew me, I knew that we could easily know ourselves. I respond to him, I knew him to be a Rwandan before he stood up, just by looking at him, he was tall and slender with black shining skin.

He suggested that because most of the time I was alone there when others went around, it was better to let him help me carry the bags and be there with him, when my co-passengers came back they would see me. It was a good idea, we went to where he was, he told me that before I sat, I had better go inside the hotel and have a tea, he would pay for me.

I thanked him but told him that I had a tea already, he said that he knew that I had one before, but OK let him go and bring a milk for me, he was sure I wanted milk.

He was right I wanted milk, but how come he knew about the tea I had in the house of the policeman? What was happening there in Kayanga?!

When he gave me the milk he asked me if it was not me who spent the night at the police station.

"It was us, we were many, others who were going other places went, but we who were going to Bukoba all of us we were here," I told him.

"No," he said, "I am talking particularly about you and your patriotism!"

Now I had to ask him what he was talking about.

"I was told everything that happened to you from Murushaka up to Kayanga until morning, those young policemen they are my friends, it was them who woke me up, they were too surprised, and they told me that they didn't know that our sisters were like that. After they told me the whole story, proudly I told them that was how we relied upon our daughters in case they met someone different from what they had seen, she might get that behaviour from somewhere else."

"You give us a good name which it might last here at Kayanga for some time. I was praying that you would not go without me seeing you. And you give that Mucaga man something to learn which he will never forget."

I asked him, "You mean that man who gives me that entire problem is Mucaga?"

"Yes," he said, "he is Mucaga and is a high officer in the immigration office here in Kayanga and his wife is Rwandan." I didn't ask his name I had no reason to know him...

He introduced himself as Nkubito, I thanked him and he said, "Nothing to thank me for I am always here where it is a way of many passengers, but I talk to few, even you it is because of your braveness, and I will get a car to take you to Bukoba, don't worry, now count on me as your brother, since my house is one room, so in case if you will not get transport that will be your home, and you will not spend any money here at Kayanga until you will go. I will be happy to do that for you, I will move in with my friends until when you go."

I told him, "You can't know much about transport here, and I can't let you do that for me for a time until I don't know when. My father has given me enough money for transport."

Nkubito said, "Look my sister remembers that it is one of our cultures to help others especially like now, when you are a traveller and you meet me." When it was 1:00pm he told me to go to the hotel which was there near, "Come, I take you to have your lunch, eat whatever you want if the car comes now there will be no problem." He took me and told them, "Give my sister whatever she wants I will pay," he turned to me and told me, "relax and eat, if the car comes, I will come for you."

When I finished I was almost stood up and I saw him come running, "Come Bamurangirwa, you are not going to believe that I got lift for you it is my friend's car and I told them the hotel where they are going to take you, and you will not pay anything, don't worry I know all of them, they are my people, go with peace." I was too happy, and I thanked him and told him that I trusted him. I was inside the car; I started my journey back to Bukoba, meaning that in a few days I would be in Nairobi, to start my new life.

On the way we didn't have any problems we came with a lot of stories like if we known each other before.

I spent that night in one of the hotels where Nkubito told them to take me, the next day was the day of the ship Victoria going to Mwanza, so I spent the next night in the ship. Most of the time when I was coming from Tanzania to Kenya I liked spending time in Mwanza so that I could give myself time to relax, because I believed that the problems I had ahead of me concerning tranport from Tanzania were limited, as far as I finished the journey of Kagera depending how much money I had, I would have liked to go to a Mwanza hotel.

I thought that the bus station might open their office at 8:00am so it was better be there at 7:00am, so that there could be no one, because I wanted to be on the Kenya side at last that day.

When I reached there I got a big surprise because there were a lot of people, as if they had spent the night there! But the people who were there before or who came after were the same, I didn't see any difference because when they started to give people the tickets, a big number of people who were strong were at the window and everyone was fighting to get them first. So if they were going to the line according to how people came, I could understand, but that was depending how strong you were not what time you came! Some were standing on top of others, then I went a bit far and looked at them to see how they were fighting for the tickets, I looked like I was enjoying looking at them, but the truth was I was confused, telling myself that if I was going to spend another night there because of the way they gave passengers tickets, it showed me that was how it would always be, meaning that I would never get one, since I would never be able to manage that fight.

I stood there hours without looking at any other place, without going anywhere, where I stood was the same place without even having to turn my head to look aside, I didn't know what I was waiting for, maybe I thought that they would reduce passengers, so that I could be able to get a chance to get my ticket.

In front of me was a man who stood there for all of that time. I thought he was not a passenger maybe he had other reasons why he was there, so I thought that seeing me there in the same place like a picture, he knew that I was new in that situation and maybe he felt sorry for me, and he came to where I was and he told me without asking me anything, "My sister, to get ticket here in peace you have to bribe," (dada kupata usafili hapa kwa usalaam nimwendo wakuruk).

"Now who can I give that bribe to, how can I know who is a genuine one, or if he is one of the thiefs who tell people that he can help them so that they can give him money and then he get lost, and now he saw me and knew that I was foreign and said he found someone who was going to give him money for free."

I didn't say anything, after some time when he came back he saw me where I was in the same position, and he came to where I was again, and told me, "Look my sister if the situation here is hard to you then you better go to Musoma, all the buses which are going to Tareme they pass there so they drop passengers off in Musoma and pick others who go to the border. There is no problem of transport there and the small cars which are going to Musoma are many, if you like, come, I will show you where they are."

I thanked him and I saw that it was a good idea. I went to Musoma, when I reached there, I asked other passengers who were there, if there were buses which passed there from Mwanza to Tareme yet, and they told me that not yet. I saw that I came before it, so. I relaxed and waited for it. It was between 11:00am–12:00 midday, sometimes lorrys or pickups were coming and I would see people go to talk with drivers, negotiating, then they would go with whatever came. It was like that until evening, but I was still waiting for a bus and thought that those who went with lorrys and pickups might be relatives of the drivers. I thought that the bus maybe got some problems but they would send another one, so I didn't even go to get something to drink let alone to eat! The whole day I was standing in one place, where the bus from Mwanza had to stop.

But I had no worry because in front of me was a hotel which looked to be a good one, but there were many people standing in front of it, others were sitting there and I knew that soon I would go inside the hotel and have a shower, and do everything and relax until the next day.

When I was almost going to the hotel after giving up, and seeing that there was no bus, in front of me came a lady who greeted me. I responded, then she asked me if I was new in Musoma, at that time I thought that the woman might be a kind of thief and she wanted to know if I was new in that area so that she could get me somehow, so I wanted to show her that I knew town life, she was not going to be able to take anything from me.

I told her that I was not new there.

"Again what are you waiting here for?"

"I am waiting for a Kenya bus!"

She laughed for some time and I was wondering what was funny. After her long laugh she said, "Yes, you are not new indeed, to stand here in Musoma and wait for a Kenya bus!"

Ooo my God that was what I told her?! I asked myself and said that now no more lies, she got me.

She started to tell me why she wanted to talk to me, "Look my name is Judith I live in Tareme, I came here to visit my parents, so me too, I was waiting for the bus because I had things I wanted to take with me, I saw you here when I came. If my brothers came up with my things I would have gone, but I didn't know what happened to them, many cars went when I was here and everyone knew that you were new here because of that, you are a passenger and you don't go with those which take others, because you know that it is only a bus which you have to go with. So now I am going back home I will start my journey tomorrow, I didn't want to leave you here because you could be in trouble."

Now it was my turn. "What trouble? If I don't get the bus I will go to the hotel, and start the journey tomorrow, that is what I planned."

"In this small town you can't get somewhere to spend the night at this time of hour, already all the hotels are full," she told me, "and the thieves they are waiting for you, they know what you think, that is the hotel you had in your mind." I was confused if I believed her or not, I was not going to ask her to escort me to see if I could get a hotel, she couldn't get that time, she could tell me that it was my problem if I didn't trust her, and what if she was telling me the truth, what could I do in case after she left I didn't get a hotel, yes I could die there in Musoma then."

Before I gave her any answer, five men came, some of them were there in front of that hotel, in front of where I was standing, they looked to Judith with stone faces and asked her what she wanted from me, and they told me that I didn't have to hear her, I didn't have to go anywhere, that they would help me with whatever I wanted!

Now it was a case between them and her, she asked them if I asked them for any help or if they knew me anywhere!

After five minutes there was a fight between themselves with words. I didn't know if the woman and the men still were one group, so if they would do that, I could fear being on my own, and go with her, then after she could take me to them without any problem, but I didn't know what to do. I didn't know what to choose, in that confusion she asked me, "Are you coming with me so that we can go together tomorrow in the same way or are you staying on your own here?"

I chose to go with her if she took me to them, fine, I told her that yes we would go together.

She told me that it was not near, I had to be ready to walk, I said that it was no problem with me. "You don't have other bags?"

"No I don't," I said.

"OK let us go," she said.

We started our walk to Judith's parents, after seeing that our walk was a long walk, I believed that she was not taking me to the thieves, it took us between two and three hours, their home was near Lake Victoria, she introduced me to her family, and asked me what I wanted, I asked her if there was somewhere I could have a bath so that I could relax after. I was too tired because of the way I was standing for almost the whole day, she took me to Victoria side and I used Victoria water to clean myself.

We had our dinner and slept, she gave me her watch and told me what time I would wake her up, so that we could prepare ourselves for our journey, she thought that because she was tired, she might sleep and forget. That was when she told me about her life in Tareme, that she was with her police husband. We did everything together, we slept in the same bed, you could think that I was their visitor. I was happy to be with her, she was my angel, I think the conmen when they saw Judith take me, they saw that they had a bad day and regretted why they didn't try me before she came.

I didn't get any other problems on the way, I had a fresh mind now, happy to see my father, ready to go ahead with my new life, at home Batsinduka was going on with his school. After getting my monthly support from the U.N. I paid everything I had to pay, I got more money because of Batsinduka, then I saw that was enough to go to Uganda to bring more children. I had no time to visit Mukabagira then, but I came with Batsinduka's sister, Ilibagiza Mukakigeli, Muvunangoma son of Rusingizandekwe and my son Manzi. I had four children now, and I knew that they were my responsibilty. I had to know that in Nairobi I was their mother and their father. I had to be grown up enough to manage a big family like that. I said that let me wait after a short time

I would bring others. I was happy to see that I was doing the job I wanted. Giving a chance to the young generation.

I had to get a big place which could be enough for all of us, I knew that it was not easy work to look after them in a good way, a respectful way, in order to be able to make them respectable people in the future. I knew that there were many things I had to do which I wouldn't mind when I was alone, I knew that was some kind of sacrifice especially for my age.

I wanted my children to be good people in the future, not drinkers, not easy going, down to earth, seeing everyone as equal, having their confidence, and loving themselves before loving others, so that they were be able to know which love they could give to others.

I was young and I had volunteered for the hard work which I had to do, as any young woman of those days, I had to go out for a drink and dance, I was single, so I had to have boyfriends. But now I would not go out, I would not drink, and I would not have a boyfriend, at least not this and that. I had to choose very carefully, and in that way of choosing, I had to try and see that the man I would introduce to them was good enough. Not a man who could shame me in front of them or in front of everyone if I could be that lucky.

In Nairobi, in my community, I was one of the people who had a big family, according to the culture of our community, and African culture in general, culture of unity, we were together as a community, when one of us had a problem, someone passed away or when one of us had a ceremony, I had to act like any other old person who had a family, to be there whenever they needed me. So to this point since I was a patriotic person who loved my people, and a social person, it was easy to me and it made me happy by being with others.

In that volunteering in general in our community, sometimes they needed some people to spend the night there. I had given myself a timetable what I would be able to do in the community, since I didn't have any money when it came to contributing money, I was only giving my time and doing whatever I could do, only what I would never do, was to spend the night anywhere no matter what.

372

Why? Because I didn't want to let my children be by themselves at night, it was one of my principles. I wanted them to know that I was there for them always. The only time I was outside of Kenya, when I went to visit our relatives was when they would spend the night alone without me. Day by day my children grew up and they were my first good friends, we were a strong family, and we were proud of each other, people outside admired us.

ME AND MY NAMELESS MAN

I liked reading whenever I got something to read, as long as it was something of interest to me, especially concerning what was happening around the word and life in general.

I liked writing letters to different people, who I knew or I didn't know, all over the world, I was not choosing men, women, country or colour. I used to get addresses from what I was reading; it helped me to feel that I was connected with people around the world.

I was writing many letters but sometimes only a few would reply to me or no one, or I was getting good communication with some of them for some time and then communication stopped without good reason, some of them we managed to go ahead with our communication, after we saw ourselves as if we knew each other for a long time.

The first countries I got good and strong friends in were Canada and Norway, where some of them came to meet me when it was their first time to come to Africa.

At that time, women who went to the U.N.'s officers with a request for study, it was the season of taking them to dressmaking whether you liked it or not, that was my time and that was where they took me, I didn't like it but it was better than nothing.

Though it helped me because I was making my dresses and my children's, something which would have been difficult if I had to go to buy ready-made from the shop.

Sometimes I had temporary jobs since to be in a permanent one was not easy, because I had to deal with those U.N. offices and some other things in immigration, it was like a job itself.

There was one time in 1978, that day it was morning when I went to the hospital. I had an appointment for Muvunangoma, we were sat on the bench waiting for our turn to go to see his doctor, we were tired of waiting, in front of us was an old man, who too, was waiting and he had a Swahili newspaper, but he seemed to be tired too. He put down his newspaper, I asked him if he could lend me his newspaper and he said that was no problem, he gave me his newspaper, it kept me busy for some time. I was almost about to give it back to him when I saw a page where there were pictures of people who were looking for friends, but in those pictures there was a white man too, who said that he was in Kenya, it was the first time I saw a white person looking for friends through Swahili newspapers.

I had an idea that this man must speak Swahili, which could be much easier for to me to communicate with him. In case he had an interest to communicate with me. I decided to put his address in my notebook, and said that I would send a letter to him and see if I would get his reply.

I had a job to look for a house for Mukabagira and her sister who were in Maraba in Kenya side, but didn't want to stay there, they wanted to come to Nairobi, they were refugees, running from Amin at the time.

I too was happy to have them near me, I got the house, it was her brother-in-law who came to see it, on behalf of his family, because they were staying together with Mukabagira as family, he liked it and they moved. After moving we were settled and happy together, I came to remember that I had an address of a German man in my notebook, I sent him a letter with few words, with a lot of doubt if I would get his letter back, like many, some replied some didn't.

After a few days I received the letter from him, telling me that soon he would be in Nairobi, he would have a meeting, he told me the hotel where he would be in, and that he would wait for me there, and if I would not be able to come there, he told me where he would be in the meeting, he also said that he was looking forward to meeting me because it would be his first time to meet any Rwandan person.

So I got the reply from a German man, who was looking forward to meeting me after the next two weeks, what else? Nothing at all, let him come, I had nothing to add or to change to the life I had, I was not ashamed of anything, I would dress as I always dressed, if he wanted to see where I lived first, I would see what kind of person he was, if he was good enough to take him in front of my children. I was not yet close with white people, according to stories from friends who stayed with them, they said that many times they liked to ask questions concerning life, past, present, and maybe future, if so then it depended what his questions would be, but otherwise what would I have to tell him? If he asked me about my past, would I have to try to get his sympathy by telling him that I was born in my country Rwanda but grew up on the way going here and there, and now my job was to be in the door of the U.N.'s offices, to see that my children could get better studies for a better future. Which might be ridiculous, he couldn't do anything about it, and maybe wouldn't even understand it.

By that, meaning, that I would be trying to show him that I was not happy with the life I had. I couldn't hide that I was a refugee, I couldn't be ashamed of that, instead I had to be proud of what I was doing to prepare the younger generation who would take me back to my country tomorrow, and I had no reason to count on him for anything, to be good to me, by going ahead to meet him, it was my opportunity to see the other side of life through him, it was a kind of business, and to learn.

I believed that white people saw any black person to be a fool no matter what, even educated ones he or she were the same, just because of the colour. And I thought that if I was right, it could be ridiculous, ignorant, selfish and cruel, if it could be so, I couldn't blame some of them, since it could be the seeds planted in their mind by their great, grandparents. I also wanted to give myself a chance to see the truth. On the other hand I thought that whatever it was, they couldn't be the same, all of them.

In those white people, who had that understanding of ignorance to black people just because they were black, some who got a chance to go to Africa, and meet the society there, they saw a different picture of what they had in their mind, because of how they took good care of them willingly, and were happy to do that because they were their visitors. According to the way they had been taught since they were young, that they had to be good to anyone they met especially visitors.

In this African society, some they did that because of their culture, and others they did that because of the seeds they had planted in their heads by their great grandparents, that they had to be servants to white people. Or on the other hand, they were hoping that this white person could save them from the poverty, which they believed they had, even if they were not poor. And some even thought that to be with a white person, everything was different to them, some thought that even where they came from, and they were created differently from where she or he knew, or they could see that it would be more respectable to the community to see him or her with white person.

On the side of the white people some appreciated the way they were welcomed and recognised their social life and generosity, and were happy to be with them, and wished to be there forever, wished that everyone they loved could come and see for themselves.

Those kinds of white people knew why some of their people had ignorance to those black people, the only reasons were selfishness, power and greed. And these people were those who would fight for equality for everyone. These people most of the time they knew the history and present between white and black. To see the generosity of those societies many times made them try hard, to show them a different picture of what they had concerning white people. So at last they could show them that not every white person had ignorance to them just because of who they were.

But others who still had those seeds of hate and ignorance, they saw that it was how it had to be for black people, always they had to be behind, had to work for them anyway, and they didn't have to mix with them in other ways, a part of business, otherwise they had to be the boss for them and that was it.

What was in common for these two people who had a different

understanding of African people, was when their time to be in Africa came to an end, and now they had to go back to their original place, not all of them looked happy, you saw them as if they had lost something important in their life, something maybe which was good and a big chance in their life, still they had different reasons why they were not happy to be going back to their home.

Some of them they were not rich people and they loved Africa and African people, they saw that they might not get a chance to come back again to that good place to see those good people, people they saw in a different picture from what they had in their mind from their parents, a good place, and good people, in a way they had never thought it could be. People who were happy to be with others, people who were happy to give their time to help…

Others couldn't be happy to go from there, a place which was the source of them to be rich or richer, a place where they had servants who worked for free or for little. Or they would not get again where other people saw them as if they were king and queen everywhere they passed.

In my mind I believed that most white people were selfish and racist, especially when it came to anything concerning profit of any kind, they could even become cruel.

In my mind came pictures of life in South Africa, and I thought about Red Indians, native of America, I heard what happened to them in the hands of white Americans.

I was thinking about the history of Aborigines, native people of Australia, what happened to them soon after Europeans came to their country, then you could see me saying that it was not surprising to see Belgians cut hands of Congolese people to scare them up, so that it could be easy for them to make them their slaves, which was one of their ways of colonising.

Now here I was, because of those reasons. So then I thought that I had good reasons to see them in that picture, and yes Africans they had their mistakes too.

I believed that the environment of life could change someone and put a person in a direction according to what kind of life you had, some could make you lose your confidence and hate yourself, maybe because you saw that no one could recognise you if you did right or wrong, to them it was always the same. Sometimes life could force you to believe that people around you had ignorance to you, to whatever you did, even if you tried to do the right thing, always to them it was seen to be wrong.

That could be dangerous, after seeing yourself to be useless, because it could damage someone by making them lose confidence that much, it could turn the person rough, and make them not fit in to the community or anywhere.

Me too, I had an idea that I couldn't involve myself in any way with a white person because I believed that white people couldn't give me a chance to prove my intelligence in front of him or her.

Then I came to remember that to have hate which couldn't give space to think of other positive sides was not brave, and if I believed myself to be intelligent then, I couldn't be holding that history in that way, and me too, us, we might have made some mistakes, it was better to give myself a chance to know my mistakes, our mistakes, and see why all of that happened, and see if we could do otherwise.

And I remembered was what Malcolm X said: 'it is not a case of good or bad blacks or whites it is a case of good or bad human beings'.

I believe that whenever you do anything bad when you are aware, and happy by doing it, you give punishment to yourself somehow in the future.

Once, in the court in 1962, Mandela said: 'we were treated courteously by many officials, but we were very often discriminated against by some and treated with resentment by others. We were constantly aware that no matter how well, how correctly, how adequately we pursued our career of law, we could not become a prosecutor, or a magistrate, or a judge. We become aware of the fact that as attorneys we often dealt with officials whose competence and attainment were no higher than ours, but whose superior position was maintained and protected by a white skin.'

I asked myself, all of that and others similarly like that or worse, which happened and still happens in some places, which are to blame? More than other between white who were given the way to go and kill and take all which they wanted to take. Can I blame those white people who use their power and money to get wherever they want from there, when most of the time they got that money from the same country where they were doing all of those horrible things. Or can I blame the people who give them a way to kill their own people and take wharever they want from themselves?

The natives of the country who turned up to sell away their countries and their people, many times they knew the consequences, but at that time they became blind by greediness, and the fact was, I think, they had never had money before, it blinded them enough to the point that they didn't mind if it was blood money. Whatever they wanted to do, which passed in those ways always were wrong things, sooner or later would be dangerous to society, and those consequences would damage the whole continent. When they were selling out their people in different ways, most of the time by keeping them in a culture of poverty, sometimes or always, it came back to the history of colonialism, to be a reason for that greediness and foolishness, but still, excuses like this would be here until when?

I thought about some of our rich countries like Sudan or Congo… with petrol, gold, coltan, copper etc… but instead of their society being rich and happy in their beloved rich countries, they were always poor, miserable and in unnecessary wars forever!

When you asked former colonials why they still did that, they would say, look, African people wanted independence, and we gave it to them, what now? It was about them knowing what they were doing for themselves. Yes, indeed, it was about them knowing what they were doing for themselves.

But it could be about them too, to let it go, this sweetening, richness of Africa, and they could deal with African people in a clear way, be clear and be in clean businesses between both of them, so that could stop blood and evil money on both sides.

They could think and feel ashamed when anyone could think how Belgian people treated Congolese in the 1880s, when they didn't mind doing anything, even if it was to hurt them, so that it could be very easy to get them as their slaves, to use them to steal their resources that could build their Belgium quickly.

But still I thought that if all black people had that hate I had to white people, and all white people had the same to black people, we could have a big problem on our small planet, because it is our world and whether we like it or not we are here to be together everywhere we will be.

Then I decided to meet that nameless man, and see him, and judge him as him, according to how I would see him, but not see him in a mirror of history.

If I saw him as a person who was looking for black people to play with, because maybe in his mind he believed that black people were less human, at that point I would be with him just for some minutes, but if I saw him as someone who could see me as me, who could see my behaviour as my behaviour, not our behaviour as black people, especially when it came to the point of wrong ones.

Then at that, I would give him a chance if he would want it, so that we could maybe get a chance to know each other more.

I saw that there was no need to go to his hotel, that I would wait and go to the office.

I had one more week to meet him but I had some feelings in me, of looking forward to meeting him, something which was not understandable, something which I couldn't even talk with my friends because I had no point or reason to have that excitement just because I received one letter from someone, it didn't mean anything at all. So I kept it for myself. But I had to tell my children since I had to tell them almost everything.

I refused to think that it was because the man was white, since I always believed no matter what all people were the same.

The day was Saturday which I would go to meet him for the first time.

In case if he would want to visit me, I couldn't change anything, he would come where I was, in my one bedroom wooden house, in the dust area when it was dry, and too much mud when it was raining.

I dressed in a long green skirt and red top with long sleeves the gift I was given by Mukabagira.

When I was there I asked someone, to see if I was right, and he told me that I was in the right place that was where Germans had their meeting.

When I reached the door I was nervous, I started sweating, and I was not brave enough to knock, with many different questions, though I would not go back without seeing him, after a few seconds I came to remember that in the other offices someone might see me standing there like a picture, so I knocked. I heard a woman's voice tell me to come in, in English. I was not trusting myself with my English, so I had doubts if it was going to be easy for me to communicate. On the part of the nameless man, I assumed that he was speaking Swahili, though on the other hand that was not a big deal, since for them too, English was not their first language. I thought that some of them might not be perfect in it, which would be understandable only I believed that, they had to come here when they were able to speak English, because Kenya on the other hand was counted as an English-speaking country.

Whatever it would be, the only important thing was if we would be able to communicate in any way.

Inside was the lady who looked to be too smart and too beautiful, something which scared me and I thought that she was one of the people who could be ignorant to others, or racist. But the way that lady welcomed me in a respectful and polite way, it made me feel comfortable and I liked her there and then, the nervousness I had concerning communication finished. The problem I was left with was only what was going to happen after seeing him.

The lady asked me what she could help me with and I told her why I was there. She showed me where to sit and after one minute she went in another room when she came back with her soft smile, which made me more comfortable, she told me that they were still busy, but that he gave her a message to ask me to wait for him if possible.

She gave me many magazines to keep me busy, those magazines were in German, but she knew that I might not know the language in those magazines, so she told me that even if I might not know the language, I could just see the pictures and she told me to try not to be bothered because she had to go, I thanked her and she had gone.

She had already made me feel much more comfortable, and it was like I knew her before, she made me see that if you were a good person to others, you could be medication to them in a way. All of my complex I had before concerning my colour and the language was over. I was asking myself how she could be that good to me, I thought that might be her nature or she was a good actor.

The time came when at that door where the lady went when she took my message, there came a white man, and the picture I saw in the newspaper came in my mind and I saw that he was the nameless man I came to meet at the first time.

I was in that room alone, where the lady showed me to sit, behind the table where staff were supposed to sit, so that it could be easy for me to choose those magazines. At that time I was nervous again like the way I was at the door when I was coming in. But I tried hard so that this nameless man couldn't notice that, he came where I was with a smile and he stood in front of me. He stood like a soldier, just looking down at me without even bending his head, and he asked me if I was Bamurangirwa. I said yes I was. He introduced himself. I stood up and we shook hands.

He was the one who started to talk and he told me that he was happy to see me and that he saw me the way he thought, when I asked him how he thought, the answer was, "Just like the way you are now."

He was still standing in the same way, and he told me that the meeting was still going on, he asked me to be patient and he turned to go, but when he reached ahead he turned and said that he was waiting for me in his hotel last night, I didn't say a thing and he asked me why I didn't come.

The answer was that I had a visitor he used his head and eyes to agree with my answer, and he was gone.

We were talking in Swahili.

When I saw him, as if he was a black man, I had to think that he was related to Tutsi people according to his height. He was tall and slender, like seven foot tall and maybe between seventy-five and eighty kilograms, in those few minutes he was in front of me I liked the way I saw him. It would be very good if his understanding and behaviour were good like his looks too, maybe I would know, but now I didn't know anything yet.

I started to ask myself many different questions with many pictures of my future maybe with him! To that point I was laughing at myself, I didn't know anything about him at all yet, now here I was giving myself a future with him! Crazy ended.

He looked to be mature maybe forty to forty-five years old. I was sure that he was not married yet, or he was divorced, otherwise he couldn't try to meet other women, unless he was one of the men who enjoyed to be with different women wherever they passed when they could get them, even strangers, sometimes be with them a day or so, and forget them the next day, and be proud of that.

In my mind I thought that to be alone without even a girlfriend was out, especially in Africa, who he was, he could be alone only if that was how he chose to be. But because of reasons I said before how the majority of Africans believed that when you came across with a white person you should count yourself to be blessed, let alone being in a relationship, to both sides, to men, or women. And yes sometimes it was true when you were lucky enough to meet a good one.

I didn't understand some who had a hobby of not being satisfied with one woman or one man. Those people I believed that they had their kind of problems.

After being on my own with my children, I had peace, I was happy whenever I saw that my children were happy, I had to do whatever I could, to see them happy, no matter what, as far as the things I had to do would not hurt anyone in any way, and would not reduce my respect in front of them, and in front of my community.

After seeing him I was confused I liked him as soon as I saw him, something I didn't want to hold me so soon, before talking to him and seeing what kind of person he was. He might have been one of the people who liked to show off, that they were this and that, they had this and that, so that people around them could give them respect, and people like that when they talked about themselves, they looked to be too proud of themselves and tried hard to make sure that you heard what they were telling you. When most of the time they were telling you about wealth.

And many times they wouldn't give others time to talk.

I knew that love at first sight was normal, and I knew too that sometimes love could be blind, but all of that, between two people, the important thing was the steps which would follow after. When they were lucky to have a good future, as a result of their love, they always remembered their first day, when they met and how they met, nothing made them happy like to talk about that day: but when their love was not successful, and sometimes when they came out to be an enemy to each other, they regretted knowing each other, and hated the first day they met, seeing that was by bad luck and was a bad day. Some others could be bad enough to the point of wishing to see the other die, if it was not to kill them or to try to kill them.

Or it could be a reason for them to commit suicide.

All of the time the nameless man went back to their meeting, I was not bothered, my mind was busy with him, I asked myself many different questions with my strong principles, and without promising myself anything yet, though I saw that I might change something in those principles if things would go the way I had in my mind.

The time came and my nameless man came out with his friends who were together in the meeting, there was more than ten people, in those were three women, he did introductions to his friends, and after greetings, he asked me if I was in a hurry. I told him that I was not in any hurry because I had told my children that I might come late, we went out where their cars were, and he showed me which car I would board and he told me to go behind the seat, he came and sat with me, we were alone in that chair, and he was talking to me in Swahili on the way, he told me that we were going to the home of one of those people to have a dinner.

We didn't talk a lot, the way we were sat there was no disturbance, we were quite relaxed, and they were driving us in that long line of cars, it was tight traffic, in that short time my mind had no sign of my past, there was not those priest's interviews back home, or any memories of Magengo… it was only him and me.

Where we were going was not near, and I wished our journey to be longer…

At that time it was my first time to be with many white people at once, when I was the only black person, but I was not thinking about their colour or mine, or if we didn't know each other before, though on the other hand, I did not mind much about anyone, it was like we were together for years. I was free to him more than the rest of them.

Concerning language they were too polite, they knew that I didn't speak German language, and they were speaking English and Swahili to the few who knew it.

The lady of the house was a good person, she tried to see that I was comfortable, and she was explaining to me what I didn't know, in them there was one man who didn't look smart and neat like the others, he was a big man and he was eating quickly, and in bad manners. I looked at the nameless man and forgot that he was one of them, I wanted to make a wink to him so that we could have something to talk about after, but when I looked at him, my mind came back and saw that he was one of them, that I was alone. I realised that on the other hand all of us we were the same, we were people, we were human; they had people with poor behaviour everywhere!

The time of our dinner was a good time, then the nameless man excused himself to others, we went to town, he wanted to meet his friend who had his car, we met his friend, and when he asked him why he didn't come before, his friend told him that he had a problem to get the address.

To that, he told him that he thought that it was me who he thought might get lost because I didn't know correct English, but he had forgotten that Swahili there was the language spoken by everyone, and Nairobi was my hometown.

The nameless man did an introduction to his friend and his friend too told me that they waited for me at night. He asked us where we wanted him to take us, if it was to his hotel or we had somewhere else. At that point my nameless man looked at me as if he was asking me where I wanted us to go.

First I had to go to see my children, and tell them my day and together see what was next. I decided to take him home and let them see him and help me to judge him according to his look and especially his conversation.

I was aware that my children for some reason might not be happy to see that I was going out with him, and in that case it would be so, I was going to choose not to hurt my children, and yes I would not go anywhere with him. I would forget him, until I met someone who both of us were happy with. Me and my children.

I told Matano my address and we were at home, outside looked to be a cheap area but inside my house was clean, with a few things which were not expensive but good and in order, though it was a wooden house but still you forgot how outside looked alike, normally when there was rain, that time we had to go with two pairs of shoes, one which we would put on after reaching a good road. It was easy for me to keep my house clean, because my children were clean like me, with or without visitors, we stayed clean, they didn't give me any problem with that or anything, something which encouraged me .

In the room which I called the sitting room were two small chairs which were wooden chairs, for one person each, and there was a double bed which always was covered with a good bedcover, and when we were inside, I told them to sit and showed them the chairs, but the nameless man didn't sit, he stood for seconds looking here and there, and finally said that there were many Kenyans who didn't have a place like mine. That made me feel relaxed somehow.

It showed me that he meant that I was not too bad maybe according to what he had in his mind, but on the other hand, it showed me that maybe he thought that all Rwandans in Kenya were in my situation, I wanted to tell him that it was my home not the home of all Rwandans who were in Nairobi. That there were others who drove Benz with a lot of Kenyans who worked for them. After being satisfied with what he saw, he chose to sit on the bed.

After they sat down I asked them if I could give them something to drink, but both of them told me that they were fine, I sat near the nameless man, and he told me that he had a hope to be with me twenty-four hours ago, now if I too was happy to go out with him, yes, he was looking forward to that. I told him to wait, that soon I would give him the answer.

I called the children to greet them, and I did introductions, then I excused myself, I went in the room to talk with my children. I asked the children how they saw the nameless man and if they saw it to be OK for me to go out with him. Together at once they said yes, yes mum, that was how I was to them, on one hand I saw them as my friends. I gave them respect enough to ask them permission or advice before doing something, even having a boyfriend! "Better go at last, you too can go out for a change." They looked to be excited, they helped to get what I would wear, and after a long argument all of us we decided a sleeveless navy blue, long dress, which fitted me up to down from the hips where it started to be wider up to my feet, the dress I made myself. I had a red soft wider scarf which I put on my shoulder, matching with shoes and a handbag, with a long blue four in one beautiful necklace which I made myself too, and I made my hair again, then the children checked me and said yes I could go. They wanted me to be happy. When I came out of the room, they said at once that I looked beautiful, I thanked them and they stood up ready to go. I turned and talked to my children and told them to lock the door, that I might be late, but in my heart I had some strong thought like I was disappointing them, but to look in their faces they looked to be more than happy, that gave me strength, I told myself that in everything had to be the first time, and you had to be strong at the beginning.

I had received letters from many penpals before, but when I received the letter from him I had some strange thought in me. It was like I knew him, and there was something I was waiting to get from him, like if there was something he had promised. I was worried if there would be some reason which would make me not meet him, all of that I saw to be crazy thoughts, I thought that I couldn't tell anyone, because I didn't know how to explain them, sometimes it was making me confused, how and why I thought the way I thought about him, as if we had met already, it was not understandable to me either.

When I saw him I saw that I was right, it was the right man I could love if I would be lucky enough to be loved by him, and asked myself if he was the man who I was waiting to give me peace and love?

On our way I didn't talk, they had their stories and he took his friend to his home, and we returned to his hotel. We sat outside and we had a drink when we were talking, he was the one who told me about himself, and I thought that he might tell me the truth, maybe not everything but it might be a big percentage of truth or he was a good convincer, but now what could I tell him, I didn't get part of my past to tell him.

That I missed education because I grew up on the way running here and there, or that my mother died in Nyabyondo Congo because she had no proper food to eat, or that after my family ignored me I found out that I was in prostitute's land. What part to start with now? Better to wait and if I would tell him anything at least not now.

I was a person of few words, so he was talking a lot and I was talking less. I was not ashamed with my past because all of that journey, had reasons why, what happened, and I was counting myself as a brave girl because I tried to fight for my right, and when I was in deep problems I managed to come out of it too, without losing control, without doing shameful things. I managed to stand to my respect and be seen as a respectable person wherever I was. So if it was needed then, I would tell him my past.

He liked to use Swahili because he wanted to know it more, and I liked to use English because I wanted to know it more, so we were using both languages though we used Swahili more.

The time came when he told me that it was better if we went inside the room and we asked for something to eat. I saw that his plan was that I would spend the night with him, and yes I too wanted to spend the night with him that night, but I had to be a proper respectable lady and show him that I didn't jump into bed with men just like that, and give him time to struggle because he was a man. Even when a woman wanted a man, many times they would try to show the opposite side, so that the man would struggle, and make a woman feel loved.

But I didn't want anything to make him upset in any way if I could help it, so I had to tell him in advance that I had to go back, something on the other hand was to test his patience, and see if he was listening to women and respecting their wishes.

I told him that although he was tired me too I was tired, inside we would eat and drink, then I said that I had to go back home, something which shocked him somehow, and he asked me if I had a man friend who I didn't want to betray, I told him that I didn't have anyone, but we needed time to know each other before we engaged ourselves in other stages.

He told me that if that was my wish he was OK with it, so he was there for a few days he would wait for my time, though he would be coming to see me and if I wanted him to come and be spending the night at my home he was OK with it too.

I told him that I couldn't find space at my home for a visitor like him, better let us wait for the right time. He suggested that we go somewhere before he took me home, and we went in other hotels, we sat and talked, he was looking at me non-stop, and he was asking me if I was telling him the truth about being by myself without any boyfriend, to him it seemed something which surprised him, but I tried to assure him, his view was that a beautiful woman like me couldn't be alone, but after I told him that there were many beautiful women who even I didn't have one quarter of their beauty, and everything had its time. He looked to be relaxed and believed me, but also that made him laugh, and he told me that it depends who looked at you, and how that person saw you. On my side to be with him at that time in that way was a blessing.

He told me to be free to tell him when I wanted to go, then I said that we could go, at home after opening the door I turned to say bye to him, but he was holding me so tightly, and kissed me. Something made me not want to go away from his arms, we said bye to each other, and he said that he would come the next day to take me out with the children in the daytime. He asked if at night we would go together at his hotel, and I told him that we would talk.

He went and I was inside my house. The next day when he came we were waiting for him. I had already told my children that he was coming to take us out, it was Sunday, and they were on holiday so it was no problem, after showing him where to sit, I asked him if we could offer him anything, and he said tea, so we had a tea together, and he asked if we were ready to go. I told him that after a short time we would be ready.

We were out, he took us to many good different places, I was more happy to see how my children were happy, the time came when all of us were tired, even the children were tired, but they wanted still to be around, so we gave them more time and we told them to tell us when they wanted to go back. The time came when they told us that they wanted to go home.

He took us to the hotel first, after having dinner we took them home, now it was more understandable than before, they were happy, and it was like they knew who he was for that short time, the whole day and it seemed that they got used to him and liked him, so it wouldn't be strange to see him go with their mum.

I asked them if they would be OK by themselves so that I could go with him. And all of them at once said that was no problem.

I had the green light to try and enjoy a friendship with the nameless man, and see where that relationship would take me.

The next day we went home in the morning and we had our breakfast and lunch at home, but he told us not to cook we would have dinner out, and that was what happened for the whole week. I was with him, after one week he went back to his job up country.

The last day, to be with him was not easy to me, I was wondering how I would manage by myself without him, in case if I would not have him forever. You could think that I was with him for years, and I had forgotten how I was without him. I loved him unconditionally. I thought that he was the first man to love almost to the love I had with Alex.

I realised that at times like that, sometimes, you couldn't get time to see, to think, if there might be any reasons which could make someone regret that he or she loved, or time to remember to choose because of this and that, or to mind anything concerning wealth, only you had peace to see that you loved especially when you believed that you were loved. Where there is someone you love that kind of love, they can't be far, you could go anywhere no matter what. Because at that time that love is your master, you do what the love tells you to do.

Sometimes it can come to you like lightning when you see that person, and it is not easy to say no, because you assure yourself that you are very careful with your judgment, and you know what you are doing. By good luck it gives you good results, but by bad luck, when you get a negative result, it can shock you and sometimes make you sick, because, you would make mistakes to assure yourself that you are an expert for that kind of judgment, and no one could stand in front of you and tell you anything, unless if that person wanted problems from you. Because you see the person who is trying to give you a warning, to be your enemy number one, because you don't want anyone to tell you that you will be the victim of love.

And when you are lucky to have it as you hoped, or as your judgment showed you, you see yourself to be rich, even when you don't have a lot. But to have each other in trust and in an honest way, that you see to be enough, to let your heart settle and be happy, which is rich, more than those who have a lot of any kind of wealth, but are alone.

When I was thinking how I lost Alex it made me nervous, in case if I could lose him too, and on top of that I had to remember that I didn't know him yet enough to trust him one hundred percent, so it was better to stand by, and be aware for anything any time, that things might change and go in a direction I would not like to see. I didn't want to ask him if he had a girlfriend, in case he said yes, because if he had any, I didn't want to know, as far as he had assured me that he was not married yet, that was only what I wanted to hear.

Back home he did what he promised me, he sent me a letter, which was telling me that he was happy and had a good time with me... that letter gave me the green light to send him a letter because I wanted to send one before that but had to hold on to see if he would send one before me, luckily I had no communication of phones at the time. I think if I had, maybe it would be hard to be able to hold on and wait not to call him many times with unnecessary calls.

We went ahead to be together when he came to Nairobi to meetings, and he had to come at least once per month.

Our communication was only letters, he was trying to send me a letter at least twice a month before he came, and I had to go everywhere with that letter, in my handbag, until when I would get another one, because I was reading it whenever I had time.

I had a good time, I had him, I had my children, and I had my best friend with me, Mukabagira. She had seen him and she said that what I had to do was only to wait and see what and how he would drive our relationship, otherwise concerning looks, there was no shame to go with him anywhere, any woman could be proud to be with a man like him beside her.

But what mattered more to everyone was personality and behaviour....

Mukabagira was like a daughter to her elder sister, her brother-in-law liked her too and both were happy to look after her, in whatever they could do to see her happy. Being the only girls they were too close like twins since they were young. So Mukabagira too was doing everything to see them happy.

In Kenya she was with her elder sister and her family, her husband and her two children, a boy and a girl.

Between us, Mukabagira and I, it was like in the 60s, when I had just come to Uganda and met her, again we were together for whatever we had in our lives happiness and sadness. In Kenya their life was like the life of any refugees who were there, they were dependant on some organisations which supported refugees, but they had other new ones which came up just for those Ugandans who ran away, since Amin was well known by countries for his careless behaviour. They had more aids from those countries.

She got a scholarship to study design, she was happy to get that chance because she liked it even before. Those Ugandan refugees mostly were Langi and Acholi who were followers of Obote and they didn't want to be out of their country for a long time, so, they started to fight Amin, the guerrilla war which started from Tanzania supported by Mwalimu Nyerere.

To go to war was voluntary, Mukabagira's brother-in-law was a good person who loved his family, his people, and his country. Being an officer in the army, and patriotic for his country, to him it was his responsibility to fight that war too, but when he thought that to go might be the end between him and his family being together, and taking care of them and seeing his children grow up, it was a big test, he loved his wife and he always didn't want anything which could hurt her, let alone giving her the responsibility of becoming a single mother.

On the other hand if he had to choose between him and his wife who could die and who could survive for the children's benefit, he was telling his friends that it was better if he chose to die, because he trusted his wife to be strong and hard-working, and an intelligent woman who could take very good care of the children, more than him.

But since him and his wife had no interest of going out of Africa no matter what.

So he had to fight for his Africa, for his Uganda, so that his children could get a better education in Uganda not elsewhere, but to sit down and watch other fighters fight when they themselves had also left their family behind, that was not him, he talked with his family especially his wife and he decided to go to war, so he went to Tanzania to start the war and fight for his children, and his people in general.

When Idi Amin took over power in 1971, Uganda was yet to have proper peace since Obote took over from Kabaka Mutesa on 24th May 1966. That is when Ugandans started to see a strange life, to them they had no idea that could be their life, a life of war and unnecessary wars. Something which surprised them to see when Rwandans ran from their country in 1959, when they saw them in big numbers, some ordinary people were telling them that they were cowards, otherwise they had to stand and fight for their king not let him run, and then ran behind him, it was something some did not find easy to understand. Maybe because in all their life they had never seen themselves without a king, and couldn't understand how anyone else couldn't fight for their king no matter what.

When Amin took over from Obote, 25th January 1979 Obote stayed out, then as a refugee, but he didn't keep quiet, he fought back with his people. Mukabagira's brother-in-law was a commander from Tanzania which was his post he had from back home, and on 11th April 1979 it was Obote II. Amin was out that year which gave Uganda the history of having three different leaders.

When it was Yusufu K Lule who was not the leadership even for two months, then Godfrey Binayisa who saw the leadership almost a year, and gave it to Paulo Muwanga to hold it for Obote so that he could finish out the election which he was a winner of on 10th December 1980.

But that war was not good to Mukabagira's family, her brother-in-law was not lucky enough to survive, they got bad news that their boat had disappeared without trace, they didn't known if it was the enemy or bad weather, but still Mukabagira had to go ahead with her studies, when her sister and her children wanted to go back to Uganda in protection of Obote II.

Mukabagira who was single since Amin's men killed her husband, she was always telling me that she had fear of involving herself with any man, maybe what happened to her before could happen again in other ways. But I was always trying to encourage her and tell her to think positive, after her sister went back to Uganda Mukabagira was good in the financial area, because she had big pocket money from her scholarship.

She was in a good place, in her single bedroom apartment, she came to meet the long school mate, they were together in school some time back in Uganda, he was Musoga man. The man Paulo was in America for study at the time. They started communication until when he finished his studying and came back to Africa, and he decided to stay in Nairobi and look for a good job there.

So that he could be near with Mukabagira and see if their communication could come out with something better than that. Paulo his name, tried to show Mukabagira that he loved her by giving her gifts and so on, even Paulo seemed go ahead and try to show her that he loved her, but Mukabagira seemed that she didn't love him as much as he did. At least they could be just friends, but for some reason she was not capable of being herself yet maybe to any man. And she knew that the love she had to Paulo was not enough to compare with the one she once had with her two men in the past, but yes she had to give it a try with him, with the hope that step by step as far as Paulo was so kind to her, she would learn to love him.

The time came when Paulo proposed to her and Mukabagira said yes. The wedding day, which had to be a simple ceremony, after going for signing at the registry office, Paulo had to call his mum to be there for him, for his special day, a day of getting Mukabagira as his wife.

Paulo was a short man compared to Mukabagira, he was like five foot three inches, too black like Acholi people, with a short and wider face, he had white teeth, so when he smiled you saw that his smile brightened him and he was somehow handsome.

Since Paulo's mum came in two days I was not there yet to meet her, but we were already finished the plan concerning the wedding, so I was only waiting for the day to meet them and be with them. When I met them, Mukabagira didn't look to be happy and I was confused, but I had no time to ask her what was going on, we went ahead for what we came for, her wedding.

When they asked her to put the ring on Paulo's finger she said that she had forgotten it, but the ceremony went on and finished.

Then I happened to get Mukabagira to the lady's, she was there crying! I was confused and I had to ask her what was going on there, when she saw me she cried more. I had to give her time and wait for when she was going to be ready to tell me after calming down.

She started to talk to me a bit calmer and tried to make me get her point, and she said that even at the moment she had nothing, but she was not going to count herself as Paulo's wife. "I didn't get a quick way to stop it but I don't want to count him as my husband," she said.

"I can't, it can be too much to everyone on my side not only me!" I was in the dark, I didn't understand what she was trying to say, she knew that I didn't understand her. After a short time, she told me that when I would come to his home I would understand what she was telling me, but now I couldn't come and see his mother had come, and then I thought that his mum might have done something to her, I asked if she did anything to her and she said nothing, but insisted to come that was when I would understand.

I said, "OK I will come, but his mother is his mother, he is the one who is going to be your husband not anyone else in his family." We didn't have any more time to talk.

We went out and went ahead with our normal plan, it was evening time when I went to her home she was out and she took me inside. In the corner, there was an old woman who was sat down on the mat. I greeted her before sitting, we had a short conversation when she came up with wine, she did introductions and I greeted her again. Where I was, one time I was looking at the old lady for just a second, and seeing how she was I started to think why Mukabagira didn't like her to the level of she didn't even deserve to be one of that family, though also to her that was like a good excuse, but I thought that was easy to her to get that excuse because she had no proper love for Paulo.

She was a fat old lady, too black like her son, but the way she looked and the way she smelled, it showed me that she might have had a shower a long time ago. She had many clothes on her body, which seemed that some of them she had never washed them since she bought them. I thought that she had a problem with her eyes, she was not looking at us for long without her eyelids working so hard too quickly up and down, when in her eyes you could think that she was crying, because there were tears mixed with other thick dirt, white and yellow, which she was wiping out many times using her clothes. To look at her, it was easy to make anyone feel uncomfortable.

The big problem was that sometimes she was using her hands to wipe her eyes and nose, they had free water, and I was wondering why she couldn't have a shower! I thought that they could help her to look better than that, and if she needed medication then they could do that for her too. To me she didn't look well, so until I talked to Mukabagira then I didn't know yet why all of that was.

We didn't want to go into many stories in our language in front of her, so that I could ask her all of that concerning her mother-in-law, when she was escorting me I asked her why she looked that way, why she didn't get a shower and why they didn't take her to see a doctor if she had a problem, according my judgment.

To the question of having a shower she told me that she had asked her and the answer was that she didn't have any strength to do that.

Concerning taking her to see the doctor she told me that she had told her son that suggestion, and the answer was that she was OK, she doesn't have any problem which needed a doctor that was always how she was.

Concerning her clothes when I asked her if she didn't have other ones to change so that she could be able to wash those for her, for that she laughed, and told me that she didn't ask her that because she wouldn't be able to do that for her, that she couldn't wash them when vomiting in them too.

"So Paulo did well to bring her and let me see her so that can be the example of the rest of their family, meaning that simply they are not my type."

"But it is Paulo who is your husband not his family," I told her.

"Look you are not understanding, it is over, how can I go and have my children with those people? Tell me if my mum can go there and visit his mum and stay there even one day? Tell me if her too who is supposed to be my mother-in-law can go and visit my mum? Where can she put her? What use is a marriage like that, when normal marriage means to unite two sides of a family, without that it is useless."

"We will survive, already now we are survivors, now our mum still has her good house, our brothers have good education, and we two girls had enough education to help ourselves tomorrow, so now is not time to force myself in that situation, that time is over."

"But I can't tell him anything now not soon. I will finish my studies and go back to Uganda, when I will be with my sister. I will tell him when I am there in Uganda, because there I will be under my sister's protection. She is a big person there under Obote's guide, now Uganda is going according to who you are, it depends on your tribe, to say anything or do anything, so widows of officers who were fighting with Obote there they are well in many areas, especially like my sister who was well educated, she had support from the government including a guide, and she has a good job, a good house and they guide her too, she is a well respected lady there, so he can't do anything to me when I am there he will have to do as I say. But here I don't know what he can do to me if he knows that I don't want him."

Now I was used to being with my nameless man when he was in Nairobi, if we didn't have anywhere to go we simply relaxed at home in the daytime and at night we would go to his hotel. The neighbours now were used to seeing him, he got along good with the children, and after some time I decided to relax, and believe that God, my God had answered my prayers. I had the man I loved, and who loved me, I had lovely children, why couldn't I put my past back and sit down, relax and be happy.

Sometimes I was not even thinking of him being white, and when I remembered that in fact he was white, I had to laugh a secret laugh, or in my heart make a joke of it. I knew that people were people, they could do what they could do as people, plan this and that, even some could believe that they were capable of everything they wanted.and hear them say me, me, me, but sometimes it can't work as they think it will work.

That gives me a hope that one day people will work together as people, not look to anyone as masters or slaves, just because of poison in their mind, not to have any idea that you can use anyone, not any fear of anyone, just so and so has to be master, that people will work together as people, in that time everyone will use qualifications not colour.

My children Muvunangoma and Manzi were still too young to give me any advice, but Ilibagiza and Batsinduka whatever I was doing concerning the welfare of our home we had to talk. Yes they were young too, but at least they were good enough to give me satisfactory ideas. Always I was seeing them as clever children and I was proud of them and too happy to have them and wondering about life without them in case I hadn't brought them over there.

The area I was, it was not a good area, but I was lucky my children had no friends from that area, and the few they had from there, they had to know which kinds of families they came from, and it was easy, because it was themselves who decided not to mix with those children. So when they came from school, most of the time they were inside their house doing housework, and their school work, and sometimes they would teach me too, they were my teachers in many different things. I could say that I had been home schooling, which was very successful, my children were unique, to the level of they were examples to many in the area, to some families with both parents, even to some of my community. That helped me to put them together in a good manner. And was one of the good reasons which made me be well known to people around me, and be respected in that area and with my community who knew me.

According to my income: I had to be very careful with my budget, to see that we would be able to eat properly and dress well, luckily they didn't need transport, their school was near, it was only me who needed it, so sometimes I had to walk to see that I would manage those two important things, food and dress. On the side of dressing, being a dressmaker helped a lot, I just had to buy material which most of the time was not expensive, as far as it was me who would make it in any fashion we wanted, both of us were happy for that.

Concerning how we ate: we saw that there were some other types of food which we couldn't bother to eat, and could be problems for our health, but still we had to have them in the house in case, for our visitors. We decided not to bother with it those, one of those was sugar and meat, only Batsinduka didn't manage to have porridge without sugar, so he had the green light for that.

When I got my support from the U.N., the first thing I had to do was to stock food enough for one–two months, or sometimes more, like maize meal of twenty-four kilograms, fifty kilograms of rice, ten to twenty beans, and peanuts with other things as snacks, and some different vegetables. This was cheap and fresh... I believed buying things in wholesale to be much better, in that way, I had no stress, sometimes I was helping others who didn't have something to eat, because many times I had a lot of food at home. There were even some other times when I was going to a big market in the city centre well known as Malgiti, and buying larger sacks of potatoes which could last for a long time too. I knew what to do to make them stay in a good condition for a long time.

The refugees who were in Nairobi five to ten percent had a high life some were good business people, some had a better life which many Kenyans had never dreamed of.

The rest, most of them, were surviving only by support from the U.N.. These two different levels of people did not mix much, concerning Rwandans, they still had their good culture of helping each other when someone was in a kind of trouble, or when there was some kind of ceremony. At this point all levels would be together without any hesitation.

That second level, some of them turned themselves to be drinkers, or they had to ask for help from friends, or simply from people they knew so that they could be able to survive to finish the month.

I thought that the reason was that they were not careful enough about their badges to see what they had and use it accordingly.

In my case concerning money when they saw that I had never asked anyone for any help, and if they visited me, and saw how I welcomed my visitors with a lot of food, and saw or knew what a big family we were and saw how we dressed, most of them, believed that I was not surviving only with the U.N.'s support like them, that I might be keeping secret of my income.

When they saw me with a white man then they thought that now they knew my secret, he was the one who took care of me all along.

Some of them including Kenyans thought that I was working with Rwandan government, at the time which was Habyarimana's! And I stayed in that cheap area to confuse people! This to me was abusive and was too far. Anything which could make me betray my people was impossible. Though on the other hand I was happy to see that they didn't know about my life, since it couldn't help me in any way, if they could think that they knew me more it was up to them to think what they wanted.

But others thought that I was a prostitute, and that was how I came to meet my white man, and probably I even took my children, girls, to sell them. The style of my life confused many outside for so long.

All of this they were talking about it when they were by themselves, and making arguments, when some wanted to show others that they knew me better than others, and it was others who believed that I dealt with stones, like gold… but a part of my life, and how I managed, the good thing was that my community trusted me, and you could hear them say that there was no one who could do this and that like me! And some of them came to me when they needed some ideas. I did not understand why they saw me to be more clever than them, when all of us we were in the same level of life.

I was trying to do a lot, but many would not come out as I wanted to, though the people who were near me they didn't want to notice when I failed, they always noticed when I succeeded, and said that nothing could be wrong on my side because of that cleverness they saw in me!

One time the education officers of the U.N. the way they were treating us came to be too much to the side of our children and their study, by making them be late to go back to school, to putting them in bad colleges, or simply not putting some of them anywhere.

Something which they were doing just because we were who we were, foreigners, refugees, and sometimes some officers could tell you, 'what do you think if your children will not go in those colleges because they are bad, who else do you think will go there?'

I tried to tell other parents that it could be better to take our stories to the media and we could choose one of the good newspapers which were well known and read by many.

NATION OR STANDARD and we chose STANDARD since even the head office didn't want to listen to us, and it could be good if we could come in big numbers, and do our demonstration, and those who did not want to be put inside with his or her picture was no problem.

They saw that was a good idea, we planned where we would meet and a time, all of us we argued.

I didn't get them so I went to the media's office to wait for others there, I told them our stories and they saw that they were good stories which had a good point, but they told me that if others didn't give me the green light to talk on their behalf I would have to wait for them.

I told the officers that the others were on the way coming, so they showed me where to sit and wait for them. I waited for them, no one came out, so the time came when I too had to give up and go back home without doing anything.

The next day one of them who counted herself to be my friend, told me that they came, and when they were almost near the media's office, they changed their mind, because one of them came up with the idea, that Bamurangirwa was trying to put them in trouble, because after the stories were out, the U.N. might cut out the support of those who did it, and then, it was them who would suffer, since me I had no problem. I had my ways of getting income, and I could afford to bribe the officers and get what I wanted. There was nothing that I could do which could make them believe that we were on the same level, with the same problems…

In those refugees there were some who were experts to know where there were new things which came to help, and they would tell only their friends. At that time it was those new organisations from rich countries, which came to help Ugandan refugees, but others from other countries sometimes would get some help too. But the problem was how you would know, I did not like to go everywhere I was told, there were other places to go, there I saw that it was to waste my time.

And they were telling me that I couldn't go in things like that simply because I was not that poor like them. So the time came when I said then, if they saw me to be better than them so be it.

When Mukabagira came near me she was the one who was helping me to that point, telling me which better place I could go, somewhere I could get something, at least I was not going to waste my time just sitting and netting.

The nameless man went ahead visiting me and I saw that I loved him, even if he could tell me to be with him anywhere, it wouldn't be a problem to me, he was not giving me money and I was not asking him for any. I didn't want anything which would make him think that I wanted him for any other reason; I wanted him to notice that I wanted him as him. I believed that the best things in life aren't things, but peace of mind.

Sometimes he was giving me a little money to buy some few things, when many times I had everything at home; there were times he asked me why I didn't ask him for any kind of help. And I told him that he could help when he could for what he could. I was telling myself that if he wanted to help me for anything, he could do that without having to be asked, since he saw my situation.

I wished that I could be able to protect him from whatever could hurt him, mentally and physically. I wanted to see him happy forever, I had pure love towards him, and I assumed that he loved me the same, that he would do everything he could, to see me happy, so when I saw that he didn't say anything, I thought that he was planning something for me, maybe he would move me from there, since when he was there when it was raining time it was a problem for him too, and yes I wished to move from that area, though I was lucky to have good children who were not affected with the area, but still if there could be some reason to move me to a better place I could be happier for it.

But some other times I thought maybe his salary was not enough for him and his mum because, he told me that back home he was poor, he didn't have even a house, and he was the only child to her. I thought that he was the one who had to take care of his mother, which was what I knew to be normal in Africa. So I didn't have to ask concerning that point. I thought that was how it was everwhere.

At that point I felt sorry for him, and told myself that no problem we would work and we would be whatever we wanted to be in the future. The time came when I was not feeling good, and when I went to the hospital, they told me that I was expecting a baby.

I was very happy to have a child with the man I loved, it was a good time because at the time, I wanted to have another child, it was only a matter of getting someone who would be the right man to have that child with. As African women we believe that children are a better future, at the time you don't have to think much about how you will manage, always concerning our future we had to put our God ahead, and somehow relax, and when things went wrong, we tried to find something else to blame, that was evil or that was how God wanted, (you, to be in trouble, or poor…) and waited for tomorrow for the change. When the same God wanted you to have the better change.

On the other hand, the baby I had in my body was a white man's baby, the man I wished to have forever, but it was the person who we had different understandings and different cultures, especially the point of family. Yes I was brave enough once to ask him if he was married, but I didn't ask him if he wanted a child. Though he told me that he didn't have any yet, that couldn't be the answer that he wanted them, according to the stories I had from my friends, that to some white people, children meant nothing, or they had to plan to get them after doing this and that. If they were lucky to those who wanted them, they got them according to their plan, or they would go on with life and forget that time was running out and when they woke up it was too late.

Now what if he could tell me that he loved me so much and wanted me with him forever, but at the moment he didn't want children, or he was not sure that the baby was his, and told me to abort my baby? How could I manage that big test? Here I wanted him and I wanted the baby? Could I choose my baby over than him or could I choose him over my child? I had the right and power to do whatever I decided to do, to have this baby, or to kill in the name of love!

But that was no big problem, at least for that I had an answer, that whatever he would tell me I would keep my baby, if it meant losing him then so be it. I am an African woman, and I will follow my head not my heart, to me nothing could be as good as my child, not even the love I had towards him. So I would choose my baby if he chose to go, my baby would be my future, that was what I had heard from my mum, to make it easy, I myself, normally loved children more than anything in life.

Sometimes all of that could turn to be rubbish thought, instead my baby could be the one who could be my key to open my lucky door tomorrow, why couldn't I think that as soon as my nameless man heard that I had his baby, he was going to be more than happy, and propose to me there, and then we could be married. And he would start planning how he could take me out of this place that was where my baby who was inside me was going to take me.

I was in those questions, sometimes I had questions, and sometimes I had none, but I was on stand by, it was better to be aware that things might not come out the way I would like them to be, and if so then, I could only know that even from the beginning. I was just lying to myself, he had never loved me, it was just a wish I had, and I wanted to believe that he loved me because that was what I wanted. And if it came up in that way, also, no regret. I would have my child, and take care of her or him together with the others, maybe in hardship, but I would do it and I would be successful. I would even die if it meant saving my child.

I didn't tell him in the letter, I waited for him to come so that I could tell him when we were together, the time came when he came, and when he came he had a new story, that from now on, we were not going to spend the night in the hotel, he would be coming to my home! Something which shocked me, my house was small, I never thought that I could come with a man inside the house, I had high respect for my children. There was nothing good there, not toilets, the place to have a bath was a separate old wooden room, and he knew everything there, so I didn't know why he decided that. Maybe he wanted to show me that he could be wherever I was, or he wanted to be used to being with the children, or he wanted to save the money he was paying to the hotel. I was confused and I couldn't say no.

When I told the children they were shocked too, we were there doing housework, once per week we were used to being with him, and the children were used to being with him, he seemed to be happy with home-cooked food, more than hotel's, my neighbours were used to seeing him as their neighbour too.

Before Christmas day of 1978 was the day I planned to tell him the news, almost the whole day we went to Masai area crimping mountain, and he was with his friends. At night we took the children to Bomas of Kenya to see dancers, so it was busy all day. I didn't get time to talk to him.

All the time I wanted to start the story so I was coming up with something, and I wanted to tell him before he went back, so that I too could know where I was. On the other hand I was asking myself why he had never asked me if I could visit him at his home. Maybe he might have a woman where he was, who stayed with him, and maybe he was only not married yet, and other times I asked myself why I couldn't trust him so much anyway. I started to blame myself somehow, and saw it to be too late, I had to throw down a bit of doubt since it was not going to help me anyway and first wait and see where things would go.

And the next day I had to get a way to tell him, so I took him out for a walk.

Outside we got somewhere to sit as always when we were out, he didn't think that it might be anything special. I started my story up to the end, I was looking at him so that I could judge him through the body language, he was listening without any interruption. But he didn't change in any way, he was not angry or happy, he remained in a normal situation.

When he started to give me his view, he seemed to be in quite deep thought, he said, "Look, I am not young anymore, I thought that I wouldn't be able to have a child. I have had many girlfriends before, I don't know how many, maybe if it is not a lot it is two hundred, but not one has told me that she has my child, one who tried was lying, so me too, I would like to see how my child might look, let us wait and see."

All my fear went; I was relaxed, now I knew where I was. He had to come every month, because of his job, and when he came we had one week inside my house doing housework, with our stories and sometimes we would go out.

One day in January 1979 he came as always, when we were by ourselves talking this and that, he told me that he had something he wanted to ask me, I came near him and waited for the question.

"I was wondering if I move you from here and put you in good house, but you alone and leave these children here, can that be OK with you?!"

I didn't say anything, only I turned my face and looked at him with shock which I think he noticed that he had asked me the question in the wrong way. So he had to collect himself, and he said, "No, I mean that you can come with Manzi, so that you can be helping others when they are here."

At that I didn't turn my face to look at him, I felt a big disappointment, it showed me that he didn't know me yet, enough to know that those children to me were no different with Manzi, and he would never know me, he didn't even love me, because if you love someone, you love the one he or she loves too. Before I thought that he too loved me and gave me respect for that, because of how I managed to take good care of them and put them together as one good family.

I thought of the picture of myself after to going and leaving them in that wooden house, which would be the first step, next could be to go to Germany and leave them for themselves, at that age, in primary school, just because I wanted to be with a man and I loved him too much! That can't be me.

I believed that man with no time could change and I could be disappointed with a lot of regret, always remembering those children I left behind. Whatever the situation I felt them with, if I left them, no matter what, I couldn't have peace in the future, my heart couldn't allow me to do so, simply I couldn't do it.

And I gave him the simple answer that I couldn't.

He saw that his question in all the ways was not going the way he maybe planned. Again he asked to buy me a piece of land, or a house, which I could choose, I told him that if he could buy a house for me, I would appreciate that. Again he went back in deep thought for some seconds, and told me that, if I wanted a house it was not bad, but I would wait for a while.

I thought that he was giving me some kind of test now he knew who I was.

Again I started to ask myself silly questions like why was he asking me about moving me now. Simply he could ask me to marry him and we could do our things together, but yes letting me have the baby first, that was when things would go on the right side, after seeing his child, that was the beginning. Even these questions came after knowing that I had his baby, I didn't want to think there that could be any reason, which could make us not be together.

I just wanted there to be one reason which was only love.

But after that, after showing him that wherever I would be, that was where all of my children had to be, I didn't see him every month again, and the letters started to be fewer, not twice a month or more. I went ahead writing as before asking him what was the problem, I was worried that there might be some problems where he was, or simply

409

a lot of work. At that point, I was feeling sorry for him, and wished that I could be there and help him for other things, when I saw him or I got his letter, he told me that he was sick, or had a lot of work, and I knew that soon I would be with him and help him, maybe he didn't have a houseworker.

The time came when I received his letter telling me the day his mum would be in Kenyatta airport, and he would pick her up from there that day, he would bring her to visit me.

I asked Mukabagira to help me with the preparation of welcoming the lady I had a hope to be my future mother-in-law. Mukabagira was there for me by teaching me this and that, to do everything to show her that her son had chosen well, and so she would be happy to have me as her future daughter-in-law. And since I had no mum I wanted her to be both to me, my mother-in-law and my mum too. So I had to try anything to see her happy when she was with me.

When she was there both of us were happy to see each other and she told me that she knew us through the pictures her son sent her, she was a simple person, and we talked as if we knew each other before, all of us and the children we had a good day.

I was already prepared to go to a hotel since we couldn't find a place for his mum at my home, so I thought that all of us we would go to the hotel, or we would take his mum and come back.

We went for a walk, when we were back his mum was tired and needed a rest, and I didn't want to make her wait for long so I went to the room to be ready to go.

The nameless man called, and I told him to give me a little time, I was preparing myself to come so that we could go, and he told me that because of his mum he was going with her alone. I thought that I didn't understand so I told him, "If you are going to take mum, yes, let me come we can take her together and we can come back no problem."

He saw that it was not going to be easy to make me understand what he was telling me, and once more again he called me by my name, "Look Bamurangirwa, I am sorry but today it is only me who will go, my mum wants to be with me, so that I can get a good time to take her to many places because you can't, it is not good to make you walk around for so long." I was six months pregnant with my baby.

I didn't want them to be that kind to me, to refuse me to be with him, and think that I was happy for it because they were sorry for me, but there was nothing I could do, so I had to say yes. I thought that might be their understanding, so I couldn't blame them for that. Our communication didn't improve. I got his letter once in two months and I didn't see him for that time either. I was always feeling sorry for him, how busy he was.

I wanted him to be near me when I was having our baby, I was lucky to be given a chance to have my baby in Kenyatta National Hospital. That hospital at the time was the best in the whole country, to get that chance was lucky, because of the way they would take good care of their patients, especially mothers, to that point they were good even more than big private ones, like Nairobi Hospital. They were offering mothers there from other areas only when they had some complication or when they had a good doctor. That was how I was offered there, to be sure that I would be in good hands so nothing would happen to me or my baby like before.

The day of my appointment came, it was on a Saturday. I told my children that in case I did not come back, they didn't have to panic, the doctor might hold me there. I went using public transport, as soon as I was at Kenyatta Hospital, they made a checkup and told me that I was not going back.

To me I was OK but on Monday they took me to the labour ward, how the nurses welcomed me and how it looked to be clean made me feel relaxed and happy, and have a hope of being in the good hands of those people who were around me.

I was not alone, every time, at least one–two ladies had to be beside me, with good words of encouragement.

It was Monday afternoon on 2nd July 1979 when my beautiful baby girl, Niwegaju has born; the first person to visit me was Batsinduka. And he told me that he asked permission at school to come and visit me, he was so happy to see the baby, he looked at her, and called me mum, and said "Our baby is beautiful."

I said, "Yes my son, she is, thank you." He was sitting on my bed, holding her, and I saw that he might forget that he had to go back home, and I reminded him that it was almost night, better to go. And I told him that they didn't have to struggle by coming to see me, better to wait for me at home. I didn't want them to be in that stress.

When he stood to go I heard him scream, I asked him what was wrong, he told me that they pickpocketed him the money he had saved for a long time, he just wanted to give it to me when I had a baby. He looked so upset, and I asked him how much they took from him, and he told me that it was 20 K sh. I told him not to worry. I had enough to pay the hospital, and to take me home, I tried to calm him down.

My beloved son went but looked unhappy and maybe he had started to save for a long time after noticing that I was expecting a baby.

After two days, the nameless man came, when I saw him beside my bed, I felt peaceful, and felt sorry for him for that work which was too much for him, to the point that he didn't get time to be near me, to welcome his daughter when she was coming to our world, and tell her that he would be there for her as her father, he would protect her and give her all the confidence that she would need from him, that she was not alone, she had both her good parents who would love and be near her in all her life.

After greeting me in silence, he went straight to where the baby was in her small bed near mine, and he took her in his arms, he looked at her with that long silence. I was looking at him to see body launguage, after a few second he held his chin in a way of deep thinking. I didn't know if he was happy or sad, but he had too strong thoughts, I tried and managed to give him all the time he needed without any interruption. He was still looking at her when I was looking at him at the same time, after time he looked up at the roof of the hospital, and it was like he was talking to himself. He said, "That is my child no question about it," and he was looking at her then and then the roof a few times, without remembering that I was there, though he didn't said any other words, I was happy to see how he was serious with his child, and he noticed that it was his, without any problems, which was my wish.

412

I thought that he didn't have trust in me one hundred percent, which could be understandable, he thought that the child might be someone else's. I couldn't blame him since he didn't know me enough yet to trust me that much, and maybe he was too happy and he didn't have a way to handle it.

Still like he was talking to himself, or there was someone who asked him the question, he said, "Yes, this is my child."

After a few seconds he was like he was back now with me. I asked him why he said that the child was his no question about that. Was that because he doubted her to be his?

The question woke him up more clearly, and he looked at me quickly, he started to look at me and talk to me, and said, "No not that." It was a short answer of no, and me too I didn't want any other answers concerning that point.

He went out and came back with English magazines with one Swahili newspaper, he knew that I liked reading, one of magazines had the title *TRUE LOVE*, when I saw that I told myself that was to show me the love he had for me to be a true one. Even the time he told me to wait to buy me a house, had come, it was the time to take out his daughter and the woman he loves who gave him a beautiful daughter out of that area.

I went ahead in my heart and my head planning our future with the nameless man, by putting things together, that since he was the one who told me about buying a house it meant that even if we could go back to Germany, we could rent it, and also we could get somewhere to be when we were back, instead of going to the hotels, so in any way there would be no loss.

When he was going he gave me 200 K sh, it was more than enough, it was the first time he gave me that amount of money, that was enough to pay out the hospital and left some. I was happy for that. Things were not bad on my side; I had a boy Manzi and now I had a girl Niwegaju. I had my good big family in general, now I had a man I loved, what else?

Nothing changed at home, it took him time to visit me and when he came he was leaving me with a little money as before, once he asked me why I didn't tell him what I wanted him to do for me, and my answer was the same, he could support me in the way he could when he was happy to do that and I didn't say that again. I hated to ask someone to give me this and that, I thought that it could look like I was materialistic when I was not, and on the other hand it could look that I was commanding him to do it. When I wanted him to help me willingly and be happy to do that.

Something I believe is that can show respect and genuine love.

Sometimes it is not good to tell people your problems, it can depend who, otherwise you can tell someone who was waiting to hear that, so that can make him or her happy to see that you are down, when sometimes it is not going to do anything for you. Or even if he or she would do something to help, it would make the person feel so proud and they might even advertise it, that you know: it is me who did this and that to so.

But to the nameless man's case, always I didn't want to think of him in the wrong ways, I was telling myself that by being a European person, he didn't understand what kind of life I had, because he had never been in that kind of life, poor life, though I was able to feed my family, but the big problem I had was where I was.

Luckily when the time to discharge me from the Hospital came, Mukabagira was there visiting me, and she was the one who took the baby. We used the public means to go home, with our baby, so that I could save enough for other needs at home. People started to talk about me getting a baby with a white man, to them it was a big step ahead, and some started to say that they knew me from the beginning, that my future would not be like everyone else!

It was not easy to be a mother when I had to breastfeed my child, here many days I was in town almost the whole day, without eating anything, seeing that I could take nothing with me from what we cooked.

But my community and my neighbours around there, now they had a good reason to be sure that I was better than them, now they had proof. It was no longer a secret, no pretending anymore, now I was with a white man it was as if I was already married to him, they started to be asking me for help, meaning to ask me for money for this and that, or for bus fare.

Sometimes I was doing foolish things, and thought that it was to confuse them forever, and gave them some from the little I had, but still, always, my life was my life and my family, there was no one who had to know how I lived.

The problem with Rwandan girls in my generation and our elders was that seventy-five percent didn't get a chance for high education, the education we had, was our nature, our background, our heads and our beauty.

And there was a lot of responsibility ahead of these girls that was why they did what they did, to reach their goals, to see their family well and happy.

Me too I was happy to do everything to see my family happy, to see all my children look healthy and happy.

I came to realise that my breasts were not enough for my baby, I didn't want to wait to see my baby lose weight, I started to feed her other things, I started to lose weight and feel weak without knowing why, I went ahead doing everything I was doing, it was my responsibility.

I told Mukabagira how I felt and she suggested to escort me to the hospital, they did a check up and saw that I didn't have enough blood, they wanted to hold me for a few days but she managed to tell them that I had a new baby, they asked us if I would be able to do what they told me, yes, we told them.

But when I was outside I fainted, something had to hold me for the whole day until later that evening, when she got a taxi to take us home. I was at home for a few days without going anywhere, Mukabagira was the one who was helping about housework and the new baby, my children looked to be shocked and sometimes they were crying, but I promised them that I would be OK, I knew the mistakes I made and I was going to change.

I started to change the way I was taking care of myself, so that I could be able to take care of my children properly, instead of killing myself and leaving them by themselves, and knowing that if I would not take good care of myself, it would not do any good for any of us especially my children. I changed the way of eating and in a short time I was fine and strong.

On 25th October 1979 in the evening, my baby was three months and eight days old, the nameless man came home without any notice, which was the first time for him to come without telling me before, I thought that was no problem, what I wanted was to see him.

I was OK, so I didn't tell him anything about the problem I had passed through, I asked him what I could offer him, and he said that he came from the hotel so he was OK. What I wanted was to be on his side, I missed him.

But I had questions of why he went straight to the hotel without telling me and came home as before, why this changed. When I thought that it was because of his child yes there were going to be changes between us, which would be changes of more love, responsibility, and happiness! But I wanted first to hear what he would tell me, there might be a good reason for all of that, as I always didn't want to judge him in the wrong ways.

I was on his side, we were playing with the baby, and he asked me if I received the letter he sent me, and I was not yet to get any, so I said no. He told me that it might take a long time to go and to check.

I told him that I was at home for the whole week…

"That is why you didn't have it yet." I forgave him because I now knew that he had told me everything in that letter why he would come straight to the hotel.

"That is why I didn't know that you were coming?"

"No I didn't say anything in that letter concerning coming, because at that time I didn't know yet that I would come. I was inviting you to come to visit me with the baby, and I was giving you the money to use for the transport. And I was telling you that I got married to a Kenyan woman, who had a baby girl two weeks older than Niwegaju."

After telling me that he went ahead talking about things which I didn't hear, it was like someone put something in my ears, which was like a drum with a beat and had a long sound. My eyes were seeing stars. I wanted to visit the toilet, I had an uncomfortable stomach, and I felt that I was almost going around and around, and I wanted to vomit. I went quickly out, and I put water on my head and washed my face, and I was crying, I wished that I hadn't heard properly. After visiting the toilet, then I was a bit better and I came back with water, which I was drinking slowly, and sat down.

I started to hear what he was saying, but I knew that I had heard clearly, and I wished that he could go that second. I didn't want to see him near me, I didn't know how I was going to talk with him, I didn't want to. I wished that he could keep quiet until when he would go, I told myself that it was better to keep quiet and be patient, the time would come for him to go.

I sat down and talked with my heart, I asked myself what love meant, and why sometimes it was there? I saw that love could be a liar, why love didn't give me time to judge and know who and why I was supposed to love, why that love was chosen for me and why I trusted it, that my heart knew what it was telling me? I had no answer and I had no one to blame.

I saw that love could have power to direct someone and refuse the person to get a little time to see and judge for him or herself, and the same love can use that power to command the victim of love, to be proud of the person you love which your heart chooses for you, and be happy to show him or her to everyone, because you are proud and trust that person and believe that the passion your heart has, will feed the mind, then lift the spirit at that time, you feel properly human and happy to be alive.

After you could find out, sometimes, after a long time together, that the person who you believed to be an angel and brave, and thank your stars to be lucky enough to have him or her, the truth about that person who you believed to have only many good things which anyone would be happy to see with someone he or she loves, the person you were with, and you thought that you would be with her or him the whole of your life. Little did you know that the same person had a double life in different ways, sometimes they might even be not only a liar, lazy, selfish, thief, cheater, the person also could be a killer!

Yes, the person you love can surprise you, by turning into anything, even a killer.

My ears were clear and I was listening without saying anything, he was telling me many words, why he did it, how he was sorry for what he did, asking forgiveness, but the first words he had told me were enough. I didn't want to hear another one, and whatever he was saying meant nothing anymore, and I had no reason to say anything either, and I couldn't believe whatever he was saying, only what I wanted was to see him go.

He started his story, "I didn't marry that woman because I loved her, it was just because I had her as a friend, then she told me that she was expecting my child, when you told me the same thing at the same time. I didn't know who was telling me the truth, and if both of you, you were telling me the truth, I was going to get two children at once, if so then my government can't help me with both children when I didn't marry any of you." To that point I wanted to tell him to be brave enough and tell me that he chose her because she didn't have the family with her which was depending on her, even if she did she had her parents with her who could hold it for her when she needed that help, and give her a chance to try her future.

Or she was the one who he loved in the first place, nothing to do with my family, which also could be understandable, and that was what only he had to tell me, to show me that by marrying her was another kind of business, it was not for love. Which to me I didn't care anymore about the reasons.

He went ahead talking, I thought that he wanted to see how I would react, so that he could enjoy it and maybe get the stories to tell his wife and friends. I saw that I didn't know him at all, and I didn't know what he was capable of. So I tried to keep quiet and to act normal in front of him as possible if I could.

He came up with a different story now, "Bamurangirwa I am asking you if you can come and stay with me and my wife, so that I can have two wives, because I have a neighbour who has two wives in one house, and both women have children, I saw that here in Africa men can do it."

I turned to look at him but didn't say anything; he asked me the same thing again. I thought that when he comes to see me he has other plans too, of trying harder to make me crazy or something, I didn't know. I didn't want to talk but I saw that if I did not talk, he would not go, so it was better to talk, and see that he could go from my house.

I said two words, "I can't."

"Even my neighbours, his family, children and wives they are always fighting, and my wife didn't want it, you too, you don't want it, meaning that it is not possible. Though my wife she has some kind of fear, that you will take me away from her because you have my child!"

I didn't ask him why, when she too, had a child, but I didn't want any stories from him. Whatever it was with his wife it was their problem not mine.

The time came when he said bye, and I said bye, but I didn't stand from where I was, so he went out of the house, and out of my life.

But I thought that still I would have a long story with him, because I would not manage to punish him as I did to Seleman or Nyilimanzi, but I had a hope that if he loved that woman he married, I hoped and wished that he loved her true love. So by good luck, that woman could be married to him because of other reasons, maybe because of business, but inside her heart, she had another man she loved, true love, or in the future could get another man who she might love true love, at that, she could punish him for me. I prayed and hoped that in the future, someone would punish him for me and make him a victim of love. That was when he would know what he did to me, when he would have that terrible pain, from someone he trusted. And I wished that when it happened, if it would happen when I was still alive, by luck, I would be able to know about it.

My children loved me and they didn't want to see me unhappy, so

I didn't tell them what happened. I didn't want to stress them in any way. I wanted them to be focussed on their studying without any interruptions, so I had no one to talk to. Mukabagira had a lot on her own, but still we had to take our problems together, and be there for each other, there was no one else we had to trust, I had to survive for myself, and more for my children.

I was sometimes thinking of the nameless man and his wife with their baby in his arms happy walking in the evening, it was troubling me, but the time came when I had to move on, and not kill myself because of someone who would never care if I died or not. Instead if I damaged myself because of him, it would only be a way of making him proud, and getting a story in life, that when he was young, he was too handsome to the point of an Africa woman killing herself, just because she was rejected by him.

My sister Kankuyo had a daughter Gahongayire, who was at home and refused to go ahead with her studying, and I thought that maybe if I could bring her over there, I could be able to convince her to take some course, in case her parents would be happy with the idea. It would not add anything to my work, with Gahongayire or without her,

I always going in those U.N. offices so it could be profitable to us as a family, if I could add her and be successful.

Gahongayire came and when she was waiting to join a college, she was taking care of Niwegaju when I was not at home. That was when I came to see how good it was, to have friends, people to talk to when you are in trouble, because when you are with others and talk to them, many times, you get some others who have passed through a lot more than you can think, and it helps you to know that people pass through many different problems. There are different betrayals out there, otherwise you could be there always thinking why you, why you?

After being settled and forgetting all of that, I had forgotten about the nameless man's letters, and even that he had mentioned something like buying a house for me. It was me and my children again.

One evening the nameless man came home, I didn't knew that he would come, and didn't care if I knew before or not, or if he came at all, inside the house he sat down. After a short time, I asked him if I could offer him anything to drink. He told me that he was fine, he was there for some minutes without me talking to him, and then he asked me why I didn't ask him about his wife.

"To ask you what? I don't have anything to ask you about her, but if you have what you want to say, say it I will listen."

"Indeed," he started, "my wife her work was gambling, 'arikuwa anafanya kazi ya magendo', but now she is working in the office, and she is always telling me that you will take me away from her, because of the baby!"

Because I didn't want to talk with him, I didn't ask him anything, though I wanted to ask him about that baby he was always talking about, what was wrong with her baby, and how could she be insecure by me because I had a baby with him, when she herself, had a baby too, and which kind of 'magendo' his wife was dealing with, but I was not brave enough to be able to talk to him a lot. He seemed like he was talking to himself, talking without comments or questions, and he had no problem with that, he went on, and said, "My wife also told me that you will give me black magic so that you can be able to take me away!"

To that point, I turned to him quickly and looked at him, thinking that I hadn't heard him properly. (I did – kwirahira) since my father was my friend, and I saw him as my master too, his name was the name Sinzi, it came to me automatically when I was shocked in any way, when I mentioned my father's name in Kinyarwanda, and that look I had in my face, a face of surprise, I asked him again.

"Yes," he repeated it again, and went ahead with the story, and yes they had a neighbour who seemed like he was stupid, he said, "And my wife told me, that was because of that black magic which a woman gave him." And that was what he thought I could do to him.

And I asked him if he believed her. I thought he looked that he had a lot to talk about his wife if I gave him a chance.

To my question, he said, "Yes, I believe her, that is why I can't eat anything here, and one day when you gave me a tea, I threw it out when you went back to the room!"

421

I didn't know how to handle him, what kind of person he was! I wanted to tell him that if there were things like that, then, he was not normal anymore; she had done it to him already!

I told him that he didn't have to worry about things like that on my side, because I didn't want to be with him through force of any kind, a part of love between both of us.

I didn't blame his wife in any way; he lied to both of us, and both of us we didn't know each other. The point that she warned him that I would poison him, I didn't blame her for that either, she might have had a good reason to be insecure, maybe she loved him, or as many African girls, she just wanted him because he was a man, and white, so in her mind he might be her radar for her future, she wouldn't want to lose him. Especially when she heard about a woman who had his baby, though she had the baby too, 'but it was a question mark'.

Or she believed in that black magic, and she was using it, and believed that everyone used it too, she had to warn him in case mine was stronger than hers, and would take him from her. I told him that it could be a good idea if he didn't come at all, if he believed that he couldn't be safe with me.

The time came and he said that he was going; I said yes, he stood up and left. I saw how things could turn to another picture quickly, to see how he stood up and went when I was where I was without being shaken at all, instead I wanted to see him out of my sight as quickly as possible!

I knew that what he did, had nothing to do with white and black he did it as a man; he did it as him.

After years I came to be involved somehow with the nameless man again, that is how and when I came to know why any time he was with me, he was talking about how his wife was insecure that I might take him from her because I had his child. It was because when she had the child he was telling me that she was two weeks older than my daughter, the child was not his; she was a child of another man, a pure black man! What happened to them after that, those were his problems. But so far, my prayers had been answered.

What I learned from this, was that: sometimes, the worst things that ever happen to you, can also, eventually, be the best things that ever happen to you.

I went ahead for everything with Mukabagira; she had left for a short time to go back to Uganda, wondering how I would manage to be without her, with my fellow Rwandans who thought that they knew me when they knew nothing about me. And I was happy to be with them in that way, we could be there for each other, for whatever came up, but not inside of my life, I preferred to tell my secrets to other friends if I could have them.

I MEET FATHER MARIO

Mukabagira went ahead by helping me in any way she could, she was the one who had the chance of knowing the place where refugees got good things, many came for Ugandans who were still there, and I was going to get some when I had time. I had a family of six children, and I was busy most of the time.

One day she told me that, at their place were missionarys they were giving people money. I told her that I didn't go well with those missionary people, and she had a long laugh, and asked me why. I too asked her if she had never heard about them when they were giving match boxes to burn Tutsi's homes in 1959, and going to tell some other people that to kill Tutsi was not a sin? To that she said that I was going to see them for my benefit not theirs, if I would not go it was not going to reduce them anything. And they didn't know me and they would not care less anything about me forever anyway. "Who are you to them?" she asked me, and I had no answer, I was nobody.

The day came when she took me there, there were many people because that had to be the particular day to see people. Some were in small groups, some were just walking around there, and most of them were Rwandans. After a short time in the office came out a white man, he looked to be a strong man who might be forty to forty-five years old, like five and a half tall, maybe eighty-five to ninety kilograms. He had black trousers, and a black sleeveless shirt, which was open three buttons from the top, and you could see his strong chest which was full of hair, and his arms too were full of hair, with a nice haircut.

I thought that this was an officer who was working there, he stood there looking at us, in silence for seconds, and he smiled to us, and you could see his good smile with two golden teeth which were either side on the top sides, he greeted us. Then he went in another house in front of us that was when people there told us who he was, to those who came there for the first time, that was Fr Mario who was director of the project.

The young man who was in our group said something like he was asking us, or telling us to look at him, the way he looked at us, he seemed that he was so kind to us, or was that one of their ways of getting people to pretend to love them? The old man was like he was giving him the answer: "You know my son; it is not easy to know about these people."

We were in other stories until when he came back and stopped in front of us again, that is when he asked us if all of us were Rwandans. One of us said yes. "We are," he told him.

Again he asked, "All of you are a Tutsi?!"

We looked to each other and no one said anything.

He smiled, and left, like to tell us that they knew everything about us, or maybe when he didn't get any answer from us, he realised that was not the right question to ask. After being inside his office, that old man who told us that you couldn't know about them, he looked to be upset, maybe with the question, and started to talk like he was talking to himself. "Look this son of Vatican, he is happy to see us in front of his office, when we look useless, when he sees us like beggars, he can or he can't give us what we come for, it can depends on the mood he has today, but that is not enough, he still jumped to our tribe, what do you think he meant by that?"

No one said anything for a short time, and then the young man told him that maybe he meant nothing by that.

"No," he said, "they always mean something, and enjoy seeing many around them who they manage to make them believe that they mean nothing, in that way; it gives them time to reach where they want to go. And always it is a big mistake to listen to these people who show you the Bible before other things." It was a laugh for all of us, and we

425

asked him if it was the Bible which told them to do all of that. That made him upset.

The answer was, "The Bible teaches them to kill, in fact it teaches them the genocide!"

"How?!" all of us asked him.

"Go and read Ezekiel 9:1-11 some wrote those," he said and said that they would try to get the Bible and see.

He went ahead and said that you would see how their God told them to go and kill everyone, old and young, even those who would be in the churches.

There was an old lady who was just listening but not saying anything since those stories started, she came near and in a quiet way, said that better people could be good if they could judge after finding out things in a careful way first.

"That part in the Bible you are talking about, we, born again people, we know that, and believe that, God is one God, who is God for everyone, and according to that part he said that people have to be killed because they were wrong to him."

The old man told them that he didn't believe that the God we believed in, was the same God these religious people were talking about, who they were preaching to us, God whatever it is, he or she, we believe to be a God full of love to his or her people, who he or she created. The same God can't punish them with such genocide, so, to him, they might be preaching another God known by them.

We said that it was better to leave alone the argument concerning religions because it was not easy, always it would remain with belief and understanding of individuality.

Other ones there said that, anyone could know the history of Catholics, in case by bad luck if you could know it you could fear to be near them at all, we asked him at once and he simply said that it was a sword which helped them to make it strong in Italy and Spain, when they were even using fire to kill position after 700 years, everyone was a follower. "That is why even they involved themselves in the

Second World War, to them killing is like a culture that is how they can protect their government."

At that time Gahongayire had joined a course of dressmaking and she loved it, my life at home was easier than before too, mainly because of my baby, Gahongayire and I, we were going out in turn. I was not going out with Niwegaju any more, or leaving her alone in the house to be checked out by Ilibagiza when she had a school break.

My time to go inside to see Fr Mario came, and he was sat down, when I was inside he stood up, with a big nice smile, which showed me his two golden teeth, and gave me his hand, a sign of greetings, we greeted, and he showed me where to sit. I sat and he too sat down, I didn't know if that was how he was welcoming all of the people who came in his office, or maybe he only had respect for women, or it was like that young man outside was saying about their acting. To me he looked to be an ordinary man more than a priest, he held his chin and looked at me, I too, looked at him, waiting to be given the questions, there was a silence between us for some seconds, and he was looking at me non-stop, when I saw that his eyes were directly on me for that long, I put mine down.

Maybe that reminded him what he had to do, and he started to give me some questions, my names, about my family and where I lived, when I told him that I had six children, he seemed to be shocked, and he asked me if I was with the father of the children, I told him that I was a single mum.

He told me that, he had a lot of people, better to contact him next time, so that he could give me an appointment and see if he could do something for me, he gave me his telephone numbers, and I was out for that day with a hope of when I would see him the next time.

Outside the lady who had to enter the office after me, held my dress as a sign of stopping me, I turned to ask her what she had in mind, and she asked me to go back inside with her so that I could help her for translation.

When Fr Mario saw me inside again quickly he asked me why I was back and I told him why, he was understanding, then he looked to

427

be relaxed, but he didn't stand up to greet the old lady I came with. That to me there was a question why he didn't stand for this lady to greet her when she was old? And why me? I didn't like it. The office was a small room and there was one chair, I had to give the chair to the lady, she was old and she was the one who was supposed to be seen.

I stood at the side of the table waiting to do what I came for; the English I knew was not good but it was enough to help me understand between me and other people.

He started to give her an interview, the time came when I was tired of standing, and I used one arm to hold on the table to support other parts of my body.

As soon as I put my hand on the table, our priest covered my hand with his! Because his hand was big, mine was not seen, you could know that my hand was there just because of my arm which was standing like a stick from my shoulder to the table. I didn't understand what he meant by that, but I didn't like the picture it showed: quickly I wanted to pull out my arm, but I remembered that I would come back to see him, that still I wanted to get something from him, yes my arm was there covered by the priest's, in a Catholic office, because I was a refugee who was there to survive. I asked myself why at last he couldn't respect that old lady who was in front of him! And I promised myself that if he was one of the priests who liked women, then I felt sorry for him, I had already heard some of them who had children, or who had helped their girlfriends get abortions.

I told myself to wait, that I would know about him next time, my hands were there, he was using one arm for other things, until he finished dealing with his client and we went out.

When we were out some people said that the white people were very clever, now he saw us quickly to put us aside and the only lucky ones were the people who were going to get something from him.

That made me upset a bit, and I asked them, until when they had a different mentality, and thought that to be clever or not to be, it had nothing to do with the colour of anyone, where someone came from or anything like that. "Yes white people they are ahead of us, but it is because they were the first ones to have problems, and learn from their problems and their mistakes, that is what you too have to do, learn from your problems and your mistakes. And also I think it was because they were the first ones to know about money, now you think that you can't put yourself in another picture in the future, or is this sitting in front of their door enough for us? Or you will always be blaming them for this and that and waiting for them to be there for you forever?"

After a few days I called Fr Mario and asked him for any appointment, the day and time he told me to go, I was there, he was outside standing near his car and when he saw me he apologised, that he had got other urgent things and he would not be able to see me, but if I passed in town he could give me a lift up to there, and he would tell me another appointment later on the way.

I was beside him in his car, he started the car and we went for some time in silence until when he turned and looked at me, and called me by my name, I turned my head and listened to him. He asked me the question I had no idea that he could ask me, "Do you dress like this when you are by yourself always?!"

I was wearing my black long dress, which I made myself, it was open at the chest and was held by a small black slide to one shoulder, I had a soft scarf and a black beautiful necklace. I was used to wearing fashions like that, and first I was confused with the question, and I had to ask him again.

"To wear something which is open at your chest?"

"Yes," I said. "When it is hot, I wear that," I told him.

"Don't do that, it is not a good idea."

I had to ask why then, I asked him why.

"Because by bad luck you can meet a bad man and he could do something bad to you."

I had to say something. I said that I had never thought about that, if so, then, I would not do that.

But I didn't take his idea seriously, and I told myself that he didn't have to mind of how I dressed, unless if he had other problems himself. We went without talking to each other, after some time he put his hand on top of my hand, where they were on my lap, like he did in his office, we went like that, he took away his arm only when he wanted to use it for driving.

And I told myself that now I knew him, and maybe I would see more, but I knew how I would deal with him. He told me to come back the next day, at the time he told me, I was there. When he saw me he was in the window, he came out to welcome me, he seemed to be happy to see me in time, and said that it showed that I liked to keep time.

I said yes, I like it, unless when I had other reasons, he said that he too liked to deal with people who kept time, by that it was easy to do what you wanted to.

He told me that he didn't want to tell me to wait for long, it was not polite that is why he told me to come back that day, and that time, so, he wanted me to take him to my home, to see where it was, and see the next step he could take after that, we would talk about the rest in the car, he said. He went inside for a few minutes, and came back, we were in the car, going to my home.

In the car he called me, I responded, and waited.

"What I will ask you, don't be scared to give me an answer."

"If I will know it, I am going to tell you."

"Is it true that the father of your last born is a white man?"

It surprised me why he took his time to try to know anything about my life, and about the man I had a child with, to be a white man or not, why this now? I didn't understand why that could be any point at all. At least not to him.

"Who told you, you were right, yes, my child's father is white, and you will see that, I am not hiding the identity of my child. I am not ashamed of it."

"I can understand, but the man, I heard that he is a priest too?"

"No, that is not true."

"No, don't be afraid of that, maybe you think that if you tell me I might not help you, I can still do whatever I can to help you."

I saw that no one had ever at last seen me with the nameless man going in the church, or coming from there, and from nowhere they just made up that he was a priest.

So about this he might be the one who was making it up, or it was him who had his idea after hearing that the father of my child was a white man, or maybe he was preparing me in a way, to be ready that even priests they have feelings for women, and sometimes they can even make a woman pregnant. So when the time would come, for him to use men's words, to tell me that he had never ever seen a beautiful woman like me… so that couldn't shock me.

I had heard many stories concerning priests before as I said. Now I was sitting with him in his car, and according to the way I saw him, I had a thought, that he might planning it to be me, who would have his baby, maybe he had reasons… but not me, he would go ahead and get someone else who would give him a child, the children I had were enough I didn't have to mix my family with Vaticans.

But if he wanted my friendship in other ways, there would be no problem with that.

He was not convinced and he asked me again twice the same question, he was getting the same answer that it was not true.

In the end to try to satisfy him in case if he was told so, I told him that the father of my child was still in Kenya, if he wanted to find out by himself, I could give him his contact, but before communicating with him for that point, it was better to be aware that he might laugh a lot, since he had nothing to do with religion at all.

He seemed to believe me after a long way.

"What do you do?"

"I am dressmaker."

"Do you have a machine at home?"

"No I don't."

"What do you want me to help you with?"

"Whatever you can."

We were at home, it was afternoon, all of my children were at home, it was Gahongayire who came to welcome us, we showed him where to sit. I was hungry, they gave us tea and bread. Father refused to eat but after we insisted he had a cup of tea. All the children were in the other room, with no time Father lifted my face and put his lips on mine, I was shocked and asked myself in case any child saw us kissing what could I do about it?! He did it quickly and let me go. I had no time to warn him, but now I had to warn him in a polite way at least there couldn't be a next time. I didn't want him to think that I was encouraging it.

He said that he wanted a child to the car to help him with something.

They came back with a big bag of green hard material, I was surprised to see that he came with anything at all, and I thanked him, but he told me first to see what it was. I opened and it was good materials, bed sheets, and bed covers, girls and boys' clothes, all were good and new. I think he went where they were, maybe those things which were supposed to be given, and he chose the new one for me.

After all of that, I came with the albums to show him the pictures, because I had nothing to talk with him about, and he was not in a hurry to go, when I was showing some pictures he came up with other questions.

"But Bamurangirwa how old you were when you had these children?"

"Some of them are children of my sisters and brother," I told him.

"So you lied to me by telling me that they are yours?"

"No I didn't lie to you I know that they are mine."

"This made me love you more, it is you who is a proper Christian, a person who has love for others, and concerning your children I am asking forgiveness, we need Christian people like you."

I didn't understand the word Christian what it meant for him, if it was a person who was a follower of religion, or it was kind people who were patriotic and determined.

"Your first born, you were married to his father in the church?"

"No we used our culture way."

"Do you go to the church?"

Now I had a problem here to that point, I had anger and wanted

432

to talk, and be what it would be, if it was going to make him disappear, to hell with his help.

I was angry for myself, because I had another thought to lie to him, because he was a priest and I wanted his help. (No: I didn't have to do that to myself), I couldn't forgive myself forever, so yes I had to tell him the truth and let him know who I was.

"The truth Father, a part of that can't be easy for me because of transport on Sundays, but I am not a follower of any religion, because I don't know anything about them yet, then, I can't just be a follower of something which I don't understand. But I believe in God, maybe because my great grandparents and my parents believed in God, though I believe that God can hear prayers anywhere, even here, and anyone has a way to communicate with God, if she or he wishes to do that, but can go according to the belief of the person, and I believe that God is there to listen to his or her people wherever they are," I told him in a calm and polite way as much as I could.

When I was telling him all of that, he was looking at me non-stop and his eyes were bigger, but he gave me time to talk until I finished, without any interruption. When I finished, he said, "Look Bamurangirwa, you changed my understanding towards refugees, I knew them to be a lie, yes I think that some they lie to get what they want, but I thought that whatever the reason was, now I can see that not all of them have to lie even for that reason."

"Now to tell me your belief like this, when you know who I am, and when you want help from me, it surprised me and it made me happy, because it is you who told me so, and no one else who said it behind your back, this shows me your nature you are not a liar, you are an honest person, and perhaps if there can be something which can force you to lie then, you can do it but you can't be comfortable with it."

I wanted to tell him that maybe it was his first time to meet a refugee who had anger with life.

He went on, "Now this made me love you more, I loved you as you in the first place, and then when I saw how you managed to take

433

very good care of your children, now this, you're honest. I can promise you that you are not going to be a reason not to help you; instead, it made me happy to help you in any way I will be able to manage. I have to go now but if you will be here tomorrow afternoon I will come back."

I told him that I would be waiting for him.

I escorted him and he was in the car, in a respectful way, I had to wait to see him go. After he was ready to drive, he turned his head and looked at me without a word, we looked at each other in that silent time, and he seemed that he had a lot on his mind to tell me or to ask me, after time he touched in his pocket and came out with money, which he gave me without seeing how much, maybe he knew how much. And I took it and thanked him and he was gone.

Inside the house, I opened my hand and was surprised to see that he gave me 200 K sh which no one individual had ever given me that much money before. Even the nameless man, apart from when I was in the hospital, and when he thought that would be money for the journey to his home.

I asked myself why he could give me all of that money, just at the first time he met me, it might be the money which was there to give away to people who were in need, or he might have had other reasons in his mind, maybe he thought that because I needed money, he could buy me! I hoped not, and I told myself that it was not good to judge so quickly, better to wait and see.

I planned that my children were going to eat good, at least for a few days, meat which normally was only eaten at Christmas and new year, and all other types of food they would eat when we had visitors.

The next day in the afternoon I had a knock when I opened it was Fr Mario at the door. I told him to come in, and he said that he was not going to come inside, he wanted someone who could help to bring something from the car, and it needed two people.

I asked what that was and he said that I would see it.

I asked my neighbour with his son to help me, we went where the car was and when they opened it was a sewing machine!

After my neighbours left I looked at Fr Mario, and didn't know what to tell him, and how to thank him, and I was in his chest holding him for some seconds, and thanking him, he looked to be relaxed, and it was like he was talking to himself, it was not a question, he told me, "I can see that you are happy."

"Yes," I said, "I am happy. I know that I couldn't buy something like this for myself, so I am happy, but I don't know how I can show you so."

He sat down and started to ask me simple questions, like "Have you gone anywhere today?"

"Yes I went to town for a short time and came back because I didn't know what time exactly you would come."

"Meaning that you were waiting for me?"

"Yes I was waiting for you."

"Meaning if I didn't come it would be a mistake?"

"Yes," I said.

"I will try to do whatever makes you happy and there is nothing I want from you apart from good friendships."

When he told me that, I took out all the opposite thoughts I had towards him, he might have been sent by God to calm me down, after all of that the nameless man did to me.

I believed that Fr Mario was a Father only when he was in the church wearing a long white uniform to direct any kind of ceremony, after, outside he looked like any ordinary handsome man, and my neighbours saw him as my boyfriend, though they were wondering where I got white men from! My child's father was gone, now soon another one was here!

Fr Mario visited me regularly and sometimes invited us to his home or took us out.

Gahongayire liked sewing more than I, though we were doing it together depending who had time for that, the money we got from our sewing was good enough to move us to some other place, not too expensive, but at last we could go out of that mud.

I told Fr Mario that I had an idea of moving from there, and he saw that it was a good idea but he thought that it could be expensive to me, so he decided that any time he would still be in Kenya, he would be giving me 300 K sh monthly, so that it could be easy for me to take care of my children, with a hope that in the future things might change itself. It surprised me because that was the same amount the U.N. gave me monthly too.

I told him, that, as I had told him before, I couldn't thank him enough.

We moved to a better place it was still a wooden house, but it was near the road, and had all other things like a bathroom which was outside, but was in good condition, the garden and other parts outside were cemented, so it was the opposite with where we were.

I came to find out that he was happy and satisfied just to be with me that time when I warned him about kissing me, the answer was that it was because I was a good Christian. Any time when he had time he was at my home or we were together somewhere, when he was going with us or with only me, wherever he wanted us to go.

And when he had time he was happy to take me where I wanted to go, even to my Rwandan friends he looked to be proud and happy to be with me.

Some who had not yet seen my daughter's father, thought he was the one, or to those who knew him they thought that he was his relative, and to the ones who asked me, I told them that he was my friend the priest, they had their doubts and their judgements.

Since I knew that sometimes he was not comfortable with how I dressed, I was giving him the green light to choose for me what he would like me to wear and things like that which was making him more than happy. The time came when he was taking care of us, as if we were his family who depended on him, he had already managed to make me free to him enough to tell him what I needed at home. When he came home he was asking what we needed and going for it or just coming with things needed at home on top of the money he was giving me. I sometimes saw him and said that if he was a family man he could take very good care of his family, he could be a good father and husband.

I didn't see him in any colour or as a priest, I saw him as a good person, and I loved him for that, I had him as my good friend. He was my angel.

The time for Mukabagira to go back home came and we knew that it would be a problem between us to see each other, but we were not going to get lost between ourselves like before. When we were talking about me it was always a good topic when we started to talk about Fr Mario. And she was joking that she got me a friend. The answer was, "Yes thank you so much for that, he's a good one indeed."

Sometimes Fr Mario was telling me that a good person like me had to have sacraments. It was not making me angry, instead it made me laugh, but I had to show him that I was serious as the way he seemed to be when he came up with the point. I couldn't know if he was forgetting who I was, or was trying, but I told him then, if he wanted to see me get it so much, then he could be the one who would do that for me. To that, he said that we knew each other so much he couldn't, better to go and get others. I told him that if he couldn't then better to forget it and that was it.

I knew that the time would come when he would go and I even might not see or hear from him again, according to the poor communication at the time, and their job too. And I was asking myself why the nameless man was not the one who showed me this kind of love and life, at that, I was giving myself the answer, that the nameless man was a nameless man, and now this was Mario they were two different people, and I had to thank my God for putting Mario in front of me for whatever time I would be with him.

All that time he was in Kenya, I, and my family we were under his good care no matter which part of Kenya he would be, and the time came when he pushed us to the good level, which was not easy to go back. The time came for Fr Mario to go back to Italy, and we communicated for some time through letters then there was no communication at all, I didn't know what happened to my angel. But he had done a good thing and come to my life when I needed someone like him. He managed to put me in a good step in my life

Thanks to him.

Now I had lost the nameless man, Mukabagira went back to Uganda, and my good new friend, my angel, Fr Mario went back to Italy, what happened to me and my family after?

ME AND MY CHILDREN

After Mukabagira and Fr Mario left me and moved from Kenya, I was alone but not lonely. I wanted to have a friend who I could talk to, and still trust that would not take out my life, since I was enjoying seeing people outside always thinking that they knew about my life when they knew nothing about it. I wanted still to be that way, because I knew that even if they could know exactly how I was, there was no one who could help. Though I loved my fellow Rwandans they were my people, and I knew that no one could see me in trouble and leave me there, as me too I couldn't do that, but not in normal life. So better to go ahead and see me the way they wanted to see me, by thinking that they knew everything about me and my life.

I was not lonely, I had my children, and concerning the situation we had at the time, it was not bad. We had reached other steps, as far as I was concerned I was a student and a good one, what I could call home schooling, I liked reading different books and magazines of different types. I was asking questions to anyone who I saw that could give me the answers I wanted, especially my children who were my good teachers. They were happy to see that I wanted to know more, one day Muvunangoma told me that I was better than some who went to high school, so I didn't have to go ahead thinking that I missed a lot, because I didn't go to high school. That made me feel happy and have more confidence and see that I would never regret taking care of my children.

From those magazines I read, I came to know that to have a friend to talk too, was some kind of medicine, because sometimes when you talked with them, you might be there thinking that you had problems, when sometimes you could hear someone who had more than yours, and that one, many times gave you strength, and you knew that it was not only you, as you were thinking before, when you were asking yourself, why you, why you. I remembered the two ladies I came to know when I was with Nyilimanzi, and we were very good friends and after we lost contact for no reason, and I knew that it was my fault and it was me who had to make effort to get them back.

My mind went back to February 1972 when I saw them for the first time, I was outside taking the clothes out, when I saw a car, taxi, since I knew that many times taxis came with visitors, I waited before going inside the house to see if I could be lucky enough to get a visitor.

Inside the car came out the two respectable ladies and they seemed to be strangers in the area, they looked like Rwandans, but I waited to hear when they spoke to each other, so that I could see if they would talk in my language, and to my surprise they talked in Kinyarwanda. I knew that it was only me who was Rwandan near there, so even if I saw that I had never seen them anywhere, I would approach them, if they were not my visitors, then I might know who they were looking for.

After hearing that they were Rwandans, I put back the clothes where they were, and went to where they were standing, they started to struggle by taking up their long dresses to find the money from their pockets. I greeted them on the way going to where they were standing, and they both at once looked at me and greeted me back.

Then I told them it was better to come inside my house, and find the money, and put their bags there too if they were happy with that, and after paying the taxi man, then we could see other things after, both they looked to be happy with the idea, and quickly without any questions they carried their bags and the taxi man helped, we put the bags inside and they found the money. The taxi man went and we were by ourselves.

They told me who they were looking for, it was a Rwandan man who was on the other side behind us with his wife and their little daughter, behind side, was not the prostitute's side, just one line, the man who they were looking for, in the daytime he was not at home, he had to come back late in the evening from work, and his wife had gone on a journey, so I told them that they were in the right place, but they would wait until evening, and I told them the reasons. So since they couldn't have a shower and there was no bath there, I gave them tea and told them to wait for proper food and then go to the bed and have a rest.

That was what they did because they were too tired; after we had our lunch they went to bed and fell asleep at once.

I knew Emile, the man they were visiting, he was alone, without his wife, meaning that to take care of visitors might not be too easy, he might also not know that he had a visitor, so I made sure that they ate the leftovers before they left, and I told them that any time they would be there, to come and share with me everything from breakfast because it would not be a burden to me, instead it would be helping me because I was on my own all the daytime. By being my parents' age, and the way they looked to be respectable, I loved them and they made me feel like I was with my family back home, they reminded me of my mum too.

The names they were using were the names they used to be called where they were at their home in the neighbourhood area, they were Rwandans who were residents in Uganda Kampala, they were nicknamed with one of their children's names, according to the culture of where they were, particularly it was the part of respect to old people, they believed that it was not right to call an old person's name now and then. Especially when they had children. So one was called as Mama Zainabu (Zainabu's Mum) and another one was Mama Rukia (Rukia's Mum).

All the time they were there, both of us, Emile, our visitors and I, we were happy, everyone who wanted to see them was coming to my home to see them, when they didn't have to go anywhere we were at home the whole day, on the other hand little did they know that every time they were there was a bonus to me, it was like a holiday. I had a very good time because even Nyilimanzi was a different person.

441

Their time came to go back and they told me that in case I came to Kampala or I passed there I didn't have to spend the night elsewhere, from now on, I had to think of them as my family.

After some time I came to get a few people who were coming from Kampala when they find out that I was Bamurangirwa, some were too surprised to come across with me, someone who was too kind who did this and that for others, according to the stories of Mama Rukia and Mama Zainabu, when they reached Kampala, they told whoever they met about my kindness, but if someone asked me what I did for them which made them so happy, I was telling them that nothing I could remember which was that special, everything I did was normal things people did always.

To me those two ladies were good people too, because not all people saw and noticed that someone did something good to them, and were that thankful, some could think that yes, you had to do it, or what you did was just a normal thing, or simply, they didn't care if someone did whatever they did, it was up to them, especially when it came to volunteer things. To me all of that was normal anyway.

After some time Mama Zainabu came alone but that time she didn't stay for a long time like before, and she told me that one of her daughters was planing to move to Nairobi, that her husband bought the houses in Nairobi and warned me to be aware that her daughter was lucky her husband came up to be one of the richest people in Uganda. Being in one room of a mud house, couldn't make me fear her because she was a rich woman, since I was sure that nothing could make her ignore anyone. "I know my child to be down to earth, she can't forget where she came from, always she gives everyone respect, I saw that here you are in this bad area, in this house, but you are not hungry, when it is different with how I raised-up my children. Sometimes I had nothing to feed them, and even when she maried her husband, he didn't have the money, so things can come any time and can go any time."

After a few months I had a plan to go to Uganda to visit my family, but before going ahead to Masaka, I had to stop over to say hello to my new friends, but when I was yet to start my journey one morning

I was inside my house, Mama Zainabu was at my door with a young handsome man, inside she told me that they were in a hurry she just wanted to show her son where I was, because they had moved already in Nairobi, they were in Muthaiga area, he was with his sister, and she wanted us to be in touch.

And she told her son to give me their contact, so that when we were ready we could call him and he would come and take us to see where they were living, and she was insisting to her son by telling him that they had to be in touch with me, and she was sure that I would be happy to have them near me, unless if they were going to be too busy to give me their time. And she was saying it in a serious way with a lot of doubt that her children would disappoint her, you could see her on the other hand she was making it as a command.

Soon after that, I was in problems, up and down with Nyirimanzi, then I had a new life, then what I had in my thoughts was only things which were in front of me.

After feeling somehow settled, when I was with the nameless man, I came to remember about them and I had lost their contact, I couldn't know if maybe they tried to find me in Magengo, and I saw all of that to be my fault since they knew that they gave me their contact, there was nothing else they could do more than that, and it was me who had to try and see if I could get them.

I had the name in my mind of a lady who they were visiting, and she was well known, though I was yet to meet her, but I had already heard many people talk about her so I had confidence that to find her would be easy, she would be the one who would tell me how I could find them, that lady was their family friend. But I didn't know if they would understand my reasons, why I got myself lost, people directed me to that lady, she was a Rwandan lady, people nicknamed her Nyirakibuno, that is only the name I knew too mean big buttocks.

When I was at her home she was a beautiful lady with big buttocks, then I knew that was why they nicknamed her Nyirakibuno, she looked clean for everything around her, dressed well too, in a beautiful big wide dress like Sudan's lady she had covered her head too.

443

She welcomed me very well, showed me where to sit, and gave me something to drink, as soon as I told her who I was and why I was there, she stood up and was dancing here and there, then she was asking me over and over if it was really me Bamurangirwa?!

The way she took it was a surprise to me, I wanted to know why she was so excited that much! Then I had to ask her, and her response was simple, she was happy to see that Mama Zainabu finally would get the good news because she had tried everything to know anything about me without any success. It made me feel guilty, and I asked myself why I did what I did. Nyirakibuno was asking me but it was like she was talking by herself when she was asking what had I done to her that made her that happy to make her love me that much?!

I told her that I knew nothing which I did: which had to be that big. She told me that both of us we were lucky because it was a coincidence, Mama Zainabu was in Nairobi, she rang the phone and when she was talking she was laughing a lot, then she gave me the phone, when I heard how Mama Zainabu was happy to find me again. I was happy and both guilty too.

She asked me if I was not in a hurry so that she could send someone to pick me up. I told her that was no problem, other things could wait, but I wanted to see her. After a short time the driver came. I thanked Nyirakibuno for her help and I was at the home of Mama Zainabu's daughter.

It was my first time to see a home like that, after the guide opened our car, Mama Zainabu saw us and she was standing on the balcony, waiting for the car to stop and finally meet me. We greeted, and she took me inside, she did an introduction to her daughter and her grandchildren, all of them were happy to see me.

She told me how much she missed me and everyone looked like they were happy, all of them looked to be surprised to see me, maybe they thought that according to the way Mama Zainabu told them, maybe they thought that I might have other looks. Not a short and small woman like me.

When they were asking her if it was me Bamurangirwa, she was

444

proud when she was saying yes. And telling them that now she was happy they saw me and we knew each other at last.

Uzamukunda her daughter was a beautiful lady, mixed race with a white man, too beautiful, and too young to see that the six children who were around her, though both looked to be still young maybe between six and twelve years old, I thought that she might have got married when she was still young.

She was in a navy blue long dress, which was fitting her from her chest to her hips, then started to be wider up to her feet. The dress was wide open at her chest and shoulder with her curly black hair, and her soft brown skin which was shining; around her neck was a big gold chain, with a number of gold bangles on her arms. I wished that I could get a way when I was sure that no one would notice me, I could look at her non-stop.

She had few words, I was asking myself if it was her nature, and if so it couldn't be a problem, or if it was ignorance which also might be natural to some of people, or it could be because of that richness I saw she had.

To look outside, there was a wider space which was cemented in a unique way of its own beauty, but near the flowers there was other beauty with small good stones, there was a fence of stones which had a broken bottle on the top of it, at the gate was a man who was in uniform, he was a guard, and had a small shelter near the door where he sat, there was another man who was working in the garden. Near the car I came with, were another three cars, two were Benz another was a Jaguar. The driver was sitting in the car in case they wanted to send him somewhere. Inside the house were two young men and one girl, who they were sending to do this and that.

It was a big house which the wall I saw was only glass. When you go wherever you go you see yourself everywhere, to go to the toilet, I had to be with someone, so apart from hotels it was the first time to see a home like that of an individual person.

All of that was too much to me; I didn't know how I could be close to someone like her. I was wondering if she could even understand me at all. I saw that her mum loved me genuinely, and I loved her too, though I had no problem with her daughter since I didn't know her character yet, but simply I had my complexes. Yes, her mum knew that might be a problem, that it could be too much to me, and she tried to prepare me in advance for that, but that was not a kind of richness I had in my mind. So many times I was talking with Mama Zainabu, after all she was the one who I knew, so I thought that maybe Uzamukunda wanted to give us time since it was us who knew each other. Or she was giving her time to know me too, I had many different guesses and judgements about her.

But whatever it was I had already made my decision, that I would be coming only when Mama Zainabu was there, though they were giving me their contact again. The driver took me to my home. Again I kept quiet I didn't make a phone call and I didn't tell the nameless man anything about them.

After a long silence I thought that it was not a good idea to hide myself and get lost as it happened before, so I made a phone call and it was a big coincidence Mama Zainabu was there again.

I told Uzamukunda about the nameless man and she invited us for lunch the next day, there they received us with respect, after our lunch, I was with Mama Zainabu alone with our stories, stories made me love her more and feel more close to her. I needed someone to tell the truth, for a long time I was like the boss in many ways, so it was not easy to get someone who would talk to me directly and tell me exactly my mistakes.

At that time Mama Zainabu looked at me and asked me why I was not even making phone calls, she said that she didn't know how she would find me since the driver who dropped me at my home was no longer working there, I said nothing, she went ahead but was not happy, she was serious and angry and she told me off.

"Look Bamurangirwa even last time when we were here I saw you, when we were talking; your mind was not settled. And always blaming Uzamukunda that she didn't make any effort to be with you, but now I can understand that it is not her fault at all, it is you who is scared of yourself, you see that you can't fit in to her life, that you are not the type of the people of that level."

"That is a big mistake and is ridiculous, I told you everything about my past, and told you that things are like wind, which can come and go, so from now on, be free don't hide yourself, you are young, it is important you have good health and you look to be an understanding young woman, so you don't know about tomorrow. Don't ever lose hope about the future, better to know that people there are the same no matter what."

Yes she was right and I told her so, and I was ashamed, there was nothing I had to tell her, unless many thanks and genuine promises now, that I would never see again that anyone was above anyone, ever.

When I went home Uzamukunda's mum wanted to go with us, so in case she could know where to start if I would hide myself again, she didn't want to trust me much. It turned to be a joke, she told me that we were going with her so that she could trust me herself, after all she was the one who was my friend, though she could be happy if all of us could be friends, and be one family.

After being on my own with my children after I lost the nameless man, and Fr Mario went back to Italy, and my good friend Mukabagira went to Uganda, that was when I saw that it was only Uzamukunda I could start to talk to, even if she would see it to be a joke or shame, whatever my problem was, I had to have someone to talk to, and still my life remained to be a secret to my fellow Rwandans.

She was the right person, because even if she would make a story from it, the people she would be talking to would be the people who didn't know me and maybe would never know me, so I did not care for that.

I called her and asked her for any appointment, she seemed like she was used to my silence, she told me when to go to see her, at her home she told her workers to put my drink in another room so that we could have our privacy.

I started to tell her why I wanted to see her by apologising for why I was not communicating with her the way it was supposed to be. I told her that all of that was my foolishness, which made me too scared of her because I saw her to be rich. "I judged you to be ignorant to people like me, just because we are not on the same level, even after mum tried hard to make me understand that is not how you are, and I am not supposed to judge you and be away from you."

"I thought how you had tried to find me, and how I had tried to be away from you without giving myself time to know you, and finding a reason why I had to be away, and now I decided to come and say sorry."

"Since mum always wanted us to be together as good friends without seeing or thinking of materials of any kind, only us today and tomorrow, now I am here to tell you what I have passed through, not that I want to change anything, or go back to my past whatever, but to hear your view, and see that maybe things like that they can happen to others or if it is only me, and see what advice I can give anyone who can come to me, in case with the same problems."

When I finished telling her my first reason why I came to see her, she seemed to be happy and relaxed.

She started by thanking me, "Look Bamurangirwa I am happy to see you finally, you come and tell me this yourself, you did something good and you are brave to be able to come and tell me the truth. I love my mum and I can do whatever she told me as far as it can't hurt anyone. Let alone to have someone like you as my friend or more than that, because I know she can't tell me the wrong things and she has had enough experience to judge people, so for that point I trust her."

"The way you welcomed them, made her love you, you did it as if you were their child, and the way she always talks about you, made all of us love you even before seeing you, but after seeing you, I was surprised to see that you didn't want to be close to us, it was hurting Mum thinking that I hadn't made enough effort to welcome you, so, now this made me feel relaxed, because I am sure my mum will be more than happy to see us together, that was her wish."

"Second, I was born poor as mum told you, sometimes we had nothing to eat, and when I married my husband, we had nothing either, so to have all of this you see, can't make me forget my past, or that I can also be without anything, things can turn into another picture in seconds. You are welcome."

Yes I did it at last, I saw that I did something good, and for that I could say that I was brave.

I told her my second reason which made me come to see her, I told her my past, my life with Nyilimanzi and the nameless man, from the beginning up to the end, she was listening without any interruption, when I finished, I saw that she seemed to be sad, and she told me that things like that didn't happen to me only, and she didn't know if she could call it normal, but it was happening to many women the same, few men too, anyone could betrayed and be a victim of love.

"The good example I am going to give you is mine. I was raised-up by my mum without a father, but my mum was the best mum I have ever seen, she did whatever she can to see me safe and happy, she didn't manage to put me in school apart from a religious school, I grew up with Islamic beliefs and culture."

"We married when we were still young, I was sixteen years old when my husband was eighteen years old, we had nothing apart from my mum was who took care of us at her home for some time. In a way both our parents were helping us at first until when my husband got a friend who introduced him to a different business..."

"He came to be good and powerful businessman, to the point of now we have all of this you see, and much more, he have houses in many countries even in Europe, many cars, he have a private aeroplane, which at this time is unusual to an African person to have a private aeroplane."

"Me and my husband we didn't get a chance to go to school, but almost all our workers have finished university, and I can't tell you how many workers we have around the world. Only here at my house I have six workers, the gardeners, cooks, drivers, guard..."

"According to our religion I was aware that my husband any time can marry another wife, but he was always telling me, that though his brothers and friends had more than one wife, and were telling him to marry another one too, but he didn't have any intention to marry another one, by telling me that I am the woman any man can dream to be with, I am beautiful, I gave him the beautiful children, boys and girls, I treat his visitors with respect and good manners, and at his home everything is perfect from cleaning, cooking... no complaints. What else could any man want to have? What in God's name can I get from other women which you don't have? I love you for what you are and I am satisfied for what you do, you are better than many, many educated women, your nature is enough to hold everything which is in front of you in beautiful ways."

"We were rich together, and we would be together. This encouragement and loving words went on for years. I was satisfied and happy with life. I loved my husband we grew up together up to now. I have never cheated on him and he knows that."

She went ahead by telling me her husband's sweet words, "In our conversations he was telling me about men who married many wives that many were just showing off, that he did not understand them. We started to have a family after one year of our marriage, but we started to get money in recent years, that was when his relatives started to tell him to marry other wives, something which was upsetting him and telling me those stories, I was wondering why they pushed him to hurt me."

"The good words stuck in my mind, that he loved me enough to be with me no matter what, they were going to try to push him to marry another woman, he would never listen to their cruel advice, we would be us and only us forever. When I had this youngest child you see, all of that changed in a quiet way, without any notice at all, he just disappeared and she grew up when she didn't have a father, she didn't know him, she grew up thinking that she didn't have a father at all."

"Normally we used to be together at dinner time and the first times when he started to get lost were strange to me. I didn't have any idea what was going on. I was staying without eating, without sleeping, waiting for him and worried to death, thinking that something terrible might have happened to him."

"When he came sometimes he came too late, when I tired to go to sleep, sometimes without eating anything because of worries, and there were times I was making myself look beautiful and sitting waiting for him, so that my husband can come and see me when I am still looking perfect, when I did all of that for him, sometimes he started to come in the morning time, without any explanations."

"Then I started to try to find out what was going on, through his friends who I know that they can't make up things which are not there, and who I trust that they can't be happy to see us break our marriage."

"After knowing that all of that was because he has other women around, it shocks me because I trusted him one hundred percent, so I was not aware that he can cheat on me at all. I didn't know if it can be better to be with a man without trust and always be aware that he can cheat on you, or more than that. Something which I think, that is not a good idea, since trust is needed in all areas of life."

"And it made me think that when some men have money it changes them and pushes them to women. True what my husband once said, it is part of showing off, and makes them feel like proper men."

"This house and all of these things you see here, there are times I didn't see them to be important, and when I see my workers outside happy with their wives, I wish that I can be one of them, I wish that all of the things we have can get lost and go back to our past life, but to have back our love and peace in my heart, that is when I came to know that things without proper love, without peace is nothing."

"The time came when his friend tried to talk to him and now at last I can see him at home not like before, but better because the children can see him, I had not put some of the money aside to hide it, I saw everything to be ours as a family, if I had some capital on my own I would have left him at that time, but I had nowhere to go with these children, that is why I am still here. Now he has already married, he has another wife."

"That is my answer, that can happen to everyone, thank your God, the nameless man showed you who he is at a very early stage, think if you went with him and he turned into a monster when you were there alone, when you have no one, maybe you know nothing yet about their life over there, and maybe you don't know yet even their language, what could happen to you at that time?"

I was happy with what I did, that talk I had with Uzamukunda was the best counselling I had ever had, and I knew that it was not only me who had problems like that, problems of betrayal, I had to go ahead with my life and look ahead, but first before everything I had to go to see my father who had lost his young wife from a short illness.

I thought the support I could give my father was to adopt his last born three boys he had with his wife, I came with Gahenda, he was eight years old, though he was a bit old I put him in a standard one primary school, with other children he was good at home and at school. Now I had a family of seven children.

We went ahead to be a good example in many ways, some people loved us for that, and some were jealous of us, my children gave me many friends local and international.

Batsinduka when he finished primary school he was in the few children who passed with high results in the whole country, and that gave him chance to go to one of the best schools at the time, Nairobi School, which was only for white children at the colonial time.

And at that time it was receiving students of three different types.

No 1: children who had very high results.

No 2: children of leaders.

No 3: children of rich people who could get enough money to buy the place for their children.

After Nairobi School he chose to go to Utali College, which was still the best around in Africa at the time, because he was not allowed to be in university. Though few of our children managed to go to universities.

Utali College had many different courses, he chose tourism and languages.

In 1982 he was in the few Scouts who were chosen to go to Britain.

Ilibagiza chose to be a hairdresser, and got a chance to be taken by Kenya school of hairdressing, which was only good for that course in Nairobi at that time, and the majority of their students were Asian and white because it was them who could afford the fees.

And how I came to be lucky enough to convince the education officers of the U.N. to pay for her, since I couldn't get enough money to bribe them, I had things from Tanzania which I got when I visited my father, just for that purpose of giving them to the education officers when I needed help from them, that was still bribing then and corruption, but if I wanted to survive and get what I wanted from them, I had to go with the system, something which came out as culture too, things which I knew that they couldn't get in Nairobi, and were cheap but looked to be good and expensive, and were making them happy, when many times I got what I was after.

Muvunangoma wanted to deal with computers and went to Strusmore College, after he was a lecturer.

Gahongayire was a good businesswoman and designer, she was one of the few people who had big shops in Mwingi in Ukambani area where she was married.

Manzi he was a professional dancer, he was well known as Yellow Boy in Mombasa especially Bora Bora.

Niwegaju was one in a few students who were chosen because of their good results and given a chance to go to Norway, to join an International School, after that she went ahead well and they renewed her scholarship which took her to join a university in Britain, in Preston University.

It was only Gahenda who didn't go well with his studies and he died young.

In that journey, the time came when my children moved me where Fr Mario left me, at that time they put me in Kangemi, but another area, with other new life.

Most of the things I had, some I gave them to other people, others I destroyed them because they were too old to give them to anyone, so that I could move with new ones, then I had all the things I was seeing in my friends' homes when I visited them, and some were good more than that, my house was self-contained of three bed rooms, it was like I had moved from another country, with another life, we changed in many ways, even our budgeting changed. We had suffered enough for a long time, and thanks to our patience to be able to hold on, and reach that time.

At that time Congo which was still Zaire, was like a country without government, so business people took different things from around the world there because there were no taxes, what was needed was just to bribe soldiers of the area where you wanted to take your things, and other business people were going there to buy what they wanted for a cheap price.

I too was going there sometimes to buy clothes and sell them, but first I had to choose ours, though we were known for how we dressed in a unique way even before, and sometimes it made me get what I wanted from the U.N.'s offices. I had what to give them, or to fail to get what I was supposed to get, when the officer was one of the people who were always jealous of us, it was easy to be jealous of me because of how I dressed, sometimes they could tell me so openly or talk behind my back.

Things like that were happening to me many times, I was coming to know what happened why sometimes I got some kind of problem, and did not get what I was supposed to get from those officers, was sometimes through other officers, who were not happy for that, maybe they were there when it happened, or were proud that the officer told her or him about it, that she or he enjoyed to make me suffer, by telling me to come tomorrow when he or she knew that I would never get anything from her or him. On the other hand to enjoy me. According to them just because I didn't look like someone who needed help, I was just showing off.

My style was to wear a long dress always, and one day in the evening when I was coming from town, from the bus stop someone greeted me in Swahili, I had to respond after seeing who greeted me, when I remembered to do so.

I saw that it was a tall handsome man who I had never seen, and he looked like a Somali man, he asked me if I was Somalian, and in a joke I said yes I was, but I didn't speak Somali language.

In a calm way, he asked me why I didn't speak the language, I told him that I grew up in Tanzania, again he asked me in his calm way, how I grew up in Tanzania, and I told him that my mother took me there when I was still a young girl.

All of that I took as a joke; I didn't know why I came up with such jokes to stranger.

The man he jumped with joy in a high voice, and said, "Yes, yes it is you."

It surprised me then; I asked him what he meant by saying that it is me.

"Yes it is you," he repeated the word because he looked to be too happy.

At that time he offered to help me to carry the things I had in my hand, which I couldn't go ahead carrying when I was with him.

I refused his offer, and he told me that better let him help me because even if I could refuse to show him my home it couldn't help, already he knew where I lived!

It gave me some kind of fear, and I asked him how and why he came to know my home.

That young man, who I didn't know his name, told me that he knew me for some time now, almost since I had moved to that area, and it was his responsibility to know where I lived too.

Then I had to ask what I had done to do all of that, and now he was here saying that it was me, who did he think I was.

He saw that I was panicking and told me to take it easy, and started to tell me the whole story. He didn't ask me my name and I didn't ask his either. He went on: "Look, we have a child who grew up in Tanzania, she went with her mother when she was still very young, and we heard rumours that she was no longer in Tanzania, and in fact had moved somewhere here, and one of our people when she saw you here, she saw you to be different with people over here, the way you

455

dress and the way you look, and we have some people in our family who look exactly like you, but we had to take it easy and be very careful before we made any approach, and that is why I am over happy to see that we get back our sister!"

It shocked me how I told him that fake story and now in coincidence it matched with their story, so I had to try to make him believe that I was joking, and make him forget me, otherwise he might tell his relative that he found their lost daughter.

I said that I was joking then. "I am not a Somali." He looked to be surprise and turned to me with shock question as if he wanted me to repeat what I said, with hope that he didn't hear me correctly, or I was not going to repeat it again, maybe I was going to say that I was joking again, but the truth I am Somali girl, that was what he wanted to hear. I said it again that I am not a Somali girl!

"Where do you come from then? Are you Borana, Ethiopian or Eritrea?"

"I come from Rwanda. I am Rwandan," I told him. He looked to be unhappy and he seemed that was his first time to hear the country with the name Rwanda, wherever he didn't want to see me go ahead trying to insist that I was someone else, so he thought it was only for some reason I was not ready to meet my relatives, so he tried to calm me down, I don't have to fear, no one wanted to hurt me, he was just looking for their relative, and I happened to be the one who had the same story with who they were looking for, though I said that it was not me there was nothing he could do. And he said bye and he was gone.

Soon when I was inside my house, I was looking for other clothes to change from what I had, the children outside called me, that on the gate they were old men who wanted to see me. I asked them where they came from, and they told me that they looked like my relatives, and I told them to tell them to come inside the house.

The children came again and told me that they would not come inside, they wanted to see me outside, so I thought that they were in a hurry, and since I didn't want to keep them waiting for long, I had to

456

go quickly. I tied one piece of cloth from my chest and I covered another piece of the cloth to my head which was covered all over my shoulders.

On the road was like ten old Somali men, who had big scarfs on their heads, with long beards which they dyed in red, with a few young men including that one who I was with, all of them had a long decorated stick, and to some who knew the secret of that stick, they were swords. And I knew too, so I saw that they were prepared for anything which could come in front of them.

I was too scared, and wanted to go back inside the house, and hide myself, but I thought that it couldn't help, I believed that they were not going to go without me if they believed that I was their child, they would kidnap me.

What worried me more was that I had never heard that there were Somali people in that area, meaning that maybe they were there for that mission. On top of that I had heard stories that Somali people, they didn't joke with what they believed to be theirs.

But I told myself that better let me go and maybe finish this problem for good. When they saw me all of them they looked to be happy, some were jumping here and there, and talking many words, though I did not understand what they were saying, but they seemed to be happy, maybe because I had covered my head too! All of those things were a coincidence!

I was shaking and sweating, knowing that my children would never see me again, finished.

I was like in a deep bad dream.

I started to think how they would take me somewhere like prison and teach me and force me to love their family telling me that it was my family and maybe see me as sick person, according to what they believed. All of the children who were around there, came and rounded us, to see what was there, and why all of that, when they saw that I was scared and almost falling down, one of the older children who was there, gave me her stool which she was putting her container of things she was selling on the road, to sit on. I sat and also was supported by the fence on my back, waiting for what would happen, they were still busy talking for themselves.

When they finished what they were talking about, one of the old men came where I was sitting and pulled back the cloth I covered my head with, and pulled a little part of my hair and showed others, this also came to be a big deal, they talked for a long time again were jumping here and there, like before, maybe saying that "You see, she is the one, even her hair is like ours, and she still has the good manners of covering her head, she is the one then. We got her."

After talking, another one came and put my hair back and covered me again. I was like a picture, I couldn't do anything for myself, I felt helpless and too scared.

Now it was time to be given an interview, some were aside waiting, and others were around me, with men between us who were interpreters in Swahili.

They asked me if I was their daughter who grew up in Tanzania. I said that I was not the one, they told me that now they had me, though they saw that I was not happy to have my original family back, nothing which could take me out from them again, so, there was no need to try to lie to them, nothing which was going to help, not even my husband if I had him, no one who would stand in front of them, I couldn't even run away again, and they didn't want to harm me, they only wanted to show me my relatives who I lost and would be happy to have me back.

They were talking non-stop without giving me time, the only time I had was that to say my answer which was no, and quickly I got other questions, "Are you Boran?"

"No."

"Are you Ethiopian?"

"No."

"Are you Eritrean?"

"No."

Then there was a pause and I got time to tell them who I was, that I was Rwandan from Rwanda. Some of them it was their first time to hear Rwanda, and others seemed to know about Rwanda and Rwandans, and told me that I was saying that because I heard that in Rwanda there were people who looked like them, and I was still trying to be clever.

The man who said that gave me a good idea which might save me from being kidnapped, when he said proudly, "How can we know that you are who you are saying you are? A Rwandan?"

It was only a few weeks before the Kenyan government gave us foreign identity! Which was a small green book written behind ALIEN with my passport photo inside, my heart jumped to it; thinking that since I had my photo and written that I was Rwandan it might save me.

I had my energy back again, and told them that I had my identity which I could show them, they looked at each other and then at me, looked to be surprised! They asked me if I was sure of what I was talking, that in my ID it had where I could show them where it was written that I was Rwandan?

"Yes," I said without shaking now or sweating. I stood up without asking any permission they warned me once more, that I had to come back, no need even to try to pass through the back door! I told them that I was going to come back. I came back with my ALIEN proudly I gave it to them, the first one who held it looked at it, it went around up to the last one who gave it back to me, and without any other word they turned like school children in the gymnastics or soldiers, they went in a line without turning their heads.

The first one went and the others went behind him with their sticks on their shoulders. I sat there looking at them, they went without even saying any other word or telling me bye, I think they had a big disappointment, and they had the anger of losing their time with maybe big hope.

On my side I thought that if the Kenyan Government had not yet given us any ID with our photo inside it, it would have been the end of my family, the next day I had to be in Mogadishu. It was like I was in a big dream, which was a lot of confusion, what I thought to be jokes, full of coincidences, almost turned out to be dangerous. It was my last time to try that kind of joke with strangers.

I was Rwandan, and had no reason again to joke that I was someone else. That time was a time of war between Museveni and Obote II, the war which was known to everyone in those countries, that he was fighting together with Rwandans, and sometimes they were coming in Kenya Nairobi for their reconciliation meetings. There were areas where other Rwandans lived around Nairobi in big numbers, some natives there knew that they were refugees, many times from drinkers who were telling them, and some had different understandings to that point, and told them that they didn't have to say anything to them, because they were living for their money, Kenyans's money. But where I was living I was alone, so there was no way native people there should know who I was, or anything about my life, and they gave me respect to see that wherever I worked, was good enough to keep my family together, and better than many of them.

In those U.N.'s offices, it was our place of meeting people from different countries, why we were going there were different reasons, but known to most of us, the big point was education for our children, and a few grown-up people, and other reasons were for support in different ways, so there sometimes you could get a friend, and sometimes be good friends, or enemies.

One day I was sat by myself, when an old lady came and sat near me, after normal greetings she told me that her daughter, she told her in case she would see me before her, to tell me that she wanted to see me, that she had something she wanted to talk with me about.

I knew that old lady to be Ugandan, but I didn't know her name, nothing at all I knew about her, not even if she had any child there with her. I asked her who her daughter was, after trying to see if I knew her, but without any success, I told her that she might tell me the message which was not mine, she insisted it to be me.

Then I asked her again how she was sure that it was me who her daughter wanted to see?

"Yes it is you," the old lady told me, "she told me the short

Rwandan woman who is dressed nice every day." I laughed for a long time at that, and asked her if it was only me who they saw in that entire group of people who was dressed nice?

To see that it made me laugh, she saw that it was like to tell her that it was ridiculous, she said, "No, no, others they dress nice too, but not every day like you."

The next time, after some time a woman came to where I was and after greetings, she asked me if her mum gave me her message? I was forgetting about the old lady and the message, and I had to ask her who her mum was, and what message.

She repeated the message and I said yes she told me, "So are you?" I asked her, and she told me that it was her. Sometimes I was seeing her like everybody in those offices, sometimes we were exchanging greetings, but no more than that. I didn't know her name too.

Yes now was time to hear what she wanted to tell me, she had finished seeing the officer she came to see, and she told me that she would wait for me, after we went and sat somewhere, she told me that her name was Rose, I told her that mine was Bamurangirwa, but she told me that already she knew my name! I asked her how, and she told me that she asked my fellow Rwandans. Only why she was interested in me might be a question, but the truth was that question didn't come into my mind. I didn't know what to think concerning this lady.

She told me that she was lucky to know many places where they helped in many different ways, and she liked me, and decided to ask me if I was happy with it, when she knew something to be telling me, so that we could be going together!

It surprised me and at the same time it made me happy, and I saw myself to be a lucky one, because she had chosen me to be her friend, though I knew nothing about her yet but still I could call it lucky.

We said where we would meet next time, and we met, from that time we were meeting at least once per week, a part from my name I came to realise that she knew a lot about me and my life before meeting me, and I told myself that the reason she gave herself that struggle to know me more, was because she liked me.

461

Always I was the first to be where we had to meet, and one time she apologised for being late, and told me that the next time, she would be trying to come in time since in my nature I didn't like to be late. I asked her how she came she knew about that, and she said that she knew that through the people who knew me, and yes she saw that it was right since every time she came to meet me I was there before her, this also didn't tell me anything!

We went ahead with our friendship, when I was waiting to be told about new things. But every time we met she was also asking me about myself one by one.

And to that, I thought that she wanted to know which type of help she could direct me to, she asked me if I sometimes went out of Kenya, and I told her that sometimes I went to Tanzania to visit my father, when she asked me if I had a family in Uganda and if I visited them too. I told her that yes I had family there but I couldn't visit them when they were still at war.

One day she asked me if I went to a Nyayo house in twenty-four floors, I told her that I had a friend there sometimes I would go there. Nyayo house was known to be place of immigration works, but twenty-four floors, known by many at the time to be for the Special Branch only.

Little did I know that all her questions had a reason, in all her questions she came to see that my big problem, like any other parents was my children's education. My son Manzi liked to dance, and I worried that the education officers might not support him for that course, so when she got where my worry was, she held there, by telling me that I didn't have to worry, she would help me for that.

That she had a relative who had a school for dancing in Mombasa, and he had donors, his students didn't pay school fees, and when she went to visit him, many times she would get a lift with her friends or his friends, who came over to Nairobi for their business, and when she was there he put her in good hotels, because he gave her respect, and they were good friends, apart from that he had a lot of money. So she would tell him about me and he would handle everything financial for that trip. I didn't have to worry about anything.

She asked me if I dealt with value stones from Tanzania. I told her that I didn't, to this point, she told me that she had a friend, a woman who was working in Shinyanga hospital, when I would be ready she could make a plan with her, and I could visit my father then go to see her in Shinyanga. Rose could give me money to buy the stone and she had the market, so we could divide the profit, and next time she could be the one who could go there. And with stone or not, since normally to go to Tanzania was a problem, because Tanzania had closed their borders at that time. I had to go when I was prepared to pass in different problems, she told me that she would be helping me by giving me a lift with her friend who was working in Tanzania side, so that he could even be helping me to pass to the border.

To point of that I couldn't go to Uganda because I feared the war, she was sorry for me, to see that I couldn't visit my relatives, and told me that if I would like to visit my family, she could plan that for me too, because the problem was to go.

To come back was no problem, so she could get a lift for me when her relatives came over there for their business.

So I saw that she was a well known person that was why every side to her was so easy to get lifts!

To point of visiting my family in Uganda, I promised myself to wait until when the war would be over, because I heard many stories of people from Kenya who went there especially Rwandans, who had big problems there, tortured even killed just because they were Rwandans. Because they believed that they were helping Museveni, I had no hurry to go to Uganda.

But to point of Tanzania, yes I was prepared to tell her next time when I would go to visit my father, even without any other business of stones, I could be happy just to get someone who could help me to the border. I was happy that I was going to give my son the education he wanted without a lot of trouble. Yes I was ready to grab that chance.

The time came when Museveni and his position would come to Nairobi for their reconciliation meetings, and Rose asked me if I would go to meet Museveni, but I told her that I didn't have any reason to meet him, she told me that she was in a group of women who would go to see him and tell him their problems, if I wanted I could join them.

But I told her that I would not join them since I had no programme to meet him, I loved Museveni as anyone who was hungry for peace, who believed that if he would win, the Great Lake area would have peace, I loved him as any Rwandan refugee who had a hope that if he would win we would get a way of our solution. But I was no one on any level to meet him.

The time came to go to Mombasa, on her side things seemed to be ready, I told Uzamukunda my happy story of going to Mombasa, that I might get a sponsor for Manzi, her mum was there too, come to visit her, so Uzamukunda was happy for me and she suggested that since it was a school holiday, all of us we could go together and the children. So her suggestion was to go by bus all of us, with my friend too, she was sure that the children would be happy to travel with a bus, so it could be our holiday together, and we could tell my friend that she could join us where we would be instead of the hotel, and we were sure that my friend she would like the idea.

Yes it was a good idea, and I was happy to have a big and good holiday when at the same time doing something for my child.

The time we had to meet with Rose was the first time she was there before me and waiting for me. We had to meet and talk about our last programme of our journey to Mombasa. Uzamukunda offered all of us tickets; I said that my friend might come without money since she didn't know the programme.

We went with Uzamukunda's mum and we met Rose. I introduced her to them and I told her our new plan, and she said that it was not bad and thanked Uzamukunda for the offer of a ticket, but told her that she had the money so we would go to make the booking for our tickets.

When we were at home Uzamukunda's mum was not happy, we asked her what was wrong and she asked me how I came to involve myself with Rose?

I told her the whole story, she told us that even though Rose these days she had a scarf on her head and wore glasses, but she saw that she knew her in Uganda back in Amin's time, they put her in newspapers with her pictures and put her picture everywhere, she was a big wanted person at that time, said that her mother was Muganda and her father was Muhima, and she married either Acholi or Lango. She was a big killer who was capable to kill in many different ways, they were telling society that anyone who would see her should be far from her, only to report her to the police, but after they heard rumours that she ran from Uganda to Kenya. "So be very, very careful with her she might be the one."

I said, "That can't be, I know her she is a refugee like all of us, she can't be that monster, she is just a beautiful lady who is struggling with life like us."

Mama Zainabu said, "It is OK, let us wait we will see the end of it."

The time to go to Mombasa came and when we were at the bus station, they told us that our friend came back and took out her money, that she changed her mind she would not go any more!

I went on holiday, but I had many questions about Rose. My mind started to go back to all of her help of lifts everywhere. I was scared of her, but I didn't know how I could judge, and I had no conclusion yet, I had to try to find out the truth about her, and see if Mama Zainabu was my saviour, but how would I be able to do that was a big question.

Some of the questions I was asking myself was that it might be true, if she had married either Lango or Acholi when I heard it, I had no doubt about it, because of her children I had seen, they didn't look like their mother, they looked like those people, either Lango, Acholi... Rose looked like Hima people, with a long beautiful face, beautiful figure, she didn't look like her mother too, her mum looked like pure Muganda without any mixture, and why she tried to know me even before meeting me, she wanted to see if I might be the right person as maybe she thought I was, the proper one, so she could use me for whatever she wanted to do with me.

Why she was coming late when she already knew that was not my character, I thought that if always I could wait for her, then it was enough to show her that I needed her and she had me. By always talking about giving me lifts for wherever I would be going, and sometimes remembering to tell me Benz, and talking about the good hotels where we would be, maybe she thought of me as a high person who liked the high life.

So all of her job could be easy since she would put me in the car by name of a lift, and take me where she wanted to take me.

And when she asked me if I went to Nyayo house in twenty-four floors, I thought that she wanted to see if I dealt with something concerning governments.

And when she asked me if I was preparing to meet Museveni she wanted to make sure if I was working for him in any way.

Back to Nairobi I prepared my mission to know about Rose, there was no other way then, since she was dealing with the U.N. as a refugee, this U.N. might know her secrets, and still protect her, something which couldn't surprise me.

I knew the old lady my counsellor, Mrs. Kamau, to be one of a few senior officers of the U.N. in Nairobi. I trusted myself that I would be able to ask deep down Mrs. Kamau and get what I wanted from her concerning Rose, if she was in any kind of gang who were killers, she might know and she would tell me. I would use all of my intelligence to make her talk and tell me that secret of the U.N.. I normally knew that they loved killers and protected them directly or indirectly everywhere in all stages of life around the world.

The day and time came to see Mrs. Kamau, inside her office she showed me where to sit, if I wanted to be listened to by her: normally I had to ask her about her daughter Mary, and how her husband betrayed her, and in general listen to her problems before telling her mine.

After all of that I started like I was giving her some kind of interview.

"Mrs Kamau you know that it is you who I have here in Kenya as my mother, not true?" I asked her.

466

Mrs. Kamau said, "Yes, yes my child, you are my daughter who I love very much."

"Now today I come here in front of you because I trust you that you can't be happy if anything happened to me. And what I come here to ask you is not a normal question, or normal stories as I used too. It is far different, but I had to come because there was nowhere else I had to go. I thought that if I did not ask you, and maybe something happened to me, then it will be my fault, and I understand that this question I am going to ask you, is something which you don't have to tell me, because it is your responsibility to keep secrets of your work. I believe it to be a secret because if it is not then, I should just know in other simple ways. But I can't."

In those offices they knew me with the names I got from Nyilimanzi, as Winnie Mukaneza, all of that time, she was listening with an interest without any interruption, she was looking at me non-stop, after a long story then she said, "Winnie ask me and if I have an answer I will tell you."

Then I started to give her questions one by one as if it was me who was the officer.

"Mrs Kamau in these offices do you have a person who is spying for their countries, and you know them, and have they got your ID like any other refugees?"

Mrs Kamau without hesitation said, "Yes, we have them."

"And head office knows them and knows what they are doing?"

"Yes, the head office knows everything about them."

"Do you have Ugandans?"

"Yes, we have them."

"In those Ugandans, they are women?"

"Yes there were two, but now one has gone we are left with one!"

To hear that, if I was standing I would have fainted and fallen down, but I still fainted in the chair, Mrs Kamau to see how I am, she stood up and came back with a bottle of cold drink and gave it to me, and commanded me to drink it.

Yes she was right, after drinking it, it was like my life came back, I started to tell her the whole stories how it started up to the end. She asked me how she looked and her name, I told her, and then she told me that I had a very long life!

She told me to stand up, I did what she said, and she took me to the window, she showed me outside the yellow small car and asked me if I saw it, I told her that I saw it, she said, "That is the one in their cars they use to kidnap people and take them to sell them, that is the enemy of their government, you can imagine what they do with them!"

She ordered me to sit down again which was what I did, she got a magazine from her drawer *WEEKLY REVIEW,* she showed me where it said a Ugandan man Kiza who I knew like anybody who came in those offices,was one of the people they tried to kidnap. That when they kidnapped him it was in the daytime in the city centre, when he was with his two children, and he left the children in the middle of the road, but he managed to run from them when they were in Nakuru on the way to Uganda!

She asked me if I knew her addresses, I told her that she gave them to me, I was on the way to visit her, she asked me those addresses, but all of that I thought to be a pretence, since they knew everything about them, even the cars they used to kidnap people!

I shouldn't ask her why they protect them to that level, since maybe the answer would be that it was how the job had to be done, or that I didn't have to know that.

Yes that was our U.N. which tried everything to protect the people on our planet one hundred percent, to give us the peace we deserved, to my view things like that showed me that if we could have peace one hundred percent, to them it could be a big loss, many couldn't get what to do.

She gave me the idea of not visiting her or showing her that I found out who she was, though: Rose too, since then she was away from me, maybe she guessed that I knew her already, or she thought that somehow, on my side I was stronger than her.

When Mukabagira went back to Uganda we were communicating through letters, she was with her sister in her house when Paul came, she told him the truth that she wanted a divorce because she didn't love him, and since she was in the protection of soldiers, there was nothing Paul could say, the solution was to give it to her in a smooth way.

Her sister introduced her to a soldier relative of her late husband, who was a polite man and too kind almost like her late husband, so Mukabagira loved him for that, he gave her everything, almost like what she had before Amin's men killed her husband. Mukabagira was happy once more again.

Rwandans in Uganda had a different life concerning time and who was the leader, the first ones who came in 1920-1940s most of them were settled with their cows and were comfortable, that was the Rwandans who ran away from Rwanda either because they didn't want to beat others, or to be beaten, according to the Belgian law at the time, of system of society had to be beaten, beating themselves too hard, for whatever they were doing for themselves, or for the Belgians, in the name of improving the country and making it modern, so if they made you be chief and you couldn't beat other Rwandans, then it would be you who would be beaten. This made a big group run away and go to neighbouring countries.

But the ones who came from 1959 maybe because they came with their King Ndahindurwa Kigeli, King Kabaka Mutesa of Uganda recognised them more and saw them as their relatives, since the majority were a Tutsi, group of Rwandan prince and princess. Though, even the first ones most of them were a Tutsi too, because according to Belgian mathematics, it was to make a Tutsi the leader, and give them the hard stick to beat other Rwandans, which they had to be beaten until the skin came out, so that the ones who were beaten, could be very easy to see that these Tutsi were bad people, they were bad leaders. These beatings were to all ordinary society Tutsi, Hutu and Twa, and when the time would come it would be easy to tell them that they felt sorry for them and they would give them help to fight for themselves and kill those bad people (Tutsi).

In 1963 when Rwandans who were in Burundi took a war in

Rwanda as Inyenzi (cockroach), the name resembled the way they were hiding themselves and shocking their enemy without knowing where they came from. On the other hand the side of the enemy was to abuse them, they used Bugesera as their way, they almost took over the government, but they missed, and were not successful, it said that was because of poor preparation, and they said that they were not supported by all Rwandans who were outside, they seemed to be in a hurry and believed in themselves. This war was when one of Francis Rukeba's sons, Kayitare, who was one of the commanders died in that war, with many others too. Something which made his father to be more patriotic, some had rumours that his original was Mushi from Congo side, but that to him even if he was Mushi, nothing could stand in front of him to fight for his country Rwanda. Rukeba was in the few who did many things which others couldn't, because of fear of Belgians, like to change his appearance and manage to visit (umwami Musinga to Congo), and to announce that King Mutara Rudahigwa would not be buried before announcing who would be the next king, according to Rwandan culture. Which was planned by Kayihura and Kayumba who crowned him and who had to come from a particular clan, 'Abatsobe', according to Rwandan's culture, concerning the ceremony of crowning King (kwimika Umwami). Francis Rukeba was loyal to the king's family from Musinga to Ndahindurwa Kigeli, but in general he loved Rwanda.

All his wives were a Tutsi, one day in Nairobi, he came where we were and he asked a group of young men that he heard that some of them got permission to move to Canada. They said yes, thought that he was going to be happy for them, but to him they were like a loss.

He asked them, "Now our young people you are happy to go ahead to go far and far away from your Rwanda, who will help Rwanda now?"

They saw how sad he was when he asked them and they gave him a serious answer too, "Don't worry, we are going to find a future, when the time will come of helping Rwanda in any way, nowhere will be far, we will come as soon as possible, and do what we have to do."

When he saw how they told him in a serious way, he looked to be relaxed and told them: "Yes how you will reach there, that is how you will come back." Rukeba died in Nairobi and he was loved by Rwandans, there were big numbers in hundreds who came to give their last respect. Inyenzi war of 1963 and R P F's war in1990, were related somehow because both had the same reason, to rescue their country. But R P F were very careful before starting their war, they didn't want to make the same mistake.

When that war came in Rwanda in 1963 for a short time made the Rwandan government kill the Tutsi who were inside the country between 1963-1964 January was killed more than 10,000 Tutsi but no one said anything.

When Obote took over the power from King Kabaka Mutesa in the mid 1960s, to Rwandan side, also things changed to be bad, but when Amin took over from Obote in 1971, to Rwandan side, things were good, he put the young men in the army, he brought back their King Ndahindurwa Kigeli who was in Kenya… to support him in his politics if he wanted to.

But again when Obote II came back, he had his good reasons to hate Rwandans, now more than double, they were helping Amin to fight him, in 1982 he used his Lango and Acholi army to terrorise them wherever they were in Uganda, they took away their animals, destroyed their property, killed some, especially those who tried to fight for their cows or other property. They raped women, and some died on the way running, some mothers were having their babies on the way when some died there for loss of blood… Some who ran on Rwanda side, there things were worse, more than seventy percent of Rwandans who were in Uganda at the time, they had problems in different ways.

There were some who came to be well known how they were cruel to Rwandans at the time, like leaders who came to be well known for their clued they did to them, and you could hear children sing their names in the villages, like Minister Chris Rwakasisi, and Rubaihayo former lecturer in Makerere University.

Though to young Rwandans they had the idea that in the future, they had to go back to their native country Rwanda, but the Obote war in 1982, to them it pushed them so quickly to put their wish in to practice, when they joined Museveni to the bush in big numbers.

You could hear one of them who came to be powerful Rwandans Patriotic Front leader, the army Chief of the general staff, General James Kabarebe, when we were in Kigali in a conference in 2004, he told us his story in brief, how he joined Museveni to the bush in 1982, how him and his friends ran in Rwanda side, knowing that they were going in their country, but authority in Rwanda told them that they would not recognise them as Rwandans, and if Uganda also didn't recognise them, meaning that even God didn't recognise them then, from there they went where other Rwandan refugees went in Rwanda side, and saw how they died in hundreds because of the situation they put them in, from there next was to go to the bush with Museveni.

In general wherever Tutsi were in neighbouring countries and inside Rwanda they had no peace.

In Rwanda to be able to do something useful at the time, or for your child to go to high school, you had to buy a Hutu identity, or your daughter, your sister was wife to Hutu who had some power and it was what helped Tutsi to push time somehow. Though the time came when their government made a law that Hutus who were working with the government they were not supposed to marry Tutsi girls, but still big numbers of Hutu especially who were rich married Tutsi girls, something which was a problem to Hutu girls, seeing that their brothers didn't see that they were there. This was one of the reasons Radio Rwanda told Hutu girls in genocide time, when France came to help them, 'all of you Hutu girls, prepare yourself and go to welcome French men, we have killed all Tutsi girls now you have no competition.'

To their cousins in Burundi, Tutsi still was in power there, but Rwandan children had to have their different marks with Burundian children to be able to go to high school!

In Uganda, Rwandan children had to have Ugandan names,

speaking their languages, with their names, it was easy to pretend to be them to get a chance of high schools.

In Kenya, the U.N. had to choose for them the course they wanted them to take, but not the course the children wanted, and it was not easy to go to university. There were very few who managed to enter university. When also their officers were another problem, with their greed of bribes, or the men trying to force women to take them to bed.

Mukabagira was one of the Rwandans who lost relatives in that Obote war in 1982, she was married to the side that was killing her relatives, her husband was too good to her and to anyone who was near him, but she was angry with his people, with Obote and with politics in general.

In 1986 when Museveni was winning his war Mukabagira's husband was commander and he was killed fighting Museveni, who was helped by his wife's relatives.

Mukabagira left with her little beautiful daughter, and went on with life, but when R P F went in Rwanda in guerrilla war in 1990, Mukabagira went with them to fight for her original country, she was one of very few who married Acholi or Langi who supported R P F, to the level of going to the front line, they saw them as the enemy, because they were fighting their husbands. But Mukabagira had to leave her daughter with her sister who seemed to be the opposite way. That kind of horrible life some Rwandans had inside and outside of their country was reason enough to take R P F to war and was the same reason that took Mukabagira to war and made her forget that R P F was the one who killed her husband.

She sent me a letter and we were not sure if we would see each other again she went to war not a kind of party or other visit.

So me behind, like every Rwandan who was out, and some who were inside Rwanda, our responsibility was to support our soldiers in all means. How and when R P F was born you will find in my book *RWANDA YESTERDAY*, when our children went to the front line, training Rwandans as carders of R P F in a secret way, was uniform around the world.

473

But still some had thoughts to think that I had a secret life, that maybe I was working for the Rwandan government, meaning that I was opposion to R P F, some went ahead of thinking of me in that way or to be dealing with value stones.

One day the headmaster of the school of my children wanted to see me, but when I was there, what he wanted to see me for was completely different with what I thought. Instead of telling me anything concerning my children's education he asked me if he could join me in stone dealing! I tried to tell him that I had no idea of that business, though; I didn't know if he was satisfied with my explanations.

One day I gave some papers concerning Rwandan history to one of my family friends who was one of the R P F leaders in our area, but at that time I was yet to join it. Kenya and Rwanda R P F like in other many parts of the world were working in big secret because of security, they were very careful so there was a very small chance to be known. To the level even if someone joined in a family other family members couldn't be told until when his or her time would come.

So that was when I was not yet to be welcomed to join R P F in an official way, when he showed them those papers, when they asked them where he got them from, he told them that it was Bamurangirwa who gave them to him. I came to know that those papers were a big deal in that meeting, they asked themselves how I could be able to get papers like that and why up to that time I had not yet joined them for the struggle?! Some of them had the conclusion that I was a spy of Habyarimana and it was simply an argument, they asked themselves where they thought my finances came from…. He tried to defend me and since he was sure that I had nothing to do with Habyarimana, one of those who was in that meeting told me that story, it was the law, of no one who had to know what was in the meeting when he or she was out. But the person trusted me to that level.

That was how I came to know that there were some Rwandans too, who thought of me in that way, that I might be working with the enemy (Rwandan government at the time). I was told before by native people, just because of how they saw me and my family, one told me personally, told me that by being in a cheap area it was only to confuse people so that they couldn't know that I was working for my government as a spy. They didn't know that I was a refugee.

The time came when I was invited and welcomed officially to join others for the struggle. That was when those who had doubt in me; concerning my patriotism, they had a chance to know me better. I did a lot of different things but I was not alone, we were doing what we chose from ideas of all of us as a group, sometimes they chose people who could stay for some time, work at night depending what the leaders or majority said. All of that was because of secretive things.

And sometimes the group could move someone to another group depending what capability they saw in that person.

There were times I was given the post to be a leader of the women of that area and the last I was moved to group of information, it was us in the area that had to know what was happening around us and other areas or countries in the world when it was possible.

The people I got in that group were respected in Rwandan community since 1959, the good educated old man, who had worked with King Kigeli in those years, and who was well known by politics leaders in Rwanda in the 1950s and outside of Rwanda, Kayihura Michel.

There was another one Munyengabe Heza in our group who nicknamed me Iyamarere this name many came to know me as Iyamarere which normally was the name given to R P F because of their braveness. Heza had his reason why he gave me this name, I didn't ask him. I thought no matter who I was talking to them in the way I saw things, in a clear way, and I liked to keep time for whatever I did, and talk about it in a serious way to anyone who didn't do so.

I was opposing postponing a thing which it was us who would do it, my ideas were 'do it and rest after to know that you managed or you failed'. So many loved me for that. I was in three people who were chosen to go to check the songs of women in the Kawangware area, and see if we had to give them the green right to put it out to all Rwandans around the world, they were struggle songs which were part of educating Rwandans, and fundraising for our soldiers.

475

It was Muzee Kayihura Michel, Charle Kayitana and I.

We gave the songs the green light to go ahead. Every month people were giving the money according to how much they promised that you would manage to get, and had to keep a clear record of how things went, each group had their leaders and other people who held other positions, but all of them had to use nicknames because of security in case a file was missed.

And in case those who were responsible for keeping the money were not serious and in cases of misuse, all of the world they knew that if someone could do some serious mistake, they would be called in Byumba and would be punished accordingly, so they had a fear of Paul Kagame, because they knew that if you made a mistake, then it was a mistake, no matter who you were as far as he was concerned, anyone was like everyone, so it was simple to do the right thing.

Peter, one of my penpals from Canada in early 1992, came to visit me when it was his first time to come to Africa. Like anyone who came to Africa for the first time he wanted to see and know some of the things in that continent, but more than that he wanted to meet my father too, the man I had told him about. My father at the time people believed that he was more than one hundred and ten years old, still a very clean man, still his mind was very sharp to the level of you could sit with him and write history. He looked weak somehow, a little blind, and deaf but good health according to his age, still with all his strong teeth when he had never visited any dentist.

And Peter wanted to meet any senior officers of R P F too, so I promised him that I would do those two things for him.

In my mind I thought that he wanted to see my father himself because, maybe he didn't believe that an African person could have that long life still with good health. And I was proud of my father, happy that anyone could meet him. He wanted to see about my people over there up country where some of them still used dirty water, and went without shoes... I told him all of that, to the point of meeting any senior officers of R P F I thought that being a western person, he was planning to make any contribution to us concerning our struggle so I was happy for that.

He wanted first to go to Toro, first we were in Kampala for one day, then we went to Kasese for one day, all of these two places we were with people I knew, some places we were welcomed by friends, from Kasese we went to Fort Port for one day, but there I didn't know anyone, from there we would go where my family were in Kamwezi Toro, but I didn't know well about transport there, so we missed the car which went to that area, though I was speaking the languages of natives there, so I had confidence that my speaking with them would help.

They told us that we couldn't get any other transport for that day until the next day which was not good for our time, but they told us too, that if we could, we could walk it was not that far, so yes we could walk but Peter had a big bag of fifty kilograms and didn't know that anyone apart from soldiers could carry that weight all of that distance which I thought might be between ten and twenty miles or more, and to the native people they saw it to be near for walking, so I had to think of a solution. It was still morning hours, and we had finished our breakfast, we were on the road just walking and looking outside, we came to meet a man and to me he looked to be a Rwandan, to this point I had to use my Africanism and trusted our culture and tried this man. I greeted him in Kinyarwanda and luckily enough he was Rwandan, then I told him our problem and asked him if he could give me any ideas.

After telling him the problem we had, he asked me what kind of bags we had he said that was simple to him, it was not far, we could walk, but not with that bag, so he could look around where he could get a bicycle, and he could go with the bag, when we walked and we would reach there after him.

When I told Peter what my stranger Rwandan man said, first he had to ask me if I knew him before. I told him that I didn't know him, it was my first time to see him, when he saw the confidence I had, it made him relax, but with a big surprise, and many questions of how could I just trust him enough to give him the bag, it was his bag, but now that bag was my responsibility, and yes, for the reason I didn't know apart of culture, I trusted him anyway.

The Canadian man was under my guide, so there was nothing else he could do he had to surrender his bag, we gave it to the man, he knew the direction, what he needed was the name of the owner of the home where he was taking the bag.

We started our journey, I had to ask where we passed, but there was no problem with that, it was a good time for walking, it was not too hot, the first time before we were tired, it was enjoyable to walk when we looked at the beautiful green mountains. On our way I was asking people, according to them, it was encouragement that it was still early we would reach there, but in my heart I had some kind of doubt that we might not.

We were passing homes which looked to be clean with good permanent houses which had big farms around them with banana trees and other different types of food, so I was stopping to normal greetings before asking them directions.

And Peter anywhere we passed, stopped to talk to the people he had to remember to ask me if those people were Rwandans. And yes they were Rwandans I was telling him, what about these homes and farms, theirs too? Yes I was telling him, that was theirs I was telling him, but he was not forgetting to ask me if they were a Tutsi too, something I didn't like much, and didn't see the point of his question, but I had to give him the answer and see why he asked the question in the first place. Yes I was telling him that most of them they were a Tutsi. Questions and questions concerning those Rwandans, it seemed that the life he saw with them was not the life he had in his mind.

What surprised him more was when we came to pass where there were many cows, the cowboys were teenage handsome boys, to see that I was talking with them too, he was asking me the same questions, if those boys were Rwandans, Tutsi, and those cows were theirs. Which to all the questions the answers were, yes, yes, yes.

I came to get the shock of my life when we reached the top of the mountain, it was a beautiful mountain, good weather, a nice place and clean, where you could sit or sleep and relax if you wanted too, that was where my Canadian visitor slept there and then, he told me that he was not going to go any more steps from there! To him that was it! The reason was that he was hungry and if he did not get something to eat he could get diarrhoea!

I was hungry too, but was still strong enough to go ahead with my journey. We had nothing, everything went with the bag, we had our money with us, but nowhere there to buy anything, and I didn't know how we forgot to carry something little with us.

Now what could I do, there were no shops there nothing at all, no phone to try to get any help. And where we were there were no homes near there, I should have gone and asked for help.

I couldn't carry him, which was a joke, let alone that he was a big man and tall, even if he was a small one I wouldn't think about it. Now what next? He slept down, like to tell me that it was up to me to know what to do.

And yes it was up to me indeed. Though at that time he told me that since he saw that I could talk to everyone there, even if I could get uncooked food it would be helpful.

Then I had the idea to leave him there and go around in the distance where I saw homes and could ask for help or anything.

After a few minutes when I was still putting together what to do, I almost wanted to tell him to wait for me there, then came an old man walking slowly, showing that he had no hurry, he was just in his village and he just passed his time maybe going to friends.

When I saw him coming in my heart I knew that he was the one who was going to help us, when he reached where we were he just greeted us in a normal way, he didn't have the intention to stop, he was still going ahead as soon as I finished my response to him. I told him that I had a problem, he had his stick in his hand which most old men liked to be with anywhere they were, so he turned and looked at me when his stick was steady down and it was like it was supporting him though he was strong enough without it, it was like if to tell him that I had a problem which needed his help surprised him.

A Rwandan woman with a white man in his village, and now what kind of this problem might it be?

He was waiting to hear that problem and I told him that my visitor was too hungry. I told him where were going and that our things went before us and we left without anything, and anything could help cooked or uncooked food, so the old man was in deep thought, after a few seconds he told me that it was not easy because the home which was near was a new one, not yet to have necessary things which could help, unless to go in the distance where there was everything, otherwise yes, it was understandable that the help like that we had to get it, and I remembered to tell him that I was a stranger to that place too, just coming to visit my family.

When he said that the home was far I thought that might say that it was not easy, in a second I had a fear that he was telling me that there was nothing he was going to do at all, but he went ahead and said that unless if he went there. But soon after saying that came a group of children like between ten and thirteen years old, who were running and they even didn't have time for greetings or at last to look at the white person as many times children did when a white person was seen in any village in Africa, these children were busy and had no time to be surprised because of a white man, so our old man had to stop them and they stopped, he told them our problem and they said that it was very simple, they turned where they were coming from, again they were running, it was a car which turned to go back, they ran then in a time of maybe ten minutes or so, they came back again running with banana leaves which were on plates, and a kitchen knife and different fruits.

They prepared our fruits, we ate and left some, and then Peter asked me how much he would pay them. I knew that what they did were not for sale, but I had to ask them, to show him that it was not my judgment.

So I asked them and the question made them laugh, with questions of surprise that how could anyone ask payment for help like that to someone who was passing by! When I told him why they were laughing then he was sure that they did it in a genuine way which showed him that it was part of our culture.

They assured us that where we were going we would be there soon, they went their way, we went ours, after one hour we were there, the children of neighbours saw me and one minute many children were there and they were aware that I was on the way coming, because the man who helped us with Peter's bag was there already, something that surprised Peter and he was happy for that too. They welcomed us, since before when he was still in his home country I told him everything about their life there to decide if he would still go ahead with that programme of visiting there or not, he was prepared for what he could, he had candles, a tent... we were there for three days. I had to be with my family and Peter seemed to be happy, he was saying that to him it was a very good holiday to be somewhere quiet, no TV or electricity.

But we came on bad days because my sister-in-law Mukakabano had passed away, it was a big loss to the family, on the other hand I was lucky to be there at that time so that I could be with others in those sad days. So many people, neighbours were coming in big numbers turning to help with this and that, some thought that I knew what happened and that was why we came, Peter saw a different culture with his own culture where he came from. Of how we were together in that way when we were in sad days like that, when western people when they were in days like that, they could be happy when they were on their own, sometimes they said that they needed their space.

The time to go back came, we had to go back with Muvunangoma who had to go back in Kampala to his school, many people escorted us to the train and when we were inside the train, that was when we had our time to talk and I asked Peter how he saw my people up country where they were in a foreign land?

I told him that the way he saw them was an example of all Rwandans in neighbouring countries.

Apart of one child who he had his pictures, the boy had poor health because his grandmother was sick and couldn't take proper care of him, unless if he could choose to show that, and say that it was an example of all of them, because there were some people who enjoyed to show the bad side only. But otherwise he told me that in general

Rwandans who were outside of the country had a good life and they were rich in all ways, he started from how clean they were, to their body and their dress, and that they had good health up to their teeth, which he said that their white teeth had life, because he didn't see even one who had damaged teeth in any way, and all of those who he asked if they attended a dentist, they told him that they had never done that. They had never had a reason, and they didn't have anything to use to clean their teeth, apart from some kind of small trees from the bush.

But he came to tell me something which surprised me and made me angry with him, and all who might have that mentality to us, he told me that according to the way he saw us, we had everything and we were better than many in some of the other continents if I wanted to know. And he did not understand people like us with beautiful children like who he saw, how we could send them or themselves to go to the war when they knew very well that they would not win it! Since they were fighting with full government which had a budget and would have a lot of different support from the outside.

Since he was a Canadian man who told me that, it showed me that some white people saw us like him, to me he was meaning that because we were Rwandans or simply because we were black people, African people, we had to keep quiet and have whatever life we had no matter how life was. Because we were poor and concerning that war I saw, he was telling me that we didn't know the value of life!

I had to tell him what I thought about his view. But first I asked him by telling him a story that Rwandan President Habyarimana refused us to go back willingly, and said that the country was small. "What would you have to do if that were you?" I asked him.

The answer was, "Yes better to go ahead and be where you are as long as you have a good life, instead of your children going there to die."

I was almost talking in a harsh way but I managed to calm myself down and asked him the meaning of the picture which was in his bag.

The answer was that it was the flag of his country.

The question again was, "What does that flag mean to you and why are you going with it everywhere?" I asked him.

"Because that is my country," he said.

"Do you love your country and it seems that you might be proud of it then?"

He looked to be surprised with the question, and was like questioning me instead of answering. When he said, "What a question, of course I do," he told me with big surprise!

I had to try to tell him how I saw his view, and try to make him understand us. I told him that it was one of ignorance and it was abusing to us in general.

"Because we love our children and they didn't hate themselves either, so they know what they are doing and why, and no matter what they will win, because they are fighting for the good reason. Because we too, we love our country, and want to go everywhere with the flag of our country too. To have this and that in foreign countries doesn't matter, when we still miss important things in life for our future generation! Who else will do it for us, and when, and why not now? Because of your understanding towards us, thank you for letting me know how you think about us before I made any introduction to any R P F officers, otherwise if you told them the same things you told me, when it is me who made the introduction to them, they could ask themselves why I took someone like that to meet them in the first place!"

He saw that I was quite serious for each and everything I was saying, and he asked forgiveness by telling me that, now he understood more, the money he would buy his visa to go to Rwanda would be a contribution to buy the guns, so instead he changed, he would go to Burundi, so he asked me to let him meet an R P F officer.

In Kampala I managed to make him meet Gahima, they talked and Peter asked him which kind of help they needed, and Gahima told him that whatever he was able to give them they would be happy for it.

Back in Toro were some children he had promised to sponsor them in their studies, all of this made me happy to see that it was good to know someone who could help my people.

The time for Peter to go back to Canada came and he went,

though we went ahead with our communication, the children in Toro when they started to ask me about their support I gave them his address and told them to deal with him directly that it was not a must to pass to me. I was starting to lose trust in him concerning any of his promises, because not the children, not Gahima who was told that he would see what he could do to help our struggle and he would be in touch!

I didn't want the children to think that maybe their support came and it was me who didn't want to give it to them.

When I was asking Gahima that he had never communicated with him I felt ashamed, to see that Gahima thought that I introduced him to someone who was not serious who was capable of talking, just the matter of talking. So once I wanted to hear Gahima's view concerning Peter because I felt guilty for making that introduction. I asked him when we were talking normal stories, "But Gahima what did that Canadian man want by asking what we need when he knew that he will never do anything?" I asked him.

The answer was, "Me too I can't know what he wanted from us."

And that was how I forgot about him and with wondering why anyone could make any fake promises when he knew very well that he would never do it! Because I knew that there were people like that everywhere in different life.

R P F's head office which was in Byumba inside Rwanda, the earlier in 1993 got the idea that Rwandans in Kenya didn't have to be behind so they had to take a carder school there, which they did.

They had to plan it before, had to prepare the people who would bring things from outside, because the student had to be inside the house without going outside at all, unless for good reasons, and had to be one not in a group, they knew who had to be welcomed to take that course, which was one month, the people who took the course had to be official followers of R P F, they could be students, lecturers, officers, business people.... Only had to be who they saw was a better person to take it, according to their judgment, at that first school of its kind for Rwandans in Kenya. Students came from around the country. I was one of the chosen people, and was happy to take it.

What they were teaching us was history, leadership, human rights, philosophy, we were working many hours because we had many different lessons which we had to take, and we had time of only one month, it was a short time, so we had to work hard, but we were very happy with each and everything we were doing. That was where I came to know better about Thomas Sankara who was President of Burkina Faso.

The young man Rwandan Bakusi Alfonsi, who was sent by head office from Byumba, was a hard-working young man, we nicknamed him hard Master, he was serious but according to the high experience of the R P F work system he had, he was a good organiser. I believed that was why they chose him for that job. So we loved him and he made everyone relaxed after hard work and we liked what we were doing. We were getting different lecturers, from all steps, most of the students and lectures were holding Masters or PhD in different things.

In all students which were almost twenty, there were two women. We were not short of anything, there were people who volunteered to make shopping for us, and we were cooking for ourselves in turn. Two each time.

We were enjoying our break time, that was when we had time for different stories and you could see us laughing or dancing, and we didn't want our school to come to an end.

Our time to finish came, with the help of one of my friends who had permission to visit us from outside. I organised young children who would dance for us on our last day, in the dancers my daughter Niwegaju was included, normally she was a traditional dancer with other children, which was one of our good sources internationally, of getting money to help our soldiers. They didn't expect that there would be any entertainment, though I had to tell our hard Master to put it in the programme, but to the rest it was a surprise, and they were more than happy for that.

Our Headmaster according to his way of organising things, he told us that any student had to know how he or she did the work, he or she did, so, we too, we had the marks and how we followed between ourselves according to our knowledge and understanding.

485

At that time, I was number one.

Followers of R P F had already passed a very hard test and we were strong with a lot of confidence that we would win and we had to win our war with Rwandan government.

The hard test and bad one was when they invaded Rwanda with their commander who was loved and respected everyone knew him or heard about his hard work, equality to everyone with his braveness Gisa Fred Rwigema, after reaching there they lost him in a way which was big confusion to many.

This was a big loss to the soldiers and to all the Rwandans outside Rwanda and inside especially to followers of R P F.

It was beyond our understanding how our war would go on, if that would be a reason to fail it was something which we didn't want to think that way, we had to believe that the solution had to come out.

It shocked some, to the level of going to medication, the soldiers were almost losing control until when Paul Kagame came to rescue the war, and he was brave enough to put the soldiers together and the war went ahead in a normal way.

Some Rwandans when I asked them what they said about the death of Rwigema, they said that the last time they lost an important person to them was when they lost the King Mutara Rudahigwa.

But still it was not an easy one, since the Rwandan government had a lot of countries to come to help them, some to the front line, like Congo (Zaire), Kenya, Angola, S Africa, and France, other countries supported the Rwandan government in many different ways, though western countries they helped Habyarimana in one way or another, but didn't mean that they were losing their sleep because of Rwanda's problems, they had problems which impacted them more than African problems, problems of Yugoslavia. It was only France who had to do everything they could to see that Tutsi couldn't come back to power.

The time of our children to go to fight for their right caused many different dramas in families of followers of R P F, because it surprised and shocked many, they didn't know that their children had that plan and to those who knew they didn't know when, some they saw that their children disappeared, and those who said bye to their families, they didn't expect that their parents would be happy to see them go to fight, so they were just telling them that they were going to fight for their country, they were not asking permission, even though they had high respect for their parents, but they did not listen to some who could try to stop them.

Those who went to that war from outside and inside of Rwanda, were young Rwandans from all levels, well educated ones, doctors, lawyers, teachers, and others who had good different qualifications, students from all levels of colleges, and cowboys, in all of these levels were girls and boys, and they went in surprise ways, most of them, where they were working or where they were students, came to know that they were not with them after being missing people for some time, then when the war came to be alive with the media, that was when and how, they came to know where those people, their co-workers or friends, or loved ones were. This was something which surprised many; they had their good reason, why someone could forget his or her good position to go to the bush to fight.

There were other groups of young boys thirteen to sixteen years old, this group knew that if anyone could know that they wanted to go, no one at all could allow them to go. And they didn't want to be left behind, so those children's solution was to hide themselves and go anyway, follow the old ones. When their brothers and sisters saw them there, it surprised them, but it was too busy to take them back, and somehow they could come back again anyway, so they had to train them and give them some responsibility. They were given the name as 'kadogo', Swahili word meaning small.

Being in a country where they didn't know its geography properly, sometimes was a big problem and of course even death, when they passed where no one had to pass there, and death was there with different reasons, disease, weather when they were in mountains… and other reasons like any other wars, so we lost a big number of our young people, but we were aware of that. Since always war is war.

Outside of the front line in the whole world including inside

Rwanda, we had our uniform system to get money which would help our soldiers, though, one of the big things which helped to support R P F was fundraising. We knew that, our children, friends, sisters, and brothers went to the war, they were our responsibility, for everything, food, clothes, medicine and we had to take very good care of our girls, who were there in the bush for whatever necessary.

And followers did many different business small and big ones, to be able to reach the goal.

People who needed serious treatment had to go out of Rwanda in neighbouring countries or western countries depending what kind of treatment was needed.

But Rwandans who were in neighbouring countries to Rwanda did extra work, many times the strong young people who were left behind were carrying the food for the soldiers, and many times they would walk in those mountains, people there were killing their cows and making dried meat with other kinds of dry food for them.

Though in some areas where they were only by themselves, this was helping them to be able to do their things in their comfortable ways.

People there had big problems, because a big number who left there were only old people, and when something came up which needed strong people which normally were the young ones who had to do it, that was one of the things which showed them how that war had a big impact on them.

I saw that late in 1993 when I visited one of my friends in Uganda Nakivare Rwagikara area there was near the border to Rwanda, so it was easy to many younger Rwandans to go, and it was an area of only Rwandans. I didn't get a problem to reach there, because who I was asking were well known in that area. When I reached there my friend was not at home but there were other people who welcomed me and they told me to wait that she was not far, but they couldn't call her for me and they couldn't tell me to go there, she was in a meeting and it was a big secret, strangers were not allowed even though I was Rwandan but they didn't know me in that area.

Automatically I knew that it was R P F's meeting, and I waited, soon she came and we were happy to see each other, it was a long time since we had been together, she was there alone all her children had gone to the war, like many other Rwandan parents who all their children went to the war, sometimes they went there straight from far in other countries where they were working or in studies, and you could imagine their hearts, when parents he or she were aware that they might not get a chance to see some of their children or even might not ever see all of them again, my friend had good neighbours, they were like her family.

She took me in her house, soon when she was still asking me about my journey we heard many people talking but we didn't know where the noise came from but we came to realise that the people who were talking they were not far from her house.

We had to go out to see what was happening, outside were many people like more than twenty were old men and women with small children, and they were near her house, so we went to see why they were there. There was a cow which had fallen in the deep hole which seemed to be there for a long time without knowing it because the grasses had covered it, and they said that even a child or a grown-up person could fall in. Tutsi people being cow lovers, were in deep confusion and looked to be very sad to see how the poor cow was struggling. So they had to try anything to see that they could save it, but the entire trick they tried was not successful because out of all of them no one was strong enough to help the cow.

There came a child of fourteen years old and he went inside the hole to put some ropes on the cow so that they could pull it up, but that was not successful either.

Then I told them, "Why can't you get a strong young person can't you see that out of all of us here there is no one who can be able to do this?"

All of them they looked at me their eyes telling me that yes you are a stranger indeed, and you don't know the life we have these days, life as Rwandan parents here. Maybe they saw that I didn't know at all what was going on about the Rwandan struggle in general, and they didn't know what to tell me and they didn't want to keep quiet, because it was not polite, so they had to tell me something.

One of the old men told me, "My child these days we don't have young people with us, the way you see us here is us, even if we lost someone it is only us who have to take care of everything!" He was too sad when he told me that and I blamed myself for what I said because that time was when I remembered that we had war, and I was on the border of Rwanda. I was ashamed to ask a question like that. I had to know what was going on concerning young Rwandans something which was known internationally at the time, but yes I knew and I was in that struggle myself in other ways, though in Nairobi we didn't have that effect because we were not in big numbers like Nakivare or other parts bordering Rwanda.

They came to remember one young man who was in the area, he came for some reason from the front, and he was the one who came to help.

From there I had to go to Toro Kamwezi to visit my father who was with my brother Rusingizandekwe and his family after moving from Tanzania.

When I was there for two days, their neighbour's daughter was sick for some time according to their story, had passed way, and left behind her child of four years old, and they told me that she died of AIDS, meaning that the parents at that time, lost their children on the front line and when back home they lost others from AIDS.

The next day was the day of the burial, so to that ceremony, the people I saw, were the same as Nakivare, there came old people and the women had to help, something which before was not allowed, to bury the dead, before that was the men's job, but that time I kept quiet, there was no question like what I asked in Nakivare. I knew why. I only seeing that old people there on that sad day how they had a lot in their hearts.

Inside Rwanda, there was a different effect, to some Tutsi women who were married to Hutu men, it was not happy for their relatives who came from outside, they saw R P F to be their enemy who fought their husbands and made their home be upside down. Some of their husbands were killed or were in prisons, so they were upset like some of their sisters who married Acholi and Langi in Uganda

And some of the Tutsi who were inside Rwanda after genocide, some of them saw their relatives who came from outside that there was nothing else they wanted, apart from their property. Some relatives when you asked them how he or she survived genocide, then the person saw that to ask that question was because you would be happy if no one was left behind, so that you could be free to have everything they left behind. And say that before that they had a happy life, meaning that it was them who caused misery, so they had to be where they were and kept quiet!

And to the side of those who came from outside, when they saw the Tutsi who survived genocide, some of them they had no trust in them, on the other hand they were wondering how they managed to survive, and judged them that they survived just because they helped Hutu to kill relatives, and yes some few did, when they were told that by helping them to kill their relatives they were not going to kill them or their families, when sometimes that was not true. After forcing them or lying to them and making them kill their people, they were killing them and their families too. There were just a few who survived because of that, though, also the Tutsi who had such problems to be forced to kill their people were a small number because most of them who were forced to do that they refused and they were killed there and then.

And these people who came from outside from different countries, they had no unity between themselves too, as how they were supposed to be, they nicknamed themselves names, which were the names to be able to know where so and so came from.

Like:

'Abatizedi' when they meant those who came from Tanzania.

'Dubai' when they meany those who came from Congo (Zaire).

'Basaija' when they meant those who came from Uganda.

'Abajepe' when they meant those who came from Burundi.

'Abasopecya' when they meant those who were in Rwanda, survivors of genocide.

And they were doing things in groups concerning where they came from, sometimes they were fighting because of the property like houses, things which they was called 'kubohoza' and **sometimes** there were even some cases of killings between themselves.

So that was another problem the government had to deal with, and the government managed to solve all of that and put them together.

Genocide which happened in Rwanda in 1994 had a lot of similarity to Jewish in the Second World War in the 1940s.

LAST PART

TESTIMONIES

Genocide has been there always even though some went beyond people's imagination. For example genocide made during slavery on black people has become so difficult for any writer to describe. In fact Ku Klux Klan came to the conclusion that. What westerners did between 1882-1930 no one knows exactly the numbers of black people who were killed. It was only the supreme court who said on what was known as cruel Joke on Black that black people who were killed might be ninety-four percent. (*Klan: Lutla Feb, 2008*)

Despite these atrocities, Red Indians native of America were killed as well as if all of us were not created by the same God in his image. Instead of being a sad history, some people such as Christopher Columbus made it easy. In his own words: 'to govern these people you have to do it as it pleases. Make them work to death in mines and plantations. Do not fear them because thousands of black people can be led by three white people. They are strong but they do not have weapons, therefore, they are easy to use as anyone wish.'

This understanding made black people, especially women and little girls, to be in slow death, as they were raped at any time and when the masters wanted. Moreover, they were forcing black men who were strong to rape young girls as a way of having strong children. What was wrong and a bad experience for girls was to force a man of forty years old to rape a child of ten years old until when she would be pregnant. Once pregnant she was left alone until she delivered, because the guy was given another girl. Therefore, many girls suffered post-natal trauma and depression, which resulted in death and no one cared.

It is true that the Atlantic slave trade had a positive impact on the US but, there are no words or expression that can describe the effects it had on African and its people. For instance it is estimated that between 1450-1900 there were at least 11,698,000 slaves exported from Africa. (*Atlantic slave Trade P.170 Hasp nick American Historical review-82.1 2002*)

This number does not include many who died during the capture or during the travel towards the port of departure. Many more died and were thrown into the ocean as they could not eat or drink properly. No one will ever know for sure how many died and were thrown into the ocean.

In conclusion, the Atlantic slave trade was a dominant factor in the market sector and has boosted western economy even though it was built by people's blood. This kind of greed has been a way of not bringing the main power from Africa only but, other weak western countries could be used as well. This led the west into the First World War in 1919. It is after this war that the U.N. was created as a way of having a peace maker and for the safety of everybody and every country.

Are we going to have a population of one million blacks in the commonwealth or are we going to merge them into our white community and eventually forget that there were ever any Aborigines in Australia? (AO Neville in First Australians page: 264 Edited by Rachel Perkins with Wayne Ackinson)

We have driven the black fellow away from the water, we have denied him the right to secure game, from all fertile land he is prohibited, and generally speaking there is less care for him than for a horse or beast. If he rebelled (which in the natural order of things he would) he has been met without hesitation by powder and shot. (From First Australians page: 214-215)

WHY AND WHEN
U.N. STARTED?

It was in 1919 after World War I, an organisation called the League of Nations was conceived for all countries wishing to join and the aim was to achieve safety and peace. Unfortunately it failed to prevent World War II. Therefore, there was no need of its existence. After World War II another similar organisation was created, and was given a name of United Nations (U.N.), but had the same name, objectives as the previous. On June 26th 1945 an agreement of creating the U.N. was signed by representatives of fifty countries.

Since the U.N. was created, more than fifty-two million people have died because of war. The former secretary of the U.N. Koffi Annan said that: 'we feel agony of knowing that our countries lost so many of its Jewish citizens.'

More than ten countries have nuclear weapons, from highs of 65,000 active weapons in 1985, there were about 20,000 active nuclear weapons in the world in 2002, many of the decommissioned weapons were simply stored or partly dismantled not destroyed. As of 2007, the total number was expected to continue to decline by thirty to fifty percent over the next decade. (*Wikipedia, the free Encyclopedia*) However, until now, nuclear power keeps going up and no one knows if it will destroy our world as it has been a threat in Japan after the events of the Tsunami. Now it is said that this can be the result that some people are already dying in Germany as the vegetables have been contaminated. The same is now starting to affect Britain. Indeed, 'Anti-Nuclear campaigners argue the government to abandon Britain's commitment to the nuclear programme after Germany announced it is to shut down all its reactors by 2022'. (*Metro: 2011, May 31*) In case this happens it will be a good beginning for others to follow in order to save our world from a sure disaster.

Genocide has been always there and I don't see what will stop other genocides to happen in our planet. Since the U.N. started it has never stopped any war or intervened on time, whenever there has been a war. Each time, you may think that the U.N. arranges how people will be killed, and how the country will be given the leader from those they will choose for them.

The example of Bosnia Herzegovina (1992-1995) is still fresh in many memories. In fact, the massacre started on 11th July 1995 while the U.N. troops protecting Serbia during three years siege stepped aside, allowing the genocide fascists aggressor to take over staged a final week of mass murder. (*Bosnia News Daily Top News from Bosnia, Friday 11th November 2008*)

The U.N. existed when the Khmer Rouge killed around 1.7 million people, a quarter of the South East Asian nation's population at the time. (*A question of Genocide in Orbadiah: According to Southeast Asia July 26-2007*) The Armenia of World War I is sometimes called the forgotten Holocaust since; it happened some ninety years ago. One asked how you would react if I claimed that Serbian's ethnic cleansing is imagination. Would you be outraged, if I told you that I could prove the Holocaust never happened? You would probably point to all the evidence, and say that my statements are utter nonsense. (*The Armenia Genocide Guest Colum by Armewn Vartinia*)

What I would like to show in some genocide has been committed before the creation of the U.N. and after it was reinstated. Nowadays, the U.N. has more than 200 countries that are members. I am not sure that these countries will be able to stop genocide unless they deal with the root that causes genocide that is mainly greed and power.

There is no genocide that is good. Those who have been killed died an atrocious death, and those who remained have unforgettably traumatic lives, which will never be healed. Sometimes they overlook what happened in order to survive. It is Aline Umugwaneza in her book called: *From Tragedy to Triumph* who said that:

I accepted Jesus in the month of December 1994. I was going through so much at that time. I have confessed to him with My mouth, but I did not let him reign into my heart as Lord and Savior of my life. I was filled with bitterness and unforgiveness in my heart, due to emotional wounds. (Aline, 2008, 69)

Indeed, many people live with those kinds of wounds without any hope at all of recovery. Not many people can be as brave as Umugwaneza. In case the U.N. can't stop genocide or intervene in time and save lives, no one will ever believe in it. If whenever the U.N. goes for peace-keeping, things become worse instead of stopping war, it looks like as if they make everything possible so that the war may last longer in order to get paid for being there. Then there is no need of having just the big name of the U.N. Moreover, because of its hidden 'interest' they overlook people dying, in order to reach their goals, instead of the local interest, then no hope in the U.N. As a matter of fact, the U.N. is a big looter and seller of illegal guns. During Saddam Hussein regime, the embargo was taken against Iraq. However, Saddam sold more oil than when the embargo was not there. Sada George who was working for many years in Saddam's army says that:

After a dozen years of sanctions, the Iraqi people became experts at how to work the system. Millions of tons of oil went through the Persian Gulf under the noses of the U.N. and multinational forces. There were days where dozens of barges loaded with contrabands would sail out of our port. And each one was carrying anywhere from 1,500 to 2000 tons of oil. Because of the restriction on oil Saddam had to sell it very cheaply. But because of the volume of contraband going out, the profits were enormous... I can say without reservation that the sanctions imposed on Iraq by the United Nations were one hundred percent failure. They had a disastrous effect on the people of Iraq and absolutely no effect on Saddam
(Sada: 2006, 207)

Recently, BBC *Panorama* has shown how the U.N. is involved in looting in D R Congo while natives are being cleansed purposely. The way things are looking they will end up by giving Congo to those they wish to. My view is most of the blood that is being shed worldwide is the U.N.'s responsibility, as it allows stupid wars to happen or to carry on unnecessarily. Genocide happens because people differ in their thinking and philosophy as far as leadership is concerned. Others prepare and carry on genocide because they want to make a name no matter whose neck they step on. It is true that people diverge in their thinking but there are those who enjoy being racist, others don't enjoy peace of others. Even if all people around talk about what is wrong, these kinds of people don't care as long as they reach their goals. Most of the time the goals are wrong and out of human understanding, they prefer to sacrifice human beings by killing those who diverge with them. The essential for them even if they have to die, they believe that they have made history and people will remember them. In case no one writes about them they create bad things, so that they may be on major newspapers.

We can name in these categories people like Hitler or George W. Bush. Bush was able to go in Iraq to destroy that country and kill uncountable innocent people. Before starting the war in Iraq, many people in the USA and elsewhere around the world, were against the war. This is because all the motives given in order to invade Iraq were wrong or non-existent. For instance, he accused Saddam of having nuclear weapons and being an undemocratic leader. By removing him, George W. Bush will save the world and will restore peace and democracy in the Arab world. All these reasons were false as no nuclear weapons were found in Iraq, and he was never associated with Osama Bin Laden. The real reasons were in Bush's mind as he wanted to achieve what his father started and to try new weapons, looting Iraq and controlling Arabs. Those who were associated with this war without believing any word of Bush went just for the interest of oil.

While in Kenya Nairobi on 11 April 2003, I had an interview with BBC Swahili Service in its headquarters in Bush House, London, through the phone, concerning the war in Iraq. I said that it is wrong to start a war as a way of teaching democracy. If someone wants to help people he can do that by helping them to go a step ahead, rather than imposing through war as we are living in a modern era and civilized world. War will never teach, but will destroy and people are going to die. War has to have a very good reason, not only the show of power and greed. I told the BBC that he is going for his economic purpose and power, but the consequence of the war will be to divide Iraqi people, and no one will be able to number civilian victims as the war will take too long as the Iraqi people will not be defeated easily, and Iraq will take years and years to be normal again if that time will come.

People who have no mercy will be born always; therefore, there will be genocide always. Today, my prediction before that war seems right because according to Abdul Rahman Munif and Abu Abbas each day at least forty people die in Iraq and on the top there is no democracy. (*Wikipedia: 2004, March 8th*) Moreover, people are more divided than ever and many Iraq people confess that better the rule of Saddam Hussein than the western reign. What is so sad is the Iraqi's infrastructures that are being destroyed easily and yet to rebuild and to reach the level they have reached will take years. Moreover, in order to rebuild the trust among different ethnic groups in Iraq and have good relationships it will take at least one hundred years or will never happen again.

That is why Jan Eliasson who is Deputy Secretary-General of the United Nations said that: 'what is happening in Iraq is beyond human imagination, and people should never allow such things to happen again'. That has prompted the word to say 'never again'. This signified that the past crimes will never happen again as it will be prevented in the future.

Rwandan genocide has been like any other genocide that happened in our world, as people were killed and others bear the wound that will never get healed. The only difference is that Rwandans' genocide took a very short time to kill such a mass of people, even though no one will ever know for sure how many victims were killed. Some think that less than a million were killed, while others said that one to two million were killed. Indeed, no one counted those who were thrown in the toilets or river. To be honest people just keep guessing. There are villages that all the people were swept away, even the killers moved away as they were afraid of the bush growing as no one could work in the gardens. For instance, no one knows how many people lived in the villages, except that Rwanda was among the country that was super populated. Philip Gourevitch in the introduction to his book says that the dead of Rwanda accumulated at nearly three times the rate of Jewish dead during the Holocaust. It was the most efficient mass killing since the bombings of Hiroshima and Nagasaki. *We wish to inform you that tomorrow we will be killed with our families. (2000 by Philip Gourevitch)* Accumulated we can confirm that Rwanda genocide differed to others in two ways. First of all, it was the first genocide that happened in an African continent, since no other African country knew genocide before. Secondly, this will be the first African country to take a European country to the International Justice court, in The Hague, if French government will not bend to Rwandan government.

I am aware that genocide is happening in Sudan, but no one has the courage of accusing those who perpetuate the massacre. In fact, we have witnessed in our own days a categorised indifference in action that took us down the unspeakable genocide in Rwanda. This is because that genocide was preventable; no one can say that we did not know. Now in Darfur more than 450,000 Darfuri have in this genocide attraction. The media have been repeating this for months now years. Those 2,000,000 have died, but the recent evidence of 450,000 that are dying is not comprehensive. This is because those who are writing are not writing as a matter of abstract statistics, behind it is a real human being with a name, a family and identity. As the student posts continue to cry out to save Darfur rallies: if not us who, if not now when? *(Jerusalem Post-opinion.jipost.com)* Meltdown in Darfur – what happened to 'never again'?

Since for many years, millions of people are dying because of unnecessary wars brought up by greedy people. Yet we have enough to satisfy everybody on this earth, if the wealth of the world is well shared. However, some people who benefit from chaos will always be there. They enjoy inequality of people and greediness; they create wars in order to sell guns, no matter if the result is genocide. In addition, they do not care about those who die with hunger, sicknesses, and stress and so on. People keep rebuilding from zero what the war destroyed, just because those who start war would like to show how powerful they are, while their ambition is to recolonise others physically, psychologically or economically. Even those who try to rebuild again have no assurance of not being attacked again, therefore, good projects are kept in cupboards waiting for when there will be real peace.

I disagree with Gerald Prunier in what he wrote in his book: *The Rwanda Crisis*. For instance, he says that: 'One of the reasons the Rwandan genocide of 1994 happened, is the lack of enough land to share'. The size of the country can't cause genocide at this modern time, we still have other small countries around the world with big number of their population but they don't kill each other as chicken. For example, Prunier's country is small and has many people and two ethnic rivals, (Walloon and Flammand), but they do not kill each other let alone genocide. The real reason was one among the political propaganda used by Hutu with their masters while planning the genocide. When we met General James Kabarebe, he told us that while at Arusha in Rwandan conference, the Hutu general Bagosora told Kabarebe who is a Tutsi that, no Tutsi will step again in Rwanda before 1000 years. General Kabarebe responded that, the Arusha talk will stop then, the only language of gun will talk, and for the moment we are at Byumba already, which is inside Rwanda, we know that we will never go out of Rwanda again the way we went out in 1959.

The Canadian General, Romeo Dallaire, who was in charge of U.N. peacemakers in Rwanda, was close to them. Even if he did not understand what was going on, he saw that they were angry and ready to fight, then, he went between them. General Kabarebe told him that for us, (R P F), we were against people thinking like you and all other ideologies that exclude others. We do no not want such Rwanda. According to Kabarebe, once the genocide started, he remembered what Bagosora told him, then, he understood that Tutsi who were living in Rwanda at that time, to Bagosora were seen as if they were not alive, as they were already on the plan of being killed, therefore, to Bagosora and his people, they were dead, and no other Tutsi who would come in Rwanda until maybe after 1000 years ahead. He carried on telling us that: "It is not necessary to read books in order to know Rwanda and its history. I talk to my people and those who write get stories from us and our elders too. Even though sometimes they write what they want to write and interpret what they their mind wants."

Moreover, our ancestors did not write as they had never been to any school but they were very brainy and able to store information in their minds. They didn't have much to worry about in their lives. I think that is why they lived so long and remembered details of things they had heard and seen. It was easy for them to transmit information as it happened or how they were told. Once an elder died in Africa, it was a whole library that was destroyed. Indeed, sitting with any elder was the best way of writing a book as they spoke historical facts with accuracy. Sometimes I write things told by my grandma or my dad, concerning my country and my people. Most of the time westerners can ask me for the evidence. Surprisingly, the evidence asked for is from the books written by foreigners even though they have never been to Rwanda. Whatever stories they write it is something other Rwandans told them. As far as I am concerned I write as an evidence myself because I am Rwandan who writes what I lived and what was transmitted by relatives and elders.

I think when they had the plan of making Rwanda genocide, to be able to manage without much problem. It will be easy to set each other just using the problem of little **space**. Next, they made Congo bigger as they needed their wealth that was plenty in that country. Without fearing anything or any shame, they named an African country 'Belgian Congo'. They knew that maybe the genocide would not happen in the near future, but it did not matter as they knew that they would not leave Africa before many years, if it would happen. They felt that Rwanda would become their **toy**. It is Gerald Prunier who wrote that, Rwanda and Belgium were the same size, and the last Belgian vice governor general, complained that the U.N. was short sighted when it forbade physical punishment after his visit. Yet I am sure that the use of physical punishment 'Ikiboko' was the major source of enmity between Tutsi and Hutu in 1920. There is nothing that shows that the U.N. has intervened anywhere before people died and lost their wealth and belongings.

As said, Belgium made everyone who was poor a Hutu but during the killing they did not check who was poor or not, they killed according to what someone looked like. We were surprised to see some we knew as Hutu, being killed by their neighbours as they knew their origins. It was true that when they were killing, they were given drugs and alcohol in order to kill under drunken effect. However, no one ignores that when they were planning they were not drunk. Even when they were given guns and were learning their use they were not drunk, and that makes me believe that whatever they did came out of their clear conscience. Especially the planners. The most terrific act was to teach people that any Tutsi and anyone born through mixed race should die, so that Hutu who will bear after will be asking: what a Tutsi looked like? And those in need of knowing Tutsi could read history books and see them in pictures. It is true that many people died during genocide, but what is so disappointing is the way they were killed after a lot of mockery. Those who were lucky were shot. According to some who survived, ladies were begging those who were assigned to kill them in a good way. Then, the killers were laughing saying that, "Tutsi you are used to living a good life, even when you are dying you still want to die in a good way! We will not shoot you as you must die slowly in order to know what suffering is."

Such is a case of a lady who used to live in the region of Butare in the area of Matyazo named Tamasha, she had been opening pregnant women using a knife. She had an objective of knowing weather Tutsi babies had the normal position as other children, according to survivors, as if she had opened others before! Those who were not pregnant she used to cut their breast while they were alive! Another man living in the same area, named Ruben, made his name as a special killer. He never used his machete twice in a person. Just one machete used to separate the head from the neck, and the people had been applauding him. Those are just some among many examples that normal people could not do but it happened in Rwanda to the level that some babies were crushed alive!

There had been two single sisters who were neighbours of Ruben. Everyone did not want to kill them because they were nice people and used to get on with all their neighbours. One of them had a child of six month only, so, Ruben went in their house and killed both of them. As he killed them, the child was smiling to him. This image troubled him and he became like a fool as he went running out of the house. After three metres people saw him going back in the house running. When he looked at the child once more, the child smiled to him and opened his small arm as if he was inviting him to carry him. He took the child, ran away and threw him in the toilet! When he went to join his team, they asked him what he did in that house as they saw him running as a mad person. He explained how he killed the ladies, but failed to kill the child as he was smiling at him. Others said that they will have to help that child because the ladies were so nice. He told them that he had already thrown him in the toilet! Since then, everyone who saw him had been saying that he became mad as he said that the image of a child smiling to him keeps haunting him.

When you talk to survivors you realise that what happened in Rwanda genocide was beyond understanding of a normal person. Normally ladies were known as kind and merciful people, but in Rwanda women became killers, to the level of some killed their own children, in case they were mixed between Hutu and Tutsi.

Women were involved as well in genocide when we knew that women normally had mercy. One of the examples given by those who were living in Kaduha is that, a teacher at the school of Nursing of Kaduha is from Cyangugu, when this girl arrived near the hospital, she quickly jumped over the gate of the hospital to get into the compound. She didn't even wait for the gate to be opened. You can see the enthusiasm this girl had for finishing off these sick Tutsis! She had a machete and went into the hospital with the other killers. She made all the sick Tutsi go outside. Then, they killed them with a strike from the machete. However, there was a Burundian Priest called Nyandwi who was in charge of the parish of Kaduha. He was selling refugees foods instead of helping those in need. He is the one together with Interahamwe from Gitarama who killed people who were in the Parish after ten days after the genocide started.

Hatred had made them kill even those who fled with them and yet both were refugees. They began by killing all ladies who were not Hutu, most of the times their wives, mothers or step-mothers. Then, they turned against anyone who looked like a Tutsi meaning they started killing their own children who were mixed race. The reason being: since they had Tutsi blood, they couldn't be trusted. Moreover, when they grew up, they might want revenge for what happed to their mothers.

I wanted to see by myself what happened to my people back home, I knew that was satisfaction of plans from the beginning.

'If you were using one of your own to hunt down, you couldn't get a better weapon than that.'

(By Berg, Founder, Koori Heritage Trust. Gunditjamara Nation in First Australians page: 133)

In 1996 I went to Rwanda having in mind to talk personally with those who escaped genocide. For this I got help from my relatives who were survivors, like Mwavita Imerance Nyiramashashi, Gasengayire Solange and others including Hoziana choir in Kigali where Mwavita were a member, who took me to Bisesero. There were those who were happy to talk about what happened to them during genocide. Others refused to talk saying that there was no need to talk about their miseries, it is a matter of the past and talking about it will never change anything in their lives. No one was going to give them back what they lost. Still others would not talk, as they thought that the interview is involved in a big business, therefore, without giving them money, they chose to keep quiet. However, most of those I met, felt discharged as they felt that I was concerned, as from time to time I was crying. True enough, when you talk to people who have problems, they discharge their burden on you, which gives them peace of mind and rest, since before they thought that no one could understand what they went through. What I have seen among those who escaped genocide, is that: to recall what they faced was so painful to the level no one was willing to talk without taking a deep breath. Others could not talk as they felt that it was like living the event anew.

Gasengayire Solange the girl who was in the roof of Hutu family for three months, with her sister-in-law and her baby cousin, she refused revenge, soon after the war was over, when they took her where used to be her home with her family, what welcomed her was only the bad smell of her relatives' bodies. She knew that they were killed by Hutus, but she was saved by Hutu.

That is confusion of Rwandans and their unity. And that is how it starts to be able to manage to try reconciliation.

DAVID KARASIRA
AT KIGALI

Karasira used to work with the Red Cross of Rwanda. He said that he will help NGO's companies concerning some of the cars taken by force, if they chose to defend their case in court. For instance, NGO's cars were used for killing innocents. Indeed, killers took cars by force pretending that they were going to help those in need. Those who were hidden used to come running believing that they will be helped. Unfortunately, they were killed without mercy. That is why some among those who escaped accused some NGOs of helping the killers. But what I am sure of is that NGOs knew the planning of genocide a long time ago before it happened. As a matter of fact, in January 1994 a young girl who was a colleague, from one of the western countries, brought a big stick, and showed it to me. The shape of it was round and big at its end with nails at that ending. She asked me if I knew this stick I responded that I knew the kind of stick, but not having nails. She told me to watch out because this kind of stick will do unthinkable things. I asked her what she meant, but she did not care to answer. The only thing she said was, "I am already resigned as I am going back home."

"Why do you have to resign?" I asked.

"You will see," she said. I thought that she feared the war between R P F and the Government, or she thought that the situation would become worse. She did not explain properly and I did not care, because I knew that R P F would conquer the country. I had never thought about any genocide. I believed that R P F went to war knowing what was awaiting them, therefore, they have prepared in consequence. I knew for sure that they would not make the same mistakes that Tutsi made in the sixties, when Inyenzi were defeated by Rwandan Government.

The other event that I witnessed before genocide was when I went to the clinic. The responsible of our clinic was a western lady. One morning she was making rooms in some stores. I asked her what she was doing; she told me seriously that she was making rooms for wounded people to come! "Where will they come from?" I did ask, but she walked out as if she did not hear my question. I concluded that western feared as they could see that R P F would soon be in control. When genocide happened I recalled all the memories about my conversations with my western colleagues and knew that NGOs and western countries in general were deeply involved in one way or another and I realised what they were telling me. Indeed, they had more details about genocide before it happened. And I can believe that if our country had oil by now we could have a different story.

Even though we believed that R P F would take over, most of Tutsi living in Rwanda at the time, had secret relatives fighting on R P F side, and therefore a big percentage knew what was going on, but there were some few Tutsi who knew nothing at all but used to follow what they heard on R P F's Radio Muhabura or a very little number who just followed Radio Rwanda only.

And most of us who were outside of our country, we knew that R P F had tried to come back peacefully, but the President Habyarimana refused. We were happy to go back where we came from, and at least be home, and others were keen to be content with getting the nationality of the place where they were living. They were happy to have just the right of their country. However, most of us had suffered as refugees, thus we never digested the fact of living outside of our country. As far as I am concerned I think people who go to war with a real justification I support them, and I believe that they always win. Indeed, looking at R P F's motivation and the reason advanced I knew for sure that even though the Rwandan government would get friends to help them, they would be defeated.

VIRGINIA NYINAWABEGA KANYAMIGANDA

I talked with Virginia when I was in Butare at her sister's home. Virginia was originally from the district of Butare in the region of Ruhashya village Kirwa, she told me that her mother had advised all the children to be separated while running away or hiding from Hutu killers. She felt that if they remained together they would get killed together, but by being separated, they would stand a chance to have some who would escape death.

We had chosen this option and we separated in order to survive. I went to hide during the night to our neighbour who was a Hutu lady and I thought that she was too old, hoping that she would not be able to kill people. Moreover, she had been a friend of our family for a long time. When I came, her house was wide open. When she saw me, she became very surprised. She asked me, are you still alive? Yes I answered. Do you know if some of your relatives survived? I don't know any news, I said. Run quickly under my bed before anyone sees you and kills you, she told me. I had spent four days and nights under her bed.

She used to feed me under the bed, during the night she used to wake up and ask me if I needed any toilet, in case I needed one, she would go first of all out and check if there was no one around, then she would take me out. The fourth day I heard many people talking and was near her house, I began to pray as I thought that they knew that I was in the house, the only question was how they knew that I was there as the old lady had never gone out since I came in her house. At that time no one could be trusted one hundred percent.

They were inside and began to tell her what they did during the week. As they did not mention about me, I became calm, knowing that they did not know anything about me. However they reported that: we found those girls of your neighbours Bidabali and Kanyamiganda. We killed some who wanted to run away, but the rest of them and their mothers were brought together. Then, we made them naked and each one of us began to rape them. When we finished, we began to beat them and finished by burning them. The old lady broke her silence by asking them if they burned them while alive! Of course, they said! They were so evil that no one among them did cry or ask for forgiveness, they were like dead trees. Probably they told her as she was too old and could not follow them in the field, and see what was happening or help them. We did not find one, at that point they mentioned my name, maybe she was killed somewhere else. I felt my heart fainting as I said in myself that she was going to tell them that I was under her bed. She did not say anything.

The group went on telling her stories of how they killed in detail how they killed families including mine, my uncle's family and others. Do you know that our girls are beautiful as well like Tutsis? After making them naked we told our children to dress in their clothes and they became beautiful and shiny, you can't believe. They were proud of telling these stories and were laughing from time to time. They finished their stories by saying that: when they were exhausted and no one else wanted to rape them again, then, we began to kill them as they could not run away but we buried them in order to make sure they were dead. The more I heard them talking, the more I felt that she would make me be killed, but still she did not tell them about me. They went out, she told me to be ready and go out when it was dark, and I do not want you to be killed in my house she said. I went out and did not enter any other house. In my mind I wanted to reach Butare as one of my sisters was married to a Congo man, and I believed that she would not be killed. I used to walk during the night and had to be very careful, sometimes I had to sit down in case I felt that someone had seen me or the bush was moving. I used to go in the people's garden at night hoping to find anything to eat. I did not know how many days or night I had spent in the bush, as I lost the concept of time and the lack of listening to any radio. I did not know that R P F took over the power, as I kept living in the bush. When I reached Butare I waited in a bush until it was dark despite people talking and laughing. I was too traumatised.

When R P F stopped the genocide, it reminded me the history of Rwandan war at the end of 1880s. During that period Rwanda had the army feared by neighbouring countries. The motto used was that: 'Rwanda invades other countries but can't be invaded'. When Bushubi was in trouble, (now Tanzania), they asked King Rwabugili help, he did send soldiers to settle matters using five battalions Nyaruguru, Inyange, Abarasa, Abahanika and Uruyange under the command of Seruzamba son of Kinani grandson to Biraboneye from Baryinyonza.

The problem was that two sons of King Kibogora were fighting for power. As Rwabigamba wanted to take over the kingdom by force, when it was known that the kingdom was given to Nsoro. Rwandan soldiers came back after a while, even though few remained there for security purposes of the king. This kind of fighting did not happen once, you could say that Rwanda was the peace maker in that area at the time.

Another typical example was the King Ntare of Ankole in Uganda, had started fighting hoping that he would conquer Rwanda because they had guns from western countries. One Rwandan who was a refugee in Ankole and friend to King Ntare told the King of Ankole, not to fight Rwanda as they had a tough army. King Ntare refused to stop the war because he knew that Rwanda didn't have guns. It did not take too long before guns were quiet. Joyfully the King Ntare asked Kinyamakara a Rwandan friend saying: I can't hear any shootings of guns, do you think all Rwandans are already dead? No Sir, he answered, I think it is wise to take children and your wives out of the palace before they get killed when Rwandans catch you. In my view those who were shooting were no longer living because Rwandans never failed. Indeed, it happened, at that time Rwandan soldiers went far, up to Masaka seventy-four miles to Kampala. That war happened more than one hundred years ago, but Ugandans are still talking about it, (a true story from my elders).

It is known that the Rwandan Army used to hide themselves in their style and could take adversaries by surprise and they had good spies. That is one of the reasons why they were able to defeat enemies even when some had been using guns. Until now at this modern time, it was known that Rwandans were good in work of spies, and in general they had a good army respected internationally, and no one knew how they fight. Indeed, many Africans know that Angolan soldiers were good fighters, who have a lot of experiences as they fought several years. However, when they fought with Rwandans, they were defeated, and most of their heavy guns and cars were taken by Rwandan army to carry sick soldiers and supply to others. R P F almost captured more than thirty big heavy weapons and guns, but before going back home, after finishing that area, they burned all weapons they captured from their enemy so that the enemy couldn't use them.

There was a time when the enemy tried to burn the airport which the R P F captured in Angola, so that everything in it could be destroyed by fire at that point could kill many of them too. So, they had thrown a tank full of petrol and then they tried to shoot the tank the missile sent did not touch the tank nor explode. Instead, this helped R P F to have enough petrol to use. Among aeroplanes that fought them, they had been one helicopter that they had been able to shoot. It belonged to the Zimbabwean Government, as they were helping Congo. This helicopter had rank officers who died, but Zimbabwe did not claim or ask for the remains of their people. All foreigners agreed to leave Congo, but war was not yet over. There were parts of that country where the war was still tough. Places such as Kabalo and Pepa in Katanga where many soldiers died, but Pweto was the most tough and the last war in Congo at the time. As Rwanda could not finish the war, it was necessary to have negotiation as South Africa was advised to drop guns. Angola was helping Kabila as an old communist friend, but Rwandans defeated them like other countries which came to help Congo. In fact, they had many heavy arms but before reaching Kinshasa, R P F had already taken more than thirty percent of their heavy weapons and many guns. Then the last aeroplane that took back home R P F commanders was the one that took James Kabarebe and Alex Kagame. All stories concerning what happened in front line war were told to me by a fighter who was involved directly but did not want his name to be mentioned.

EMMERENCE MWAVITA NYIRAMASHASHI KIGALI

She was newly married and had a newborn baby. They were hidden in one of their friend's houses together with two other families, when killers came; they said that they will kill all men except the owner of the house because he was a Hutu. He told them that you know all of us here and you know that we are not Hutu not Tutsi, but children of God as we are saved. If you have to kill, kill all of us together. Therefore, they took them and they were killed. The rest of the women and their children left from that house as they believed that they would come back for them. While running, hot porridge spilt on Mwavita's leg. The fear took over to the level she did not even check she was telling others that she was shot in the leg. Other ladies asked how it happened as she did not fall down. She replied that she only felt the bullet entering her leg as it was so hot but now it was hurting. When she wanted to give the child her porridge then she discovered that it was the porridge that burned her leg instead of being shot. After, this became one of the jokes that used to remind that horrible moment. Fortunately, R P F took them to Byumba until the war was over. What is sad is that she was very disappointed so that she refused to marry as she did not believe to have someone who would love her the way Lambert Bitanuzire did. Moreover, she was not sure that somebody would love her child Louange Bitanuzire Igihozo; like her father did in the short time he had her. This child would like to be a peace-maker, as she said, I don't wish to see any child growing without having a father or relatives just because of the war.

Even though Hutu killed Tutsi in that horrible manner, there were some Hutu who did hide Tutsi, by God's grace, a big number of them survived. They felt too bad when people said that all Hutu were killers.

This is the case of a Catholic priest; a Hutu called Celestin Hakizimana who managed to protect many Tutsis from the killers in the church Saint Famille Kigali, (Holy family). I was told about him by some survivors, saying that he saved their lives. When a Father Wenceslas Munyeshyaka whose Mother was a Tutsi and father was Hutu, was busy around there with selections of Tutsi refugees who had to be murdered and to rape many young women when he gave away their brothers to be killed. I tried to get him and talk to him as a matter of curiosity. He looked to be calm and had confidence, and looked to be simple. He told me that he was lucky not to be killed. When asked why he did risk his life, he said that he does not believe that human beings should take the life of others just because they do not share ethnicity or any other reason. Moreover, during 1959 when Tutsi were killed, I saw my dad hiding many Tutsi, he said, at the end they became good friends. It is good in life to think that you have saved people, instead of walking with guilt of being a killer. I did ask him about the accusation against the Catholic Church being involved in genocide, he answered that each one should be responsible of his or her acts. Concerning western religions that removed traditional religions, he said that it was a mistake because they could modernise traditional religions instead of banning them. I asked him when you hear Tutsi saying that all Hutu are killers, how do you feel?

"It hurts," he said.

"It makes you think that if you knew you couldn't bother to save them?" I asked him.

"No I will always help when I can, especially when it means life," he said.

"Is it because you are a priest?" I asked him.

"Not at all, it is a common sense. My dad was not a priest but he did hide Tutsi. There are people who help without having any religion. And now they have a peace of mind." I thanked him he stood up and shook hands and I left.

CONSOLATE UMWIZA CYANGUGU

During genocide, the killers began to lose the battle in favour of R P F. As a result, they began to flee to the countries that share borders with Rwanda. Most people had chosen to go to Congo DRC as Mobutu was a friend of Habyarimana. They felt that they would be well protected. More than one million were refugees in Congo DRC and a considerable number went to Tanzania, very few went in Burundi. While running away, they were doing propaganda against R P F in order to make all people follow them if possible. The aim was to leave R P F without society and in future they could use them to return.

Umwiza is a Tutsi who followed them because she was told that R P F were not normal human beings, as they were born in the bush and grew up in the bush together with beast. For instance, they told people that they were not fully developed to the level their ears were not like other people and they had tails. Moreover, they were wicked more than any beast as they killed and ate human beings. This made people who didn't know much about R P F follow killers as they feared to be eaten by R P F's soldiers.

Those who planned knew that if all people followed them, Rwanda would be empty; westerners would help them to come back as the country couldn't be a country without people living in it. That was how Umwiza went to Goma as she believed everything she was told by leaders.

It was not easy for R P F but they won the war with a big struggle, they brought back their people from Goma. In 2004 Major General Rwarakabije a Hutu who was one of the high commanders in Habyarimana's government that fought R P F came back freely to join R P F. All had been called to come back in their country without fear. We met him in a conference organised by General Kabarebe, where he said, "Most of my fellow Hutus don't believe that I came back in Rwanda. Some think that it is propaganda from R P F and others says that it is someone else who looks like me, and the last group confirm that R P F has corrupted me as they have a lot of money. However, I have chosen to come back in my country. After fighting for all of this time, I asked myself three questions: what is the reason behind what I'm doing and the benefit of it. In analysing R P F's political thinking, I believed that we will never defeat them."

Indeed, what surprised me was that they used to capture our soldiers. Normally we knew that they would kill them. Surprisingly, they used to take them to the hospital, treat them and then re-educate them about R P F philosophy and why they were fighting. The aim of R P F was not to fight brothers but to bring back all children of Rwanda in the country, so that together they may build their country. In order to reach this level everyone needed to be integrated in the society. Those who were not willing to come back in the country we would still fight them as rebels. Those who accepted this philosophy were integrated into the R P F army and sent back to fight those who were still in the bush. This is because the primary goal is the security of those who have chosen to live in the country as R P F decided not to let any other war happen in the country.

You could see these two Rwandan generals, General Kabarebe and General Rwarakabije talking together, when they look back in their war time especially about genocide time. When General Kabarebe was asking him, "Do you remember when I was telling you that you better stop your soldiers killing society because it is not going to help in any ways apart from destroying and killing?" General Rwarakabije was answering every question, that he didn't know that he was telling him the truth at the time, and I think he had some kind of regret about the time he lost in the bush, but on the other hand said that it was better late than never.

Many Rwandan refugees who went to Goma died following several reasons. Some died because of cholera and lack of clean water, sicknesses, to be millions in a small place. Moreover, some citizens were afraid of killers, then, they poisoned them, and much more reasons. Moreover, genocide was a cause of many deaths, to the level that some called it 'Africa's First World War', because many countries were involved such as Congo, Burundi, Kenya, Tanzania, South Africa, Angola, and Zimbabwe. There were western countries involved as well, physically, and others supported by giving money and guns. Asians and Americans were involved as well…

A Congolese lady who lived in Congo and didn't want to be known told me that they had killed many Rwandan refugees in Congo through foods that they had been selling to refugees who were at Goma. Indeed, they used to mix bread flours with rat's killer medicine and this had killed many according to her. They believed that since they were killers, after they would kill them too, so it was better to kill them first. Others had died in the bush because the bush was so big and they did not know where to go and how to come out of it. Therefore, hunger and thirst killed many. Savage animals and snakes were killing as well. Some died being raped by guerrillas, and they were eating anything to survive so some were eating poison. Others were throwing their own children after being tired, and ferocious animals were eating them. In summary, many people died even though journalists keep talking about different numbers of those who died during genocide, but those who survived and saw what happened said that those who died are more than double of what they think, the number was far more than three million if you can count all inside and outside Rwanda.

In fact, in Goma they could not find enough land where people could be buried. Therefore, they were throwing them in a mass grave. One of those mass graves became full to the level it became like a mountain. That mountain is still there and it is called after Clinton, the

American President of the time. These people walked by foot more than 5,000 kilometres, and you can imagine how many died in Tingitingi.

Between April and May 1995, there had been a massacre at Kibeho, that journalists called the second Rwandan genocide. For instance, Kibeho village had the biggest displaced camp within the country. The R P F decided to destroy that camp because of a lot of soldier activities that were going on but covered by civilians. It was necessary to destroy it even though many people died. This is because the government feared to be attacked from inside the country. Moreover, the scars of genocide were too fresh and Rwandan soldiers refused to go outside the camp willingly, when we proposed them to come out peacefully. The government tried to convince them to let those who were not soldiers disassociate with them. As civilians were taken as scapegoats they refused them to go. Hence, there was no other option than to fight and destroy the camp instead of waiting to be destroyed by them. In that camp many guns of all kinds were found. I was told this by General Kabarebe when I was at Nasho.

As usual all newspapers and international radio said about it, at that time I was in Nairobi Kenya. One of my friends, my friend then, up to now is still a good friend Uta Fager, told me that if R P F had done that, then, there must be a serious good reason. In addition she said that R P F soldiers were too careful to be correct. The only problem was that international people chose to ignore the real reasons that pushed R P F to react. The same happened in 1997 when the government of R P F was forced to go to Goma in order to bring back its population that was captured by killers. It was necessary as some people were running away from their captors. No one else could free the people unless the Rwandan government acted, and quickly. As no one helped R P F to win genocide, then they knew that they were not waiting for anyone to do it for them. It was another short war, it was a hard one, but R P F had to fight it too. What was important, they took back their people as they did not have any other choice because life was too tough in a foreign country. Some were not sure if once in

Rwanda R P F would not kill them for what they did. Still others knew that for sure there would be consequences as they committed genocide, but they felt better to die in their country. Moreover, they knew that it would be hard to find those who would accuse them as they believed that they had killed everybody. They didn't know yet that there were some who came back from the dead!

The last group decided to carry on fighting and had chosen to go far away in the bush hoping that they would conquer Rwanda again. But others walked more than 5,000 miles until they reached a place called Tingi Tingi. Not all of them remained there because some carried on and went in other countries such as Angola, Congo, Brazzaville, and Central Africa and so on. This was the last war in the eastern part of Congo at the time, even though it was genocide. This was because of the scale of the people who died that could not be numbered. No one knows the exact number of those who died it is known that genocide which was planned for Tutsi, its consequences killed big numbers of other people too. Hutu and Congolese died too. All of them were African people who were dying because of unnecessary war. Many innocents died without knowing the origin of the war. When the war ended, the so-called super power countries began to show up themselves by bringing the aids. Some were sorry by asking forgiveness, others were offering free money and others were promising to participate in rebuilding Rwanda. At the end they concluded that, 'genocide never again'.

To be honest all western powers and the U.N. have contributed toward Rwanda genocide of 1994 in many different ways by ignoring signs which was a big shame, and then by reducing the U.N.'s presence at the time when it should have been reinforced. You can see or hear Romeo Dallare a man who saw it all when he talks, who was there when it was happening looked helpless when he couldn't do anything to help when he was in the uniform as general commander of the U.N. forces, forces which came to make **peace.** In his book, he says, *even now, a sensation, especially a smell, can send me back to scene from that slaughter. I hear a stick, tacky, tacky sound, and then flash to decaying bodies* *slithering like fish in the net of an open mass grave, and I am briefly unable to extricate myself from this quicksand of memory. I felt I owed the people of Rwanda as retribution for the failure of the international community to come to their aid. (P.5 Introduction of: They Fight Like Soldiers They Die Like Children by Romeo Dallaire)*

In addition. France compounded the problem by protecting Hutus knowing that they were protecting killers. Moreover, by creating refugee camps in the Congo to the border of Rwanda, it was an invitation to the 1997 attack on the refugee camps by Rwandan government and therefore, could avoid another genocide from the Congo side, or it was an invitation of another genocide by France inside Rwanda and R P F Rwanda government did it first before them.

THE LADY WHO DIDN'T
WANT TO BE KNOWN

I met this lady who didn't want to mention her name but she told me her story.

People keep asking us to talk about what happened to us, what is the benefit of it as perpetrators of genocide live free among us? She went ahead asking me while looking at the floor as if she was talking to herself. Then she looked at me as if she wanted an answer. Don't you think that they will finish us one by one? Now they are majority, they did it, and yes they have success for that, she repeated the same word, now they are the majority. And when in our neighbourhood on the road, they look at you in a way that you feel real menace in their eyes.

We are living under permanent fear and threat, said the lady. She became silent for a moment while looking down, when she lifted up her head; she saw that I was still fixing her, waiting quietly to hear how she escaped genocide. The lady who introduced me to her, told me to be careful not to push her. Normally she does not want to talk about what happened to her, no one knows yet how she escaped when all her children were killed.

After a minute, instead of talking she began to cry. As I did not know what to do, I approached her slowly and gave her a hug. Without knowing I began to cry as well. We spent around three minutes and then she began to shake. I told her not to worry I was there just to support her by sharing with her that horrible time she passed through. At this moment she began to talk and said that: when genocide began, my husband had already died a normal death. He was ill and was lucky to die in a normal way before seeing all of these evils.

What you can't understand and I did not understand is that people who came to kill us were people who we used to live with, those called our best friends. All the young ones grew up with our children and were friends. They came at home having all kinds of weapons, such as spears, arrows, machetes and many different kinds of weapons. They had special sticks, big, sharp and long, other sticks had nails at their end. Two among the killers had guns and three of them had grenades, as they told me. At that time I lost all notion of dates and time, but I think it was between the 1st and 10th of May 1994.

They began by pulling my daughters with the intention of raping them in front of all of us, meaning their brothers and me. I prayed, saying that God should allow them to kill me first and my sons before we see those taboo. I didn't know what stopped them, then, they told us to go out of the house. Once out, one of them told others not to touch us as we are good people, he said. Let another group deal with them. Another asked me how we wanted to be killed as we are friends. I told him that, if we have their favour, let them shoot us. He said that I am a fool as bullets are very expensive. Then, he showed me something saying do you know this? I said no! This can kill all of you quickly more than a gun. Just look to what will happen to that house, then, threw on the house, in a minute all the house was burning after a big blast. One among them said, let us give them a chance if they have money. They burned one of my houses since I had two in one compound. I have money in the house I told them. Go and bring what you have. I went, brought money and handed to them; at that point they went running without another word. We were relieved.

I told my children that we needed to move from the house because if they came back or other groups came we would not survive. In the evening we went to hide in the bush in the middle of mud. After three or five days, children began to be more and more weak as we were eating some small things from the garden at night. I began to encourage them that we needed to resist because R P F would come soon to our rescue.

The next day it became even worse. As I felt that they would die, I decided to go and beg one of my friends who was a Hutu for some food, hoping that she had not yet changed to the level of becoming a killer.

I told my children that if I spent more than two hours before returning, they should know that I was killed. Therefore, instead of giving up, they must start eating grasses as I was sure R P F was not far searching for survivors since we would finish what we could eat from the garden which was around there. I went and hid in my friend's garden of bananas before having the courage of knocking their door. This lady did not have any children and was living only with the husband. After a while I saw the husband coming home having blood everywhere and meat which was hung on a big stick that he had on his shoulder. I began to think if they were eating people's flesh. Anyway, he knocked the door and his wife opened. He went in the house and few minutes later came out and went. After observing that the lady was alone, I went and knocked the door. She opened the door but nearly fainted when she saw me. She told me to go out of the sight and took me back in her garden. She told me that her husband would not last and if he saw me he would kill me. They are now crazy, she said. She asked me if all my children were killed. I answered that they were still alive and I just came to ask any food for them as they were dying of hunger. She went in the house and came back with a big pot of porridge. She told me to come back at the same time and as long as we were alive. Never knock my door again but I will be coming out if my husband is not in the house or he is asleep.

The lady fed us for almost a week. During the day, we heard as if somebody was moving slowly. I told the children to remain calm and quiet. Then we saw a big snake moving out of where we were sitting. I have never seen any big snake like that before as it was around two metres long or more, and too huge. Moreover, the snake has created a nice way as it used to pass there. We lived all this time with a snake beside us. We was too surprising and too fearful thinking that when it comes back it will kill us. The children wanted to leave the place straight away, but I convinced them to wait until it was dark, otherwise we would be seen and get killed. They have accepted but any winds that shake grasses we knew that it was back and everyone was shaking. Fortunately for us, it did not come back until night and we moved from that bush in mud and went to the bush in the land.

We knew that it was very dangerous to hide in the bush outside the mud as we could be seen easily but we could not live side to side with that snake. After a while I went to see my friend in order to have food. She was there with a big pot of food but told me not to come back in the banana garden again. She said that, last night after meeting you my husband went to check in the banana garden and I don't know why he was suspicious. I don't want to see anyone of you killed in my sight. To be hidden in the mud was better than in the bush in land. This is because, every time there were people who were passing in order to search if there were survivors so that they may kill them. Once someone was discovered, we knew it was killers, they would shout, sing, and rejoice before killing the person.

Then we heard many dogs running after people as if they were trained for the job. We knew that we would not last as dogs would discover us. Indeed, dogs discovered us and killers began to shout insults, singing and saying many unspeakable things. Some were saying that we thought that we are too intelligent but they were more clever than us.

Then they asked me if I wanted to say anything before they did what they had to do. I told them that it will be good if they could kill us quickly in good manner, starting by me. They began to laugh saying that: you are too beautiful and you need to die in a beautiful way as well? At that level I did not say anything again. One of them told everybody to find a way of killing quickly. One man who was talkative became quiet for a minute then, went ahead with his story without looking at me as before. He took my oldest son; put him in the middle of the road, he posed for seconds, with his machete, he hit only once, I saw the head falling down and the rest of the body felt with a big shaking. I think the part of his body had life for a few minutes and had pain and shock.

The same person took the youngest girl, my last born and made her naked. He made her kneel down and then pushed a sharp long stick in her private part and began to push. The child was crying for help and crying calling mum, mum. Without mercy, the stick came out of her head as if he wanted to roast her, and that was her end as she was thrown in the river.

All of this his friends were looking at him as if he was their hero. They were singing for him hero songs. You may think they were watching a good game of football.

The others were busy beating my older other son and all the attention was on him as he was badly beaten. They killed him with beatings until they were sure he was dead. I remained with my two teenage daughters to be killed. They removed their clothes and began to rape them, each one of them having a turn. I began to cry with them now as I felt guilty and begged them to kill me first but they were laughing. I felt that if I began to insult them they would be angry and kill me quickly, but my voice could not speak only tears began to run. When they saw that I was crying, they came to me while others began to insert a sharp tree inside my daughters; they didn't throw them to the river as they did to the others.

They tied me in the big tree which was there in the position they wanted and started to rape me, I don't know how many raped me. After I was excused and dying they left me, and were looking at me as if I was a film, as I became semi-conscious. They brought the bodies of my daughters and put them beside me and I saw that they were still alive. As I was still naked, some passed time to time to rape me again even though I was like a dead persoon. I don't know how long it took my daughters to die, even though I could not help. I heard a lot of raining and people running away from me but I went into a coma. I don't know how long I was there or how I came from there because when I woke up I heard people telling me not to worry I was in good hand and in hospital. I don't have any idea of how I got there. Those who did these atrocities are our neighbours except very few that I did not know. Until now I met with some of them as they are free in the villages. I have never accused anyone and I will never accuse anyone. I asked her if she took any AIDS test, she said that she will never do it as she thinks that what happened has happened. How can a crowd rape you including street boys and expect to be safe, she said. I asked her what the most painful moment of her life was even though everything she passed through was painful. She said that the most painful was to see her children dying slowly without being able to help them. Everywhere I am, walking or sleeping I see those images.

MARY MUNGANYINKA-
KIGALLI

This girl was like Nyinawabega, separated accidentally from the rest of the family, even though, her case was very different.

I went hiding wherever I found a big bush. Sometimes, I could see killers coming with a group of people who looked like prisoners and then, kill all of them. After I would leave from that bush to another, but only when it was dark. During the day I would see how people were being killed and those who were killing them. In killing they were using an axe by chopping people as if they were firewood, from the head to the bottom until they separated the victim! There were times when I was scared to death to the level I wanted to scream.

I did not know where to go except to find a pastor friend who was a Hutu. I believed that he will never become a killer, not only because was a pastor, but because I knew him as good person. It is true that I have seen many changing but this one was my only a hope. I believed that no one would search his house. Indeed, when I reached the place I found four other Tutsi hidden in the pastor's house. Two young men, and a lady who was my aunt and her teenage daughter who had one of her hands chopped off. We were surprised to meet there in that situation but had no time to ask questions, only our hearts were talking to them. This pastor was married recently and did not have any children yet. His relatives were known as killers without mercy. We had spent two months in that house without going outside, but he used to take our toilet outside. Several times killers used to beg him to follow them in order to kill at least one Tutsi but each time he refused. Most of the time, when this pastor heard people talking he used to rush out and talk to them as he avoided anyone entering his house.

One evening came another group of killers including his brothers. They asked him to go with them otherwise there was something he was protecting and he would get killed himself. He told them that he did not know why people were being killed. Moreover, as a man of God, he was not given hands in order to use them for bloodshed. At that point they killed him. When the wife heard the shooting she went out and asked her in-laws: How can you kill your brother? They told her, we need to search your house or you will die as well. She said that, I have repented, I am saved you can kill me; it will not mean anything as I will go to heaven. Since you have killed my husband I wish to go with him instead of giving away innocents to be killed for no reason. If it is okay for you to kill, then, go ahead and kill me, then they killed her too. The house was open, surprisingly, not one of the killers did enter the house instead they went away running saying, you cockroach, know that we never joke, we will be back to finish you.

Then we thought of running away from that house but my auntie advised not to try going outside as we can't go beyond one mile. It was better was to wait until they killed us in this house. Killers did not come back, but we became weaker day after day because of hunger, since no one went out after the pastor and his wife's death. If R P F did not come, we could die one by one just by hunger. We remained in the house until we heard people shouting and talking outside. We felt that it was our last day of living. We were lucky as it was R P F. I think they were searching house by house in order to find any survivors. So, they got us, but we were very weak to the level they had to carry us on their backs, after some time, I met both of my parents but I will never forget what I have seen on the way, the killings, and the death of the pastor and his wife.

THE PERIOD THAT OVERWHELMED ME

NO 1:1995 MEETING THE SON OF MY ELDER SISTER ANTOINETTE KAMASHARA.

I had received a letter from the post office. The content of it was telling me that the son of my sister wanted to meet me. I read and re-read the same letter without believing it. This was because he was in Rwanda during genocide and I did not expect to see anyone from my family. Before even meeting him I was overwhelmed by joy and I could confirm that all days were not Monday. Indeed, days are not alike as they are full of surprises and one can experience new things never seen before. I have tried to write before to my relatives who lived in Rwanda, to the level that I passed the message to the Red Cross so that they may help to find anyone from my family. As I did not get any response or communication, I knew that everybody was killed.

During this period they did not have any other means of communication than writing although I had a telephone at home, they did not know my number. In the letter I received, this son gave me the address where to find him. I decided to stop every programme I had the next morning, as my priority was to find him. I did not sleep that night as I was too excited. Early in the morning I went to find my son. The address given was a theological school which was well known.

When I was there the first people I asked did not know him. The second man I asked told me that he didn't know him, but the one he presumed was a family man when I was looking for a single man. My last solution was to ask for any Rwandan as I felt that I could get the help I was looking for. I was shown a Rwandan family, and when I asked them if they knew him, they offered to bring him to me.

It did not take too long before I saw him. My eyes could not believe seeing someone from my family. He was a tall man big and mature. In him I saw all the people I left years ago in Rwanda. I began to imagine in him people I knew and my relatives I did not know but heard their names only. I wished it was in my house so that I may turn him and see every corner of his body in order to identify him with those I knew. Finally, he took me to his home where I began to ask for news concerning the family that I left thirty years ago. He told me what happened during genocide and how they escaped a certain death. I felt very happy, as I believed that I was no longer alone. I thanked God as He can't allow everybody to die at once in a family. Since then we began to share everything we could do.

NO 2: BATSINDUKA

When Alloys BATSINDUKA married in August 1999, most Rwandans had already gone back home to Rwanda. There had been still few remaining in Kenya and they were more united as before conquering Rwanda. This is because once we had any event we used to be so many because our daughters who married Kenyans had to come with their families and friends so that no one knew that others went to their country.

I had been friends with the acting Ambassador of Rwanda called Alfonci Mbandahe Mbayire. After observing my life and what I was doing, we became partners in some matters concerning our country, to my side it was voluntary work. After having the date of marriage, many people offered to help. Those who offered help were my friends, Batsinduka's friends and friends of my other children. In addition, we had Kenyans who grew together with my children, studied in local schools together and were working together.

Like everyone who would have a big ceremony like wedding, they had regular meetings in order to raise money to be used on the wedding day and to make plans how things would go. This included everything which would be needed such as: the hall, transport, foods, drinks and the group of cultural dancers. This organisation was the most important as it was in charge of assigning tasks. The Rwandan Ambassador became the key person even though we did not expect him to do much. He became more involved to the level that some others felt that they were lazy. The more he got involved others became more active as well, some maybe because of competition or because they felt ashamed as the new arrival was more involved and yet he was their leader.

In brief, together they did a good job ever dreamed. On my side, the ladies did a big impact as well, because they were involved in how to receive those who came from far, as many from my family came from Rwanda and Uganda. They were in charge of arranging cultural dancers who were admired by many. They had to organise their rehearsal and their uniform. The plan was to start in the church where a Rwandan priest could bless the marriage. Then, going to the hall where all the people will be received while enjoying Rwandan cultural performance. Lastly, the married would go home in order to rest a bit and have a change. Then, during the night they would join friends in a hotel with the last performance of our cultural requirement in marriage known as 'gutwikurura' or giving the wife the right of cooking and doing other domestic works, and be free as wife, then, rejoice with friends.

Everything went according to the plan. During the matrimonial service, around one hundred people came, but in the hall prepared for reception, many people came to the level some of the people could not enter and some who were able to enter did not have any seats. People enjoyed and came out saying: we have not seen this kind of wedding for a long time. In our African culture, when you get many people in your event and are able to satisfy them with food and drink and entertainment, then, you can claim to have a good day. I have never thought that my child can have a wonderful wedding, so I was a happy mother and thank my God.

Many people came from Rwanda and Uganda and outside of Nairobi. After the wedding, my relatives including Kantamage, Batsinduka's mother, said that you are so wonderful in making friendship. You have proven it to us by the crowd that came out to support you. If anyone has a choice of giving birth or making friendship you can be the best choice. I responded to them that I was not special more than others, but I was blessed to have people willing to be friends. It is possible to be good and willing to have friends but it is sometimes difficult especially when they are not willing to associate with you. Some can be complicated, or are not willing to live with you. This can push you to give up some friendship. Therefore, people who choose to live with me are good people too.

NO 3: THE SCHOLARSHIP OF NIWEGAJU IN 1997

Niwegaju was a good and intelligent student while studying at Aga Khan High School in Nairobi. From the beginning of her secondary school she was getting high marks. Uta Fager was a lady from Germany and was one of my few good friends for many years. She knew how much I would like to see my children go further in their studies. She advised me to seek for a scholarship. As she knew which door to knock, she introduced me to a priest called Father Fr Eujen who took me to Sister Rouse. She was the one who started to support all my children in secondary school. Moreover, when Niwegaju was almost at the end of her secondary school, she was among the few students chosen to go abroad through scholarship.

Niwegaju was sent to one of the Red Cross United's school in Norway. As far as I am concerned, it was a miracle to hear that one of my children would go abroad for further studies. I never dreamed that one of my children would study abroad. The only thing that gave me hope was to remember that Batsinduka studied in a good college of tourism called, Utali College in Nairobi. When he was in Nairobi school he went to the UK as a scout and spent weeks there. Since then, I told myself that everything is possible as long as one is living. That which can be seen as a small thing, to me was a good sign. Uta was one of a few good friends to me which opened my door the lucky door which was our lucky way as a family. My goal and wish was not to see my children going abroad for the sake of going, but to reach at least the level of a first degree in university.

The school that Niwegaju attended was an international school where students came from all over the world. That made her interact and make diverse friends and this was a high step as a family. While in Norway, her father, a native of Germany knew that she was studying at World College. Therefore, he invited her to visit him in Germany. When she went there, she found that her father was married to a black lady, a Kenyan, and had three children, two with her father and one was the same age as her, but she was black girl. As Niwegaju looks like her father and has a light skin colour, and uses her father's name, this family began to have strange bahaviour maybe they thought that she would create a big disorder in the family by claiming her right in the family. I thought that, they believed that she knew everything about the other child and her mother. We knew that the nameless man was married and had three children, but did not know that one of them did not belong to him 'in reality'. She did not know more than that about this family, nor was she going to claim anything. On the contrary she discovered that they did not live a good life as a family.

After a few days, all the family were happy because they discovered that she did not disturb anyone, instead, she became a good friend to the girl they thought could be a reason of misunderstanding between Niwegaju and their family. When she came back home she told me that according to what she had seen, that we were lucky as we did not follow her dad to Germany, and she was happy and proud with her family where she grew up. When she told me about the black girls, especially the one who had the same age with her. I came to realise that was why every time he was telling me that his wife was always worried that I would take him from her because I had his child!

Niwegaju passed with good marks and was given another scholarship to go ahead with her study in Britain. Where she was until 2009, when she moved to Australia to join her husband. People were telling me that I was lucky to have a western daughter as her father pays for her in Europe. On the other side her father wrote a letter to me saying that: he knew that I was able to sponsor Niwegaju to study in Europe. This is because the Rwandan government was the one who was sponsoring her and he thought that I might become now more rich than him because of Kagame who was now in power. It was like a comedy to me to the level that I went to show the letter to our acting Rwandan ambassador Alphonse Mbandahe. He commented that he didn't see how that nameless man could involve Kagame in all of that. I thought that maybe it was because he knew that I was patriotic, but there are many, many patriotic people anyway. I didn't understand, and when I asked Uwe what he meant, he told me that Kagame is a Tutsi, and therefore, he is supporting me because I am a Tutsi as well! I didn't explain more as I felt that it may be hard to make him understand that millions of Tutsi will not become rich in a day or that Kagame can't know each and every Tutsi: he is there for all Rwandans and for Rwanda, not for one group of Rwandans.

That is not why they fought. He didn't say anything.

And Rwanda as a country was young at the time and couldn't sponser anyone abroad.

MUVUNANGOMA'S
SCHOLARSHIP

It was my joy when my son Muvunangoma got his scholarship to carry on his further studies. For instance, I had a German friend called Mrs. Pandiko. She was the one who supported my son Batsinduka to study Tourism. Pandiko had an organisation that used to help children who were intelligent but had no one to support them. I went back to this lady and pleaded for Muvunangoma, so that he may carry on further studies.

She was so comprehensive and accepted to pay his scholarship as he has passed with high marks. That was how he went to study at Strathmore College his IT. From this college he had a good job and became a teacher of IT while in Nairobi. When R P F took power he had to go back to his country for the first time. In Kigali he was given a job in one of the best colleges of the country as a lecturer.

SAD MOMENTS IN MY LIFE

LOSS OF MY MOTHER

Loss of the person I loved with all my heart. Loss of my mum at an early age, I believed to be one of the big reasons for my struggle in all journeys of my life.

THE DEATH OF FRED GISA RWIGEMA IN 1990

Most Rwandans will never forget his death. Some loved him because he was just a beautiful young man, a humble man, very intelligent and committed to the change of the country. Moreover, he was capable of taking R P F back to Rwanda because of his determination in fighting in the name of democracy for all Rwandans, Tutsi, Twa, and Hutu. Being a child who grew up in exile, he was most fighting for Rwandans who were outside of their country for years and years. He wanted to fight for some those who were inside the country and they were living like prisoners in their own country. Indeed they were living in permanent fear of being arrested without any reason at all or being killed because of talking with their brothers living outside of the country. Others who were not Tutsi, but loved Rwanda, were sympathetic because they had hope in him because he was a moderate young man who believed in power sharing and unity as Rwandans as Africans, indeed: politically he was recruiting everybody, meaning Hutu including non-Rwandans born in Rwanda. Therefore, they knew that his death would change much as far as power sharing and unity was concerned. They didn't trust if the other who would take over would have the same philosophy. Hence, his death was a worry for them.

Others would never forget him as they believed that once Fred was dead, all the rest in R P F would be discouraged and therefore, no change would happen in Rwanda as they would be defeated. This made all young people who were outside the country join R P F as a way of supporting his idea of change and refusing to go back as defeated people. For the opposition, his death will never be forgotten, as it was a day of a great joy for them. They believed that there would be no more war between them and R P F that they were a winner until when Paul Kagame surprised all of us including the opposition when he came and rescued the R P F by rescuing the war. Rwigema became an icon that will be remembered forever in Rwandan history, as he became a hero.

RWANDAN GENOCIDE

I heard about genocide when I was traveling from Nairobi to Masaka in Uganda. I slept in the bus from Nairobi to Kampala, then, I took the second bus to Masaka. It is in that bus from Kampala that I heard on the radio about genocide. Then, I saw on T.V how crops were being taken out from the Lake Victoria and how bodies were floating. I become very ill straight away as if I was being chopped as well. When I reached Masaka I couldn't even walk or see where I was going. Other passengers had to hold my hand in order to move out of the bus. The pictures we saw about Tutsi who were being pushed and then killed made me feeling as if I was dead. Those massacres will never go away not only in my mind but in the mind of many Rwandans who lost their loved ones. The same is true in the mind of killers for the horrible things they did which keep haunting them.

THE DEATH OF JANE ILIBAGIZA ON 7TH SEPTEMBER 2003

Ilibagiza was a beautiful grown-up girl who had a very good character. Moreover, she had a good job and had enough money. If she wanted to, she could rent her own house and live quite well, but she has chosen to follow Rwandan culture in remaining at home. Indeed, according to our culture, a child is always a child and has the right of living with the parents no matter her or his age, most of the time she goes out of the parent's house once married. Each parent wishes that a girl should have somebody who loved her and took her with honour by marrying her and having her own family.

This culture and understanding is good but has some bad sides as sometimes it holds girls who would like to have children without bothering getting married. Like some single mothers can afford to raise-up children and give them everything necessary they need. However, because of this Rwandan culture and their honour they feel that their family will be ashamed if they have a child before marriage and the pride of the family will be lost. The consequence of this culture is that, some of the girls become too old and unable to have children when they would like and love to have them. As far as Ilibagiza was concerned, she took home as her own house. For instance, she was the one who has to take care of visitors and other issues in the house. For example, in case somebody came from far to visit us, she will be the one to find something to give as a gift. As for me she used to buy new clothes that were in fashion each period of the year. Sometimes I used to refuse gifts from her, because I felt that she was using a lot of money unnecessarily. I was very happy about her generosity to the level I wished her to get a nice husband and have her own family. I didn't care that I depended on her in many areas, but I knew that even if she went and had a good family I would benefit, as there would be two living together and caring for me. The fact of knowing that by marrying she could be happy could make me happy.

Ilibagiza was a born stylist so that every clothes she wore were perfect and so she used to buy new clothes. My little children Niwegaju and Manzi used to take her clothes, thinking that she did not know. Most of the time she used to laugh in showing me and saying that: by wearing my dresses, they think that I will never know. However, I know all my clothes even though I have many. I would wish to see them asking for what they want, as I can give out but, I understand how children act. I knew that Ilibagiza loved people in general, but she loved her family more. I was sure that once she got a husband she would have a good and a nice family. This is because I could see how she organised my house on every level such as shopping, cleaning, buying or changing furniture in the house. All of these were her responsibility even though others used to help her or do what she asked them to do.

Therefore, I wished with all my heart that she would get married and have children. This is because she really loved children. As a matter of fact, each time we had visitors who had children, she could do whatever in her power to satisfy them. Sometimes she was happy to take them out in specialised places for children. Personally, I felt that she was delaying to have a child whatever means as felt that I would support her. Some single mothers can raise their children better than some married mothers. Moreover, I wished to see her children while I am alive, so that I may help to raise them, instead of becoming old without marrying and without a child. I have seen many girls finishing this way, or marrying too old to the level they could no longer have children as I said.

What was so special for Ilibagiza she lived her life, like a girl of our generation more than a modern girl. Indeed, she used to respect any grown-up people. For instance, I have never seen her being angry against me or raising her voice when talking to any grown-up. During our generation no child could become angry against his or her parents as he or she knew that: no parent would make a child angry on purpose even though it may happen. Sometimes you may find a bad child, who was born in a very good and nice family. Among the children, one may become so evil to the level that neighbours question if the child belongs to such family. A Rwandan proverb says that: 'you only give birth to the body, not the heart', meaning that you never give to the child a personality you want.

Most of the time when the children grew-up they didn't like their parents to advise them as they felt that parents looked down upon them or they looked on them as if they were still small kids. They thought that if parents spotted something that was not right, they should do it rather than to tell children what was wrong. Even though by doing it some still felt indirectly offended. This happens especially when children are already married. This is because they would like to do it their own way in order to show that they are capable. On the other side, parents would like to keep parenting by showing what is good and bad according to them.

Sometimes children gossip about their parents by exchanging what is good or bad with their parents. Most of the time they agree how they will be responding to a particular situation that arised from parents. Being children, most of the time they make it a subject of laughter. When a parent does exactly what they were discussing, they run to their point of meeting and share what happened. Each child learns through others, especially when a child has good company, it helps them with how to deal or respond to their parents. As far as I am concerned, none of my children has ever raised a voice while talking to me. Though normal children they don't live or behave alike, but each child is unique. You just raise them in the same house and in a same way, but each one develops his or her own behaviour.

In our house, I gave my children the right of correcting and teaching me what they felt good in their generation. This made our family have solidarity and unity, and good friendship between ourselves. As for Jane Ilibagiza, I had never seen her angry or offended by what I was doing. She was the one who took almost care of us by using her money, even though we were doing our things as a team. Even though I used to tell her that I didn't wish to dictate what she did with her money, she used to seek advice of how to use what she had. This is because I did not want to take advantage of her personality, and she loved me for that. I was not greedy of anything and that was my nature, and it helped me a lot. I wanted her to be happy for whatever she was doing, and feel free with her life. She used to discuss what seemed to her unclear. This was a sign of love, trust and togetherness. She liked too much our close and extended family. There were people who used to approach her because they have problems. Each one of them had a solution to the level that she had people she accepted to be in her monthly charge. She did all she could in order to make people happy.

She began to be ill in 2000, but not something serious as she used to go to work. She had enough money to pay for her treatment at Nairobi Hospital; it was among the best in Nairobi. In 2003, she began to be seriously ill to the level she could not go to work several times. Moreover, her skin began to have rashes and yet she used to have beautiful skin desired by many girls. I began to feel sad and sorry and began to develop some kind of fear. I began to pray for her and our family, and one day I went to her doctor to enquire about her problem. I didn't want to challenge her face to face by asking directly what was going on with her health. I knew that she would tell me in case there were any serious sicknesses. Moreover I did not want to hear any worse news even though I knew that if it was a bad news sooner or later I would have to face it.

I was sure that he would not refuse to tell me the truth concerning the health of my beloved daughter. He knew that she was my child and most of the time in Africa, doctors normally at the time didn't like to say the truth when things were wrong. They try always to give patients hope that things are okay. I went in his cabinet and greeted him. After greeting I became silent for seconds as many thoughts were passing through my mind. I was fearful for what maybe I was about to hear. I thought that Ilibagiza could have an incurable sickness, which I would not be able to help. Then, I was thinking if it was necessary to ask about her sickness or not. What if I discover that it is incurable sickness, everyone had already known about AIDS, and that was the only thing that came in everyone's mind in a situation like that. I am going to accept it, or will I die before her and therefore, fail to help her in the moment she needed me most! After that short silence with determination and ready for whatever will be, I broke like a bomb shell and asked the doctor, what the problem of Ilibagiza was. And the doctor looked at me for a second and told me that the problem Ilibagiza had, according to the time we were living in, it was not surprising because she had AIDS! The doctor told me that not to worry since there are drugs even though it is expensive but at least not like before.

Yes I had that guess before, even though I didn't want to believe it, but now it is her doctor who is telling me this, meaning no more doubt, and I have to believe it. I need just to be strong and brave enough in order to be able to help her, and satisfy her for all areas needed. After hearing the answer of the doctor I could not hear what he was telling me. For seconds or a minute, I felt something like a wind pass in me, wind of confusion, and I could see her immobilised in her bed while weak, and the last time, the end of her life. The doctor gave me all my time until when I came back on earth and stood up, thanked him and went.

I had seen many others, who died with AIDS, but I didn't have any idea that this killer would even come in my house to my children, the children who we shared good things and bad things together. She was a good example in the area and community, to all who had known us. I saw that this disease had no kindness, fear or respect at all. To make us suffer through our Ilibagiza we love, and make us soon be alone without her was so sad.

I went back home, sat down and started imagining people in the condolence time, they would be trying to make me understand that it happened and we do not know how and why. Only God knows why he wanted this child to die this kind of death. I didn't want people to tell me anything concerning God's name as I felt that he is a cruel God. As far as I am concerned I believed in a God who has power and is kind not cruel one, who can kill Ilibagiza, and kill her with AIDS. I believed that she or he could only do good things.

Where did this AIDS came from and how and why? Can it be a biological weapon as some people say? 'Can it be a creation of Robert

Gallo who wanted to kill black people? Was it Christopher Colombus who wanted to kill Indians?'

Some other rather controversial theories have contended that HIV was transferred cryogenically (via medical interventions). One particularly well-publicised idea is that polio vaccines played a role in the transfer. Or in life during the late 19th and early 20th century in Equatorial Africa and the Belgian Congo, the colonial rule was particularly harsh and many Africans were forced into labour camps where sanitation was poor, food was scarce and physical demands were extreme. These factors alone would have been sufficient to create poor health in anyone, so Simian Immunodeficiency Virus could easily have infiltrated the labour force and taken advantage of their weakened immune systems to become HIV.

Some say that HIV is a conspiracy theory or that it is 'man -made'. A recent survey carried out in the US for example, identified a significant number of African-Americans who believe HIV was manufactured as part of a biological warfare programme, designed to wipe out large numbers of black and homosexual people. Many say this theory is the belief that the virus was spread (either deliberately or inadvertently) to thousands of people all through the smallpox inoculation programme or to gay men through Hepatitis B vaccine trials.

While none of these theories can be definitively disproved, the evidence given to back them up is usually based upon supposition and speculation, and ignores the clear link between SIV or the fact that virus has been identified in people as far as back 1959. *(The origin of AIDS and HIV and the first cases of AIDS. By International HIV and AIDS charity.)*

Whoever did it, for whatever reason he had, what name can I give this God, him or her? Only that can be more than evil. To put this genocide to our world, which no one knows when it is going to stop killing? Real God couldn't allow this to happen to us. This is not God's will. As people like to say for whatever happened to them.

Unless there is someone else that is in the position of God, and this person or whatever, had some other power of its kind which has all evil powers. And can be using God's name as propaganda in order to attract people to him or her but in reality it is evil. Here they tell us that it is the God who brings the earthquake, flooding, wars, sicknesses, hunger, poverty and people die probably because of him or her. In the understanding of many people, we think that those who taught us about God, know exactly who brings this disaster otherwise they tell us that God is loving and merciful. How then, can he become a killer of people he created? Probably, they have been lying to us about the real thing they are serving and prefer to call it God because it is easy for people to understand and believe without questioning.

How can I believe this God? Is he or she what we believe or do we have to follow what scientists say about this life and the world? When I believe that we are God's children and that God loves us and has all powers. With that power, why can't our God use that power to protect us from all of these evils which hurt our hearts in our life? I believe that no parents who can make his or her child suffer that much in the name of testing the trust of the child, unless if the parent is a cruel one. Sometimes I hear them, preachers saying that it is how our God weighs our trust and love towards him or her, if so then, it is too much to us as human beings. This can be a hard test, which is torture to us. People, who pretend to answer all of this, are those who claim to know much about God. But when it happens to anyone he may doubt God.

In case a democratic vote is proposed between God and the position, God can get very few votes as we know that he is the one who makes evil things happen including all curses that we are facing according to how the preachers told us that whatever happens to us is God's wish. The people who are teaching us about God and religions which tell us about heaven and hell should be clear when they teach in telling people who is that God they are teaching. Maybe there are things done by people who are agents of evil. Probably, it is known by few among them as they trust and believe in him or her and it is why it is using them for their evil purposes. However in order to hide it or to confuse some they teach about God when in reality they serve something else that they call God.

This was C. S. Lewis's problem as he struggled with his grief following the death of his wife from cancer. In *A Grief Observed* he wrote, 'Not that I am (I think) in much danger of ceasing to believe in God. The real danger is of coming to believe such dreadful things about him. The conclusion I dread is not "so there's no God after all", but "so this is what God's really like. Deceive yourself no longer"' He then asks 'Is it rational to believe in bad God? Anyway, in a God as bad as that? The cosmic Sadist, the spiteful imbecile?' It was also Gerald Sittser's problem following the death of his wife, mother and daughter in a car crash:

'Theres appear to be two possible answers: Either God is powerful but not good, and thus a cruel God who causes suffering; or God is good but not powerful and thus a weak God who cannot prevent suffering, though he would like to. Both answers have problems because they appear to undermine what we want to believe about God, namely that he is both powerful and good.' *(P.309, RWANDA the Land God Forget? By Meg Guiillebaud)*

So I would not like to meet people who will tell me that they understand the problem of that suffering, and know how much it hurt. This is because no one will ever understand how much the loss of Ilibagiza hurts me. I knew that she would be my second important person who I would never forget, after my beloved mother. Probably I am selfish as I know that Ilibagiza was precious to all of us as a family, even though I feel that it is a personal matter and hurts me more than anyone else. In my wish I did ask my God not to let her suffer as I have seen some other patients, and God heard my prayers. After losing weight and getting some rashes on her face, she started to look beautiful again and she gained her weight back. She became normal even though she was not eating enough, but even before being ill she used to eat little. It was not as I wished but at least it was keeping her living even thought she was still weak but looking good. By being the child of my elder sister Kantamage, who was in Uganda, I wanted to be fair to both of us, and I asked her if she wanted me to take her near her mum and take care of her when she was there. She told me no, she wanted to remain with us. I was happy with the answer because it showed that she was happy and satisfied with what we were doing for her. I called my sister to come and see her instead, whatever I was doing I was asking her if it was okay with her. Sometimes I used to talk with her and laugh as before. One day she told me, mum, (the way all my children use to call me), please don't worry yourself, because of what you are doing to me, I am happy and grateful the way you are taking care of me, only God will pay you back, mum. When we had visitors who we trusted, she was telling them to talk to me, that I didn't have to worry too much. So I noticed that she was worried about me, though I tried not to show her that I too was worried. As always she didn't want to see me unhappy for whatever reason. When I knew that she was worried about me being worried, I made an effort, not to show her my side of worry, but it was killing me, to see that, still, she wanted to take care of me. I knew that, as family, her death was a big loss as she was a person who was always happy to see others happy. Moreover she was a person who used to show satisfaction when you did something for her.

She was admitted in Nairobi Hospital for two days and came back home. At home I tried to give her at least two glasses of milk a day, some food I thought she would like and porridge. I was trying different things every day, and she was trying hard to eat something which I came to realise that she was doing it just to please me. Indeed it was making me happy in a way, when she was able to eat something. She was at home for a few months, then, came the time when she was too weak and could not eat like before. She was now surviving by milk and porridge only. She reached the point of walking with help and I began cleaning her, this took a few weeks, but we were happy for that. It was as if we were used to this situation and accepted it. Sometimes when I was giving her a bath you could hear us joking and laughing, but she didn't lose weight or her skin did not have problems again. After a while she was not speaking properly, and this worried me a lot. This problem came about so quickly even though I wanted to remain with her, even if it meant years. I was happy to do whatever needed to her, but I could see that her life was slipping through my fingers.

My children Muvunangoma and Batsinduka were always on stand by when I needed them, they were doing everything possible. Batsinduka had a car; I called him and told him how I saw changes. We had a visitor who told us that it was better to take her to the hospital, something I didn't want at all. Almost at forty years I still remembered my mum as if was yesterday, the last person I loved and lost, when she went to the hospital that was it. She didn't come back home alive. This memory made me fear hospitals and I felt that Ilibagiza too, could die once taken to hospital.

In case someone died at home in Kenya it would be a police case that could be worse. Then, when Batsinduka asked her if she wanted us to take her to the hospital, she said that she didn't want, she only wanted to be there with us at our home. We told her that we wanted to take her to the hospital so that they could help her. She accepted, we took her to Kenyata Hospital for one day. This was because Kenyata Hospital was no longer good in terms of taking care of patients, then; we decided to take her to a private hospital.

All the visitor's time, we were with her for one week until Saturday 7th September. This Saturday I was there for the whole day and was going in and out according to the visitor's time. Moreover, I was waiting for other friends who were coming so that I may direct them to where she was sleeping. I was the last person to see her alive, when I was with her, giving her what I called the last drink. I saw her becoming too weak, but I was happy because she looked happy. She was trying to drink and she was smiling showing that she recognised that I was with her. She looked very beautiful as before at her normal happy lifetime. I believed that my God listened to my prayer concerning Ilibagiza's sickness and death. As I prayed that she didn't suffer as I saw others suffering for a long time with this sickness and look horrible. I believe God did it because she did not have any problem with people and she was so kind to others in her short time she had life.

I also believed that good God heard my prayer as it was seen during her burial. That ceremony like others we had been doing, according to our culture was the responsibility of our friends to organise and to help as they could, and people were willing and happy to do it. The announcement passed to one of the newspapers in Kenya and Radio Rwanda as many do. Some people had to come from Uganda and Rwanda, we wanted that ceremony to be perfect as much as we could and the organisers did everything they could. The lady who was her employer came and told Batsinduka that, as a last respect for Ilibagiza, her part of contribution for that ceremony, would be the offer of the coffin. This made Batsinduka uncomfortable because he had already planned a very nice coffin for his sister, and he was not sure what she would offer was good enough. He tried to tell her that they had paid the deposit to another one but the lady was insisting that it was the only contribution she planned to give including the car that would carry the body. Batsinduka and other organisers saw that it was what she wanted to do, and they told her that as long as she brought something that would be good enough, then, no problem.

To Rwandan women's side, I asked them to wear our cultural dress, known as 'umushanana' or 'umukenyero'. Normally, in exile, we dressed like that when we had other ceremonies only such as weddings or other feasts. In addition, I asked them to make themselves look beautiful as much as they could, as I felt that this was her wedding too. And I told the one who was responsible for her dress to make her like a wedding dress which they did. I had a special relationship with Our Ambassador his excellence Kamanzi, and his first secretary Mr. Mugwiza. A part of their responsibility was to be with their people in their special times, happy times or sad ones, but in this case they were very involved. The burial was planned for Saturday, the day was chosen because many people do not work.

The day chosen came, and the College Hekima was chosen to host the first part of the ceremony. College Hekima was one of the best Colleges of Kenya that used to teach theology and had a church. Beside the college and a church, the college had some young Rwandans who were studying there. It was them who organised everything there. It was known that Africans didn't like to be somewhere on time but when they want to do a positive thing, they can be on time. There were many people, Rwandans and Kenyans and cars were everywhere. All of us were still outside including Embassy's staff. As the college had many activities on Saturday such as sports parties and so forth. We thought that there were some other groups, which came for other things, because we were so many in the compound and some didn't know each other. After a short time we heard a lot of horns, and we saw many lights, which were going on and off. It was like some kind of music, there was a nice new black car followed by other cars, with a lot of lights that were on and off many times until they stopped. Where I was, I just waited, but people were asking who that could be, maybe there were other ceremonies and that could be somebody else's body brought in the church. The others felt that it may be a rich person, or other Kenyan authority in power, because no one could imagine that those expensive nice black cars were the cars that brought the body of our child.

In most of what happened, I was just contributing some ideas of what I felt should be done, but things were done by organisers chosen for that task. That was why I did not recognise that it was our child that was coming and yet I did wish to make her last wedding. However, when we checked the time, it was our time, so we were confused. After a few minutes we saw the young man who was chosen to carry the coffin coming out of the new black car and he was in a black uniform as planned. It was only then when we came to realise that it was Ilibagiza's body. Once more it was too hard to me, to the level that the woman who was near me had to hold me firmly. When the coffin came out of the car we were surprised all of us. The church was not enough for all the people, because those who remained outside equaled those who were inside even though the church was so big. This surprised everyone including myself because it was a long time without seeing crowds of people coming together in order to pay their last respect to a Rwandan in Nairobi at least not after Rwandans went back to their country. Those on the street, who saw diplomatic cars, came to conclude the person who passed away was a foreigner. Many people couldn't know the difference of countries just through the flags. Since our cars were going very slowly, it was easy to hear what people were saying on the way that, the person who passed away, came from one of the rich countries. This is because maybe there were many cars, and probably the way people were dressed especially women. When we reached the cemetery of Langata, at her final journey, the staff who were working there, took Batsinduka and one of his friends aside, and told them that better not to go from there, without cementing the grave where Ilibagiza sleep. This was because thiefs could steal that coffin as it was too expensive. It is like the one that they had used recently to bury Vice President of Kenya Kijana Wamarwa!

When I heard that it surprised me but I concluded by saying that, all of these were a gift from God for what Ilibagiza was in this world, especially what she did for others. Indeed, no good act has no effect, if not immediately but later God remembers our good deeds. And on the other hand, it was my gift as well because God was honouring me by giving a gift of being respected. I had never thought that someone like me could be recognised at this level. There was no way a member of my family could get the last respect like the one Ilibagiza had and in a foreign land! I told other children the reason of Ilibagiza's death but I was not brave enough to tell anyone among my friends. I said to myself let those who will guess have a guess, but I am not ready yet to tell them anything about the illness. True enough, at that time AIDS was a sickness that brought shame to the entire family as people believed that only prostitutes had it, and people that had it were cursed. We did not try to know how she got it even she could have got it from washing people as she used to work in a beauty therapy shop and yet most of the time they did not see the importance of using gloves. Or if she had a boyfriend and she saw that I didn't have to know him yet, or if she got it from the hospital. Though wherever she got it from, that did not matter anymore, she had it and it took her from us. What is the matter now, what worries me more, is that, this killer is still here, is still killing people around the world, until I don't know when. (When?) After now to turn up to be a big business to many.

The Vatican Council of course promotes a social doctrine based on Christian love, justice and solidarity – in other words equality. In the words of Pope John XXIII, 'love is the driving force of the economy, the hallmark of the Christian social doctrine.'

(God for a Secular Society: The Public Relevance of Theology, By Jurgen Moltmann, SCM press)

You can see how people become disappointed when they ask me my religion or which church I go to pray in on Sundays. I come across those questions many times, I realised that they see me as being a mature African and almost everyone is aware that most of African people's religions have disappeared a long time ago, so the expectation is that, I must be among those who do everything to be happy in their second and last life, so that they can be able to go to heaven after death. They expect from me to say that, "I am born again, in the name of Jesus Christ."

When I tell someone that I have no religion, some think that they didn't hear me correctly, and they ask me again to make sure that they heard me properly.

When on my side, I don't understand them either, but since I don't want an argument with anyone concering their religion, I ask myself if it is a must for my beliefs to be made public?! Did I have to belong to a religion so I can become God's friend and be heard by Him or Her? Why can't my relationship with my God be my own business? Did I have to communicate with my God only when I am in a particular place with particular people? Did I need to join a religion to be taught that love is the driving force of the economy? I think not.

One day when I was in Birmingham, I visited my GP; my doctor was a man who knew Africa and African people very well. He too, asked me the same question the second time, this was the end of 2013, but this time he looked to be in a relaxed mood more than the first time. I gave him the same answer as I gave him the first time, though maybe he did not remember that we had the same conversation before.

After telling him that I didn't have any religion, he looked surprised, and with a smile, he told me that he knew African people to be God-fearing people, and recently Africa is leading in Christianity internationally.

But when he was telling me this, that smile he had, it was telling me something else, I saw in him, that he was telling me that: you old lady, what are you trying to say here? That you don't have any religion! You alone, what are you going to change? We have you, finished.

'Pride, cruelty, honour, grace, good guys and bad guys. Religious blindness, love, hatred, jealousy, generosity. All the elements that make history. Read original sources and wonder about your country'.
(First Australians, edited by Rachel Perkins and Marcia Langton)

'I have travelled across the length and breath of India and I have not seen one person who is a beggar, who is a thief such wealth I have seen in this country, such high moral values, people of such qualities that I do not think we would ever conquer this country, unless we break the very backbone of this nation, which is her spiritual and cultural heritage and therefore, I propose that we replace her old and ancient education system, her culture, for if the Indians think that all that is foreign and English is good and greater than their native culture and they will lose their self-esteem, their native culture and they will become what we want them, a truly dominated nation'.
(Lord Macaulay Address to the British Parliament on 2nd February: 1835)

'There is not a remarkable featuring in the country without a special tradition. Why, it is the very breath of their nostrils that is it was before the white man came amongst them and trampled tradition and everything else that was good out of them'.
(Frank Gillen in First Australians, page 181)

'Someone wants what somebody else has, and they are prepared to murder to get it. The hands do the taking, but the hearts and minds have to justify acts that the Bible prohibits: killing and stealing'.
(Bruce Pascoe in First Australians, page 117.)

NIWEGAJU VISITED US – WAS A HAPPY TIME TO SEE HER

After three months of Ilibagiza's death Niwegaju visited us with her husband who we had never met. Niwegaju like everyone else in the family had a big loss concerning Ilibagiza's death. They grew up together as sisters and they were good friends. Moreover, the memory of how she used to spoil her was still fresh.

Niwegaju's email that she sent as condolence was the only thing Muvunangoma read at the time of her burial, because Ilibagiza told us before her death that she didn't want anyone to say anything during her burial, concerning how good or bad she was. According to her, the reason being that if someone is good to you let the people know your appreciation when that person is still alive, she said, not when that person passed away.

That is why they read that email from Niwegaju, because it was like she was talking about herself, instead of Ilibagiza, and she didn't manage to be there, though it made people cry a lot.

During this period we were not doing very well financially. For instance, Muvunangoma had a job but his salary was not enough. Batsinduka was married just a few months before this death, and his wife had no job. Normally, Batsinduka used to work for ten years in a good company with a very good salary. Unfortunately, when the president Kibaki took over the government, he tried to make changes in all economical areas as a way of stopping corruption. In so doing, Kibaki closed many companies including United Touring Company, where Bastinduka occupied a good position. When the company closed, some of the staff were dismissed without being paid anything, and yet they did work for more than three months without being paid. So to say, as a family we were in a bad position financially but we had hope.

Concerning the visit of Niwegaju and her husband we had no special plan of welcoming them, and they did not expect any. At that time I met one of my good friends called Mrs. Jane Kagenza. I told her that Niwegaju and her husband had come and she knew that it was the first time her husband visited Africa and it was the first time to meet Niwegaju's husband. So Mrs. Jane Kagenza asked me about the plan of welcoming them. I told her that I had no plan at all. She looked very surprised, but after telling her our situation, as she was an understanding person, she advised me to seek help from friends. I told her that I couldn't do that after all the sacrifices people did during the funeral of Ilibagiza. This was because I knew that friends had used a lot of money and time during that funeral and I did not want to add more burdens to them.

She insisted that the same friends who helped were the same friends who would be involved and this was true friendship. There was nothing wrong with asking for help when in need. However, it was not easy for me to face anyone asking for help and this was for two reasons. First of all, I felt that it was not necessary to receive my children beyond our means. Secondly, this was not the last time they would visit us, therefore, we would do better next time when we would have enough money. Jane Kagenza advised again in saying that, as you have good contact with our Rwanda Embassy, go and talk to them just in order to hear their view before making a conclusion. You do not have to tell them the whole concept, just tell them that your children are visiting and let them speak. Maybe you will have other ideas from what they will say. I accepted the idea and went to talk to two ladies Teddy and Edith who were staff there and were friends for so long. I told them not only because I was advised to do so, but, it was in my obligation to share with them good news.

When I told them the news our Embassy staff, these two ladies, were happy to hear that my daughter came to show us her husband. They still knew that I was affected by the loss of Ilibagiza as normal; everyone knew how much I was close to my children. After listening they asked me the same question as Jane Kagenza did. What is the plan to welcome them? I gave them the same answer that I can't manage to do anything because of all we went through, and I can't ask people to help me for that. It can look to be too much. Edith said straight away that if that was the only reason, then, better to leave everything to us, just what they would like to know is when they planned to go back. I told them that they had one month, Teddy said that they would take care of women's side meaning in Rwandan community, what they wanted me to do was to talk with Mugwiza. Mugwiza Desire was a young tall black handsome man, who was a serious and hard-working man, the first secretary of Rwandese Embassy in Kenya at the time. I told them the same thing, that I didn't know what to tell him. They said that, just go and tell him that we have suggested doing something in order to welcome the children. Wait for his reaction, then, from there you will get what to tell him. The rest will be our responsibility.

When I saw Mr. Mugwiza I told him about my visitors and told him about Teddy and Edith's idea. However, I told him as well that it was hard for me to ask our community for help, because it was too soon, after all they did during the funeral. Mugwiza answered quickly that according to our culture, it was normal to do what they did. To welcome their brother-in-law and show him that his wife has a family where she comes from is one of their responsibilities too. In addition, the funeral and welcoming someone are two different things with two different names. Come back tomorrow after I have spoken with the Ambassador I will be able to tell you what I will do. This conversation gave me hope that once more I could manage to do something good for my children through people, through friends and see myself that I am blessed to be loved and respected something I didn't know before that it was that much.

In doing all this, I did not tell Batsinduka that there was anything to welcome Niwegaju and her husband in a special way. When I began just to tell him about it, he was shocked as he thought that I was ignoring the hard situation we were passing through. I told him not to worry because I did not initiate to do anything because of our situation that I knew better. Then, I began to tell him the story about what made me accept this kind of plan. When I finished the whole story, he became calm and was happy. The only thing he said was that: let us wait for the reaction of others and the last decision.

When I went to see Mugwiza the next day, being a patriotic person and pure Rwandan, he knew that any type of event for Rwandan people, the important thing was drinks. He told me straight away that he was ready to buy all types of drinks for one hundred people! By hearing that I almost fainted and told him that I thought that he would plan for ten people. He replied that Rwandese living in Nairobi were not only ten, and Niwegaju was born and grew in Nairobi, she had friends too. When I left the Embassy I was overwhelmed by joy and began to plan to announce to other Rwandans about the event. The first one that came in my mind was Salam the daughter of Uzamukunda. I went to her office and began to tell her the good news and told her how the plan started and who gave the idea. When I finished the story, she said that on her behalf, she would cook for one hundred people and that would be her contribution. It was as if he knew what Mugwiza planned it even though I was not yet to tell anyone about the numbers of how many people would be invited or how many people Mugwiza mentioned!

When I told this message to Batsinduka, he was so happy and he started to go to his friends too. He got many different contributions, and was given a tent and musical equipment to be used on the day. On the other side, women they gave me 20,000 K sh, which was collected by Teddy and Edith. When I gave the money to Batsinduka since he was the one who had to be in charge and he was the one who knew what was needed, he told me that he didn't need any money that everything was fine. I could use the money in other things. Mugwiza told me that he hoped children would dance for her. When I told this to Rwandan women, they said that it was right, since Niwegaju was one of the dancers before, it would be good to dance for her as well.

At the ceremony, more than two hundred people came but all of them drank and the food was enough for everybody. As for the entertainment Rwandan dancers performed excellently, and other African type of dancers performed too. In addition, our Rwandan ladies were dressed in our cultural costumes and were beautiful as ever, it was like a wedding. Niwegaju was dressed as other ladies but in white and was so beautiful. The car that carried her was chosen and decorated by one of my friends. During the ceremony, one of my friends came where I was sitting, and told me that I was lucky to have my children. I asked her why, since she had grown-up children too. She told me that Niwegaju was asking her: if everything was good, and if I was happy as well. She answered that the way she saw it, I was happy one hundred percent. I came to realise that, whatever she was doing, she did it to make me happy. I knew that my children loved me, but to hear that my daughter was thinking of me and wished to see me happy for what she did, made me feel happier than before.

I moved to Europe. When I left Africa, Muvunangoma went to Kigali where he got a good job.

EUROPE IN MY EYES: HOW I SAW BRITAIN

It was in November 2004 when I left Africa for the first time, I came to Britain where my daughter Niwegaju lived. When I came, she had a two-month old baby Uwera. I was not scared because I was going far from home without being sure about the life I was going to face. I believed that I knew quite a lot concerning the life in Europe, since I had many friends from that continent, and I knew other things from what I was reading. But when I was in Britain I realised that I knew nothing about their lifestyle.

For instance, I lived in Kenya in the city of Nairobi. In that part of Africa like any other big city, you find different people having different cultures according to where people came from. Moreover, no one has time for other people as each one minds his own business. Though Nairobi people were not comfortable to associate with others who they do not share the same ethnic background. For example, Luhya even if they are Kenyan, they will not associate with Kikuyu although they are Kenyan as well or Lou etc… at least not much. This was not the same for Congolese, Rwandese, and Tanzanian, Ugandans and so on… Where I was passing in Britain people could live for so long without knowing the name of their neighbours, as each one enters his house without minding the next door. However, people from each culture or each part of the world could come together occasionally or when they have an event or some cultural matter to deal with. For example, Rwandans could meet once in two weeks or in a month, in order to teach young people cultural dance or other things of common interest and so on. What happened in Kenya was the opposite of other African countries such as Tanzania, Uganda and others where people used to come and greet any newcomers in the area. This is the attitude that is found in many parts of Africa. But you get this behavior in capital Nairobi.

When I left my so-called poor continent Africa, Britain was my first country to visit. I knew that I was now in Europe as I could see good and smooth roads without any hole everywhere I passed. There were many people on the road walking freely without any fear and many houses built in the same style and size. Without knowing the name of your road and the number of the house you can get lost as the houses are so similar. When coming from Africa you may think that the houses do not have a good plan. This is because I lived in a big house that had only one bathroom. I thought that it might be because of economical reasons behind the building.

What I liked the most, and what showed me that I am in an industrialised country, I was happy to see that in fact everyone has a place to sleep and food to eat, even those who do not work. Yes, it should be like this, otherwise to be in an industrialised country can be meaningless. Indeed, there are some charities which provide food and sleeping places for homeless and not only feed them but provide clothing as well and all these for free. I could not believe that in many countries in Europe, even if you do not work or do nothing, still you have the right to have somewhere to sleep and foods from the government's budget. That is why I came to realise that Europe is one or more steps ahead of where they still have a name of 'third world countries'. This is what we call good parenting in a family when a parent can provide all needs for his children.

However, this system of having everything for free is being abused by many and so taken for granted by some people. They do not bother to search for a job as they know that they have a life guaranteed through benefit. What is so bad is that this kind of life is being transmitted to some young people as they think that to live without working is normal.

This is what is very different from the other parts of the world. In my continent Africa, there are until now during this modern era people who die with hunger. For instance, most of the crimes that happen in Africa are due to hunger or trying to escape from poverty. Up to now you can get some parts where children have no chance to go to school. Even if someone gives them access to a school, they can't afford to buy books, pencils, rubbers and so on, therefore, 'poor forever'? Answers are with only African people. The truth is that these kinds of families have never worn shoes, and yet they have talent that will never be used.

At first I was able to talk to some people, but the communication was a problem because of my accent. It took me time to be used to western culture. Back home I used to say hello on the street, but here when I say hello to someone, sometimes they look at me as if I was crazy. Instead of talking to me they prefer to go back and talk to their dogs! Don't expect that your neighbour will knock on your door to say good morning, and don't try that to them, because they might call the police if you knock at their doors. It is Kamran Mofid an economist and writer who remarked that:

In the process of modernization and industrialization we have become more and more individualistic, more secular. We have lost the art of empathy and sympathy. Progress has been at the expense of comradeship, solidarity, concern for others and a sense of the common good. (Mofid: 2002, 5)

Having said this, it is not all of them, because there is a small number of people who are happy to help, and if you did ask to go somewhere they were ready to show or to take you anywhere. I read in one of the newspapers in 2005, that in Germany, they wanted to start schools that would teach people how to laugh because they had forgotten about it. Then I thought that even in Britain, they need a school like that, because more people have the same problem. There are some who are left only with the so-called smile; this is to pull their lips to the sides for half a second. I came to meet a lot of old people who told me that they have never had a family for themselves and that was their choice. Instead, they look as if they don't have enough contact with people and the good friends they have are their animals. Maybe that is why some leave fortune to animals when they die. Others have separated from their families for many years and they have forgotten each other. Someone told me that if he met his children, he wouldn't know them even though they still lived in the same area! One of my friends told me that she doesn't know if her mum is still alive or dead! She doesn't know anything about her for more than twenty years! And when you talk to a person like this for some time, no matter how much money he or she has, they do not have a happy life. I have seen in the news some children age fifteen and below, gathering in big numbers and enjoying killing old people or other children! They go forth advising parents to carry their babies in their chest in order to keep them safe.

However, back home in Africa we were taught that the back of ladies is the best side and comfortable for babies. I have never seen this kind of life in Africa because, there are no worries like that concerning any kind of attack so you are sure that your baby is safe and comfortable on your back anyway. I feel sorry and it hurt me to see some young Africans who came here and forgot even their own people where they came from, but I had thought that in the near future the majority of our young people are going to be happy and proud to stay in their continent in order to build their countries. And when you have a British passport they are very careful in reminding you, and want you to remind them too, who you are, over and over, each time you fill any forms, you have to tell them your origin. So don't think that if you get it you are recognised as full British, which I saw that to be very good to those who maybe, can be too comfortable and might forget where they came from.

In the past it was taboo and a curse to kill someone except in times of war. I came to realise why in Britain they give a medal to anyone who has been good to others. It is a way of encouraging people to make every effort to be good while dealing with other people or neighbours. Something that is culturally natural to Africans even though some bad seeds of hatred have been planted, a neighbour is always considered as a member of the family. Therefore, at least ninety percent have responsibility to help each other and the least, history is judging them.

Rwandan genocide in 1994 happened in sight of the whole world as everybody was watching like a movie. After this event, Rwandans had started a hard process of reconciliation which was successful day by day, and this was helped with the history of unity they had before. In fact, Alison in the book called *War has Changed Our Life, Not Our Spirit* says that:

'*After the genocide in Rwanda, Tutsi widows (who the husbands has been massacred), began coming together as they faced the same sort of problems. They worked together on their small projects, and their group expanded. They were approached by Hutu widows whose Tutsi husbands were also killed in the genocide. So they took them in. Then, they saw other Hutu women struggling alone, unable to send their children to school. These women had Hutu husbands in prison, accused of genocidal crimes. The Tutsi widows expanded their association to include these women too… Women can become leaders of reconciliation. They realise what they have in common and stick together.'* (Des Forges: 2001, 13)

It was a very hard step but they had to do it, and it was successful day by day. I have hope because more is yet to come.

On the other hand, in Britain there are some families who have different lifestyles, compared with the majority of society. Their children do not have much freedom at home and they know that their parents have the right to punish them, when they can't call the police which to me this is how it has to be. But other parts of society where they were forced to give their children freedom, to me this kind of freedom is like to abuse freedom or on the other hand is premature freedom. But all of this is because they don't trust the parents which is something that comes from far sometimes from parents and grandparents who grew up in care and missed something in life as children. But these other families who know that children have to be under their parents most of the time they took their children to private school, or they took them to schools abroad.

On the other hand these parents are not parents who came from work and first passed to the pubs, they go straight to their families and try to be able to get time to spend with their families as much as they can.

In the street the first time when I saw the people with their dogs, you could think that they were following their orders given by these dogs, to see how they were walking with them, because when they were stopped the owner also stopped too, when they started to walk the owner walked. In Africa, there are different cultures, according countries, and sometimes, some parts of the country. But there are many cultures which you will get everywhere in the whole of Africa like socialisation.

The way I saw some Europeans, concerning culture of loving animals I believed that you could get it everywhere you go in Europe, or anywhere in west countries, but the problem was that sometimes some of them can forget that they are animals: yes they are their friends, but they are still animals.

I get this idea when one French woman Isabella Dinoire in 2005 her dog ate her and damaged her very badly. She was thanking a family of the donor who gave her new lips, a chin and nose. The world's first face transplant showed off her new features in a room full of reporters and cameras. According to *Birmingham Post,* Tuesday 7 February 2006. Later after there were many different cases where dogs were killing people especially children when those dogs were the pets of those families.

While walking around in the city, several times I met with people having different kind of foods in their hands, running and eating! And when I saw those people, most of them seemed to be respectable people. When I asked why respectable people would eat on the street, I was told that they do not have time to sit and eat properly; therefore, they redeem their time. There were others who were a surprise to look afar and see someone walking hardly like a person. In approaching those creatures I came to realise that it was indeed people except that they had been transformed by being overweight. The way they looked you may assume that they have been bitten by bees on their faces. You recognise that they are people as they can talk and are dressed like any human being. In addition, you can't guess their gender unless you approach them or hear them speaking.

In case it is a man his chin, jaw, and throat look like one thing all together. To look at his chest, he has big breasts more than women! Those breasts are hanging on the top of the stomach. The stomach itself is too big more than an expecting woman. As this stomach is down to his thigh, it makes it very difficult to walk properly; he has to walk very slowly, maybe because of his weight that holds the legs down. So I wanted to look at them non-stop but couldn't because, I thought that they could become angry in case they found out that I was observing them.

In my ignorance I thought that it was a kind of illness and when I asked what kind of illness it was. I was told that it is the result of eating too much and some of them die! It surprises me to know that there are some parts of the world, where people can die because of eating, when I knew that there are people who die because of hunger. In the city centre most of the people seem to run instead of walking. This made my life so difficult when I was still new in the country as no one was willing to stop and listen to my question. Yet I was struggling in finding my way around. I had to try several times to stop someone until when I would get anyone who was kind enough to give me his or her time. One day I wanted to ask a lady, who was with a man in Manchester, but they went inside their house before I reached them. It was in the afternoon and began to become dark. I decided to knock on their door and ask for directions. They tried their best to explain but failed as I could not understand the map properly. In the end they discovered that even if they directed me, still I might be in some kind of trouble. Therefore, they decided to put me in the lady's car and take me to the address and I was so grateful.

Once or twice a week, I saw in the news someone who was killed or had been beaten badly. I asked myself if in Africa where I came from, there is a similar situation or we don't see such situation by lack of strong media. For instance when I was coming to Europe particularly in England, I had a very different picture of England. I was thinking of going to a peaceful land where crimes do not exist, as most people are civilised and teachers of human rights. I assumed that they are capable to guide society no matter how people may behave. Unfortunately, I came to realise that people are the same; the only difference is that the societies in western countries are well organised in terms of helping their people. I am saying this in regard of social services where no one can die of hunger and everybody who is old gets help. While in Africa eating properly is the privilege of some and others die with hunger.

Having said this, old people in Africa even though they are poor they die happier because they die within the families. This is different from what I have seen in this country. When someone is old it seems to me that he has no value anymore to the level that he or she is taken to home care in order to wait for his or her death, but there are few families which they are happy to take care of their parents at home. When in Africa an elder person is gold, anyone wants to be near him or her, they are respected in the community and he or she is consulted by people when there is an issue that matters in the community. But what I saw in Europe is that others took their parents to the homes to die there. Some of them they were raised in homes where they put orphans or simply homeless children. Sometimes someone like that who grew up in those homes, and later after staying by him or herself without a family on his or her own, is a person who has never got chance to know the value of family. This person if they are able to have some qualifications he or she will be going to work, pass the pub and pass the ready food, and go home, to be welcomed by the pets and the TV. That is the life they know. When they have problems, other friends where they will go to talk to: is a counsellor, but these counsellors will give their patients time to be with, next, is to go to depression medication. I came to see that they believe that a big number of old people had to have dementia, which to me I don't see it that way, I see that one of the reasons it is like that, is one I said before. Because like Africans, in that poverty life, but the old people in big numbers they die without dementia to the level that Africans didn't know about this problem, even if it is there, it is in a small number which is known only by families of patients and close friends.

DEPRESSION IS UK'S BIGGEST SOCIAL PROBLEM, GOVERNMENT TOLD

Around fifteen percent of the population suffers from depression or anxiety, says Lord Lanyard, emeritus professor at the Centre for Economic Performance of the London School of Economics.

The economic cost in terms of lost productivity is huge – around £17bn, or 1.5% UK gross domestic product.

There are now more than one million mentally ill people receiving incapacity benefits – more than the total number of unemployed people receiving unemployment benefits, he writes in the *British Medical Journal*

By Sara Boseley, health editor The Guardian – Friday 28 April 2006.

Article history.

That kind of society at the last time of their life, I was told that some who don't have their own family they left their property with charity, or if they are people who can make friends, they can leave what they have to their adapted family if they have them, or simply to their pets. All of this was new to me, according to where I was coming from, where everyone knows that, his or her life is to be with a family.

I came to see that Europe know and respect human right, especially to women and children, you can say that it is a better place to women and children, on the other hand sometimes women they use these rights they are given in abuse of men, and men know that they have to be very careful if they want to have their marriage and their property. To foreign women, those coming from outside of that continent, since where they come from places like Africa or Asia in this part of our world, women are second citizens. Not Rwanda at this time of R P F's governing, where women hold more than half parliament seats since the R P F time. This came to be the only country in the world to have a big number of women in the cabinet. Something they see as one of the rare and unprecedented breakthroughs in women leadership. This helped women in the whole country in all of steps of life.

So some African women when they are in Europe see that they are on top of their men, to them it is something they have never dreamed of, and their men, then, they have to know that they are in trouble, which to many can't be easy, when they are still held by their culture and know themselves as leaders of their family, when their wives saw it the other way around. In that case, few marriages would survive, because normally, according to their culture men are the head of the family and most of the time, the breadwinner for the family, but in Europe then, with or without him, they will survive, for that reason, their patience and respect which normally needed in marriages.

But some of them, after throwing their husband out, they would regret it and try to make them come back, but, some were not easy to win back because the shock they got, it wiped out the trust to their wives. They can't afford to carry that shame again of being thrown out by women.

QUOTE OF THE BOOK

Largely the British community is broken up into three parts. The older generation, the very young and the 'able-bodied'. The young are kept in little room most of the times to 'stay out of the able-bodied way' the able-bodied need to 'live their life'. The old are locked up in nursing homes, or in their houses with their carers, cut from the youngest and the 'able-bodied'. The 'able-bodied' spend their time in offices or in other working arrangements 'working their life away'. The young never get a chance to spend quality time with the 'able-bodied' and older generations.

These three groups need each other, the young need to learn from the older generation and it keeps the older generation 'young at heart' and it gives more meaning to their lives, it gives the young the chance to become better human beings, the 'able-bodied' need both the young and the older generation to have a well-rounded life.

In short the society has been broken up like this in order to make money; it is to make the human being a machine with no real meaning to life. The 'able-bodied' work their lives away and work hard to pay for homes that they eventually use to pay for carers and nursing homes. The nine-to-five culture is a main thing used to control; the education system is crushed and the youngest have no option but to follow in the footsteps of their predecessors, they have no inclination to take it upon themselves to take care of them as there was no real connection that was established in the first place. Only the very lucky escapes this vicious cycle. The human essence, spirit and real potential have no place in this society.

By Niwegaju Sinzi Greiner.

Most of the parents they came back from work very tired and they passed in the pub or somewhere else, the children grew up almost by themselves, the result is the children became more independent in premature time, they don't know how to deal with grown up people, the coincidence is that when the parents try to punish them as parents, they will call the police because that is what they were told by the teachers, they will see it to be abuse.

On the other hand because the parents have a lot of stress because of the work and sometimes they will see the children like they stress them too. So these parents will not talk with the children in a friendly way.

Between them will not be friendship. Next some of the children will see that they are unwanted children, will go to the street and will become homeless, and it will be possibile for them to be taken into care with other homeless children.

In that process, and sometimes, that person will not know anything like respect on the street or simply to respect the older people. And this person will have grown up with anger seeing himself or herself as an unwanted person, someone who had never got someone who was close to him or her from an early age, from his or her family home.

Next will be hush to almost who came across to him or her
No respect on the way sometimes to anyone.
Will get problem of anger management.
Will go to drugs; think that will help him or her to feel relaxed.
Will have depression.
And sometimes will be a killer.

KILLED BECAUSE HE HAD NO MATCHES
Metro, Wednesday 26 June, 2005 by Oliver Stallwood.

> *A father of three was beaten to death by 'hoodie' troublemakers yesterday, after he was unable to give them a light for a cigarette.*
> *Mugilan Suthermen a non-smoker was called names before being battered about the head and body. One hooligan kicked his head as if it was a football.*

KNIFED BY THUG FOR SAYING HELLO
The Sun, Wednesday 15 June, 2005 by John Troup.

A yob has been caged for two years for beating up a man and slashing his head with a knife just because he said 'Good morning'. Security guard David Harwood, 59, always greeted passers-by on his 20-minute walk to walk...

£20,000 BILL AS GIRL, 17, RUINS HOUSE
Metro, Friday 13 April 13, 2007.

Revellers from across the country wrecked a family home after a teenager inspired by TV series Skins issued a party invite on MySpace.

Around 200 partygoers caused £20,000 of damage to the house in a quiet cul-de-sac, and seven police cars were called to the scene. Now the mother of Rachel Bell wants her 17 year old daughter arrested.

TREATED LIKE A DOG, USED AS A PUNCHBAG, THE LIFE AND DEATH OF A BABY BOY CALLED 'SMILEY'
Daily Mail, Wednesday 12 November, 2008.

Baby P's happy smile masked months of pain and terror inflicted by his mother and stepfather.

The toddler was speaking his first words and had already learned to call his mother's boyfriend 'dad'.

In return, he was used as a punchbag by the sadistic thug who trained him 'like a dog' – the child instinctively put his head to the floor when the brute approached.

Known to family as Smiley, the toddler would be wrapped in layers of clothing until he began sweating and gasping for air. His fingernails were pinched – and possibly ripped by pliers – until they fell off...

SLAVES WERE BEATEN AND HELD CAPTIVE BY 'INVISIBLE HANDCUFFS'

Daily Mirror, Saturday 23 November, 2013 by Andy Linnes and Russel Nyers.

Three women held as slaves for 30 years were subjected to beatings, police revealed yesterday.

Last night Home Office minister James Brokenshere said slaves could be hidden in almost every London neighbourhood. And he warned that as many as 6,000 people could be captive across the UK.

BRITAIN'S BIGGEST COFFIN. 60 STONE DAD'S CASKET IS 7FT 11 BY 4 FT. 6.

The Sun, Friday 10 August 10, 2007.

A dad who weighed around 60 stone has buried in the biggest coffin ever made in Britain.

Mark Bamber's mahogany structure tipped the scales at more than half a ton the casket — 7ft 11ins long, 4ft 6ins wide and 30ins deep was too big for a hearse and had to be taken to the cemetery on a horse-drawn flat, back cart.

OBESITY EPIDEMIC MAY TRIGGER 12,000 CANCER CASES A YEAR.

Science Correspondendent The Guardian, Tuesday December 5, 2006, Ian Sample.

ARTICLE HISTORY.

Cancer specialist used the most recent figures on obesity from the Department of Health to calculate the number of people at risk of developing cancer.

According to the health department figures, there were 24.2 million obese or overweight people in the UK in 2003, a number the department predicts will rise by fourteen percent to 27.6 million by 2010.

BRITAIN IS BECOMING THE 'OBESITY CAPITAL OF THE WORLD'

Lga Press Release, 15 August 2008

It has been estimated that in England, by 2012 one million children will be obese, by 2025 around a quarter twenty-four percent of boys will be obese.

One day I visited my friend and she had a girl who came at her home as a refugee, she was a thirteen year old girl, her mum was trying to force her to sleep with men so that she can start to have babies instead of go ahead with school, because according to her mum, they can get more money (benefit) this is type of greedy ones who never know or care for the future of their daughter.

Other group of parents who wants their daughter to go ahead with their education, help them by gives them contraception, from age of ten years old.

MAGNUSSON PAID PRICE FOR HIGH WAGE BILL.

Exclusive by Paul Smith Sundaymirror.co.uk 16/12/2007

I come to see that British people they like sports especially football some obsessed to it, some can think about their team 80 times a day. And seven per cent of fans are so obsessed they think about the game once a minute, a survey suggested.

Disregarding sleeping time, the average fan drifts off into their own fantasy football world once every 12 minutes.

Sheffield United fans top the league when it comes to soccer obsession, thinking about their club 110 times a day on average. The Virgin Money survey revealed.

And it is the £110,000 a week wages paid to Freddie Ljungberg
almost treble his Arsenal deal that sparked Gadmundusson into action.

About the youngest, the first time to see how they treated them, to me, they were like 'prisoners' children can't play outside by themselves and come back when they are tired and hungry, just to ask their mum for food, this is what I knew from children where I lived, to be a child, then even to go to school, they are escorted by old people, and from school is the same thing.

Is it breaking the law to leave underage people in the house by themselves?

When I asked I was told that all of that is because of the safety of the children, because bad people they are everywhere and can harm them in different ways or simply can steal them.

ARMIN MEIWES FROM WIKIPEDIA, THE FREE ENCYCLOPEDIA

Meiwes (born 1, 1961) is a German who achieved International notoriety for killing and eating a voluntary victim he had found via the internet.

After Meiwes and the victim jointly attempted to eat the victim's severed penis, Meiwes killed his victim and proceeded to eat a large amount of his flesh. December 25 2001 Meiwes in his home amputated Brandes penis and the two men attempted to eat the penis together before Brandes was killed. Because of his deeds, Meiwes is also known as the 'Rotenburg Cannibal' or 'Der Metzgermeister' (Master Butcher) Meiwes was arrested in December 2002.

AFRICA

I asked one of my friends, who came from Africa, and was in these developed countries for many years, about his view concerning life in the developed countries, how he saw these behaviours which I called strange ones.

He told me that it was how it had to be, because when the country was busy with developing life, there have to be other people who will be left behind; they will be doing their own things which no one can understand. Because sometimes, they see that there are no other ways they can be known.

Yes when I look back in big cities in Africa, and see how life is changing so quickly, some they don't have enough time with their families like before, it shows me that it is how things start to change slowly slowly, and it can be easy in that way, when people will realise what is happening it can be too late to turn it back.

I have friends back home in Rwanda who live in the countryside. When I spoke to them in 2013 they told me that the children who live and work in the big cities used to come to visit them regularly and bring them their grandchildren to see them. However, since the era of the mobile phone began and they bought one for them, things changed drastically. They would talk almost everyday, but sometimes it would be two to five years to actually see each other physically. I told myself that if it started to happen in that small country, where it only takes some hours to drive to any part you want to go, then, that is the beginning.

If it will go ahead like that with internet in every house, which slowly in fifty to one hundred years, I can't imagine where Africa will be. Only now some parts have started to fight for their right, which is to be open about their homesexuals, like gay… Only what I think is that they will not change enough to be Meiwes, Josef Fritzl… or someone to go out naked when they have no mental problems.

I am not saying that African people in their Africa they only do the right things, there are many; many good things African people have to learn from outside of Africa. Like to know the value of time, to be happy to improve someone who has talent… without waiting for only someone who is related to them or the person to buy that support… and know that by supporting the person they are not supporting individuality, they are developing the whole country etc.

To ordinary people there are many horrible things they do, which can't be known because the media is still behind.

Like some people who believe in witchcraft, and believe that by doing everything they are told by so called witchdoctors, they will get what they want, which most of the time is to try to escape poverty in one way or another.

Some they asked them to come with parts of human beings, some they are told to come with particular parts of albino or of small boy, girl, head etc…

The same thing to women who have a fear to be apart or be divorced by husbands, many times not because they love them so much, but, because they have a fear, how they will survive without them, especially when it is them who is the breadwinner.

All of this shows me that, some African people they have lost their confidence and believe that they are poor even when they are not. The problem now is to get proper leaders who will work for their countries not for themselves.

The leaders who will sacrifice themselves and say no, now enough is enough, no more orders, no more bribes from outside or inside. No more excuses of the past. I am here now to work for change. I am here to work for my country, for my Africa, if it means to die then I will die but I will be a good example for tomorrow and others will go ahead from where I will be.

African people can ask themselves what they have done after independence. What was missed and how they used the richness they have, if they used them very well or not, and why? Africa can jump to superpower if they treat themselves well.

- Naigeria: oil, metals.
- Libyia: oil.
- Sudan: oil, chromium, gold gypsums.
- Angola: oil.
- Gabon: oil, mangonese, uranium.
- Tunisia: oil, phosphates.
- Congo D R C: diamond, cobalt.
- Congo Brazaville: oil.
- S. Africa: gold.
- Tanzania: diamond, gold.
- Sierra-Leone: diamond, gold, rutile, (titanium ore).

Among others from source:
SOURCE: PHILIP'S ENCYCLOPEDIA (2007), OCTOPUS PUBLISHING GROUP, LONDON.

Some Africans they still give people positions following how they know them not qualifications, I can understand that Africa is one part of the world, its richness supposed to benefit its people before benefiting someone else, and go with the proper international law in all levels.

So that Africans can work with others, not to work for them, not to be used to kill themselves and their continent.

Not to wait for anyone from outside to come with sweet words, sympathy, and think that they love them so much more than how they love themselves.

Nothing strong like (unity) Africans have to wake up and know that they have to work together.

And forget to force unnecessary respect for them, and learn from outside of their Africa.

Don't waste time of people who want any service to them. Maybe to make them feel respected or powerful. Some leaders in some parts of Africa, when MP visited some areas they will close the shops, the schools, so that they can go to see the leader, when this leader will come, there will be another ten cars or more behind his or her, something you can ask yourself if it is respect or a waste of time and money.

Africa needs proper leaders like Thomas Sankara who was considered by some as proper patriotic to Africa an African 'Che Guevara' who wanted to give the continent in general and the countries in particular a new socio-political dimension. Once before he was murdered, he said that 'while revolutionaries as individuals can be murdered, you cannot kill ideas'.

A leader like Kwame Nkrumah, after getting independence for his country said that, 'we are going to see that we create our own African personality and identity. We again rededicate ourselves in the struggle to emancipate other countries in Africa; for our independence is meaningless unless it is linked up with the total liberation of the Africa continent'. And once said that he had no arms to fight the Americans, the British nor the France, but he had an inspired weapon that is the 'truth', 'truth will forever prevail' so long as some of them live. Thomas Sankara in Burkina Faso once said that revolutionary person don't die. Muammar al-Gaddafi in Libia. Patrick Rumumba in Congo, Micombero in Burundi and King Mutara Rudahigwa in Rwanda who were determined to do all they could to see that Great Lake became independent and Africa in general. These are some of the African leaders who were killed because of their ideas but what they died for will never die, to give Africa proper freedom.

Leaders like Paul Kagame who managed to win Rwanda genocide and build the country in less than twenty years, to become a role-model in neighbouring countries and beyond. On the occasion of the commemoration of the 20th anniversary of the genocide against the Tusti in Rwanda said that: 'there are stories whose truth must be told in full, no matter how uncomfortable'.

Africa is still in struggle.

Some parts of Africa I don't know which is a better time between colonial time and now, like D R C. In the colonial time they suffered a lot when Belgians one of the systems they had to boost their rubber production was simple, to go to villages and brutally butcher them, cut up their hands, one hand or both, so that others would fear and do whatever they were told to do.

But after 30th June 1960 when they got their independence, being one of the biggest countries and rich, it is still in one of poorest countries when the society live with a lot of problems, there was a time when I was watching BBC1 *Panorama* programme was in Ituli in Congo D R C where there was a war and the U.N. was there to protect people but the reality according to an interview with the soldiers, the same U.N. staff were coming with guns for fighters, they were promoting the war so that they could be busy because they had another agender of taking gold.

To see like this researchers, International Rescue Committee.

A new IRC survey has found that 5,400,000 people have died from war-related causes in Congo since 1998 – the world's deadliest documented conflict since WW11.

The vast majority died from non-violent causes such as malaria, diarrhoea, pneumonia, and malnutrition, easily preventable and treatable conditions when people have access to health care and nutrition!

One big and good lesson Africans can and have to learn from Europe is the unity they have now, and think where they came from. To see America, it is United States of America. That is what Africa needs.

It can be good if they can wake up now when they are still having their culture.

One day, in 2003, in Kenya Nairobi, when I was with Batsinduka at his home, his American friend Brian visited him with a group of his friends, some of them it was their first time to come to Africa, they were in Africa for two weeks, in our conversations I asked one gentleman who was near with me: how he saw Africa?

He told me that Mr. Brian gave him a very good gift to be the one who made him visit Africa, because now he sees where paradise is, somewhere God came for relaxing after many problems at his continent!

I asked him again why he says that and simply he told me that is how Africa is, it's geography, weather, but especially the culture and behaviour of people in general.

I thought that yes in a big part Africans are brave in many ways, compared to some parts of Europe where they are still poor when up to the 2000s a woman could be pregnant just to sell her baby soon after birth, and sell the baby for $20! Acccording to one of my friends from Eastern Europe I talked to in 2005… I think I can't compare their life and behaviour with poor people in Africa.

Though, I still think that Africa might be somewhere better by now more than where Africa is now. And I believe that African people don't do enough yet.

Now if by chance Africans can wake up now, and correct their mistakes, when in other parts of life around the world in general people are seen according to qualifications not colour. And when Barrack Obama the boy who was born to a Lou man from Kisumu Kenya and an American girl became president of the USA, the man many saw him as the first black president of the USA with his wife the daughter of black Americans, the people who originally were Africans but were brought there as slaves. When there are others who believe that John Hanson was the first black president and first president of the USA, when George Washington was definitely not the first president of the USA. It says that he was the first President of the USA under the constitution the USA follows today.

(macquirelatory.com/first%20Black%20President.htm)

But all of this shows us that anyone can do anything.

Today many parts of Africa, although rich in human as well as natural resources, remain among the poorest regions of the world, with the highest debt burdens in the world.

In recent United Nations publication on the global distribution of income, it was noted that the richest 20% of the world's population received 82.7% of the world's income, while the poorest 20% receive only 1.4%. After so many decades of economic development, industrialisation, modernisation and globalisation, global economic prosperity has rarely filtered down to the poor. In another study it was noted that the richest 360 people in the planet own as much wealth as the poorest two billion.

What this means is that globally, we have a situation of economic apartheid in which the proportion of the haves to the have-nots is roughly 1:4.

Consider also global energy consumption, C02 emission, the amount of waste produced, pollution and other environmental factors, and it becomes clear that the same 20% of the global population is also responsible for some 80% of the forces of destruction of our planet. Dr Mofid Kanram in GLOBALISATION (36-37)

I am sure that African know that the history of liberty is the history of resistance as Martin Luther King said "if a man hasn't discovered something he will die for, he isn't fit to live." They know that they need change, that is why they started to stand for themselves by asking freedom from the ICC, that is good beginning.

The Master of Universe has taken good measure of Africa's importance in world affairs and has rightly concluded it doesn't amount to a bushel of beans. Comment from 00:43:37 Sunday 17th November 2013 mwene Kalinda (The Sunday Times Rwanda)

MY LAST STRUGGLE

While I was in Britain, like everyone 'foreign' some of them, concerning why. I had to struggle to get permission to stay in the country, sometimes to many of them, it is not that easy, unless if you are lucky, first, some they will pass to people who are known to be experts, and have experience of situations, and teach them how they have to deal with that new life they are preparing themselves to enter in, especially how they will deal with the officers who will meet them at the first stage. So they will create a story for the person in need, some might change their identity if they need to, these people will be friends or relatives, and some will trust their story, and no need of forge one, as far as they know that is a genuine one, and strong enough to anyone who can listen to it.

These two people who have different stories, a created story, and genuine one, they go to the officer who is concerned, surprisingly, sometimes the concerned officers believe the created story, and refuse the genuine one!

Indeed according to the experience of the officers, how can they know who to believe? So it is a matter of luck. Unless it can be very strong and maybe a dangerous one, officers, then, can go ahead with their hard work of deep research, which definitely, at that point will know who this person is.

But that takes a lot of money and time, they can't do that kind of research to all of the thousands and thousands of cases a year.

And if you are lucky and your case is accepted, you will get the permission to stay in the country without a fear, even for a very short time. And at that point you will be a friend to many people around you, because they will see you as a clever person, who can fight for her or his survival.

But if they refuse your case, you will start to suffer in different ways, especially when you have no permit to work, and you have no other kind of support, at that time you might even lose friends, sometimes if you have relatives around, some can go far from you, because they fear that you might cause them some kind of problems, or you can become a burden to them.

At that time some of these people, though, they knew that to work without a work permit is a big risk: but they would work anyway, for survival, most of the time cleaning or if they are lucky, caring for old people…

One day my friend had a job in a big company, she was a very hard-working lady, her boss told her that he wanted to see her in his office, when she entered the office there were two other people who to her were new faces, they gave her a seat, but in her mind, it was telling her that, somehow, they got information that she was working illegally, and they were there to arrest her.

In the office, first they asked her if she was happy with her work, when they were talking with her, she was like she was not there with them, because she started to become sick, she was sweating, her stomach inside was like it was mixed up, feeling dizzy. They asked her if she was OK, and she said yes she was OK. But she was not.

They noticed that she had something which was troubling her, but they didn't know which one, they came with water for her to drink, and they had to wait for their interview, they went out, and they were just walking around there, to give her time for whatever it was, so that she could relax.

She went to the bathroom with the intention of trying to see if she could get away and run away, but she was not successful to get anywhere to pass, so she had to come back.

When their meeting started again, they told her that the new officers came from head office to see her because she was a hard-working lady, and they wanted to promote her. They wanted to take her as their permanent staff too! And they told her the next day to come with her papers, so that they could do what they had to do according her new promotion.

Still she went out but that day was her last day, because she didn't have proper papers to come back with, and she couldn't come with her forged papers. Simply she disappeared.

And many times ignorance and selfishness can be a dangerous thing. This reminded me again of the book *Unscrambling Africa Reconciliation Process Europe & Africa.* 'The fail of development in some of Africans nations was caused by our robbing their resources. We cannot change the past but maybe we can change our hearts instead of seeing these migrants as a threat to our standard of living *(P. 38)* I saw how the war over power, resources and influence began and Europe fell short of fulfilling God's plan for itself. In not serving Africa to find God's identity we lost our own revelation about it as well. But more than anything else we failed to help the African people come to grips with their divine destiny and have instead robbed them of their dignity.' *(P.38-40 by Segun Johnson, Roger Michael, Samuel Rhein Michael Schiffmann and Chris Seaton)*

To me too, it was not easy, I was up and down for five good years. At the first time when I gave myself that struggle, from my daughter Niwegaju and Uwera her daughter's home in Preston. They took me to Bury a small town in Manchester, for some time, they sent me refusal letters, telling me that I am no longer their responsibility, no support no shelter. Better to go back where I came from, or they will take me back by force.

No one had told me before about that system of throwing people out to the street. When their cases went wrong, the system I came to know, some people they called it: Blunkett's law. So it was not easy for me to understand it, I was lucky to have my daughter, but surprisingly, I was not brave enough to tell her that bad news! For something like that to happen to me I saw it as shame to me.

I didn't know how I could tell it to anyone let alone my child.

I had no hope of anything, but I had to hold on and wait, sometimes I had the foolish idea that since I am an old lady, who has never broken any law anywhere, and has no intention to do that in the future, they will see that I can't harm anyone, and that will give me immunity and Blunkett's law would not touch me.

Though I tried to ask advice from the few friends I had, they gave me many different pieces of advice, I tried to find someone who could give me somewhere to sleep for some time in case I might not get that immunity, but I was unlucky for that too. Everyone I was telling my problem and asking for help or room to sleep for a few days, it was the last time to have communication with him or her, including some Rwandan family I had known there who were almost my neighbours. But I had big hope in a Rwandan young man who was settled in Manchester, who once I kept him in my house back home for some time with his relative, when they had some problems, him too, like everyone else, after telling him my problem, that was the last conversation I had with him, next he would not pick up my phone again! I had a hope that to keep him at my home or not, only to be a Rwandan and know me back home, he would be happy to help me. But I was wrong.

Though concerning Niwegaju, I knew that something like that could break her heart, and maybe she would blame me for that, by asking herself why all of that in the first place? So because of circumstances like that, I told myself to try on my own some other things without having to involve her.

True indeed, the date came for me to go out, I had nowhere to go then, I didn't know what to do, and even when I saw officers with their keys to throw me out, from where I thought to be my home, my mind was still dumb, couldn't help me to move on, the same mind couldn't let me tell my daughter either.

The officers were good enough to offer to keep my things for some days, so that I left with what I could carry, and could go wherever I wanted to go.

Outside without knowing where to go, but I had to go. I went with a small suitcase to the library, where I used to go whenever I wanted to go and pass my time. But that time it was not to pass time, it was to try to hide myself from my mind which was not helping me at all. I was like I was in a deep sleep and I was dreaming.

Dreaming that I was on the street without knowing where I was going to sleep when the dark time was there.

Normally I had people who I used to meet in the library, and we used to say hello, but at that time, maybe, because of that suitcase I had, or maybe the way they were reading me through my face, no one wanted to talk to me, when they saw me they would pass far from where I was!

But the time to close the library had to come; when it came like everyone, me too, I had to go out, with my small suitcase. I went to sit on the bench in the bus stop, after sitting there for thirty minutes, it was like I woke up, and had my normal mind back.

I asked myself what I was doing there, and at that time I remembered the lady who I had seen once, a friend of the Sierra-Leone girl I was sharing a house with, this lady was from Zimbabwe, Mrs. Trisha Gumbo who I came to know that she was the same age as my daughter, it happened for some reason when I saw her, I asked her mobile phone number and she gave it to me, so I decided to try and call her and remind her who I was, and tell her what had happened to me. When I thought about the Rwandan young man, the way he disappeared, even though I helped him, it was not the point, simply I assumed that knowing him from home, only could be a good enough reason to be number one, to rescue me.

It was a matter of trying then, it was the last solution, I had no hope for this Zimbabwean girl, but I did it anyway. She was the one who picked up the phone, after telling her my story, she sounded like it shocked her, at that time she told me to stay where I was, and she was coming to my rescue, in a few minutes she was there with her husband, it was my first time to see him, they greeted me with a lot of respect, they were calling me mum, and they looked to be very sorry for me.

Though it was not far and there were a lot of buses, they hired a taxi, inside the taxi no one talked about anything, at home she showed me my room, and she tried to tell me a lot of good things to make me feel relaxed. She gave me a long time of counselling, and brought me a Bible and showed me where to read, and she went on by telling me to feel at home, and see her like my daughter, and see that house as my house. And she told me to stay as long as I wanted, that they were happy to have me at their home, I didn't know if the things she gave me were in the house or if she went shopping for that purpose.

Because everything she gave me to use was new, and she gave me everything necessary, I was comfortable with her and her family, her husband and their young daughter, she was my angel, who rescued me from the streets of Bury, and I forgot all about those Rwandans who hid themselves from me and others, and said God had something for me in his or her store, and I did not regret what I did for him (this Manchester man), I was paid through Trisha. I will always help when I can, because I saw that you can be paid in other ways, with someone else, not exactly the same person who you helped.

That is how and when I came to Birmingham. My GP directed me to Community Integration Parternship, it was a college where mainly there were women who were asylum seekers and refugees. There we were doing many different things. In that round with my case; in Birmingham I found many friends, who were directing me here and there. But through Dally who was director there, and a lady who was happy to help when she could, to whoever came to her, she directed me to the office of David Fobles so that he could help me with my case. He tried to do everything possible he could do, something his clients liked in him, he was giving me hope and encouragement, life in Birmingham was better than Bury, but again through friends I came to know Geoff Wilkins. To help me more with my case, but this gentleman came to be my right hand, not only to my case, yes, concerning the case like all his clients, he was loved by all who came across him with that kind of problem, he will do whatever he can, and if needed he can ask ideas from his friends, so that his clients can be successful, no matter what. To my case Clare Short, being my MP at the time, she contributed as much as she could. I will always thank these kind people who gave me their time when I was in need.

But Geoff, he was there up to the end with it, but there were other times, when he was worried a bit, he didn't know what would come up, that you could see was hard time to him, he didn't want to discourage me either. By seeing him in that situation, I knew that I had him, who was carrying my burden, and that gave me encouragement, and less stress, because I knew that I was not by myself, he was a fighter, and refused to give up, he tried all ways possible, and at last he won.

On the other side, when I asked him for ideas about my writings, he was happy to help me too for that matter, his encouragement made me go ahead and believe that, yes, I could. To be able to put together this book which parts of it, I had in my suitcase for more than thirty years.

This lady Dally was the one who connected me with Writers Without Borders, the group of writers, as soon as I saw them I loved them for their unity and solidarity. In the chances she gave me, one was to let me meet people in high positions in the government as one who looked to be a respected person.

She was preparing to meet ministers and officials from the EU.

I was one of the very few people she chose to go with her at the time, but what surprised me, was when after a few days I got a letter from presidency, which according to it, it showed me that, by meeting me, they took it as a big and good chance!

The letter was like this:

UK
PRESIDENCY
OF THE EU
2005

Dti
Meg Munn MP
DEPUTY MINISTER FOR WOMEN AND EQUALITY
December 2005
Commuity Interation Partership
Ground Floor
Newland House,
137–139 Hagley Road
Edgbaston B16 8UA

Dear Patricia,

I wanted to write to express my thanks to you for playing such a vital part in the success of our meeting of Gender Equality Ministers earlier this month.

The inspirational stories that you were able to tell our European colleagues served to illuminate our discussion the following day and made me very proud to be a UK Minister. Through you we were able to demonstate the good practice that exists in the West Midlands and to encourage an exchange of ideas that will last long after November 2005.

I know that meeting you was the highlight of the ministerial meeting for them. Indeed one colleague said that meeting you reminded him of why he went into politics. Another minister said that this was the best thing she had ever seen in the UK and she didn't want the discussion to end.

We couldn't have hoped for a better result and I know that Commissioner Spidla was very impressed by the vitality and innovation of the projects.

I was particulary impressed by the way you were able to demonstrate the commitment and independence of the women involved in your project and the steps you have helped them take to achieve both economic and personal empowerment.

I hope that you enjoyed the day and meeting the ministers and officials.

Thank you once more again on behalf of myself, and my officials in the Women and Equality Unit, who found it such a pleasure to work with you.

Yours sincerely,
MEG MUNN.

To some people like me, I saw this to be a chance which comes once in lifetime.

I CRIED.

I cried so hard for so long.

That phone call.

On that morning on 23 August 2010.

Geoff Wilkins my Lawyer called me and told me, "Bamurangirwa I have good news."

What news? Just ten minutes before he called me when he was reminding me that I was moving.

Now he was telling me good news?!

Though I was almost used to moving anyway, after moving thirteen times.

What was a big test, I had to choose between two things. To go back by myself where I came from. Or to go mad where I was.

And now it was fourteen times since the five years I had been here in Britain!

Did he think that I enjoyed these moves?

But I knew that it was not his fault, he was only doing what he could.

I was stressed with that moving. I didn't want more stories. At least not at that time. Maybe what others thought to be good, to me might be bad. So what a story?

"Yes I am listening," I said.

"You know what?"

"I am waiting for you to tell me. What?"

I gave a lot of respect to my lawyer because of who he was. To me Geoff was not only my lawyer he was some kind of angel... with a golden heart and he saw everyone to be a proper person. But if it was someone else, I would say otherwise.

But I had to be patient and listen.

Since the time I was told that I had my support back. And I had to move when they would get a place for me. Normally I had to be happy, because I had that support back.

Meaning that I would have some kind of card which had £35 per week instead of £10 per week from the charities. The card showed me that I was not allowed to hold the cash, because I was in section four!

What section four means? Don't ask, that is another story. In short, it is a person who is waiting to be deported back home.

And these people they would not want to be taken back home in that way: when they were guided by guns, and maybe their hands tied on their back. And they would not like to go by themselves because of the reasons that made them come in the first place. Which is rubbish politics, or rubbish economy in their countries, though some, yes, they were fed up with that life of torture, and would go back by themselves.

These lives made some marriages break up, when one of them came over here to be in that kind of prison for ten years or more. Something which was not easy for a wife or husband back home to understand that much. But me: that moving… I was like an African farmer in the past, who would go with cows where there was grass to feed them!

"You have got indefinite right to remain in Britain!" he said.

The reply he got in his ears was an automatically hard and very strong cry!

The only the word I managed to say was, "God bless you Geoff."

That drama took some minutes. He tried to say something to cool me down, but couldn't help.

It was the same song as it started, until when he gave up and hung up the phone.

Yes somehow it was normal in some circumstances, to some people to cry when they meant happiness. Which they call tears of joy! But in my case were they tears of joy or was it something else? To me, I was mixed up for many reasons.

In the first place why and how did I end up being in Europe and in this entire drama?

Was it because it is a rich country and I hate my continent Africa and my country Rwanda?

Of course not, ever.

Then what?

And now can I say that I am genuinely happy because I am now on my way to being a British citizen when I am Rwandan? Did I have to pass through this entire struggle to get this?

The truth was that I was crying for anger. Anger of my continent. Anger of my people past and present, my African people and my history, **our** history. Anger of what happed in those years and years. And what is happening now! And anger of how it happened and why. Anger of why we came in this way and passed through all of this. Anger and I asked myself, when now, when again would the African continent which has everything almost more than everywhere. When again is it going to become a super power?

The last time Africa was a super power, it was only at the time when a Jewish baby boy was born, in danger of being killed, the only place his parents had to take him as refugee, where there was peace, was Africa, that was the time when Jesus Christ was born. You can see how young people from poor countries or countries which have unnecessary wars risk their lives in dying in the ocean trying to go to Europe.

Now I am waiting for tomorrow and yes with a hope, for a second coming.

A lot of thanks to Geoff Wilkins and Mr. & Mrs. Anthony being there for me in a hard time when I need someone to understand me.

And I am genuinely happy to be British when I am Rwandan. Settled in Birmingham UK with good friends around me. Writers without Borders, Hope Gardening, Cross Point and with my Rwandan community. I have love and peace.

Try not to be too busy making living and forget to make life.

Life itself is a good teacher, it is not easy to forget someone who helped you in difficult times, it is not easy either to forget the one who left you in a horrible situation or the one who put you in a difficult situation.

But always hope, patience, love, respect for yourself, and others around you, is richness and the weapon in life.

BIBLIOGRAPHY

American Historical review 8.1 (2002).

(Atlantic slave Trade p.170).

Armewn Vartinia the Genocide Guest Column.

Andy McSmith, *The Independent,* Thursday 9 August 2007.

R. Woolley, A. C. Bishop and William Roger Hamilton, Editor Lester Hawksby, Source: Philip's Encyclopedia (2007) Octopus Publishing Group, London (2007).

Bosnia News Daily Top news from Bosnia Friday 11 November 2008.

Birmingham Post Tuesday 7 2006.

David Wilkes, *Daily Mail,* Thursday 2 August 2007.

Dailaire Remeo *They Fights Like Soldiers They Die Like Children,* first published in Canada 2010 London house in 2010 by Hutchinson.

Daily Mail, Wednesday 12 November 2008.

Daily Mirror, Saturday 23 November 2013.

Guillaud, Meg. RWANDA: *The Land God Forgot?* London: Monarch book, 2002.

First Australians. Edited by Rachel Perkins and Marcia Langton. With Wayne Atkinson, James Boyce, RG Kimber, Steve Kinnane, Noel Loos and Bruce Pascoe.

Gourevitch Philip, *We wish to inform you that tomorrow we will be killed with our families.*

The Guardian, Tuesday December 5, 2006.

Klan: Lutla Feb, 2008, *What Western Did Between 188-1930 With Black People.*

Mark Ellis, Foreign Editor *Daily Mirror* Saturday 9 September 2006.

Mofid Kamran. *Globalisation For The Common Good*. London: Shepheard.

METRO Friday 13 2007.

METRO Thursday 15 May 2008.

Mirror.co.uk.sport Sundaymirror.co.uk 16 December 2007.

Oliver Stallwod, *METRO* June 2005

Nelson Mandela The Man and the Movement by Mary Benson.

Prunia Gerald, *The Rwanda crisis, history of Rwanda genocide* first published in the United Kingdom by C. Hurrst & Co (publishers LTD).

The SUN, Friday 10 2007.

The Sunday Times Rwanda 17th November 2013.

Sarah Hills, *METRO,* Monday 18 July 2005.

Southeast Asia July 26 2007.

Sugun Johnson, Roger Mitchell, Samuel Rhein Michael Schiffmann and Chris Seaton, *Unscrambling Africa, Reconciliation process Europe & Africa.*

Umugwaneza Aline, *From Tragedy to Triumph who said that.*

Ella, Danielle, *War has changed our life, not our spirit.* Roma: Jesuit Refugee Service, 200.

Walwyn (Publishers LTD).

ACKNOWLEDGMENTS

I thank my parents Bagorebeza and Sinzi, who gave me a proper foundation of life with unconditional love. I was lucky to have wise parents like them. I want to thank my children who were good friends, and good teachers. Batsinduka, Muvunangoma, Manzi, late Ilibagiza, late Gahongayire, Niwegaju, and late Gahenda.

To the side of teaching me and encouraging me, I am extremely grateful to Batsinduka, Ilibagiza, Muvunangoma and Niwegaju. Without their patience and love I wouldn't write this book today.

In a life of struggle I have to remember to thank a few good people who were there when I was in need to go a step ahead. I will always thank Khadijah wherever she is if she is alive or dead to notice that I was in trouble and needed someone.

I thank Senzage for being there for me and encouraging me to be strong and stand for myself. I remember late Madam Adela, for the single advice she gave me in August 1994, was a key of my confidence, when she told me that: it is me, who has to be number one to be responsible for my problems.

I thank Peter Omaya and Mrs Oyuwa who were immigratin officers at the time, for serving me as me, for years and years, without 'kitu kidodo'.

I thank David Maina Duke and Jane Gatitu, for the encouragement they gave me to go ahead and write the first part of this book in the 1980s.

Thanks to my good friend of years and years, Uta Fager, a German lady, with a golden heart, who was my director, she was a lighter of my whole family, she gave me a way of my vision, vision of the future, without her I wouldn't be where I am now, doing what I love most, writing.

Many thanks to the late Alfonci Mbayire Mbandahe for recognising me and giving me the high respect, when I thought that I didn't deserve it.

Thanks to Desire Mugwiza for giving me a big and good chance, a chance, which took me high, where by myself I wouldn't dream to be able to reach.

Thanks to Uwera Monica Kabanda, and Jane Kagenza, for being there for me when I was in a sad and hard time, and when I was in a happy time too. I can't forget that time.

Thanks to Rose Mupende and Mary Rwamushayija, for being my good and trusted friends.

Thanks to Salam Saad, for being ready and happy to help when needed.

Thanks Geoff Wilkins for believing in me and encouraging me. Many thanks to Phillomene Nduwimana for encouragement.

Many thanks to Rose Mukamutara Masozera for the advice and correcting me in my writings.

Thanks to my beautiful daughter Niwegaju and my wonderful son-in-law Dylan W. Chown for corrections and advice.

Thanks to Dally Panesar, a lady who works with equality for everyone, for many things she did, she is the one who introduced me to Writers without Borders.

Thanks to Hope Gardening and Cross Point for being good to many people.

Thanks Writers without Borders to my good friends and for opening my door of writing which was a dream come true.

Many thanks to Pastor Mwanza who volunteered his many hours shaping this book.

Thanks to my parents' angels, who always look down on me.

But more than that, many thanks to my God who gives me patience and HOPE.

Note: 'some names in this book have been changed'.

I owe this book to my parents, my children, and my grandchildren and to all the girls around the world, from my generation, before them and after, who were denied a chance of education, **just because they are girls**.